Bendicksen

Bendicksen

INVITATIONS

INVITATIONS

Changing as Teachers and Learners K-12

Regie Routman

IRWIN PUBLISHING
Toronto, Canada

HEINEMANN
Portsmouth, NH

Heinemann
A Division of Reed Publishing (USA) Inc.
361 Hanover Street, Portsmouth, NH 03801-3912
Offices and agents throughout the world

Published simultaneously in Canada by
IRWIN PUBLISHING
1800 Steeles Avenue West   Concord, Ontario, Canada L4K 2P3

ISBN 0-435-08578-6 (Heinemann paper)
ISBN 0-435-08593-X (Heinemann cloth)
ISBN 0-7725-1850-5 **(Irwin paper)**

Credits for reprinted material are on page xv.

Library of Congress Cataloging-in-Publication Data
Routman, Regie.
       Invitations : changing as teachers and learners K–12 / Regie Routman.
           p.   cm.
       Includes bibliographical references and index.
       ISBN 0-435-08578-6 (paper)
       ISBN 0-435-08593-X (cloth)
       1. Reading (Elementary)—United States—Language experience
approach: I. Title.
       LB 1573.33.R67   1991
       372.4′1—dc20   91-9304
                                                                    CIP

Canadian Cataloguing in Publication Data
Routman, Regie
       Invitations : changing as teachers and learners
K–12

Includes index.
ISBN 0-7725-1850-5

1. Reading (Elementary)—Language experience
approach.   2. English language—Composition and
exercises—Study and teaching (Elementary).
I. Title.

LB1573.33.R68 1991   372.4′1   C9I-093830-X

Cover photo by Kevin G. Reeves:
       WEB reading program: daily book check and independent reading
       in Joan Servis' grade 4 class, January 1991

Cover design by Jenny Greenleaf.
Designed by G&H SOHO LTD.
Printed in the United States of America.
93   94   95   9

For Frank, Elizabeth, and Peter

Contents

Permissions

We are grateful to the publishers and individuals below for granting permission to reprint material from previously published works.

Page 13: Cambourne's Model of Learning. From *The Whole Story: Natural Learning and the Acquisition of Literacy in the Classroom* by Brian Cambourne. Copyright 1988, Ashton Scholastic Ltd., Auckland, New Zealand. Reprinted by permission.

Page 25: Response to "Boycott the Basals." Reprinted by permission of Richard C. Owen, Publishers, 135 Katonah Ave., Katonah, NY 10503.

Page 64: Jelly on the Plate. From "Jelly on the Plate." Modern Curriculum Press. Reprinted by permission.

Page 142: From *Jamaica's Find* by Juanita Havill. Text copyright © 1986 by Juanita Havill. Illustrations copyright © 1986 by Anne Sibley O'Brien. Reprinted by permission of Houghton Mifflin Co.

Page 254: "Am I Becoming a Good Speller?" Reprinted by permission of R. D. Walshe, for the Primary English Teaching Association, Sydney, Australia.

Page 282: From *Zoo Books 2: Alligators and Crocodiles*; copyright 1986 by Wildlife Education Ltd., 930 West Washington St., San Diego, CA 92103. Reprinted by permission of the publisher.

Page 306: "Evaluation Data Gathering Profile." Adapted from a form developed by R. Anthony, T. Johnson, N. Mickelson, and A. Preece. Reprinted by permission.

Page 322: "Concepts About Print." Adapted from "Concepts of Print" test in *The Early Detection of Reading Difficulties*, 3rd ed., by Marie M. Clay. Copyright 1985. Heinemann, 361 Hanover St., Portsmouth, NH 03801. Reprinted by permission.

Page 44b: From "Champions by Rebel Williams." Reprinted by permission of The Wright Group, 18916 N. Creek Parkway, Suite 107, Bothell, WA 98011.

Page 92b: *Amos & Boris* Teacher's Guide. Reprinted by permission of H. P. Kopplemann, Inc., 140 Van Block Ave., Hartford, CT 06141–0145.

Page 93b: *Journey to Topaz* Teacher's Guide. Reprinted by permission of H. P. Kopplemann, Inc., 140 Van Block Ave., Hartford, CT 06141–0145.

Page 103b: Getting Parents Involved Letter. From the Fall 1988 newsletter of the Whole Language Teachers Association, 16 Concord Rd., Sudbury, MA 01776. Reprinted by permission.

Page 109b: Parents as Allies in Children's Education. Reprinted by permission of Shary Rea, 850–1001–13th Ave., S.W., Calgary, T2R 0L5. Canada.

Page 115b: Book Club Form. Reprinted by permission of Nellie Edge Seminars, Inc., P.O. Box 12399, Salem, OR 97309.

Other credits for work in this book include:

Page 235: Chapter 10, "Integrating Spelling into the Reading-Writing Classroom," is an expanded and revised version of an unpublished manuscript that was co-authored with Linda Cooper and Elaine Weiner.

Page 263: Chapter 11, "Setting Up an In-School Publishing Process," derives largely from the work of Marianne Sopko.

Page 29b: The annotations for "Journals" were co-authored with Dawne Boyer.

Page 77b: Appendix A, "A Folk/Fairy Tale Unit," was co-authored with Joan Servis.

A Note on the Use of Pronouns

To maintain a personal and objective tone, the use of he/she and him/her has been alternated and balanced throughout this book.

A Note on the Use of References in the Body of the Text

When a professional resource or children's book is cited only once in the text, the author, date, and publisher are included along with the resource cited. When that reference information is not provided in the body of the text, consult the index to locate full publishing information. The boldface page number in the index indicates the page where full publishing information is located.

Acknowledgments

I owe a debt of gratitude to so many educators, students, and parents in the Shaker Heights, Ohio, City School District whose voices are woven into this book. Most of all, I am grateful to the many teachers in my school district who have welcomed me into their classrooms each day and have made my own growth and continued learning possible. Although the written words in this text are mine, the ideas have emerged from continuous sharing and working with my colleagues and the children in their classrooms.

I am grateful for the support and trust of the principals in the buildings where I worked from 1987 to 1990—Don Coffee, Rebecca Kimberly, Margaret Lennard, Bernice Stokes, and Larry Svec—as well as Jean Sylak, director of elementary education, and Mark Freeman, superintendent of schools. I am also appreciative of their allowing me the freedom to take risks and find my own way as a teacher supporting other teachers. I am deeply thankful especially to Bernice Stokes for her encouragement, trust, support, and friendship. As the principal in the building where I am based, she has supported me daily and made it possible for me to continue to grow professionally. To Delores Groves, the principal in our grades 5 and 6 building, I am thankful for her ongoing support and friendship.

The writing of this book has been an enormous effort and could not have been completed without the assistance of many people. First, I am greatly indebted to those who thoughtfully and generously took the time to respond to one or more chapter drafts: Richard Allington, Pam Anderson, Bonnie Daniels, Paul Daniels, Dollye Finney, Peggy Gerhart, Margie Glaros, Joseph Grimes, Robin Grimes, Vicki Griminger, Jim Henry, Theo Husband, Rebecca Kimberly, Carol Lyons, Loretta Martin, Bill Newby, Ellen Potter, Mary Pryor, Jeannine Rajewski, Peg Rimedio, Kathy Roskos, Ellen Rubin, Lee Sattelmeyer, Jim Servis, Sam Sexton, Cheri Shapero, Karen Sher, Marcy Silver, Marianne Sopko, Bernice Stokes, Rob Tierney, Elaine Weiner, and Kathy Wolfe. Their feedback contributed significantly to my revision process and made the book clearer, more accurate, and more readable.

Second, the following people took the time to talk with me and share ideas and materials: Cheryl Ames, Patsy Bannon, Julie Beers, Deanne Blackburn, Reg Blue, Ruth Blumenthal, Dawne Boyer, Donna Brittain, Connie Brown, Darla Carlson, Jean Church, Charleen Civiello, Kittye Copeland, Anna Cresswell, Sylvia De-

Marco, Judy Detunca, Marie Dingwall, Jacqueline Douglass, Kay Dunlap, Hilda Edwards, Marilyn Eppich, Nancy Erkkila, Frank Gabbert, Susan Gardner, Bill Goepfert, Onajé Grimes, Sheri Grossman, Dede Hall, Jerry Harste, Tom Hatch, Judy Heiskell, Betty Hess, Ann Hogsett, Karen Horton, Lois Hudson, Bob Justice, Tom Kelly, Barbara Kittrick, Beth Lazerick, Carol Lindow, Susan Long, Susan Mears, Marisa Mercurio, Ella Moore, Dick Needham, Lori Oczkus, Donna Ostberg, Jim Paces, Maria Padovani, Michael Pellegrino, Robyn Platt, Joyce Pope, Debbie Powell, Linda Powers, Billie Price, John Ridley, Kitty Rose, Joyce Russell, Linda Salvadore, Nancy Sargeant, Debbie Schaedlich, Bob Scholl, Susan Scheps, Nancy Schubert, Karan Shelley, Peggy Sherman, Karen Shiba, Karen Smith, Barbara Speer, Brenda Spivey, Tudy Stewart, Sylvia Tallentire, Bob Thomas, Colleen Thompson, Nancy Tuttle, Sally Wilson, Jill Wisneski, Maryann Young, Bonnie Yousif, Deborah Zinn, Donna Zorge.

Some people deserve to be on both lists, but I have simply listed them in their more major role.

Most importantly, I am thankful to the special people in my life who have supported and sustained me through the long, arduous writing process of this book. Andrea Butler read a major portion of the manuscript and gave generously of her time and knowledge. Her honest feedback helped me regain a necessary perspective I had lost and cleared up confusions I was struggling with. I am indebted to her for her warm friendship and kindness as well.

While many teachers generously gave their time and support, several also sustained me throughout the writing process. Their voices and input are major contributions to this book. Holly Burgess continued to offer to read chapters and give honest feedback from the perspective of a high school teacher. Joan Di Dio read and gave valued input to many chapters. For her insights, time, honesty, and ongoing friendship, I am continually grateful.

I am also grateful to Joan Servis, from whom I have learned so much and whose classroom community of learners has been an ongoing source for my own professional development. Joan read and responded to several chapters and was always available to answer my questions. Our friendship as well as our weekly professional sharing continue to be a welcome and necessary part of my own growth.

Linda Cooper read and reread almost the entire manuscript. She tirelessly and generously gave me excellent suggestions and honest feedback. Her daily friendship and support have been a major sustaining influence throughout the writing of this book. Additionally, many of her own teaching ideas are an integral part of this text. I will always be grateful for both her knowledge and her caring ways.

I am also grateful to the secretaries in all the buildings in our district for their unfailing kindness and cooperation, and especially to Beverly Scoby and Linda Mendelsohn, the wonderful secretaries at Mercer School, where I am based. I am thankful, too, for our district library media office, which, under the leadership of Ellen Stepanian, has been constantly helpful in providing me with copies of journal articles, meeting any special requests, and obtaining information I needed. Thanks also to Lois Markt, who was largely responsible for my training and follow-up support as a Reading Recovery teacher.

With *Resources for Teachers* in the blue pages, I was most fortunate to have the help of many talented educators whose considerable input and expertise have greatly enriched this book. Susan Hepler generously shared her extensive knowledge of children's literature, wrote most of the children's literature annotations, and responded to a chapter draft. Our many hours on the phone together and our frequent correspondence discussing book titles, as well as discussing our personal and professional lives, were a highlight in writing this book.

I was also most fortunate to have the talent of Vera Milz, who shared the writing of annotations for the recommended professional books. Without her time and vast knowledge of professional literature, that section would be far less complete.

I am grateful for the title suggestions from Mary Krogness for the grades 7–8 recommended literature, as well as for her support as a fellow teacher and writer. For the recommended literature for grades 9–12, the input and suggestions from Don Gallo—expert in YA literature—have been invaluable. Thanks also to Dana Noble, a talented high school English teacher in our district, for taking time to read and consider most of Don's suggestions along with his own, to thoughtfully write the annotations for the grades 9–12 lists, and to respond to several chapter drafts.

In facilitating the publishing process, I am most appreciative of Philippa Stratton, editor-in-chief at Heinemann, for having respected my voice as an author and for taking so much time to patiently conference with me over the manuscript. The friendship we developed as a result of our time together has been an added pleasure.

Thanks also to Cheryl Kimball, production editor at Heinemann, who supported me through the arduous final stages of the book. Her flexibility, knowledge, support, and humor went a long way in easing tensions.

To the staff at G & H Soho who worked conscientiously to edit the manuscript and produce the book under a tight deadline, I am grateful.

I am also appreciative of the efforts of Leslie Schwarz of Heinemann Services who facilitated my writing process through her friendship and by taking care of so many small details.

Ultimately, I could not have completed this book without the support and love of my special friends and family. I am grateful for the constant friendship and love from Harriet Cooper. My aunt, Gloria Mills, has cheered me on. Susan Neuman—my stepsister, colleague, and friend—has encouraged me in so many ways. Our parents, Mildred and Manny Leventhal, have been constant supporters of my work. And Margaret Marshall has offered her continuous support and pride in my work.

My son, Peter, supported me throughout the process and took the time to read and comment on many chapters. His honesty, gentleness, and encouragement have meant so much to me. My daughter, Elizabeth, helped continuously with the final copyediting process and gave me valuable suggestions in so many areas. I have benefited so much from her writing talents, clear insights, and generous help. Most of all, I am thankful for my husband Frank, who offered his constant love and support and who put up with a wife who was always working and feeling stressed. Without his affection, help, and patience, I could never have written this book and continued teaching at the same time.

Finally, while its inadequacies are mine alone, I believe that this book is truly a collaborative effort, made possible by the generosity, support, and openness of teachers, administrators, librarians, parents, students, and my friends and family. To all of them, I am deeply grateful.

January 1991

INVITATIONS

1

Beyond Transitions

Invitations in grade 1:
choosing to read during independent work time

I am a teacher. I don't say "just a teacher" anymore because I feel proud of the job we teachers do and of our ability to have an impact on students' lives as well as on our own.

In the early 1980s, when I was experiencing success using literature and meaning-based strategies to teach reading and writing to all learners—including at-risk students—I thought other teachers could benefit from my story of what had happened in one elementary building. Somehow, I had the notion that perhaps I could write a book for teachers. At the time, the idea seemed outrageous. I had never even had an article published. I did not consider myself a writer, and I was an "unknown." I was—like so many teachers—quietly and diligently working in one classroom, largely isolated from other teachers. Still, something inside me persisted, telling me to at least try. Over the next several years, my book proposal received a series of rejections, but I continued to look for a publisher. While there were wonderful books for teachers on whole language written by educators from New Zealand and Australia, there were no books written by an American teacher. I believed I had a different perspective to offer that would be useful for teachers in the United States.

In the spring of 1988, my book, *Transitions: From Literature to Literacy*, was jointly published by Rigby in Melbourne, Australia, and Heinemann in Portsmouth, New Hampshire. The response to the book has been gratifying. Teachers across the country have read the book, reflected on their teaching, and made changes. Many teachers have written to me sharing their concerns, questions, changes, hopes, and struggles.

When I wrote *Transitions*, I was teaching in an elementary school where the majority of students were part of a minority, lower socio-economic population and where many students were failing to learn to read successfully with traditional methods. In my book, I told the story of what happened in the primary grades in

1

one school when we moved from the basal text and worksheets to a literature approach to reading and writing. That story took a new turn in the fall of 1987 when our district began a reorganization effort as a result of declining enrollment and racial imbalance. At the same time—because of the leadership of parents, teachers, librarians, and administrators—our board of education made a district-wide commitment to move toward more meaning-centered approaches to reading and writing. This approach was to be implemented largely through the use of the best of children's literature. Teachers across our district began working to integrate the language processes—reading, writing, speaking, listening—and move toward what has become known as whole language.

While *Transitions* was written to give support to teachers in beginning the change process, especially as it relates to the use of literature in the classroom, this book, *Invitations: Changing as Teachers and Learners K–12*, begins where *Transitions* left off. It was written to support and encourage teachers in their further transitions in teaching and learning. As a teacher working with teachers and students, I share what I have observed, and I discuss connections, insights, and reflections other teachers and I have made. My hope is that reading the book will promote some self-reflection, risk taking, greater understanding of the principles of language learning, and a closer tie-in between theory and practice. The book is about changing as teachers and learners and is meant to be a series of invitations and possibilities to facilitate literacy in the classroom.

While the book was written to be read from beginning to end, it can easily be read in any order. Each chapter is complete within itself. You could begin with "Evaluation" (Chap. 13), "Integrating Spelling into the Reading-Writing Classroom" (Chap. 10), "Components of Whole Language" (Chap. 3), or whatever topic you are interested in. It is a long book, and I am respectful of the time constraints we teachers have, so use the book to suit your own purposes. The "blue pages" at the end of the book comprise an extensive annotated *Resources for Teachers* section meant to supplement and support the teacher as a professional, especially in the use and selection of children's literature and professional literature.

It was not my intent to write such a long book, and I have wrestled with the length of *Invitations*. In the end, however, I decided not only to include reading and writing topics but also to address the issues we teachers all struggle with, and to do so in depth. If the change process is to be successful, we teachers must lead the way by becoming knowledgeable professionals. I have devoted a chapter to the importance of establishing support networks since most of us work in school districts which do not have strong support systems or ongoing staff development plans. Chapter 14 presents many strategies for working with learning disabled and at-risk students since they are a part of every classroom. An entire chapter is devoted to journal writing so that teachers can implement it and sustain it in a meaningful way. Since so many of us struggle with classroom management, Chapter 15 discusses many specifics for successfully organizing the whole language classroom.

In writing *Transitions*, I tried to stay away from the term "whole language," fearing its overuse and misuse. While I still have those concerns, "whole language" has become such a widespread, accepted term that I now use it as a point of common reference. It is to be hoped that some day there will be no need for special terminology. When I was visiting a school in Auckland, New Zealand, I used the term "whole language" in my conversation with some teachers at lunch, after having spent an exciting morning in whole language classrooms. One New Zealand teacher, never having heard the term, asked, "What's that?" The principal responded, "That's what we do."

Beyond Transitions

Since the fall of 1987, I have been serving as a language arts resource teacher, assisting and supporting teachers in our five k–4 buildings in their transition to whole language. I am in each of these buildings one morning a week where I work with teachers on an invitational basis. In each building, I have organized and facilitated a weekly, before-school language arts support group where teachers meet to share issues and ideas in their teaching and to tie theory and practice together. These voluntary meetings have been invaluable for staff development and for teachers to collaborate and share ideas and concerns (see pp. 465–472).

Each morning I also go into classrooms at the request of teachers. I demonstrate lessons in reading and writing, conference with teachers, coach teachers, and provide and suggest teaching strategies and resource materials. In the afternoons, I am based in one building where I work daily with students, supporting and supplementing their reading-writing program in coordination with the classroom teachers. Rather than pulling students out of the classroom, I work in the second grade rooms (see pp. 144–146).

Recently, my role as a resource teacher has occasionally extended to our grades 5–6 building, our middle school, and our high school. What began in our district as mostly a primary grades focus on whole language has now begun to extend to the secondary level. The transitions have been slow, but the movement to more meaning-based and student-centered approaches is growing steadily.

Because of my daily work with teachers in classrooms in my district and my communication with teachers across the country, I became aware of a need for guidance and support for teachers who had already made the transition and commitment to more meaning-centered approaches. Teachers were asking for more assistance in going further with literature and whole language once they had taken the initial plunge. I also became aware, because of my interaction with secondary teachers in my own district, that the whole language process is the same from kindergarten through twelfth grade and that the elementary model has much to offer secondary teachers. The issues we struggle with in the elementary grades— using literature meaningfully, giving up some control and allowing children more choices, writing for authentic purposes, considering holistic strategies for at-risk students, establishing a collaborative classroom, evaluating, questioning our teaching—are critical issues for the kindergarten teacher as well as the senior high English teacher.

I believe the experiences of teachers and students in our district are representative of many school districts around the country and apply to many teachers and classrooms. Our school district is an "inner-ring suburb" of just under 5,000 kindergarten through grade 12 students, half minority and half nonminority. In terms of economics, families range from poor families on public assistance to extremely wealthy families. We deal with the same problems of student achievement that most diverse districts experience. *Invitations* concerns the issues we all think about and struggle with in our efforts to make our teaching more relevant to our students and ourselves. This book moves beyond transitions in one elementary school to include the continuing transitions of many teachers across a school district.

Reflections

Recently a teacher asked, "How can I know if I am really becoming a whole language teacher?" I could not give her an answer because it's one she'll have to find for herself. The best I can do is share my own and other teachers' experiences and reflect on current research and theories of literacy learning.

Perhaps, more than anything else, whole language is about all learners feeling whole and able and part of a community of learners. It is about belonging and risk taking and feeling successful as teachers and learners. It is about the power of collaboration to break down the isolation of teachers and to establish communities of belonging and learning for all students and teachers.

I recognize that change is difficult and risky for most of us. Whatever we do for the first time, whether it is small-group guided reading, shared writing, integrating spelling, or holistic evaluation, we are bound to bungle it at the start. This is natural behavior for all new, comprehensive processes and procedures, and we need to be forgiving and patient with ourselves. The main thing is to begin, to give it a try. Once you have made that first attempt, you can make modifications. One group of undergraduate students told their professor to go easy with them because they were in the "rough draft stage." Becoming a whole language teacher means being prepared to always be in a draft stage in some areas. However, you can't make revisions and improve at a task until you have first tried it. Don't worry too much about getting it "right." Decide what it is that's important for you to change and have a go at it. Adapt what seems right for you and your students. Go slowly, and add only one new component or procedure at a time. Continue to read, risk, and reflect. Trust your intuition. Slowly your confidence will build and your competence will grow.

I invite you to reflect on your teaching and begin to make meaningful changes. I wish you good luck and a safe, exciting journey.

2

Becoming a Whole Language Teacher

Language arts support group: establishing criteria for schoolwide holistic writing

"What About the Skills? Shouldn't I Be Teaching Them?"

When I saw Maria in the fall of her second year of teaching, the change in her demeanor and outlook was absolutely striking. Full of broad smiles and enthusiasm, Maria Padovani was a teacher who exuded confidence. Her classroom was a joyful, collaborative community where the teacher and learners supported and learned from each other. Every day she and her students were reading, discussing quality literature, and writing for a variety of authentic purposes. Skills were being learned and taught as much as possible in the context of genuine reading and writing experiences.

Maria had not started out that way. Despite the fact that she had received university training in whole language and had done an exceptional job in her field experience and student teaching, a "skill and drill" philosophy dominated her thinking during her first year of teaching. Because almost all of her schooling—from kindergarten through college—had been based on a skills model in traditional classrooms, that model initially prevailed in her first year of teaching.

Although Maria had *seemed* well prepared to teach, what she was prepared with was methodology. She could make up activities to go along with books; she could do journal writing; she could take children through the steps of the writing process; and she could teach a skills lesson—all as long as someone else laid out the framework.

In an effort to become as competent as possible, Maria sought out colleagues for advice and support, worked at school most evenings until 7 P.M., and continued working at home late into the evenings and over weekends. Nonetheless, she continued to feel overwhelmed and inadequate, and she often ended the day in tears. No matter how hard she tried, things didn't seem to come together for her. "I saw what some other teachers were doing, but I had no idea how they were arriving at what to do. I just thought they must be spending hours planning."

That first year Maria felt tremendous pressure to do everything, and to do it well. She was afraid of disappointing people and worried about not measuring up to the standards of her colleagues. She was constantly looking at what others were doing and not giving herself credit for what she was doing well. Whenever she walked down the hall and saw a new bulletin board or walked into another teacher's room and saw "something," she wondered if she should add it to her lesson plans. Initially, too, Maria felt she should go to every workshop that she heard about, whether it was on literature, writing process, spelling, or management.

Most of all, Maria was preoccupied with teaching "skills," and one of the hardest things for her was to decide what skills to teach and how to teach them. She was constantly asking, "Shouldn't I be teaching skills? I see so-and-so doing a lesson on verbs (or capitalization or grammar). Shouldn't I be doing that?" I did not have the answers for Maria, and we struggled together. When she would ask, "Why do you have to teach grammar or punctuation?" I asked her, "Why do you think you have to teach it?"

Maria later said,

> The questions made me go back and reflect, reason out and modify what I was doing. Also, the suggestion to pick out one thing to concentrate on and not try to do everything was helpful. Last year, I chose to focus on making my questioning more meaningful in reading groups. This year my focus will be on integrating the skills into writing.

Maria also noted the positive influence of a whole language summer workshop. After the sessions, she had felt inspired to read many journal articles provided by the workshop as well as several recommended professional books. She noted, "The reading made me question the way I was doing things. I saw how contrived a lot of my teaching was. I began to move toward experience-based writing instead of just assigned writing and to really think about my teaching."

Before Maria could offer children choices in decision making about their own learning, she had to find her own literate voice—slowly and thoughtfully. She had to examine and determine what she believed about how children learn before she could make thoughtful, ongoing decisions about her teaching. Once Maria could combine her strong educational background and experiences with a clear theoretical literacy model, she was on her way to becoming a whole language teacher.

> I realize now that I was missing a clearly defined philosophy. Until you have that and it's your own, you continue to struggle. I integrate a lot of different people's ideas. I think about what Calkins and Graves and others say. I continue to read, explore my thinking, question my ideas, and share with colleagues. Now, however, I have the understanding of the philosophy, and the ideas and activities just come to me.

Maria continues to value the time she invests in professional reading, attending workshops, and participating in our district-level whole language support group. She has been instrumental in helping fellow teachers in a nearby school district begin their own support group and has felt rewarded by being able to help other teachers. She continues to choose one focus for her teaching and learning and accepts the fact that she cannot be an expert at everything. She is still concerned about "skills," but is feeling more confident about integrating skills into her teaching. She often feels she wants to be doing more, but she does give herself credit for what she does well. She also accepts the fact that there will never be enough time to do everything. She is now most concerned with having her children develop a love and appreciation of reading and writing.

"I'm the Only One Having Difficulty"

Walking into Loretta Martin's second grade classroom, one sees children reading books of their own choosing as the mainstay of the reading program, buddy journal writing, spelling as part of the writing program, a child-centered room where children are productively in charge of their own learning, and a relaxed teacher clearly enjoying herself and her students. Loretta is a confident whole language teacher, but she did not start out that way.

When Loretta first began to make changes in her teaching, she felt isolated in her struggles: "Every time I tried something new, there was always some snag. The lesson didn't flow, and the immature kids didn't catch on. I was upset, but I wasn't comfortable sharing my failures. It seemed as though everyone else was talking about their successes."

While she felt good about some of the changes she was making in her teaching, Loretta was also extremely frustrated.

> When you have workbook pages for phonics, spelling, handwriting, and reading and you're trying to add literature, as well as teaching all the other subjects, you feel very stressed. I felt that way for three years. I was so busy getting through all those required skills and workbook pages every morning. The kids were worn out with all the work I gave them.

Loretta knew she wanted to have a whole language classroom, but she was aware that she lacked an understanding of the philosophy. With twenty years teaching experience in grades k–2, Loretta considered herself a traditional teacher but an eclectic one who incorporated many approaches. She was known as an excellent teacher who held high expectations for all her students. She always read aloud to her class and incorporated literature into her basal program, but literature and reading were "entirely separate." Reading was what she did when she used the basal and did skills work. Literature was the pleasurable time, for enjoying books and talking about authors, that came after the reading work.

Loretta began making changes in her teaching about five years ago. She began by adding chart poems in enlarged print and children's books to her reading program. Gradually the excitement of the kids and the support of the parents encouraged her to give up the basal entirely. She credits a supportive principal, the intervention of Mary Krogness—our district writing expert—observations of colleague Elaine Weiner, and an observation of the first grade literature program at Moreland School (see Routman, 1988)* for beginning her transition. "I couldn't get over the comprehension, fluency, and excitement of first graders reading *Ira Sleeps Over* (by Bernard Waber) in late fall," Loretta observed.

The turning point in Loretta's transition to whole language came when she attended a week-long conference—"The Pursuit of Literacy: Creating the Whole Language Classroom"—in Geneseo, New York, in the summer of 1989. She was inspired by speakers Lucy Calkins, Dorothy Strickland, Charles Chew, and Violet

*See index for pages giving full publishing information.

Harris as well as by many teachers she met. At the conference, Loretta was able to share her frustrations and failures with other teachers who were also looking to understand the whole language philosophy. "Until that conference, I thought I was the only one trying new things that didn't work," Loretta commented.

During the conference, she also went to a bookstore and purchased many professional titles.

> I had seen most of these books but knew I didn't have time to read them during the school year. I recognized the covers from seeing them at our language arts support group. I had already read and been very influenced by several books on whole language. I was especially impressed with books about minority children who became successful readers and writers. As a black teacher, the success of black children was really important to me.
>
> I spent a lot of time during the rest of the summer doing professional reading. As I read, I wrote down what I wanted to do in my class—a message board, a daily morning message, reading by choice, abandoning spelling workbooks and phonics pages. That fall I was able to implement lots of changes in my teaching.

Loretta sees one of her biggest changes as focusing on the positive. To her that means not only noticing what kids can do but also what they are doing. In the past she relied on tests to tell her what kids couldn't do and structured much of her teaching around those results. "Now, even when the child has only written a few sentences and I know they can do more, I am accepting of what the child has done. I know they've learned a lot more than what they put on the paper."

Today, Loretta continues to attend conferences, interact with other teachers at those conferences, and share with her colleagues. She is an active participant in our weekly language arts support group meetings, and she has begun to share her knowledge with teachers in other districts. While she has gained many ideas and perspectives from attending workshops, she notes: "It wasn't the workshops that led to major changes in my philosophy and teaching. It was taking the time to do the professional reading and reflect on my teaching."

Understanding Language Learning

Loretta's statement is true for me too. I am largely self-educated in whole language, and most of that education has come from the professional reading I have done and continue to do. While professional workshops and interaction with colleagues have been extremely valuable, it is, most of all, the reading that has caused me to reflect insightfully about my teaching. Professional reading has led me to confirm directions I am heading toward, question present practices, and continue to make changes in my teaching. Looking at the books that have had the greatest effect on my teaching and learning, I see they are all a combination of theory and practice. Those are the books that have enabled me to make the vital connections between the how and the why of teaching-learning and to think, "Aha, so that's why that works."

As a result of putting theory and practice together through my professional reading and more than twenty years of teaching experience, I have come up with my own theory of learning and teaching. My theory is still growing and constantly changing, but it is where I am now. My beliefs are based on my daily interactions with students and teachers in classrooms and on observations I have made. I continually apply my beliefs and connect them to whole-life contexts.

Underpinning my beliefs is my understanding of the necessary conditions for language learning. Here I have been largely influenced by the research and teachings of three educators: Don Holdaway in New Zealand, Brian Cambourne in Australia, and Kenneth Goodman in the United States. Additionally, in formulating my learning theory, I have been greatly influenced by the work of Frank Smith, Jerry Harste, Donald Graves, Marie Clay, Andrea Butler, and Nancie Atwell.

Some major understandings include:

- Literacy acquisition is a natural process.
- The conditions for becoming oral language users are the same as for becoming readers and writers.
- Young children enter school with much knowledge about literacy.
- Becoming a reader and becoming a writer are closely related.
- Optimal literacy environments promote risk taking and trust.
- Becoming literate is a social act and a search for meaning.
- Literacy development is continuous.
- Genuine literacy acts are authentic and meaningful.

Holdaway's Developmental Model

In the 1960s and early 1970s, Don Holdaway, the New Zealand educator responsible for developing shared book experience, theorized that the ways children acquire oral language could be used as a developmental model for all language learning. He found certain conditions to be common all over the world in learning spoken language, and he translated those conditions into a "Developmental Model for Language Learning" (*The Pursuit of Literacy: Early Reading and Writing*, Michael Sampson [ed.], Kendall/Hunt Publishing, 1986). Holdaway's model has had the greatest influence on my teaching. I carry the model in my head, and I try to employ it in every teaching situation. When my teaching breaks down, I go back to the model.

Developmental Model for Language Learning

1. Observation of "demonstrations" In learning to speak—and to read and write—the child observes competent adults that he admires as genuine users of the literacy act. The act that is modeled is authentic and purposeful. The learner is a spectator with no pressure to perform.

2. Participation The child is invited to participate and collaborate because he has a need for and genuine interest in learning to talk or mastering a particular skill. The "expert" welcomes the "novice" while explaining, instructing, and demonstrating what to do. The act becomes collaborative, as in a confirming conversation ("Oh, you want juice? Here it is.") or in a shared reading or shared writing.

3. Role playing or practice The learner is given the opportunity to practice the skill without direction or observation by the demonstrator or teacher. This is the critical trial and error period when the learner independently engages in the literacy act and attempts to self-regulate, self-correct, and self-direct his own learning. The competent user or teacher is nearby if needed.

4. Performance   When the learner feels competent, he voluntarily becomes the demonstrator, and the model or teacher becomes the audience. This is the time for the learner to share what has been accomplished—whatever the level of development—and to receive approval and acknowledgment.

Applying the Model in My Life

The model became significant to me when I was learning how to use a word processor. My son Peter, a computer whiz, handed me the Macintosh manual and said, "Mom, anyone can figure out how to operate the Mac by reading the manual." I picked up the manual and tried to pore through it, but I couldn't make sense of it. What may have been clear to someone with a computer background was totally unclear to me. I felt stupid and frustrated. "Peter," I said, "you're going to have to show me." I watched carefully as he demonstrated for me. He sat right next to me and encouraged me to try while he was right there to help me. He slowly took me through the steps I needed to know and showed me over and over again until I had some glimmer of understanding. Probably the most important step was when Peter left the room. Only then could I work out the difficulties and take as much time as I needed. I was embarrassed to have my son see what a slow learner his mother was on the computer. I needed to practice, make mistakes, and get it right on my own, without him looking on. If I got into trouble, I knew Peter was in the next room, and I could call on him. Then, when I felt ready, I proudly called him in to show him what I could do on the word processor. His smile and my pride were big rewards.

Demonstrations need to more than just take place in our teaching. When learning occurs—in any area of the curriculum—the learner engages with the demonstration.

Engagement with Demonstrations

1. Doable by the learner
2. Purposeful for the learner
3. Learner feels safe to take a risk
4. Works best if learner admires the demonstrator
   (Adapted from Cambourne, 1988, pp. 54–55)

Looking at both the developmental model and the conditions for engagement—and applying them to my experience in learning to use a word processing program on the computer—I see that a number of interrelated factors contributed to my success:

1. I had a need for and an interest in learning how to use the computer. I was writing a book while working full time, and I had a publisher's deadline to meet.
2. I had someone I trusted and admired available (but not ever present) to guide me.
3. I had time to practice independently.
4. I was rewarded for my efforts. I was proud of myself; my son was proud of me; I was able to revise my writing more easily and write more efficiently.

Analyzing how I learned to use a word processor made me especially aware that one demonstration is rarely enough. I can remember when I used to think that because I had shown students something once, they should be able to do it. However, most of us need to be shown over and over again, especially in those areas that are difficult for us.

I believe that when students aren't learning, it's because the demonstrations we are giving, or not giving, are not adequate and/or are seen as not meaningful or necessary to the learner. This idea seems especially significant at the secondary level where many students are apathetic or turned off. Students become engaged with teacher demonstrations and begin to take responsibility for their learning only when they have meaningful curricular choices that relate to their interests and their lives.

For some young children, phonics worksheets and workbook pages are not doable even when the teacher explains how to do them. Not doable either is learning a weekly set of spelling words or memorizing long lists of vocabulary words. Whenever we expect students to complete tasks that do not have a meaningful context, we can expect some students to experience great difficulty.

I get very nervous around audiovisual equipment, especially when I am doing a presentation. If the slide projector jams or the microphone doesn't work properly, I am helpless to fix it. I especially worry about the overhead projector malfunctioning because I use many overhead transparencies to support my talks. Recently, just before I was to begin a presentation to a large audience, the audiovisual man came up to me and said, "Sometimes the bulb goes out on this projector, but don't worry, there's a spare. Here's what you do to get it in use." He then proceeded to demonstrate how you slide one lever over, lift another lever up, move something else down, and let the bulb drop into place. When he was on step 2, I was already confused. It was such a simple procedure, but I needed him to show it to me at least two more times. Feeling foolish about needing to be shown again, I was embarrassed to ask him. What went through my mind was that if there was a problem, I would ask someone from the audience to help me. I simply stopped paying attention because replacing the bulb did not seem doable to me, and past experiences with mechanical equipment made me feel insecure about fixing a malfunction myself.

How many students in our classrooms simply stop "tuning in" because they feel the assignments are not doable or relevant to them?

Applying the Model to the Classroom

I believe the conditions that are present for acquiring oral language need to prevail for all literacy instruction across the curriculum. What has particularly impressed me about Holdaway's developmental model is that there is no place in the model for competition, exclusion, criticism, or coercion. The model includes only cooperation, acceptance, approval, and an invitation to join in. Implicit in the model are teachers as real readers and writers; a curriculum and materials that are interesting, meaningful, whole, and relevant to the learners; and a safe, nurturing environment that promotes social interaction and collaboration. "What we're concerned about in whole language is setting up the organizational, intellectual, and social patterns that allow acquisition to occur." (Don Holdaway, address at the annual meeting of the International Reading Association, New Orleans, Louisiana, May 4, 1989).

Cambourne's Model of Literacy Learning

In the 1970s, the Australian researcher Brian Cambourne spent hundreds of hours carefully observing young children who were becoming successful literacy learners. He documented what he saw happening and translated his observations into a set of conditions for learning: immersion, demonstration, expectation, responsibility, use, approximation, response, and engagement. Engagement occurs when the first seven conditions are present. (See Figure 2–1 for an explanation of these conditions; see also Cambourne, 1988.) "Cambourne's conditions," as they are often called, are necessary conditions for all effective language learning. They operate simultaneously in every successful whole language classroom and provide the context for language learning. Cambourne's work helped me understand the importance of engagement with demonstrations.

Goodman's Reading Research

In the mid-1960s, Kenneth Goodman observed first- and third-graders and documented what they did in the process of reading. He noted, among other things, that when the children were asked to read a whole story, they could read words in context that they could not read out of context; they expected print to make sense, and they attempted to read for meaning, as evidenced by the approximations and self-corrections they made. Goodman noted the "miscues" readers made as "something unexpected that the reader does in the process of reading," as opposed to "errors" or mistakes.

Goodman's research showed us that it was not necessary to introduce and drill words out of context, teach phonics in isolation, teach reading in a hierarchy of skills to be mastered, or use contrived reading materials. In relation to understanding the reading process, Goodman's work was revolutionary.

My Learning Theory

My Beliefs about Language Learning for Teachers and Students

Based on the work of notable educator-researchers, on my daily classroom experiences working with children and teachers, and on where I am now in my own teaching-learning process, I hold the following beliefs and attitudes. I see these beliefs as necessary for optimal learning for both students and teachers. Once I had these beliefs and attitudes in place, concerns about the skills and activities fell into proper perspective.

I share my beliefs only as a way for you to think about your own beliefs. Each person's learning theory will be somewhat different, based on individual life experiences, observations of students, interactions with colleagues, professional reading, knowledge, and interpretation of the research and understanding of language learning. There is no one correct set of beliefs. My beliefs and attitudes

Figure 2-1   A Schematic Representation of Brian Cambourne's Model of Learning as It Applies to Literacy Learning

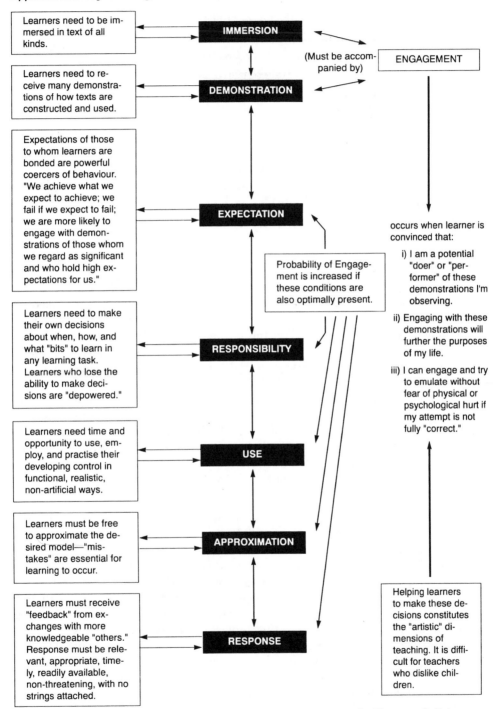

From *The Whole Story: Natural Learning and the Acquisition of Literacy in the Classroom*, by Brian Cambourne, published by Ashton Scholastic Ltd., Auckland, New Zealand, 1988, p. 33. Reproduced with permission.

continue to develop and change, to be integral to all areas of my teaching, and to influence the way I approach children, the curriculum, and learning.

- The developmental level of the learner must be respected.
- All students and teachers can learn.
- Focusing on the strengths must come first when looking at learners.
- We teachers need to demonstrate ourselves as "joyfully literate."
- Learners need many opportunities for "languaging."
- The learning process is highly valued.
- Evaluation is ongoing.
- The goal of education is independence.
- Learning is lifelong and requires thoughtfulness.
- The teacher is a facilitator and colearner.
- Curriculum is negotiated, and learners have choices.
- "Demonstrations" are necessary for learning.
- Sharing is an important part of all learning.
- Sufficient time is needed for optimal learning.
- Collaboration and social interaction foster literacy development.

• *Respect for the developmental level*   I believe that all children enter school at their readiness level and need to be instructed wherever they happen to be in the developmental literacy process. I see this as true for older students, too; we need to instruct them wherever they are in the learning process. When I design a program to fit the student, rather than trying to fit the student into a predesigned program, the student usually learns successfully.

For us teachers, too, respect for the developmental level means welcoming, encouraging, and accepting all teachers—wherever they happen to be in the process of moving toward whole language. I have found that when teachers feel accepted as they are, they are usually open to change. I believe respect for the teacher-learner and student-learner is primary. Our tone of voice, behavior, and attitude must value and kindly regard all learners. The "literacy club" must be open to all, with no special entry requirements.

• *Expectation that learning will occur*   Regardless of the child's language or background of experiences, I believe every child is capable of learning to read and write if he or she is viewed as a learner who possesses fundamental abilities. In two decades of teaching reading, I have *never* worked with a child who failed to learn to read. I expect the child to learn, and I give off that expectation.

Interestingly, when I go into classrooms and do demonstration teaching, I usually don't know the individual children—who are the supposed bright ones and who are the perceived dull ones. Often, following a lesson, teachers will tell me they were surprised by a particular student's participation and comments. This has happened so often that I think the only explanation can be expectation on the part of the teacher. Because I have no prior knowledge of children's abilities, I have the same expectations for them all. The children sense that I expect them to be able to participate, and they do.

Too often we give the message to students and parents that a child cannot learn or that, at best, he will learn at a slow pace. The mother of Onajé, a learning disabled (L.D.) student who became a successful reader, was told by the local Association for Children with Learning Disabilities that "Your son may never learn to read" but not to worry about it because "When he's older he can have access to a secretary and tape recorder." Chapter 1 and L.D. programs, where the usual expectation is for the child to receive services for the entire year (or for a substantial part of his school career), could drastically reduce their numbers if administrators and teachers changed their expectations of what these students can do. One of the powerful messages of Reading Recovery is that the program's high "recovery" rates document that children's learning can be greatly accelerated when we expect it to happen. Just as important, Reading Recovery demonstrates that expectations about "remedial" learners can change.

As teachers, we also need to have high expectations for ourselves as learners. I once heard a well-known publisher say he believed that only 30 percent of teachers were capable of becoming whole language teachers, that the rest of us weren't smart enough. I've thought about that statement for a number of years, and after working with many teachers, I'm convinced he's wrong. It's my opinion that becoming a whole language teacher has as much to do with openness and flexibility as it has to do with intelligence.

• *Focus on the strengths*   One of the hardest shifts for teachers is to focus on the strengths. I think it's almost a cultural phenomenon that we notice what's wrong before we see what's right. When I was visiting schools in Australia several years ago, I hung onto an empty potato chip bag for two days before I decided where to discard it. On the back of the bag was printed, "Please dispose of this thoughtfully." Here we say, "Don't litter." The positive wording, "Please dispose of this thoughtfully," played over and over again in my head and encouraged me to act in a responsible manner.

As a Reading Recovery teacher working with at-risk first-graders, I have had to write a diagnostic summary of each child after an initial evaluation. If the only thing the child could do was write his name, then that's how I was taught to begin the narrative. "The child *can* write his first name." Anecdotal records, individual education plans, and reporting to parent forms need to note the child's strengths before noting the weaknesses.

It is not just focusing on the child's strengths that can be difficult. As teachers, we tend to be very critical of ourselves. We are quick to point out all the things we are not doing. We need literally to pat ourselves on the back for what we are doing well. "Are you reading aloud to kids?" Great. "Are you trying to give students some choice?" Wonderful. "Are you thinking about your teaching?" Bravo! "Have you added literature to your program?" Fantastic! So often we are doing important things and not valuing them. We need to notice and value what we are already doing.

Focusing on the strengths also means focusing on the possibilities, appreciating and valuing students' cultures and getting rid of the "Yes, but . . ." mentality that says, "Whole language might work in your school, but we can't do it here because . . . we have too many students in our class, . . . our kids are too diverse, . . . we don't have funds available for books, . . . there's too much content we have 'to cover,' . . . our parents don't cooperate," and on and on. Focusing on the strengths means getting rid of the excuses. With a positive attitude, a group of kids, paper and pencil, and access to a library, teachers probably have enough going for them to be successful.

• *Display of joyfulness*   Don Holdaway has often said that we must display ourselves as joyfully literate readers and writers if we expect our students to become joyfully literate. I have also heard Frank Smith say that it is our responsibility as educators to make school so interesting that students will want to learn. The only way students will choose to read and write beyond the school setting is if they view reading and writing as enjoyable and purposeful.

Recently some visitors to our school commented that while students in their own classes spent time reading books, students at our school seemed joyful about their reading. They spoke of observing one of our young students walking through the front door enthusiastically reading a book. I think this has happened because our teachers are genuinely excited about books.

• *"Languaging" encouraged*   Language learning is an ongoing, social, active process, and students need many opportunities to interact in reading, writing, listening, and speaking with each other. "Languaging" must be purposeful; language is best learned through its use and not its practice. The actual room arrangement— how desks are clustered and where the teacher is—contributes to the languaging that does or does not take place.

It is not only students who need time to talk together. We teachers also need to be encouraged to interact. We have spent so many years working isolated in our own classrooms that it is a new-found experience to have engaging, professional, and social conversations with our colleagues. This really hit home for me after a visit to Australia.

When I returned from New Zealand and Australia several summers ago, a colleague asked me what impressed me most about the schools. When I responded "morning tea," I surprised myself. I had not realized until then what an impact that event had made on me. Morning tea occurs each morning at about 11 A.M. After teaching for two uninterrupted hours, teachers meet for fifteen minutes in a common area where they drink coffee or tea, have a snack, and talk with each other. While the children are outside for a recess, the teachers have a chance to complain about how certain students drove them crazy that morning, what they did last evening, what was on the news. The point is, they socialize, and they enjoy it. I never saw so many smiling teachers as I did in the several schools I visited in Australia. I thought about what would happen if we made time for morning tea in U.S. schools. Most teachers would stay in their classrooms and grade papers. We continue to work in isolation from one another.

• *Process orientation*   Process orientation refers to noticing and valuing what the student (and the teacher) does in the process of reading, writing, listening, and speaking. For us teachers, this means valuing the process as well as the product, because it is in the process that the learning takes place. While the product is still important, emphasis shifts to how the student arrived or is arriving at the final product or goal. It means expecting students to hand in a final copy with all the drafts and revisions attached. It means record keeping that notes a student's strengths, weaknesses, and needs. Process orientation also means not over-emphasizing correctness. For the young child, a totally error-free paper may not be realistic even in a final copy.

Perhaps, most of all, process orientation means not just tolerating predictions and approximations but celebrating those that show evidence of thinking and learning. Students need to be encouraged to approximate and try out words, meanings, spellings, and conventions. Valuing the process means recognizing and trusting students to learn.

Process orientation applies to us teachers in transition, too. We need to value ourselves in the learning process even if we are not "there" yet. Implicit in process orientation is lots of risk taking, which acknowledges that learning happens gradu-ally over time. Teachers moving toward whole language need to feel safe to take risks, try out, and make mistakes.

- *Ongoing evaluation*   I believe that evaluation, not just of students but of our-selves as teachers, needs to be ongoing. Evaluation focuses on the value of what students and teachers are doing and notes growth over time.

In particular, evaluation is reflective. That is, the learners—both the student and the teacher—develop the ability to observe themselves carefully in the teaching-learning process. (See Chap. 13, "Evaluation," for a complete discussion of the topic.)

- *Independence fostered*   I believe in promoting independence by not doing for learners what they can do for themselves. This is part of the notion behind invented spelling, prediction in reading, and expecting students to take responsibility for tasks such as editing their work, choosing their topics, and establishing classroom rules. The goal of education needs to be independence. Learners read meaningful material and use all the systems of language to work through a challenging text. Independence means that learners are able to examine and monitor their own behaviors in the learning process. Traditional education has made students and teachers dependent on texts and other people for solutions and curriculum.

Dana Noble, a ninth grade teacher moving toward whole language, comments, "I particularly enjoy pushing my students towards independence in their writing, 'putting them in the driver's seat,' as Nancie Atwell calls it, in decisions about what their writing should do or accomplish. After a while, they begin to take pride in their new-found independence."

- *Lifelong, thoughtful learning*   I believe whole language teaching is about stu-dents and teachers who can make intelligent choices, think and analyze critically, and choose to go on learning—in all areas of their lives—even when they are not in the classroom or taking formal course work.

A colleague who recently returned from a conference said that *for the first time* she disagreed with some of the points a speaker made. She had been attending conferences for years, taking in everything she heard as "truth." But now she had some knowledge of her own; she had been reading, thinking, and talking to colleagues and making changes in her teaching. She was no longer a passive learner. She had begun to question and analyze. She felt exhilarated at being able to "sift out" what she found to be irrelevant and incorrect for her. We celebrated her new-found "thoughtfulness." Whole language teaching and learning is about becoming an articulate and critical reader, writer, speaker, listener, and thinker. That's not just kid stuff. That's for us teachers too.

• *Teacher as facilitator and colearner*   I moved from teacher-as-director to teacher-as-facilitator several years ago. Only recently, however, did I make the transition to teacher as colearner. I added "colearner" after I was able to give up even more control and share the responsibility for learning and teaching with fellow teachers as well as with students. As a colearner I do more listening and less talking. I am an observer, encourager, participator, and respondent. I am a coach.

• *Negotiation of curriculum: The importance of choice*   For us teachers and students, negotiating the curriculum also means finding our own answers for what should be taught as well as working through problems in our own way. It means deciding what to read and write and being able to make responsible choices and decisions.

While lesson plans and general goals are established and clearly written, I capitalize on the teachable moment and "go with the flow." If something comes up that needs to be taught or an unplanned discussion arises from a topic, plans are altered to fit the needs of the class.

Being able to make choices is an integral part of whole language. Students and teachers must be free to choose their reading books and their writing topics most of the time. In many classrooms, especially where students are in remedial programs or are placed in lower-level tracks, freedom to engage in meaningful literacy acts is still very restricted. Choice implies trust of students and teachers, and this trust does not come easily.

When my own children were at our district high school, there was a required summer reading program. Each summer, students were expected to complete two or three required books that usually comprised about one thousand pages of challenging reading. During the first days of school in the fall, they were tested to be sure they had done the reading. I suggested several times to the English department that they might want to consider having only one required book and letting students choose two others from a list of about a hundred books. I was told, "How will we know if the students have read the books?" It all came down to trust. That required reading hung over my kids all summer like a curse. I could never get them to pick up another book "just for enjoyment" because they felt so bogged down and restricted. Not until after they graduated high school did they become readers—that is, people who choose to read when they have some leisure time.

High school teachers who take the risk of giving students choices express their surprise and delight when they see the results of allowing students—even low-achieving students—to read any book. A group of teachers at our local high school found that when students could choose any book to read independently, nearly all students read and kept a journal with little in-class guidance. They noted that previous assigned reading had never been as successful in getting students to read independently.

Negotiation of the curriculum also means sharing the responsibility for learning with the learners. I no longer feel responsible for providing all the activities or all the questions to go along with a book or unit of study. Students are capable of developing their own questions and projects if enough modeling has been done. Teachers are capable of developing meaningful plans if they have a solid theory and a philosophy of learning.

• *"Demonstrations" taking place*   The word "demonstrations" was coined by philosopher-educator Frank Smith. I have heard him say, "Either you tell the child, 'Great job,' or you say, 'Let me show you how to do that.'" Without a doubt the biggest visible changes in my teaching are reflected in the demonstrations I do— many of them over and over again. I do most of my demonstrations on the overhead projector because it is an easy to use audiovisual machine that helps me grab and sustain the kids' attention.

A fifth grade teacher noted, "I'm not comfortable with modeling. It's real scary for me. But I know that if the kids see me taking risks, they'll begin to take risks too."

I strongly believe that we must go through any process we expect our students to go through and that our students must see us work through the process. One of the biggest differences between elementary and secondary classrooms is in the number of demonstrations taking place. Many high school teachers skip steps 1, 2, and 3 in Holdaway's developmental model and go right to step 4—performance. The assignment is given and the student is expected to do it on her own. The English teacher, or last year's teacher, is supposed already to have taught "that." However, if teachers *in any subject area* expect students to complete an assignment thoughtfully and independently, for example, a research paper, teachers themselves must also be willing to do a research paper and share their own thinking processes, note taking, drafting, revising, preparing final copy, or whatever else they expect of their students.

I demonstrate my mental processes by thinking aloud: I demonstrate I am a writer by writing with and in front of students and teachers and by sharing drafts of my writing. I demonstrate that I am a reader by sharing and discussing books I am reading and by talking through the process I use to figure out unknown words. I demonstrate revision and editing by taking my writing or a student's (with permission) and showing the students what I have done or how to do it. The more complete and relevant my demonstrations, the greater the students' understanding and the more independently they can eventually work.

Demonstrations need not come only from the classroom teacher. Older students can effectively demonstrate for younger ones; students can demonstrate for each other; and teachers can demonstrate for one another.

• *Sharing*   I believe that sharing should be an integral part of every whole language classroom. There may be daily whole class share time where students and teachers set aside time for responding to ideas and concepts expressed in print and oral language. One such time is shared book experience, where the class gathers as a community to read and reread rich literature. There is small-group sharing through reading and writing conferences with peers and with the teacher, book sharing, project sharing, or acting out plays and scenes. Group share time promotes more interesting writing because students hear one another's ideas and writing styles. While the teacher is an important audience, the teacher is only one audience and, very often, not the primary one.

An important part of sharing includes teachers sharing with teachers—by grade levels, across grade levels, throughout the district, across the state and nation. In our school district, teachers from kindergarten through twelfth grade have an opportunity to share in our evening district support group, which meets every six weeks. That has been a stimulating and valuable time for understanding processes and concerns across the grade levels. It also promotes collegiality among teachers who would not ordinarily work together.

In general, I find we teachers need a lot of encouragement to share with our colleagues. We feel self-conscious about spotlighting ourselves, and we assume other teachers already know or do what we do. Yet whole language is possible only when teachers generously share their knowledge and network with each other. It can be too overwhelming to try to work out everything yourself.

• *Valuing time*   For teachers and students, time refers to time for reflection, time for sharing, sustained time for reading and writing, wait time, and time for collaborating.

Whole language does not just happen. It develops slowly over time. I believe we teachers need time for reflective observation of ourselves and our students and for understanding what whole language is all about. We need long chunks of time over vacations and summers to engage in professional reading. Students need frequent and regular time for sustained silent reading, even at the high school level. Students need wait time when reading—time to work out trouble spots and figure out solutions without being interrupted, and they need time to think before responding. Students also need blocks of time for writing. Teachers need the freedom to work out schedules so that meaningful blocks of time can be created, and they need occasional release time during the school day to collaborate with colleagues.

• *Collaboration and social interaction*   Collaboration is closely linked with "languaging" and is one of the greatest benefits of whole language. Becoming a whole language teacher can be a difficult process. The process seems a lot more manageable and possible when ideas of what's working and not working are shared with colleagues and when teachers jointly plan literature and thematic units. Our weekly language arts support groups foster collaboration and sharing (see Chap. 16, "Establishing Support Networks"). Some teachers find that by combining their two classes occasionally they can create a workable opportunity for teacher collaboration. Other teachers find that by getting together after school or during common planning periods collaboration of ideas is possible. With collaboration, students, teachers, administrators, and parents work together. In keeping with the developmental model, competition is absent, and there is a spirit of true cooperation.

Collaboration also means administrators and teachers working together in a democratic fashion, not in a "we-they" manner. In Australia, some principals go back to classroom teaching after five or six years, and they do not consider it a demotion. On the contrary, they seem to welcome the opportunity to work more closely with teachers and students.

I agree with Jerry Harste, who sees collaboration as even more desirable than cooperative learning. He writes, "I discovered what it means to collaborate rather than cooperate. When we cooperate we work towards some mutual goal, but when we collaborate we expect to go out changed in the end, to become a different person" (Watson, Burke, and Harste, 1989, p. 65).

I am a different person than I was years ago when I worked in isolation. Collaborating with teachers and students has changed me and my views of literacy. With genuine collaboration—where there are no fixed rules—there are always surprises and new insights. Collaboration with my colleagues continues to be a joy and a privilege that suppoprts me in finding my own literate voice.

Finding Our Literate Voices

Before I found my own literate voice and could apply my beliefs to teaching, I had to learn to trust myself, allow time for change, and give up some control—all of which I continue to struggle with.

Trusting Ourselves

"First you have to believe in yourself. Then the answers will come as you interact and learn along with your students, your colleagues, the professional books and journals you read, the courses you take, the reflection and self-evaluation in which you engage" (Bird, 1989, p. xi).

I have been in the process of becoming a whole language teacher since the mid-1970s. I continue to question my teaching, read professional articles and books, attend workshops, talk and interact with my colleagues, and try out new ideas. One of the hardest things has been to trust my own intuition, to believe that what I am seeing or doing is valid and appropriate—or to be able to decide that what I am doing is not appropriate and needs to be set aside. I think the reason it is so hard for us teachers to trust our own instincts is that we have had years of pre-conditioning and pre-packaging that gave us the message that the plans and answers are in textbooks and manuals. We bought the notion that people and publishers who did not know us or our students somehow knew more about our students and teaching than we did.

Over time, I have slowly learned that the answers are not in the books. The books and the experts can cause us to reflect and give us new ideas, but they cannot be used as prescriptions. The most highly acclaimed book and the most knowledge-able expert are, at best, useful resources. We teachers have to find our own answers and tailor our lessons to our particular group of children and ourselves. This is no easy task. Most of us have received training and methodology in the courses we have taken as opposed to education that promotes thinking and decision making. Frank Smith stated it well when he said: "Many teachers are trained to be ignorant, to rely on the opinions of experts or 'superiors,' rather than on their own judgment" (1983, p. 5). Indeed, we have been well taught that the answers lie outside of ourselves.

Even as I am writing this passage, I am thinking, "What do Ken Goodman, Don Holdaway, and Jerry Harste say about becoming a whole language teacher?" I have to stop myself from reading their thoughts and summarizing their writings and focus on what I think. After all, I am in the classroom every day working with children and teachers. I spend a lot of time reading and reflecting. I am a knowledgeable practitioner. Still, sometimes it is hard to trust myself.

We have to trust ourselves and value and adjust our own thinking even when the suggestions and ideas come from a highly reputable source. This idea really hit home with me when I was demonstrating a lesson for a colleague. She had asked me to do a writing lesson with her intermediate grade class—"something that will get them motivated because they don't like to write." I had just finished reading Don Graves's book, *Investigate Nonfiction* (1989), which is full of inspiring, practical ideas. I seized on his lesson of having the students write a letter to someone in the school community requesting a change in policy or practice. It seemed like a wonderful idea, and certainly the examples he presented spurred me on without question. Instead of adapting the lesson to fit my particular context, I adopted it exactly as Graves presented it.

What I had failed to take into consideration was this particular group of students. Given the opportunity to talk first about possible people they could write to and concerns they could write about, they used the lesson as a gripe session. Even when it was apparent that the lesson was degenerating and students' comments were clearly out of line, I forged ahead. After all, the idea came from a renowned author. This is not to say that the idea was not an excellent one for another group of children, perhaps even for most children, but for these children it was a disaster. It was only after I read through some of the negative letters that resulted—letters that would have caused an uproar if we had sent them—that I finally let go of the idea. Because I failed to trust myself to adapt an idea to my specific context, I was unable to redirect the lesson.

"First you have to trust yourself."

Allowing Time for Change

I believe that the transition to whole language is at least a five- to ten-year process. When I say that publicly, teachers breathe a sigh of relief and administrators gasp.

I think we need to be honest about exactly how difficult the transition is. So many teachers read about how whole language classrooms are supposed to look and function, and then they worry that they're not measuring up. They wonder what's wrong with them because they are still struggling and full of self-doubts. Let me say it loudly and clearly. I don't know any teachers who are not struggling, and I don't know any teachers who have it "all together." I struggle daily as I work in classrooms with teachers. Some days I even feel like an imposter. When a lesson goes badly, I feel inadequate. However, it is in the struggle that the learning takes place. I may feel better when a lesson goes well, but there's no doubt that I have learned the most from the failures. It is the failures that make me re-examine, change focus, and add a different dimension.

A high school English teacher with fourteen years of experience expressed his uneasiness about moving toward whole language: "It's a lot easier to do things the way I've always done them. I used to know what to expect. My plans were in order, and there were few surprises. Now I sometimes feel inadequate and unsure of what direction I'm going. The whole process is very unsettling, and yet, I know it's right."

It's not easy to struggle, but we need to know it is a normal and important part of the process for us all. Researcher Brian Cambourne has stated:

It seems that any learning associated with creating meaning through any medium typically involves some kind of struggle before the full potential of that medium is under control—art, music and mime, as well as print. Furthermore, there appears to be something genuinely pleasurable derived from the struggle which is experienced in these situations. Remove the struggle and you remove the pleasure. (1988, p. 5)

In my struggle to make literature-group discussion time more meaningful, I believe it has taken me more than ten years to ask the really important questions to go along with the books. Having milked the basal for skills for many years and having been conditioned to listen for right answers, I have found it difficult to use the literature *just* for pleasure and appreciation and to make connections with our lives. It has also been difficult to learn to redirect discussions so that the students—not the teacher—have ownership of the meaning making. This does not mean I was not a good reading teacher before; I was. However, I am a better teacher now because I am guiding students to construct and validate their own meanings.

I think there is another message that needs to come across. I am in and out of classrooms every day, and I have yet to see a "pure" whole language classroom, whatever that may be. I do not see every subject tied together by theme and children's needs, and I have rarely seen a totally integrated program. The totally integrated classroom takes many, many years to achieve. Even then, I'm not sure it is always possible.

I used to feel I didn't measure up because I wasn't integrating everything. Andrea Butler helped me some years ago by reassuring me that I was a whole language teacher. Now I believe that if I am integrating the language processes in meaningful, authentic ways, that's whole language. The ideal integration—across the total curriculum—is still a goal, but I'm not a failure because I'm not there yet.

I am privileged to work daily with a group of public school teachers whom I consider unusually dedicated and talented. Most of us work way beyond contract hours, and we take time to reflect on our teaching. We are all struggling to weave in demands of the curriculum and required objectives along with trying to become whole language teachers. In addition, we are adjusting and juggling schedules for children leaving and entering classrooms throughout the day for various special services. We are dealing with a diverse and challenging population in school and are leading busy private lives and taking care of our families outside of school. We need to give ourselves credit for all that we are doing well and for the growth we are striving for in our teaching. If we are integrating reading, writing, speaking, and listening in a natural, meaningful way—even part of the time—we are whole language teaching.

Teachers, parents, and administrators need to be realistic about how long meaningful change (not just cosmetic change) really takes. There's often an expectation that if a district or school makes a commitment to whole language, everything should be in place in one year. I have never seen that happen. Typically, I notice that teachers feel comfortable adding one new component to their program each year—perhaps shared book experience the first year, journal writing the next year, an independent reading program the following year, shared decision making about rules and curriculum the next year, and integrating spelling after four or five years. The thoughtful, slow change that is occurring may not always be visible, but it is change of the highest order—stemming from a greater understanding of the philosophy and of the literacy model of learning and teaching.

Finally, I believe we need to be kind to ourselves and accept and acknowledge that the kind of deep change we want to make takes time, lots of time. We need to go slowly, let ourselves make mistakes, and, most of all, give ourselves credit for what we are doing well and for the risks we are taking.

Giving Up Control

Giving up some control has been my most difficult transition in becoming a whole language teacher. To gradually move from directing a classroom, where no one speaks without a raised hand and being called upon, to being a colearner in a cooperative environment where students freely express their opinions was unsettling at first. To slowly change from an environment where all comments are directed to the teacher to a more flexible setting where students have some choices and respond to one another, as well as to the teacher, has not happened easily.

Initially, the kids don't really believe we teachers want them to make choices. They have had years of conditioning: in writing for the teacher, in answering to and for the teacher, and in looking for the "right answer" they think the teacher holds and wants from them. To write and think for themselves is a totally new experience for many of them, and at first they do not believe this is really the desired goal. At the secondary level, where quiet classrooms with lecture formats have been the norm for a long time, trying to move to a more democratic setting can initially be unnerving for both teachers and students.

Part of giving up control has been adjusting to a different model—an interactive, collaborative model of teaching and learning instead of the traditional, transmission model which has us teachers as the source of all knowledge. High school teacher Holly Burgess comments, "My big fear was I wouldn't be a real teacher if I wasn't teacher centered and directive. It's so hard to get away from that after being tied to that model for so many years. When I get nervous or apprehensive, I still retreat to structure."

Some teachers fear that giving up control means giving up on discipline, but I do not see that as the case. I see giving up control as referring to giving more ownership and choice to students and trusting students to be responsible. It may take a while, but teachers report being pleased with the results when they begin to let go. High school English teacher Dana Noble comments:

> I conducted a writing workshop based upon the Atwell model and found that a pair of students seemed always to be talking and laughing, generally very excitedly when they should have been writing (as I often reminded them). However, when they completed pieces I found evidence of their positive influence on each other. I had (and still have) trouble giving up control.

Mary Pryor, a second grade teacher, noted that she had changed her procedures for her annual autobiography project. In the past, she had sent home written directions for writing the final page, "About the Author," and students received help from their parents. This year she modeled what an author page looks like and gave the responsibility to the students to do in class. She was delighted with how well the children did. In addition, she had previously done all the final proofreading herself. This year she modeled some proofreading expectations and was pleased to see how much the children were able to do themselves.

Joan Servis, a fourth grade teacher, has her students work in groups to write reports on prairie wildlife to go along with their literature study of *Sarah, Plain and Tall* by Patricia McLachlan. She had always set up the format for the reports, but this year she let the children choose their own formats. She states, "Ninety percent of the students came up with a better format than mine."

I found that when I began to give up some control and became less directive, not only were my professional relationships enriched. Improved relationships extended outside the classroom. For myself, when I finally stopped having all the answers, I became a more effective parent and developed a healthier relationship with my children. Now when a problem is presented I am not so quick to give solutions. Rather, I am more likely to ask, "What do you think?" and then listen to what my family has to say.

Giving up control also includes giving up being controlled by materials. It refers to taking more responsibility for the materials we teachers are using and how we are using them. As long as publishers' programs are determining how and what we teach, the materials—and not the teacher and students—are controlling instruction.

"The Basal Is Not the Enemy"

"Materials in the hands of a teacher who holds a skills model are skills materials. Materials in the hands of a teacher who holds a whole language model are whole language materials."

That highly significant statement was made by Paul Crowley at the annual meeting of the International Reading Association in May 1989. While quality literature and materials are necessary for excellent instruction, the materials we employ are only as strong as our theory of language learning. It is the way we teachers combine theory and practice that determines the effectiveness of our materials.

In some school districts, whole language has erroneously become synonymous with giving up the basal. It has become common to hear teachers say, "We're doing whole language. We're using literature." I recently overheard a teacher say, "I teach reading in the morning. I *do* literature in the afternoon." While this teacher saw herself as a whole language teacher because she was using literature, her statement indicates that her theoretical beliefs have not changed. She still views reading as the basal and skills work—and literature as something "extra," to be done after the reading work is out of the way. She is clearly giving her students the message—whether she states it or not—that reading is getting the skills.

It is not unusual to see classrooms with no basals but where books of literature are read whole class, round-robin style. Seatwork consists of packets of vocabulary words to look up and lots of questions to answer in written form for each chapter. Even though literature is being used, children have few actual choices during reading time. Using literature, reading Big Books, and doing journal writing are not enough. Unless we also know why we are doing what we are doing, the way we do these activities may be no different from the skills-based, fragmented, teacher-directed basals we have set aside. Conversely, it *is* possible to take a basal story and use it meaningfully.

Undoubtedly, we need to examine basals closely and continue to put pressure on publishers to make them better. The teachers' manuals and workbooks need to be used judiciously—if at all. If they are used, attention needs to shift to the enrichment section, with little or no focus on the segmented, required skills. When basals are used, I believe they must be heavily supplemented with authentic books, self-selected reading of all types, and genuine oral and written responses. At the same time, we also need to be looking very carefully at whole language materials—if there is such a thing. Some whole language companies are producing so many materials that it's beginning to be difficult to distinguish them from the basal companies. One company goes so far as to say, "If it's not from _____, it may not be whole language." Teachers need to be knowledgeable enough about language learning to choose how to use all materials appropriately.

Educators need to guard against the common tendency to pit whole language against basal texts and to set up whole language as an orthodoxy. We must take great care not to give the message that there is only one right way to be a whole language teacher. Perhaps, most importantly, we cannot ignore the very practical issue that many teachers do not have the option of giving up the basal textbook. Basals are still mandated by many, indeed probably most, boards of education.

In talking with teachers around the country, I worry that the whole language movement may be promoting exclusiveness. To imply that one can be a whole language teacher only if no basals are used or only if certain specific procedures are followed is dangerous because this places far too much emphasis on materials and methods. When I first gave up basals and workbooks, I spent years as a "basal basher" with minimal tolerance for basal users and publishers. As a literature "purist," I spent a lot of time pointing out the bad features of basal texts. Over the past several years, however, I've come to realize that the basal is not the enemy. The basal text is, at best or worst—like any material—a resource. In the hands of a knowledgeable professional, it can be used holistically and intelligently, particularly if the worksheets are set aside. Becoming a whole language teacher is not conditional on the materials the teacher is using; it is conditional on the teacher's theory of how children learn. It is the literacy model the teacher holds that determines the type of instruction that actually goes on in the classroom.

Whole language is not just about giving up the basal. Rather, it is about having teachers and students decide together what is worth knowing and how to come to know it. It is about setting up a learning environment that is purposeful, authentic, and based on both the children's and teachers' needs and desires to know.

One strength of whole language is that the teacher is a decision maker. To tell teachers they cannot use basals or any other commercial material is as directive as the school district that mandates their use. I don't like being told I must do something in order to gain acceptance. I prefer to look at the evidence and make my own decisions and choices based on careful evaluation, reasoning, and sound judgment. That is, after all, what we are hoping children in our whole language classrooms will be able to do.

Transition to whole language is a very slow process. Most teachers seem to need to hang on to their basals for a while as they gradually move toward a literature and meaning-centered approach. We need to be supportive, accepting, and encouraging of all teachers who are choosing and attempting to move toward whole language. We need to remember that becoming a whole language teacher-learner is a humbling experience; the process is ongoing, probably for life.

Stages in Becoming a Whole Language Teacher

In examining my own behaviors in moving toward whole language, I see myself as going through the following stages:

1. I can't do this. It's too hard, and I don't know enough.
2. Maybe if I find out about it, it's possible.
3. I'll do exactly what the experts say.
4. I'll adapt the experts' work to my own contexts.
5. I trust myself as an observer-teacher-learner-evaluator.

Like many of us, I started off feeling overwhelmed and inadequate, and becoming a whole language teacher seemed out of reach. Part of that feeling stemmed from defensiveness and a reluctance to change. Gradually, because of curiosity and wanting to grow as a teacher, I moved to stage 2, where I took the time to explore—mostly through professional reading and attending conferences. Listening to educators at conferences and interacting with teachers in process made whole language seem like a possibility. At that stage, however, whole language seemed possible only if I could get all the activities in place.

Looking back, I see that initial preoccupation with activities as normal. For myself and others, becoming a whole language teacher seemed so initially overwhelming that we looked to get the materials and activities in place for some comfort and security. One teacher described herself as having spent an exhausting year "scrambling for activities." After a year of attending our district support group—where much time had been spent talking about learning theory—she realized that she had changed her activities while holding on firmly to a traditional philosophy. She excitedly announced her insight at our final spring meeting and said she was now ready to begin to do some professional reading and think about why she was doing what she was doing.

As I continued to attend conferences, read professionally, reflect on my teaching, share ideas of what was working and not working with colleagues, and observe children, I slowly began to feel that meaningful change was possible for me. I came to realize that the process is not about activities and covering curriculum but about ongoing thinking and analysis of educational philosophy and teaching methods.

I have spent the longest time at stage 3. Jerry Harste has called a similar stage "adopting a guru." After I read Donald Graves, I taught the writing process exactly as he wrote about it. When I read Frank Smith, Ken Goodman, Nancie Atwell, Marie Clay, and many other experts, I did not question anything they said; I simply adopted their stances. I did not yet have the confidence or well-developed theory base to take my own stand, and I had not yet become a kidwatcher.

Gradually, after many years of teaching, reflecting, observing, and collaborating, I began to feel confident about my own beliefs about literacy learning. While I am still highly influenced by many great educators, I have begun to adapt what I read to my own learning-teaching contexts. Because I can articulate my own learning theory, I can apply my theory to what I read and observe and make thoughtful decisions about my teaching.

The last stage builds on stage 4 and is where I want to be. It makes me a part of a community of learners that recognizes that for all of us—even the "experts"—beliefs grow and change. I am now as influenced by my fellow teachers as I am by the great educators. Because of my observations and ongoing evaluation of myself and students, I am better able to trust my beliefs and adjust and apply them to new contexts. I recognize that I will always be a learner. I welcome the fact that I will be in the process of "becoming" all the years that I remain a teacher.

Resources

The following resources have been particularly helpful in furthering understanding about whole language and in developing a personal philosophy. They have also proved useful and thought provoking in group discussion. See also "Themed Journals" (pp. 27b–29b) for complete journals devoted to whole language. For a complete listing of recommended resources see *Resources for Teachers* (blue pages in this book and in Routman, 1988).

Braunger, Jane. Fall 1988. "Whole Language Teaching: Support from Instructional and Research Models," *Oregon English. Theme: Whole Language*. Portland: Oregon Council of Teachers of English, pp. 71–75.

   The author, a language arts specialist, summarizes recent research findings supporting a meaningful, integrated model of literacy and offers insights about the effective teaching of reading and writing. An important article for aiding understanding of various models of literacy instruction as well as of how a teacher's theory of literacy learning affects students.

Butler, Andrea. 1987. *Whole Language: A Way of Thinking*. Crystal Lake, IL: Rigby Education. (videotapes)

   This sequential four-part staff development series on whole language is an outstanding aid for understanding the theory behind whole language and applying it to the classroom. In video 1, Andrea Butler explains Brian Cambourne's conditions of learning. Video 2 discusses the application of these conditions to the classroom. Video 3 examines the ten components of a whole language classroom. Video 4 explains and demonstrates shared book experience.

Cambourne, Brian. 1988. *The Whole Story: Natural Learning and the Acquisition of Literacy in the Classroom*. Richmond Hill, Ontario, Canada: Scholastic-TAB Publications Ltd.

   For teachers ready to take the time to understand the theory behind whole language, this text (201 pp.) offers detailed insight into the language learning process. The in-depth discussion of Cambourne's eight conditions of learning is thought provoking and applicable to the classroom.

Edelsky, Carole, Bess Altwerger, and Barbara Flores. 1991. *Whole Language. What's the Difference?* Portsmouth, NH: Heinemann.

   See annotation, p. 6b.

Goodman, Ken. 1986. *What's Whole in Whole Language?* Portsmouth, NH: Heinemann.

> *This excellent, short guide (79 pp.) for teachers and parents explains what whole language is all about. Ways to make language learning easy are given; the learning theory behind whole language teaching is discussed; principles of whole language instruction and learning are listed; implementation objectives and specifics are concisely noted.*

Harste, Jerome C. November 1989. "The Future of Whole Language," *The Elementary School Journal*, pp. 243–249.

> *This is a provocative commentary for thinking and talking about how whole language theory is changing and what the implications are for all areas of the curriculum. Harste suggests criteria for judging the success of the whole language movement in the future. "(1) Did the movement allow us to hear new voices? (2) Did the movement allow us to begin new conversations? (3) Did the movement help us to establish structures whereby those conversations can continue?" (p. 249). Don't miss reading and rereading this article.*

Holdaway, Don. Winter 1989. "The Big Questions Behind Whole Language," *Teachers Networking: The Whole Language Newsletter*. Katonah, NY: Richard C. Owen Publishers.

> *This is a wonderful article for understanding the theory behind whole language. Holdaway explains what is meant by natural language learning, how it operates, and what the implications are for educational practice.*

Holdaway, Don. 1979. *The Foundations of Literacy*. Portsmouth, NH: Heinemann.

> *This classic text (232 pp.) by the originator of shared book experience is a must reading and rereading for anyone wishing to understand the roots and rudiments of whole language. Holdaway gives many examples of how to induce the development of literacy strategies that respect the developmental learning model.*

Newman, Judith. October 1987. "What Is Whole Language Really About?" in *Whole Language Newsletter*. Richmond Hill, Ontario, Canada: Scholastic-TAB Publications Ltd.

> *This one-page statement about whole language gets to the heart of the matter in a succinct and intelligent manner.*

Newman, Judith (ed.). 1985. *Whole Language: Theory in Use:* Portsmouth, NH: Heinemann.

> *Canadian teachers share their experiences for teaching and understanding reading and writing. Particularly useful for increasing theoretical understanding are the articles by Judith Newman: "Insights from Recent Reading and Writing Research and Their Implications for Developing Whole Language Curriculum," "Using Children's Books to Teach Reading," and "What About Reading?"*

Smith, Frank. 1983. *Essays into Literacy*. Portsmouth, NH: Heinemann.

> *This is a book you will want to own or have in your school library. Smith gives us lots to think about concerning how we are teaching reading and writing and how we should be teaching. This is an absolutely terrific book for understanding learning theory and for helping form one's own philosophy of learning and teaching.*

Smith, Frank. 1988. *Joining the Literacy Club*. Portsmouth, NH: Heinemann.

> *Smith's second collection of literacy essays discusses the teacher's role as critical in facilitating all students' entrance into reading and writing clubs. By "literacy club" Smith means the social nature of literacy learning and children's natural desire to be part of the community of learners. This inspiring, thought-provoking reading contains lots of specifics for fostering club membership.*

Watson, Dorothy. November 1989. "Defining and Describing Whole Language." *The Elementary School Journal*, pp. 129–141.

> *Watson describes whole language and includes the content of the classroom and the beliefs whole language teachers support. This article comes as close as you will get to giving a satisfactory working definition of whole language. Excellent for discussion.*

Watson, Dorothy. Fall 1988. "Reflections on Whole Language: Past, Present and Potential," *Oregon English Theme: Whole Language*. Portland: Oregon Council of Teachers of English, pp. 4–8 (available through National Council of Teachers of English in *Oregon English Theme: Whole Language*).

> *Watson, a leader in the whole language movement, traces her history and understanding of whole language giving both personal and national perspective. Excellent source for discussion and perspectives.*

Watson, Dorothy, Carolyn Burke, and Jerome Harste. 1989. *Whole Language: Inquiring Voices*. Richmond Hill, Ontario, Canada: Scholastic-TAB Publications Ltd.

> *See annotation, p. 20b.*

Watson, Dorothy, and Paul Crowley. 1988. "How Can We Implement a Whole-Language Approach?" in Constance Weaver, *Reading Process and Practice: From Socio-Psycholinguistics to Whole Language*. Portsmouth, NH: Heinemann, pp. 232–279.

> *This is a very useful resource for getting a comprehensive picture of what goes on in a whole language classroom. Excellent tie-in of theory and practice.*

Weaver, Constance. 1990. *Understanding Whole Language: From Principles to Practice*. Portsmouth, NH: Heinemann.

> *See annotation, p. 20b.*

3

Components of Whole Language

Sustained silent reading

The purpose of this chapter is to present possibilities and raise awareness of what constitutes a balanced literacy program. Components of a whole language program as organized by the teacher and students are discussed and include:

- Reading aloud
- Writing aloud
- Shared reading
- Shared writing
- Guided reading
- Guided writing
- Independent reading
- Independent writing

This chapter is meant to encourage teachers of all grade levels and subject areas to look at their teaching and think about incorporating and integrating the various components in ways that both suit their purposes and respect a whole language view of teaching and learning. For clarification and organization, the balanced reading and writing programs are delineated. In actuality, however, there is little or no separation between reading and writing. And while literature is viewed as the mainstay of the literacy program, literature is meant to include fiction and nonfiction and to encompass the content areas. Implicit in the various approaches to reading and writing described here are many opportunities for speaking, listening, sharing, and evaluating.

A Balanced Reading Program

A balanced reading program includes the following components:

- Reading aloud
- Shared reading

31

- Guided reading
- Independent reading
- Language opportunities to respond critically and thoughtfully

Each of these components or approaches is part of the ongoing reading program through the grades. While most of them can be integrated into a daily program, there is much room for flexibility. Shared reading, guided reading, and/or independent reading are sometimes missing from the reading program. By discussing these various approaches in depth, options and opportunities may seem possible and desirable. (For an excellent description of the above approaches to reading, especially for kindergarten and grade 1, see Mooney, 1990.)

A Balanced Writing Program

- Writing aloud
- Shared writing
- Guided writing
- Independent writing
- Language opportunities to respond critically and thoughtfully

Each of the above approaches—in natural combination—make up part of the daily writing program. These approaches, which include demonstrations by teachers, offer lots of opportunities for student choice, involvement and response, and teacher guidance. The examples presented are meant to encourage a wide range of possibilities.

A Balanced Reading Program

Reading Aloud

Reading aloud is seen as the single most influential factor in young children's success in learning to read. Additionally, reading aloud improves listening skills, builds vocabulary, aids reading comprehension, and has a positive impact on students' attitudes toward reading. It is the easiest component to incorporate into any language program at any grade level. Reading aloud is cost effective, requires little preparation, and results in few discipline problems. Nonetheless, it is sometimes neglected just because it is so easy and pleasurable. I can remember for years feeling uncomfortable about spending daily time reading aloud—the children and I were enjoying it so much. It took me a long time to accept that one doesn't have to suffer, do hard work, or require written responses for an activity to be worthwhile.

In kindergarten and grade 1, much of what we read aloud may be repeated readings of favorite books and poems. Teachers find when they place the read-alouds in the classroom library, children often choose these books to read. Reading aloud should take place daily at all grade levels, including junior high and high school. With limited time periods at the secondary level, the read-aloud may be a poem, excerpt, or short story used as a read-aloud or shared reading. The read-aloud is completed in just a few minutes at the beginning of the period and helps set the tone for the class. One middle grade teacher begins each afternoon with a poetry read-aloud, with each student being responsible for a week of poetry reading. The teacher has lots of poetry books in the room all year, from the library and classroom collection, and students choose favorite poems and practice reading them before presenting them to the class.

Frank Smith tells us that everything we need to know about reading and writing we can learn from authors. I believe this strongly, along with Nancie Atwell's notion that we have to make students "insiders," able to see the way the author has chosen to put the text together. Reading aloud is a powerful technique for promoting story enjoyment and literature appreciation and for noting what authors do in the writing process so that students can make similar choices for themselves.

Shared Reading

I define shared reading as any rewarding reading situation in which a learner—or group of learners—sees the text, observes an expert (usually the teacher) reading it with fluency and expression, and is invited to read along. The learner is in the role of receiving support, and the teacher-expert accepts and encourages all efforts and approximations the learner (the novice) makes. Each reading situation is a relaxed, social one, with emphasis on enjoyment and appreciation of the stories, songs, rhymes, chants, raps, and poems. The literature is carefully chosen for its high quality of language and illustrations and often includes rereadings of favorite stories and poems. Following shared reading, students have opportunities to reread the literature independently. When enlarged texts are used, little books of the same title are always available.

While shared reading has traditionally been associated with beginning reading in the primary grades and the use of delightful stories, poems, and songs in enlarged print (especially predictable Big Books with rhyme, rhythm, and repetition), shared reading is appropriate and desirable for children of *all* grades, even through high school. Some secondary foreign language teachers have successfully used Big Books and shared reading as a way to reinforce language and add motivation and interest. Second language learners (ESL students) pick up rhymes and sight vocabulary and develop reading fluency from nursery rhymes and predictable books with repetitive patterns. In addition to enlarged print in Big Books and on charts, regular-size print can be made visible to all students by using transparencies of several prechosen pages on the overhead projector. As in all shared reading experiences, the emphasis is on enjoying and appreciating the text.

Shared reading is one way of immersing students in rich, literary-level language without worrying about grade level or reading performance. For young children who have had limited exposure to the language of storybooks, shared reading and discussion of stories provide a framework for literature and language. For reluctant and struggling readers of all ages, shared reading offers a nonthreatening approach to reading that strengthens skills and enjoyment. High-frequency words and the conventions of print, seen over and over again, are learned naturally without boring drill. Poems that are reread for pleasure provide a way for students to build reading fluency and confidence as well as develop an appreciation of poetry.

A variation on the technique of shared reading that works well is to introduce nursery rhymes or poetry orally first. Once students become accustomed to hearing the language, reading the text visually follows easily and naturally. Listening to the language first works well for beginning readers as well as for older, reluctant readers.

Shared book approaches may include:

1. Teacher reading
2. Student reading
3. Paired reading
4. Tape recorder

Teacher Reading

In a shared reading experience, the teacher gathers the students together—often on the floor in front of her—and invites students to read along with their eyes or aloud with the teacher. Some of us have a designated carpeted area; others ask students to move desks to create such an area. A rug can be rolled out or individual carpet squares can be used; even the plain wooden or linoleum floor will work. Students sit together in a relaxed, informal manner. An engaging Big Book, a chart poem, an overhead transparency, or a copy of the selection or book is available for each student to hold or see, and students join in on an invitational basis. With older students, where shared reading is likely to occur with the use of the overhead projector or individual copies of the text, shared reading works fine with students seated at their desks. Usually the selection is read first by the teacher. On the next reading—or even on the first reading—many students will attempt to participate orally or will follow the text with their eyes. In kindergarten and grade 1 especially, to promote one-to-one matching and letter-sound links, the teacher points to each word at the same time the word is spoken.

The introduction of a book is always carefully done to invite predictions and excite the imagination. Before reading, the teacher will point to the title and author, front and back covers, book jacket, and table of contents and ask the children what they think the book will be about. The teacher may go through the pictures and ask children to predict what is going to happen. Some typical questions might be: "What do you think the focus of the book might be?" "What do you think the author is trying to tell us about . . . ?" All responses are valued and accepted. This is a time for encouraging oral language and having children listen to one another. Enough wait time is given for children to formulate their responses. Guided questioning continues throughout the story to maintain student attention, involvement, and participation. Typical questions are: "What do you think will happen next?" "What might _____ do to solve the problem?"

Shared reading is an effective way to vary the daily read-aloud book or assigned silent reading. Instead of reading an entire chapter from a book, the teacher may combine reading aloud with shared reading and/or silent reading. Or the teacher might begin a chapter with several pages of overhead transparencies (that have been made by reproducing the text). The children see the print and are invited to read along, silently with their eyes or aloud. Cloze procedures (explained on p. 141), where the teacher pauses and invites students to fill in the words orally, may also be used as long as the emphasis is on group enjoyment and participation. The chapter might then be completed by having students read aloud or silently or by combining these approaches.

Shared book experience is always a joyous time, with each child treated as a reader with no pressure to perform. We welcome children's predictions and interpretations. A sense of community builds as teacher and students share favorite literature. It is important to keep this time just for reading, responding, and sharing. Shared reading is never the time to go over assignments or seatwork.

Student Reading

A student may volunteer or be selected by the teacher to do a shared reading. Poetry works particularly well here. A student has practiced a poem of choice over and over until he feels he can read it smoothly and with expression. Copies of the poem are distributed, or the poem is put on the overhead projector, and the rest of the class follows along visually and joins in.

In Linda Powers' second grade class, students lead the daily shared poetry sessions. Usually two or three poems are read in about five to seven minutes. While the sessions begin early in the school year, with the teacher reading the poems on the overhead projector while moving a line marker down the page, our students happily take over the job after several weeks. Putting students in charge creates ongoing enthusiasm for reading poetry in the classroom. Students are always on the lookout for favorite, new poems to add to the classroom collection. The classroom notebook, where the poems are kept, is also available for student reading throughout the day. Adding new poems to the notebook—as well as locating old favorites—has also been a natural way to teach alphabetizing.

Paired Reading

Shared reading may also be paired reading, with one person reading and another following along. This technique is a powerful one for supporting less able readers. Usually a more competent reader is paired with a less competent one. For example, a teacher might read with one student or a student might read with another student. The more able reader (the expert) reads the text aloud while the less able reader (the novice) follows along. The less able reader, with no pressure or expectation to read, follows the text visually and enjoys the story.

Some of us are beginning to use this technique regularly as a way to promote heterogeneous grouping and give all students access to literature. The student who is unable to read all the words of the text independently can now join a reading-group discussion of a book that he is able to comprehend orally but may not be able to read silently. Paired reading can take place with students in the same class or with an older student reading with a younger one (see pp. 477–478).

Paired reading is also an enjoyable way for two students to complete a reading assignment or share a story. The students might go into the hall or to a designated spot and take turns reading: One reads and the other follows along, with the students supporting each other as necessary.

Tape Recorder

Many of our primary grade classrooms use cassette tapes to accompany favorite picture books. At listening posts, students follow along visually with the commercial or teacher-volunteer–made recordings. While the focus is on reading for pleasure, repeated listening and rereading of favorite stories aids fluency, development of sight word vocabulary, and story comprehension. The tape recorder is also a powerful and nonthreatening tool for struggling middle grade or older students. By having a volunteer tape book chapters, students can follow the text at their own pace to get phrasing, fluency, and meaning.

Some teachers find time to tape a single page of a text for a poor reader. Especially if the child is already familiar with the text, listening, looking, and following along without pressure builds fluency as well as self-esteem. Often, voluntarily rereading a page the student already comprehends helps the individual to become a better reader.

Reading that students cannot accomplish silently on their own may be accomplished with the support of a tape. Students may be encouraged to follow along a short section repeatedly and then be prepared to read the section orally the next day in reading group. Hearing themselves able to read more fluently is a tremendous confidence booster for students.

Strategies for Shared Reading

Shared reading leads quite naturally into innovations on books, dramatic or musical interpretations, and meaningful literature extensions that often utilize the visual arts and relate meaningfully to the text. Shared reading is also a natural way to teach skills and specific features of print. However, caution is necessary. In all cases, the text should be read and reread several times purely for enjoyment. We have observed that students request to read and love to reread favorite stories. Then, on the third, fourth, or fifth reading some teaching strategies can be utilized. Andrea Butler recommends making not more than one or two teaching points in a shared reading session. On a first reading, I often do not even use the pointer. I might slide my finger or the pointer along loosely, but at this time I am not concerned about one-to-one matching and specific words. I simply want to share a piece of literature I love and have the children savor the language, imagery, and story.

On subsequent occasions, I might do some work with specific features of the text. Repeated exposure of students to rhyming words in books and poems—with occasional use of an oral cloze procedure—makes the use of isolated rhyming worksheets unnecessary. Sometimes, I pause when I get to a particular word or phrase and let the children fill in the expected language. Some teachers use Post-it™ notes to mask (block out) high-frequency words or conventions of text so that children fill in the missing text.

Shared reading is also an excellent time to help children discover features of text—letters, phonemes, punctuation, and high-frequency words as well as do innovations on text. I use a sliding mask (see Appendix E) to highlight features of the text and naturally blend word parts in context. Specific procedures, rationales, and many examples of using Big Books and shared language experiences are provided in depth in *The Foundations of Literacy* by Don Holdaway (1979, pp. 64–80 and 126–146). (For procedures and ideas for shared reading for older children, see Adrian Peetoom, *Shared Reading: Safe Risks with Whole Books* [Richmond Hill, Ontario, Canada: Scholastic-TAB Publications, 1986, 32 pp.])

Figure 3-1   Creating Songs for a Shared Reading Experience

Tune: "Oh, the Preacher Went Down to the Cellar to Pray"
Lyrics: Joan Di Dio

The second graders went down (echo)
To the classroom to read (echo)
They picked out their WEB books
And were HAPPY indeed!
  (We're gonna read and read . . . and read some <u>more</u>!)

} Repeat, higher

Now, Amelia Bedelia (echo)
Is one of the friends (echo)
We meet in our reading
So the fun never ends!
  (We're gonna read and read . . . and <u>read</u> some more!)

} Repeat, higher

We're reading Beverly Cleary (echo)
Who can't be beat!
And then, of course,
There's the great Bill Peet!
  (We're gonna read and read . . . and <u>read</u> some more!)

} Repeat, higher

Now, the <u>Little's</u> series
Is so much fun!
Their world is so tiny
But they get things done!
  (We're gonna read and read . . . and <u>read</u> some more!)

} Repeat, higher

We're gonna read <u>some</u> WEB books fast
We're gonna read <u>some</u> WEB books slow
But they're ALL gonna help us grow.

Don't forget the <u>JOURNALS</u>!

Oh, we write in our Journals (echo)
Almost every day
"Cause a second grader
Has SO MUCH to say!

} Repeat, higher

Refrain:
    Yes, we write in our Journals
    About how we feel.
    Sometimes it's "made-up"
    And sometimes it's real!
    We're WRITERS, now
    In second grade!

A Specific Example: Reading a Poem

I like to use the overhead projector and an oral cloze procedure with favorite poems from my childhood or favorite poems the children choose. Using two 5 by 7 inch index cards, I employ the bottom card to cover the text completely and move down the page one line at a time; I use the top card to expose the text gradually, word by word, as the card moves to the right across each line. With rhyming words, we need show only the beginning consonant, digraph, or blend for students to complete the rhyming couplet. An example of an old favorite is the following:

> I had a nickel and I walked around the block.
> I walked right into a baker shop.
> I took two doughnuts right out of the grease;
> I handed the lady my five-cent piece.
> She looked at the nickel and she looked at me,
> And said, "This money's no good to me.
> There's a hole in the nickel, and it goes right through"
> Says I, "There's a hole in the doughnut, too."
> (From *A Rocket in My Pocket*, Holt, 1988)

Despite the fact that my grown children have warned me not to sing in public, I sing everything that has a tune to it or that the music teacher will set to music. Children love to sing, and following the words along on the overhead, in the text, or on individual printed sheets makes the reading/singing fun and easy. One primary teacher used the daily literature as a springboard for a song that became a class hit (see Figure 3–1). For older, reluctant readers, favorite songs and raps with acceptable lyrics can be used for a shared reading experience. Children enjoy adding their own sound effects and dramatic movements to the songs.

Guided Reading

> In guided reading the teacher and a group of children, or sometimes an individual child, talk and think and question their way through a book of which they each have a copy. The teacher shows the children what questions to ask of themselves as readers, and of the author through the text, so that each child can discover the author's meaning on the first reading. Guided reading is dependent on the teacher being aware of each child's competencies, interests, and experiences; being able to determine the supports and challenges offered by a book; and accepting the role of supporting learning rather than directing learning (Mooney, 1990, p. 11).

Guided reading is the heart of the instructional reading program. Here we meet with students to think critically about a book. Selections that have been assigned for silent reading are discussed, with the children responding to the text in open-ended and personal ways. Most of the time with the group is spent in discussion, in appreciating and enjoying the language of literature, and in sharing personal and group insights. Often there is oral reading, but not round-robin reading with emphasis on getting the words right. This is oral reading for pleasure, for emphasizing particular descriptive passages or settings, for backing up a statement in discussion, and for noting strategies that children are employing. Even at the secondary level, students request and seem to need to read aloud. There will be teachable moments—for example, stopping to examine a concept or a feature of the text—and specific teaching for strategies as the need arises. During this time, vocabulary, as it relates to the text and children's lives, is discussed in the context of the book. Relating a book to children's lives, to other books, and to other authors are worthwhile connections the teacher guides. (See Chap. 6, "Responding to Literature," for detailed information on literature response logs, asking important questions, literature discussion groups, and various responses to literature.) While guided reading as discussed here refers to literature in the reading program, guided reading also needs to extend to texts and informational books across the curriculum.

While I believe strongly that small groups should be heterogeneous (see Chap. 4, "Grouping for Success: Taking a Close Look at Ability Grouping") and grouped according to interests and not abilities, for me the exception is first grade, especially early in the school year. To try to meet all students' needs, I find that small groups based according to ability that meet for fifteen to twenty minutes a day to develop specific strategies and reading fluency are appropriate. For the teacher it can be extremely frustrating to have small-group, literature sessions that include students who do not yet have one-to-one matching (of spoken word to printed word) along with students who are already reading or on the verge of reading. Even in first grade, however, the majority of reading time is heterogeneous, whole-class shared reading. And, once children are reading fluently and have moved to independent silent reading, most of the small-group reading time can be spent on discussion, and mixed ability groups are desirable. This can happen toward the end of the school year.

Although there may be some short-term ability grouping in first grade, all books in the classroom reading center or library are available for all students to choose to read independently. Additionally, it is always advantageous to invite small groups of interested children to "read" and enjoy a book together.

I see guided reading in kindergarten as being invitational and an opportunity to explore books and print. Students who have enjoyed a shared reading of a Big Book may choose to "read" it with the teacher or with the teacher and a small group.

Whole-Class Guided Reading

In whole-class guided reading, all students read and discuss the same book at the same time. Each student has a personal copy of the book, and the teacher guides the literature discussion. While this is often a transitional stage for many teachers, there are benefits in whole-class reading.

I have observed that as teachers have moved into literature and away from the basal text, whole-class reading seems to be the norm. Most of us initially feel overwhelmed at the thought of reading all the new titles, planning activities without the aid of a teacher's manual, and managing three reading groups and the accompanying independent work assignments. Whole-class reading makes reading instruction time manageable. At times, and in moderation, whole-class reading is an excellent way to get to know the children, observe strategies and attitudes, and build a reading community. I have always liked starting off the year with each student having a copy of the same book. It is an opportunity for me to model good questioning techniques, encourage open-ended responses, observe the students' reading abilities and attitudes, and promote the enjoyment of the literature in a relaxed, congenial setting.

In time, however, I believe there should be opportunities for small groups to meet so that all of the children's voices are heard. I have found it impossible to have an entire class of twenty-five children involved in a discussion. The same seven or eight children tend to dominate, and you never get to know all of the children as readers. The only way to involve all children in meaningful discussion and to observe the strategies they are using is to meet in small groups of about six to nine students or to meet with individual children.

In my own district, the first year we moved into literature-based reading I was surprised to find most teachers doing whole-class reading most of the time. It took me a while to understand the dynamics. It was not that teachers were taking the easy way out—far from it. They were working harder than ever. Teachers simply did not yet have the confidence, the management techniques, and all the activities they felt they needed to break into small groups. Reading and teaching just one book without the aid of a detailed teacher's manual was initially very time consuming and emotionally demanding. It was the working together in the buildings—in our weekly support groups and with each other—that gradually encouraged most teachers to move into small, guided reading groups. The impetus for change also came from the frustration teachers had experienced when it came time to write report cards as they found they could not give specifics about individual students' reading.

For most of us, the transition to two, three, or four guided reading groups has taken at least several years. This is important to keep in mind because it would be easy to just look on the surface and judge ongoing whole-class reading as a lack of effort on the part of teachers. In rare cases this may be true. However, for almost all teachers I have worked with, whole-class guided reading is the beginning of the transition from the basal to literature.

Even with whole-class reading, the format may be varied. A reading period may begin with the teacher reading aloud while students follow along visually in their own copies. The teacher can take this opportunity to "think aloud" and make thought processes and strategies visible to students. For example, the teacher can think aloud about how the meaning of a word is inferred from text and background experiences. Students may then be asked to read some pages silently for a specific purpose. A page of text can also be put onto a transparency and placed on the overhead projector. Part of the page may be read as a shared reading and part may be read silently. Students may be asked to read to answer a specific question or to note the author's purpose. Students who read quickly and finish early may be told, "Find the line that tells us . . . " or "Find the sentence that lets us know . . . ." The transparency may also be used with a sliding mask (Appendix E) to note specific vocabulary or do word analysis. Within whole-class reading and discussion there may also be paired reading or individual silent reading of text, followed by whole-class discussion.

Small-Group Guided Reading

In the small-group guided reading session, most of the time is devoted to high-level discussion, with the teacher and students reacting to all or part of a book. (This topic is discussed in detail in Chap. 5, "Responding to Literature: Early Transitions" and Chap. 6, "Responding to Literature: Later Transitions.") In first grade, the guided reading lesson is geared mostly to developing fluency, confidence, and early reading strategies and to promoting independence. In secondary classes, guided reading allows all students to develop insights into theme, style, divergent opinions, higher-order thinking, and various forms of literature.

Guided reading groups may also be the place to do direct and indirect teaching of vocabulary, phonics, and word-attack skills. As the need arises, we develop strategy lessons for particular skills. Many of these lessons will occur on the spot. Small-group guided reading sessions are also used with struggling readers to teach and reinforce strategies. For example, students who are successfully contributing to a heterogeneous discussion group because they have received support reading the text (usually through a paired reading) may be called together at another time during the day to practice reading portions of the text and receive guided reading at their instructional level. (See "Teaching for Strategies," pp. 138–144, for specific examples of small-group strategy lessons.)

Individualized Guided Reading

Some teachers are very successful in combining an individualized reading program with whole-class shared reading experiences. The program is individualized in that students self-select fiction and nonfiction books, self-pace their reading and performance, and conference with the teacher. In place of small-group instruction with the same book that the teacher may have selected, in an individualized guided reading program the teacher either meets individually with students or guides small-group discussions with students who share reactions to different books they have read or are reading. In conferencing one-to-one, the teacher may ask the child to do some oral reading, retell a story, or answer some questions to assess comprehension. On-the-spot teaching of needed strategies will take place. (See David Hornsby, Deborah Sukarna, and Jo-Ann Parry, *Read On: A Conference Approach to Reading*, [Portsmouth, NH: Heinemann, 1988] for suggestions and procedures.)

While an individualized reading program is terrific for placing important emphasis on self-selected reading and children's interests, my personal bias is that small-group guided reading—discussing the same book—is necessary to reach the high level of critical thinking and interaction that can evolve only from in-depth discussion of a book that a group of students are reading or have read. And without teacher guidance and encouragement, some worthwhile books might never be picked up and come to be appreciated by the students on their own. Additionally, a totally individualized approach can be difficult to manage. Finding the time to meet regularly and in depth with every student can be a real challenge to any teacher.

Depending on a particular group of students and their needs, the combination of approaches will vary. There is no one right way or best way. As long as your reading program is balanced, with a variety of reading-writing-listening-speaking possibilities that include guidance, choice, and response, there are many options.

Independent Reading

Opportunities for students to read self-selected books is an indispensable part of a balanced reading program. In independent reading students are in charge of their own reading—by choosing their own books, by doing their own reading, and by taking responsibility to work through the challenges of the text. "The teacher's role changes from one of initiating, modeling, and guiding to one of providing and then observing, acknowledging, and responding" (Mooney, 1990, pp. 72–73).

The importance of voluntary reading cannot be overstated. In a study of fifth-graders' activities outside school, it was found that "time spent reading books was the best predictor of a child's growth as a reader from the second to the fifth grade" (Richard C. Anderson, Paul T. Wilson, and Linda G. Fielding, "Growth in Reading and How Children Spend Their Time Outside of School," *Reading Research Quarterly*, Summer 1988, p. 297).

Since there is no question that reading achievement is positively influenced by the amount of time spent reading books, we must provide time in school—even at the secondary level—for students to read books of their own choosing. According to the research study just cited, even ten minutes a day of independent reading can increase reading proficiency.

Providing a wide selection of all types of fiction and nonfiction books through school and classroom libraries is essential. Our available books include both familiar books and new titles and are representative of children's interests and reading abilities. Books are changed and added to as needed to promote high interest and meet the demands of the curriculum. Guiding students to select books and gain familiarity with authors is necessary, especially at the start. When I bring lots of books into the classroom library, I take time to do brief "book talks." I tell just enough about the book to whet students' appetites and give them some guidance in self-selection. Even when I have not read the book, by looking at the synopsis of the book on the jacket flaps or back cover, I can give some useful information. For introducing students to books, having students "sell" their favorite books to classmates also works well.

Setting aside time for reading, with us teachers as reading models, must be a priority in all classrooms. For some students, school is the only place where quiet reading time and the possibility of developing the reading habit is conceivable. Outside of school, video games, video cassette recorders, movies, music, telephone calls, and television often preempt what could be time for reading.

In some classrooms, individualized reading of self-selected books may be the mainstay of the reading program. In others, it is a small but vital part of the total reading program—often taking place after lunch or at the end of the day, when students and teachers find pleasure in a favorite book. While quiet is desirable for voluntary reading time, silence is not necessary unless the teacher and students prefer it. Young children—for example, kindergartners—enjoy reading a book together, talking about a book, or dramatizing a story during their voluntary reading time. Some teachers call this sustained shared reading time.

Many teachers find it works well to begin with five to ten minutes a day of SSR (sustained silent reading), RR (recreational reading), DIRT (daily independent reading time), DEAR (drop everything and read), or whatever the teacher chooses to call this time. Then, depending on the ages of the students, in-class time when the teacher and students read quietly can last up to twenty to thirty minutes or more daily.

Quiet reading time of self-selected books is also a desirable and appropriate alternative to workbooks and skills sheets. We no longer need to feel guilty that students are "just reading." Reading is probably the most worthwhile activity students can be doing. As a part of independent work time, many teachers now encourage and expect students to read.

WEB Reading: A Home-School Independent Reading Program

In addition to daily time set aside for in-class reading, we also expect students to read voluntarily outside of school. Until children can read independently, the expectation is for parents to read to and with their children. What we call WEB (*Wonderfully Exciting Books*) reading is part of our balanced reading program. WEB helps create a community of readers. Students recommend books to each other and share book information and responses in daily interactions and interviews. Most of our students seem to get "hooked" on reading through daily expectations for independent reading. Our goal is for books to become a relevant and pleasurable part of every child's life.

With a voluntary reading program, it is important not to stress the number of books read because books vary in length and difficulty. However, when beginning WEB for the first time, some teachers like to keep a tally of the books each student reads. When a student reads ten books or a multiple of ten, a special incentive may be added as a motivation to continue to read. Eventually, the reward for reading should simply be enjoyment of the book itself.

Selecting Books

Students select books from multiple sources: the classroom library, the school library, the public library, the home, the bookstore, a friend, or any other available source. Finding out what children are interested in, helping them choose books at library time, and introducing them to books by an appealing author may help them with the selection process. Students are encouraged to select any book they like, and affirming their selections creates a climate of encouragement and trust. "Book talks" or sharing a Big Book, with little books available, greatly increases the choices for many young readers. Besides the teachers' introduction of books, students are also motivated by their peers to read books they might never have selected on their own. Some teachers note that about half the books students choose to read have been recommended by other students.

While students are free to choose what they like, they are also guided to read a wide variety of literature and to choose books at their independent reading level. Independent level means that students recognize 95 percent of the words used in a selection and comprehend 90 percent of the content. This is the easy reading level, where students read without teacher or parent help. Reading lots of books at this level promotes comprehension, vocabulary development, fluency, and overall reading facility.

Some students will choose books that go beyond their independent level— because they heard the story and loved it, because a friend read it, or just because they want to try it. I no longer tell a child, "This book is too hard for you." I may jot a note to the parent saying that the child will need help reading the book or will need to have it read aloud, and I may suggest to the child that he read it with a parent or sibling. Children often surprise us. A book that seems too hard may sometimes be read by the child if motivation and engagement are high enough.

At the same time, when children consistently read books that are too hard for them, they will not be able to tell much about the book. These students need to learn how to select appropriate books for themselves. Learning how to do that may first mean choosing some difficult, inappropriate books. Though we need to offer guidance, we also need to let students go through the selection process—and make mistakes—so they can learn to choose appropriately for themselves.

In selecting books, it is common, and beneficial for young students to choose to reread a favorite story. Not only do young children enjoy rereading stories; they actually have a need to do so. Rereading a story aids fluency, comprehension, and familiarity with the language and structure of the story. Older children, like adults, occasionally like to reread a book, and they should be allowed to do so.

At times, students will need to be encouraged to raise the quality of their reading. However, like adult readers, they must be allowed to read light, unsubstantial material for a time if that is what interests them. Above all, we want them to choose to read.

The parents of a group of third grade girls "hooked" for months on dime store novels became exasperated by the poor quality of the books their daughters were reading. In their desire to lead their children to some notable authors, the mothers finally asked the teacher, "What are some authors you would recommend?" The teacher sent home a list of authors such as Roald Dahl, Judy Blume, and Beverly Cleary with a list of the books they had written. The parents' involvement eventually led the students to respected authors.

WEB Procedures

Students are expected to read twenty to thirty minutes each evening, to be responsible for bringing their books to and from school daily, keeping a record of their daily reading (as soon as they are able) and of books completed, and being prepared to be interviewed while reading and/or upon completing each book.

Parent involvement is an integral component for a successful WEB program. A letter is sent to parents at the start of the school year (later, for first grade) explaining WEB reading and inviting parents' cooperation (see Appendix J3). When necessary, parents are asked to become involved to encourage students to take more responsibility for completing independent reading. In addition, our principal lets teachers, parents, and students know that daily WEB reading is a school expectation for all students.

In the early grades, WEB reading is a significant part of children's learning to read successfully. Many of the books children choose will come from the classroom library and will be books heard and read during shared book experience. In addition to pleasurable reading, daily practice on familiar books builds sight vocabulary, fluency, and confidence. (For more information on WEB reading in the primary grades, see Routman, 1988).

In the intermediate grades, on the first day of school or in early fall the children are introduced to the daily routine of logging in their self-selected independent reading. In Joan Servis' fourth grade class, WEB takes place for approximately the first twenty minutes of each morning throughout the school year. The students enter the room, hang up coats, unpack book bags, and open their literature response logs. They use the last section of the log to record their daily book reading.

Figure 3-2   Sample of a Daily Record of a Fourth-grader

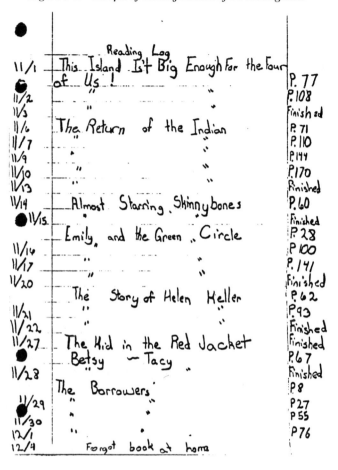

A separate recording log or folder could also work well. Students write down the date, name of the current book, and page number where they stopped reading at home (see Figure 3–2 for a typical student's record). If they have completed the book, they write "finished" and sign up on the chalkboard for an oral interview by the teacher or a peer who has also read the book. Students then read silently or select a new book from the classroom book spinner or school library. (The latter works if the school librarian has some available time when students can come to the library for book selection.)

Monitoring independent reading   Teachers try to make time to check WEB reading daily or at least several times weekly. In the early grades this means meeting with students one-to-one, listening to them read, and/or checking comprehension. As students get older and more fluent, the daily check may be only a quick look to see that they are keeping track of their daily reading in their logs. Often this check is done first thing in the morning while students are settling in and doing independent reading or at the end of the day or class period.

Fourth grade teacher Joan Servis uses an interview process to check understanding and appreciation of the book read. The interview follows a demonstrated format (see Figure 3–3). Each child has a copy of the WEB format in a separate WEB pocket folder (which also holds books completed each month). At the beginning of the school year, the teacher demonstrates, whole class, how to interview a student about a completed book. After several demonstrations, the teacher encourages several students to demonstrate peer interviews. When the class seems familiar with the process, all students may volunteer to interview independently during WEB time.

After successfully completing an interview, the student puts a check after her name on the board and records the book title on a monthly book list in her WEB folder (see Figure 3–4 for a typical monthly list). This list of completed books, collected monthly, is very helpful in evaluation of students' progress. The teacher can see at a glance the amount of reading a student has done, the level of difficulty of the books read, the genre of the books, and whether a student needs help in selecting books. Students also look at their book lists to note the authors and types of books they are reading. In addition to keeping a record of books read, some students and teachers keep a list of "Books I Want to Read."

Monitoring independent reading in reading group   Some teachers prefer to do the WEB check as part of the guided reading group. This is time well spent. While one student is briefly talking about a book, others are listening. In this way, many students have learned about—and been influenced to read—books they would not otherwise know about.

Students come to group with their WEB books. The teacher does a quick check and writes on the student's record card what page she is on. Some teachers keep a file box (with a 4 by 6 inch card for each student) at the reading table. If there has been a problem or a particular observation, it is briefly noted on the card. For example, the teacher might suggest the student reread a section for better under-

Figure 3-3   WEB Interview (Created by Joan and Jim Servis)

FICTION

1. Name of book
2. Name of author
3. Illustrator's name (show examples of work)
4. Why do you think you picked this book?
5. Describe the setting
6. Tell about the problem, but don't give away the secret of how it was solved!
7. Would you recommend this book? Why or why not?

NONFICTION

1. Name of book
2. Name of illustrator or photographer
3. What is the book about?
4. What did you learn?
5. Would you recommend this book? Why or why not?

Figure 3-4   A Monthly Record of a Fourth-grader

Dina   September

1. The Diamond Champs - Matt Christopher
2. Thank You Jackie Robinson - Barbra Cohen
3. Song of the Trees - Mildred Taylor
4. The Dog that Stole Football Plays - Matt Christopher
5. Johny No Hit - Matt Christopher
6. How to Fight a Girl - John Robbins
7. Four in the Family - Enid Blyton
8. The Great Quarterback Switch - Matt Christopher

standing. Or if the student isn't enjoying a book, a new one may be selected. If a new book is being signed out, the title is noted. With the occasional student who continually chooses another book, an interview may be necessary to determine the student's interests and concerns and to give guidance in book selection.

In a reading group of seven or eight students, WEB check takes about ten minutes. For some students, the check is merely noting where they are in the book. For others, the check will involve asking a question or two. (See "Open-ended Questions," p. 107, pp. 117–119, and Figure 3-5 for suggested questions that have worked well.) It is not necessary for the teacher to have read a book to be able to determine if the student has understood it. By asking open-ended questions while looking through the book and listening to the student, the teacher can get a feel for the student's understanding, engagement with the text, and enjoyment level.

I have found that it takes teachers at least a year to incorporate this kind of quick WEB check without feeling rushed. Students tend to want to talk a lot about a book they are enjoying, and teachers are reluctant to cut them short. However, the purpose of this brief check is to acknowledge interest in the reading the student has

Figure 3-5   Some Suggested Questions for Checking WEB Books

1. Why did you choose this book?
2. Would you recommend it? Why or why not?
3. What was the most interesting part?
4. Why do you think the author wrote this story?
5. Did anything strike you about the author's style or the way the author put words together?
6. Did you learn something new?
7. Are you like any of the characters in the book? How or how not?
8. What was your favorite part?
9. What was the problem in this story?
10. If you could change one part of this book, what would it be? Why would you change this part?
11. Will you read another book by this author? Why or why not?

done and to check that the book is on a level the student can easily read and understand. Once I feel confident about that, I may gently interrupt the student by saying, "That's great. I can tell you're really enjoying the book," and I move on to the next student.

Asking questions   One of the guiding principles that has helped me the most in asking worthwhile questions with WEB books is, "Are these the kinds of questions I would ask my friends if we were having a discussion about a book we had read or a movie we had seen?" I have never yet asked a friend to give me the main idea for a particular chapter and the supporting details to go with it. Nor have I ever tested friends on their factual understanding of the book. Rather, we share insights about characters, talk about why certain passages or sections were memorable or boring, share emotional reactions, try to make connections to our own lives, and clear up confusions we might have had while reading. We need to be asking questions in school that allow for those kinds of connections, and we need to listen to the varied responses of our students.

Mike Pellegrino, a new third grade teacher, says he found the open-ended questions especially helpful in eliciting more interesting and insightful responses. At first, he was asking literal questions and questions the students answered by just reciting the story. "I didn't get any insight into the students' thinking. Now we're getting more deeply into the books." He admits to being surprised by how easily students were able to answer open-ended questions. He has especially liked the following questions—and the thoughtful responses they have evoked.

"Is this story like any other story you have read? Why?"

"Think about the characters in the story. Are any of them the same type of character that you have met in other stories?"

We also want to ask questions that make students aware of what authors do so that they can think about doing similar things in their own writing. In checking Michael, a second-grader who had read the first few chapters of *Ramona the Pest* by Beverly Cleary, I learned he had paid careful attention to the text.

ROUTMAN: Did anything strike you about the way the author puts words together?

MICHAEL: Sometimes she writes the words over and over again, like on page 10, "This is a great, a great day, a great day!"

ROUTMAN: Why do you think the author does that?

MICHAEL: To make the book interesting and sound like singing.

The Teacher as a reading model   One of the most important parts of WEB, or any independent reading program, is that students see their teacher as a reading model who reads in the classroom at the same time they read. That means not just observing the teacher read but also hearing talk about the books the teacher is reading. When I demonstrate the WEB check for a teacher, I also demonstrate myself as a reader. I bring in the books I am presently reading and talk briefly about them to the students. Students are always fascinated to learn about what the teacher is reading. I briefly mention something about why I chose the book and what I am getting out of it. If the book is a mystery, I might tell them that it was hard for me to stop reading the night before. Just as students' reading needs to be balanced with different genres and authors, I try to balance my reading to include adult fiction and nonfiction along with children's books and professional books.

Attitudes of teachers and students   Fourth grade teacher Joan Servis says WEB is the favorite classroom activity of most of her students. Some comments from her students have included, "It's so much better than SSR because you get to talk with someone about your books" and "WEB has made me become a lifelong reader." It has not been unusual for entering new students who are poor readers to become proficient readers through daily WEB. An accompanying boost in self-esteem is also noticeable.

While initially it can seem overwhelming to be adding WEB reading to an already full program, the benefits are worth the effort. Third grade teacher Karen Horton tried WEB reading for the first time two years ago and notes that it has taken her most of that time to feel comfortable and confident with the management of the process. She has this to say:

> Having some suggested questions to start with was really helpful. It gave me a place to begin. Then I could go from there, add my own questions and make the procedure my own. I've seen tremendous value with WEB reading. It helps kids become readers and teaches them the use of leisure time. Overall, I am very pleased with the way students have learned to remember to bring their books back and forth between school and home and to talk about their books.

Finally, our own reading attitudes are critical to the success of the independent reading program. Merely putting books in the room and expecting children to read is not enough. Unless we take a personal and sincere interest in what children are reading and display ourselves as joyful and excited about reading, many children will not actively participate. Additionally, we have to be careful not to turn independent reading into a tedious, required program. While we want to encourage, we don't want to push so hard that we turn students off to reading. There is a difference between mandating reading and having high expectations that it will occur. The latter, gently and firmly fostered by a caring teacher, can make all the difference.

Evaluating Books

Students enjoy rating and evaluating the books they have read. Thinking about what makes an excellent book helps make students critical readers and writers. Some teachers have student include their ratings with their record of books read. To help students determine what makes a good book, a whole-class shared writing works well. (See pp. 59–66 for a discussion of shared writing.)

The following "What Makes a Book a 10?" is the first draft from a grade 3 class:

Beginning	Keeps reader interested
	Introduces main characters and setting
Ending	Reader wishes there was a sequel or wants to read the series
	Reader feels satisfied
	Reader wants to read more books by that author

Whole Book	Should be on reader's level or below
	Print should not be too small for reader
	Story should be exciting in some way
	Story should have an interesting plot
Characters	Should be very interesting
	Should have a problem of some kind
	Should be well described so you feel you know them
Setting	Should be so well described that reader can picture it
Pictures	Should go along with the story
	Reader should be able to feel what the picture means

Teachers enjoy working with their own students to write classroom guidelines. Based on students' knowledge of literature, responses will vary.

Critic's corner Another way to evaluate books was suggested by a fourth-grader in Joan Servis' class. The student was inspired by "Critic's Corner" on "The Today Show," where Gene Shalit discusses and evaluates movies.

"Critic's Corner" occurs weekly and is an opportunity for a student to recommend a book to the class. The student sits in the author's chair and tells the class about the book, stressing why she recommends it. The children may ask questions or make comments. Often other students affirm the "critic's" choice, telling the class that they read and liked the book also. "Critic's Corner" often promotes a book that will then make the rounds of the entire class.

"Critic's Corner": student evaluating a book read independently

A Balanced Writing Program

While various approaches to writing are discussed here individually, in reality, these approaches are intertwined and interdependent. In a balanced writing program, writers regularly interact with and overlap all of these approaches.

Writing Aloud

Writing aloud is a powerful modeling technique at any grade level for getting students' attention and demonstrating various aspects of writing. Writing aloud occurs when the teacher writes in front of students and also verbalizes what he is thinking and writing. As children observe the teacher in the act of writing, the teacher makes explicit what he is doing—the thinking, the format, layout, spacing, handwriting, spelling, punctuation, discussion of vocabulary. Writing on large chart paper, the overhead projector, or the chalkboard, the teacher verbalizes his thought processes as well as the actual transcriptions as he is doing them, and students relate the spoken word to the written word.

For older students, even at the high school level, writing aloud offers students a framework of what a good essay, short story, or report might look like before the student is assigned to write one. Writing aloud increases students' interest and motivation in writing as well as the quality of student writing. Writing aloud demonstrations can take many formats, and several are demonstrated on succeeding pages.

Writing a "Morning Message"

I first saw this approach demonstrated by second grade teacher Loretta Martin, who picked up the idea of "Morning Message" at a whole language conference. The teacher writes a message to the students about what will be happening that day in terms of activities and schedule or about what has happened or will be happening in the teacher's life. Some teachers use writing aloud in place of a daily schedule written on the chalkboard. "Morning Message" is an excellent way to connect news of the classroom or news about the teacher to reading and writing. See Figure 3–6 for a substitute's message and a teacher's message.

The teacher thinks aloud while writing the message on the overhead projector. Students read along with their eyes and may also read aloud along with the teacher. After the message is written, the teacher takes a few minutes to ask children questions and familiarize them with conventions of writing. I might ask,

Why did I capitalize . . . ?
Why did I begin a new paragraph here?
Why did I use a comma . . . ?
What do you notice about . . . ?

Instead of the teacher explaining and giving the answers, students are asked to think and figure out the reasons for the conventions used.

I have demonstrated "Morning Message" for many teachers. They are always amazed at how students become totally engaged and how much can be written and

Figure 3-6 "Morning Messages"

Good Morning ‾Oct. 5, 19 ¶
I am here for Mrs.
Martin. She is in another
State today-New York. Sh
is attending a conference
with 2,000 other teachers.
She will be gone today and
tomorrow.
You have gym this
afternoon, so don't forget
to change your shoes.
Have a good day ☺!

November 29 1989
Nov. 20, 1987

Good morning,
    Thanksgiving is a special
time for families. I know that
many of you will celebrate
this *holiday* with your families,
in town or out of town and
even out of the state of
Ohio.   city   state
        I will go to *Chicago, Illinois*
to visit with my mother and
her family. My mother has
twelve brothers and sisters! There
will be lots of good food,
children, adults, music, and
probably not enough CHAIRS!

talked about in a very short time. The whole activity takes about five to seven minutes and is a fine and enjoyable way to reinforce skills—spelling, punctuation, grammar, paragraphing, capitalization, or any parts of writing you want to bring to the children's attention. Because I believe it is important to write in our best form and demonstrate what competent writers do, I do not deliberately make errors for children.

Second grade teacher Loretta Martin comments, "I feel writing aloud with my students clearly puts so many of the conventions we want to teach children in the proper context of written language without teaching skills in isolation."

One teacher who had said, "This sounds great, but I can't see it happening on any kind of regular basis with our tight schedules" was surprised how easy "Morning Message" was to implement and how little time it took once she tried it.

Writing a Draft from an Assigned Topic

In moving toward a more democratic (student-has-ownership) style of teaching, many of us initially have difficulty allowing students to self-select most of their writing topics. One way to get involved in the writing process and engage students who say they do not like to write is to choose a topic that everyone knows a lot about and can relate to. For students who are unpracticed and lacking confidence in writing, writing a draft that is short and focused can serve to loosen them up and help them gain confidence with the written mode. However, even when the topic is assigned, lots of leeway for meaningful student choice is provided. Later, more choice can be given, with several topics assigned and students having the option of choosing one.

Beginning with a whole-class brainstorming session seems to help get some students started. In that way all students have something to write about. See Figure 3-7, "A Bad Day," for one example of an assigned topic and the preliminary brainstorming. Unless there is an authentic reason to do so, most of these drafts do not go to final copy because the purpose here is to focus on writing interesting content. At a later date, some students may choose to develop a piece into more final form.

Figure 3-7   Brainstorming an Assigned Topic

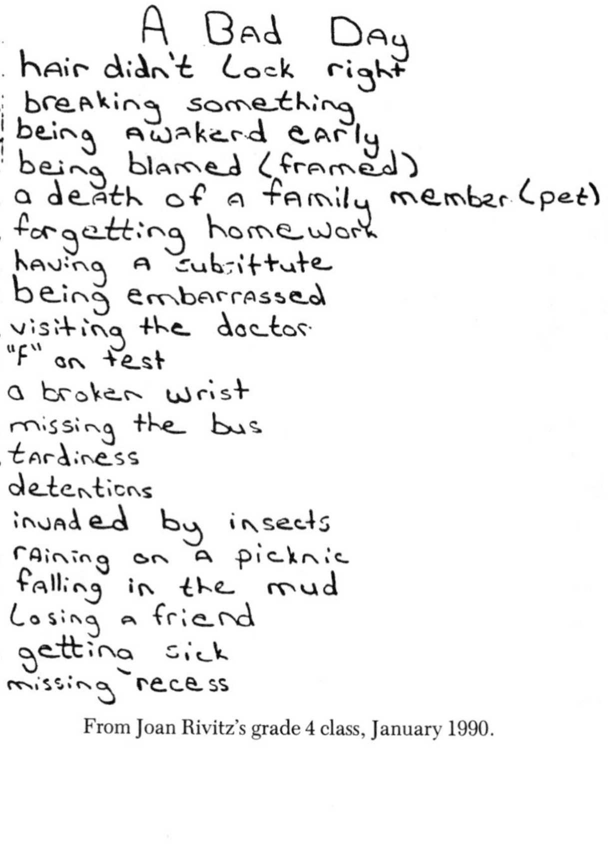

A Bad Day
1. hair didn't lock right
2. breaking something
3. being awakerd early
4. being blamed (framed)
5. a death of a family member (pet)
6. forgetting homework
7. having a subittute
8. being embarrassed
9. visiting the doctor
10. "f" on test
11. a broken wrist
12. missing the bus
13. tardiness
14. detentions
15. invaded by insects
16. raining on a picknic
17. falling in the mud
18. losing a friend
19. getting sick
20. missing recess

From Joan Rivitz's grade 4 class, January 1990.

Being an Expert

One writing topic that has proved successful across the grade levels—even for reluctant writers—is writing about being an expert at something. The idea for this topic came from second grade teacher Elaine Weiner, who heard it suggested at a whole language conference she attended. This is a particular favorite because the writing focuses on the strengths of students. As teachers and students learn about one another's unknown talents and gain appreciation for individual aptitudes, a sense of community builds.

This is also a good topic to take to final copy because it is often short and focused. We often use students' completed and illustrated pieces to put together a class book of "experts," which is shared with parents at open house. We sometimes use the copying machine to enlarge pieces and make a Big Book of expert writing. The book is always a classroom favorite. Students enjoy reading about one another's areas of expertise. The entire writing project takes several weeks from start to finish.

Brainstorming and drafting   With our expert writing, I begin by brainstorming (on the overhead projector) some things that I am an expert at. My list changes regularly, depending on what I've been doing. I want to show students that being an expert does not have to refer to something major. A recent list of mine follows:

Putting a meal together quickly
Cleaning a bathtub
Loving my dog Tobi
Making jam
Killing flies
Teaching reading and writing
Keeping Frank's socks together
Taking care of plants
Shopping for clothes on sale
Making turkey gravy
Losing my gloves and my glasses
Writing letters

Students then brainstorm their own lists, and those that would like to share do so. See Figure 3–8 for two "expert" lists from fourth-graders.

Next, I select one of my own expert areas to write about and brainstorm what I might want to include in my paper. Depending on the ages of the students, I might do a semantic mapping where categories are kept together, but usually I just jot down possibilities (see Figure 3–9).

I also write down three areas I will include—and that students are to include—in the piece of writing:

- How I became an expert
- What I do that shows I'm an expert
- How I feel about it

Figure 3–8 Two "Expert" Lists from Fourth-graders

1. (playing basketball)
2. making things out of foil
3. making poem and my own card
4. (trashing my room)
5. playing tick ball
6. (getiny mad quick)
7. dancing
8. staying up late and geting up at 7.00
9. cooking ...
10. playing with the cat
11. playing the recorder
12. playing the clarinet
13. (drawing) ✓
14. checkers
15. roler skating
16. bowling
17. riding my bike
18. reading book

1.taking a long time
2.making friendship bracelets
3.drawing
4.keeping my room messy
5.talking on the phone
6.watching T.V.
7.swimming
8.skating
9.cooking
10.fighting with my brother

Figure 3–9 Possibilities for One "Expert" Topic

Killing flies

glass & paper method
problem in my house
fly swatter
wrist actn
mess on wall
average number per day
exterminator
wet towel
describe flies
my feelings

Listing what's required helps students organize their writing and provides a framework for those not used to choosing their own topics. Students' writing will often include three paragraphs, one for each of the areas listed.

I begin by writing my first draft in front of the students on the overhead projector. I think aloud, reread what I've written, and discuss possibilities. Then I ask students to choose which expert area they want to write about and to brainstorm their own possibilities. After checking these ideas to be sure students have enough information—and conferencing with them when necessary—students begin to write their drafts.

Modeling Response. After the first drafts are completed, I model the response process aloud in the following manner:

1. I ask for a volunteer to read his piece.
2. For the first reading, I just listen and try to get the overall feel and message.
3. On the second reading, I listen more critically and take notes.
4. I take my notes on the overhead projector so students can see my thinking and the comments I am making. Because this must be done quickly, I write down just enough to jog my memory so I can give constructive feedback. I divide my response paper (the overhead transparency) into two parts, one for noting what I liked and the other for noting questions, confusions, and suggestions.
5. I begin by making specific, positive comments such as "I liked the words you used to describe . . . ." "I like the way you told how . . . ." With questions or confusions, I word my comments carefully: "I wondered why . . . ." "I was confused when . . . ." "You might want to think about . . . ." From the start, it is important to demonstrate that general comments such as "I liked your story" are not helpful to the writer.

I try to demonstrate specificity by noting particular words or ideas that grabbed my attention or specific places where clarity is needed. Being a helpful responder requires very concentrated listening; it is a difficult task which must be carefully modeled before one can expect students to try it. It takes us teachers a while to feel secure and knowledgeable with the response process. Teachers that try it find they become more skilled with time and practice.

With each suggestion or question raised, the writer is guided to use a colored pencil or marker and write a note to herself—something that will signal her to look carefully at part of the writing for possible revision. Time is not taken now for the writer to defend or explain ideas. The writer merely makes notes for later consideration. Students will tend to want to "answer" the questions that have been posed to them. To save time, we are firm about having them just write the question and consider changes later.

I now call for a second volunteer, and I model the process once more. This time students and the classroom teacher also participate. I coach students to make positive, useful comments. I give feedback from my notes, again taken on the overhead projector in front of the class. Many demonstrations will need to take place before students become skilled responders. I also place my draft on the overhead, read it, and take questions and comments from students. They see me write notes to myself that may determine later revisions. More important, students see that their comments and suggestions are taken seriously. Figure 3–10 is an example of the beginning of a draft.

After drafts have been revised, some students volunteer to show how and what comments affected their revisions. They read aloud and explain to the class the actual changes they made. I also share my changes. Finally, with permission, I reproduce several revised drafts, make tansparencies, and model the editing process on the overhead projector (see pp. 177–179 for editing demonstrations).

Because peer response is difficult to do well, I believe it works best when teachers guide the process. As much as possible, students need to see and hear over and over again the kinds of comments that are helpful to a writer. Until students are well practiced in skillfully responding to drafts, merely putting students in groups to respond to one another is not useful in the revision process.

In modeling the response process, an effective approach is for two teachers to combine their classes and respond to each other's drafts. Students are very interested in the kinds of comments made and in their teachers' reactions. English teacher Dana Noble noted, "My students were very concerned about my feelings when a teacher suggested changes for my choice of words until I said I welcomed it!" Authentic teacher demonstrations, where teachers verbalize their thinking aloud, encourage students to model similar responses with their peers.

Figure 3–10 Demonstration of an Early "Expert" Writing Draft

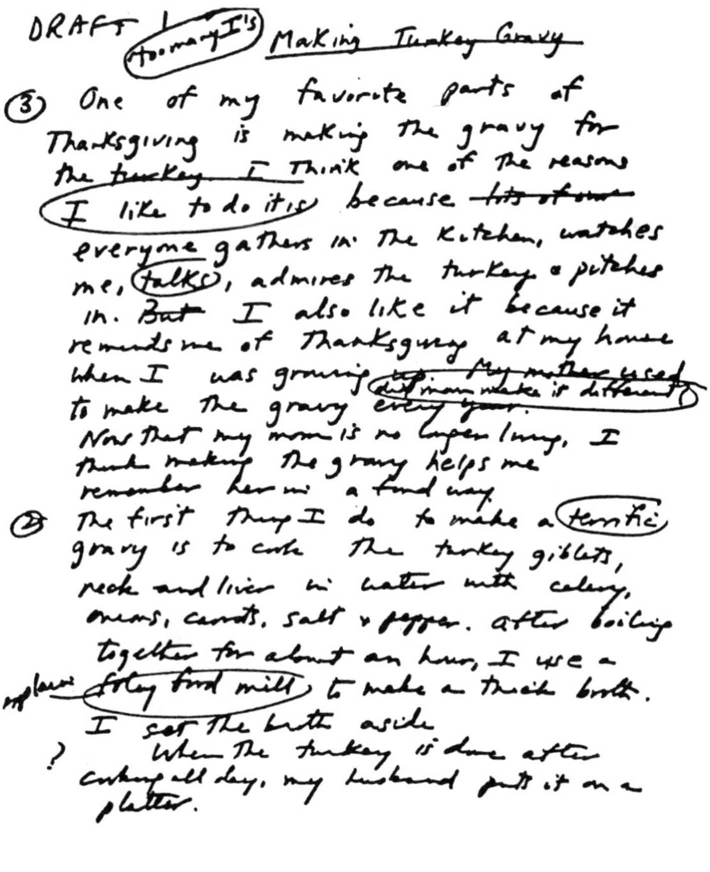
DRAFT 1 (Too many I's) Making Turkey Gravy

(3) One of my favorite parts of Thanksgiving is making the gravy for the turkey. I think one of the reasons (I like to do it is) because lots of everyone gathers in the kitchen, watches me, (talks), admires the turkey & pitches in. But I also like it because it reminds me of Thanksgiving at my house when I was growing up. My mother used (did mom make it different?) to make the gravy every year. Now that my mom is no longer living, I think making the gravy helps me remember her in a fond way.

(2) The first thing I do to make a (terrific) gravy is to cook the turkey giblets, neck and liver in water with celery, onions, carrots, salt & pepper. After boiling together for about an hour, I use a replace (foley food mill) to make a thick broth. I set the broth aside.

? When the turkey is done after cooking all day, my husband puts it on a platter.

Narrowing the focus of a draft   One topic that has worked well is to write about something that is or has been difficult to do. Again, I begin by brainstorming, but here I also try to narrow the focus. When students choose football, math, or babysitting as areas that are difficult for them, I ask them to choose one small aspect of their topic and tell about it in detail. In my demonstration, I have talked about how hard writing is for me and have narrowed my focus to one aspect that is especially trying for me—getting started. Following is a recent rough draft as I wrote it on the overhead projector in front of a group of fourth-graders.

> I wake up thinking about how I will begin. My stomach feels tight and uneasy. I get into the shower and try to put the beginning sentences together, but they do not come. I eat breakfast, read the newspaper for longer than usual, get dressed slowly, make the bed, clean up a bit. I look at the clock. 8:30 A.M. I've been up since 7:00 A.M. It is time to get to work.

Figures 3-11 and 3-12   Draft by a Fourth-grader about Something That Is—or Has Been— Difficult to Do

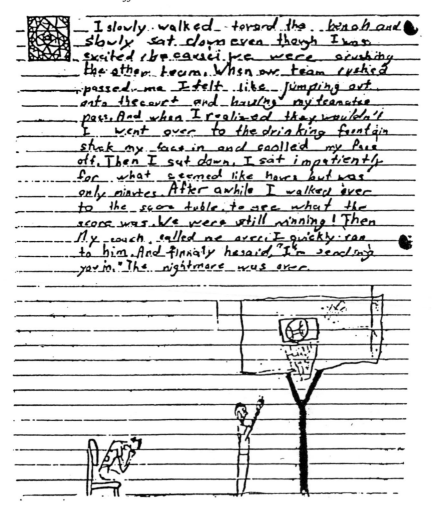

Figure 3-12

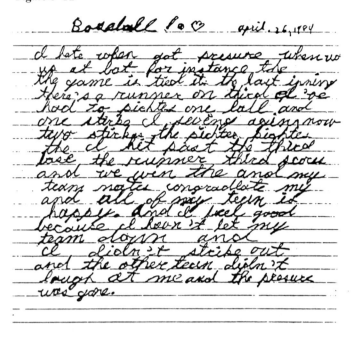

Reluctantly, I drag myself over to the computer, sit down and turn it on. I flex my fingers up and down, in readiness to use the keys. I move papers out of the way, adjust the chair to just the right position. It is time to start.

The blank screen is in front of me, gray and empty and beckoning. I stare at it for what seems like a long time. How to begin. The words do not come. I move my hands together, squirm around on the chair and stare at the screen again. The room is silent. I look out the window and watch a bird starting to build a nest. I must begin!

I place my fingers over the keys. The silence continues as my fingers gently rest on the keyboard. And then the gentle clicking noise begins. My fingers are moving across the keys, and words start to slowly pour forth onto the screen. It does not matter that the words will have to be changed and rewritten. I have done the hardest part—just getting started.

Figures 3–11 and 3–12 are examples of drafts written by two fourth grade reluctant writers following the writing-aloud demonstration. The first talks about an agonizing wait before being sent onto the basketball court by the coach, and the second describes pressure to perform in a baseball game. These were significant pieces of writing because they came from students who rarely invested in their writing.

Shared Writing

Frank Smith has said, "The most direct and relevant way to demonstrate to a child the power of writing is to write with the child." Shared writing, where the teacher and students compose collaboratively, with the teacher acting as a scribe and expert to her group of apprentices, is appropriate for older as well as younger students. Shared writing goes beyond language experience in which the teacher takes dictation from the child's language. In shared writing, the writing is a negotiated process with meanings, choices of words, and topics discussed and decided jointly by students and teacher.

As in shared reading, in shared writing the teacher's role is an enabling, supportive one that encourages and invites students to participate and enjoy writing experiences they might not be able to do on their own. Shared writing is a relaxed, social time where the teacher and students are gathered together informally, sometimes on a rug or in a designated floor space, as in shared reading.

Shared writing often develops naturally as a response to shared reading. Younger students who have become familiar with favorite texts often opt to create their own innovations and stories with guidance from the teacher. Eventually some of these new texts become enlarged, illustrated texts for shared reading and wall stories posted around the room before they are bound into Big Books. As is usually the case with stories the children create, they choose to read these stories over and over again. We may also suggest topics for shared writing as a way to show children various possibilities.

With the teacher collaborating with students and acting as a scribe—and not expecting students to create texts on their own—children learn that writing opportunities are available to them. Because children are focusing on the composing-thinking process without the additional task of transcribing, shared writing frees their imagination and helps them gain confidence in writing independently.

The language we teachers use in the shared writing context is critical for a genuine, participatory experience. For example, instead of saying, "I don't feel that sentence fits," I might say, "What do you think about . . . ? Does that fit?" to make the process more democratic. Or instead of saying, "Let's put this in dialogue," I might try, "What do you think about using dialogue here?" While teacher input is important, we don't want to take over. The teacher's voice should guide rather than dominate.

Shared writing may take many forms:

Wall stories and Big Books

Stories, essays, and poems

Original story endings

Retellings

Class journal entries

Class observations of pets, plants, and science experiments

Shared experiences, such as field trips and special visitors

Class rules and charts

Weekly newsletters to parents

News of the day

Curriculum-related writing

Reports

Information books

Evaluations of books and activities.

Advantages of Shared Writing

Because shared writing is a powerful approach for promoting development and enjoyment of writing—yet one that is seldom employed, especially with older students—its many advantages are listed with the hope that more teachers will give shared writing a try and realize its benefits:

- Reinforces and supports the reading process
- Makes it possible for all students to participate
- Encourages close examination of texts, words, and options of authors
- Demonstrates the conventions of writing—spelling, punctuation, and grammar
- Provides reading texts that are relevant and interesting to the children
- Focuses on composing and leaves writing (transcribing) to the teacher
- Helps students see possibilities they might not see on their own
- Recognizes the child who may have a wealth of verbal story material but be unable to write it down
- Gives both teacher and students confidence in their writing ability
- Gives the reluctant-to-write teacher a supportive environment

Many teachers are terrified to write. For most of us, our education in writing focused on the editorial aspects rather than on the creative, composing parts. We were trained to write correctly and for the teacher. For teachers who don't like to write or who are fearful of writing, shared writing is a nonthreatening way to become personally involved in the writing process. The support teachers receive from their students is often enough of a boost to give most teachers confidence to begin writing themselves.

During the first week of school, shared writing can be used to establish the rules and procedures for the classroom. Rather than having the teacher post the rules ahead of time, children enjoy working them out with the teacher. With the teacher acting as scribe, students are actively involved with the teacher in the decision making process. When students have some ownership of classroom expectations, they tend to act more responsibly in respecting the rules. The final, revised charts may be written out by the children so that the reading material on the walls is by the children.

A Shared Writing Lesson in Grade 1

Shared writing is a powerful way to demonstrate to children that their own observations, along with guidance and self-questioning, can markedly improve the quality of writing. I was invited into a first grade classroom where the teacher was frustrated by the boring quality of the daily journal entries. Most of the children were writing short, simple entries like "I went to my friend's house. We played together. I had fun. Then I went home." I suggested we write together about something the class knew a lot about, such as a recent shared experience. Several children wanted to write about the class pet, the rabbit that lived in a cage at the front of the classroom. Working through the story together provided natural opportunities for elaborating on the text and demonstrating how much the children knew about their subject. What follows is the shared writing experience—the thinking, composing, and scribing about the class rabbit. (*T* stands for teacher—me—and *S* stands for a student responding.)

T: How should we begin? Can someone start off our story?

S: We have a rabbit in our classroom.

T: (*Writing slowly and orally stretching out the sounds of the words*) "W-e h-a-v-e a r-a-b-b-i-t i-n o-u-r cl-a-ss-r-oo-m." (*Silence*)

T: What does the rabbit look like?

S: She is brown all over.

T: Yes, she is brown, but take a good look at her. Is she brown everywhere?

S: No, her tail is white.

T: How about if we say, "She is brown all over except for her tail, which is white."

S: We need to tell that her bottom is light brown.

T: Good. Let's add it here. "She is brown all over except for her tail, which is white, and her bottom, which is light brown." Anything else?

S: She likes to nibble things.

T: What does she like to nibble?

S: She likes carrots, paper, crayons.

T: "She likes to nibble things likes carrots, paper, and crayons." Oh, I put an *s* after that second *like*; that shouldn't be there. I'll just cross it out. That's what writers do when they make a mistake. They just cross it out. What else can you tell me about your rabbit?

S: She has brown eyes.

T: Where do you think we should we put that? (*Silence*)

T: Can someone find the part that tells what the rabbit looks like?

S: Where we say "She is brown all over . . ."

T: Yes, that's right. How about if we put, "She has brown eyes" right after that so we keep the parts about what the rabbit looks like all together? (*Puts in a caret and writes and verbalizes, "She has brown eyes"*) This is what writers do when they need to stick something in. They make kind of an arrow like this; it's called a caret.

S: (*Calling out*) She has *small* brown eyes.

T: O.K. How should we add that in?

S: Put a caret after *has* and write in *small*.

T: Yes, that's right.

S: The rabbit has pointed ears, too.

T: Where do you think we should add that?

S: We could say, "She has small brown eyes *and* pointed ears."

T: I like the way you combined two related things into one sentence.

s: I want to add, "She has *long*, pointed ears. Use a caret and put in *long*.

T: That's great. You really understand how to use that caret. When you are writing on your own, and you get an idea you think belongs before something you have already written, just use the caret and write it in. Anything else about your rabbit?

s: She has a lot of accidents. Once she peed on the carpet. (*T writes it down while verbalizing*)

s: When she stands up, she looks fat.

T: (*Writes it down while verbalizing*) Anything else you want to say about your rabbit?

s: When she yawns, we can see her teeth.

T: (*Writing and verbalizing*) "When she yawns, we can see her teeth." What does your rabbit do all day?

s: Sometimes she knocks over her food bowl.

T: What happens then?

s: We have to clean it up.

T: (*Writing and verbalizing*) "Sometimes she knocks over her food bowl, and we have to clean it up."

T: Why does she knock over her food bowl?

s: Because she's mad.

T: What is she mad about?

s: She's mad because we won't let her out.

T: How about if we write, "She does that when she's mad because we won't let her out."

The completed text appeared as follows, and children eagerly read and reread it:

> We have a rabbit in our classroom. She is brown all over except for her tail, which is white, and her bottom, which is light brown. She has small brown eyes and long pointed ears. She likes to nibble things like carrots, paper, and crayons. She has lots of accidents. Once she peed on the carpet. When she stands up, she looks fat. When she yawns, we can see her teeth. Sometimes she knocks over her food bowl, and we have to clean it up. She does that when she's mad because we won't let her out.

The first grade teacher reported enthusiastically that there was an immediate improvement in the quality of the children's daily journal writing, especially a noticeable addition of descriptive detail. Shortly thereafter the first grade teacher felt confident enough to do her first shared writing, an account of a class field trip to the art museum.

A Shared Poetry Writing Lesson in the Primary Grades

Inspired by a lesson I saw in an Australian classroom, the poem "Jelly on the Plate" from *Jelly on the Plate: An Anthology of Poems,* collected by June Factor (Modern Cirriculum Press, 1987) became a model for children writing their own patterned poetry in a second grade class (see Figure 3–13). We began by repeatedly enjoying

Figure 3-13   Patterned Poetry Model

Jelly on the plate,
Jelly on the plate,
Wibble wobble, *wibble* wobble,
Jelly on the plate.

Paper on the floor,
Paper on the floor,
Pick it up, pick it up,
Paper on the floor.

Piggy in the house,
Piggy in the house,
Kick him out, kick him out,
Piggy in the house.

Traditional
2

the rhythm of the poem together in shared reading and discussing the illustrator's choices to go along with the poem. We then talked about how the poem was written—the style, format, rhythm. In a shared writing draft, I recorded everything the children discovered about how the poem was put together. Notice all the information they garnered about how the poem was constructed without the teacher telling them. If they failed to notice something, I prodded them with a question like, "Do you notice anything about line . . .?" or "What does the poet do to show . . .?" Our draft follows exactly as we wrote it:

2 beats per line

Commas at end of lines 1, 2, 3 and in middle of line 3

Line 4 ends with a period.

Every line starts with a capital.

Line 3 is different—uses action words and different print

All 4 lines are on the same basic idea

On line 3, words are repeated

Lines 1, 2, and 4 are the same: A, A, B, A

First word of lines 1, 2, and 4: 2 syllables

Last word of lines 1, 2, and 4: 1 syllable

Using Holdaway's developmental model (pp. 9–10) and the illustrations on the page that the poet did not include, I demonstrated—with student participation on an invitational basis—how other verses might be written. On large chart paper I wrote:

Lego on the floor,
Lego on the floor,
Build it up, build it up
Lego on the floor.

Monkey in the tree,
Monkey in the tree,
Swing on down, swing on down,
Monkey in the tree.

For the next stage, the practice phase, students broke into groups of four and wrote original verses using the illustrations on the poem and the guidelines on our draft. Classroom teacher Mary Pryor and I walked around and gave guidance as necessary. These verses were then shared with the whole class. Figure 3–14 is an example of one group's work.

The following week, when I was back in the classroom, we chanted the poem "Jelly on the Plate" several times again; and, looking at the illustrations carefully, we talked about in what room of the house the action of the poem might have taken place. The students speculated it could be a playroom, child's bedroom, kitchen, or den. I then told them that they were to choose a room in their house to write their own poem and illustrations for. First they were to take a careful look at that room and note everything in it. I modeled first by choosing my kitchen and coming up with the following list:

cookbooks, jelly, window, flowers, refrigerator, dishes, silverware, platters, crack in ceiling, cups, napkins, pepper mill, towels, coffee, glass jars, pots, pans, hanging plants, turkey, stove, cupboards

Figure 3-14   A Group-written Verse

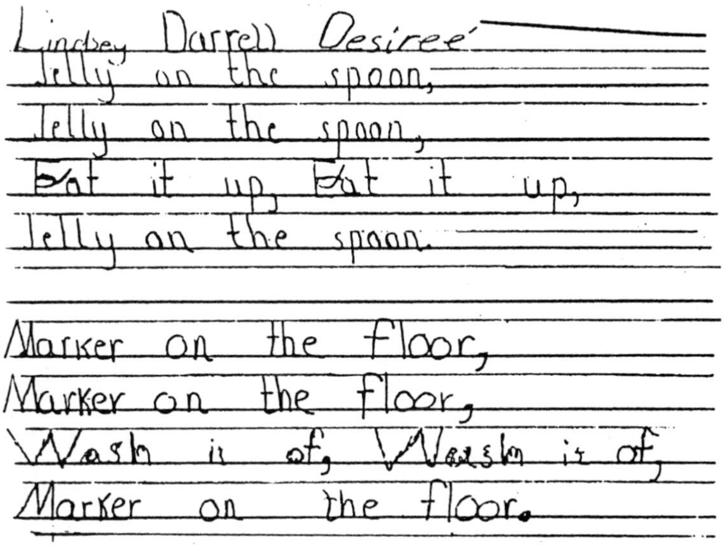

Lindsey Darrell Desireé
Jelly on the spoon,
Jelly on the spoon,
Eat it up, Eat it up,
Jelly on the spoon.

Marker on the floor,
Marker on the floor,
Wash it of, Wash it of,
Marker on the floor.

Then, in front of the students, I wrote three verses to go along with some of the items. One verse follows:

> Pepper in the mill,
> Pepper in the mill,
> Twist it hard, twist it hard,
> Pepper in the mill.

After students carefully observed and wrote down what was in the room they had selected, they were ready to work individually on drafting verses to go along with room items. Before showing their verses to either Mary Pryor or me, they were expected to use the original poem and the chart we had written to check their poems carefully for form, punctuation, capitalization, choice of words, and so on. We expected students to correct whatever they could on their own by using our classroom chart.

Next, students were given large chart paper to use as a "sloppy copy" to lay out in pencil their poems and illustrations. Once those had been revised and edited, they worked on large chart paper to write the final copy of their poems in their best handwriting and with carefully done, colorful illustrations. Individual pages were then spiral-bound into a class Big Book, which became a year-long class favorite for rereading and enjoying.

The entire project took place over several weeks and was a great success. We noted especially that low-ability students felt a particular pride and joy in their work. I emphatically believe that the amount of demonstrating, opportunities for participation, and practice that students received *before* they were expected to work on their own was vital for the high level of achievement that resulted.

Guided Writing

As in guided reading, the teacher's role in guided writing is to guide students, respond to them, and extend their thinking in the process of composing text. Also, as in guided reading, where the student holds the book and does the reading, in guided writing the student holds the pen and does the writing. By contrast, in writing aloud and shared writing, the teacher does the writing.

The teacher's role in guided writing is one of facilitator, helping students discover what they want to say and how to say it meaningfully with clarity, coherence, interest, style, form, and individual voice. Teachers are supportive rather than directive, suggestive rather than prescriptive. Ownership of the writing always remains with the student. Our role is to empower writers to discover their own meanings.

Guided writing is the heart of the writing program. It takes place when students have time to write and the teacher is available for guidance. It may occur during whole class, small group, or one-to-one as part of writing workshop, story writing, journal writing, content area writing, letter writing, report writing, or any other form of authentic writing. Guided writing, like guided reading, occurs after students have had many opportunities to see writing demonstrated aloud and in shared contexts. Also, as in guided reading, there are opportunities for choice, decision making, and peer response and for making connections to students' lives.

Demonstrations in selecting topics, drafting, responding, revising, editing, and other minilessons that have been done by the teacher in writing aloud and in shared writing are now incorporated independently by students—with teacher and peer guidance—into their own writing. Mechanics or skills are taught strategically, as the need arises, in the context of the genuine writing situation.

My own insights on the teaching of writing—especially the rationale and procedures for conferencing, response groups, revision, and editing in guided writing—have been heavily influenced by the work of Nancie Atwell, Donald Graves, Lucy Calkins, and Jan Turbill. Their major works are excellent resources for establishing authentic teaching-learning-writing processes in the classroom. (See Jan Turbill, *No Better Way to Teach Writing!* [1982]; Nancie Atwell, *In the Middle* [1987]; Donald Graves, *Writing: Teachers and Children at Work* [1983]; and Lucy Calkins, *The Art of Teaching Writing* [1986]. For secondary teachers, add Tom Romano, *Clearing the Way* [1987] and Steven Zemelman and Harvey Daniels, *A Community of Writers* [1988]. All of the books were published by Heinemann, Portsmouth, NH.) These sources give clear guidelines and procedures for revision, editing, conferencing, classroom management, minilessons, publishing, and lots more. (For examples of guided writing, see Chap. 8, "Authentic Contexts for Writing.")

As with all language learning, the role of guidance in writing is to lead the learner toward independence: " . . . every conference trains writers for the most important conferences of all. Those are the conferences writers must hold with themselves during the writing process" (Murray, 1989, p. 124).

Independent Writing

The purpose of independent writing—like that of independent reading—is to build fluency, establish the writing habit, make personal connections, explore meanings, promote critical thinking, and use writing as a natural, pleasurable, self-chosen activity. In independent writing, the student has opportunities, many of which are student initiated, to write without teacher intervention or evaluation. The student takes responsibility for working out the challenges in the writing process. Writing experiences may include, but are not limited to, journal writing, responding in a log, and freewriting. (See Chap. 9 for information on journal writing and Chap. 6 for information on literature response logs.)

Writing to Learn

"Writing to learn," often done in a learning log or curriculum-related journal, can be a form of independent writing. "Writing to learn may be defined as short, spontaneous, unedited, exploratory, personal writing that's used not to affect an audience but to channel, crystalize, record, direct, or guide a person's thinking." (Zemelman and Daniels, 1988, p. 103; see pp. 103–113 for specific examples of writing to learn in the classroom.)

I see writing to learn as one of the most powerful techniques available for developing critical thinking. While I have heard and used the terms "writing as a thinking process" and "writing to learn," their meaning became clear to me only in the process of writing this book. While I began with an outline and general idea of what I wanted to say and accomplish, I had no idea how a chapter would turn out—or even what it would finally include—until I struggled my way through it. It was in the process of writing that I cleared up confusions, worked through problem areas, organized my thinking, checked references and notes, and synthesized my thoughts. It was through writing that I learned what I wanted to say. The actual process of writing forced me to think about concepts and come to some understanding and conclusions. It was not just that I wrote what I already knew. In the process of writing and thinking, I learned what I knew, what I didn't know, and what I needed to know. In using writing as a vehicle for thinking, I was able to clarify and extend my knowledge. Even more than that, when I was finished, I found I actually knew more—and felt smarter—because of the hard thinking and learning the writing had forced me to do.

Based on my own experience, I am convinced that we must provide many opportunities for writing as a thinking process across the curriculum—in mathematics, art, music, science, social studies, foreign languages, and more. (For specific procedures on how this can be done, see *Resources for Teachers*, especially Atwell, 1990; Murray, 1989 and 1990; Zemelman and Daniels, 1988; and the index entry "Learning logs.")

Figure 3-15   A Fifth-grader's Freewriting

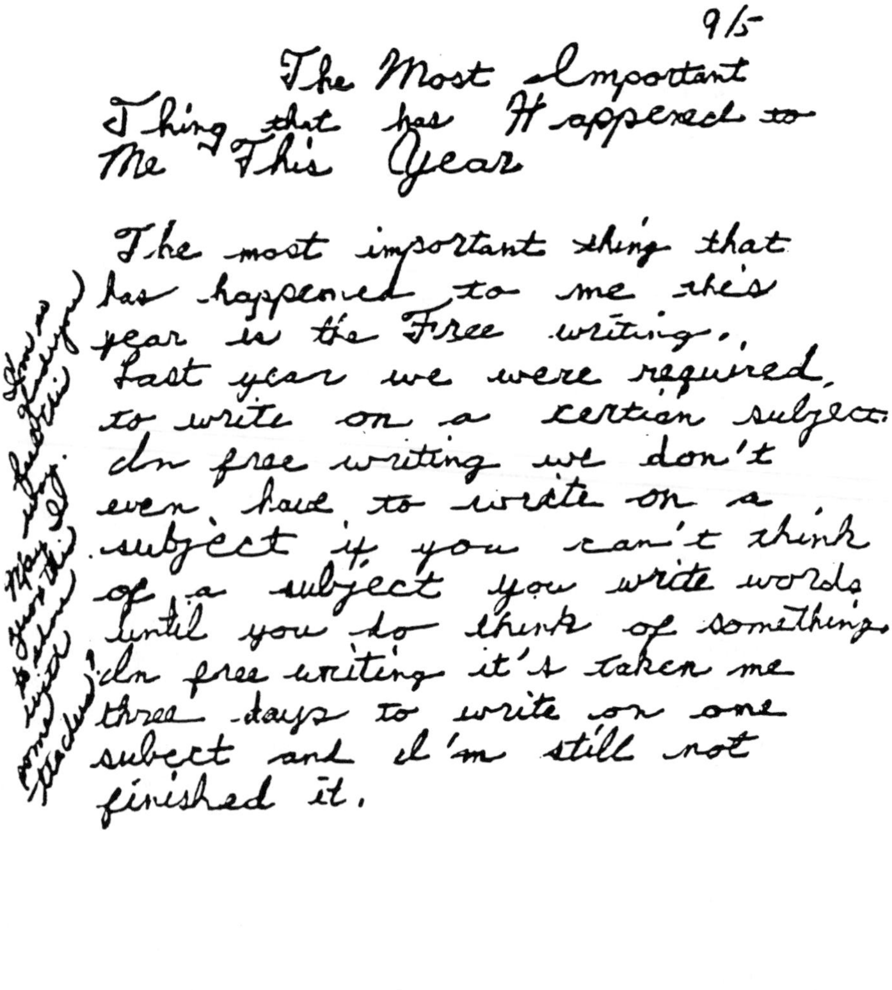

9/5

The Most Important
Thing that has Happened to
Me This Year

The most important thing that
has happened to me this
year is the Free writing.
Last year we were required
to write on a certian subject.
In free writing we don't
even have to write on a
subject if you can't think
of a subject you write words
until you do think of something.
In free writing it's taken me
three days to write on one
subect and I'm still not
finished it.

Freewriting

Freewriting allows and encourages students to write without interruption in any form they choose. For a short, timed period, students write as quickly as they can without worrying about spelling, grammar, and correctness. For students who have been used to writing everything for the teacher and worrying about correctness, freewriting can help develop confidence and fluency in writing. Once students relax with it, they enjoy and value freewriting (see Figure 3–15 for a fifth-grader's comments). Focused freewriting can be used for "freeing up" students' prior knowledge and is a valuable strategy in the content areas. (See Bayer, 1990, for suggested procedures.)

Reflections

While the various approaches to reading and writing have been separated for purposes of clarity and demonstration, this separation is artificial. In reality, reading and writing are connected and flow together.

In our whole language classrooms, reading and writing topics are relevant to students' lives, interests, and the school curriculum. Conferencing, responding, revising, demonstrating, and encouraging are ongoing with students and their reading-writing processes. The classroom environment encourages collaboration, risk taking, responsibility, and reflection and provides time and space to read and write.

I have found it takes most of us many years to achieve balanced reading and writing programs. We need to allow ourselves time to try out and incorporate the various approaches/components while recognizing the importance of moving toward an integrated and balanced literacy program.

In looking at the various approaches to reading and writing, it is the degree of teacher intervention, support and choice that determines the type of approach being employed. While we need to begin reading and writing with lots of teacher demonstrating and scaffolding (reading and writing aloud and shared reading and writing), gradually students take more ownership and responsibility for their own learning processes (guided and independent reading and writing) as teachers guide students toward independence.

Grouping for Success

Taking a Close Look at Ability Grouping

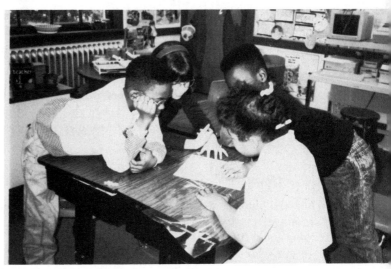

Students collaborating and taking responsibility for their own learning

When Elliott was invited to be part of a mixed-ability reading group in second grade, the experience dramatically changed his view of himself and his life in school. As a very poor reader in the first grade, Elliott's instruction had focused on skills and structured readers. Now, for the first time, he had the opportunity to read a whole book, the same wonderful book his classmates were reading.

At the end of second grade, I interviewed Elliott:

ROUTMAN: What was reading like for you in first grade?

ELLIOTT: I had a lot of trouble with big words. All reading was very hard for me.

ROUTMAN: What was different about reading this year?

ELLIOTT: I was part of a reading group.

ROUTMAN: How did you feel when your teacher first put you in *Charlotte's Web*?

ELLIOTT: I felt very happy. I'd never been in a very hard book before. I could read some hard words but not all.

ROUTMAN: Were you worried about not being able to read hard words?

ELLIOTT: Mrs. P. says, "Go back. Does that make sense?" If I couldn't figure it out, she would tell me.

ROUTMAN: What was it like discussing a book?

ELLIOTT: Answering questions was really hard for me at first. But it's not hard for me now. I like to tell what I think.

ROUTMAN: How did you feel being in the *Charlotte's Web* group?

ELLIOTT: I felt like a person who would never get as far as *Charlotte's Web*, so I was really surprised when I got that book. I thought I would never get finished with the book when I saw all those chapters. Sometimes

I could do the reading by myself and that made me happy. I was amazed when I could do some reading all by myself.

ROUTMAN: That surprised you?

ELLIOTT: Yes. It made me anxious to go on by myself.

ROUTMAN: Did it make you feel smarter?

ELLIOTT: Yes, because it was a very hard book, and I felt smarter for having read all those hard words.

ROUTMAN: Do you feel you can read hard books now?

ELLIOTT: Yes, if I get some help on the hard words.

ROUTMAN: How do you feel about reading?

ELLIOTT: I think that I'm getting better at reading, and I'm starting to like it better. I feel better about school because I can learn, and I'm getting smarter.

Elliott is a literate person. He became a reader, writer, and thinker when he was viewed as a capable learner. He was fortunate to be in a classroom with a teacher who was questioning traditional grouping practices and attempting to move away from a subskills approach to reading. His teacher was in transition, reflecting on her teaching and adjusting her theory and practice based on her professional reading, interaction with colleagues, and observation of her students.

Elliott is typical of the large population of learners who have traditionally had separate, segmented, and less challenging instruction—often because of their cultural and economic backgrounds, perceived deficits, and language differences. His experience illustrates the far-reaching potential for literacy when we begin to examine and change our teaching to include equal expectations for all students. As Elliott's story demonstrates, whole language and the best of children's literature are not just for some students. *All* students and teachers that I have worked with and observed learn more easily and feel more confident when they are engaged in meaningful enterprises and are part of a collaborative community.

The practice of grouping students by ability, especially for reading and math in the elementary grades and for all major subject areas in secondary schools, is common. Once they are in a lower track, however, students receive separate and unequal instruction, are treated differently, and are unlikely to move to a higher group (see Bloome, 1989; Braddock and McPartland, 1990; Goodlad and Oakes, 1988; Slavin, 1988). Because ability grouping is pervasive in classrooms, we need to examine its effects carefully and explore possible alternatives.

Transitions

All the years I was a classroom teacher I grouped children by the level of their ability in reading and math, especially as was determined by a standardized test. Homogeneous (ability) grouping was the norm, and, frankly, I never thought much about it. In teacher training, even on the graduate level, I don't recall being exposed to any research that was against ability grouping, and I certainly didn't believe I could be harming children by segregating them by ability. I was a caring teacher who believed ability grouping aided achievement. The thought that I might be contributing to impairing the attitudes and self-esteem of students placed in the lowest reading group never entered my mind.

My positive attitudes about ability grouping were also influenced by the fact that, years ago, my own children were in the top reading groups in the elementary grades and in the advanced tracks at the high school. I admit, although not proudly, that I believed that the "highest-ability" and "lowest-ability" students were best served in homogeneous groups. Although I often felt a twinge of conscience when I saw so few minority students honored for high achievement at awards ceremonies and graduations, I wasn't ready to see grouping as a possible culprit.

I began to have doubts about ability grouping in the late 1970s when I began to take a serious look at what was happening to students who failed to learn to read successfully. I was working in an elementary school as a reading specialist with mostly minority students, and I saw firsthand the damaged self-concepts of these children after only one year of failing to learn to read as well as their peers. I saw the methods and materials being used with these students as the main cause of their failure. The basal textbooks, worksheets, and isolated skills approach were to blame. I sought to teach reading and writing in more meaningful ways and began to teach small groups of remedial students with children's literature. The positive results and far-reaching effects of that endeavor are related in *Transitions: From Literature to Literacy* (Routman, 1988).

However, it was not until the mid-1980s that my views began to change. Our district reorganized as a result of racial imbalance and declining enrollment. Four elementary schools closed, with the remaining five buildings housing all kindergarten through grade 4 students. (A separate building housed all fifth- and sixth-graders.) Mercer School was located in the highest socioeconomic area of the district and had a predominantly (over 90 percent) white population. Moreland School, located in the lowest socioeconomic area of the district, had close to a 90 percent black and transient population. The majority of students from Moreland School, where I had been teaching for twelve years, were bused across the district to Mercer School where I was assigned.

In order to avoid potentially explosive relations between the school and the community, some teachers began to re-examine their grouping policies. After the reorganization, if teachers at Mercer School had continued to organize their reading groups as they had always done—homogeneously by ability—the "highest" groups would have contained almost all white children and the "lowest" groups almost all black children. While there were black children reading at the highest levels, they were few in number. This was not a black-white issue but rather a socioeconomic one; nevertheless, the groupings would have appeared racist. In addition, sensitivity was needed because the Moreland community already felt slighted by the closing of a well-loved school.

When several teachers first decided to group heterogeneously, an amazing thing happened. Children who had been predicted by standardized test scores to have difficulty reading did better than anticipated. By incorporating shared reading, paired reading, and the use of tape recorders for assigned silent reading—and by including all children in group discussions of their assigned books—many of the children began to "read" books that were above their test levels.

The children proved that when reading is viewed as constructing meaning from text rather than just decoding words, then most students of average intelligence become capable readers. When vocabulary is discussed in the context of the story, students see the relevance of word meanings and are enabled to read the text more efficiently. That is, when the focus of reading and group time is discussing a book and reacting personally to it, most students—even if they have needed assistance with reading the words—can participate on a high level. The children also showed that when the teacher is gentle, caring, and has high expectations for all students, every student has the opportunity to become a capable reader.

Students' Attitudes

In the spring of 1989, I interviewed some former Moreland School students who had been among the first in our district to be immersed in a reading-writing classroom in first grade. As fifth- and sixth-graders now, I was curious about their attitudes toward reading and writing. The main results of these interviews are given in "Taking a Look at Teacher and Student Attitudes," (pp. 365–370). Here I address the unexpected and unsolicited information that came out about grouping. The insights of these young people are cause for reflection.

> Jolene was a proficient reader who made sense out of print despite her difficulty using phonics cues. On our standardized reading test, she scored in the 99th percentile in reading comprehension in the fall of second grade. She was reading challenging chapter books that she understood, and she loved to read. However, in December of second grade, Jolene moved and was placed in a classroom with a phonics-based teacher. Because of her inability to complete phonics worksheets, she was put in the lowest reading group, and she received daily pull-out support from the school's reading specialist. (Jolene is discussed in Routman, 1988, pp. 209–210.)

JOLENE: In second grade, I was put in the lowest reading group. I didn't feel good about myself. I had higher expectations for myself. I knew I was smart. The teacher just didn't know I was smart. In third grade, I transferred to a new school, and it was hard to adjust. I tried to tell the teacher I was a good reader, but she wouldn't listen to me. She kept me in the lowest group. That made me feel bad. All my friends were in higher groups. In fourth grade, my teacher knew all kids had ability. She really encouraged all the kids.

My mother was my biggest influence. She taught me that I could do and be whatever I wanted. I think I'm in the medium reading group now. That doesn't phase me because I know I'm good.

I think grouping is unnecessary. It makes kids feel bad, like they can't be as good as the next person. I think there shouldn't be any grouping.

Jamaar had been one of our best readers in first grade. However, he often exasperated his teachers because he did not work up to his potential, and he failed to get assignments done. I was surprised by his spontaneous and candid comments about grouping.

JAMAAR: I don't think grouping is fair, because if a person can't read fluently, the teacher puts them in a lower group. If they can read semi-good, they should be in the top group. Kids in low groups feel bad. The teacher puts that group down because they can't read good. He doesn't work with that group much, or explain the book. He just assigns worksheets and makes them read books on their own and never checks the worksheets. He spends a lot of time with you if you're in the top group or the middle group.

If I were a teacher and a kid couldn't read, I'd help them. I wouldn't put kids in groups.

Nicky had always been a serious, hard-working student. In sixth grade, she was still a top student and in the highest reading group.

NICKY: I think grouping is childish. People in the low group feel bad, like they don't know as much. If I were a teacher, I would do away with grouping.

Hard to Reach Students: What Can Happen When the Grouping Structure Is Changed

Mario entered third grade at Mercer School as a virtual nonreader. He was streetwise, socially adept, and totally uninterested in school. He was moody, his behavior was disruptive, and he had difficulty completing assignments. Although he appeared to have at least average intelligence based on his fine verbal and social skills, school seemed to have no relevance in his life. At home he was "boss," with few limits set. It was not unusual for him to rest with his head on his desk, or even to fall asleep in class, because he had been up past midnight watching videos.

In first grade Mario had been in the Reading Recovery program, and in second grade he had the services of the Chapter 1 program. He had caring teachers, but he was failing to learn to read and write. He found academic demands overwhelming and school very boring. He had always been in the lowest reading group, and he knew it.

Mario's third grade teacher grouped him for reading with other students—but not by ability. The first book read was *The Comeback Dog* by Jane Resh Thomas, and it was done whole class. After that, Mario was placed in the group reading *Mr. Popper's Penguins* by Richard and Florence Atwater (Little, Brown, 1938). He could not read most of the words but he could enjoy and appreciate the story. For silent reading assignments, he was paired with a strong reader who read to him while he followed along in his personal copy of the book. Occasionally, Mario would attempt to read a paragraph or so to his partner. After initially just listening during group discussion, he eventually began to participate. His comments and perceptions were accepted and encouraged. Mario also began to take risks and make predictions based on what had been read and discussed. After a while, his whole demeanor changed. During reading time, he was most often on task, eager to respond, and smiling. Unexpectedly, his actual reading skills began to improve. His Chapter 1 teacher reported being very surprised when Mario volunteered to read a paragraph from *Mr. Popper's Penguins*. Sensitized to the language and the author's style, having heard the passage already read by a peer, and having met success as part of a reading group, he felt confident enough to try it himself.

I had been Mario's Reading Recovery teacher. Initially confident of his potential for success, he had been one of my most frustrating students in many years of teaching. In spite of intensive instruction, frequent communication with his parents, and genuine caring, I had failed to reach Mario. When his third grade teacher enthusiastically described his participation in reading group, I reverted to my traditional background and put her on the defensive by asking, "What are you doing about the skills?" The truth of the matter was that by immersing him in quality literature and including him in the reading community, she was doing more about the skills than any of his previous teachers had done. As he became involved and accepted in the reading process, Mario began to see himself as a reader and could begin to see the relevance of using and needing reading skills.

This is not to say that Mario became a good reader in the traditional sense; he was still severely reading disabled. By the spring of third grade he received one-to-one reading support from the learning disabilities teacher. In addition, he remained part of his classroom reading group. However, it was through the pleasurable act of reading and group acceptance that Mario acquired the desire to read and the confidence in himself to try. Without that desire and effort, there could be no chance for success. After that, it was not just Mario's reading that was positively affected. The acceptance and respect he received from his reading group spilled over into other academic areas. He began to see himself as a valued and participating member of the community of learners in his class.

As a first-grader, Elliott (whose interview begins this chapter) had barely functioned in the lowest reading group, where he spent most of his time on skills sheets and "sounding out." By the end of the school year, he was lacking in self-confidence and was not a risk taker. He saw himself as a very poor reader. While the better readers in his class were involved in delightful children's books along with the basal, the poor readers had only the basal and its accompanying structured activities. Elliott's first grade teacher believed, as many teachers do, that literature was all right for the good readers, but the poor readers needed the basal text to learn how to read.

In second grade, Elliott was placed with a teacher who had decided—for the first time—to use literature (and no basals or worksheets) with all of the students, not just the good readers. It was a big risk for her but one that would have a permanent, powerful effect on both herself and the children.

She began the year with homogeneous grouping, finding the challenge of using only literature initially overwhelming. The four poorest readers began with *Frog and Toad* books by Arnold Lobel, and they remained with this series for several months. All of the group discussion, skills work, silent reading, oral reading, repeated readings, and written assignments came from these books.

In February, the teacher decided to try mixed-ability grouping. She was determined that Elliott and all her students should have the opportunity to read the most challenging book in the literature collection for second grade, *Charlotte's Web* by E. B. White. She invited me into her classroom weekly to provide support, to demonstrate lessons, and to answer questions and dispel doubts. It was not only the children who benefited; as teachers, we grew professionally. For each of us, these times represented a positive learning experience as we shared ideas and concerns, closely observed students without at the same time having to teach, and took the time to carefully examine the teaching and learning that seemed to be taking place.

The emphasis in the guided reading group was on story enjoyment and responding to the text with skills being taught in the context of the literature as the need arose. Because the text was too difficult for Elliott to read on his own, before he came to reading group he was either paired with a student who read the text to him as he followed along or was asked to follow along with a tape the teacher had made. The tape recorder proved especially beneficial because he could reread a chapter at his own pace.

At his teacher's request, I sat next to Elliott in reading group for many weeks. She was worried that he might not be doing well enough. Was he getting the meaning and developing the skills? Did I think he was over his head? Initially Elliott was over his head. He had never participated in a group focused on high-level discussion, and his answers to questions seemed confused and off the mark. But after several months of daily group discussion, he began to respond meaningfully, and it became apparent to us that he was a capable child. Eventually, Elliott was also able to complete reading assignments independently and answer written questions in his reading spiral notebook.

When Elliott was initially handed *Charlotte's Web*, he was wide-eyed and incredulous. Each week as I observed him in his guided reading group, his growing confidence and pleasure as a reader and member of the class community of readers became more and more evident. I doubt that he would have had the same chance for success and confidence building if he had remained in the lowest reading group. Looking back, what I remember most vividly about Elliott is the smile on his face while he was participating in reading group. Like Wilbur in *Charlotte's Web*, he was absolutely radiant.

What Does the Research Say About Organizing Classes by Ability?

In summarizing the research on the achievement effects of grouping at the elementary and secondary levels, Robert Slavin, who has done a comprehensive analysis of the data available on ability grouping, states that "every means of grouping students by ability or performance level has drawbacks that may be serious enough to offset any advantages" (1989, p. 68). Other important findings are as follows:

- Studies of whole classes grouped by ability, special education, and gifted students show "no benefits for ability-grouped class assignment or special education assignment and only inconsistent and flawed evidence in favor of special programs for the gifted" (Slavin, 1989, p. 71).
- Within-class grouping by performance level for one or two subjects, if students are heterogeneously grouped the rest of the day, may aid achievement in those subjects. (Research in this area has been mostly limited to mathematics achievement in the upper elementary grades.)
- Self-contained classes in the upper elementary and middle grades are favored over departmentalization—where students are taught a major subject by another classroom teacher. (Research here is limited.)

At the elementary level, where ability grouping in reading is standard practice, Hilda Borko and Margaret Eisenhart studied reading groups in four second grade classrooms in a small town/rural public school. They concluded that the reading groups function as social and linguistic communities that can promote or hamper school success: "the content of reading instruction, student conceptions of reading, rules for participation in literacy events, and teacher expectations and evaluations differ across ability groups" (Borko and Eisenhart, in Bloome, 1989, p. 120).

Taking Another Look at Ability Grouping

If we are to be knowledgeable, conscientious professionals, we need to carefully re-examine the homogeneous grouping practices that are widespread in the United States. Ability grouping, especially as it has been applied to reading in the elementary grades, needs to be changed. Although some teachers are grouping heterogeneously and encouraging cooperative learning groups, based on my interaction with teachers in our school district and across the country, this seems to be the exception and not the norm.

Since the best-known studies of ability grouping at the elementary school level have not demonstrated higher student achievement for either high-track or low-track students, teachers need to re-examine their grouping practices. At the high school level, where almost all schools have some tracking, results are less clear—partly because so little research exists. At the very least, educators at the secondary level need to be looking at less tracking. Alternatives to tracking that include cooperative learning techniques have proved effective for both high- and low-ability students at all levels. Well-known researchers strongly suggest consideration of thoughtful and workable alternatives to tracking to provide quality education for all students (see Braddock and McPartland, 1990, and Goodlad and Oakes, 1988).

Other teachers and I have found that when students are grouped heterogeneously in a cooperative learning environment that respects and values all students, it is not only the lower-ability students who benefit. Gifted students can sometimes explain something in a way that is easier for students to understand than if the teacher explains it. With peer tutoring and cooperative learning, the gifted student has to evaluate what students already know, rethink and reorganize concepts, and demonstrate and explain ideas clearly. In doing so effectively, gifted students clarify and extend their own thinking. Additionally, we have noticed that providing opportunities for all students to work together creates a classroom community of learners and promotes the self-esteem of all students.

Given that the research about the questionable benefits and possible harmful effects of ability grouping has been around for at least fifty years, why do most teachers ignore the results of that research? Looking at my own teaching practice, I think I failed to take the research seriously because:

1. I believed all children in my classroom were being taught well.
2. I had no university training that presented the relevant research.
3. My administrators supported and encouraged ability grouping.
4. There was no parental pressure to move toward heterogeneous grouping, especially from parents whose children were in high-ability tracks.
5. Initially I did not really believe the research—or I chose to ignore it—even when I read it. Only after much soul searching, observation of children, and rereading of relevant research was I able to make a philosophical shift that translated into teaching practice.

While most of the research on ability grouping deals with achievement, the long-range psychological effects on students cannot be ignored. Based on my own experiences, I see this as perhaps the area in which most of the damage occurs. What has become especially clear to me, as I continue to struggle with the issue of homogeneous grouping in a context beyond reading in the elementary grades, is that students in low-ability tracks feel alienated and suffer feelings of low self-esteem. I believe the damage to their self-concepts may be irreparable and lifelong. In addition, I have observed that these students, as compared with students placed in high-ability groups, often have lower standards set by their teachers academically as well as behaviorally. The material they are given to read is often less interesting; the questions they are asked are less demanding; the wait time they are given for responding to questions is shorter; and they are interrupted and corrected more often when reading orally. All of these practices on the part of teachers contribute negatively to students' feelings of self-worth and competence. If our job is to teach and develop whole students, not just teach academic subjects, then we must begin to structure our classes more heterogeneously and treat all students intelligently and with respect.

5

Responding to Literature

Early Transitions

A literature extension in grade 2

Moving into Literature: The First Years

In the fall of 1987, after a district-wide reading committee composed of teachers, administrators, and librarians had been meeting and planning for one year, our district made a long-range commitment to move toward a literature approach to reading and a process approach to writing. A holistic language arts philosophy for kindergarten through grade 12, written by the committee, was adopted by the board of education; and in place of new basal texts, multiple copies of quality children's literature were purchased for kindergarten through grade 6.

Learning to Use the Core Books

We began with about six core books for each elementary grade. These core titles were carefully selected by the reading committee with input from the grade-level teachers. Enough copies were purchased for the books to be used whole class and for each teacher to have a personal copy as a teacher's edition. The core books would serve as the mainstay of the reading program, with questions, activities, and discussion centered around them. While many supplemental titles also became a part of the literature collection in each elementary building, it was the core books that teachers were expected to introduce children to.

How the core books were used was decided (and is still decided) by individual teachers. Books were read whole class, aloud, with small groups, independently, or with any combination of these approaches. There was no mandate that these books had to be "covered." If a teacher did not like a title or didn't have time to get to it, the book might simply be available in the room for children to choose to read independently.

At the same time, the teacher could continue to use the basal text and workbooks. The use of workbooks, however, was highly discouraged by principals, and after two years no new reading workbooks were purchased. Many teachers chose to use a combination approach for several years.

To facilitate the transition to literature and whole language that first year, we were granted release time by grade levels for two half days. The first in-service focused on understanding the theory and research underpinning whole language. The second concentrated on the use of the core books. Without teachers' manuals we were very concerned about management, and we wanted questions, and especially activities, in place. Under the leadership of Rebecca Thomas, a knowledgeable librarian and authority on children's literature, teachers worked together by grade level developing folders of meaningful suggestions and activities to go along with our literature collection, especially the core books.

Teachers made visual brainstorming maps, or webs, to highlight key areas for discussion. For example, second grade teachers created "Bill Peet: Getting to Know an Author/Illustrator." The web included suggestions for activities, such as taking a close look at Bill Peet characters and their characteristics, personification and imagery, ecology and math tie-ins, and suggested extension activities. Looking back at the folders several years later, I see that we probably had too many activities for some books, but we had made a good start, and we needed the security that putting ideas in writing provided.

Besides the webs, the folders that have been developed for our core books contain information that individual teachers and librarians have contributed over the years. These include excerpts about the book from other resources, ideas from other sources for questions and extensions, information about the author, and activities that teachers and librarians have developed and used successfully. Every elementary school teacher in our district has at least one folder for each book in our core collection. The folders have also been helpful to new teachers and teachers who have changed grades in getting started with unfamiliar books. However, not everything in these folders is excellent. It has been up to the teacher to be knowledgeable enough to pick and choose what is appropriate.

Beyond activities to go along with the books, in some buildings teachers used the weekly language arts support groups to work through a core book together. For example, in one building we read and discussed *Danny the Champion of the World* by Roald Dahl. We decided a week ahead of time what chapters we would focus on at the next meeting. Teachers then read the chapters and wrote in the margins of their copies questions, activities, and vocabulary to highlight. Some teachers also noted particular pages that would be good for reinforcing certain skills—for example, a page with lots of contractions, possessives, or compound words.

When we came together as a group we talked about what we thought was important, what were good questions for particular chapters, and what activities we might use to introduce the book or tie the whole book together. We added to and changed what we had done on our own by writing in additional suggestions/questions in our personal copies. We discovered that by working together and learning from each other we could come up with a very good book guide. The group was also an effective way to build confidence in our abilities to plan approaches on our own.

Many of our teachers now write what used to go into a separate book guide or folder in their personal teacher's editions of a core book. The space above the opening of each chapter, the margins, and the space at the end of the chapter all provide room for writing in important questions for discussion. The inside back cover may be used to list "Related Activities." Having the guide in the book makes it handy for the classroom teacher or substitute.

Beginning Transitions in Using Literature Meaningfully

Despite the fact that we had the literature, folders of activities, and some in-service, many of us still had difficulty deciding what questions and activities, and how many, were appropriate to go along with the books. It was common initially to "basalize" the literature by asking too many questions and requiring too many written responses, too much vocabulary study, and too many activities. Considering our past training, that was almost to be expected. Certainly, I am among those who at one time "killed" a good book by dissecting it for every possible skill and activity. It was not unusual to hear a teacher say, "After months on that book, the kids hated it and so did I."

After being wedded to the basal for so many years, I think it is part of the normal process of change to teach literature poorly before teaching it wisely. The change from the basal, with all its teacher-directed activities and manual instructions, to literature where there is no manual and the teacher and children choose the stories, questions, and activities can be overwhelming. Not used to making decisions and giving children choices, many of us did what we had always done. In planning for instruction, we created guides and worksheets every bit as burdensome as the basals we had just set aside. Only with the gradual development of our beliefs about language learning has our confidence developed in using literature thoughtfully.

In the first few years, most core books were read and discussed whole class. Many teachers felt they couldn't manage the new literature approach and also worry about independent seatwork. At the same time, when there was grouping, it was usually homogeneous, ability grouping. That has gradually changed.

After three years of using a literature approach to reading, more and more teachers are beginning to use small-group discussion, and increasing numbers of teachers are using heterogeneous, mixed-ability grouping. Some teachers have begun by having all students in the class read the same book. However, instead of one large class discussion, they divide the class into three or four groups. Initially, using one book has allowed teachers time to work out the management of having a literature discussion group while the rest of the class is working independently. Gradually, with confidence and time, many have moved to having several books going at one time. The books may or may not be related by author or theme.

At the same time, many teachers are now beginning to worry less about focusing on activities and are spending more time on developing critical thinking and encouraging children's personal responses to literature. As our knowledge and understanding of whole language has grown, we find that book-related activities present themselves naturally to us and the students. What has become the larger challenge is to ask the really important questions and to encourage the kinds of responses to literature that promote and integrate reading, writing, discussion, listening, and thinking on the very highest levels.

Chapter 6, "Responding to Literature: Later Transitions," addresses these concerns and describes the efforts some of our teachers are making. (For more information on early transitions into literature by some teachers in our school district, see Routman, 1988.)

While our district moved directly from the basal to literature, based on my experience, that is not typical. Recognizing that most school districts seem to begin their transition process to a literature approach by maintaining the use of a basal text, what follows is the story of a school district that used a basal approach but supplemented it with more meaningful activities and trade book literature.

With the hope of promoting more thoughtful responses to literature, the rest of this chapter examines how to use a basal story more holistically, demonstrates how to make a meaningful book guide, and provides examples of worthwhile literature extension activities.

Looking at a Basal Story and Using It Holistically

A local school district recently decided to "move into whole language" based on the decision of a reading/study committee composed of teachers and administrators. Multiple copies of trade books were purchased for guided reading. At the same time, the district adopted a new basal series. Funds were available for both purchases because of an anticipated reduction in the use of basal workbooks. As contradictory as it sounds, I know of several school districts that have followed a similar course. A group of teachers and administrators make the decision to move toward whole language but don't want to rattle the school community and the board of education. One assistant superintendent told me, "We weren't prepared to do away with the basal. The basal offered a comfort level that most of the staff and community still needed, and we wanted to take everyone with us."

As facilitator for a whole language institute for the teachers and administrators, I suggested that we look at the new basal text to see how it could best be utilized. I asked the reading specialist to select what she considered to be one of the best stories, and she picked "Keep the Lights Burning, Abbie" from the grade 2, first semester basal. The story, based on a real-life event that took place in 1856, centered on a young girl, Abbie Burgess, who kept the lighthouse lamps lit during a fierce storm while her father went to get needed supplies. The nine-page story was adapted from the forty-page book by Peter and Connie Roop (Carolrhoda Books, 1985).

At the time I read the story, I had no idea it was an adapted version. Nowhere in the basal is there even a hint that "Keep the Lights Burning, Abbie" is not an original story. The acknowledgments section says, "Reprinted by permission . . . ." Not only does the adapted version lack the mood, detail, setting, and language of the original, but most of the charming watercolor illustrations by Peter Hanson are missing. Also missing is the informative page "A Note from the Authors," which gives background on lighthouses as well as factual information about Abbie Burgess.

Additionally, wonderful classics such as *Daniel's Duck* by Clyde Robert Bulla (Harper & Row, 1979), *Frog and Toad Together* by Arnold Lobel, and *Dandelion* by Dan Freeman (Viking, 1964), which our first-graders read in original book form—are needlessly adapted in these second grade basals. While the newer basals are much improved, with many stories by notable authors, there are still far too many adapted versions.

With the basal, besides being aware of adaptations, it is also important to realize that students spend only about ten minutes a day actually reading the text if the teacher's manual is followed. Therefore, it is imperative that teachers become selective and critical of the basal selections they do use. Furthermore, the basal must be supplemented by authentic literature with lots of time available for reading and discussion. If children are to become readers, they must spend most of their reading time reading. Additionally, teachers need to become judicious in selecting what is worthwhile from the text and the teacher's manual and to make sure that the questions and activities employed are worth the children's time and attention. This can make the difference in whether or not students come to enjoy and value reading.

In order for teachers to feel they could use the required basal in a more meaningful way, all participating teachers in the workshop were asked to read "Keep the Lights Burning, Abbie" and take a critical look at the accompanying teacher's guide and workbook pages. I was amazed and upset to find that the teacher's guide "lesson organizer" for that story is twenty-six pages long and includes sixteen possible worksheets! It took me well over an hour to study the guide, far longer than the time it took to read the story, and I remember feeling what a waste of a teacher's time it was and how insulting such manuals are to teachers' intelligence. The focus was on unimportant skills in isolation and not on meaning.

While some of the questions the teacher was directed to ask were good, there were far too many of them, sometimes as many as three or four for one page of text. There were fill-in-the-blank worksheets available for "teaching" characterization, comprehension, using new words, filling in correct words, vocabulary, critical words in the story, time lines, unstressed vowel sounds, words with r-controlled vowels, reality and fantasy, main idea/details, keeping a log, and capitalization. The worksheets did not require any real thinking and were not worth the time they would take to complete. All of the skills could be taught meaningfully in the context of reading and discussing the story.

At the top of the worksheet on "teaching characterization" this advice was given: "Remember: To understand a character in a story think about what the character says and does. Also think about how the character speaks and acts." Sentence 1 stated, "Makiko's friend Carmen laughed a lot. She always had a smile on her face. Carmen was _____ (surprised, naughty, or happy)." (Student Workbook, "Garden Gates," Morristown, NJ: Silver Burdett & Ginn, 1989, p. 39.) The simplistic worksheet used names that were not in the story and was really a cloze exercise that could be answered through the context of the sentences. Surely this cannot seriously be called "teaching characterization." The way for students to understand characterization is to talk about the actual characters in the story!

As is often true in basal teacher guides, the suggestions in "more ideas for selection follow-up" are the best. Yet this is the section most teachers skip because it's extra and not required. This section includes open-ended questions, a suggestion to reread the story as a play, and ideas for role playing and keeping a log. Unfortunately, more practice skill sheets were also included. With the assistant superintendent in attendance, I urged teachers to skip the worksheets and most of the teacher's manual and develop their own questions and activities. We would first do that together by trying to develop a meaningful guide.

Developing a Guide for Literature

Once teachers have had practice in making and using guides for literature, they can develop their own framework for a good guide. It is important to know what makes a meaningful guide, not only for doing it yourself but for being able to look at commercial guides and deciding whether or not they are worth your, and the children's, time. Now that teaching with literature is big business, commercial publishers have responded with slick, seductive packages to lure unsuspecting teachers. Unfortunately, most of these guides are poorly prepared. They include too many questions and activities, as well as isolated vocabulary study, and go off in unrelated directions. Additionally, they usually cost too much money.

In moving into a literature approach, the first guides that teachers create are often just as poor. Based on the training many of us have had, this is a natural transition, and we should not be too hard on ourselves. In a sincere effort to cover all the important concepts and skills, initially we do too much. I know many well-meaning teachers who have worked hours creating literature packets for their students. They use these as management tools for conducting the reading group and for assigning seatwork. In addition to skills activities, multiple choice questions, and vocabulary words to look up, these all-inclusive organizers often contain every conceivable kind of extension activity related to every aspect of the curriculum. I have seen teachers take E. B. White's *Charlotte's Web* and have students do research reports on spiders as well as read about and study pigs and farms and then create math problems to go along with them all. One teacher even brought a live pig into her classroom. While none of these extension activities are inherently bad, they take children away from the book's potential impact on the reader. As far as good literature is concerned, we could do well to heed the maxim "less is more" where questions and activities are concerned.

We were fortunate in our district to have Susan Hepler, a well-known literature consultant and an expert in constructing literature guides, available to teachers for a recent, full-day summer in-service. Although I was not able to attend, colleagues shared their notes, and at a later date, Susan responded personally to my questions about making a guide. Susan has provided the most useful information to teachers on guide making that I have come across (see Hepler, 1988).

The following suggestions and format for making a teacher's guide for a book are adapted from Susan Hepler's work. In making a worthwhile guide, keep in mind that questions and activities should enhance readers' enjoyment of the book and bring them back to the text for reexamination. Time spent with a book should be worth the effort, actively involve the reader, and be true to the book's intention.

Since making book guides takes thoughtful time, titles should be chosen that are quality literature. (See "Recommended Literature by Grade Level, K–12," in the *Resources for Teachers* section for suggestions by grade level and Appendixes B and C for specific examples of excellent guides for a picture book and a chapter book.) A book guide is not meant to be used as a rigid formula. Rather, it should be a flexible framework for the teacher for using a book holistically, for promoting critical thinking, for enjoying a story, and for allowing readers to examine their own feelings.

Framework for a Meaningful Book Guide

Summary

Include author/illustrator credits.

Give a brief summary of about two sentences.

If relevant, mention something about the plot, characters, artwork, theme.

Initiating Activities

Book introduction; keep brief.

Have students make predictions regarding setting, characters, and possible content from available information—book jacket, chapter titles, opening pictures, dedication.

Thinking Critically

Picture books: 6–8 questions

Chapter books: 3–5 important questions per chapter or reading chunk

No more than 30 questions for a chapter book

Ask questions that stay with the book, relate to the artwork, or deal with understanding the characters, major themes, or the book's impact on the reader.

Phrase questions that invite many responses.

    What are some ways . . . ?

    What clues does the author give to . . . ?

Phrase questions that ask for evidence.

    How can you tell . . . ?

    How do you know . . . ?

    Why do you think . . . ?

Related Activities

For complete book: 4–6 activities

Allow students some choice and collaboration. Out of the 4–6 activities (some short, some long term) students select (or the teacher assigns) 1–3 activities.

Activities should lead students back to the book and require some work in depth: examining plot, character change, author's style.

Most activities should include a written component in a suggested format: diary, newspaper article, explanation, description, poem.

An activity may include extending critical thinking through discussion based on reacting to the book as a whole.

Some activities should include illustrations. Well-done artistic interpretation is valid, enjoyed by students, and is a change of pace from writing.

Some activities may take students beyond the book by involving other books by the same author or on the same theme or by making connections to their lives.

As a clarification, the answers to the questions included in the book guide are not meant to be written out by students; they are for teachers to use in guiding discussion before, during, and after reading. However, a response to a question might be written if it is part of the related activities at the conclusion of the book. The number of questions and activities depend on the length and depth of the book, how much time is being spent on it, whether discussion is whole class, small group, or one-to-one with the teacher, and whether discussion is taking place as the book is being read or after the book has been read through in its entirety. For the latter, there would be far fewer questions, and they would be more global; for example, "What is friendship?" "What is courage?" "What have you learned about . . . ?"

Creating a Book Guide

After discussing the framework for a meaningful book guide, teachers and administrators in the aforementioned summer institute worked together as a whole group. We created the following guide in about fifteen minutes. (Since everyone had read the story, to save time we omitted the summary.) For teachers who had never done this before, their questions and activities were more meaningful than the basal teacher's guide and took 75 percent less time to prepare than to read the instructions in the teacher's manual.

Book Guide for "Keep the Lights Burning, Abbie"

Initiating Activities

1. Look at the title and pictures and predict. How is the girl dressed? Where do you think this story takes place? What do you think it is about?
2. What do we know about lighthouses? Provide necessary background information. (For example, Gail Gibbons' *Beacons of Light: Lighthouses* [Morrow, 1990] would work well here.)

Thinking Critically

How do we know that Abbie is responsible?

How do we know Abbie was brave?

How did Abby react when the storm came?

What makes this story seem real to you?

Why was it important that Abbie keep the lights burning?

Related Activities

Write a journal entry as if you were Abbie. How would you have felt?

Compare the basal story with the original book.

Discuss how you think Abbie changed as a result of this experience.

For teachers creating guides for the first time the hardest part is to avoid the tendency to overkill. Initially teachers found it difficult to believe that the guide was long enough and involved enough. One teacher said, "I would have been inclined to have students create a journal showing a week out of Abbie's life" (instead of a day). While the activity was a good one, it would probably have added days to the time spent on only a nine-page story. Without the usual amount of written products it takes time to feel that reading instruction and comprehension have truly taken place.

Following the guide we produced as a whole group, teachers met in small groups by grade level and constructed guides for some of the picture books and chapter books that had just been purchased for the district. Each group's draft of its guide was written on an overhead transparency and shared with the entire audience. Typed copies of all guides were later distributed to all in attendance. Many teachers commented on how valuable and doable the guides seemed and how much they appreciated the opportunity to work with their colleagues.

As I talked with teachers a year later, many remarked that one of the direct results of the workshop was the realization that the basal could be used differently. Teachers who in the past had felt "skills driven" and compelled to do every workbook page now felt knowledgeable and confident enough to choose the stories and workbook pages they saw as worthwhile. The comfort level of most of the teachers seemed high. With few exceptions, teachers were choosing to use a combination of the basal text and trade book literature and were incorporating more meaningful strategies in their teaching. Several teachers mentioned that the guides constructed at the workshop had been extremely useful. Additionally, both teachers and administrators emphasized that the use of workbooks had been substantially reduced in all the buildings. Clearly, teachers were focusing more and more on the meaning and enjoyment of stories while gaining confidence that students were learning the skills. High scores on basal unit skills tests and students choosing to read constantly confirmed this.

Literature Extension Activities

To assist the creating of meaningful book guides and responses to literature, the following section presents various activities that can be used to extend and enhance the understanding and enjoyment of literature in the classroom without resorting to worksheets. A worthwhile literature extension activity

- grows naturally out of the literature
- encourages students to thoughtfully re-examine the text
- demonstrates something the reader has gained from the book

Activities can be done individually, with a partner, in a small or large group, or whole class. The majority of activities should be explained and in some cases demonstrated by the teacher before students are asked to work independently. Taking the time to explain and demonstrate the assignment raises the child's confidence level and increases his chances of doing a successful job. Students should also understand the purpose of doing the activity, and there should be ample time for sharing and displaying completed projects.

The activities and strategies that follow are presented with a strong caution. In no way are they meant to be all inclusive or used as a "recipe." They are merely suggestions that have proved successful over time. They include ideas for dramatic, artistic, and written responses. Activities that are overused, or always assigned without choice, can become boring and meaningless for students. Too much response can turn students off to a book and to reading and writing. Indeed, we need also to recognize the importance of continued silent reading, or silence, as a response. You don't always have to do something with a book in order to enjoy and appreciate it.

The most important caution, however, involves understanding educational theory about how children learn and our role as teachers. Merely incorporating different activities without an accompanying change in beliefs will result in no real, meaningful change. Always we need to be connecting learning with the activity by asking:

- What is my purpose in selecting this activity or strategy?
- How does it fit with my beliefs about learning and teaching?
- How will this activity enhance the students' appreciation and knowledge of the literature?

While we all admire creative teachers who come up with great ideas that children enjoy, we need to be sure that we know the purposes behind those ideas. Students, too, should be able to tell why they are doing a particular activity.

The main response to literature in the classroom should always center around personal enjoyment, discussion, and activities that help connect the literature to the students' lives. Above all, we want the students to continue to choose to read and write. If the literature and related activities are well chosen, not only will comprehension be extended but students' lives will be enriched.

Tried and True Enterprises

Frank Smith (1988, p. 70) prefers the term "enterprises" to "activities," which he sees as an overused term. Many of the most worthwhile enterprises arise from collaboration, from teachers planning together and students working together without pressure and restrictions. (Besides the list that follows, see "Writing for Authentic Purposes," pp. 170–171, "Literacy Extension Activities," pp. 35b–39b, and Routman, 1988.) The enterprises on the following pages are not listed in order of significance.

- Rewrite or retell the book or story as a play, short story, picture book, folktale, soap opera, parody, or television script.
- Write an introduction, epilogue, different ending, or an additional chapter.
- Design a bookmark, book jacket, or front and/or back cover.
- Make a poster that advertises the book, depicts favorite scenes, or describes a "wanted" character.
- Keep a diary from the point of view of one of the characters.
- Write an original dialogue between two characters.
- Make a diorama, mural, or filmstrip depicting scenes or major settings from the book.
- Act out a favorite scene, perhaps with simple puppets (such as "lunch bag puppets") or as a pantomine.
- Write a letter to the author or book character with questions and suggestions.
- Advertise the book through a commercial, Reader's Theater, or radio show.

- Dress up as a character and discuss/justify your behavior and actions.
- Illustrate the settings of the book as a visual map, travel brochure, photo album, or poster.
- Make a comparison chart of several versions of a tale, different illustrations in similar versions, or various books by the same author.
- Make a Big Book, picture book, or wordless book from a chapter book.
- Using a folded paper booklet or sheet divided into eight sections, illustrate the major happenings of the book in sequence, and include with each picture several sentences that sum up the event.
- Make a class graph of favorite characters, books, or authors.
- Create a dictionary for specialized language or facts learned from the book.
- Find and read original reviews of the book. Give a summary report. Write your own review.
- Research information about the author.
- Create an enterprise that demonstrates your enjoyment, appreciation, and understanding of the book.

Making an Eight-Page Book from One Sheet of Paper

This is a fantastic, favorite resource that students are able to put together on their own from grade 1 upward. Using any size piece of paper, and cutting and folding according to the directions below, an eight-page book is created without staples or tape. The standard $8^{1}/_{2}$ by 11 inch sheet is most useful because it is plentiful in most schools as copy paper. Also, when this standard size book is opened and flattened, it can be copied on the Xerox machine—allowing for multiple copies of text for reading, writing, and illustrating.

Teachers and students alike love these eight-page books. We have used them for note taking on field trips, making picture books from chapter books, collecting true facts from a novel, creating individual vocabulary booklets or skills booklets (for homonyms, compound words, synonyms from books), sequencing main story events, summarizing, and illustrating favorite sections of a book. The possibilities are endless. Directions and samples follow.

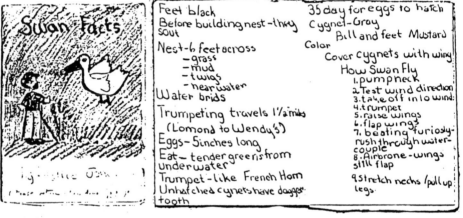

Cover and two pages from a third-grader's book of "Swan Facts," as found in *Trumpet of the Swan* by E. B. White.

MAKING AN EIGHT-PAGE BOOK FROM ONE SHEET OF 8½" BY 11-INCH PAPER

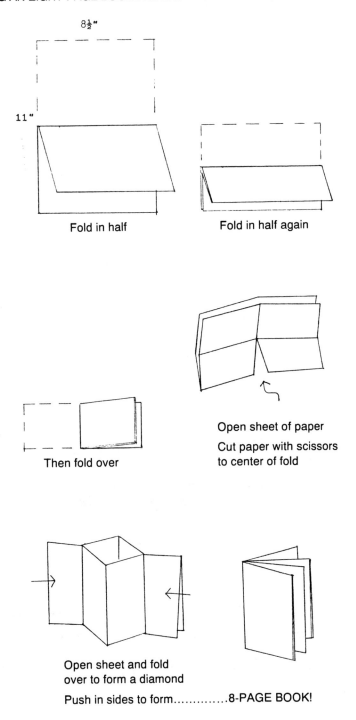

8½"

11"

Fold in half

Fold in half again

Then fold over

Open sheet of paper
Cut paper with scissors
to center of fold

Open sheet and fold
over to form a diamond
Push in sides to form..............8-PAGE BOOK!

Flip Booklets

Flip books are easy to put together, and young children enjoy them. They can be used to depict events, feelings, personal histories, scenes from a book, or anything you can think of. Using 8½ by 11 inch paper, two or more sheets of paper are folded and then stapled on the common fold with a long-arm stapler. Directions and a sample follow.

Fold three sheets of 8½ x 11" paper
this way:

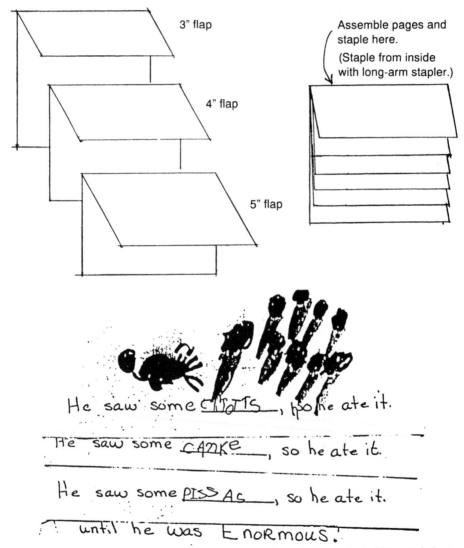

Based on an idea by beginning first-graders after hearing/reading *The Fat Cat* by Jack Kent (Scholastic, 1971).

Creating Take-offs on Favorite Stories

Many books for young children work naturally as springboards for writing. The stories naturally suggest themselves as writing models, and children use the basic structures to create original texts. This is very different from restrictive, patterned writing, which is sometimes overused. (See Wason-Ellan, 1988, "Using Literary Patterns: Who's in Control of the Authorship?")

Following are some texts that have worked well. (For additional titles, see "Books Which Invite Writers to Write"— "Recommended Literature," blue pages, and Routman, 1988, p. 76.) Excerpts from first-graders' take-offs are included.

Gelman, Rita Golden. *Why Can't I Fly?* (Scholastic, 1986)
Heller, Ruth. *Chickens Aren't the Only Ones* (Grosset & Dunlop, 1981)
Kellogg, Steven. *Can I Keep Him?* (Dial, 1971)
Wells, Rosemary. *Noisy Nora* (Dial, 1973)
West, Colin. *Have You Seen the Crocodile?* (Harper & Row, 1986)
Viorst, Judith. *The Tenth Good Thing About Barney* (Atheneum, 1971)

Ten Good Things About Nipper, our class Ginea pig

adapted from The Tenth Good Thing About Barney
by Michael

Nipper isint normlee to brad to cuch. Mabye its becus he is yuostou me sins I give him a deesint amount of atentin

Crocodiles arnt the only Ones.
by Christen

Crocodiles' arnt the only ones. Ducks swim too.

Adapted from *Chickens Aren't the Only Ones*

Picture Mapping

Picture mapping sequences the major events of a story without words. Students who prefer drawing to writing especially favor this activity. Small groups enjoy working together and re-examining the text and illustrations to decide whether an event is a main idea or a detail. Usually not more than ten to twelve pictures are included in a picture map.

Intermediate grade students have had great fun doing circular picture maps of William Steig picture books because a number of his stories begin and end in the same setting. Note the picture map below of *Brave Irene* by William Steig (Farrar, Straus and Giroux, 1986), done whole class. Picture maps done in small groups or individually yield different interpretations. As long as students can support their decisions from the text, all reasonable responses are accepted.

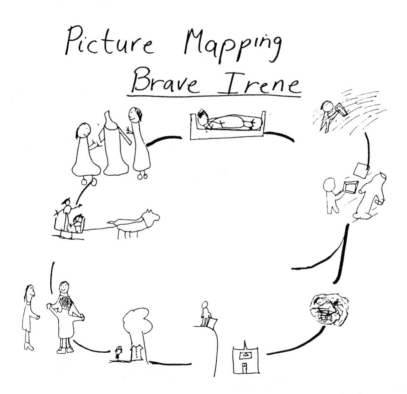

Venn Diagram

The Venn diagram is a visual device for comparison that uses two concentric circles. Concepts in common are denoted in the space created in the intersection of the two circles. The diagram can be used to compare two books, two versions of a fairy tale or fable, two different mediums for a story—a book and a videotape—or two characters. Phrases are used to note characteristics of a story or character. For very young children, pictures may be used instead of words. The Venn diagram may be used from kindergarten through high school—whole class, small group, paired students, or individually for older students. Because it is so visual, it is easy for students to grasp.

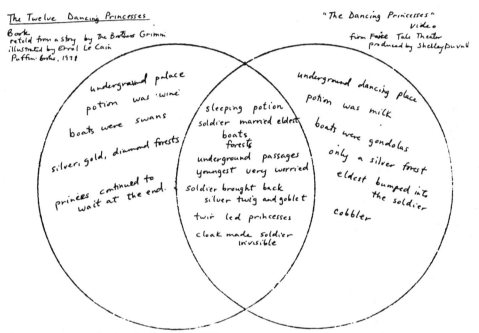

The Twelve Dancing Princesses
Book retold from a story by The Brothers Grimm illustrated by Errol Le Cain Puffin Books, 1978

"The Dancing Princesses" Video from Faerie Tale Theater produced by Shelley Duvall

underground palace
potion was 'wine'
boats were swans
silver, gold, diamond forests
princes continued to wait at the end.

sleeping potion
soldier married eldest
boats
forests
underground passages
youngest very worried
soldier brought back
silver twig and goblet
twin led princesses
cloak made soldier invisible

underground dancing place
potion was milk
boats were gondolas
only a silver forest
eldest bumped into the soldier
cobbler

By Karen Horton's third grade class, 1989–1990.

Storymapping

Various formats may be used for storymapping. The purpose is for students to recognize and analyze the structure and elements of a story by noting the setting, characters, problem or conflict, events, and resolution. Storymapping helps students internalize the structure of stories; it is useful for aiding understanding of new stories and writing original stories.

Many of these elements will be viewed differently by the reader, depending upon one's point of view and personal interaction with the text. Note the storymaps of several first-graders for *There's a Nightmare in My Closet* by Mercer Mayer (Dial, 1986). All responses are different; all interpretations are valid.

THERES A NIghTMaRe
Book Title
IM MY closeT
setting: In his room
characters: The BOY and The nightmare
problem: Th A BOY Gets sKard.

Event 1 he was mad BuT hot
To Mad
Event 2 The nfenTMARe
Gets In Bed
Event 3 The monSTer
CrIse

resolution: That The Boy
Let the monSTer
I nhTs Bed

THERE'S A Nightmare
In My Room
Book Title
setting: House
characters: a little boy and his dad and monsters.
problem: There are monsters in his room.

Event 1 Monsters loeknedid in bed room.
Event 2 Get rid of them.
Event 3 bok for the monsters avry were.

resolution: find mensters thay were bad gis.

Good woRk, Michael ☆

There es a Nightmar
in myBook Title Closet
setting: Bedroom
characters: A Boy and his Nietmer
problem: The Nietmer gets woond id

Event 1 The Boy hs chi rin uv a NieTmmer
Event 2 He gets redey to shoot.
Event 3 The MonsT re Krise.

resolution:
The Nietmer maexs freneeds Wit the Boy

Reproducing Photographs from a Shared Experience

A delightful remembrance of a field trip, classroom visitor, or any shared class experience can be captured by taking pictures of the event. On the school copying machine the teacher reproduces the color or black and white photographs. The photos may be selected and sequenced by the teacher and made into individual booklets or a class Big Book. Students write and read their own text. The photos help students focus and recall main events and details.

The example below shows books produced by first-graders (near the end of the school year) after a visit by a doll maker. Working in small groups with teacher guidance, the students wrote rough drafts, revised them, and produced their own final copies for the first time.

 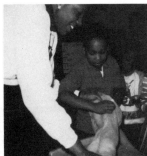 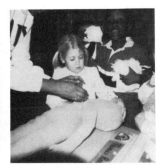

Mrs Eady Visited us. She took us to The rug. And she had some doll Skin And she was holding the Skin up.

Guess What, they're doing? They're Stuffing Alot of Cotton. Mrs. Pope And I Like The way Terry And Terry's mom Work.

Now Beth is Stuffing The head So The head will Look Real. Jerome is Not Going to Eat That. Is he? No!

Pages 1–3 from "The Making of Elizabeth, a Doll" by Raquel. Idea developed by Joyce Pope.

Reader's Theatre

I first learned about Reader's Theatre when I heard Lynn Rhodes describe it at a national IRA conference. I have been using it and demonstrating it to teachers and children ever since.

Reader's Theatre involves creating a script from a narrative text and performing it for an audience. Students work cooperatively to write a dialogue, rehearse it, and read it to the class. Props are minimal. Interest and involvement are high.

We have used Reader's Theatre to dramatize and retell one scene or chapter of a book, to highlight the personality of particular characters, or to advertise and promote a favorite book read independently. After the script is written, the writer or writers choose students to practice and read the character parts.

Below is a Reader's Theatre from *More Stories Julian Tells* by Ann Cameron, as written by a group of third-graders after I modeled and talked through a scene from the book on the overhead projector.

Robert, Amanda, Alison

characters: Gloria, Julian narrator   pp. 25-27

narrator: It was seven-o-clock at night. and Julain was waiting for Gloria to call. (the phone rang) it was Gloria.

Julain: hello Gloria

Gloria: look out your window

Julain: I dont see anything unusal.

Gloria: Whatch the wall across from the window.

narrator: Julain watched a yellow circle of light on the wall

Jalain: It lookes like the sun

Gloria: It is the sun. look out your window again

Julain: Your right Gloria you win.

narrator: The End .

Creating Simple Story Frames

Kindergarten and first grade children can demonstrate their comprehension of a story by illustrating and/or briefly noting their characters, setting, problem, and solution in a picturebook story. Such open-ended frames allow differing points of view and encourage students to think about the problems or events that they feel are most important. Note three first-graders' responses to three different story frames.

Story	Problem	Solution
Mouse Soup	The weasel caught the mouse and the mouse was going to be mouse soup	the mous. tricked the weasel.
Tikki Tikki Tembo	Tikki fell in the well and he was in there a long time.	the old man got tikki out of the well.

Story	Characters	Setting
If you give a mouse a cookie	boy / mouse	House
The Carrot seed	mom dad boy Big Broter	otside lauree Elen e-h

Name LAUREN
Date 1 18 0P
Title THE TROLLEY RIDE

• I drew the story in order

Idea developed by Peg Rimedio.

Writing Feature News Articles from Book Events

A feature story, with a headline, is written about a main event in a book. The feature is written as if it had been found on the front page of the newspaper where the event takes place. Students will first need to be familiar with how feature newspaper articles and headlines are constructed.

Then, taking on the role of news reporter and putting themselves at the scene of the event, the students need to tell succinctly what happened. The first sentence should reflect the headline, and quotations should be from eyewitnesses to the event. Students will need to reread the text for key events and phrases. This activity could also take the format of a nightly news show, with students reading their headlines and stories. Another variation could be to pull facts from an actual newspaper article and turn it into a story.

Below are some headlines and feature stories from Patsy Bannon's third grade class based on *Trumpet of the Swan* by E. B. White (Harper & Row, 1970).

LOMOND WAVE

U.F.S. TAKES VALUABLE TRUMPET

By Tori Skubic (L.W.)

Billings, Montana – A valuable musical instrument was stolen by an unidentified flying swan.

The swan rammed right into the window of a music store. The swan broke the glass and cut himself. Luckily, the swan was the only one injured.

The swan caused $900.00 in damage. The police want to arrest the thief. The police are looking for the trumpet and the swan.

WHITE BIRD ROBS MUSIC STORE

By Sharon Moffie (L.W.)

Billings, Montana – A huge white bird flew into a music store and stole a very valuable trumpet.

The bird was injured by crashing into the store's window, but no one else got hurt. A saleslady fainted when she saw the bird.

The police came and tried to arrest the robber.

There was $900 worth of damage done to the store. The owner tried to shoot the bird, but missed.

The bird flew away with the trumpet.

GIANT BIRD BOMBS MUSIC STORE

By John Pope (L.W.)

Billings, Montana – A giant swan robbed Mallard's Musical Instrument Store yesterday. The music store was robbed of a valuable trumpet.

The swan flew through the glass window of the store! The swan was injured by the broken glass. No one else was hurt. A salesgirl fainted!

One eyewitness said, "It was a terrifying experience!"

The manager fired at the bird two times, but missed. The police came, but the bird escaped. The owner complained that $900 worth of damage was done to his store.

Creating Comic Strips

Students of all ages enjoy turning a scene, event, chapter, or book into a comic strip. Students like to study actual comic strips first for format and use of color. Many teachers find the "bubbles" help students understand the use of conversation and quotation marks.

Below is a comic strip done by a third-grader from a scene in *Nora and Mr. Mind-Your-Own-Business* by Joanna Hurwitz (Morrow, 1977).

Idea developed by Patsy Bannon.

Making a Photo Album

Students enjoy putting together a photo album or scrapbook of important events, scenes, and characters from a story. This can be used to highlight settings, characters, or main events. Each snapshot or photo is captioned with a description. Corners to hold the photos in place are made with black Magic Marker in the shape of small triangles.

Below is one page of illustrated photos by a third-grader based on *Danny the Champion of the World* by Roald Dahl.

Idea developed by Sylvia Tallentire.

6

Responding to Literature

Later Transitions

Heterogeneous literature discussion group: fourth-graders leading their own discussion of Every Living Thing *(Rylant, 1985)*

Three to five years after moving from the basal to literature, some of us have begun to make a further transition to a more collaborative response to literature. Teachers are ready to ask fewer—but even better—questions, plan fewer activities, and encourage more student ownership and participation. One way to achieve this is through the use of literature response logs and literature discussion groups.

This chapter elaborates on using literature response logs, asking important questions, and facilitating discussion groups as a means for promoting high-level thinking and reasoning from the primary grades through high school. The formats given here are meant only to serve as flexible guides for many possibilities in responding to literature. Various uses of the formats are examined in detail because they have been a very successful vehicle for some teachers and students. You will want to adapt their use, choose your own formats, use certain components, try out what appeals to you, and add your own unique experiences and expertise.

Literature Response Logs

A literature response log is a journal for recording reactions to literature. It has also been called a reading response log, literature log, reading log, or reading journal. It is an excellent tool for connecting reading to writing, for extending the meaning of the text, and for giving readers ownership of their literary experience. Responding in writing to a question, impression, mood, or reaction generated by the reading seems to promote critical thinking. The response may be intellectual or emotional, personal or general, or a combination. In any case, the literature response usually goes beyond mere summarizing and factual recall.

Written responses may be in the form of responses to open-ended questions, freewriting, vocabulary words, or illustrations. Responses may also include dialogue journals—personal, written interactions between the student and the teacher or between two students.

Students' written responses can be used as a springboard and reference point for group discussion. Additionally, the literature response log can be an effective evaluation instrument. The teacher, student, and parents have ongoing, visible evidence of the student's reactions, interpretations, and thinking regarding a particular book. Finally, the literature response log is a meaningful alternative to answering traditional comprehension questions and writing lengthy, mandatory book reports.

Literature logs can be used from the end of grade 1 all the way through high school. For first-graders, I have found students most receptive to the log when they are at the point where they can read silently and their invented spelling has progressed to the stage where it is easily readable. High school students, used to directed reading assignments, will need lots of oral and written modeling by the teacher before they can honestly express their interpretations and reactions to books. Initially, they begin by thinking and asking, "What does the teacher want?" and "What is the purpose of all this?"

For the literature response log, we have used a spiral notebook, a three-ring notebook, or a booklet put together for the specific book being read. To make a booklet I simply fold sheets of mimeograph paper together and staple them at the centerfold with a long-arm stapler. Paper can be lined, unlined, or a combination of both. A different-color sheet can be included for the cover, which students design. Students are expected to date each entry and write legibly.

What we and the students look for in the reading response log is a reflective response to the literature. It is important that the focus remain on the content of the response and not on the mechanics. There is no red penciling in the log. Comments—written or oral—that the teacher or students make should relate to the content of the message. Care always needs to be taken that not too much writing is assigned or expected. We want students to continue to enjoy to read. Some days no written response is expected. Students just read and enjoy the literature. The response may be simply a personal appreciation of the literature.

As a management tool, literature response logs offer built-in independent work while the teacher meets with other reading groups or students. The students who are not in a reading/literature group read silently and respond to literature in their logs and through other activities the teacher and students have agreed upon. As opposed to worksheets, which encourage "right answer" responses and rarely expand thinking, the literature response log encourages the widest possible range of responses. The student is encouraged to interact with the text and use her own experiences and the book to interpret and construct meaning from what she reads. The student is always encouraged to go back to the text to support her response. The exception to re-examining the text would be responding to a read-aloud book or asking students to write a reaction or response following the reading.

High school teachers who use a response log format, either for guided reading or independent reading, report that they never see evidence of "Cliffs Notes." One high school teacher commented, "I have had some trouble teaching students the value of logs, but there is never a doubt about whether they've done the reading." The only way to respond personally and thoughtfully to a text is to read it.

Ways to Use the Literature Response Log

My favorite way to use the literature response log is as part of the guided reading program. The whole class, or small groups of students (up to eight), read a book and meet to discuss their impressions after reading silently. (See pp. 38–41 for discussion of guided reading and pp. 122–132 for literature discussion groups.) One advantage of the literature response log is that it encourages students to assume responsibility for the discussion. While the teacher is present to guide the discussion and model questions and responses, students do most of the talking. Instead of the teacher dominating the discussion, with comments directed mostly to the teacher, students talk with each other. Students refer to their entries as a reference to back up specific points they make. Because they have already thought about a question that has been posed, their confidence level rises, and they are often more likely to participate in the discussion. Many of us have noticed that the discussions are livelier, and students have better recall of what they have read. Often the silent reading has taken place the previous day, and the log jogs students' memories. One third-grader said, "I remember the chapter better because I can look at my notes."

At the end of the discussion time, typically about ten to fifteen minutes, I write the next silent reading assignment and requested response on a small, portable chalkboard. (If a different book is being used with each group, several small boards may be used and set aside for easy reference.) While I usually have ready an idea for a general question, I am just as likely to choose a question or issue that has arisen from the discussion that has just taken place. Students copy the response question into their logs and know exactly what is expected of them. In that way, when the teacher is with another group—that day or the following day—students are ready to work independently. Students, teachers, and parents also have a clear record of questions and responses.

For most of us who have been used to asking many questions, asking one or two questions may initially not seem substantial or engaging enough for independent work. However, the type and substance of the questions are quite different—as this chapter demonstrates—and teachers that move to this format are quickly convinced of its benefits. (In addition, students have other options for independent work. See "Classroom Management and Organization," pp. 437–442.)

The literature response log can also be used as a dialogue journal (Atwell, 1987) without group discussion. A written transaction occurs between two students or between a student and the teacher. In that case, it is recommended that the teacher also keep a reading log so students have the teacher's response as a written model. Students, or student and teacher, exchange logs, react to each other's perceptions, and write thoughtful comments to each other. The paired exchanges could vary daily or weekly. The teacher would first need to model what is expected in a thoughtful response. See Figure 6–1 for an example of a student's response to another student and Figures 6–10 and 6–11 for examples of a high school teacher's responses to a student's log.

There is no one right way or best way to use the literature response log. Vary the way you use the log with students and adopt what works well for you and your students. Keep in mind that we first need to show students, by thinking aloud and writing in front of the students, how he or she would respond to a question or give a

Figure 6-1   Literature Response Log by a Ninth Grade Student

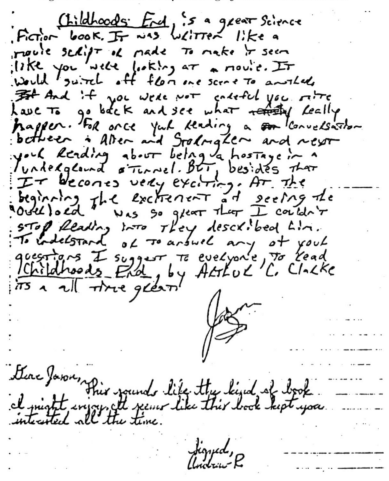

personal reaction to what has been read. One demonstration is rarely sufficient. We demonstrate again and again until students have a clear sense of expectations and possibilities. Using Don Holdaway's developmental model, I begin by giving a demonstration myself and then inviting students to participate.

Even with demonstrations, students need time to get used to the new format. Those who tend to rush through assignments may do the bare minimum and not give thoughtful responses at first. Also, students who are not used to putting ideas into their own words may also have difficulty at first. Because participation in follow-up group discussion is often based on the log, students—who all enjoy being part of a lively discussion—do not take long before they are completing their logs satisfactorily.

We have found it works well for us or the students to choose only one question or format for a particular day's response. Initially, teachers find it difficult to believe that comprehension is being adequately addressed. As teachers, we have been used to requiring lengthy responses, book reports, summaries, large numbers of vocabulary words to be looked up, and/or answers to many specific questions.

However, when teachers and students look at larger issues from literary and personal perspectives, the important details, major happenings, and themes do emerge.

The goal is not to come to common agreement but rather to share various viewpoints and interpretations. The teacher's viewpoint is also shared, but it is only one opinion in the group and is not considered more important or more valid than the ideas of the students. The teacher's role is to guide the discussion but not dominate it. The following are some strategies you can demonstrate for students in using the literature response log. They are not listed in order of significance.

- *Respond to an open-ended question.*   The question that you or the students select should reflect the overall theme or feeling of the chapter or reading chunk of several chapters. The question should be genuine; that is, one right answer is not already in the teacher's head. (See "Asking Important Questions," pp. 117–119.) A good question may elicit some surprising and varied responses. One question is usually enough. We do not want students to be overburdened with writing. If you choose your question carefully, the key points of the chapter will come out in the discussion. The question is merely the vehicle to get the thinking going. It may call for prediction before reading, a reaction after reading, and/or a response during reading.

Teachers used to asking a lot of questions, many of which have been at the literal level, need time, trust, and the ability to risk to realize that all of the important facts surface when an important question is asked. In fact, by being asked inferential and critical questions, the reader is focused on higher-level thinking, and the literal level takes care of itself.

Some examples of questions that work well are:

What else do you learn about a particular main character?

How does the character feel about . . . ?

What is (a particular character) concerned about?

Describe the relationship between . . . .

What has the author done to build suspense in this chapter?

What do you predict will happen in the next chapter?

What does the author do to make you want to continue reading?

What do you think is most important about what you just read?

Was there anything about what you just read that surprised you?

What do you think the author is trying to tell us about . . . ?

What do you hope to find out in this chapter? What did you find out?

What do you think the focus of the next chapter will be?

What do you think it means when . . . ?

What would happen if . . . ?

Again, we teachers will need to demonstrate how to respond meaningfully before expecting students to do so. Older students—especially at the secondary level—find it less threatening to talk about events in the story, as they have always done. After many years of focusing on plot, they need time and repeated demonstrations before they can begin to respond more thoughtfully and personally.

In their response logs, students are encouraged to make deductions based on the text as well as to prove their points referring to the text and applying their own knowledge and experiences. If the purpose of the log is to support students' ideas in literature discussion groups, they need only write down key words and phrases. This is also a good example of purposeful note taking. If the log is not being used with discussion groups, expecting complete sentences is appropriate.

Joan Servis, a fourth grade teacher who uses literature circles effectively, uses the same question or prompt for all students even if students are reading different books. One question may serve for one chapter, several related chapters, a picture book, or a short story. Joan has her students prove their points and concepts by noting page numbers and specific quotes to support their thinking and inferences. Hers is a terrific technique—one I have used repeatedly with great success.

Here is an example of a prompt and demonstration for Chapters 1 and 2 of *Danny the Champion of the World* by Roald Dahl. Note that complete sentences are not expected here. The purpose is to expand thinking, have students read the text carefully, and use their notes as a catalyst for discussion.

> What do you learn about Danny's father? Prove your conclusions by jotting down a key phrase or insight from the text and the page it is on.
>> Poor—did not own much, p. 3
>> Loved Danny—lavished his love for Danny's mother (who died) on Danny, p. 4
>> Mechanic—owned a filling station, p. 5
>> Storyteller—made up a different story every night, p. 9
>> Not educated—"I doubt he had read twenty books in his life," p. 9
>> Could be trusted—"was an eye-smiler," p. 9

Notice that the characteristics at the left are gleaned from the text—but not necessarily stated in the text. The student has to infer traits about the character through the author's language. When the student comes to group discussion, he will refer to his notes to jog his memory and make his points. Figures 6–2 and 6–3 are examples of fourth grade students' responses to a question shortly after the literature response logs were introduced and modeled.

You will be able to tell by the level of the discussion if the question was a high-level one. The broader the question, the better will be the group discussion. With a probing, comprehensive question all the important points of the chapter will

Figure 6-2   Response to **Sarah, Plain and Tall** *from a Fourth-grader*

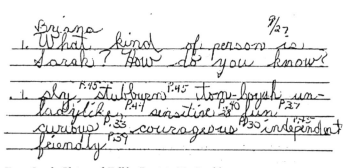

From *Sarah, Plain and Tall* by Patricia MacLachlan

Figure 6-3 Response to The Lion, the Witch and the Wardrobe

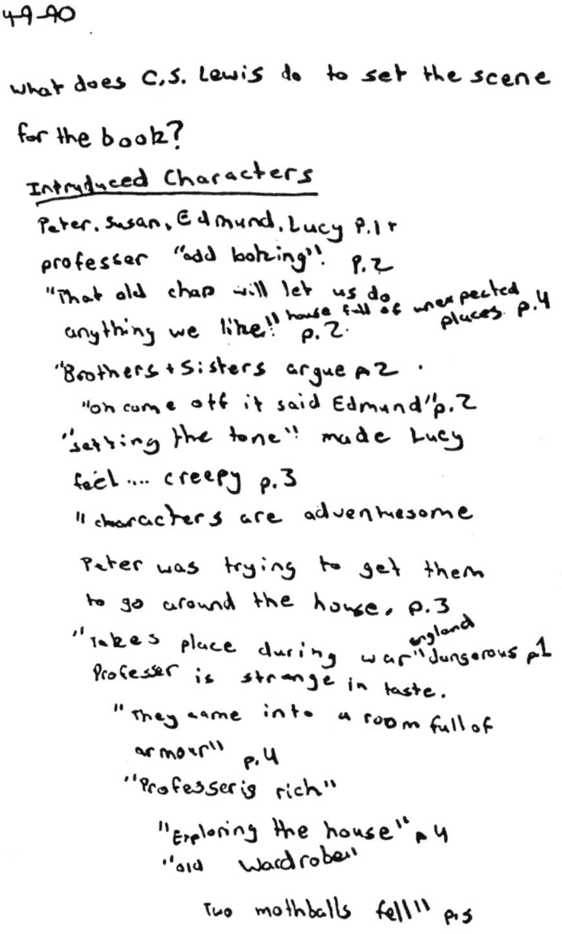

4-9-90

What does C.S. Lewis do to set the scene
for the book?

Introduced Characters

Peter. Susan, Edmund, Lucy P.1+
professer "odd bokring". p. 2
"That old chap will let us do
anything we like!" p. 2   house full of unexpected places p. 4.
"Brothers + Sisters argue p2.
   "oh come off it said Edmund" p. 2
"setting the tone" made Lucy
feel .... creepy p. 3
"characters are adventuesome

Peter was trying to get them
to go around the house, p. 3
"Takes place during war" england   Dangerous p1
Professer is strange in taste.
   "They came into a room full of
armour" p. 4
   "Professer is rich"
      "Exploring the house" p 4
      "old wardrobe"
         Two mothballs fell" p.5

From *The Lion, the Witch and the Wardrobe* by C. S. Lewis.

surface. A limited question will elicit a limited response. Students and teachers need at least several months to get comfortable with the questioning.

(For further examples of open-ended questions that work well, see the next section, "Asking Important Questions.")

• *Reflect on your personal reactions while reading.*   Based on life experiences and points of view, a piece of literature affects individuals differently. One use of the log, often employed for responses to books read independently or in an individualized reading program, is for the reader simply to write down what was going through her mind while reading. The written response can be done while reading or after the reading is completed.

Some suggested prompts include:

As you are in the process of reading, write down some thoughts that are going through your head.

Were you reminded of something in your own life as you were reading?

What were you thinking or wondering about as you read this chapter?

What was your overall reaction to what you just read?

What questions came to your mind as you were reading?

I modeled my in-process reading-thinking for a group of second-graders who had read *Stone Soup* by Marcia Brown (Scribner, 1975), a story about a group of hungry soldiers who "trick" some unwilling villagers into feeding them. I quickly jotted down phrases on Post-its to recall my immediate impressions while reading. Then, using the overhead projector, I thought out loud as I wrote:

> I was surprised that such a greedy group of villagers could be tricked so easily. I think people are like that. If they believe they will get something good for themselves, they'll believe anything. However, the peasants were not only greedy. They were curious. No harm was done. Everyone wound up eating a great meal.

When writing in front of the students, I point out that personal responses can often begin with: "I was surprised by . . .", "I noticed that . . .", "I wondered why . . .", "I didn't understand when. . . ." Familiarity with possible beginnings often helps them get started.

• *Choose several unknown vocabulary words.*   Students at all grade levels can be asked to choose several vocabulary words from the chapter (or several chapters) that they would like to know the meaning of and to write down what they think the words mean. Students are encouraged to choose words they might encounter again. This procedure needs to be modeled because students often have trouble choosing words they don't know. Once students become familiar with the procedure, it is enough for them just to write "vocabulary" in their log, but initially I give the following prompt, which they write in their log:

> Choose three words (or another small number) that you would like to know the meaning of. For each word, write the line number and page number it is found on, how it is used (partial or complete quote), and what you think the word means.

Then, when we meet for reading discussion, students refer to the specific lines, page numbers, and contexts so other students can participate in talk about the words' meanings. Very often a word can be determined by the context. When it cannot, this is the ideal time to use the dictionary. While the teacher can also choose words to highlight, it is not only the teacher's words that will be discussed.

With the teaching of vocabulary, it is unrealistic to expect students to look up, memorize, or understand the meanings of fifty to a hundred words or more per book. Several words per chapter usually means twenty to forty words per book, which may still be too much. Use your discretion based on your students' needs and ages. Just because students have looked up and even tested well on a large number of words does not mean they have learned those words. Vocabulary that is truly learned can be meaningfully applied to new reading, writing, speaking, and listening contexts.

A further recommendation is to post the important words that arise (those the student is likely to come across and use again) on a chart and to use and refer to those words over and over again in classroom conversation. In that way, students come to "own" the words, and they begin to appear in their own conversations and writing.

If I were to give a vocabulary test when the students have finished the book, I would ask them to choose a specified number of words from our list and use each word in a sentence that demonstrates the meaning is understood. I would not expect all students to be responsible for the same words or to have learned all the words. Imagine us as adults being expected to learn the same set of words from a novel we have read. Our individual needs and prior knowledge of vocabulary are too diverse to expect that a common list of words would emerge.

Another way to highlight vocabulary and lead into a discussion on the author's use of words is to give prompts such as the following:

As you are reading, note the way the author uses descriptive words and phrases. Choose some that appeal to you (with page numbers) that you might choose to use in your own writing.

What are some of the words the author uses that give insight into a character's personality?

What particular words that the author used gave you a vivid picture of the setting?

• **_Illustrate a part of the text._**   It is important to allow time for artistic interpretation as another way to respond to text. Most students, even older ones, relish the chance to draw as a change of pace. In addition, students who are not proficient readers and writers may enjoy the opportunity for artistic expression. Some response prompts include:

Draw a favorite part of the story.

Based on the author's description, draw a particular character.

Design another cover for this book.

Draw the setting as described by the author.

Select a scene and draw how you picture it.

Assume the role of illustrator for the chapter(s) you just read.

When I introduce *Danny the Champion of the World* by Roald Dahl, to third- or fourth-graders, I read the first few pages aloud and ask students to form a picture in their minds. Then I give each child a reproduced copy of the setting as Dahl wrote it. As I reread the description aloud, I ask the students to underline the parts they could consider putting into their illustrations. First, I do a demonstration and show them the parts I would underline. Often I do this on the overhead projector, inviting student participation. Below is one paragraph from the ten-paragraph description (pp. 5–7).

> The <u>filling station</u> itself had only <u>two pumps</u>. There was a <u>wooden shed</u> <u>behind the pumps</u> that served as an <u>office</u>. There was <u>nothing in the office</u> <u>except an old table</u> and a <u>cash register</u> to put the money into. It was one of those where you pressed a button and a bell rang and the <u>drawer shot out</u> with a terrific bang. I used to love that (p.5).

This is an excellent activity because it directs students' attention back to the text in a careful, critical manner. It is much harder to do than it appears. Students have to re-examine the text, think about spatial placement, layout, detail, color, size, perspective, and what is important to include. (See Figure 6–4 for one student's interpretation.) In this particular book, I show students the illustrator's interpreta-

Figure 6–4   *A Student's Interpretation of the Introductory Setting in* Danny the Champion of the World

Figures 6–5 and 6–6   *Second-graders' Responses to* Fantastic Mr. Fox

Figure 6-6

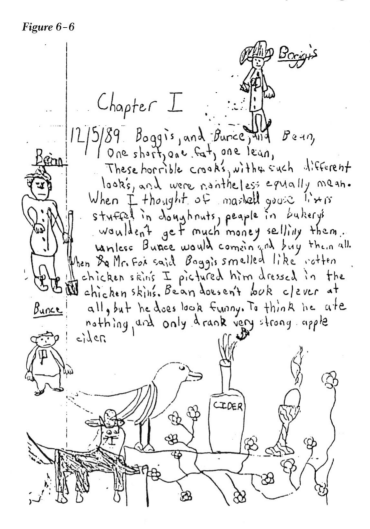

Chapter I

12/5/89 Boggis, and Bunce, and Bean,
One short, one fat, one lean,
These horrible crooks, with such different
look's, and were nontheless equally mean.
When I thought of mashell goose livirs
stuffed in dohyhnuts, people in bakerys
wouldent get much money selliny them.
unless Bunce would comein and buy them all.
When to Mr. Fox said Boggis smelled like rotten
chicken skin's I pictured him dressed in the
chicken skins. Bean doesen't look clever at
all, but he does look funny. To think he ate
nothing, and only drank very strong apple
cider

tion after they have completed their drawing. In rereading, one group of students noticed that "the square brick building to the right of the office" was pictured in the book with wood siding, an error on the part of the book illustrator.

- *Examine the author's style and motives.*

  Why do you think the author put in the minor characters . . . ?

  What is the format of this book? Is it effective?

  What clues does the author give . . . ?

  How does the author use humor (or . . .)?

  Why do you think the book ended the way it did?

  Is the author's style of writing and organization like any other you have encountered? Explain.

- *Freewrite.* Have the students write anything they would like to about the book so far. See Figures 6–5 and 6–6 for two second-graders' responses to *Fantastic Mr.*

Fox by Roald Dahl (Knopf, 1970). To encourage students to respond personally in freewriting, you may want to demonstrate how some sentences might begin with "I":

I noticed . . .
I was confused . . .
I was wondering . . .
I disagree . . .

• *Imagine another point of view.*

If you were the main character, what would you do and why?
Write a letter to the main character.
Write a letter to the author of the book with any questions you have.
Write a diary entry from the point of view of a particular character.

• *Make up one or more questions for discussion.*   Even primary grade students can be expected to formulate their own high-level, open-ended questions once the teacher has done lots of modeling. Students come to reading discussion with their question(s) written in their reading logs. After the group responds to some of these questions, discussion can focus on which questions worked well and why. One third-grader who asked a factual question commented, "My question wasn't that good because it only had one right answer. There wasn't really anything to talk about."

• *Respond to a final question when the book is completed.*   While there is nothing wrong with an occasional teacher-made test, having students draw their own conclusions after the book has been read and discussed is more meaningful in terms of learning. Because students have been active participants in group discussion, they will be able to write thoughtful responses. Older students can respond to questions they create themselves.

After small groups of fourth-graders had completed *A Taste of Blackberries* by Doris Buchanan Smith, a first-person story of a boy's coming to grips with his best friend's death, I asked them to respond to one of the following questions as a final evaluation:

Who is the main character? Why do you think so?
Why do you think this book is called *A Taste of Blackberries*?
What is your reaction to this book?

See Figures 6–7 through 6–9 for sample responses. Notice that even when two students choose the same question, their responses vary. Both extend and confirm the meaning of the book. Both are valid and can be used in evaluating students' appreciation and understanding of the text.

Other concluding questions that work well are:

How does this book fit with others we have read?
Why do you think the author wrote this book?
What character in the book are you most like or most unlike? Explain.

Figures 6-7, 6-8, and 6-9   Fourth-graders' Responses to **A Taste of Blackberries**

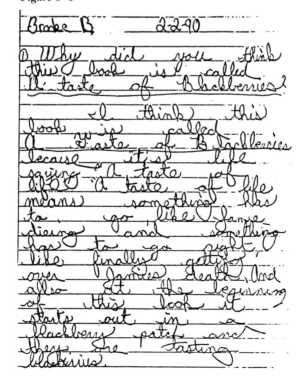

Jett M.

Why do you think the book is called A Taste of Blackberries I think it is called that because at the beginning they were going to pick the berries but they weren't ripe but at the end the narrator picked the blackberries for Jamie because he was dead and I was thinking about Jamie and wondering if he remembered the taste of Blackberries because it was sweet and sour like a taste of life or Death

Figure 6-8

Brooke B   2-2-90

① Why did you think this book is called A taste of Blackberries?

I think this book is called A Taste of Blackberries because it's life saying a taste of life "a taste of life" means something has to go, like Jamie dieing and something has to go right, like finally getting over Jamie's death. And also at the beginning of this book it starts out in a blackberry patch and they are tasting blackberries.

Figure 6–9

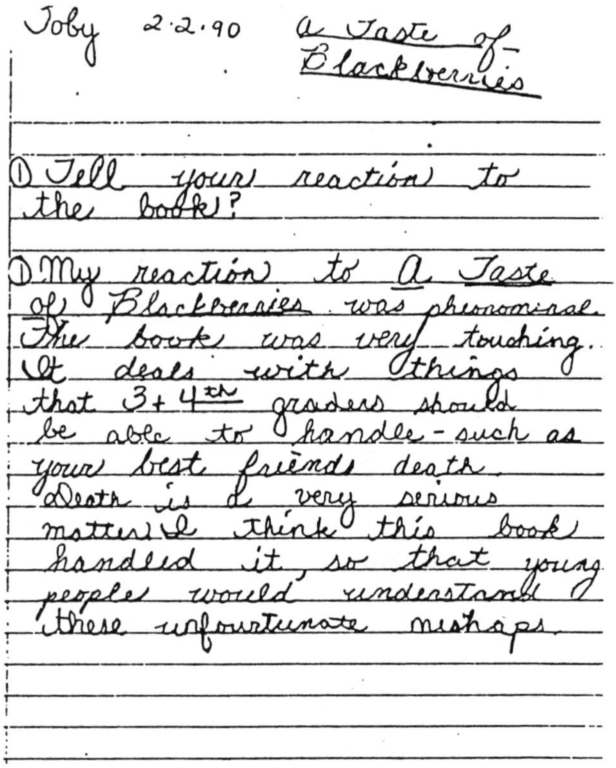

> Joby 2·2·90   A Taste of
>   Blackberries
>
> ① Tell your reaction to
> the book?
>
> ① My reaction to A Taste
> of Blackberries was phenominal.
> The book was very touching.
> It deals with things
> that 3 + 4ᵗʰ graders should
> be able to handle – such as
> your best friends death.
> Death is a very serious
> matter. I think this book
> handled it, so that young
> people would understand
> these unfourtunate mishaps.

With practice and experience, students respond in their literature response logs with intelligence and insight. As they become accustomed to sharing their interpretations, their confidence grows and the quality of group discussion improves. High school teachers note that open-ended questions help students go beyond the usual summarizing of plot.

Teachers also note a carryover to other areas. A third grade teacher said that when students were talking about books read independently, they began backing up their points with quotes from the text. One fourth grade teacher noted that her students were more thoughtful in their responses to social studies questions once they were used to responding in their literature logs. Other teachers note carryover to the content areas, especially in note taking. Jotting down key phrases in the logs on a daily basis is good practice for picking out important points in other texts. (For using response logs across the curriculum, see *Resources for Teachers*, Atwell, 1990, and "Journal Articles," pp. 233–234.)

The literature response log can serve as a reading record of the student's thinking and learning. Teachers find that students' responses not only become longer with time, they also become more thoughtful and insightful. Perhaps the greatest value of the literature response log is that the student comes to realize that what he has to say is valid and important.

Adjusting to the use of logs can be easier for students than teachers. Linda Cooper says that originally she didn't like the responsibility for having to think up a good question: "I hated it at first because it was hard for me. But the kids' enthusiasm kept me going. I saw how much they liked it and how it helped discussion. Their notes jogged their minds, and they could remember a lot better what they had read."

Elementary grade students are practically unanimous in their enjoyment of using the logs. They like the fact that the logs are for them and that they'll all get a chance to talk. They also like the idea that the teacher checks the log only to see that it's done or to respond personally but not to make corrections. That students enjoy and benefit from the logs is apparent by the following typical comments by intermediate grade students:

EVAN: I like using it because all my thoughts are together in one place.

RHONDA: It helps get the discussion going.

AMY: I like it for organization. Everything is easy to find.

TASHA: It refreshes your memory. My notes help me think better.

ISAAC: I like it when someone is talking and I can look at my notes and think of something to add.

Asking Important Questions

In order to provide optimum guidance to students in responding critically to literature, we need to be able to ask the kinds of questions that promote thinking on the very highest levels. This is no easy task. Years of directive questioning in teachers' manuals that put a high priority on factual questions and simple answers makes the transition to higher-level questioning difficult. Most of us have spent years assessing comprehension and listening for the right answers. It takes a long time, as well as the ability to risk and trust ourselves and our students, to ask open-ended questions and questions that facilitate comprehension. Broad-based open-ended questions encourage a variety of responses and are probably the highest-level questions we can ask. They encourage thinking on many levels, value students' background knowledge and experiences, and allow readers to go beyond the text in making meaning.

Open-Ended Questions

Among the best open-ended questions are prediction questions, with readers describing what they think will happen in the story or predicting an answer *before* they read. Then they confirm, adjust, or disprove their predictions before reading on. Even very young children can predict based on prior knowledge, past experiences, and what they see on the cover and in the illustrations. Older children can predict from all these factors as well as from what they already know about literature and authors. Prediction questions work equally well with nonfiction and often stimulate children's interest in a topic.

The following open-ended questions have proved to be particularly helpful for teachers from the primary grades through high school, both for questioning and as models for creating thoughtful questions. Some questions are particularly effective when a book is read and discussed chapter by chapter. Others seem better suited to a whole book when students read straight through for confidence and fluency.

1. Where and when does the story take place? How do you know? If the story took place somewhere else or in a different time, how would it be changed?

2. What incident, problem, conflict, or situation does the author use to get the story started?

3. What does the author do to create suspense, to make you want to read on to find out what happens?

4. Trace the main events of the story. Could you change their order or leave any of them out? Why or why not?

5. Think of a different ending to the story. How would the rest of the story have to be changed to fit the new ending?

6. Did the story end the way you expected it to? What clues did the author offer to prepare you to expect this ending? Did you recognize these clues as important to the story as you were first reading it?

7. Who is the main character of the story? What kind of person is the character? How do you know?

8. Are there any characters who changed in some way during the story? If they changed, how are they different? What changed them? Did it seem believable?

9. Some characters play small but important roles in a story. Name such a character. Why is this character necessary for the story?

10. Who is the teller of the story? How would the story change if someone else in the book or an outside narrator told the story?

11. Does the story as a whole create a certain mood or feeling. What is the mood? How is it created?

12. Did you have strong feelings as you read the story? What makes you think of them as you read the story?

13. What are the main ideas behind the story? What makes you think of them as you read the story?

14. Is this story like any other story you have read or watched? Why?

15. Think about the characters in the story. Are any of them the same type of character that you have met in other stories?

16. What idea or ideas does this story make you think about? How does the author get you to think about this?

17. Do any particular feelings come across in this story? Does the story actually make you think about what it's like to feel that way? How does the author do this?

18. Is there any character that you know more about than any of the others? Who is this character, and what kind of person is he or she? How does the author reveal the character to you? What words would you use to describe the main character's feeling in this book?

19. Are there characters other than the main character who are important to the story? Who are they? Why are they important?

20. Is there anything that seems to make this particular author's work unique and different? If so, what?

21. Did you notice any particular patterns in the form of this book? If you are reading this book in more than one sitting, are there natural points at which to break off your reading? If so, what are these?

22. Were there any clues that the author built into the story that helped you to anticipate the outcome? If so, what were they? Did you think these clues were important when you read them?

23. Does the story language seem natural for the intent of the story and for the various speakers?

24. Every writer creates a make-believe work and peoples it with characters. Even where the world is far different from your own, how does the author make the story seem possible or probable?

25. What questions would you ask if the author were here? Which would be the most important question? How do you think the author might answer it? (From Harste, Short, and Burke, 1988, pp. 300–301)

Open-Ended Questions for Nonfiction

Dorsey Hammond of Oakland University, Rochester, Michigan, suggests five basic questions to ask with informational articles. Students first brainstorm what they already know about the subject, predict possibilities, and raise questions about what they want to find out. Then they read the selection.

1. Did we find the answer to our questions?
2. What questions do we still need to find out about?
3. What else did you learn that you didn't know?
4. What was the most surprising or interesting thing you learned?
5. What have you learned by reading this that you didn't know before?

Teachers, of course, add their own questions to these basic questions.

Using Open-Ended Questions as a Model

High school teacher Dana Noble used the following questions to go along with *Night* by Elie Wiesel for his ninth and tenth grade students. Students responded first in their literature response logs and then in follow-up group discussions. He found the questions helped students go beyond the usual summarizing of the plot and into thinking about the book in depth. See Figures 6–10 and 6–11 for two entirely different responses to the same prompt and for the teacher's response.

Reading 1, pp. 1–20. May 24

Who is the teller of the story? What kind of person is he? Make as many judgments as you can and cite evidence for your inferences.

Reading 2, pp. 21–43. May 25

Some characters play small but important roles in a story. Name such a character from this reading. What does this character add to the story and why? Jot down page numbers for specific evidence.

Figures 6-10 and 6-11   High School Students' Responses to a Common Prompt and Their Teacher's Responses to Their Logs

Andrew P.
journal #4
6/1/90

The Jews in the camp have two serious problems. They are, should they pray to god, and the selection. On page 17 and 18, Elie and the rest are trying to decide if they should pray. Elie says to himself, "Why should I pray to god when we are in this death camp?" Most people decide to pray because they want to show god that they can worship him even in that hell hole.
The selection process was horrible for the prisoners. Prisoners were examined by doctors to see if they were fit enough to work. Those who weren't, were taken to the crematories. There was absolutely nothing for the prisoners to do except pass. Elie and his father both passed the physical, but some do not, they will eventually be killed. I can't understand how anyone could be that cruel.

Andy,   6/1
    It is incredible. I suppose we have to look at ourselves. Could we do the same under similar conditions?
    Watch the movie "Mississippi Burning" and see how Southern whites treated blacks — as recently as the 1960's!
                                                        Dn

Reading 3, pp 45–62.   May 29

Did you have strong feelings as you read this chapter? What did the author do to make you feel strongly? Support your responses by citing, quoting, and so on.

Reading 4, pp. 63–80.   May 31

What serious problems do characters have, and how successful do you think they are at solving them? Quote lines that show the enormity of the problem.

Reading 5, pp. 81–98.   June 1

What idea or ideas do these chapters make you think about? How does the author get you to think about them?

Figure 6-11

Adam

One problem that Eli faced
is his anger. His anger towards
the German army and towards God.
He said, "what are you, my God" this
disturbed me. It shows him loosing faith
and once you loose faith you die in
there. Another problem that a character
is facing is Eli's father. Eli is also
suffering in this. Eli's father said,
I'm asking this of you ..... Do as your
father says" Eli's father was going to
give Eli his fork and spoon. Eli would
not take it for he didn't want his father
to give up hope,

adam,
    I feel for Elie also in his loss
of faith, but I disagree that
"once you lose faith you die." My
thoughts are that Elie was so
angry in his loss of faith that
anger kept him alive.
    Notice how tenacious Elie
and his father are at surviving
the horrors that follow.
                        Dn

Reading 6, pp. 99–109.　June 4

Are there any characters who changed in some way during the story? If they changed, how are they different? What changed them? Did the change seem believable?

Guiding Students to Construct Their Own Questions

Embracing Frank Smith's suggestion of teacher collaboration (Smith, 1988), fourth grade teacher Nancy Schubert and I modeled creating questions for Chapters 1–6 of *The Lion, the Witch and the Wardrobe* by C. S. Lewis. We talked in front of the students as we attempted to come up with open-ended questions. We stressed that we were formulating questions that did not have a right answer but had a wide possibility of answers. We came up with the following:

1. How is the professor different from most grownups?
2. Why do we feel better after the conversation with the professor?
3. Do you know anyone like Edmund?
4. Why do you think C. S. Lewis put him in the story?
5. How could the Queen have found out the Faun betrayed her?

Students then worked in groups of four discussing and writing their own questions for these chapters. Nancy and I walked around providing guidance as necessary. Each group was asked to come to a consensus on its one best question and share it with the class. Interest for this activity was very high, and we were surprised at how well students were able to create questions on their first attempt. Their selected best questions were as follows:

1. Why didn't Lucy know it was snow on the ground when she first came into Narnia?
2. Do you think there are many passages to Narnia? Why or why not?
3. Do you think Lucy would have believed Edmund if the adventure had first happened to him? Why or why not?
4. Why do you think Lucy went with Mr. Tumnus?
5. How do you think the Queen felt when she took Edmund? Describe.
6. Why do you think time stopped while Lucy was in the wardrobe?

Important questions go beyond the text but bring the reader back to the text. Significant questions do more than just ask recall of what was read; they make students think about what they read—before, during, and after reading. If students are to become actively literate adults, they need to be asking their own questions as they are reading, writing, thinking, and discussing.

Literature Discussion Groups

The literature discussion group, as described here, goes hand in hand with the literature response log and refers to heterogeneous, small-group, student-directed, and teacher-guided discussion that occurs as a book is being read. This section focuses on procedures and formats that have worked well for a small group of teachers who have made, or are making, this kind of transition to responding to literature. However, these ideas and procedures may also be used with another format and adapted for whole-class or homogeneous small-group discussion, as well as for group discussion that does not occur until students have read the entire book. What is presented here is not *the* way, it is but one way. As with all whole language teaching, flexibility, choice, and ownership are primary. It is up to you and the students to decide what will work best for you.

Jerome Harste urges us to use the notion of conversation and voice as criteria for determining whether or not our educational programs are effective. He notes that "schools are real good at silencing kids" and that, as teachers, we must constantly be asking ourselves:

"Have I heard each student's voice?"
"Have I put in place a structure where conversation can continue?"

(Presentation to teachers, Shaker Heights, Ohio, City School District, 1990)

A literature discussion group gives every student an opportunity to speak and heard. The teacher is a member of the small group but not its president. Students take ownership of the learning process and often go beyond what is expected. Talk moves past prediction, central story, and plot happenings to critical analysis. Reflective questioning and responding, as described earlier in this chapter, encourage the highest levels of critical thinking and evaluation. Using textual references, prior experiences, and background knowledge, students state their opinions, make inferences, draw conclusions, analyze character motivation, and synthesize ideas in new ways. Students justify their opinions with evidence from the text, and the discussions are often quite lively. It has not been unusual, even with eight-year-olds, to have the students leave the group still talking about a book.

Allowing Time for Change

A genuine literature discussion, where the focus is on inquiry, does not just happen because the teacher moves from the basal to literature. Most of us have been entrenched for years, closely following teachers' manuals and asking lots of short answer-type questions. Students have been trained to sit passively, waiting for instructions, and to respond with the "right" answer. Once a student realizes her point of view is sincerely wanted, valued, and respected, she views school differently. We found that once we were able to give up some control in leading a discussion, the discussion flowed better, and more students were eager to participate.

Moving from leading the discussion to assuming a less central role has been a big adjustment for most of us. As teachers used to directing, we have needed time to adjust to a more democratic discussion format. Students have needed time, too. Students who have not had experience with in-depth interaction with a book over time may need months before they feel comfortable participating in discussions. One teacher said, "I realize now that it was the participation of the students which had to come first. We could get to the meat of the question later. But it was very tense for me at first." It is important to allow ourselves and our students lots of time for change and give ourselves credit for taking a risk and trying a new format.

It is not unusual for discussions to be superficial at first. Years of constant questioning have kept students in a subservient position, and some—often those who have a hard time sharing their feelings—are intimidated by the new process. Students who have never really been asked to think deeply about an issue also need lots of time and modeling before they begin to express their views.

Importance of Parent Education

As with any change we make in teaching, parents need to be informed—not only so they know what's going on in the classroom but also so they will foster high-level questioning and discussions at home.

A student was having a conversation with her mother about a question that had been posed for several chapters and said, "On page 52, it says . . .". Her mother responded, "I don't care about the page. Just tell me the answer."

atements rather than questions. Acting as an equal
acher can still bring out salient points, share a favorite
her opinion, but this is done conversationally rather
we ask questions, it not only directs the response to
e looking for a particular answer. For example, rather
with questions like "Do you think . . . ?" or "How do
hich direct students' comments back to the teacher,
the following: "I'm not sure what you mean by that";
as thinking about the way the author . . ."; "I was
surprised to learn . . .". The teacher can also challenge students: "Prove your
point"; "Stay on the topic."

Without being chief director, the teacher offers what he thinks by making
clarifying statements or redirecting discussion. This invites students to agree,
disagree, or take off from the teacher's comments. Eventually such modeling will
pay off, and students will lead the discussion on their own even when the teacher is
not present.

• *Allow for periods of silence.* Allowing for wait time and reflection is difficult at
first. Initially, the silence hangs heavy, and teachers are apt to jump in and say
something like, "What do you think about . . . ?" Instead, teachers might try
allowing for silences up to about ten seconds and then saying something like, "This
is your discussion. It's up to you to carry it on." After a while students get the
message that they're in charge.

Organization and Procedures

Getting Started

Grouping   Our literature discussion groups are usually heterogeneously grouped,
with five to eight students in a group. Three groups of seven to eight students each
has been the most common arrangement in our classes. We have found that more
than eight in a group does not allow for interactive discussion by all students.
However, if the class size is large, the groups may have to be larger. A group of ten
will still allow more voices to be heard than a whole-class discussion where,
typically, the same students tend to dominate. Occasionally whole-class grouping
occurs with a core book when there are enough copies for each student.

In the beginning, teachers like to choose the heterogeneous groups to ensure a
balanced mix of students. As new books are discussed, it's a good idea to change the
group makeup to promote optimal and varied peer interaction. Some teachers have
found that it works just as well for students to choose the group they will be in. If
three groups are to be formed, the teacher can give a short talk about each book,
telling just enough to get students interested. (Books may be related by theme or
author, but they don't have to be. See *Resources for Teachers*, "Recommended
Literature by Grade Level, K–12," for excellent book choices.) The books are then
available for perusal, and students sign up for their first, second, and third choices.
We have found that students almost always get their first or second choice.

Seating arrangement   Students sit anywhere around the reading table or designated floor areas. The teacher sits among them as a contributing member of the group rather than at the head of the table as the dominant leader. With a kidney-shaped table, it works well if you place several chairs at the center for students and take a seat off to the side where you can still see the entire class. The physical location of the teacher has a dramatic effect on the discussion. Having the teacher seated off to the side represents a subtle change, but it sends the message to the students that a democratic community of readers and thinkers is gathering, not an autocracy where all the decision-making power rests with the top person. Moving off center makes it easier for the teacher to be an equal voice in the conversation. With this arrangement, students also tend not to direct all comments to the teacher.

One teacher found it took her a month to move away from the center of the table. After sitting at the helm for fifteen years, it was difficult to give up her space.

Using the books   Each student needs to have a personal copy of the book. If you do not have multiple copies in your school, your school or public librarian may be able to borrow copies from other libraries.

The teacher also needs a personal copy of the book. As previously noted, in our district, each teacher receives a copy of each core book, to be used as a teacher's edition. Teachers write in questions to ask students to respond to in their logs, underline important vocabulary to be noted, and make any other comments they may want to bring out in discussion. This edition also serves as a guide for the substitute teacher.

Establishing procedures for independent work time   So that the discussion group can function without interruption and with the teacher's total involvement as a participant and observer, students not in the group need to know exactly what is expected of them.

For some teachers who have done almost all literature and discussion whole class, I have often been asked to demonstrate how the management works. I explain to the students that the teacher will be meeting with a literature discussion group and will not be available to students working at their seats. I let the students know that we, as a class, need to establish some guidelines for acceptable behaviors. I put the responsibility on them to try and elicit their responses. I let them know that we will be writing a first draft and that revisions will probably be necessary after we see how our rules are working. I might begin, "What should you do if you have a question and need some help?" I write their responses on the overhead or large chart paper. If a rule seems out of line, I might say, "Does everyone agree with that? Will that work?" I also ask the teacher if she is comfortable with the rule. She may state it another way or give additional feedback.

The end result should be a set of rules that is comfortable for both you and the students. We try out the rules and make modifications as necessary. If there is a problem one day, I might say something like, "I had difficulty hearing everyone today during discussion group. I need your help. What do you think we need to change so things work better tomorrow?"

Even though establishing procedures with the class is more time-consuming than just stating the rules, the time is well spent. Because students create the rules, they take them seriously. Once a satisfactory working set is agreed upon, a final draft is made, and the rules are posted. The rules should be brief and stated positively. The following is a draft written by Julie Beer's third grade class. The original draft stayed as written.

Independent Work Time Rules

- Whisper.
- Stay in one area away from other people.
- Do your work.
- Leave room only if positively necessary.
- Be considerate to people in reading group.

Time allowance for discussion You will find that with practice and experience, you can easily meet with three groups in an hour. Everything important that needs to be said in a discussion comes out in ten to twenty minutes. Fifteen minutes has been about average for our groups. Depending on the length of the book, a discussion group can last anywhere from a day to several weeks to as long as six weeks. Most teachers try to meet with groups daily. Some meet with groups three days a week. In classes where teachers are combining group discussion time with checking of WEB books (pp. 45–48), each group time will need to be about ten minutes longer.

Students not in group While one group is involved in discussion other groups are reading, responding in their logs, and working on book-related activities. (For specifics, see "Literature Extension Activities," in Chap. 5, and Chap. 15, "Classroom Management and Organization.") Students not in group work independently for thirty to forty-five minutes.

Procedures

Reading the book—allowing time in class Nancie Atwell's *In the Middle* (1987) legitimized reading in class and freed many teachers, especially at the secondary level, to allow and value time for reading in school. For reluctant readers especially, the results can be dramatic. High school English teacher Holly Burgess comments, "It's been so wonderful to look up and see them reading. It's such a surprise. I don't know why, but it is."

Having students do their silent reading assignment in class is the first order of business once discussion groups start to meet. Rather than assign the whole book at one time, we assign chapters, individually or in small chunks. With discussion taking place while students are reading, confusions can be cleared up. If discussion takes place only after the book is completed, memory of comprehension—rather than comprehension as it is occurring or just occurred—tends to be the focus.

While the teacher is meeting with one group, other groups are reading and responding in their logs and/or completing assigned or self-selected activities. Even if the teacher is working with the whole class, it is still important to value time for silent reading. This is especially difficult for secondary teachers who may have students for only thirty-five to forty-five minutes. Nonetheless, giving this time pays off. A struggling tenth-grader wrote in her log: "If I didn't have to stop reading for my classes, I wouldn't stop. That says something because I never read. I used to hate reading. I'm beginning to enjoy it."

Some middle school and secondary teachers who use literature discussion groups have found a workable plan is to allow Mondays and Tuesdays for reading and responding to logs, Wednesdays and Thursdays for discussion group meetings, and one day for "catch-up." (See Figure 15–7 in Chap. 15, "Classroom Management and Organization," for a high school teacher's plan.)

Students who cannot read the text easily will need to be paired with a better reader or provided a tape to follow along. The purpose of literature discussion group is to talk about the book. Opportunities to work on word-attack skills and reading fluency will happen at another time. As long as the student can listen to the story and understand it—even if he can't read all the words—he can participate effectively in group and should be given the opportunity.

What Happens in a Literature Discussion Group?

- *Being prepared*   Students come to group with their reading and log assignments completed, and the teacher makes a quick check to see that they are prepared. Anyone who is unprepared is sent back to his seat to complete the reading and log. I say something like, "I'm sorry you can't join us today. Please come to group when you've completed your work." This is a very effective management technique. Students do not like to be left out of the group and miss the animated discussion. Teachers who have been pessimistic about the effectiveness of this method express surprise at how well it works. After missing group for just a few times, it is rare for a student not to take responsibility for being prepared.

- *Setting rules for discussion*   Some teachers like to have a student leader pose the question or begin the day's discussion. Others find a leader unnecessary. As in a normal conversation between adults, students do not raise their hands. This practice takes a bit of time for students to get used to, but once they do, they are completely comfortable. If they want to make a point, we encourage them to politely let the speaker finish his remarks and then intervene with comments such as:

> Excuse me . . .
> I'd like to add . . .
> I disagree . . .
> I agree because . . .
> I don't understand what you mean . . .
> I'm confused . . .
> I'd like to expand on that . . .

Some teachers post these phrases on a chart in view of the group so students have easy reference for discussion language. Of course, this practice needs to be modeled first by the teacher. In the beginning, to elicit these kinds of comments, the teacher might comment on a student's use of language and procedures. I might say, "I like the way Ned made his point. He started out by saying what he disagreed with and then backed it up with evidence."

Having a student-led group where students talk with one another without first getting a signal from the teacher sounds questionable to some teachers at first. They wonder if the group will be chaotic. Quite the contrary. Once students are practiced in a more democratic format, they relish the change. Engagement is high, and off-task behavior is rare. Believing that students can manage a group without hand raising requires a teacher willing to take a risk, to trust, and to allow time for change.

• *Using the log in discussion*   Students have their logs open and refer to them—to confirm or disprove—when someone else is commenting. The question that has been posed serves as the catalyst for discussion.

• *Reading orally*   Students or teachers may choose to read a section from the book to back up a point or highlight the author's use of language. The only time we take the time to reread a section, either silently or orally, is when it is obvious from the discussion that comprehension has not occurred.

A Literature Discussion in Grade 3

Third-graders, new to open-ended questions, literature response logs, and leading their own discussion, were discussing Chapter 8 in *The Comeback Dog* by Jane Resh Thomas. Daniel, a nine-year-old boy who has been having difficulty coping with the loss of his dog "Lady," has mixed feelings about a stray dog he's been caring for that has now disappeared. The question for the students was, "How was Daniel feeling?" Part of the discussion follows. Notice that it begins with students not connecting to each other, but gradually they get into the discussion.

MATT: Here, on page 55, it says "He pressed his face against the glass . . . until his eyes hurt." I think Daniel was spending a lot of time watching for the dog.

SARAH: I think Daniel is being pushy. The dog is probably not ready to be close to Daniel.

DAVID: I think he was kind of worried, because when he was studying, his mind kept wandering to "Lady." On page 56 it says, "But he couldn't concentrate. His thoughts returned to 'Lady.' "

MATT: I agree. He was distracted.

QUENTIN: Yeah. He woke up in the middle of the night. (*Using his log*) "She was gone, and good riddance. He would forget her." He was glad the dog was gone.

ANDREA: I disagree. Daniel was angry and disappointed. Rather than show his disappointment, he got angry. I felt like that whey my dog ran away.

DAVID: His feelings are really mixed up. He wants her and he doesn't want her at the same time.

Beneficial Outcomes

• *Listening skills improve.*   In the past, when students addressed most of their comments to the teacher, not all other students listened carefully. Now, because students are no longer looking at and to the teacher for answers and approval, they not only listen better to each other but they come to value listening to each other.

- *Comprehension improves.*   It has been interesting to observe students come to discussion without a strong understanding of what has been read. Initially they seem lost; yet, as the discussion continues, they begin to make connections. By talking, listening, and having other students fill in gaps, what has not been understood becomes clear. Third grade teacher Peg Gerhart notes, "I can tell when students are confused, and I can see the confusion clear up. As discussion continues, a light bulb goes on."

Parents also notice a difference in their children's understanding of text. One mother said, "My youngest son has a different orientation toward books. My older children read but not with the same critical analysis."

- *At-risk and low-ability students succeed.*   One of the greatest results of heterogeneous literature discussion groups has been increased participation by and improved self-esteem of at-risk and low-ability students. With demonstrations and practice, learning disabled and other at-risk students are able to answer questions in their logs, even if their responses are mostly literal at first. We also notice that these students are more likely to initiate conversation with the log-discussion format. This seems particularly significant for students who in the past were most often relegated to phonics and skills work. In discussion, as long as students can back up their opinions with evidence, they are viewed as being correct.

Third grade teacher Marilyn Eppich states,

> Jeffrey sometimes has a hard time making connections. He reads on a very low level. I paired him with a better student for reading. During discussion, I have been surprised by his level of understanding and by the fact that he has not been tentative making comments. He takes a firm stand.
>
> Also, he's not a writer, so this process, where he only has to write a little, has been good for him. Also his writing is hard for me to read, but here, the writing is not for me. It has to make sense only for him.

It has also been interesting to note that visitors often assume from the quality of the literature discussion that the group is a high-ability one. Not only are they surprised to learn that the group is mixed ability—they often have trouble telling the "highs" from the "lows."

- *Social relationships change.*   Because the groups are mixed ability and everyone's voice is given equal weight and respect, we notice that low-achieving students are afforded new respect by their peers. Also, through the use of the logs and follow-up discussion, students realize that individuals differ in what they perceive from the same piece of literature and that it is normal and healthy for people to have different points of view.

- *Students take ownership.*   We notice that students do not easily back away from what they believe. One day a group of third-graders was discussing *Danny the Champion of the World* by Roald Dahl. The log question had been, "Describe the keeper." Diane, a former Reading Recovery student, said the keeper was "nice." She was challenged by every member of the group, who gave reasons to support the keeper's nasty, mean disposition. Diane disagreed and offered, "The keeper was nice because he didn't use his gun or chase them." From her vantage point, she backed up her view and refused to concede. We quietly cheered her independent thinking.

• *Students are more honest.*   We have noticed that students tend to be quite candid when they are talking with one another and not focusing on what the teacher thinks about their responses.

• *Teachers come to trust students more.*   We have noticed that even when the question we pose isn't as good as it could be, everything that is significant about the reading comes out in discussion. This has happened so consistently that teachers give up constantly worrying about covering everything and begin to trust the students to uncover what is significant to them and to the text.

• *The teacher has time for critical observation.*   As an equal participant in the discussion, rather than the director, the teacher can really see what students are learning. Once students have moved to leading the discussion, the teacher can sit on the fringes as a teacher-researcher, observer, and evaluator. What needs to be taught and demonstrated becomes apparent.

• *Substitute teachers find the format very workable.*   Several substitutes have commented on how impressed they have been with the level of discussion and the students' ability to carry on independently. Because students are used to leading their own discussions, the substitute teacher can sit in with the group without having to manage and direct it.

Literature Discussion Group: What's Different? A Summary

- Heterogeneous grouping
- Students lead discussion
- Teacher participates as one voice
- Teacher sits among students (not at center)
- No hand raising
- Students talk mostly to each other
- Silences in discussion are okay
- May be no consensus
- Most of the time spent on discussion (very little oral reading)

Evaluation

Students' attitudes.   One of the greatest benefits of utilizing literature discussion groups is the attitude of the students. Even struggling readers enjoy the opportunity to voice their opinions and have them count.

I asked third-graders who had been using literature response logs and discussion groups for the first time to comment on how they liked or disliked this new approach compared with their past experience where reading of literature was assigned and they then came to a teacher-led reading group (which often was whole class) with just their books. Here are some of their comments regarding discussion:

> JAMISON: Discussion is just like a conversation. It's better because you can say what you really think. As long as you have the proof, no one can dispute you.

ROBERT: I like it because you get to talk to other people.

JULIE: It's a lot more interesting. You get to talk more.

CLIFF: I like it better because you can give your opinion without raising your hand.

BRIA: It's better because there's less independent work to do at your seat.

ANDREW: I like it because you can have your ideas, and you don't have to agree with someone else's, even the teacher's.

VALERIE: I like that we get to have a longer discussion and that it's okay to say when you don't understand things or disagree with someone.

RHONDA: You have to think a lot about what you believe.

JAMES: I like it because you don't have any right or wrong answers.

Teachers' attitudes   Teachers report feeling a sense of exhilaration they have never felt before in a reading group. There are magical moments, difficult to recapture, and spontaneous comments and surprises.

Above all, the importance of genuine conversation is affirmed. Peg Gerhart, who has been an elementary teacher for nine years, sums it up well when she says the process has "made me revalue how important conversation is in the interaction between teacher and student and for student growth and development."

Peg has been moving gradually to a more meaningful literature approach. She says she began comfortably with literature using "basalized packages" and whole-class teaching. When she had difficulty writing specific comments on report cards, she realized she was not aware of the reading strategies students were using. "I'm a risk taker, and I knew I had to change," she said.

I modeled for Peg once a week for a number of weeks, gave her time to work out the kinks on her own, coached her, and gave her feedback. After several months she had this to say:

> The biggest and most difficult thing for me has been giving up control. It was very tense for me at first. It really bothered me when we weren't on the question. I bit my tongue, and then I saw something else emerging. Kids who didn't talk were talking. I was absolutely amazed by some of the responses. The level of discussion was so high. It surprised me, even shocked me. Students I thought would have been silent came up with high-level ideas. I could see thinking going on I had never seen before. I was pleasantly shocked. That's what convinced me.

Peg sees herself continuing to change and refine the discussion process. She believes teachers have to be open to suggestions and new ideas but also need to accept, "This is where I am right now." She is finding comments on report cards easier to write now because she knows her students better.

Marilyn Eppich, a third grade teacher, tried literature discussion groups and was delighted at how well they worked and how much they increased her enjoyment of teaching reading. She comments: "I can really sit back now and listen instead of always thinking about what my next question should be. That's why I'm enjoying it so much. I'm also getting to know the kids better as well as listening to their responses. Teachers don't take time to listen enough."

Self-Evaluation

Self-evaluation, for teachers and students, is an effective way to improve the quality of discussions. Notice to whom students are looking at and talking to during discussion. If students are still focusing on the teacher, the teacher's voice is still the dominant one. See if you can get a colleague to observe you during discussion group and give feedback. We have found it also works well to tape record discussions occasionally. Students enjoy evaluating how the discussion went—what was good about it and what could be improved. It's also a good way for the teacher to note her interactions, tone, comments, and conversation.

The teacher can also ask students for feedback. Linda Cooper gave the following questionnaire to her students to fill out after several months of using literature response logs and discussion groups:

1. What do you like about the way we are doing discussion now as compared to before?
2. What do you think we should change?

What Happens in the Long Run: Further Transitions

Ideally, another step in the process of moving away from teacher-directed classrooms toward more empowerment for students is literature discussion groups that function independently and simultaneously without direct teacher involvement. This step can occur only after both students and the teacher are comfortable with the discussion groups. Based on my experience, making the transition takes many years of teaching with literature. Understanding and practicing a philosophy consistent with language learning are required, as well as excellent management techniques, before discussion groups can function without teacher involvement. Teachers and students will first need to have a great deal of experience with self-management, collaboration, and responsibility in a democratic classroom.

Even then, independent groups are not common. Therefore, teachers need not feel inadequate if they continue to be part of the literature groups. In fact, as long as the teacher is only one member of the group and her voice does not dominate, I personally find it advisable to have the teacher's opinion and reactions part of the discussion. It is our job to guide the children in making connections and discoveries they might not make on their own and to continue to model good questioning and response techniques.

If the transition does occur, teachers can choose which group to join on a particular day and occasionally use student self-evaluation forms to check on how the other groups managed. Or teachers can use that time to carefully observe how a group interacts and take anecdotal records on particular students' contributions. With practice and sufficient modeling, students become quite capable of choosing their own questions (they can receive a set of selected questions to choose from or write their own questions) and even deciding how much should be read for the next meeting. (For further information, see "Literature Circles" in Harste, Short, and Burke, 1988.)

The format of the literature discussion groups can be carried across the curriculum. Students can meet in groups and discuss their findings from their research/readings/thinking in social studies, science, and mathematics.

Reflections

The way students are asked to respond to literature in school influences their development as readers, writers, and thinkers as well as their enjoyment of literature. Through discussion and identification with characters and themes, students come to understand the consequences of human behavior and see connections to their own lives. Readers become familiar with genres, authors, characters, places, new concepts, and literary language and use some of these insights in their own writing. Perhaps most significant, literature has the power to help develop students as critical readers, writers, and thinkers. As adults, these are the people who read with questions in mind, substantiate their opinions, take an intelligent stand on an issue, read the newspaper analytically, question politicians' jargon, and act as thoughtful citizens. If we are to educate students thoughtfully for the future, literature can be the vehicle for thinking on the most critical levels.

7

Teaching
for
Strategies

Putting theory into practice:
first grade teacher Jim Henry doing a
shared writing lesson in reading group

"I wonder if the kids are really learning anything."

Teachers who make the transition from the basal to literature worry a lot about whether or not skills are being taught. Additionally, many teachers feel nervous that they are not teaching enough. I have found this to be a common feeling among beginning whole language teachers. We teachers feel guilty spending reading time reading, discussing, and enjoying the literature. We have spent years teaching reading using lots of skills sheets. Without worksheets, where you can "see" skills work, it's hard for teachers to trust that the skills are in the books and that learning is truly occurring. Many of us devise activities to be sure skills teaching occurs.

Understanding the Difference
between Skills and Strategies

Because it is important to bring skills teaching to the strategic level, we need to understand the difference between skills and strategies. While skills teaching is a necessary part of all good instruction, it is our beliefs about learning combined with our approach, method, context, and timing that determine whether or not we are teaching skills so that they later become useful strategies for the learner.

In discrete skills teaching, the teacher—or the publisher of a program—decides what the learner needs, and the skill is directly taught, often in a predetermined sequence, and then practiced in isolation. The skill, whether it includes word attack, alphabetizing, sequencing, or vocabulary acquisition, is directly taught with an emphasis on practice and automatic, correct responses. The teacher or program controls how much practice or exercises students need. Application of the skill to new, meaningful contexts rarely occurs.

134

In teaching for strategies, however, skills are taught in a broader context because the learner demonstrates a need for specific skills in the instructional/learning setting, perhaps in a guided reading group. The skill is taught because the learner genuinely needs to use it—or the teacher anticipates the learner's upcoming need to use the skill. The teacher guides the student to self-determine the generalization and think through possibilities in authentic contexts. While the teacher may question and suggest, it is the learner who is encouraged to make deductions and consciously apply what is learned from one context to another. Don Holdaway notes, "The major difference, then, between 'skills teaching' and 'strategy teaching' concerns the presence or absence of self-direction on the part of the learner" (1979, p. 136).

In other words, a skill—no matter how well it has been taught—cannot be considered a strategy until the learner can use it purposefully and independently. Application of a skill to another context is far more likely to occur when the skill has been taught in a meaningful context that considers the needs of the learners. I have observed that teachers begin to focus on strategies when they begin to change the climate of their classrooms from teacher dominated to student centered and when they come to view reading and other language processes as constructive and interactive.

Applying the distinction between skill and strategy to the teaching of sight words, phonics, and vocabulary, we see clearly that merely teaching the skills in isolation and practicing on worksheets has no relation to meaningful teaching. While we may believe that a skill has been covered, until the learner can discover how to utilize the skill in varied reading and writing contexts, skills teaching is largely a waste of time. *The learner must know how and when to apply the skill; that is what elevates the skill to the strategy level.*

It has taken me many years to become convinced that all the skills are in the literature and that the literature itself can be used as a vehicle to teach skills strategically. Most of us initially need to see concrete evidence of skills teaching, and we use the literature to teach and practice the skills we believe children need. Even then, we must be careful that skills work does not interfere with enjoyment of the story and that our focus on skills results from a genuine need for meaning.

I have observed that after about five years or more, teachers seem to move away from practicing specific skills in literature to promoting strategies in the ongoing context of genuine reading and writing, as the need arises. By becoming careful observers of our students and practicing ongoing evaluation, we can determine what strategies students are using and not using. We need to give ourselves time for this transition. As our own learning theory develops, and as we begin to take ownership of our teaching and rely less on directed instructional programs, we have less of a need for a predetermined skills agenda.

Making the Transition

All the skills required in a district's course of study—such as using grapho-phonics cues, making generalizations, finding the main idea, understanding figurative language—can be developed in the context of the literature. We don't really need separate practice exercises. However, transitional activities may give us confidence and peace of mind until we are convinced that skills are being learned through everyday authentic reading and writing activities.

While courses of study designate concepts and skills to be taught, there is usually latitude in how concepts are to be taught. Even when there is a required text, the text can often be used as a resource and reference instead of as the total curriculum.

The following are examples of activities that may be used to promote high-level skills teaching for teachers who feel the need to teach skills directly but who want to do so more meaningfully. Many of these activities can be used for independent work—in place of worksheets—while meeting with a reading group.

Quotation Marks

- Have students write conversations with each other. Model the activity first through oral language, and write down what the speaker says.

- Reproduce a page of familiar conversational text from a book being read. Using white-out liquid, remove quotation marks. Make a transparency, and model—with student participation—how and where quotation marks would go. Then have students work together, or independently, to put quotation marks on another page they have already read where the quotation marks have been whited out and the page reproduced for students. Students self-check with the original text.

- Select several pages of familiar text that has lots of conversation. Students take the part of the characters and speak their parts. This will first need to be demonstrated.

Homonyms

- Students are guided to notice homonyms in literature and their own writing. A class chart is begun, and as new homonym pairs are discovered they are added to the chart.

- Individual homonym booklets can be made using literal pictures.

- Linda Cooper grows a homonym "pair" tree in her room. When students come across homonym pairs in their reading and writing, they write and illustrate the words on a double-folded paper shaped like a pear. The "pair-pears" are attached to the tree (see Figure 7–1).

- Have students write comic strips with "bubbles" and then take the message in the bubble and write it using quotation marks. Demonstrate the activity first.

Compound Words

- Students make individual compound word booklets from words they come across in their reading. See Figure 7–2 for a page from a third-grader's book.

Overused Words

- Have each student make a thesaurus to encourage the use of interesting, vibrant language in writing. For example, students can keep a record of words authors use for such overused words as "happy," "nice," "said," "walked," "mad." Words come from independent reading and group reading and are referred to in writing. William Steig and Roald Dahl are two authors that give elementary students a wealth of interesting, alternative words.

Figure 7-1   Homonym "Pair-Pears"

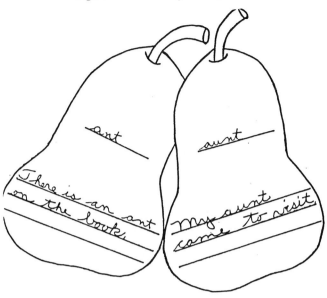

Figure 7-2   Pages from a Third-grader's Compound Word Book

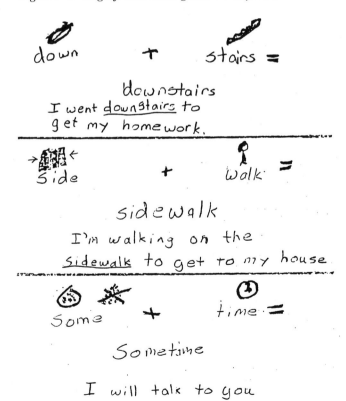

Figure 7-3   Illustrating Idiomatic Expressions

Contractions, Possessives

• Select a short, familiar passage and have students note the contractions. Some teachers like students to make their own contraction booklets, noting contractions and what they mean as they come across them in their reading.

Figurative Language

• Students note figurative language as they come across it in their reading and illustrate the idiomatic expressions (see Figure 7–3).

The skills just listed are being applied at the strategy level when students are using them appropriately and independently in new, meaningful contexts. For example, the student who uses quotation marks or homonymns correctly in a story she is writing is indicating that she understands how and when the skill is used.

Using a Picture Book to Teach for Strategies in the Primary Grades

Selecting the Book

Working with a small group of struggling second grade readers, I demonstrated for the classroom teacher how literature could be used to teach skills strategically. I selected the picture book *Jamaica's Find* by Juanita Havill (Houghton Mifflin, 1986), the story of a young black girl who finds a stuffed dog at the park and wrestles with whether or not to keep it. The book was carefully chosen for its appeal to children, its potential for interesting, meaningful discussion, its natural and predictable language and the good match between illustrations and text. It was also a book the students had never heard or seen, and I believed the readability level was just about right for these children. That is, they would be able to read the book with about 90 percent accuracy.

While it is important for young children to have lots of practice reading familiar, easy books, they must also be regularly introduced to books on their level that they have never seen before. In that way the teacher can note what strategies the reader is using and not using and give appropriate guidance.

Introducing the Book

Talking through the book together before reading it gives reluctant readers familiarity and control of language patterns and vocabulary, a motivating interest in the story, and a feeling of "I can read this." The introduction should be short—not more than five to seven minutes—and be carefully planned by the teacher so the language children need to know to read the story is included. As children become more independent readers, the introduction will become even shorter—perhaps just a sentence about the book.

For this lesson each child received a copy of *Jamaica's Find*, and we predicted what the story might be about by looking at the cover. After accepting the students' responses, I gave a short summary of the book to give them a framework for reading. "Yes, you are right. This is a story about a girl about your age who finds something that doesn't belong to her, and she has to decide what to do about it." Then, before we began reading, I went through the book page by page and talked about the pictures, being careful to put any unfamiliar or difficult words in their ears. Hearing unfamiliar language before being asked to read it builds in potential for success. Vocabulary is never introduced in isolation.

At the same time, we used this time to discuss possible solutions for Jamaica's dilemma. "What do you think she should do?" "What's another possibility?" "What might happen if she does that?" "How is her problem solved?"

Reading the Book

Whether meeting with one student or a group of students, most of reading time is spent reading the story. By giving each child an opportunity to read, or reread a page or two of the story, the teacher can carefully observe reading behaviors.

- Does the child have one-to-one matching of spoken word to printed word?
- What strategies is the child using (picture cues, visual cues [grapho-phonics], sentence structure, sentence context, rereading, memory for text)?
- What does the child do when in trouble (stop and wait for the teacher; "sound it out," reread to predict, check, or self-correct)?
- What strategies does the child need to be using?

As the children are reading the book, I take the opportunity to teach for strategies as the need arises. I keep a small chalkboard and chalk with me at the reading table as well as a slide (see Appendix E). The following are examples of teaching points made in the process of students reading.

Jason began on the first page (p. 5), which read, "When Jamaica arrived at the park, there was no one there. It was almost supper time, but she still had a few minutes to play."

JASON: "When Jamaica . . ." (*silence, looks to teacher*)
ROUTMAN: Skip that word and read to the end of the sentence.
JASON: "When Jamaica . . . at the park, no one was there."

ROUTMAN: What would make sense? Where is she?

JASON: "When Jamaica *arrived* (*reads it easily*) at the park, there was no one there. It was almost *super* time, but she still had a few . . .

ROUTMAN: Keep going.

JASON: . . . to play."

ROUTMAN: It's the end of the day. Is it *super* time? Does that make sense? Think about what would make sense.

JASON: "It was almost *supper* time, but she still had a few *minutes* (*reads it easily*) to play."

ROUTMAN: Good for you. I like the way you looked at how the word began and put in what made sense.

I did not interrupt Jason when he misread "supper" for "super." If I had told him to "sound it out," he still couldn't have read it. By letting him read to the end of the sentence, he had a chance to self-correct through the meaning of the sentence.

Meredith had trouble with the word "stains" in a sentence that described the stuffed dog Jamaica found as being covered with grass stains. Using the small chalkboard, I wrote the word "rain," which I thought she might know. She read it easily. I wanted to point out that a pattern she already knew—"ai"—could be applied to a new context. I wrote "stain" and asked, "How does it *start*?" (emphasizing the "st" to put the sound in her ear). She then read the word "stain."

Julia got stumped on "returned" in the sentence, " 'But, Jamaica, you should have returned the dog, too,' said her mother" (p. 15). Using the slide (Appendix E), I moved next to her and exposed just the "re" and asked her to read that. She did. Then I moved the slide to show the next letter, "t," and asked her to start the sentence again. She read "returned" without difficulty.

Teacher Language to Encourage Independence

Some teacher prompts that help get the child thinking, predicting, sampling text, confirming, and self-correcting include:

- Look at the picture to help yourself.
- Get your mouth ready to say it.
- Look at how the word begins.
- Does that make sense?
- Does that sound right? Does it fit?
- Does that look right to you?
- Start that sentence again.
- Skip that word and go on. Now, what do you think it is?
- Where have you seen that word before?
- Think about a word you know that has the same sound in it.
- Put in a word that makes sense, and go on.
- Is that right? Check that again.
- If that word was . . . , what would you expect to see at the beginning? at the end? What do you see here?
- What can you do to help yourself?

I always want to give the child the message that it is her job to do the reading work and that she can do it. It is also very important to verify for the child what she knows and make her aware of the strategies she is using. By praising and encouraging all attempts and noting what the child has done well, we build self-esteem and encourage the repeated use of the desired strategies. On subsequent rereadings— which are done for pleasure and to build confidence, fluency, sight vocabulary, and practice in using meaningful strategies—improvement is noticeable.

Such comments as the following may be helpful:

- I like the way you tried to help yourself.

- Good for you. I saw you checking the word with the picture to see if you were right.

- I like the way you worked out the hard part.

- I noticed you tried . . . when you had trouble. Good for you. That's what good readers do.

Incorporating Skills Work

As part of a rereading, I will sometimes do some skills work. When the story is well chosen and of high interest to the children, they enjoy repeated readings. However, I do not incorporate the skills work until children are fairly fluent with the story. Enjoyment and understanding of the story always come first, and any skills work is only a small—and meaningful—part of reading time. Care is taken not to "basalize" the literature and extract it for isolated skills.

Cloze exercises, where the student uses meaningful context to complete or fill in the part of a word or whole word that is missing from a text (see Figure 7–4), are a particularly worthwhile skills activity. The student uses thinking and meaning ("What would I expect to see?") to bring "closure" to the missing parts of the text. It is always a good idea to have students read the entire passage first so they see the value of reading ahead when they can't figure out a word. We want students to learn that the context can help them make predictions.

I wanted to firm up the children's use of consonant blends because facility with blends can help them make predictions. If the reader can begin the word by making the sound of the consonant blend, then, by using the context of the sentence, she should be able to figure out the word even if she cannot read the word in isolation. I reproduced page 8 of *Jamaica's Find* and whited out parts of ten words while exposing the consonant blend. While the general rule in constructing cloze exercises is not to omit more than one out of every ten words, I use common sense and the meaning of the passage as a guide. If the passage seems readable omitting words that are less than ten words apart, I am comfortable doing so (see Figure 7–4).

The first time I give such an exercise, we work it through together as a group. After that, children work in pairs to figure out the missing words. I rarely have them do this kind of exercise independently because I want them to problem solve, and working with a partner facilitates problem solving. The exercise may be redone independently as a follow-up activity if a child needs more practice.

This kind of cloze exercise is an excellent practice lesson for showing students how being able to read just the beginning of a word in meaningful context is often

Figure 7-4   Cloze Exercise

Then she climbed up the sl___There was a red sock hat on the ladder st__. Jamaica took it for a ride. She slid down so fast that she fell in the sand and lay fl__on her back.

When she rolled over to get up, she saw a st___dog beside her. It was a cuddly gray dog, worn from hugging. All over it were faded food and gr___stains. Its button nose must have fallen off. There was a round white sp__in its place. Two bl___ears hung from its head.

enough to figure out the whole word. I also find that this type of exercise helps children's spelling. Children self-check their papers with the book. When they proofread, they are expected to correct their answers. If they write in a word that is different than the author's but does not change the meaning, the word is acceptable. That reinforces another strategy—when you can't read a word, put in a word that makes sense and go on. However, caution is needed here. We must be careful observers of children's substitutions to be sure children are not just guessing but are actually putting in meaningful alternatives. When children substitute words that don't make sense, comprehension is lost.

Teaching Sight Vocabulary Meaningfully: A Small-group Guided Reading Lesson in Grade 1

While some children will learn to read naturally through immersion in daily reading and writing activities, most children benefit from some guided instruction. Even at the beginning of first grade, literature can be used to teach sight vocabulary, promote fluency, and develop reading strategies.

After a story has been read in reading group, some high-frequency words can be put on index cards. A student having difficulty identifying a word can be helped to find ways to help herself. She can be asked to go back to the text and find the page that contains the word. Using pictures and the story context, and matching the word on the index card to the word on the page, the student is guided to read the word. The student is always encouraged to use the meaning of the original text to help figure out the word. Teaching words in isolation, without connection to context, is not a part of meaningful reading instruction.

First grade teacher Jim Henry used the book *My Bike* (by Craig Martin) to build sight vocabulary and fluency. As in the previous lesson, the book was introduced first and then read. After the book—with its cumulative, repetitive structure about a boy who rode his bike "around the trees, over the bridge, under the branches, through the puddle, up the bank, and down the hill" before he crashed—had been read several times with a group of struggling first-graders, Jim used the text to build sight vocabulary in a meaningful way. The words "up," "down," "over," "under," "around," and "through" were written on 4 by 6 inch file cards to reinforce careful attending to text. While students might be reading the words in context through the story pattern and pictures, having to examine each word by itself forced them to attend to specific letters in the word.

While children were expected to read the words, they were not expected to do so without the support of the text. They went back to the text to find the word that fit—through context, pictures, configuration, and teacher guidance. When Rick was unsure of "through," Jim asked, "Do you know where to find it in your book?" Richard flipped through the pages, read it in context, and then read it on the card. When Caleb read "up" for "under," he sensed it was incorrect. On his own, he checked his book and used the picture of the bike "under" the tree to self-correct. When Sarah read "under" for "around," Jim asked, "could that be 'under?' What would you expect to see at the end of 'under'?" Sarah went back to the text and self-corrected.

To further reinforce vocabulary and make the reading-writing connection, Jim and the children wrote an innovation on the text. High-frequency words were written and read in a new context. Students had to go back to the text to figure out the pattern of the book and check for vocabulary to be included. Questions such as, "How will the next line begin?" "What word could go here?" and "How should we write that?" put the responsibility on the children. Jim verbalized the sounds in sequence as he wrote. After the story was written and read on a chart, individual booklets were reproduced for each child. Putting in illustrations to match the new text became meaningful independent work.

The shared writing, which the students called *My Jet*, followed the pattern of *My Bike* and included:

> On Monday, I flew my jet
> around the town.
> On Tuesday, I flew my jet
> around the town,
> and over the clouds.

The cumulative structure continued to build for each day of the week and concluded with:

> On Saturday, I flew my jet
> around the town,
> over the clouds,
> under the helicopter,
> through the sky,
> up the mountain,
> and down to the airport.
> On Sunday, I crashed!

Demonstrating How to Figure Out an Unknown Word

I use silent reading of a passage read whole class or in small groups to demonstrate how good readers substitute meaningful words and go on reading when they can't read a word. I find that some students have never been shown how to do this.

After the whole class or group has read a page silently, I ask, "Did anyone have trouble with a word while reading?" (See pp. 398–399 for a discussion of this strategy.) Robert raised his hand and spelled "distributed." I wrote it on the overhead transparency. I told him, "Read the sentence, and when you get to that word put in something that makes sense." He read, "All the drawings and papers that had been hanging around the room were taken down and 'passed out' to the various artists and writers in the class" (from Joanna Hurwitz, *Class Clown*, Morrow, 1987, p. 91). After complimenting Robert on his meaningful substitution, we did some word analysis with the word on the overhead projector.

Relating the Known to the Unknown

I often show students how familiar patterns and little words they already know can be applied to figuring out new words. Using a small chalkboard at the reading table, I write a word I think the student knows and use it to guide him in reading the unknown word. Some examples follow, with the easier word being noted first. I often underline the known pattern in the new word.

it, sit,
and, land, stand
out, shouted, about
at, that

Giving Verbal Support for Structural Words

Beginning readers often have difficulty with words such as "they," "what," "that," and "when," especially if the word is the first one in a sentence. If "they" is the first word, I might say, "What did *they* do?" Other prompts might be, "*What* happened?" or "What do you think *that* is?" Stressing and emphasizing the structural word, and putting the language in the child's ear, is often enough to get the child going on her own.

Changing the Pull-out Model: Applying Strategy Lessons to a Supportive Reading Program in the Classroom

In the fall of 1990, after four years of working as a Reading Recovery teacher, I elected—with the support and collaboration of my principal Bernice Stokes—to go into second grade classrooms and work closely with the classroom teachers to support reading-writing strategies. Believing strongly that the traditional pull-out program was not working for many at-risk children, my principal and I discussed alternative possibilities. We believed second grade was a critical year for reading success. Based on my many years experience as a reading specialist, I had found that if students were not successful readers by the end of second grade, it was unlikely that most of them would become confident, proficient readers at a later date.

While I am viewed as a resource teacher interacting with all students, most of my daily time in each second grade classroom is spent working with a small, targeted group of about five students who have been identified through teacher observation and standardized test scores as needing additional reading-writing support. While these students are included in reading and discussing the same core book literature as the other students in the class each morning I give further support to those who are unable to read the text easily and need to learn to apply strategies to their reading. Additionally, the classroom teacher and I work closely together and use similar holistic approaches in the teaching of reading.

We begin most afternoon sessions with a five- to ten-minute whole-class shared poetry reading or with "book talks," where students volunteer to talk about a favorite WEB book and why they recommend it. Then I meet with the small targeted group of students (plus several others who may choose to join us) for twenty to twenty-five minutes. The two major areas we have focused on during our guided reading time have been gaining confidence with reading and understanding the core books and receiving guidance at the students' instructional levels.

• *Reading the core books* Sometimes we read ahead several pages and discuss what is happening in the story so that students feel more confident and participate more readily in the next day's class reading and discussion. Most often, because the text is above the students' oral and silent level (but at their listening-comprehension level), I employ an oral cloze technique where I read and students follow along in their personal copies using a line marker. I pause on a word I expect them to be able to read by using the meaning of the story and the beginning consonants of digraphs and by making connections to other words they already know.

At times, I tape several favorite paragraphs of text that have been read and discussed in class. Using the listening center and headphones, students use part of their independent morning work time to listen and follow along over and over again. This technique has been terrific for building confidence as well as fluency. Students later enjoy showing off their increased reading ability when they come to group.

After students feel comfortable with a portion of a favorite text they have practiced with the tape, I make a cloze exercise out of it, as in Figure 7–4. Students complete the words in writing, then check the book to see if they are correct. Incorrect spellings are self-corrected, and students are then asked to turn over their papers and write several words they have just completed in the cloze exercise. The success rate and enthusiasm are high.

• *Guidance at students' instructional level* Using a predictable book and the strategies discussed in this chapter, I spend much of our time teaching for strategies while building confidence and fluency. As part of a balanced reading program, it is critical for all students to be guided in reading text at their instructional level where they recognize ninety out of one hundred words with solid comprehension.

• *Writing as a response to reading* Occasionally we do an innovation on the text or shared writing. Students' writing becomes their reading material, and engagement and interest are high.

• *Monitoring independent reading* I do a WEB reading check (as discussed on pp. 44–48) at least several days a week. Here I am checking for fluency, comprehension, and appropriateness of books.

Working daily in the classroom with another teacher and students has been a privilege. I have enjoyed the daily collegiality and communication, the opportunity to get to know all the children, and the increased potential for children's reading-writing success when two teachers collaborate. However, I am aware that welcoming another teacher into the classroom is no easy matter, and I am appreciative of teachers' risk taking and flexibility.

Second grade teacher Linda Powers, who joins our small guided reading group when she can, notes:

> Initially I was apprehensive about having another teacher in the classroom daily. I worried about getting off schedule and being forced into a time slot. However, this disadvantage is outweighed manyfold by the benefits I see the children deriving. I see kids building confidence early in the school year. Reading ahead in the core book gives them an advantage which allows them to participate readily in discussion. The look of pleasure and pride on Tamika's face when she was able to read a passage in *The Velveteen Rabbit* (by Margery Williams) [Doubleday, 1969] with a high level of accuracy and the self-knowledge that she was doing an excellent job made me realize this was worthwhile.
>
> I never thought I would find it fun to have another teacher in my classroom, but I have enjoyed the collaboration, and we're sure having a good time together.

Self-Evaluation Checks in Teaching for Strategies

Because most of us have had training that emphasizes discrete skills teaching, heightened awareness is necessary to move toward teaching for strategies in reading.

- Is your language fostering meaning-based strategies and independence when a student can't read a word, or are you relying only on, "Look at the letters" and "What sounds do those letters make?"
- Are you using engaging books with predictable text that support the reader, or are your texts dull and sequentially based for skills?
- Are you guiding students to apply strategies, or are you teaching for mastery of skills?
- Are you giving students sufficient wait time and encouragement to figure out words and meanings on their own, or are you quick to supply the answer?
- Do other students know it is the reader's job to do the work and that they need to give the reader quiet wait time, or do students call out words?
- After students have one-to-one matching and some confidence as readers, are you introducing students to unfamiliar text to note what strategies they have under control, or are students reading only books they have already heard?
- Are you asking important questions that follow naturally from the text and encourage more than one possibility, or are you looking for only one "right" answer?
- Is vocabulary taught in context during and after reading, or are you introducing words in isolation before reading?
- Are follow-up activities leading to further enjoyment and engagement with the text or are they merely keeping students busy while others are in group?

Phonics in Perspective

"Phonics is the rock upon which the house of reading is built."

A first grade teacher told me that recently, and I could relate well to her thinking. That was my position for at least the first fifteen years I was a teacher. I have been able to modify my thinking and my teaching only after much professional reading, reflecting, and observing of children—especially as a Reading Recovery teacher.

Phonics continues to be an emotional and political issue, and it does not seem likely that educators will ever come to a consensus. While most teachers feel very strongly about their particular approach to teaching phonics, phonics is also an area many teachers feel guilty, uncomfortable, and defensive about. Few primary teachers actually talk about how they teach phonics, and most of them teach it behind closed doors.

The question is no longer *if* phonics should be taught but rather *how* phonics should be taught meaningfully. Successful readers view reading as an interactive, meaning-getting process, and grapho-phonics is one of the necessary cueing systems they utilize (see Figure 7–5). Proficient readers function with an interdependence between the three cueing systems: semantics, syntax, and grapho-phonics. Semantic cues (context: what makes sense) and syntactic cues (structure and grammar: what sounds right grammatically) are strategies the reader needs to be using *already* in order for phonics (letter-sound relationships: what looks right visually and sounds right phonetically) to make sense. Phonics proficiency by itself cannot elicit comprehension of text. While phonics is integral to the reading process, it is subordinate to semantics and syntax (see Figure 7–5).

Figure 7-5   The Three Cueing Systems

The reading process can be viewed diagrammatically:

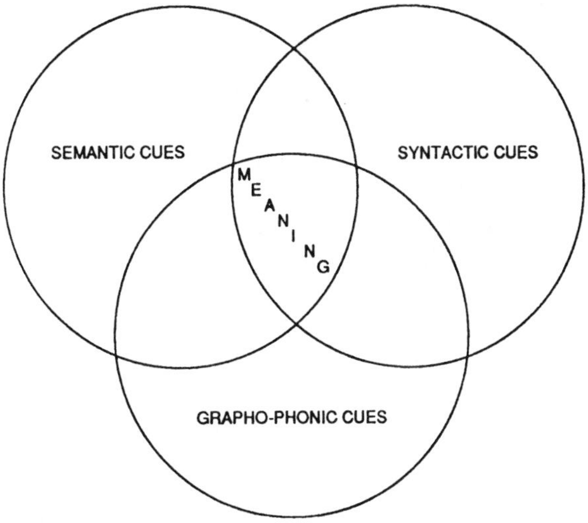

Any one area cannot exist in isolation from the others if comprehension is to be maximized.

Part of the reason some children have difficulty learning to read is that we have overattended to one cueing system, and most often it has been grapho-phonics. In addition to depriving children of more meaningful strategies, overattention to phonics takes away from time that might be better spent on reading authentic texts. Parents, too, have generally overvalued the role of phonics in reading. One mother said, "When I told my child to sound out the word and he couldn't do it, he began to get frustrated, and I backed off. I didn't know what else to do to help him figure it out." We need to teach parents higher-level strategies that go beyond phonics (see Appendix J2, "Ways to Help Your Child with Reading at Home").

[margin note: need to teach parents strategies, too]

Through critical attention to relevant research and careful observation of children in the reading-writing process, we teachers can intelligently decide how to teach phonics. For our answers, we need to look to the child and carefully observe daily reading and writing behaviors. We also need to examine the most relevant research and draw meaningful conclusions. (For a listing of significant research, see Manning, Manning, and Kamii, 1988; Turner, 1989; and Weaver, 1990, pp. 109–141.) Finally, we need to apply how children learn all language processes to the acquisition and teaching of phonics.

Issues in Teaching Phonics: In Isolation or in Context?

"I loved phonics because I came to school already reading. It wasn't a puzzle I had to figure out. I could never understand why the kids who couldn't read as well as me had so much trouble with phonics" (Holly Burgess, English teacher, conversation, fall 1990).

For many teachers, beginning reading is still equated with teaching phonics, and phonics is taught systematically and sequentially, in isolation, as a separate subject. One problem with teaching phonics in isolation is that most young children have no idea how the sounds they are connecting with letters relate to reading. For a reader who is already struggling, having to rely heavily on the least important of the three necessary cueing systems adds a further handicap. The sound of a letter is useful only in the context of a word that is already embedded in a meaningful sentence. Also, because there are so many exceptions to phonics rules, the reader often needs to see the word in a broader context to determine its pronunciation. Furthermore, and most important, in order for children to see the purpose of letter-sound relationships, phonics skills must develop from authentic language experiences.

I was in a kindergarten class recently where the teacher was flashing individual letters, and the children were doing a fine job of making the sounds (in isolation) to go along with the letters. However, when I introduced and read a Big Book to the children and asked them to find a word that began with one of the letters they had studied, they were unable to make the transfer to a real reading situation. What they had learned was an isolated skill, not a strategy. They did not know how or when to apply what had been taught. They could parrot a response but were unable to make any meaningful literacy connections.

[margin note: an isolated skill, not a strategy]

When we give young children phonics worksheets or flash letters and words in isolation, we are asking them to go from letter to sound—an unnatural and complicated task where some children have no success. Children naturally go from sound to letter, from the oral mode to the written mode, when writing and using invented spelling. Going from sound to letter respects the principle that learning proceeds from the known to the unknown. When children start with real words and what they know, they can better hold the sound and connect it to a letter in their minds.

I prefer to teach phonics strategically, in the meaningful context of the predictable stories children read and write every day. In the context of written language, phonics instruction facilitates meaning making and independence. Most of reading time is spent on reading and most of writing time is spent writing on self-selected topics, so that children develop much phonetic awareness naturally as they try to make sense of texts. However, because I am aware that some children do not just "pick up" phonics, I also guide students to discover and apply phonics generalizations by using the literature and the children's needs to determine the phonics I teach.

It has taken me well over ten years to feel completely comfortable with this approach. One thing that eased my further transition was holding onto the spelling workbooks for a while after I had long given up phonics worksheets. Knowing that the skills were still being covered relieved my conscience and helped my comfort level. Like many teachers, I did not believe children would really learn to read without a heavy dose of phonics first.

Contexts for Teaching Phonics Strategically

In meaningful phonics teaching, connections of sounds and letters are always made in real-life contexts. Beyond the book or story, we lead children to make connections in other contexts—signs, labels, charts, calendars, poems, and children's names.

Even with a natural approach to phonics, it is perfectly acceptable to call attention to sounds and words that we know students will need for reading and writing. In choosing Big Books to read, we are sensitive to the phonics and rhyming words that can be highlighted. For example, I have noticed that the Frank Asch books, some of which are available as Big Books, contain many examples of words with consonant digraphs. *Happy Birthday, Moon* (Prentice Hall, 1982) and *Mooncake* (Prentice Hall, 1983) have lots of words with "th" and "wh."

Rather than telling students what the sounds and letters are, however, I have found that an inquiry method that has the children "discover" the sounds and rules works best for engaging students in meaningful phonetic associations. I might say, for example, "What do you notice about the words . . .?" I see several words that begin with 'th.' Who can point to one?" "Can you find any other words with the same sound?" This approach is in direct contrast to that of most commercial phonics programs which tell students the rule or generalization and then present practice examples as skills in isolation rather than in the context of meaningful, continuous text.

Opportunities for ongoing phonics teaching and evaluation arise daily in the following contexts, all of which are discussed in this text:

- Shared reading
     Big Books, stories
          cloze exercises, masking (see Appendix E), blending in context

Poems
  highlighting sounds on a poem chart; for example, mun<u>ch</u>, lun<u>ch</u>
  Reading and rereading
- Shared writing
- Writing aloud
- Self-selected writing
  journals, stories
- Guided reading
  strategies for reading
  using cloze technique—powerful for group phonics connections
  using known words to work out unknown

Within these contexts, there is nothing wrong with direct, explicit teaching of phonics as long as it is done strategically. Words can be taken out of context as long as they are put back into context. Don Holdaway has developed two techniques that work well. One is the use of a sliding mask to highlight and blend words and word parts; the other is the use of a "flag" to highlight a word by taking it out of context and then putting it back into context. (See Appendix E.) The key is to remember that when a word is taken out of context to study it or break it apart, it always goes back into the context of the sentence before moving on. (See Chap. 9, "Personal Journal Writing," and Chap. 10, "Integrating Spelling into the Reading-Writing Classroom," for more information on teaching phonics meaningfully.)

Phonics Charts

Making enlarged phonics charts is perfectly appropriate in the whole language classroom. The order of sounds taught and the words used as examples are determined by the teacher and children, as the need arises in the context of reading and writing. This is very different from the use of traditional phonics charts that emphasize rules and use a prescribed sequence and fixed set of words.

For example, after *Who's in the Shed?* (Parkes, 1986) had been enjoyed over and over again during shared book experience in a first grade class, I demonstrated for the teacher how the "sh" sound could be reinforced through the book. I asked the children, "Who can find a word that begins with 'sh' [I made the sound] on this page?"

> So the sheep had a peep
> through a hole in the shed.
> *What did she see?*

A child was then invited to come up and point to a word. As the child pointed to "sheep" and read it, I used the sliding mask to blend the word parts and highlight the "sh" and the whole word. I then wrote the word on our new "sh" chart, stretching out the sounds and verbalizing as I wrote it. In the same manner, children found "shed" and "she" on that page and subsequent pages, and those words were added to our chart. I then asked if anyone's name should be added to our chart, and "Josh" and "Shelia" raised their hands. We talked about whether the "sh" was at the beginning or end of the names. Nicky volunteered that *New Blue Shoes* by Eve Rice (Macmillan, 1975) had "shoes" to add to our chart. Rosa pointed out the word "should" from one of the week's chart poems. Later in the day *Noisy Nora* by Rosemary Wells was reread, and the children discovered other words to add to our chart—"hush," "shouted," "shrub," "trash," "crash."

It has worked well to tell children, "When you find a word as you are reading, come up and put it here on the chart." Limiting the words to books helps keep the spelling on the charts fairly accurate (we also tell children to write in pencil) and keeps the children from calling out scores of words. Children easily and excitedly work together to fill up our charts, and they develop increasing phonetic awareness and knowledge in the process (see Figure 7-6).

During the first week of school in one first grade classroom, we were focusing on "t" after having read and enjoyed several Big Books together. Children searched the room for "t" words and found "August" on the calendar, "today" on the bulletin board, "Mrs. Routman" on the chalkboard, and "t" words on titles of books. We discussed where to put the words on the chart—on the left words that begin with "t," on the right words that end with "t," and in the middle words that have "t" in the middle. One eager little girl brought me a book called *Trucks* and pointed to the "t." With encouragement ("Look at the picture. What could that word be? It begins with the 't' sound.") she read the title and was delighted with herself.

Figure 7-6   A Phonics Chart in First Grade

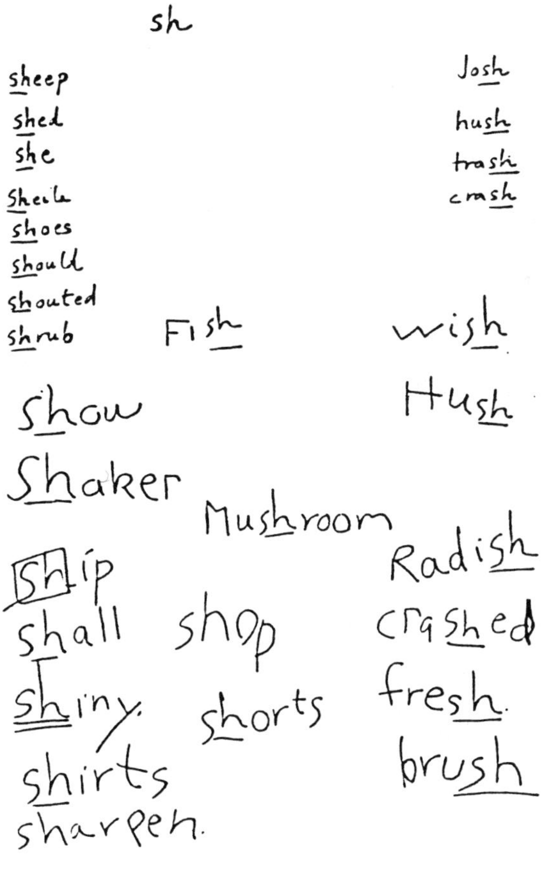

Phonics charts are posted in the room for children to add to and refer to. Separate sheets can be hole-punched and put together into a Big Book. I like to keep all the pages together for easy referral and organization in a large, spiral-bound chart tablet (24 by 16 inches). In the kindergarten classroom, phonics charts may be made with pictures from magazines with the word written next to each picture.

Personal Phonics Booklets

Some kindergarten and first grade teachers also have students keep their own sound and letter books in which students draw or paste in pictures to represent sounds for letters. (See Figure 7–7 for a page from a kindergartner's personal phonics book done during the second month of school.) Sometimes these books are also used to practice handwriting after the teacher has demonstrated the formation of the letter(s). One first grade teacher has students write optional "tongue twisters" (see Figure 7–8).

Some first grade teachers have students keep lists of words that students notice from their reading to go along with particular letter-sound combinations. Students can always read these words *before* they examine them phonetically. These booklets serve as personal phonics charts. See Figure 7–9 for a student's page from Joyce Pope's first grade class. Notice that the words come from the context of the classroom—"honey" and "hungry" from the familiar storybook *The Hungry Giant* (The Wright Group, 1980), "wishy," "washy," and "lovely" from *Mrs. Wishy-*

Figure 7-7   A Page from a Kindergartner's Personal Phonics Booklet

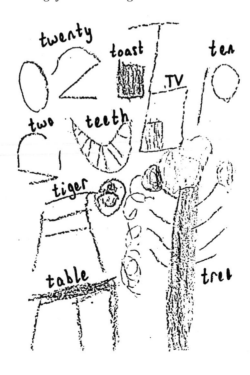

Figure 7-8   Phonics "Tongue Twister"

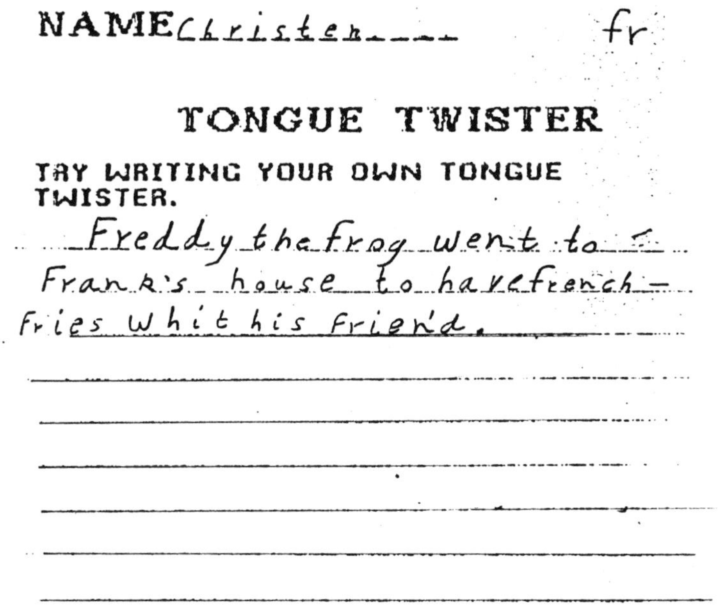

NAME *Christen*   *fr*

TONGUE TWISTER

TRY WRITING YOUR OWN TONGUE TWISTER.

Freddy the frog went to Frank's house to have french fries whith his friend.

Idea developed by Jim Henry.

Figure 7-9   Page from a First-grader's Personal Phonics Booklet

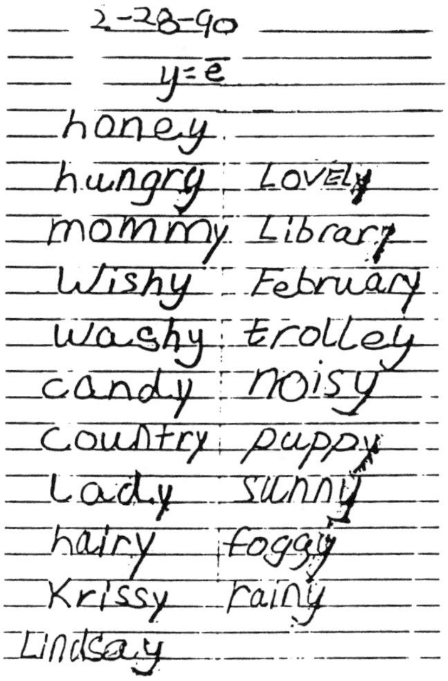

2-28-90

y=ē

honey	
hungry	Lovely
mommy	Library
wishy	February
washy	trolley
candy	noisy
country	puppy
lady	sunny
hairy	foggy
Krissy	rainy
Lindsay	

Washy; "Krissy" and "Lindsay" from children's names in the class; and "rainy," "sunny," and "February" from the calendar bulletin board.

Such individual phonics books are appropriate as long as they are a very minor part of the total reading program and students have some ownership over what goes into them. I have noticed that teachers tend to move away from these booklets once they are convinced that children are learning phonics in the normal course of daily reading and writing. One teacher said, "I did the booklets because *I* needed to see the evidence that phonics was being taught."

Teaching Short Vowels: Getting Perspective

The appropriateness of teaching short vowels to very young children needs to be re-examined. Reading the following partial paragraph, which begins like a story, helps provide some clarity. If you get stuck while reading, you should keep going, read for meaning, and put in what makes sense.

> -nc- -p-n - t-m- th-r- w-s - h-nds-m- y--ng w-lf n-m-d
> L-b-. L-b- l-v-d w-th h-s m-th-r -nd f-th-r -t th- -dg- -f
> a d--p, d-rk w--ds. -v-r- d-- L-b- w-nt t- h-nt -t th-
> n-rth -dg- -f th- w--ds, n--r th-e l-ttl- v-ll-g- -f C-l--s . . .
> (Weaver, 1988, p. 80).

I have used the preceding exercise repeatedly to convince kindergarten and first grade teachers that children can read quite well without knowing short vowels. Many teachers have told me that being able to read this paragraph with all the vowels missing forced them to examine their heavy emphasis on vowel sounds. The importance of beginning consonants, then ending consonants, and finally medial consonants is clear. Notice how important the "th" digraph is for reading about 20 percent of the words. Notice also that being unsure of the name of the village didn't affect the meaning at all.

Try an exercise like this with parents at open house to explain why vowel worksheets will not be used and coming home. Take any meaningful paragraph, delete the vowels, and you obtain the same result.

The teaching of short vowels to young children has largely gone unquestioned. It has been prescribed for years by commercial programs, most of which place emphasis on vowel sounds and their associated letters. Parents, based on their own education, expect phonics to be taught. And teachers feel they must cover all the sounds because of the perceived expectations of the next year's teachers and state and local testing requirements.

However, if teachers observe children's daily writing, they quickly notice that short vowels do not appear regularly in the writing of most kindergarten children and beginning first graders. The message that children are giving us is that they are not yet developmentally ready for short vowels. Most students are not ready to apply these sounds in reading and writing until the end of first grade. In our failure to heed that message, many young children have been labeled poor readers based on their inability to hear sounds in words—especially vowels—on worksheets. Additionally, emphasis on short vowels puts undue stress on second language learners (ESL students), who characteristically have difficulty identifying and hearing the different vowel sounds in words.

[handwritten marginal note: Short vowels don't appear in kid writing]

The blame for overemphasis on phonics cannot be laid entirely at the publishers' doorsteps. Educators have ignored the research, bought the programs, and insisted on lots of phonics exercises for very young children. John Ridley, Editor-in-Chief of the Elementary School Division of Houghton Mifflin Company in Boston, noted, "We have recognized the appropriate handling of phonics for a long time but there has been resistance through a range of pressures to have phonics taught earlier and earlier despite research to the contrary" (conversation, August 1990).

Recently there appears to be a shift in the marketplace. Teachers seem to be finally resisting the wholesale marketing of phonics through workbooks and drill sheets. Publishers have begun to respond with programs that attempt to teach phonics through the context of poems and stories.

Phonics: A Suggested Teaching Order

By being attentive to children's daily reading and, especially, their daily writing (as in their journals), teachers can easily note what phonics generalizations children have mastered and what they are ready to be introduced to. While there is no predetermined order for teaching letter-sound relationships, the following suggested sequence may be helpful when the teacher is trying to decide where to place emphasis first in the early grades. This order is based on my own observations working with young children.

- Beginning consonants
- Ending consonants
- Consonant digraphs ("sh," "th," "ch," "wh")
- Medial consonants
- Consonant blends
- Long vowels
- Short vowels

Instruction should always have meaning for the child and not just follow a prescribed sequence. After the lesson on "t" the first week in first grade, a number of children had questions about "th." Many saw the first letter "t" in "th" and wanted to add it to our "t" chart. We had just read *The Trolley Ride* (Rigby Education, 1987), in which the word "then" appears six times. Some children could already read "the" in several contexts. One student brought over a book called *Things That Go* by Anne Rockwell (Dutton, 1986). Because the children asked for it, it was appropriate and timely to move directly to "th." A discussion of whether "t" and "th" sound the same followed, and one student noted " 'th' makes a different sound." We began a "th" chart on the spot. "Brother," "mother," and "father" were added to the chart during our journal writing time. At least half a dozen students immediately referred to one of those family words and wrote it correctly in their journal entries. Even more noted "the" and incorporated it into their journal entries.

In determining what letter-sound relationships to highlight, we need to be constantly observant of children's needs and be flexible in our teaching. For example, word endings, especially "-ing," are often needed early in writing and should be taught as the need arises. It will also be necessary to do repeated demonstrations, individually and in small groups.

Demonstrations of how we are teaching phonics need to occur with parents, too. For parents to understand the meaningful teaching of phonics, we need to educate them about the current research and how we are applying it to the classroom. When parents see that phonics is still being taught and are shown the how and why, they are very supportive.

Making the Transition to More Meaningful Phonics Teaching

Kindergarten Teachers' Changes

Most kindergarten teachers in our district moved away from commercial phonics programs several years ago to the use of a "sound of the week" program, which immerses children in art, cooking, writing, and related activities to learn particular sounds in a prescribed sequence. Some kindergarten teachers have made a further transition to where the sounds that are covered for a particular week emerge naturally from daily classroom experiences. Daily reading of Big Books as well as daily writing are used to develop letter-sound awareness. A class-generated story or sentence can be the impetus for focusing on particular sounds. Teachers keep a record of what sounds have been introduced so they are sure none are overlooked.

Making the transition from "sound of the week" phonics to teaching phonics in the context of daily reading and writing is not easy. Kindergarten teacher Kathy Wolfe says,

> It was really difficult to make this change. I felt real guilty for a long time, but I was finding teaching a "letter of the week" was no longer relevant. It was an activity in isolation while I was trying very hard to teach everything in context. I saw that the children were learning their letters and sounds through all our reading and writing so I began to feel it must be okay to teach this way. Before, when I was teaching a letter, if a student wasn't ready for it, he wasn't learning it anyway. Now, I see when children need a letter, they try to figure it out through self-discovery, seeing me model, asking a friend, or looking at print around the room. I think I can finally relate teaching phonics to the way children learn to talk. I trust that it will happen.

As an example of teaching a sound in context through discovery and inquiry, a lesson that developed in a kindergarten class follows. While the teacher had decided that the day's rereadings of Big Books would be useful for focusing on the "g" sound, the children discovered the sound-letter associations. In reading through *One Cold Wet Night* (Melser and Cowley, The Wright Group, 1987), the repeated phrase "One cold wet night the farmer got out of bed and said, I'm going to be warm tonight" was used to highlight the "g" letter-sound association. "Who can find a word that begins with the "g" sound?" When a student came up and pointed to "got," I used the slide to mask the word and blend the word parts smoothly. "Say it with me: g--o--t." Before I could go on, Craig offered, "I see another word," and he was invited to come up and point to his word, "going." Other students commented that the "g" was also at the end of the word. Then a discussion about "tonight" followed after several children noticed the letter "g" in the word. They could tell that the "g" sound was not in the word. I noted, "Sometimes a letter you can see makes no sound." Because they seemed satisfied with that explanation, I made no further remarks.

Next, the children reread *Sing a Song* (Melser and Cowley, The Wright Group, 1987), which included the refrain, "Sing, sing, sing a song, Sing a song together." "Where do we find the "g" sound here?" They discovered "g" at the end of "sing" and "song" and in the middle of "together." One of the children noticed "go" on a chart poem and got up to point it out. When I asked if anyone's last name started with "g," Robin Griffith and Sam Gates raised their hands. We started a "g" chart which the teacher and children added to as new words were discovered through reading and writing.

First Grade Teachers' Struggles

Most of us seem to find the transition from prescribed phonics in isolation to teaching meaningful phonics in the context of literature very difficult and slow going. It may be reassuring to know that most teachers are struggling with making phonics teaching more relevant and applicable to reading and writing. I believe it is critical to remember that before we can change our teaching, we have to carefully re-examine our beliefs in the light of current research and learning theory.

Susan Mears has been a first grade teacher for eight years. In talking about phonics, she describes herself as "struggling awfully" despite the fact that she had done much reading and thinking about phonics teaching:

> I did more phonics in context this year, noting beginning and ending sounds and digraphs in chart poems and Big Books. The kids really liked the big charts we made where they could add their own words, but I am still struggling to find a balance in teaching phonics. I find myself feeling pressure from some of the second grade teachers who expect kids to arrive with solid word attack skills. Also, I feel guilty for not giving spelling tests. When I'm teaching all the phonics sounds, I feel as though I'm teaching spelling too. I still teach phonics separately even though I don't see kids transferring the skills. I notice that every time I pull a sound out of context, two or three kids give me an example of a word that doesn't fit the rule at all. I'm still not comfortable with the way I handle phonics.

Colleen Thompson has been teaching first grade for two years. After a series of workshops on whole language, she began to question the traditional workbook approach to phonics teaching:

> I have continued to teach phonics lessons through the workbooks, but I now see that the kids don't transfer that phonics to their reading. I had five kids who learned to read who never did catch on to phonics. I still use the workbooks, but I'm trying to use context more. If I can feel comfortable teaching phonics in context, I'd rather go that way. I saw this year that all the sounds are in the literature books. This next year I plan to spend most of reading time reading. I see I have to work with the parents too. They use only "sounding out" when working with their kids. If the child can't read the word in isolation, parents think the child is not reading and has just used memorization. I need to make them aware of the other cueing systems.

Promoting Vocabulary Development

Vocabulary development is best promoted through wide reading where new words are learned incidentally (Nagy, 1988; Herman and Dole, 1989). Therefore, we need to encourage extensive reading—reading aloud to students, guided reading with students, and independent reading by students—and teach strategies for inferring meanings of words through context. We also need to share this information with parents so they can promote vocabulary development at home.

Most vocabulary is not acquired through direct instruction and memorization. Students do not "own" a word just because they have looked it up in the dictionary or used it in a sentence. Unless they can generalize a word's meaning to apply it to a new context, vocabulary work has remained at the skills level, and transfer of learning will be slight.

In *Teaching Vocabulary to Improve Reading Comprehension*, William Nagy (1988) demonstrates the futility of having students look up unknown words in the dictionary. He lists a series of words followed by their definitions in *Webster's Third New International Dictionary* (1961) and challenges the reader to use each word correctly in a sentence. Without some prior knowledge of the word, it is very difficult to use the word correctly. "Definitions do not teach you how to *use* a new word" and "definitions do not effectively convey new concepts" (p. 6). Dictionary definitions can be utilized only if the student already understands related concepts.

We teachers can best promote vocabulary development within the context of literature when the meaning of the text can be used to determine word meaning. We can guide students to use what they know and what the author presents to construct word meanings strategically at the concept level. Vocabulary is developed during or after reading when semantic relationships can be made. The only time I introduce a word before reading is if understanding a particular word is critical for comprehending the passage. This is more likely to occur with reading in the content areas than in the literature/reading program.

In guiding students to utilize the context, we need to demonstrate how this is done. In reading *Charlotte's Web* by E. B. White, I showed a group of second-graders how the author helps the reader with word meanings. In the beginning of Chapter VII, "Bad News," White begins by discussing flies as a nuisance. "The cows hated them. The horses detested them. The sheep loathed them." I think out loud and show how "hated" can be used to infer similar meaning for "detested" and "loathed." White then goes on to say that Charlotte "always put her victim to sleep before eating it. . . . 'I always give them an anaesthetic so they won't feel pain. It's a little service I throw in'" (p. 48). I verbalize how the previous text lets the reader know that "victim" means a fly and that the meaning of "anaesthetic" can be figured out even if you can't read the word.

Students need to know they can make meaningful substitutions and continue reading. It is also important to point out that the author's choice of words affects the mood, interest, quality, and tone of the writing so that young writers will begin to think about choosing their own written words carefully.

Dictionaries are consulted when the need arises—when the definition of a word that is needed for understanding cannot be inferred. This is what many adults do. When I am reading, I rarely stop to look up a word in the dictionary. I try to glean the meaning, substitute a word or phrase that makes sense, and go on. Only when the word is necessary for understanding a major concept—or when I have come across a word many times before and am curious about its meaning—do I look it up. We need to apply the same real-life use to the classroom.

Because of the high correlation between vocabulary and reading comprehension (Nagy, 1988; Herman and Dole, 1989) and because students enjoy learning new words, knowledge of vocabulary is important. However, since drill and practice exercises account for little actual vocabulary development, I believe that most time for vocabulary acquisiton should be related to applying acquisition strategies to independent reading. Self-selection should be a major part of how vocabulary is studied; that is; students should choose most of the words they want to learn. With a full-length chapter book, focusing on several words per chapter or about twenty words per book is sufficient. Students can keep personal vocabulary notebooks. Because the words have importance for students, there is greater likelihood of recall. (See Chap. 6, in "Responding to Literature: Later Transitions," pp. 110–111, for suggestions for vocabulary instruction; see also Nagy, 1988, for procedures for vocabulary acquisition from kindergarten through college.)

8 ═══════════

Authentic Contexts for Writing

Choosing to co-author a true book about sharks: grade 1

Becoming a Writer

A colleague asked me, "What teacher influenced you in your writing?"

"I don't know. I can't remember any teacher that way," I replied.

"Surely, there must have been someone," she persisted.

No one had ever asked me that question before, and I realized I had never thought about it. Surely, there *must* have been someone. Thinking back through my school career, I could only remember writing for the teacher, diagraming sentences, being concerned about "getting it right." I was not much of a reader initially, so it couldn't have been the influence of the great authors. I read in school and completed assignments, but I didn't become an avid reader until well into high school. It was then that my mother's influence—gently nudging me to read books she had loved as well as seeing her constantly reading—finally rubbed off.

But writing? That was something else. If not a teacher, then who? Then it came to me. My grandmother. My grandmother who had completed only sixth grade because she had to work to help support the family. Living and working, not schooling, were her education. Grandma had a way with words, a cackling sense of humor, and a stubborn streak that drove much of her family crazy, but to me she was wonderful. While I was growing up, and all through my teenage years, we spent many hours visiting together. Some evenings she told me stories for hours, and the way she put words together fascinated me. Many stories she wrote down, and read to me. I can still see her reaching up into her crowded bedroom closet and pulling down a large, faded cardboard box filled with her written memories. At the time, I did not realize that she was a born storyteller or that I was her private audience. I only knew that her words, her voice, her raw emotions captivated me. She embellished stories and poems of the old country, of hardship, of a failed romance, of her children, of marriage, of getting old.

After a while, Grandma would usually stop and say, "And now you have to hear a real author." And she would select a passage from *Gone with the Wind, The*

160

Good Earth, or some classic she loved and read to me. "Listen to the words, and feel them" she would say. "They are beautiful." I still remember Margaret Mitchell's descriptions of the devastated South during the Civil War. Being read aloud to as a teenager had a powerful effect on me. I began to appreciate the depth, beauty, and possibilities of language.

When my grandmother was in her late seventies, she enrolled in a writing class at the local high school. Always desirous of more education, she wanted to become a "writer." I don't think she, or any of her family, acknowledged she was already a "real author." I have only recently realized the extent of Grandma's influence on my own desire and ability to write.

The Importance of Being a Writing Model

I sincerely believe that we should not ask children to go through any process we have not experienced ourselves. Our students must have writing models if they are to become writers, and we teachers need to be those models. Generally, we have come to believe this about reading. Almost every teacher I know reads with and to children every day—during read-aloud time, sustained silent reading, and guided reading. Not so with writing.

Most of us don't write with children or share our own writing. In fact, many of us don't like to write and are afraid to write. We have been conditioned by our own traditional schooling to view writing as an assignment by and for the teacher. Though we meticulously lead children through the steps of the writing process, we have never been through the process ourselves. Yet just as we would never consider taking music, art, or athletic lessons from a teacher who talked about the subject but had never actually done it, we cannot be teachers of writing until we demonstrate the craft ourselves. We must become genuine users and risk takers before we can expect the same of our students. This is not an easy task. Writing is tough work, even for those who do it regularly.

There are many ways to begin to become a writing model. One way is to share a copy of a letter or note written for a real purpose. Another way is to try a shared writing after a common class experience such as a field trip. Or two classes can be combined, with one teacher writing in front of the children and the other teacher providing support. I believe it's okay to tell the students we've never written in front of a class before and are feeling very anxious. We don't need to worry about botching the job. Children will respect and learn from a process if they know the teacher is sincere and cares about them. If the fear of writing before the class is too great to actually do it, try inviting a writer into the classroom. The individual need not be a famous author. He or she could be a parent, the principal, a colleague— anyone who makes writing a real part of daily life. Students must know adults who write and who are willing to demonstrate their thinking-writing-revising-editing processes for them.

Being a Writer Means Being Vulnerable

When my book *Transitions* was published, I was terrified. I didn't know that I was going to feel that way, but as the book was about to be unveiled (at the International Reading Association annual meeting in Toronto in May 1988), I felt as though I were being undressed in public. The writing of the book had been a very private undertaking, the reading of it would be a public one. All my inadequacies would be on view for everyone to see. I remember feeling sick to my stomach and wanting to go into hiding. My principal and good friend Delores Groves, who had come to Toronto to celebrate and be part of a symposium on whole language with me, chided me for the way I was dressed. I had on all dark colors, no jewelry, and little make-up. She encouraged me to "brighten up," and she was right. Looking back, I think I wanted to become invisible.

> Readers peer into the writer's very soul. They judge the depth of sensitivity, the clearness of thinking, the soundness of values, and the range and sophistication of verbal skill. If beauty and truth embody the writer's spirit, they will be revealed. So, too, will shallowness and ineptitude (Romano, 1987, p. 41).

In workshops for teachers, I have always stressed the importance of teachers writing—and writing in front of their students. I had always shared drafts of my own writing on the overhead projector, but I had never demonstrated writing in front of my peers. It took me seven years to get up the courage to do that!

demonstrating in front of kids

While giving a presentation to teachers and administrators at the K–8 writing conference in October 1989 in Columbus, Ohio, I talked about journal writing and how to make it come alive for students. I listed some topics that I could write about: needing a haircut and perm, making jam, raking leaves, driving to Columbus, being nervous about my presentation. I didn't know I was actually going to write in public until I did it. As I began composing on the overhead projector, the room became silent. I felt apprehensive because I had no idea what I was going to write or how it would come out. The audience seemed as surprised as I was by my public act of writing. This is what I wrote:

> Late last night some friends came up to my room, and we were sharing pictures from our lives. As it got later and later, I started to get really nervous because I needed some quiet time to organize my thoughts for the next day's presentation.
> I had trouble sleeping. I kept waking and looking at the clock and wondering when it would be 6:00 A.M.
> My stomach was doing flip-flops all morning—through breakfast and through Lucy Calkins' keynote talk. But once I started talking, my nervousness disappeared, and I began to relax.

My handwriting was as illegible as usual, I had several cross outs, my content was sparse, but at least it was a genuine attempt, and teachers appreciated that. Several teachers told me it was the first time they had ever seen another teacher write. One teacher later wrote to me and said seeing me write had given her the courage to begin to write in front of her students.

My own feelings of vulnerability have helped me be empathetic to students—and teachers—who share their writing and have sensitized me to the need to set up a classroom writing climate that is supportive and encouraging. We all need to feel that our writing and best efforts are valued if we are going to take the risk of sharing writing and accepting responses.

Teachers Writing Together: Taking a Risk

Some of us have found that writing in front of students becomes possible if we first go through the process with our colleagues. In one building, where our weekly language arts support groups had begun focusing on the writing process, teachers were honestly talking about the fact that they did not write themselves. Based on an idea by Harste, Short, and Burke (1988), I read *The Relatives Came* by Cynthia Rylant (Bradbury, 1985) as a springboard for triggering personal, family memories. After listening to the story, principal Larry Svec and about twelve teachers began to write a draft of a fond family memory. Because I wanted the writing to have a real purpose, I suggested that the written memory might be given to the actual person as a gift.

We took about six weeks of our regular support group meetings to write our drafts, meet in small response groups to give feedback, write final copies, and share finished pieces. Several teachers commented about how vulnerable they felt sharing their writing with peers. One teacher said she was surprised at her own sensitivity to a minor suggestion that was made after several very positive comments had been offered. "It made me realize how careful we have to be with students. I had no idea I would feel so defensive about my writing."

Third grade teacher Lee Sattelmeyer took the initiative to word-process completed pieces and, working with school secretary Judy Kalan, put together a book called *Musing: Reflections upon Our Life* and gave a copy to all who participated. The morning we received the bound books at our support group meeting, everyone sat captivated, reading privately. The response went beyond respectful silence. A community had been created. We knew each other better, trusted each other more, and felt closer as friends and colleagues. Several teachers said it was the first time they had ever written and shared publicly and that the experience would make it easier to demonstrate themselves as writers to their students.

Setting up the Classroom Environment for Writing

The climate of the classroom, both emotional and physical, contributes to students' willingness and eagerness to write. We need to examine and be able to articulate our own beliefs about writing before we can foster an environment that meaningfully engages students in the writing process. For me, Nancie Atwell has said it best:

A Framework of Beliefs about Writing

1. Writers need regular chunks of time.
2. Writers need their own topics.
3. Writers need response.
4. Writers learn mechanics in context.
5. Children need to know adults who write.
6. Writers need to read.
7. Writing teachers need to take responsibility for their knowledge and teaching. (Atwell, 1987, pp. 17–18)

I add two additional beliefs about writing:

1. Writers need to feel safe to take a risk.
2. Writers need a genuine purpose for writing.

Making the Writing Process Real

Genuinely Engaging in the Writing Process

In many writing classrooms, writing is not natural. Instead, writing is a mechanistic process that has all the how's without the why's. Many of us have bought into "process writing" without the necessary personal conviction to make it significant for students. It is not unusual to walk into a classroom today and see the steps of the writing process posted on the wall in sequential order. Certainly I remember starting that way. I took students through the steps as if following a recipe. On Monday we did prewriting or rehearsing. On Tuesday we did the first draft. Wednesday we revised. Thursday we edited. Friday we published. While this description is a bit exaggerated, I—like many other teachers—believed that I could teach the writing process by taking students through sequential steps. Only when I became a writer myself and began to write with students and colleagues could I see that "doing writing process" was not valid.

<u>My writing process</u>   When I began to write regularly, I became very aware that writers don't go through an ordered or exact process. I never get up in the morning thinking, "Today I will be prewriting." My prewriting or rehearsing goes on constantly. I prefer the inclusive term "percolating" for the ongoing, thinking, reconsidering process that takes place throughout the writing process. (see Romano, 1987, pp. 55–58). Even after I have written drafts and made revisions, I am still percolating. My percolating goes on when I am driving, swimming, eating, walking, trying to sleep, sitting at the word processor about to write, taking a shower, listening to colleagues, cooking dinner. For Romano, "percolating" is "anything done in relation to the piece of writing aside from producing a draft or revising one." That could include outlining, brainstorming, jotting notes. For me, percolating is mostly a mental process, the thinking that goes on before I write.

Once I begin to write, the percolating stops and the writing takes over. Writer Madeleine L'Engle says, "Don't think. Write. We think before we write a story, and afterward, but during the writing we listen. It is an act of focused attention, which is very different from conscious thinking." (In "How They Feel about God," by Madeleine L'Engle [a review of *Writer's Revealed* by Rosemary Hartill], *New York Times Book Review*, November 5, 1989.)

I never go neatly through steps; I meander back and forth through stages. I percolate, write a draft, revise, percolate, rewrite the draft, percolate, begin a new draft, revise a previous draft some more, and so on. I don't follow any sequential steps. I let the writing—and what I think I might want to say—lead me. As much as possible, we need to allow students the same time and latitude to find what works for them.

We also need to allow students the opportunity to set a piece of writing aside. Again and again, while writing this book, I experienced writer's block and was unable to continue writing a chapter or section. By moving to a different topic, I found I could often come back to a previous draft more easily at a later date. This is not to say we should not give students due dates, but we can build in flexibility as much as possible.

Perhaps hardest of all, we need to create uninterrupted blocks of time. I cannot write anything meaningful in a half hour. I need long, quiet periods of time. While this may not be possible in the classroom, we can look at our schedules and try to put writing at the center of the curriculum, at least part of the time. Based on my own writing experiences, I now believe that writing *is* thinking and that through writing we learn to write and think more clearly. I believe writing must become central to our teaching and integral to all subject areas across the curriculum.

Valuing Revision

Revision is at the heart of the writing process and is fundamental to almost all good writing. Students can understand revision and the need for it when revision is demonstrated as a genuine part of what good writers do. On the other hand, when it is presented as "step three" in the writing process, students rarely take it seriously.

Donald Murray calls revision "central to the act of discovery" (1990, p. 171). Revision means, literally, looking again at a piece of writing and *re*-visioning it. It is for me both the most challenging and joyful part of the writing process. Early revisions on a quickly written draft are the hardest because the writing has no clear form or direction yet. Final revisions are when I have the most fun: playing with individual sections and words and seeing the promise of the piece as a unified whole.

Revision requires careful attention and thinking and refers to any changes the writer makes in an attempt to improve clarity, organization, wording, fluency, and understanding. Revision includes changing one word for another, but it is much more. Words, sentences, and whole paragraphs may be added, deleted, or moved around. The writing is reshaped, molded, and polished.

When I go into classrooms to assist with children's writing, I try first to demonstrate myself as a writer. I bring in my chapter drafts to pass out. I tell students that when I write a draft I get my thoughts down quickly, not concerning myself with getting things right. This is the time for exploration, and I usually have no idea how a draft will turn out. I am rarely satisifed with a first draft, but it is a beginning.

For a particular chapter, I do at least five or more drafts, and I share these with students and let them draw their own conclusions. When I ask students what they have noticed about the drafts, I find it interesting that students are always surprised by the number of "errors." They view any marks on the paper—the changes, crossouts, rewordings, rearrangings—as "mistakes" (see Figure 8–1). I explain to them that this is how writers work, that no one gets it right the first time, that writing is difficult, creative, time-consuming, and tiring work, but worth it, because the finished piece brings a wonderful sense of creative accomplishment.

I always let students know how tough revision is ahead of time, and I find my honesty does not scare them off—quite the contrary. Like the pilot warning passengers that they are about to experience turbulence, letting students know that revision will be challenging helps prepare them for the work ahead.

I also talk to students about the role of response in revision and how that works

Figure 8-1   Partial "Messy" Chapter Draft by the Author

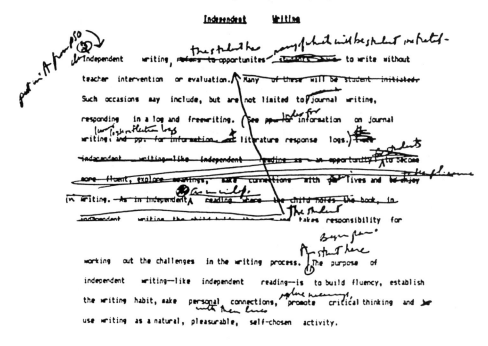

for me. I let students know that because my audience is teachers, I always have each chapter draft read by at least three to five colleagues. I sincerely want and need to know what seems unclear or confusing, missing, needing reorganization. I want to know whether my tone is invitational, whether the content is relevant, whether the information is clear. I also want to hear—and need to hear first—what has been helpful and clearly written. Because writing is such hard work, the writer always needs supportive messages along with suggestions for changes.

I explain that as only one writer-reader, I cannot possibly be sure whether my writing is clear and complete. I then show students two actual chapter drafts that I gave to teachers for reactions. The first one has no comments on it except "very good." The second is filled with comments—reader reactions, suggestions, confusions, new learnings. I ask students which response has been helpful to me as the writer, and they are quick to comment on the usefulness of the second one.

I also let students know that because I respect my reader-responders, I take every comment and suggestion seriously, and I make more than 90 percent of all changes suggested. Students see the necessity for the revision process, and they do "buy into" it. I have found that they are not "turned off" with honest talk about the difficulty and necessity of revision. On the contrary, they appreciate the honesty and realistic expectations and come through the task admirably.

While teachers may not have extensive drafts to share with students, most of us have something we write that requires revision—letters to parents, handouts to explain the curriculum, a note to a favorite person on a special occasion. When you find yourself writing something that requires going back and making changes, save it, and share it with your students.

Looking at Writing Errors as a Necessary Part of Learning

When a new student who has come from a school in which correctness and form in writing have been emphasized above meaning and exploration, enters a reading-writing classroom, the student's writing may be correct but it is also usually dull and lifeless (see Figure 9–10 in Chap. 9). Overemphasis on correctness produces unimaginative writing.

Connie Weaver said it best in a significant article entitled "Welcoming Errors as Signs of Growth" when she noted "growth and error go hand in hand" (*Language Arts*, May 1982, pp. 438–444). She cited research which showed that as writers risked new forms, they made more errors until the form came under control. For example, Weaver noted that while sixth-graders were found to have more "sentence sense" errors than fourth graders, the sixth-graders were experimenting with more complicated constructions, especially the use of subordinate clauses.

We need to notice the kinds of errors students are making and to not see them all as negative. Especially important is the recognition that as students get older and try out new, more sophisticated forms, they may temporarily make more errors as they develop insights. The amount of writing may also decrease temporarily while students are struggling to get things right. This is very much akin to the young child trying out a more sophisticated form of speech. Before getting the correct form under control, the child needs lots of time to practice and exaggerate—and needs to be encouraged and congratulated for risk taking. We need to encourage students to experiment with form while continuing to guide them in proofreading their work.

Donald Murray observes,

> Many teachers complain that their students can't write sentences. I complain that many of my students write sentences. Too early. Following form, forgetting meaning. Following language toward correctness. For its own sake . . .
>
> We don't know enough about how to write badly—and why. Syntax often breaks down when we approach a new and interesting meaning . . . (1989, p. 39).
>
> All writing is experimental. We don't know what works until we try it. Failure is normal and instructive. From failures we see ways to achieve success (1989, p. 123).

I believe we need to give students lots of opportunities for experimentation and practice without concern for grading. Only a very small percentage of writing should be evaluated, the rest should be for students to try out alternative forms, styles, and genres.

Using Published Authors for Demonstrations

Often the best way for students to write successfully in a particular genre is to immerse themselves in the literature of that genre. For example, students need to examine and appreciate models of quality fiction before they can be expected to write fiction themselves.

When reading aloud or working with a reading group, I often stop and note the way the author has created a mood, setting, or character description in a work of fiction. I may reproduce a page or paragraph and share it on the overhead projector, highlighting key words and phrases the author has used. I want to make students what Nancie Atwell calls "insiders," privy to what authors do, so students may think about similar possibilities for their own writing. Even young children can take note of what authors do and begin to apply it to their own writing.

When a second grade class was getting ready to write stories for an upcoming "Young Authors' Conference," we focused on how good stories begin. We looked at the "leads" in books we had already read and discussed—*Charlotte's Web* by E. B. White, *Sam, Bangs and Moonshine* by Evaline Ness, *Wump World* by Bill Peet, and *One Morning in Maine* by Robert McCloskey (Viking, 1952). In particular, we noted that the author made the setting descriptive and clear right at the beginning. A number of students were able to use these demonstrations to create their own interesting leads (see Figure 8–2 for two examples of first attempts). Student examples of quality writing were also used as demonstrations for other students.

I have come to believe that literature provides the best models of language. Through reading, thinking about, discussing, and interpreting great literature, students come to learn most of what they need to know about language—especially if the teacher takes the time to note the demonstrations the literature provides (for example, the leads, the conventions, the vocabulary). *The way to become a writer is through becoming an insightful reader.* That insight comes directly from Frank

Figure 8–2 ***Two Second Grade Students' First Attempts at Writing Leads***

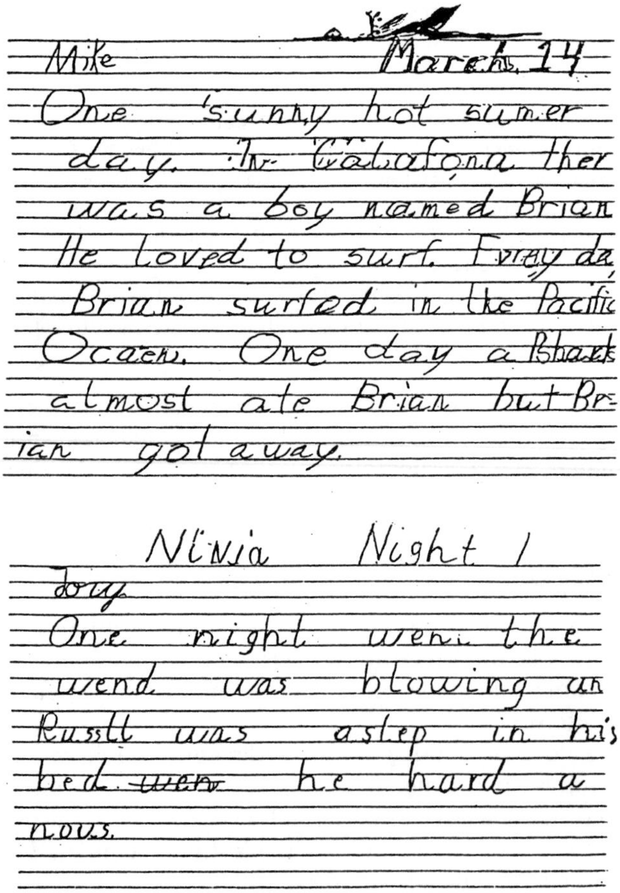
Mike March 14
One sunny hot sumer day. In Catafona ther was a boy named Brian He loved to surf. Evray da Brian surfed in the Pacific Ocean. One day a Shark almost ate Brian but Brian got away.

Ninja Night
Tony
One night wen the wend was blowing an Russll was aslep in his bed. ~~wen~~ he hard a nous.

Smith's article, "Reading Like a Writer" in *Joining the Literacy Club* (originally published in *Language Arts*, May 1983, pp. 558–567). A favorite quote that I often reread from this article follows:

> To read like a writer we engage with the author in what the author is writing. We anticipate what the author will say, so that the author is in effect writing on our behalf, not showing how something is done but doing it with us. This is identical to the spoken language situation where adults help children say what they want to say or would like and expect to be able to say. The author becomes an unwitting collaborator. Everything the learner would want to spell the author spells. Everything the learner would want to punctuate the author punctuates. Every nuance of expression, every relevant syntactic device, every turn of phrase, the author and learner write together. Bit by bit, one thing at a time, but enormous numbers of things over the passage of time, the learner learns through *reading* like a writer to *write* like a writer (p. 25).

Setting Up the Environment for Writing

I have a small room in my house where I write. All my tools and equipment are there—word processor and printer, comfortable chair, books, pens, pencils, Post-its, wire baskets to hold papers, file cabinets, drafts, loose notes, dictionary, writing notebooks, stapler, scissors, tape, white-out liquid, paper clips, rubber bands, blank paper, wastebasket, blank file folders, folders organized by topics and work samples, paintings, pictures of my family, clock, light, coffee cup.

When I begin writing, the room is neat and organized, but once I am "in process" there are papers and piles on every available surface, including the entire floor. Eventually, I encroach on surfaces in adjoining rooms, and drafts and papers take over the dining room table, kitchen table, chairs and ledges. I am by nature a fairly neat person, but not when I write. Writing is "messy." I become disorganized in order to find my organization. I need to see all the parts so I can rearrange, discard, add, reshuffle, rethink, and rework to create a meaningful whole. My writing room becomes orderly again only after I have worked through the writing challenges. I cannot put away my tools until I have satisfactorily used them.

I mention all this to sensitize us as teachers to the needs of writers. While clearly it is not possible for each student to have his own room in school, the traditional fixed space of the desk could be expanded. For example, for students who work well independently, long tables could be set up in the hall just outside the classroom to give writers more space and freedom. Children could be allowed to spread out on the floor in class. They might even be allowed to leave their "messy work" where it is if there will be another opportunity later in the day to write. Post-its, paper, pens, tape, and so on, could be readily available for student use.

Just as important, we can attempt to arrange classrooms to be as comfortable as possible for students and teachers to write (see Figures 15–1 and 15–2 in Chap. 15). Students should know where to find writing supplies and what areas of the room they may use when they write. It works well to have several areas for conferencing. A few desks pushed together can serve as well for a conference area as a larger table.

We could take a lesson from our kindergarten teachers, many of whom have created authentic spaces for writing. Children write all over the room—at the writing center, in the play area, with the teacher, with a friend, spread out on the floor, at big tables. Another lesson we can take from kindergarten is the importance of talk in learning to write. Young writers need and enjoy collaborating, and they use their talk to expand and clarify ideas. We need to make all classrooms more user friendly for writers.

Demonstrating the Use of Writers' Tools

Before students become immersed in the writing process, take some time to show how writers work. Let students see drafts with cross outs, arrows, carets, and individual cues to the writer (such as letter codes) to move a section. Many elementary teachers have found it works well to have students write on only one side of the sheet and skip every other line. This practice makes cutting and pasting and adding and deleting easier later on. We let students know that writers don't just recopy and that a messy draft is normal. We actually demonstrate how cutting and pasting is done with scissors and tape and show how colored pens or pencils may be used in the editing process.

I always show students a messy draft (see Figure 8–1). Showing a draft by a colleague or an author would also work well. In "The Author's Eye" series, Roald Dahl and Katherine Paterson (1988) share their thoughts, jottings, and writing drafts, and students can see the thinking-revising process.

Writing for Authentic Purposes

Relevant Writing

The writing that goes on in classrooms must be relevant to students if they are to become engaged in and value the process. Practicing writing through exercises, skill sheets, and isolated activities does not produce good writers and, in fact, is not real writing. Our focus must be on writing for real purposes.

This section gives examples of some of the forms of writing we use in our daily lives. As such, I believe they are appropriate forms of writing (and reading) for the classroom and can be used as guides for authentic writing. The forms or genres listed are not in any particular order and are not meant to be all inclusive. Notice that basal stories, worksheets, book reports, and the five-paragraph essay are not listed; these forms exist only in schools.

This list may prove useful for generating ideas for meaningful independent work, providing optional opportunities for writing-publishing and for encouraging communicating-thinking-learning-writing in a variety of genres. In all cases, the writing should connect with reading, the curriculum, other children, varied audiences, and real purposes.

In most cases, we will need first to demonstrate the particular form or genre by immersing students in many reading-writing examples. For example, before expecting students to write directions, book blurbs, an author page, a newspaper article, or a report, we must first expose them to many pieces of quality writing in that genre so that they become familiar with the format, style, language, and conventions.

Specific examples of letter writing, story writing, and journal writing are discussed and demonstrated following the list of possible writing forms. Because personal journal writing—where students write about their own experiences—is such a powerful vehicle for getting started successfully with authentic writing, the next chapter examines in detail the rationale, benefits, and procedures of this form, especially as it applies to the elementary grades.

Books	Dedications
Stories	Brochures
Reviews (of books, movies,	Newsletters
restaurants, products)	Anthologies
Author page (for books)	Yearbooks
Directions	Book blurbs
Notices	Thank you notes
Newspaper articles	Greeting cards
Reports	Summaries
Interviews	Recipes
"How to" manuals	Lists (for shopping, gifts,
Advice columns	parties, trips, things to do)
Surveys	Calendars
Questionnaires	Messages
Evaluations	Bulletins
Instructions	Posters
Essays	Signs
Advertisements	Charts
Memos	Letters
Poems	Postcards
Diaries	Conversations
Scripts/plays	Want ads
Comic strips	Announcements
Rules	Song lyrics
Proposals	Magazine articles
Invitations	Guides
Journals	Assignments
Crossword puzzles	Commercials

Writing Letters

I write letters all the time. I probably write fifteen to twenty letters a week—to friends, to family, to colleagues, to teachers who write to me, to my publisher. I prefer writing and receiving letters to talking on the telephone. After a long day at work interacting with lots of people, I welcome the solitude and peaceful reflection letter writing affords. I enjoy the opportunity to put down on paper thoughts and feelings that may be awkward to express over the phone. And while I usually word process letters that have a professional or business audience, I always write by hand when I want to be personal, despite my poor handwriting. I also enjoy saving and savoring letters I receive and rereading them at a later date. I treasure special letters from my husband, my children, my father, my aunt, my principal, my good friends, and my colleagues.

Letter writing is a necessary life skill. If we are to communicate effectively, we must be able to organize our thoughts on paper. For giving and receiving information, we all rely on letters to some extent. Currently, with fax machines in most offices, the letter or memo—often handwritten for quick transport—is being employed on a regular basis.

As teachers, we must demonstrate our own writing processes for students before we can expect them to take the process seriously and invest their full energy in it. Recently I wrote a letter to *The New York Times* in response to a short article I had read in the "Hers" section of the Sunday magazine section. I brought in my rough drafts and my revisions and used a third grade class as an audience for feedback on the clarity of the piece. Later I showed the children the final, finished copy with the changes I had made. Students are always amazed to learn that teachers have to work at writing, that most people do not get a written message right the first time, and that their insights can be helpful to adult writers.

Another time third grade teacher Lee Sattelmeyer, who uses letter writing across the curriculum, and I were reviewing a draft of a letter he had composed for the school's upcoming open house for parents. The letter, which was largely a philosophical statement, was to be an important cover sheet focusing on the year's curriculum (see Figure 16–4 in Chap. 16). As we were talking, I realized that this was the kind of activity students need to witness. They need to see and hear our thinking, our exchange of ideas, and our actual changes. They need to know that the final, perfectly typed version they would take home to their parents had gone through a long thinking process that began as a draft. Lee and I moved our initial private conversation over planning time into the classroom and made it an authentic demonstration for the children. While we worked out the confusions and inconsistencies of the piece in front of them, they witnessed our struggle to clarify the writing and our eventual satisfaction with its improvement.

When I am invited into a classroom by a teacher who wants to become involved in process writing or who is concerned about the poor writing of her students, I often begin with letter writing for a real purpose. Part of the reason letter writing works so well in the classroom is that it is short and focused. The amount of drafting, revising, and editing is limited because letters are rarely more than a page or two in length. As such, students are willing to invest time in the entire process. Some letters, of course, such as thank you notes to another class that need to be sent right away, are sent as first drafts, and some teachers stamp these "unedited."

Writing a Letter of Appreciation

In one fourth grade class, the teacher, Debbie Schaedlich, and I decided to have the children write letters of appreciation to a person in the school or community. We discussed the idea that most of us write or call to complain when something goes wrong, but we take for granted a job done well. We asked the children to think about thanking someone for something that had never been acknowledged. We began by brainstorming possible people we could write to, and we came up with this partial list: mailman, custodian, teacher, neighbor, coach, principal, librarian, school secretary, school nurse, parent-teacher association, policeman, mayor.

Figure 8-3   Draft of a Letter to the School Custodians

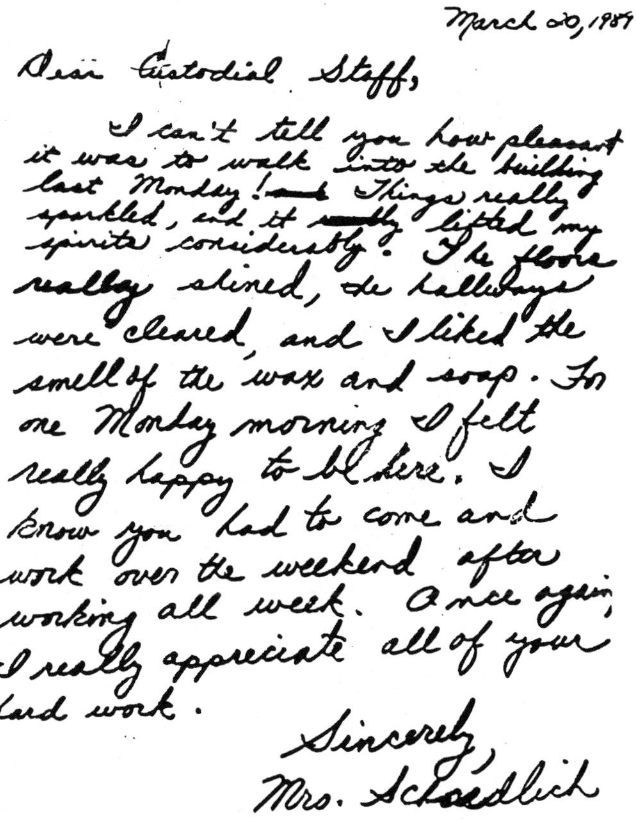

Debbie began by writing a draft of her letter on the overhead projector. While the children looked on, she wrote and thought aloud of possible people she could write to and then decided to write to the school custodians. Her draft is shown in Figure 8–3. Because the teacher modeled the process and the children could engage meaningfully in the task, they wanted to complete the assignment, and they wanted to do it well (see Figures 8–4 and 8–5). They saw that there was a reason to have clear sentences, proper punctuation and grammar, and legible handwriting. All the letters were stamped and mailed after they had been revised and taken to final copy. A number of the students received personal replies to their letters, demonstrating to them the power of letter writing.

Forms of Letter Writing

Letter writing can take many forms: letters to pen pals (students in other schools or younger students writing to older students in the same school), parents, students who are sick, classmates who have moved; notifications of and invitations to

Figures 8-4 and 8-5   Fourth-graders' Letters of Appreciation

April 11, 1989

Dear Little Caesers,

Thank you for giving us two pizzas for the price of one. There are mounds of cheese, and lots of toppings on both pizzas. Plus, there is a very short wait when you pick up the pizza. The pizza tastes great! I was wondering where you get that great taste? You should have more restaurants in Shaker Hts.

Sincerely,

Sam R.

Figure 8-5

4/11/89

Dear PTA,

I'm sorry I didn't get around to telling you how much I appreciated the ballet troupe you sponsored. It was great. I felt like I might be a dancer when I grow up. In March I got real excited because the ballet was coming to Fernway. My favorite part was when the dancers did those big short kicks. Well any ways the ballet was very good.

Yours truly,
Mark S.

174

classroom and school-wide events; and, of course, letters to favorite authors. We have checked with librarians for a list of authors (and their addresses) who generally respond to children, and we have also written to them in care of their publishers. Our students have recently received replies from Norman Bridwell, Joanna Hurwitz, Bill Peet, and Steven Kellogg.

Taking the time to write a personal letter demonstrates caring and personal interest. Second grade teacher Elaine Weiner writes letters to all of her students several weeks before school begins. She introduces herself, tells something about her summer, and says how much she is looking forward to meeting the student. Each year several parents comment on the impact the letters had on them and their children.

Writing a business letter As an authentic way for students to learn to write business letters, Lee Sattelmeyer uses writing a business letter as part of his social studies unit on the community. After studying and discussing the various parts of their local community, students are asked to choose a person or institution they want to know more about and write a letter of inquiry. Several students, who previously had done little writing, put great efforts into their letters: Their questions and interest were genuine. Most students received replies and were delighted. See Figures 8–6 and 8–7 for a typical letter and a response.

Figure 8–6 An Information-Seeking Letter

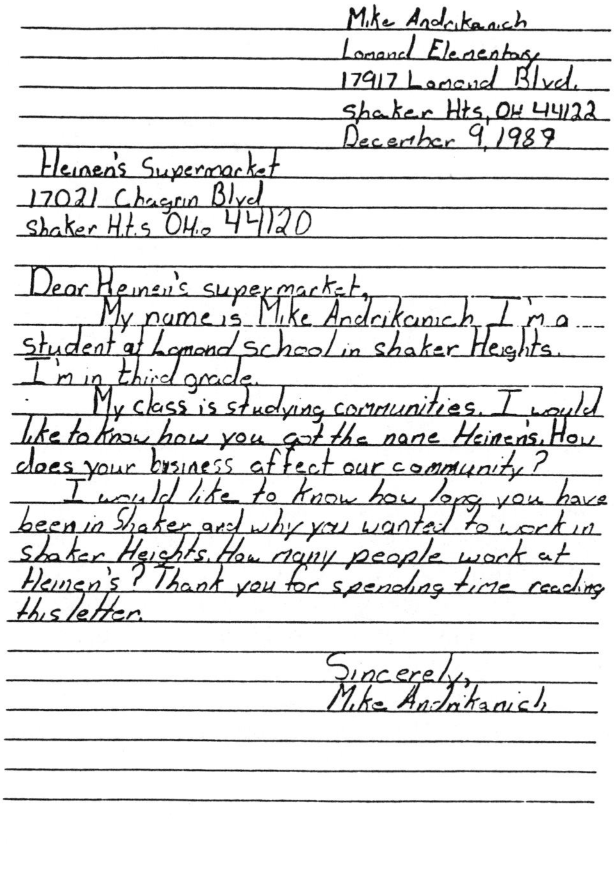

Mike Andrikanich
Lomond Elementary
17917 Lomond Blvd.
Shaker Hts, OH 44122
December 9, 1989

Heinen's Supermarket
17021 Chagrin Blvd
Shaker H.t.s OHio 44120

Dear Heinen's supermarket,
My name is Mike Andrikanich I'm a student at Lomond school in shaker Heights. I'm in third grade.
My class is studying communities. I would like to know how you got the name Heinen's. How does your business affect our community?
I would like to know how long you have been in Shaker and why you wanted to work in Shaker Heights. How many people work at Heinen's? Thank you for spending time reading this letter.

Sincerely,
Mike Andrikanich

Figure 8-7   Response to a Student's Letter

December 22, 1989

Mr. Mike Andrikanich
Lomond Elementary School
17917 Lomond Blvd.
Shaker Heights, Ohio 44122

Dear Mike,

   My grandfather, Joseph Heinen, started Heinen's as a butcher shop over
55 years ago. His first store was right down the street from where our
present store is today.

   Our present store is much different from his store, but the purpose is
the same - to serve the community with the finest foods at a reasonable cost.
Over sixty people work full and part-time to achieve that aim.

   We intend to serve Shaker Heights in the years to come and hopefully in
another few years we will be able to do it from a new store.

                              Sincerely,

                              Jeff Heinen
                              Jeffrey Heinen

JH/bjm

One form of business letter that has been very effective for engaging students in writing is the informal business letter to obtain information. Some fourth grade students who were interested in the possibility of getting published wrote to sources that publish student writing. They received a sheet listing the name and address of and general information about reputable sources that publish children's work. (For sources, see Seminoff, 1990, and Stoll, 1990.) Out of a genuine need to find out what publishers want, each child selected a source to write to. Students are always more motivated to write when they know there is a chance for publication. In this case, the act of letter writing helped students realize that publication was within the realm of possibility. (See Appendix G for publishers' guidelines for students.)

We began by brainstorming possible topics and questions to include in the letters. See Figure 8–8 for a whole-class brainstorming. Then each student drafted a letter using the business letter format laid out in the language text. Using peer response groups—after many whole-class demonstrations—students revised their letters.

Figure 8-8   Fourth Grade Class Brainstorming Session

Business letter that's friendly
What kinds of things you publish
    nonfiction, fiction, poetry - all
        kinds?   bibliography
are you interested in 4th gr. writing?
any particular kind of story?
illustrations - who makes them? Drawings? photographs?
    necessary?
audience - for little kids, what grades?
    age of author
format - typed or handwritten
    length - would take 2 p. story
    story - lots of detail?
        table of contents
        setting
        description
        dialogue
can we choose the kind of print we want?
If you don't like my story, will you send it back?
Will you make changes in my story?
    suggestions for my writing?
Can you send in more than 1 piece of writing?
If accepted, how long till published?
    deadline to get story in?
    dedication allowed?
    title?
Can there be more than 1 author in a story?

Revising. With the students' permission, several fourth-graders' drafts were photocopied, made into transparencies, and shared with the whole class on the overhead projector. First, I modeled my thinking processes aloud (as described in "Modeling Response," pp. 56–57). About a half dozen teacher demonstrations of the response process were given before students met in peer groups to conference with each other. The peer group conferencing was effective for this situation because the format and guidelines were limited enough for students to deal with.

Editing. The responsibility for editing was put on the students. First, we did a whole-class shared writing of what they needed to look for in the editing process. With some teacher probing, we came up with a comprehensive list (see Figure 8–9). Because students came up with the items, as opposed to being told them by the

Figure 8-9   Editing Checklist from a Whole-Class Shared Writing

EDITING

1. Check for misspelled words.
   a. Circle them.
   b. Try to spell those words correctly.
      Ask someone.
      Look up in the dictionary.
      Sound it out.
      Try writing it another way until it "looks" right.

2. Check for punctuation. Reread.
   Use a comma
         after your greeting.
         after your closing.
         between two sentences, before "and" or "but."
         between words in a series.
   Use a period (.), question mark (?), or exclamation mark (!) at the
         end of a sentence.

3. Check for capitalization.
   The first letter of the first word in greeting or closing
   Titles (magazine, book)

4. Indent the first line of every paragraph.

5. Check your format.
   In the business letter, the heading and closing are lined up under each other on the
         right side.
   The publication title and greeting are lined up on the left.
   Skip a line
         after the heading, greeting.
         between body of letter and closing.

6. Check for abbreviations.
   Write out each word completely—streets, numbers, months, states.

7. Neatness
   Spacing
   Best handwriting
   Legibility

8. Clarity
   Stick to the subject.
   Check to be sure you have used the best wording.
   Be sure everything makes sense.

9. Have a friend check your paper before you give it to senior editor (teacher).

teacher, they became more engaged in the editing process and took greater responsibility for their papers. The editing chart remained posted in the classroom for reference, and the classroom teacher and I were firm about not making corrections for students that they could make themselves. Students were also referred to the language arts textbook as a resource for checking format and conventions for letter writing.

Students who have become accustomed to having the teacher find and correct errors do not initially take the editing task seriously. Many students quickly brought their self-edited letters to us as "complete" when there were many editorial conventions that still needed correcting. We gently put the responsibility back on them with questions and comments such as "Take a look at number 2 on our editing chart. Do you have commas where they need to be?" Or, "You need to check the language arts textbook for the correct format of a letter. Notice how the heading is set up." Or, "I still see some misspelled words that I know you can find. Take another, more careful look."

After students have been sent back to proofread a few times, they get the message that it is their job to do the work. One technique that has worked beautifully is to put a Post-it note on the paper with a comment such as "Check the first paragraph for spelling and punctuation," or to note correctly the misspelled words on the Post-its. Teachers are amazed that when they are consistent about refusing to do the work for students, the students eventually assume accountability for the task and are capable of doing much more than had previously been thought. (See Figure 8–10 for an example of a student's draft of his letter.) Having students take ownership for the editing process takes time. In my experience, even with teacher demonstrations, students need at least several months to take responsibility for a process their teachers have traditionally assumed.

For teachers used to taking most of the responsibility for making corrections, shifting the responsibility to the students is not an easy transition. One third grade teacher noted,

> Slowly, I'm becoming more comfortable with giving the editing process over to the students, but it's been very painful. I'm so used to doing most of the work, and trusting them to do it has been unbelievably hard for me. Initially, it seems easier if I just make the corrections, but I see now that they just keep depending on me to do it, and in the long run that's not effective for their learning.

Once teachers do shift the responsibility, they feel freed. Fourth grade teacher Nancy Schubert comments, "I used to spend my evenings with a red pencil. Now that the kids do most of the work, I have some time to read professional books and children's books in the evenings."

Teachers' expectations for editing will vary depending on the age of the students and the writing purposes. However, for all grade levels we need to be careful not to emphasize editing too soon in the writing process. Before dealing with editing, we want to guide students to write interesting, clear content that reflects personal voice and imagination.

Writing Stories

Children, like all writers, write best about what they know. Writing fictional stories seems to work most successfully when children have been immersed in

Figure 8-10   A Student Takes Ownership of the Editing Process

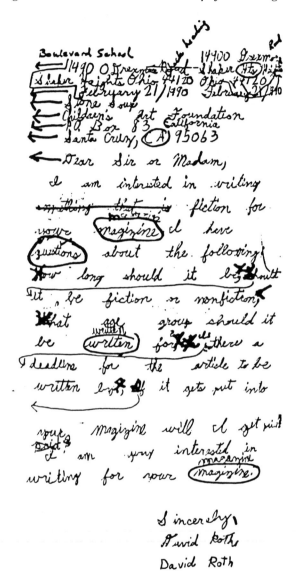

literature and language and can utilize authors for demonstrations of quality writing.

I worked with Brenda Spivey's fourth grade students, who were writing stories for an upcoming "Young Authors' Conference." Before the students began writing, we talked about how writers write from experience. The kinds of stories the children later wrote dealt with real problems for their age group—moving to a new house, making new friends, fighting with a sibling, getting braces, having problems with a teacher.

Planning for Writing Stories

I talked with students first about how authors usually have some general plan for their stories before they begin to write. Some of us have found that having students create a visual plan before they begin to write works particularly well. A terrific idea for "picturing" the character was developed by fourth grade teacher Joan Servis. The technique is excellent for getting students to think and plan for character development. Students are asked to visualize their main character by drawing a picture of him or her, making brief notes about the character, and perhaps even drawing the character in a setting (see Figure 8–11).

Brenda first created her own character on large chart paper and talked aloud as she demonstrated in front of her students. Then students talked about the kinds of characters they could create. Representing the character physically seems to help students get to know a character—his or her attributes, features, personality traits, motivations. Brenda and I also noted that because students knew one another's

Figure 8-11   Visualizing the Main Character

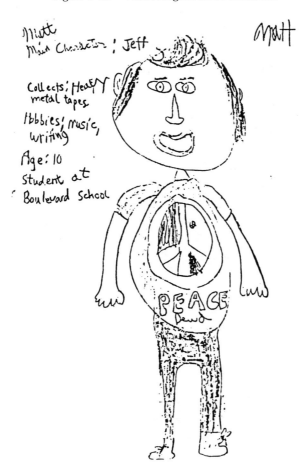

characters through the pictures and brief accompanying notes, subsequent suggestions to peers for revisions were specific and helpful.

After students' main character(s) were discussed and shared with the teacher and peers for feedback, students were expected to complete a storymap before they began writing. Again Brenda demonstrated first by creating her own storymap.

The storymapping was an important next step because it forced students to think through the main problem in the story, the main happenings, and how the story might conclude (see Figures 8–12 and 8–13 for examples). We and the students found that taking the time to plan out the characters and story encouraged more thoughtful, better organized, and more interesting story writing. As a result of conferencing with students one-to-one before they began writing, stories had better focus and development. Storymapping eliminated boring, episodic stories that rambled with no solid plot or resolution.

After the students drafted chapters, they read them to their peers and the teacher in whole-group and small-group conferences. Responding to a student's writing was modeled first by the teacher. The piece was read in its entirety; then, during a second reading, notes were taken to give feedback to the writer (described on p. 56).

While peers can be used in the response process, my personal bias is that the

Figures 8–12 and 8–13 Storymapping, in Planning for Story Writing

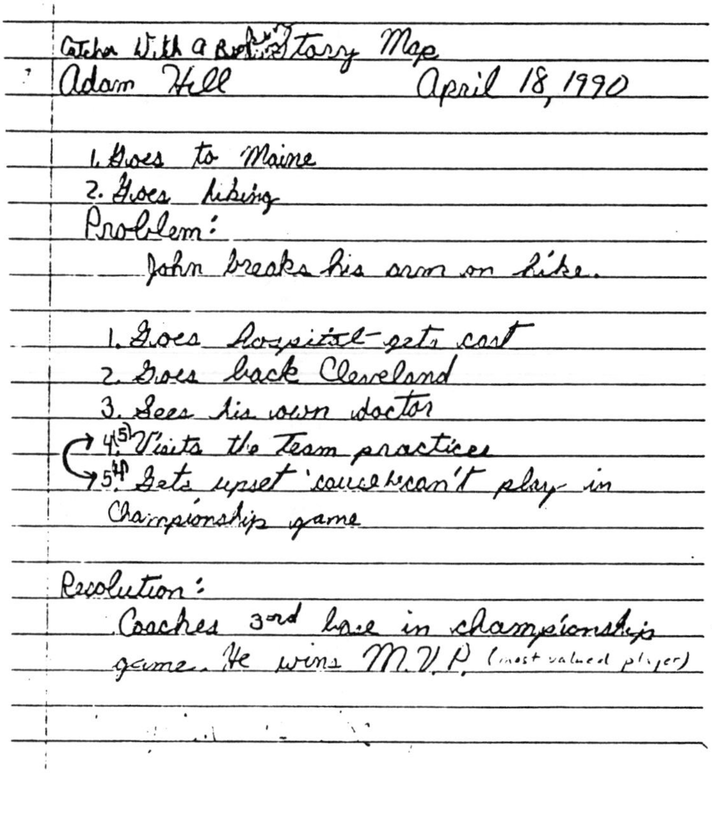
Catcher With a Broken Story Map
Adam Hill April 18, 1990

1. Goes to Maine
2. Goes hiking
Problem:
John breaks his arm on hike.

1. Goes hospital—gets cast
2. Goes back Cleveland
3. Sees his own doctor
4.(5) Visits the team practice
5.(4) Gets upset 'cause he can't play in Championship game

Resolution:
Coaches 3rd base in championship game. He wins M.V.P. (most valued player)

Figure 8-13

SAN FRANCISCO

Sarah Kim
Age 10
is Korean-American
has 2 brothers
Parents born in Seoul Korea
born in San Francisco, California
now lives in Cleveland, Ohio
ice skates
plays piano and flute
favorite food is pizza
has black hair and brown eyes

Story Mapping
Grace Lee   April 17, 1990
              Sarah
Problem: is having trouble
making friends after moving.

1. Intro.

2. People make fun of her.

3. make friends with new girl
who is like her.

4. People understand her
better.

Resolution: Makes new friends.

183

teacher is needed to guide the questions and comments. I have found the most effective response groups to be four to eight students sitting around a table with the teacher. Students note first what they think is best about the writing and then offer suggestions for improvement. The teacher demonstrates and guides the process. "It is a fallacy to think that kids can ask the kinds of questions that can evoke exciting thinking," says Mary Krogness.

Students' Observations after Revising Stories

After demonstrating revision with my own writing and with students' writing and assisting students to put revision into practice with their stories for a "Young Authors' Conference," I asked Brenda Spivey's fourth-graders if they would choose to revise in future writings. Remarkably, every student answered "yes," in spite of the fact that revision had taken lots of time and was hard work. One student said, "I'd want to make my story so good that everyone would want to read it, and you have to revise to write like that."

Here are some other typical comments:

SHARON: Revising really helped me see where I needed to make changes. It helped me cut out some parts that didn't matter or belong.

ANDREA: Without revising, the story is just not done. I didn't feel good about my story until I got some response. Revising was kind of hard, but it helped make my story better.

ADAM: Now that we've done all this revision and I understand the process, I'd probably give a new story to more than one person to read.

MARK: My story didn't sound good at first. I was jumping around all over the place. The comments I got from classmates really helped me fix up my story and make it better.

Because revision is often a difficult concept for students to grasp and apply, I wanted to hear how students defined revision after they had been immersed in the process. Some responses included:

- Suggesting things to people to make the story better.
- Getting new ideas about what you might change.
- Helping someone make a story more understandable.
- Making your story better by having others look it over so readers will understand it.

Several students went on to comment that recently when reading books they found themselves thinking about changes authors should have made. I found that insight remarkable! At nine and ten years of age they were now reading like writers, critically noticing authors' use of language:

- When I got mixed up in one chapter, I was thinking what the author could have done to make it clearer.
- Parts of my book were confusing, and I was thinking the writer needed to do a better job explaining.

Using books they were reading independently during sustained silent reading, other students had spontaneously begun using Post-its to mark specific passages that were particularly well written—or not well written—to read aloud to the class. The revision process had come full circle: We had started with writing, and the students took the process into reading, where they began thinking about how authors shape their words.

Evaluation: Teachers' Attitudes

When a teacher moves from being writing director to writing facilitator, students' writing improves and teachers' enjoyment of the process increases.

Brenda Spivey comments:

> The most important thing for me was that it took away my role as goddess of writing. Before, I was in charge of doing it all. Students would write ten to fifteen pages of boring stories, and then it was my job to revise and edit those awful stories. Now, finally, I don't have to have total control. I gave that job back to the students. I'm still involved in every story, but more as a guide and facilitator. My old attitude of "the teacher will fix it for you" is gone. Giving students ownership of the process has been very significant. The quality of writing is a lot better, and it's been a relief not to have everything fall on me.

Dana Noble, a high school English teacher who recently began to move away from his traditional mode toward implementing reading-writing workshop (Atwell, 1987), comments:

> I've felt more successful this year than I have in years. Students' writing has far exceeded what I expected. In the past, I gave writing assignments, allowed some time in class for students to start writing, and assigned the rest as homework. Final copies were turned in and graded. Until this year, I hardly looked at a draft.
>
> This year, kids do all their writing in class. That caused me a lot of stress at first. I couldn't stand seeing them not be productive. At first, I was listening only to the noise in the room and was failing to listen to what was being said. It seemed as though some kids were just "messing around," but when I finally looked at their work, I couldn't believe the improvement. It hit me that I didn't teach that. I've not taught topic sentence and paragraph this year, and I think the writing is more lively. Something really happened when I gave kids time and freedom to write and respond in class.
>
> Also, allowing kids choice has had tremendous impact on their writing. For the first time, I've had important pieces due where every child has turned in assignments. That never happened before. I've allowed students to choose their own format for writing and to collaborate in writing, and the quality of writing is the best I've ever received. The kids seem more aware of audience, too. Another change is that I no longer write on their final copies. I make my comments on Post-its or in pencil.
>
> Also, for the first time, I've started every piece of writing that I've expected them to do. That has helped me a lot with realistic expectations. I've discovered how hard it is to finish things. In the past, I've been strict about having kids meet deadlines. Now I see they need more time, and I give it to them.
>
> I went through a period of feeling, "Am I really teaching anything?" If it

wasn't quiet and orderly and the teacher directing the discussion, it was hard for me to believe anything worthwhile was going on. I still have to stop myself and just listen to what the kids are really saying. I still worry that some teachers look at me and think that I'm weakening the curriculum.

Reflections on Whole Language: Two Teachers' Letter Writing

High school English teacher Holly Burgess began corresponding with me in November 1989 after I presented a workshop on whole language to secondary teachers. Then she and I met to discuss changes she was ready to make in her teaching, including sharing more responsibility with students. At the same time, Holly began reading *In the Middle* by Nancie Atwell and *Clearing the Way* by Tom Romano, and she began to incorporate reading-writing workshop into her daily classes.

Since my full-time teaching at the elementary level left me little time to interact with high school teachers, our correspondence afforded us an opportunity to share and reflect on daily happenings and changes. The following are excerpts from some very long letters over the course of a year. Holly's letters are in regular type and mine are in italics.

November 1, 1989

Thanks for your time and encouragement yesterday (and candy bar!) Now for today's report:

Listening dialogue [discussing what good listeners do] with students went well first period! They covered all the important points and I didn't pass out the hand-out on listening. (Return to control . . . I couldn't resist r-e-a-d-i-n-g it to them. What a waste! What a lesson to me!)

. . . anyway, asked students to sustain a 15-minute write on whatever was on their minds most this A.M., talked about focus, writing what was foremost. Without exception, all were writing for 25 minutes and only one had stopped by the time the bell rang. Ready for some listening partners and "visioning-re-visioning" tomorrow.

November 2

See some real s-l-o-w down with the re-visioning stage. Students appear to think that they are done at this point, doing the sharing as an exercise in isolation, that a re-visioning is really a re-copying. Will do a modeling tomorrow with my writing and with the class as my listening partners for questions and feedback. . . . Is it merely the control issue that boxes me into thinking there is not much "productive" time? . . . I'm a teeter-totter!—weighed down at one end with time on task and on the other with providing a climate free and open enough to allow for the "dead" time that is part of creativity.

November 3

Congratulations on the successful listening dialogue. At least you realized it was a waste of time reading your hand-out to them. I find I learn best when a lesson bombs, so it's never a waste. Really, it's an opportunity for growth. Just the fact that you're examining your own teaching is highly commendable.

Perhaps the re-visioning would be more successful if the students knew and wanted publication. It's important they're revisioning for a genuine purpose— letters that will actually be sent, pieces that will be put into a class booklet, etc. I know this is very hard, but the authentic use part is powerful and motivating.

November 3

. . . I want to believe in the process, but am amazed at my "need" for immediate gratification of self as a teacher that is somehow, probably mistakenly, more "actual" in quiz scores, test grades, you know, all that "measurable" stuff.

November 6

About first period . . . some students were eager to get folders and get writing, more were interested in listening partners. Had a group of three who chased me away. One of my best story-tellers is at least started. He doesn't focus well in the classroom, but has more than once entertained with his descriptive exploits. I will have to review the process again tomorrow. Many are asking questions like, "What do I do now?" or "Do I have to copy it over?" I feel afloat, or better yet, poised on the high dive and I don't swim real well! One student asked if it was okay to write some poetry. It's all real tentative, or perhaps I'm real tentative.

9th period. . . . Students need constant reassurance that whatever they write is okay. I am made uncomfortable by the judgment that English form and fear of it has severely crippled their *believing* themselves to be writers. Need help with the publishing piece. Some threatened to not write at all if I was going to MAKE them publish, even for a class publication.

November 10

It has been an exhausting week! Would like to *see* a real, live model of writing-reading workshop. Seems like "stuff" and "management" and too small a room and my own hang-ups, history and up-tightness keep getting in the way. . . . I thought I had been working on this "letting go" process for years. Now I have discovered how little letting go I'm willing to do.

Perhaps we can meet again soon.

November 14

I have just finished reading the responses to The Learning Tree *by Gordon Parks (Harper & Row, 1963), and I am incredulous! Your students have connected their lives with literature at the very highest level—to help them make sense of their own lives. They write honestly and passionately. They expose their vulnerabilities; you are to be congratulated. They couldn't write so genuinely without the risk taking, caring environment you have obviously created and fostered. Without exception, each piece went right to my core being. These kids are struggling to make sense of their complicated, and often tragic, lives. I see that as the highest level of literacy and education—finding relevance in school to the real world. . . .*

I liked that you didn't "mark" on their writing and left it intact. You could use Post-its to comment on parts that especially grabbed you or to ask questions you have.

You're on the right track. The kids need to know how powerful their writing is because it's authentic and on topics that are highly important to them. Pat yourself on the back for all your small successes and new risks you are taking. Give yourself time. Change that is real and long lasting happens slowly, as you well know.

November 15 (first period)

Started class by "modeling." . . . When I wouldn't talk, but would just write, they eventually got the message. When Farris asked me if I was sure I was all right, Coop said, "Aren't you going to get the 'status of the class'"—and that was just after introducing the term two days ago. Discovered that I am just as impatient with re-visioning as my students are! There always seems to be something better or easier to do or "more important" than taking another look at a piece of my own writing.

It was soooo good to get your letter this A.M.! Thanks for all the affirmation. There is just so much to do and I keep getting in my own way. I'm usually "relatively" well organized, but since this (whatever this is?!) has started I feel scattered and disorganized! The teaching of a skill from the actual writing is wonderful, so why do I judge that it's not enough? What is clearly enough, though, is the positive way some kids are responding to class, whether they are reading the book of their choice, writing, or listening to a friend re-visioning. . . .

November 21

. . . I was absolutely knocked out by your students' writing—authentic, powerful, rich, unbelievable! I love the way you took the prose and helped the kids put it in poetry form. I can see why the kids were thrilled. Typing it, too, makes the writing seem more important. . . . I'm so impressed your kids feel safe enough with you to write this honestly. (I'm sure much of it could be published.) . . . [See Figure 8–14 for an example.]

You're taking so many risks; I really admire your gutsiness and intelligence. You're doing it in a highly professional way—really thinking about your teaching and learning and not just trying a new "activity."

November 27

. . . I resisted the impulse to PLAN little ditties for my substitute and gave her only the "freedom" that I had tried to establish. Although she reported that "some" refused to work for her, it seems that they were the same "some" that generally refuse to work, read, write, cooperate, etc. In other words, the students kept their commitment to the experience.

November 29

. . . Taught a mini-lesson on good leads that seemed to go okay.

I get lost in Atwell's sheets of accountability. See the need for more of it, but at the moment it is a piece that I am unable to keep up with. . . . Have enclosed a poem by one of my seniors. This is a girl who didn't think she could write. Also had another senior ask me if there was a limit to the length of his story. Made me laugh. I've been remiss about my own writing these last two weeks, and although I clearly see the difference it makes to students, I just can't seem to get started again. . . .

November 30

How wonderful that you submitted the student writing to a possible place for publication. Give yourself credit for everything you are doing. Try to stop bashing

Figures 8-14, 8-15, and 8-16   Poems by High School Juniors

In the ninth grade people said I looked like a Hawaiian.
They cracked their jokes.
No harm done.
In the tenth grade people called me a Mexican.
They cracked their jokes.
My eleventh grade year, people called me a China-man or a Jap.
They crack their jokes.
Maybe a tiny bit of harm done.

My first step-mother was from Thailand.
She's the one who took care of me.
My father and her are divorced,
But I still visit her.
I feel comfortable calling her "Mom,"
But the wife my father has now, I call her "Doris."
It's not like I don't like her or anything like that,
But she's not the one who raised me.
She's still a cool lady.

Racism.
My father is an Afro-American,
My mother (my real one) is from Egypt.
My father has had many racial conflicts...
Two white friends wanted to ride their bikes with my father.
They rode and they had fun (I guess) and
Some men stopped them and asked,
"Why are you riding around with a nigger?"
They tried to get away,
But a man threw a rock causing
My father's white friend to fall off.
The men then beat him up.

To this day my father wonders why
He didn't go back and save his white friend.

Another example.
When my father was in the Air Force (he still is).
He was shipped to Thailand,
Where he met my step-mother.
He was at a party with some of the Thai ladies.
They asked him where his tail was.
They believed that all Black men grew tails at night.

I've been through a lot of racist comments in my life,
But I'm not going to let them stop me from shining.
It's like the Bible said,
"We are a split image of God"
And that's the way it is.

Joseph Dee Crawford,
Junior

yourself for what you're not doing. Whole language focuses on the strengths, not the deficits—ours too, not just the kids'. You've taken some huge risks with some wonderful results. It all takes time. . . .

As far as Atwell and anything else you're reading, just because it's in a book and by a ''guru'' doesn't mean it will work for you or is right for you. Make adjustments based on what you believe. Trust your intuition.

December 4

Plodding along on this end. Can't seem to get a re-write together to model for them. I hear myself using their excuses! How difficult it is being a *student-*teacher and having a life too!

Have included some new writing of my junior, level 2 Humanities kids. Aren't they wonderful?

December 6

. . . I love your kids' writing—absolutely splendid, heart-wrenching stuff. Wonderful you're getting it typed. Good to hear you say they are ''wonderful.'' They are! [See Figures 8–15 and 8–16 for examples of poems.]

January 11, 1990

. . . My seniors have ''completed'' this writing project unit, and although some of the pieces of writing are quite good, their commitment to task has been less so. The bind of judging good writing against or with a look to quantify chafes. And individual knowledge of students' limitations makes me feel highly subjective about the grades. I will have a writing conference (well, actually, an overview conference) with each student next week for decision-making about the grade for the unit. I had hoped to have built-in high grades and am feeling a tug downward about my unmet expectations, which probably shouldn't impinge as much on their grades as on my own! . . .

I need to put some requests in writing for next school year regarding writing/reading approach and changes that I want to make—would like to have you *see* my room and discuss some housekeeping. For me this needs to ''happen'' before the more important changes of my own efforts, commitment. With fifteen long-legged seniors moving round the room, conferencing with others, areas of quiet or not-so-quiet tested my patience and concentration. I am more keenly aware of my limitations as well as huge areas I wish to change (areas of geography as well as soul-searching!). . . .

January 12

. . . I'm most eager to come over to see your room and your kids and see you! . . . It's wonderful you're thinking about changes for next year already. . . .

Your debate with yourself about grading and quantity of writing is a struggle. Have you thought about having kids evaluate themselves before you meet with them? Put in writing the criteria you use for grading, and ask them to give themselves a grade and give supportive comments for that grade. I think you'll be surprised. It's been my experience that the kids grade themselves tougher than we do. It could make grading easier for you.

I'm feeling unusually stressed—trying to write every day after work when I'm really too exhausted. Can't remember if I told you I'm writing a follow-up to Transitions *for Heinemann—contract deadline late September—very exciting but masochistic too. Writing is so hard—especially without adequate time. . . .*

Figure 8-15

Leave me alone

I'm not at home.
I'm not on the phone.
Please—
just leave me alone.

I'm not here.
I'm not there.
I'm somewhere.

I'm fine.
Believe this is true—
Don't call me.
I'll call you.

Orlando Makupson 12-89

Figure 8-16

Life

Born, buck-naked, out of my mother's womb
A man, cooped in a rubber room.

Times changin', time flies.
Caterpillars turn into butterflies.

A kitten grows up to be a tiger.
I grow up to be a writer.

Children grow through puberty
and they reach maturity.

Brian Cunningham   12-89

February 23

. . . I read and modeled with them [11th-graders] an excerpt from Claude Brown's *Manchild in the Promised Land* (Macmillan, 1965), and they were able to find many points in the "story" to wonder about, reflect on, connect with in a personal way. But even more wonderful are the requests over the next two days by five! Count them! Five! adolescent boys to READ *Manchild*. I had two copies of my own to lend, one actually borrowed from library and I will have two of the school's copies next week. They are openly talking about how "live" it is and if you were the least bit "liberal" in the sixties . . . it's still pretty "bold" today! This is basically an I-hate-to-read group.

Am trying to begin (God, how tentative could one possibly sound!) a combined Atwellian concept with a more traditional approach. Haven't thought it through yet and would like to get some feedback from you. I would like to teach—or whatever term works—*A Gathering of Old Men* by Ernest Gaines (Knopf, 1983) to my seniors with a dining room table kind of approach. I don't know if it is possible to do with an old, traditional all-class kind of read, but I have some sanity reasons to want more control with these groups, one of which is graying my hair and brain daily! . . .

March 3

. . . What a joy to read about your students requesting to read. BRAVO! You're doing a lot right if that's happening.

Let's talk about what you're trying—"Atwell plus traditional approach." We can talk by phone or meet after school any day.

So glad you did come to our Monday night district support group. Believe me, you're in the worst stage now. Getting started is the hardest part. It's going to get easier.

. . . One of the most exciting things about moving toward whole language is the reality that it's so hard that you can't do it without collegial support. Teachers, instead of being isolated, wind up collaborating more.

March 6

I can meet you any day after school but Monday or Tuesday. Would like to talk about *Gathering Old Men* approach with you. . . . The current plan is that we are having SSR on M, W, F (with the exception of the first 15 min. of M and F for journal writing). Tues. and Thurs. are discussion days. Any student who may be behind the general outline of pages to be read may read during this time with no penalty and join the discussion when caught up in reading. One of the already assigned journal entries for a week will be a "literary letter" to me or to another student. Students are encouraged to keep a sheet beside them while reading to jot down any questions. It is my hope that discussion will help lead to questioning. Have one excellent reader who is half-finished with the book (in 3 days) and is sharing with me some of the humor—which is often missed by my students.

No tests or quizzes. . . .

May 3

. . . Thanks for sharing your American Family unit. I like the relevance to students' lives and your communication to parents, too. A couple of thoughts that may be too late for you to do anything with:

1. I hope you also do a family history and demonstrate the possibilities, for example, writing a family story yourself.

2. I think it's important to give students choice, perhaps choosing three out of four parts to do.

3. At completion of unit, perhaps do an evaluation of the project with students. What parts did they like? Suggestions for improvement/change? It will give you an even better format for next year, and allow collaboration with students.

. . . Ha! you laughed about my writing struggles. I've been totally unproductive. I can't believe how little I get done each evening and weekend. I'm feeling really tired. . . .

June 13

I devoured "'I Have Never Read Five Books Before in My Life': Reading and Writing Naturally in High School'"!!! (in *Portraits of Whole Language Classrooms* [Mills and Clyde, 1990]. I can *see* some of my students writing these same words—and the nonwords, too! . . . think the article is the best synopsis of what I am attempting and have passed it along. . . .

Am thinking of beginning the juniors next year with the standby—*The Learning Tree*—it goes well with my students. Help me think of "creative Atwellian approaches"! Haven't decided what to do with my seniors. Since many of them will be students known to me, maybe I won't have too much trouble establishing myself. . . .

I am—for the first time ever!—excited about next year in June!

August 31, 1990 (first week of new school year)

It has been a good opening! I've included a list of student comments regarding writing. I think their comments are GREAT! . . . My two senior classes have self-selected books and are reading daily. Have begun with reading/writing workshops and am still working out the "structure." . . . I suspect that I am a little slower at jumping in than some, but I think it will help me in the long run to move very slowly. Kids seem very responsive to "ideas" so far, and I am thoroughly enjoying some of the YA fiction. . . . Call when you can.

September 12

. . . Classes are going by so well. I am successfully battling the once-in-a-while fear about no tests, quizzes, grades, etc.—at least until it's time for progress and grade cards. . . .

My biggest fault is that I talk too much and have asked kids to help remind me that whatever I am saying, I have probably spent too much time trying to say it! They are beginning to be glad to oblige. . . .

What comes through in Holly's letters are her struggles to let go of control, her ever-increasing belief in her students and in the reading-writing workshop process, her efforts to incorporate more teacher demonstrating and to give students more choice and flexibility, her desire to create a more workable room environment, and her growth as a teacher moving toward whole language. With the start of a new school year, Holly's voice is more confident and her trust in students greater. She begins by having students self-select books to read the first week of school. She is no longer the same teacher who stated that she "felt like a failure seeing kids so unhappy and so unengaged with school."

I did not really "help" Holly. I provided support, affirmation, and active listening for her risk taking, but she found, and is finding, her own way. Our letter writing served as a way for her to work through some of her dilemmas and confusions and to make personal reflections on her teaching. Teachers in process, at any level, often find that writing down their thoughts serves to clarify the struggle and give them a useful perspective.

Reflections

I no longer believe that writing can be taught. The best we can do as teachers is nurture writing, encourage it, sustain it, and give it time, space, freedom, and room in which to grow. As much as possible, writing purposes, contexts, and audiences must be authentic if we want students to engage in the process. Students must understand and value why they are writing so they see a need for clarity, voice, organization, and even completion.

Perhaps most important, we must be writing models ourselves and also give our students great writing models through literature. Our greatest challenge is becoming risk takers and writers ourselves by making our own writing and thinking visible to our students. For most of us, the shift to valuing writing and making it an integral part of our daily teaching and curriculum is a slow, gradual process. We need to congratulate ourselves whenever we share our own writing with students and whenever we make sincere attempts to write in front of the class or with the class. Until we demonstrate and value the craft ourselves, many students will fail to take writing seriously or to see writing as a tool for thinking and learning.

9

Personal Journal Writing

And one more thing. I am doing good in school. (Tara's journal, fall of second grade)

Journal writing in the kindergarten

A Look at One Student: Tara

Although Tara was considered one of the lowest-functioning children in first grade at the start of the year, she found her voice and grew as a reader and writer when she had lots of opportunities to write about what was important to her. She was fortunate to be in a classroom where she was immersed in the rich language of stories and had daily opportunities for authentic writing. While most of the writing Tara and other students engaged in happened to take place in a journal, the discussion of personal journal writing—the focus of this chapter—applies to all authentic writing.

The power and benefits of personal journal writing, as well as the impact of literature on writing, are evident when one looks at samples from Tara's journal in first grade (see Figures 9–1 and 9–2). She has moved from random strings of letters (which she stayed with for an entire month) to complete stories and from limited, invented spelling and mechanics to increasing use of conventional mechanics and spelling. Her sense of story has blossomed. Tara has not been formally taught any of these skills, but she has been engaged in authentic language activities in a whole language classroom.

Her confidence at the beginning of second grade is evident in her letter to her parents telling them about open house (see Figure 9–3).

> Mom and Dad,
>
> When you come to open house, I want you to see my dinosaur. And I want you to see my dinosaur hats. And I want you to read my writing journal. And I want you to see my clay dinosaur. And one more thing. I am doing good in school.
>
> From your daughter,
> Tara

195

Figures 9-1 and 9-2   Samples from Tara's Journal, First Grade

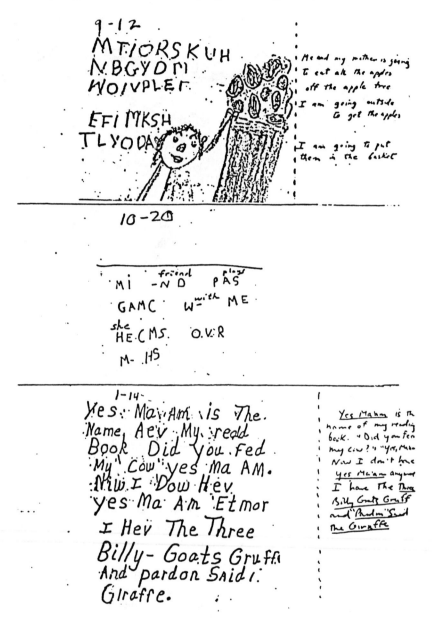

It would be easy to look at Tara's letter (page 198) and see only a child with poor spelling, poor mechanics and poor phonics skills. Fortunately, her second grade teacher saw the strengths in Tara's expressive language in spite of the fact that she still qualified for Chapter 1 because of poor performance on skills subtests of standardized tests. (See Figure 9–4 for a poem Tara wrote and Figure 9–5 for her last entry in second grade before she moved to another school district.)

Tara's second grade teacher described her as above average for content and free expression in writing. Her personal journal writing had helped make that possible.

Figure 9-2

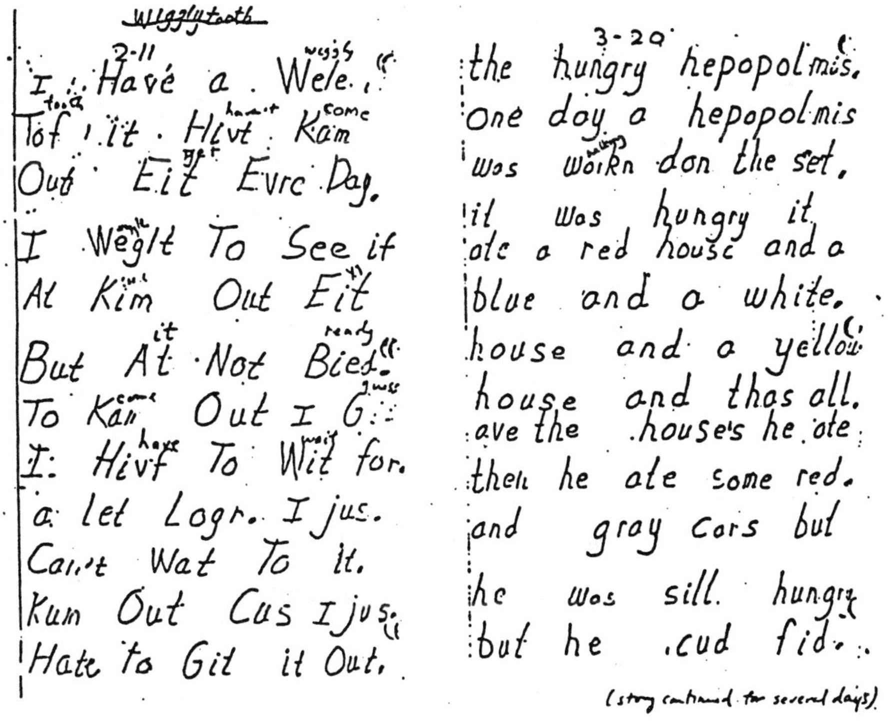

(story continued for several days)

Tara's journal entries included personal stories, stories with literary influences, retellings of stories, poems, letters, and reflections. The journal became a safe and valued place where she could explore language, feelings, and life's happenings in a variety of forms.

Benefits of Journal Writing

For teachers moving toward whole language, journal writing is a component that can be easily implemented wherever teachers happen to be in the transition process. Journals provide a nonthreatening place to explore learnings, feelings, happenings, and language through writing. They also provide opportunities to discover experiences and feelings teachers and students have in common. Teachers who use journal writing have found that when they are sensitive and respectful of students' attitudes, life stories, and learning processes, the children come to value and enjoy journal writing, and journals become an integral part of the curriculum.

I see the power of personal writing as connecting what is significant in children's lives with what goes on in school. Personal journal writing can be a means of validating each child, of saying to each child that what goes on in your life is important, that what you think and feel is relevant, and that everyday events are the things writers write about. Children are full of stories, regardless of their backgrounds, but many of them don't know they have stories to tell. An encouraging teacher can help bring out children's stories and celebrate them. In doing so, we

Figures 9-3, 9-4, and 9-5   Samples from Tara's Journal, Second Grade

Oct. 6

Mom and Dad,

Wen you Came to opne
houuse. I wot you to See
my dase. and I wot you
to See my dinrsiruc
hots and I wot yoo to
redea my widenu gov. and
I wot you to see my
Caye dinr rue and one
More thege I Im duwene goit
ch School. from your drdrea
Tara

Figure 9-4

Nov. 5

Blow wind

I See the wind blowin
away I Can see the
wind goin away yes I
Can. Oh no the wind is
push me away do not
blow me away ok wind
ok siad the wind

Figure 9-5

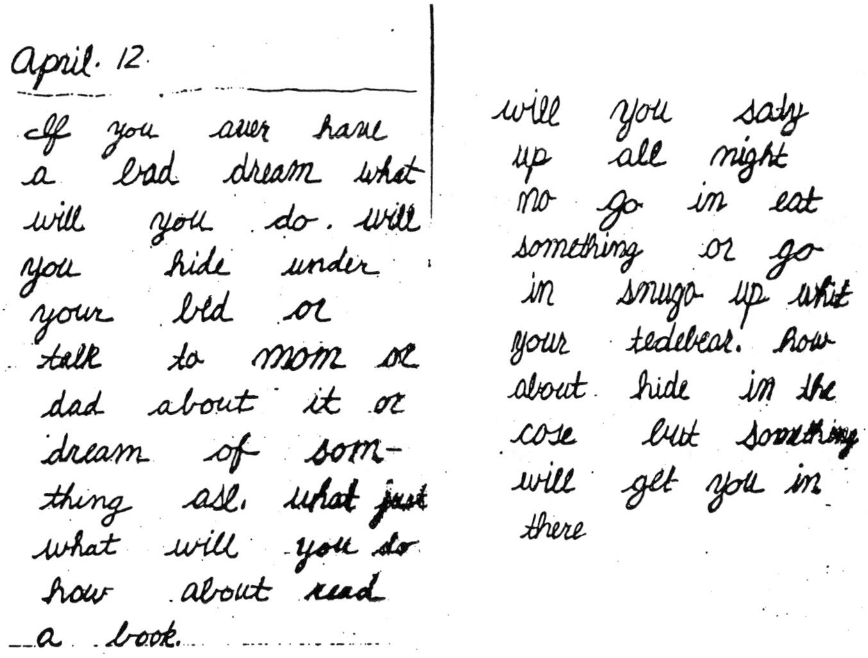

april. 12

If you ever have
a bad dream what
will you do. will
you hide under
your bed or
talk to mom or
dad about it or
dream of som-
thing all. what just
what will you do
how about read
_a book.

will you stay
up all night
no go in eat
something or go
in snuga up with
your tedebear. how
about hide in the
cose but something
will get you in
there

affirm our students, build their self-esteem, and encourage them as writers. Students and teachers also grow to know and respect one another, and a sense of community builds.

When teachers also become part of the journal writing process, our students get to know us better, and we and they see that we are all connected by our humanness. I believe the benefits of personal journal writing are significant for both students and teachers.

• *Promotes fluency in writing*   Teachers note an ease of expression and a greater facility with written language. Dan Kirby (1988) calls the journal "the most consistently effective tool for establishing fluency I have found."

• *Promotes fluency in reading*   The very first reading that some of our young students do is their own writing. When that writing is transcribed, students read it easily because it is their own language, the most predictable text of all.

• *Encourages risk taking*   Knowing they will not be corrected or graded, students write freely, exploring spellings, conventions, language and feelings.

• *Provides opportunities for reflection*   Journals encourage thinking about life and learning. Peter Stillman says, "Think of your journal as being a net for catching shining particles from the day" (Fulwiler, 1987, p. 80).

• *Validates personal experiences and feelings*   Small incidents and life events are viewed as important and relevant to the child's life in and out of school. What the child cares about and values is respected. Writing brings students in closer touch with themselves.

• *Provides a safe, private place to write*   Especially for older students, journals are a place to write for themselves. Sharing is always an option, not a requirement.

• *Promotes thinking and makes it visible*   Having to write thoughts—and learning processes—down forces the learner to recall, re-examine, and organize information. The teacher also sees what has been valued and understood or what the student is confused about.

• *Promotes development of written language conventions*   Teachers note that the sheer quantity of writing in a reading-writing classroom positively influences the correct use of capitalization, punctuation, and grammar. Many children also add chapter headings, titles, page numbers, and indexes; use dialogue; and continue a story from one day to the next without being formally taught.

• *Provides a vehicle for evaluation*   Students can look back through their journals as a way to evaluate their own writing. They can be guided to note their progress in all aspects of writing. Teachers can use journals as one way to check the child's phonics and spelling skills in addition to writing content and style.

• *Provides a record*   Years later, students can look back at their journals and see what was important to them and what they were thinking about at a particular stage in their lives.

Setting the Tone: Introducing Journal Writing

The way journal writing is introduced often determines how receptive students will be to it. By allowing sufficient time for oral brainstorming of possible topics, demonstrating the process by writing ourselves, and placing no value judgments on what students have written and where they may be in the writing process, we set the tone for a positive learning experience.

Without careful introduction, we may turn students off to writing. One upper elementary grade teacher expressed her frustration with the writing of Darius, a new student. Darius had written almost two sentences about playing football, but he had stopped when he couldn't spell "touchdown." It was important to give him the message that he could write.

I stooped down next to Darius so we were at eye level, and I asked him to read me what he had written. Then I asked him some questions about playing football. It was obvious from his smile and easy conversational tone that he was interested in the subject. I asked him if he could write down what he had told me, and he frowned.

ROUTMAN: Did you get a chance to do writing like this—where *you* could decide what to write about—at your old school?

DARIUS: No. The teacher told us what to write.

ROUTMAN: What kind of writing did you do?

DARIUS: Mostly filling in workbook pages or worksheets or copying from the board.

ROUTMAN: Well, in your journal you can write about what you're interested in. You don't need to worry about perfect spelling. Just do the best you can. I see you're stuck on this word; just put down the sounds you hear and go on. Also, your handwriting is beautiful, but in your journal, just think about getting your thoughts down, and try to write a little faster. You don't need to be so concerned about your handwriting.

I stayed next to Darius for a few minutes to encourage him to write down some of the things he had told me. When he hesitated on a word, I reminded him to spell the word as best he could and go on. Based on what he did write and on our conversation, he appeared to be a capable child. His reluctance to write was based on his previous school experiences, not on his lack of ability. It would take time, probably many months, but with demonstration, acceptance, and encouragement Darius would be able to write freely and comfortably in his journal.

With new students, and even with students used to journal writing, allowing enough time to talk about possible topics and demonstrating the journal writing process are critical. It is equally important to be sensitive and accepting, especially when journal writing is first introduced. Students not used to taking risks and selecting their own topics feel especially vulnerable. The teacher who appears disappointed with the first results may be setting the tone for the year by turning students off to writing. Our comments and body language strongly influence not only the quality of our students' writing but also their attitudes toward writing.

Getting Ideas for Topics: The Importance of Demonstrations

Many teachers that incorporate journal writing complain that students' entries quickly become stale and boring. However, teachers find that when they demonstrate through oral sharing and their own writing, the quality of the writing improves dramatically.

As with all demonstrations, once is rarely enough: Usually a demonstration will need to take place many times before more students can apply the concept. If only a few students apply what has been demonstrated, the demonstration has been successful. While demonstrations do not need to take place daily, they do need to occur regularly, as an authentic response to learning-teaching needs.

Valuing Everyday Experiences

When I go into classrooms and demonstrate journal writing, I begin by talking about things I could write about. They are ordinary things but they are important to me: my dog Tobi having fleas, my house needing cleaning, the waffles my husband cooked for breakfast, how I didn't want to get out of bed when the alarm went off, talking by phone with my dear friend Harriet, how worried I am about my aunt who is sick, how I feel about my new haircut. My list of topics is always different, depending on what is going on in my life. I stress that the topics are all things I know and care about and that the students too have things in their lives that they know a lot about.

Talking about what I could write about is the closest I come to being a story-teller. I notice that children are fascinated by the stories in our lives, and I tell mine with gusto. In talking about the waffles my husband made from scratch, I tell about waking up and smelling fresh-brewed coffee—a clue that this would be a lucky day when I wouldn't have to cook breakfast. I talk about how my husband has perfected his recipe and technique after several years. I describe the color and texture of the waffles, the butter melting into the small waffle squares, the delicious taste of hot, pure maple syrup, and my feelings of guilt about eating something so fattening first thing in the morning.

With very young children, my stories and demonstrations are shorter and less involved, but the topics are the same. Illustrations are also included because to know what they want to say young children often need to draw before they write. I want students to see and feel that telling and writing life stories are what writers do, that being a writer doesn't have to mean being a famous author or writing about an exciting place. Most of us haven't taken exciting trips, but we can make writing about ordinary events exciting. Perhaps, above all, I want them to feel that what goes on in their lives is significant. I try to inspire confidence by validating and encouraging what they know and feel and by accepting their best efforts.

Note the difference in Nathan's journal entries at the beginning of second grade when he was self-selecting his own topics but when no demonstrations were taking place. In the first entry, he writes a few sentences about his teacher. The next day, after a demonstration and oral sharing, he realizes he has a story to tell (see Figures 9–6 and 9–7).

I find that after I have demonstrated where my ideas come from and allowed time for oral discussion, children do not have difficulty generating topics. Students prefer and need to select their own topics. One fourth-grader who had previously been assigned topics told me, "I hated that. We had to write on things like 'What did you do over your vacation?' I had absolutely no interest in that."

Figure 9-6   Nathan's Journal Entry Before Demonstration

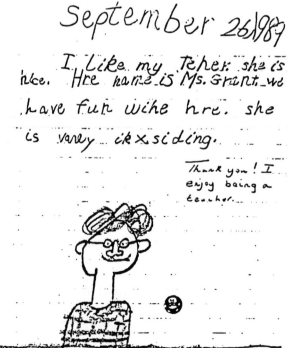

Figure 9-7   Nathan's Journal Entry after Demonstration

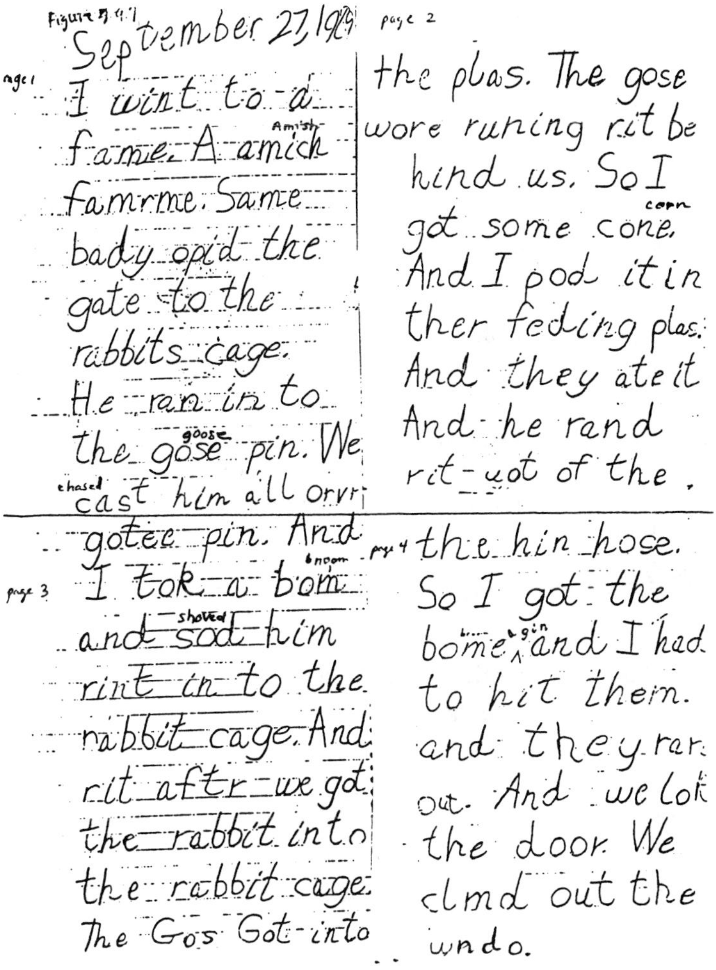

The demonstration serves to reinforce the idea that everyday topics are valid. In the spring of the year, in a kindergarten class that was doing journal writing for the first time, I talked about what I could write about—cleaning out my basement, making cookies, having to carry my dog downstairs, being tired—and wound up writing, "I was so tired this morning, I could hardly get out of bed." Following the demonstration, many students wrote about being tired. Other topics they wrote about were eating oatmeal for breakfast, being awakened by a dog barking, having an early Christmas because Grandpa would be away, swinging from a tree in the backyard, getting a new toothbrush.

Encouraging Students to Find a Meaningful Topic

I tell students they may write about anything, but I make videos, movies, and television shows off limits unless the experience has had a personal significance for the student. This rule eliminates boring recounting of events. I also encourage students to write about events that have already taken place. When students write about something that is about to happen, they tend to have less to say than when they have already had the experience. Additionally, when I find students writing repetitive accounts about the same topic day after day, I guide them toward a new topic.

Even with demonstrating, there may still be children who have difficulty coming up with topics. Jim Henry, a first grade teacher, notes,

> This past year, after I noticed that students were experiencing difficulty thinking of topics, I looked for opportunities throughout the day to help them generate ideas, and there were many. When the students arrived in the morning excited about something that had happened that morning or the night before I commented, "That would be a great thing to put in your journal!" I commented the same way to students during shared reading experiences when a story or poem prompted reflections on personal experiences.

When journal writing is introduced, and sporadically throughout the year, Jim takes the time to have students share what they are writing about. He then lists the topics that others have written about on the board to serve as an idea stimulator for those having difficulty finding a topic.

Very young children also need to be encouraged that what has happened to them is worthy of writing about. Note the following exchange with a kindergarten student who had begun to write:

KARESA: This isn't so good, but I'm trying my best.
ROUTMAN: What are you going to write about?
KARESA: I am picking apples.
ROUTMAN: Did you really pick apples?
KARESA: No.
ROUTMAN: Why don't you write about something you really did? How about when you made applesauce this morning? What could you say?
KARESA: The applesauce was mushy and icky.

What difference in language when the story was genuine! Karesa was very proud of herself, as exhibited by her big smile.

There is a marked difference in children's writing when topics are assigned and when children can choose their own. See Figures 9–8 and 9–9 for two third-graders' journal entries on two consecutive school days. The first entries, on an assigned topic, are limited and boring. The second entries, done the following day after a demonstration, are more interesting and have a personal voice.

New students who are not used to journal writing and selecting their own topics will need lots of time to take ownership of their writing. The kinds of writing and demonstrations that took place in a previous school are easily detectable by examining a child's writing. When I asked a first-grader who entered midyear if she got to write in first grade, she said "yes." When I asked what kind of writing she got to do, she replied, "handwriting." Her handwriting was fine, but her content was limited and boring (see Figure 9–10). Even at the first grade level, such students may take months before they feel free enough to write in their journals. Figure 9–11 is a journal entry by a first-grader in the same class who has been journal writing daily since September.

Figures 9-8 and 9-9   Third-graders' Journal Entries on Consecutive Days

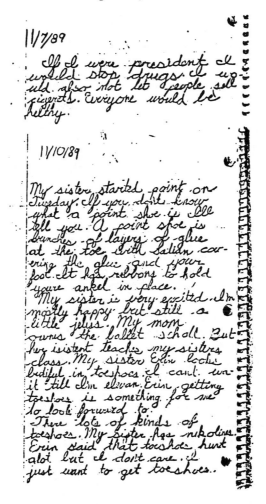

When nothing seems to work   For students who still have difficulty coming up with a topic, I suggest techniques that have worked for me:

- *Look around the room and outside the window. Something you see may trigger a thought or memory.*

    When I look up at the ceiling, it reminds me of the time the plaster crashed down from our bathroom ceiling in the middle of the night. Looking outside at the trees makes me think about all the leaves that need to be raked in my yard. (See Figure 9-12 for a fourth-grader's entry after he noticed a styrofoam plate on the teacher's desk.)

- *Think back to a special memory—a birthday, holiday, or family outing—and put yourself in the event. How were you feeling? What do you see happening?*

    Oral sharing of some of these memories, before journal writing, often gets students thinking about their own special memories.

- *If all else fails, begin writing, "I can't think of anything to write about" and keep writing about that.*

Figure 9-9

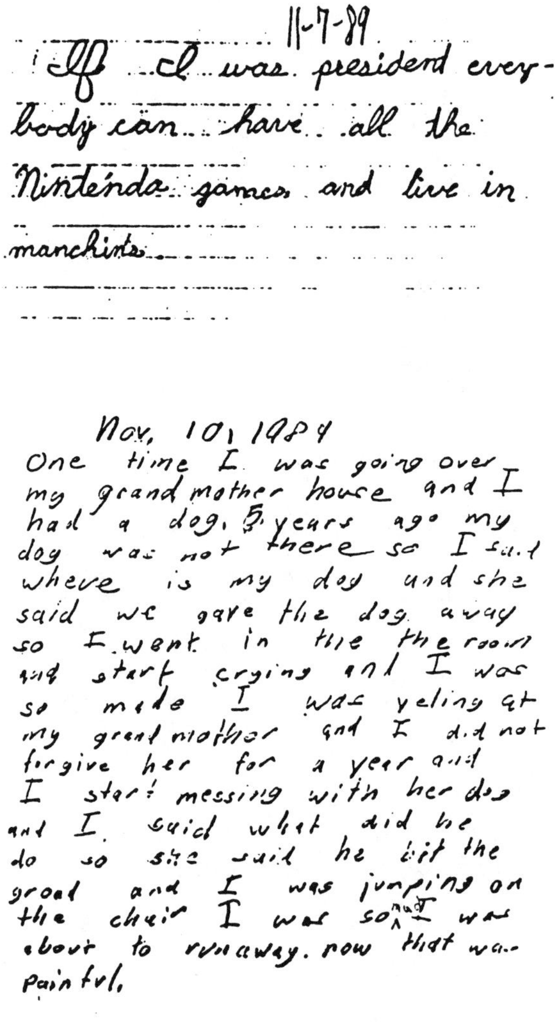

11-7-89

If I was president everybody can have all the Nintendo games and live in manchine

Nov, 10, 1984

One time I was going over my grandmother house and I had a dog. 5 years ago my dog was not there so I said where is my dog and she said we gave the dog away so I went in the the room and start crying and I was so mad I was yeling at my grandmother and I did not forgive her for a year and I start messing with her dog and I said what did he do so she said he bit the groad and I was jumping on the chair I was so mad I was about to runaway. now that was painful,

Sometimes students begin writing by writing that they have nothing to write about, which helps trigger an idea. For young children, a prompt on the board such as, "I like _____" or "I wish _____" may encourage them to finish the thought.

Every once in a while a student will be unable to write, and I accept that. I have days when getting words down on paper is so difficult I just wind up cogitating. We need to allow students the same reality.

Finding a Focus

Once students are writing fairly fluently (unencumbered by letter formation and spelling), which for some may be as early as mid-first grade, I encourage them to:

Figure 9-10 First-grader with No Experience Choosing Her Own Writing Topics

Figure 9-11 First-grader with Journal Writing Experience

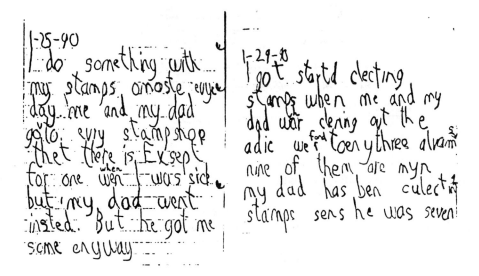

- Choose a topic that is important to them.
- Focus on one aspect of the topic.
- Tell what happened.
- Include how they feel about what happened.

I demonstrate these points orally first and then in writing.

Figure 9-12   Fourth-grader's Journal Entry Inspired by a Styrofoam Plate on Teacher's Desk

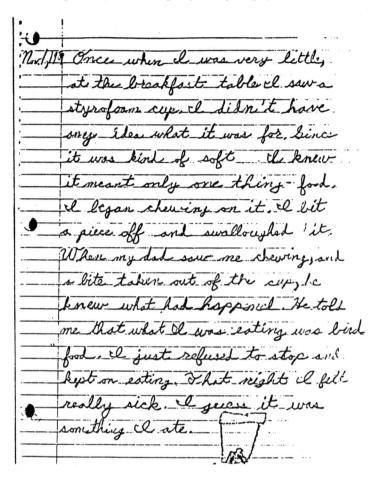

Getting students to focus brings out description and detail that do not come out when they just recount what happened in sequence. For example, when I write about my dog, Tobi, I tell about *one* aspect of my pet: his problem with fleas, his difficulty getting up and down stairs now that he is old, his playfulness, or the way he sleeps. I try to get students to do the same. That focus helps to move them away from telling everything they know about a topic and the tedious mode of "This happened, and then this happened."

Writing in front of students   As I write in front of the children, usually on the overhead projector but sometimes on the chalkboard or chart paper, I verbalize my thinking. Often I have not decided what to write about until I am actually about to begin. Sometimes I change my mind at the last minute, and I let the students know that writers do this. I try to make my thinking visible, and I let students know I have no idea how the writing will turn out. Often I find my focus *as* I am writing. One day, for example, I started off thinking I would write about neighbors (who had moved away) and having an afternoon visit with their year-old daughter. I didn't know until I had begun writing that I would wind up focusing on how the baby reminded me of my daughter Elizabeth at the same age. I let students know that a writer often doesn't know what she's going to say until she says it, a concept I grasped from the writings of Donald Murray and my own experience as a writer.

As I demonstrate, students often see me change my mind about something and cross out words. I tell them that writers cross out because it's quicker than erasing and leaves a record of their first thoughts. I try to discourage erasing and the notion of having a "clean" paper so students will grasp the idea that drafts are normal.

I point out to students grade 2 and above how quickly I can fill a page. I have them note that I write a whole page in five minutes; therefore, in twenty minutes they can certainly do the same. Even though quantity is not the goal, some students need to be shown that it is not difficult to write a whole page and more when a writer has a topic he knows a lot about and a topic that is important to him.

A brainstorming strategy   A strategy that works very well for getting students to focus on small happenings and feelings within larger contexts is brainstorming. Beginning by demonstrating myself, I list all the possible subtopics I can think of to go with my topic (see Figure 9–13). Then I choose the subtopic I want to write about today and try to tell as much as I can about it in an interesting way.

This brainstorming technique is a primary form of outlining that encourages students to group together like information. I have used this technique successfully as early as mid-first grade. Repeated demonstrations are necessary, and the strategy works best with small groups of students.

When students try this guided brainstorming, what happens is that things they might never have thought to include become part of their story. Additionally, when a student is asked to pick only one of many writing options, he tends to do a more thorough job. Figures 9–14 through 9–16 give examples of brainstormings by first-graders and some follow-up writing. Notice in "Going to Grandma's House" the last item that came out on the student writer's brainstorming was "crowded car."

Figure 9-13   Brainstorming Subtopics on the Topic "My Dog"

Tobi

✓ how we got him
what he does all day
what he looks like
his problems
     old age
       arthritis
        stairs
sleeping habits
        blanket
       dreams
what he eats
      begs for food
      change in dog food

Figures 9–14, 9–15, and 9–16   First-graders' Brainstormings on a Topic

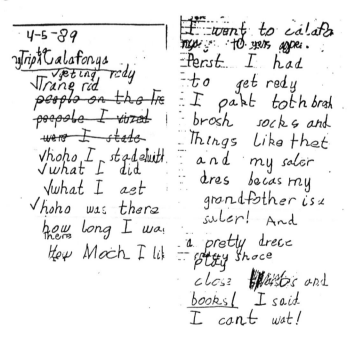

11·14·88

Christmas
vtran riding.
get Presents.
deckorat tree
wotch TV.
dad and bruthr
have dinre.
go to Chrche
goto bed.
get up,
open Prethn
cusuns,
Big teste.

Figure 9–15

4-5-89

Trip Calafonya
vgeting redy
Trane rid
people on the tre
people I vized
were I state
hoho I stade with
what I did
what I aet
hoho was there
how long I wa
How Mach I li

I went to calafa
nyu. To yers appe.
Perst I had
to get redy
I pakt toth brsh
brosh socks and
Things like thet
and my saler
dres becas my
grondfother is a
suler! And
a pretty drece
ptty shoce
close boods's and
books I said
I cant wat!

This would probably not have come out without the brainstorming. Yet it adds an interesting dimension to the story and is what the student chose to write about first. I suggest to students that they check or cross out their subtopics as they write about them. Often students use their subtopics as a table of contents for the beginning of a chapter book on their topic.

Figure 9-16

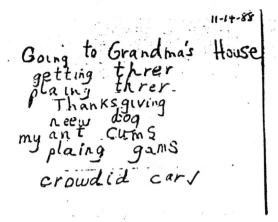

Translation

When We Go to Grandma's House

We get up very early. We put the suitcases in the car. We get in the car. My baby sister sits in a booster seat. Then we get into the car. We are very squished.

The Teacher as a Writing Model

Just as we demonstrate ourselves as readers, we also want to demonstrate ourselves as writers. In kindergarten and early first grade, these demonstrations take place mostly in small-group and whole-class settings, with the teacher writing in front of the children. However, once students can write without teacher intervention, it works well if teachers write at least several times a week in their own journals at the same time the students are writing. First grade teacher Jim Henry found that writing with students—which he felt comfortable doing about mid-year—revitalized his journal writing program. Children seemed more excited about their own writing and enjoyed finding out what their teacher had written.

Also, just as teachers do not mark papers during sustained silent reading, so too journal writing is best used only for writing if we want students to get the message that this kind of writing is a valued activity. Some teachers enjoy using their own journal writing as an opportunity to reflect on their teaching.

Besides serving as a model for students, teachers' writing and sharing allow students to get to know their teachers as people. Walking into one classroom, I discovered the teacher writing her journal entry with tears in her eyes. Her son had just turned sixteen, and she was writing about her sense of loss and her worry about her son as a new driver.

Teachers' Observations

Karen Horton, a third grade teacher, noticed immediate improvement in the quality and quantity of her students' writing after several demonstrations.

> Before that, I was getting a lot of listing and enumerating. They weren't really saying much of anything. I was amazed at how many kids wrote a whole page and more after seeing journal writing demonstrated. There was a noticeable improvement in the content of the writing, and kids showed a lot more confidence. They felt they had something to say.
>
> Journal writing is a wonderful vehicle for sharing feelings. I feel so much more in touch with the kids' lives now. Sometimes you don't get a chance to talk about things in the classroom, but they can write about it and I know what they are thinking and how they are feeling.

After a teacher demonstration, fourth grade teacher Nancy Schubert says her students were begging to have journal writing "like we did last week" (when they could choose their own topics). Nancy had moved from always assigning topics to letting students choose their own topics. She noticed a dramatic difference in student interest in writing. Nancy notes, "I know now you don't need to give starters or topics or start with a discussion of world or school events. The whole concept of 'real' is very important to the kids. Once in a while, I still assign a topic, mostly, I think, as a test to see if choosing their own topics really produces better writing."

Students' Observations

Here are some second-graders' comments after journal writing was demonstrated:

- I had to work hard to think of what I wanted to write about but then I just wrote. I didn't think.
- Usually I try to write a whole story. It was easier because I just wrote about a small part.
- I didn't know I would get ideas by looking around the room. I have another idea for tomorrow.

When I asked a group of third-graders if their writing surprised them in any way, one girl whose teacher described her writing as mostly lists of what happened said, "I didn't know I could write so much on one thing. It's easier when you focus on one thing you know and care about."

Taking Time for Oral Sharing
Sharing to Get Journal Writing Started

Taking time for oral sharing promotes language development, inspires confidence, and gives reluctant writers possible topics from which to choose. Oral language is used as a tool for learning and is integral to successful journal writing. While some students are talking about what they might write about, others are developing and practicing good listening skills and getting ideas for their own writing. The oral language time also allows the teacher the opportunity to probe and guide the student to awareness of what he already knows but may not know he knows. It is a time for hearing the personal stories of our students. The time for talk also encourages very young children to move way from common, boring topics such as rainbows, hearts, and butterflies.

After my oral sharing, I always take lots of time—ten to twenty minutes—to go around the class and ask, "Who knows what he or she could write about?" When the student says, "My dog," I probe, "What about your dog? What are you going to say?" I try to get them to note small, but significant, incidents and events and to express complete thoughts so they can get them down on paper later.

I remember Jordan, a first-grader described by his teacher as "very slow" and a child who "hardly writes anything in his journal." In our oral sharing, a number of students had talked about their pets. I gently probed, "Jordan, do you have any kind of pet?" I learned he had a goldfish that had just died. By asking him genuine questions ("How did your fish die?" "How did you take care of your goldfish?" "Did you clean its bowl?" "What did you feed it?" "How did you get your goldfish?") and engaging him in conversation, a story emerged. With guidance, Jordan proudly wrote for several days about his goldfish, and that story became his first published book. Without the oral sharing, I don't believe he would have "found" his story.

Initially, some teachers feel guilty about taking time for oral language, but oral language is critical and gives students a framework for writing. Teachers who do take the time note that the quality of student writing is much improved. Kindergarten teacher Kathy Wolfe always takes lots of time for oral sharing before journal writing, and she notes that the students' writing is lively and interesting and that everyone has something to write about.

The following were some orally stated topics—with focuses—from a fourth grade class in early fall after an oral demonstration:

LISA: going to a wedding; choosing and wearing pink and green bridesmaid's dress

NATALIE: cleaning up "junky" room—lollypop wrappers on floor, old pieces of cheese sticking to the sheet, excitement of finding a friend's phone number buried

TOMMY: worry about cat; eyes don't look right, not eating, not sure what's wrong

KARL: dog died; passing a pet shop; went in and saw two golden retrievers

ABBY: starting dancing class, nervous about how it will go

NATASHA: choosing seats at a movie and buying popcorn

Figure 9-17   Validating a Students' Experiences through Journal Writing

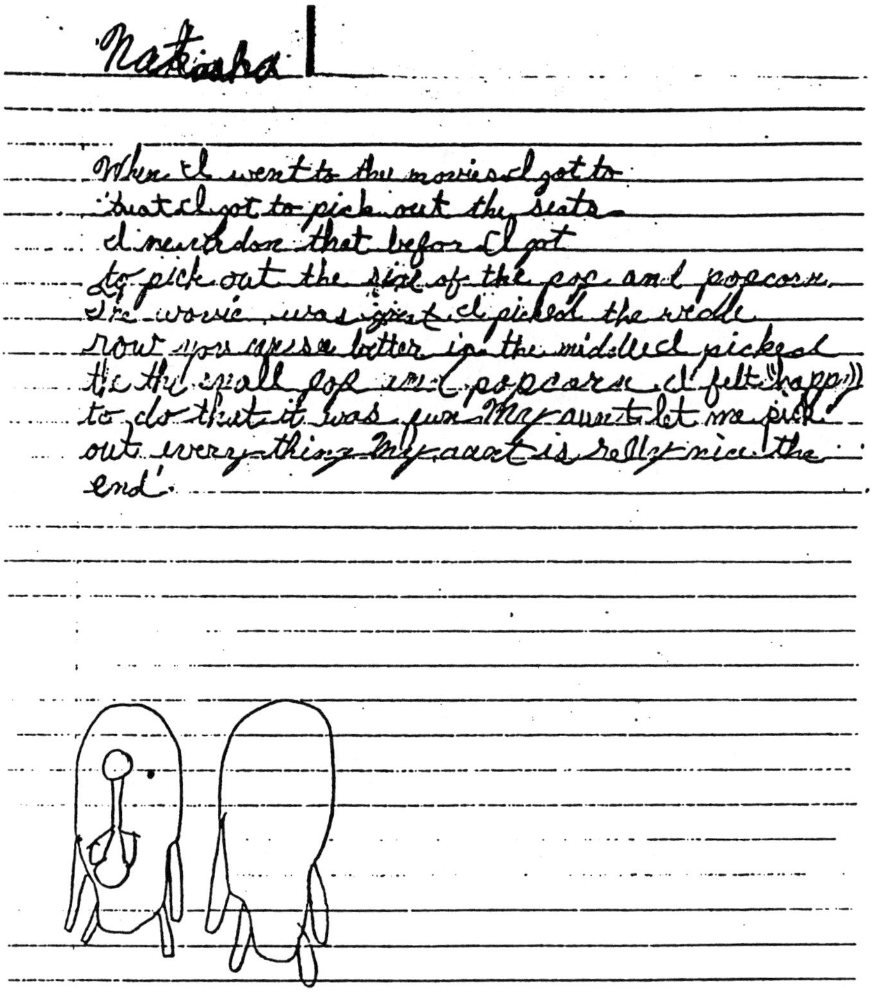

Natasha was a "low-ability" student with poor self-esteem, and her journal entry validated an important experience in her life. It was the first time she had ever chosen the seats at the movie theater, and she was elated. Journal writing gave her a vehicle to bring that experience into school and share it with her peers (see Figure 9–17).

Billy was a struggling student in the same class who chose not to share orally. Note how he is able to use his journal entry to talk about a difficult event in his life (see Figure 9–18).

Figure 9-18 Using Journal Writing to "Talk" about a Difficult Experience

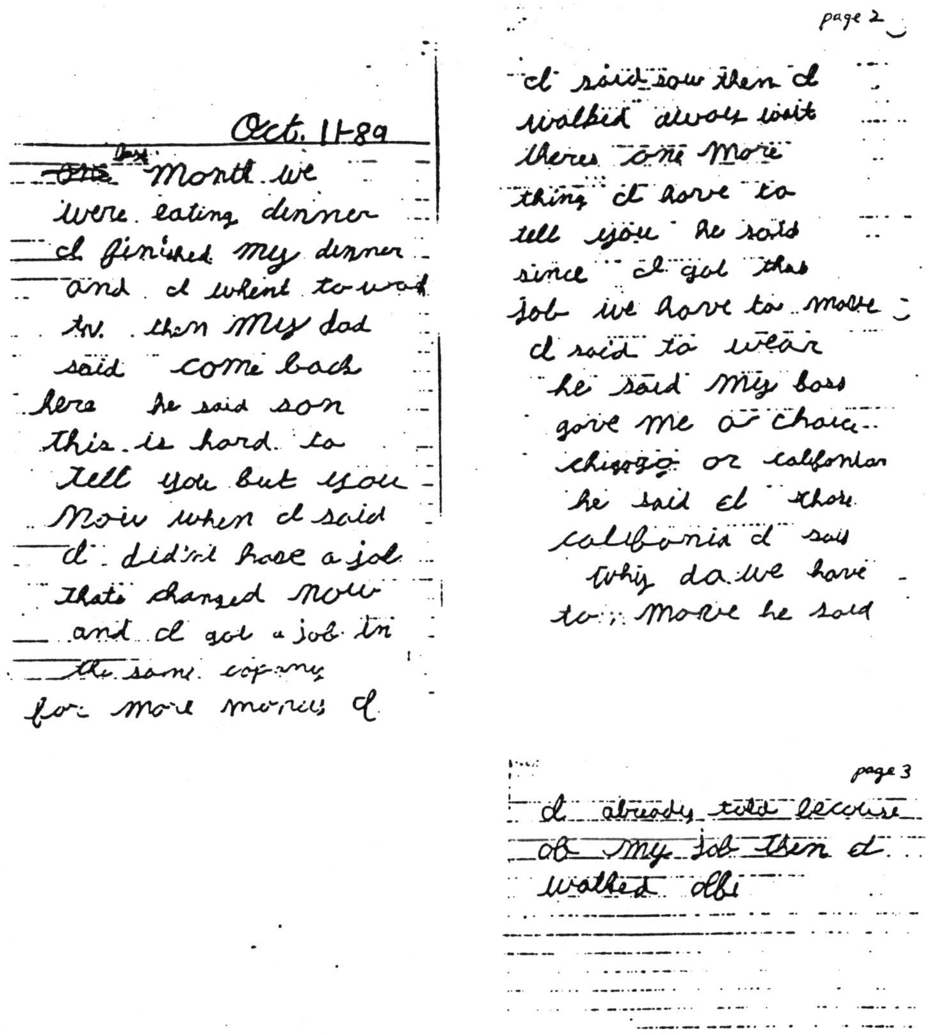
Oct. 11-89
One Month we
were eating dinner
I finished my dinner
and I whent to wach
tv. then my dad
said come back
here he said son
this is hard to
tell you but you
now when I said
I didn't have a job
That's changed now
and I got a job in
the same copany
for more money I

page 2
I said sow then I
walked away wait
theres one more
thing I have to
tell you he said
since I got that
job we have to move
I said to wear
he said my boss
gave me a choice
chicago or califonia
he said I chose
california I said
why do we have
to move he said

page 3
I already told because
of my job then I
walked off

Sharing after Journal Writing

Sharing time is important because it validates and gives children an audience. It is the "show-off" stage, the important last step in the developmental model (pp. 9–10). Almost all young children enjoy the opportunity to "read" their journal entries and talk about their illustrations. With older children, journals are often best treated as private places.

Sharing seems to work best when it is voluntary. In classrooms in which students have had to read their entries aloud, some children develop an aversion to journal writing. One fourth-grader stated, "Last year, we had to read our journals out loud, and I hated that. This year we have an option, and that makes me feel a lot better."

Journal Writing in the Kindergarten

Journal writing can begin the first week in kindergarten if writing is viewed as any marks on paper that have meaning for the child. That could include drawings, squiggles, lines, mock letters (made-up letters), random letters, or anything the child puts on paper that makes sense to her. "During kindergarten, the most typical forms of writing used in connected discourse (such as stories or letters) continue to be scribbling, drawing, and nonphonetic letter strings, with fewer children using phonetic (or invented) spelling, and conventional orthography (dictionary spelling)" (Strickland and Morrow, 1989, p. 72).

Journal writing takes place in all our kindergartens, and our teachers have been largely influenced by the leadership and guidance of kindergarten teacher Jeanette Throne (See "Journal Articles" in *Resources for Teachers*). Writing in the kindergarten extends beyond journal writing into natural contexts, play areas, and writing centers. Children's strong, early foundation in writing continues to have an impact on their writing development and their attitudes toward writing.

Getting Started

When I demonstrate journal writing in the kindergarten early in the school year, I demonstrate many forms of writing while telling them they are already writers (see Figure 9–19):

- Picture writing
- Scribble writing
- Random letters
- Invented spelling—beginning consonants to represent words
- Conventional writing

I do not give more weight to one form than to another. As in other grades, I begin by discussing what I could write about. I start by drawing a picture and telling students that many of them probably draw better than I do. I am careful to refer to drawing as a form of writing and a way of telling my story. I will then "read" my picture. Then I scribble—write my story while I verbalize it—and say, "Some kindergarten children know how to write something like this. How many of you can write like this?" Most hands go up, and I congratulate them for being writers. Next, as I write a random stream of letters, perhaps with some mock letters included, I again slowly verbalize my story and say, "Some kindergarten children write like this. How many of you can do this?" Again many hands go up, and children are complimented for being writers.

Invented spelling is demonstrated next. I might say, "Some children write letters for the sounds they hear in their stories. See if you can help me write my story, 'I cooked scrambled eggs for breakfast.'" I slowly stretch out the sounds in each word, and I accept whatever letters they give me. Then, I ask them to read with me as I point to each "letter-word." Finally, I write the conventional form of my sentence, saying, "This is what my story looks like when I write it. It took me many years to learn how to write like this." I invite them to read it with me.

Before the children begin to write themselves, there will be lots of oral sharing of possible topics. Then, whatever writing form the child chooses, from the start she

Figure 9-19 Demonstrating Journal Writing in the Kindergarten

will be treated as a writer and a reader. We must take great care to see that all children's expressions find acceptance in school.

After the child has finished writing, I say, "Read your story to me. Use your reading finger." The child moves his finger along (perhaps with teacher guidance) and "reads" the story. One little girl was following along her scribble writing with her finger, reading, "We played freeze tag. It was so. . . ." Her finger ran out at "so," and then she said, "Oh, I forgot 'fun.'" She happily added another scribble and went back to reread her complete story. She clearly understood that print contains a message.

While the teacher or parent volunteer writes down the child's story at the bottom of the page (lightly in pencil so the child's writing marks predominate), this is not traditional dictation because children cannot write. This is dictation of a story the child has written. Having children write for themselves from the beginning eliminates the need for traditional dictation. However, some teachers find it worthwhile to continue to incorporate dictation for the depth of oral storytelling that can result. Dictation allows for extensive language in spite of limited sound-knowledge or limited experience with the structure of stories. Occasionally there are children who may not view scribble writing and stringing letters together as writing. Always, respect for the child is primary, and for these children the teacher would serve as scribe for their dictated stories.

Scribble Writing

"Encourage children who are scribbling to write and scribble every day" (Hayes, 1990).

Just as babbling is a natural and expected behavior in learning to talk, scribbling is a beginning stage of writing development that enables emerging writers to explore language. Writing that may mean nothing to the teacher may be filled with meaning for the child. I see scribble writing as a way of freeing children who are not yet ready or interested in forming letters or connecting sounds with letters. Scribble writing allows all children to write from the start of school and to see themselves as writers. With scribble writing as an option, kindergarten children no longer say, "I can't write."

Several years ago I would never have demonstrated scribble writing, mock letters, or random letters. In my old way of thinking writing meant starting with letter formation, and therefore many students believed they could not write. As soon as I started demonstrating scribble writing, almost without exception every child wrote and believed he could write.

I have come to believe that when children are immersed in a print-rich, authentic literacy environment with daily opportunities for language exploration—including reading and writing independently and with guidance—they will move toward invented spelling and conventional spelling when they are ready. It takes a lot of trust to believe this will happen and to accept that children's writing is purposeful for them, even when we feel they can do more. However, as long as children are seeing lots of letter formation and conventional print through teacher demonstrations and through text, they will develop and progress as writers. In the long run, a child's exploration of shapes and lines probably aids letter knowledge and form. Although we may encourage and gently guide students to move to another stage when we think they are ready, essentially we must trust students to let it happen.

For some children, scribble writing seems to make it easier to concentrate on the story they are telling without worrying about sounds and letters. At times, it also seems to be a vehicle for supporting the very verbal child who has much to say. A case in point was Jonathan, a kindergarten student who stayed with scribble writing until mid-year. Jonathan was in Karen Sher's reading-writing classroom with lots of daily opportunities to read and write. Journal writing took place, whole class, once a week with the assistance of a parent volunteer. In terms of average writing development, Jonathan does not seem to have lost any ground by having been allowed to move at his own pace (see Figures 9–20 through 9–22). Karen reflects:

> My year with Jonathan was my first exploration with scribble writing. There were moments when I began to doubt that Jonathan would move to the "next stage." I'm so glad I resisted the urge (and *my* need) to push him, although gentle, positive encouragement *was* given when appropriate. Jonathan had extraordinary ability to express himself through art. I feel that giving him the freedom to fully explore his talent helped to make him feel confident and comfortable with written symbols he freely used by the end of his kindergarten year.

In relation to writing, children's tears are now rare—even the first week of school. When the tears do come, they are usually from a child who is not a risk taker and who won't put anything down unless it's right. One little girl who cried and said she couldn't write finally wrote "The" for the first word in her story and was upset because she couldn't spell the rest correctly. Once these children realize

Figures 9-20, 9-21, and 9-22   Development of a Kindergarten Writer Who Remained with Scribble Writing Until Mid-year

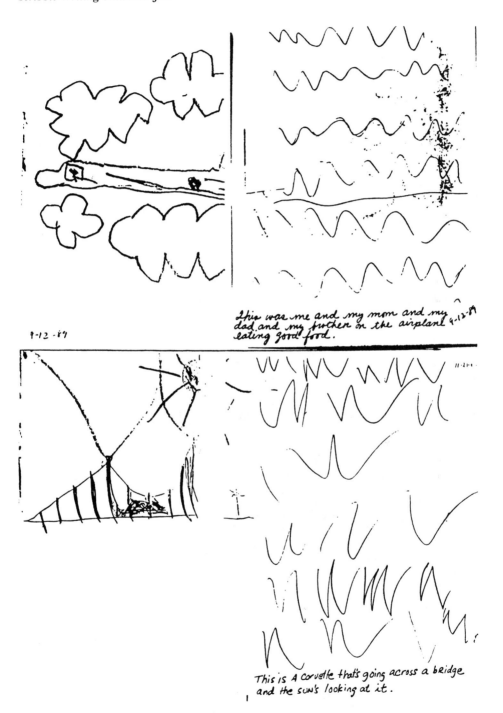

9-12-89

This was me and my mom and my dad and my brother on the airplane 9-12-89 eating good food.

This is A corvette that's going across a bridge and the sun's looking at it.

Figure 9-21

that they should do the best they can and not worry, they relax and begin to incorporate invented spelling.

Some kindergarten teachers are uncomfortable demonstrating scribble writing, thinking that it will encourage an early form of writing that may delay movement to the invented spelling stage. Also, some children stay with scribble writing for

Figure 9-22

4-10-90

"woN I
woS.
At ScdL
MY MOM
BOt ME
F IS.

When I was at school my mom bought me fish

At HOM MY
MOM GAYV
ME A MOWNY
BAYK aNd Lt
WOS KLYr

5/1/90 at home my mom gave me a money bank and it was clear.

quite some time. This can be unnerving for the teacher who is wondering whether more conventional writing will ever happen. However, children's daily writing is not always logical or sequential; at times, children may move back and forth between stages. Some of us have found that it has taken the vantage point of looking back over a whole year of writing progress to feel comfortable with scribble writing and also to feel confident that children are developing as writers. As with all forms of language learning, there is no best way or one right way; it is up to the teacher to decide what she is comfortable with.

Finally, parents need to be kept well informed about the writing program. Teachers that take the time to communicate with parents about their children's writing stages find that parents are reassured and supportive.

Organization and Management

Scheduling

Many teachers try to schedule journal writing daily for ten to twenty minutes or more. Some teachers schedule journal writing first thing each morning, or at the beginning of a period, feeling that it helps build a sense of community. Others prefer it at the end of the morning or day. Some teachers like having journal writing right before reading groups and independent work time, so that children who want more time can have the option to continue journal writing.

A consistently scheduled time with the teacher helps children expect journal writing, value it, and look forward to it. Even though students should also have options to write in their journals at other times, a scheduled time allows for oral discussion, minilessons and demonstrations, and teacher time to conference individually with students. A scheduled time also gives the teacher time to sit down and write with a group of students, which seems to encourage their own writing. By contrast, when journal writing is only assigned as seatwork while the teacher is involved with other activities, students do not take journal writing seriously or give their best efforts.

My recommendation is to schedule journal writing as often as you are comfortable with it in kindergarten, daily in grades 1 and 2, and at least several times weekly from grade 3 up. Many teachers feel that increasing curriculum demands through the grades makes it difficult to find time for personal journal writing. However, the incorporation of other types of journals—learning logs, reflection logs—makes journal writing a tool for learning across the curriculum and makes it possible to schedule it on a daily basis.

In scheduling journal writing, flexibility is important. If journal time seems to be becoming routine or forced and the children are not enthusiastic about it, think about including it only as an optional activity or setting it aside altogether for several weeks or months.

Supplies Needed

- Journals—may be spiral-bound notebooks, lined or unlined. Most teachers seem to prefer some type of bound book, but a three-ring notebook with dividers also works well, especially if learning logs are being used in several content areas.

   With a machine that spiral binds, using mimeograph paper and sturdy paper for front and back covers, blank books can be made for kindergarten and beginning first-graders. Most of our first grade teachers use lined spirals, but we tell the children to ignore the lines, and they do.

- Crayons or colored pencils—for illustrations (Magic Markers "bleed" through).

- Date stamp—or students may write in the date. Even some of our very young children write the number of the month, a dash, and the date. Writing the number of the month instead of the name saves time. Dating each entry is important for noting progress and keeping an organized, ongoing record.
- Pencils and pens

Choosing a Topic

Some teachers find doing a whole-class brainstorming of possible topics works well after the teacher has demonstrated what he might write about. Others have students do individual brainstormings and keep these in their journals for reference. Figure 9–23 gives a third-grader's personal brainstorming after a whole-class brainstorming of topics.

Some first grade teachers send home a sheet called "Topics for My Journal" at the beginning of the year, which the parent fills out with the child. Some topics that may be included are "Family," "Friends," "Hobbies," "Pets," "Special Places," "Holidays," "Favorite Activities," "Important Memories." The completed sheet is stapled into the front of the journal and is referred to by the teacher and student when the student has trouble choosing a writing topic.

If a student is still having difficulty getting ideas, you may want to suggest to the parent that possible topics to write about be a subject of meal-time discussion.

Figure 9-23   A Third-grader's Personal Brainstorming for Writing Topics

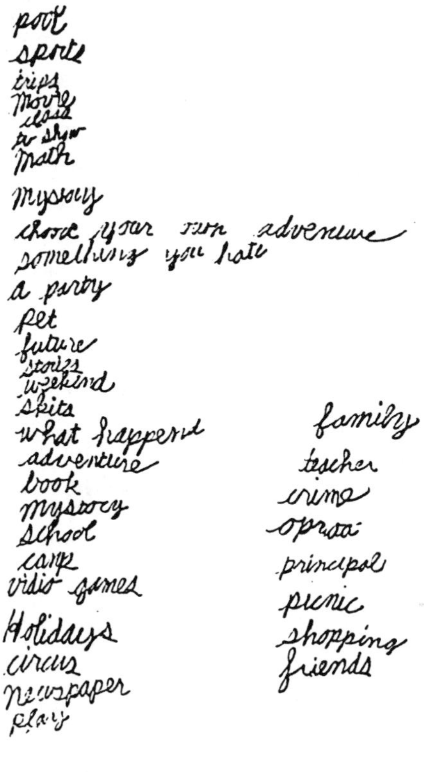

Prompting the parent to say to the child, "You could write about that in your journal" is often enough to get the child going on her own.

Illustrating

Young children often need to draw pictures before they attempt words. After children are writing easily, often by mid-first grade, they are gently encouraged to spend most of their time writing and to save their illustrations for their published books and projects as well as for independent work time. For children who are more comfortable just writing a story, we don't insist on pictures.

Using Dashes and Cross Outs

When I demonstrate writing for young children, I tell them, "If you're not sure what comes next, just put a 'dash,' like this (—), and go on." This practice frees children who stop writing because they "can't spell." I also show how writers cross out when they make a mistake or change their minds. Crossing out is faster than erasing and leaves a record of the writer's first intentions.

Encouraging Invented Spelling

The primary purpose of invented spelling is to free children to write. In a class of twenty-five or more students, the child is able to continue writing and does not have to stop and wait for the teacher. If the child asks me how to spell a word, I say, "Do the best you can" or "What sounds do you hear?" or "How can you help yourself?" When he asks, "Is this right?" I might say, "That's just fine for now." If the children are continuing to ask the teacher to spell words, they are still getting the message that the teacher will spell for them.

When I demonstrate invented spelling (or what is now also being called developmental spelling), I do not deliberately misspell. I ask the children to help me write the words, and I accept and congratulate them on their approximations. In that way, I observe and accept the developmental level of students, and I remain authentic with my own writing. I then write the sentence or paragraph conventionally (under or next to the invented spelling version), and I point out the parts of their words that are conventionally spelled. As I am writing I might say, "Good for you. Look. You got the first and last letters."

The language the teacher uses in demonstrations is very important. When I do my writing after the invented spelling, I always tell the children that it took me many years to write like this. While I am sharing the correct model, I am at the same time giving the message that I don't expect the children to write like adults. This takes away overemphasis on correctness and helps make students comfortable with using invented spelling.

Fostering Independence in Writing

It's a good idea to discuss what writers can do when they can't spell a word:

- Sound it out—stretch out the sounds.
- Ask a friend.

- Use print resources—books, charts, print in room.
- Use a dash.

It also works well to demonstrate for young children how they might use a familiar book, poem, or chart to find a word. I might say, "If you are using the word 'today,' where can you find it?" (calendar board). "If you need the word 'my,' where can you look?" (poem or chart or teacher's modeled writing on the chalkboard). To promote writing fluency, it works best if the child does not stop to look up a word in the dictionary.

For an important, difficult word that a child requests and that I know will be written repeatedly, I will sometimes write the correct spelling. For example, if the child is about to write a story about his pet rabbit, I might say, "You will be using 'rabbit' a lot in your story. This is how you write it."

Making Print Resources Readily Available

A variety of print resources in the classroom encourages children to move toward conventional spelling and independence in writing.

- *Alphabet strips and picture charts* Young children need to see the letters right in front of them for reference. It is not sufficient just to have the alphabet posted high up on a bulletin board because many children do not yet have the eye-hand coordination to copy letters from far away. Some teachers adhere alphabet strips to each child's desk; others staple a copy of the alphabet, showing upper and lower case letters, inside the front cover of the journal. Many of us also make individual alphabets with picture cues (see Figure 9–24) for each child.

- *Environmental print* Labels, signs, calendars, children's names, and messages

Figure 9-24   A Resource for K-1 Students: Alphabet with Picture Cues
Compiled by Karen Smith.

that children see over and over again in context in the classroom and at home have a powerful impact on children's writing and reading.

One kindergarten student who was just starting to use beginning consonants to represent words wrote "off" correctly. When asked how he knew the word, he said, "I saw it in my refrigerator. My mommy told me what it said." A first-grader who spelled "Australia" correctly told me, "I can spell it because 'Australia' is on my stamps in my stamp collection."

• *Family words*   Early in first grade, sometimes even the first week of school, we begin an enlarged chart of "Family Words." Words such as "mother," "father," "cousin," "grandpa," and "aunt" get added as children ask for them.

• *Content and theme words*   See "Wall Charts," page 247.

• *High-frequency words*   In kindergarten and early first grade, putting a reference card of most frequently used words at each writing table facilitates writing and gives support to emerging writers. This idea was shared by a visiting teacher from New Zealand, and it works well. By observing the words children need and are using and making them readily available, young writers are aided in the writing process. I start with only four words on one side of a card, add four more words on the reverse, and later move to a card with six or eight spaces (see Figure 9–25). Some teachers start by putting on the board one word that many students seem to be using. When there are four (or more) words on the board that children can read, a guide card is made. The short, high-frequency word list may also be clipped into each child's journal.

Words that children ask for and use over and over again can be put into a personal words section at the back of the journal. I will often say to a student, "You are using this word a lot. I will put it here for you so you can find it when you need it."

Figure 9-25   For Beginning Writers: Reference Card with Frequently Used Words

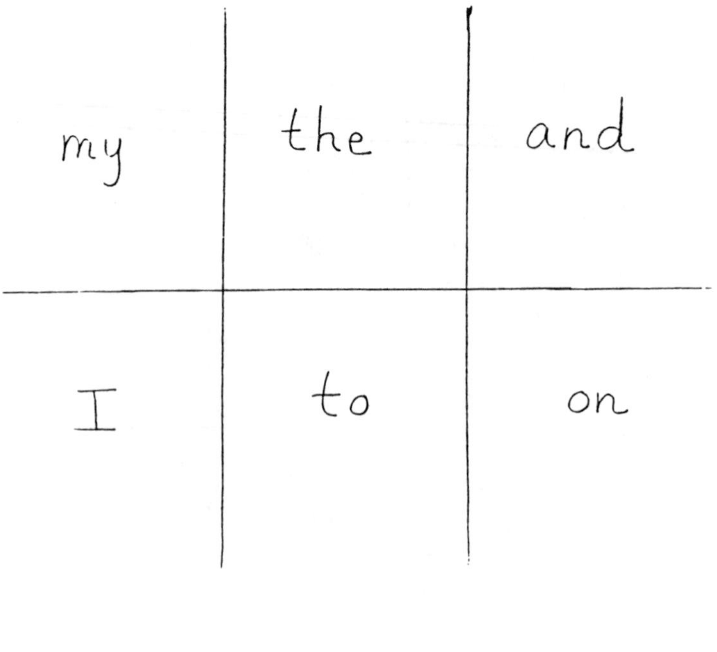

Encouraging Collaboration

Especially with young children, opportunities for quiet talking seem to promote writing development. Desks clustered in small groups allow for natural sharing ("What are you writing about?") and help with spelling ("How do you spell _____ ?"). Having some children who are strong writing models in each group offers support to peers.

Keeping Track of Skills

Some teachers like to keep a checklist in the journal of skills the child *is* using. For example, when the teacher notices that "I" is used correctly, when sentences are beginning with capitals, or when punctuation is appearing, it is noted and dated on the checklist. This practice is fine as long as the checklist is used by the teacher and student to note behaviors that are occurring naturally. We need to use caution here, however, as overemphasis of mechanics will take away from the primary purposes and benefits of journal writing.

Taking Time for Minilessons

Some teachers like to begin the journal writing period with an occasional minilesson. The lesson might be a demonstration in spacing of words, in finding a focus in writing, in utilizing print resources in the classroom, or in anything the teacher notices from looking through journals that students might benefit from.

Minilessons also occur as we quickly conference with students one-to-one during journal writing time. For a student having difficulty with spelling, some comments might include, "What do you hear at the beginning? Does it start like any word you know? Stretch it out slowly with me. What do you hear in the middle? at the end? What can you do to help yourself?"

Utilizing volunteers

Many kindergarten and first grade teachers find it valuable to have a parent volunteer present one or more mornings a week to respond to every child. Especially if journal writing is done whole class, this practice facilitates getting around to everyone.

Implicit in the use of volunteers is preliminary training by the teacher. Parent volunteers need to understand and value the theory behind invented spelling and to observe how the teacher interacts with students when conferencing. Without both the theory and the practice, parents can send the wrong message to students. I observed one parent focusing on capitalization and punctuation with a beginning first-grader, taking his pencil and "correcting" his "errors."

Setting Up Centers

Many kindergarten teachers schedule journal writing time with students once a week. They meet with a small group around a table while the other students are working at learning centers, for example, painting, pasting, completing a project, listening to tapes, or whatever the teacher has set up. Each day students rotate to a new center.

Responding to Journals

One technique that works beautifully for many of us in grade 1 and above (but no one remembers where the idea first came from) is to make four 3 by 5 inch cards carrying the following messages:

- Collect all journals (teacher checks journals and responds).
- Read entry to partner.
- Share entry with class (about three students are selected).
- Put journals away.

A student is chosen to pick one card. Students love this activity and the anticipation of which journal response will be used for the day.

Providing Time for Sharing

Young children especially love sharing their stories. Sharing should be optional and nonthreatening. In kindergarten, some teachers schedule a sharing time later in the day—either individually, small group, or whole class—and encourage students to "Read me your story."

Communicating with Parents

The purpose of journal writing needs to be clearly articulated to parents. Without understanding the importance of approximation and invented spelling as well as the developmental stages of writing, parents may think teachers are not doing their job if they see that spelling and grammatical mistakes have not been corrected. A letter to parents may be helpful (see Appendix J1). Also, because journals usually stay in school, some teachers find it works well—especially in the early grades—to reproduce one page a month from the child's journal and send it home. In that way, the parent sees the child's progress. At the same time, this could also be used as an opportunity for self-evaluation—ask the child to "choose the entry that best represents your writing this month."

Teacher Expectations

While journals are not evaluated, teachers have expectations of students:

- Entries are required. Though journals are not graded, the completion of a required number of entries may be figured as part of an overall grade.
- While beautiful penmanship is not a goal, handwriting is expected to be legible.
- Invented spelling is welcomed for words the student is not expected to know how to spell. High-frequency words, however, are expected to be spelled correctly, especially by older students.
- At times, with teacher guidance, the student needs to move to a new topic, for example, when the student writes about the same subject day after day.
- Students are always expected to do their best-quality work.

Utilizing Various Types of Journals

While the personal journal has been the focus of this chapter, there are many types of journals and various ways to use them. Some teachers use or combine one or more of the following types:

Personal. Most often this is a first person diary format, but it is not limited to this. Some students mix diary entries with stories. Young students enjoy using the structure of familiar stories to create original ones.

Dialogue. The teacher and student, or student and student, respond to the journal through written conversation. Comments are often brief, informal, private, and direct.

End-of-the-day. A quiet wrap-up before school is over. Kindergarten teachers Sue Fitzpatrick and Karen Sher find that ideas are easily generated at the end of the day. Or teachers can suggest, "Write about the best part of your afternoon."

Reflection. Students reflect on what they learned, what they still have questions about, and what they want to know more about in a particular subject or area.

Learning log. The student communicates how and what he has understood about a concept or unit of study. Students describe their learning processes—that is, "writing to learn." Some content area teachers take five to ten minutes at the beginning or end of a period for students to respond in their learning logs. Learning logs may be used in mathematics, science, music, art, foreign languages, or any subject area.

Writer's notebook. Students keep a record of favorite phrases and words they come across in reading that they might want to use in their own writing. They jot down ideas, thoughts, images, anecdotes, observations, and memories for future topics. (I keep an ongoing writer's notebook and often show it to students.)

Poetry. Students copy favorite poems, write their own poetry, and keep ideas and images for poems (see McClure, 1990).

Class. Observations about a class pet, plant, activity, or trip are kept in a common log and may be entered as a shared writing entry or as individual entries. With younger students log entries are often done in enlarged print.

Responding to Journals

Teacher's journal responses should be genuine and personal. A response may be brief, based on a quick look, or as involved as a personal, written response. Sometimes response means making brief contact with each student. With young children, I like to carry a small chair from student to student so I am at eye level. I might ask, "How's the writing going? Could you read me what you've written?" I am careful to leave the ownership and the writing with the child. I have also found that when walking around conferring with students it works well to focus on one or two students. While a "stop and go" conference will be fine for many, some students will need additional guidance and encouragement.

When I cannot read a child's invented spelling, with extreme care and the child's approval, I very lightly pencil in the words, either just above the child's writing or in the space below it. The advantages of penciling in the words are long term; when the child, teacher, or parent goes back to the early writing, the message is clear. The child also has a model for a word that may be used again. Often, when students are ready, they refer to and use the conventionally spelled word in their new journal entries.

Responding to Teachable Moments

While I believe we must be very sensitive about making any critical comments on children's writing, I also believe that we should take advantage of teachable moments when they arise. If a child we are conferencing with seems ready to deal with a confusion, standard spelling, or editorial convention, then we should teach the skill at that moment. Experience has taught me that it is best to focus on one letter or convention at a time to avoid confusing the child. At the same time, we need to keep in mind that just because we introduce a convention once, the child may not be ready to pick up on it. We may need to point out the convention over and over again.

I was invited by a first grade teacher to assist with journal writing in the classroom the first week of school in September. The teacher had introduced and demonstrated journal writing the previous day. With two of us in the room, we could easily get around and respond to each child's writing.

"Tell me about your story," I said to Brandon, as I pulled my chair up next to him. With great enthusiasm, Brandon proceeded to tell me about his pictures of Batman, Robin, and the Joker. He had not written any scribbles, letters, or words. He told me he did not know how to write. I asked him if he knew how Batman started.

"B"; he called out the letter name without hesitation.

"That's right. Put it here," I told him. He looked at the alphabet strip of upper and lower case letters on his desk and then wrote the letter "D" next to his picture of Batman.

"What else do you hear?" I prompted as I stretched out the sounds for him and said "B--a--t. . . ."

"T," he called.

"Good. Put it here," I said, pointing next to the "D." "Now, what else do you hear?" I stretched out the word again, stopping on the "m" and prolonging it: "B--a--t--mmm----a--n."

Brandon said "m," and wrote "M." We continued the procedure.

I said "Batman" again, emphasizing the "n," and he wrote "N."

As Brandon and I were going through this procedure, I was thinking about whether to say anything about his writing "D" for "B." It was early in the school year, and I was wrestling with my strong feelings of accepting all writing so the child would not feel "corrected" in any way. However, I was also feeling that this confusion could probably be cleared up easily in the present writing context, especially since I knew Brandon could write his name, which began with "B." In the past, I probably would have left things alone. Now, I decided to seize the teaching-learning opportunity.

"Brandon," I said, "Can you point to the letter 'B' on your alphabet strip?" He pointed to "D." "This is the 'B' here," I said, pointing to it. "Point to it here with me, and say it with me, 'B.' Now let's write it down here on your paper for practice. Good. Now write it again."

Brandon quickly seized the moment and said, "Should I change this?" ("D"), and he started to erase the "D" and replace it with "B."

"Brandon, you can erase it, but do you know what writers do all the time when they want to make a change? They just cross out. Now, what is the letter you have just written?"

"B."

"Good. That will be easy for you to remember, because your name starts with 'B,' just like 'Batman.' What a good job you have done! Now, read this word with me." I point to "BTMN," and we both say "Batman."

In our brief interaction, Brandon saw that he actually knew how to write letters to go along with the verbal labels for his pictures. He also cleared up an important letter confusion. Hopefully, by focusing on just the "B" at this time and not comparing it with the "D," Brandon will remember to write the letter "B" for the sound of "B."

Responding in Writing

While students enjoy teachers' written responses to their journal entries and the responses provide reading-writing models, this practice is very time consuming for the teacher. Except for very young students, it's not necessary to read every entry. Many teachers try to work out a system where they respond in writing occasionally. Some teachers collect all journals every few weeks, skim the entries, carefully read one or two that spark their interest, and respond in writing to one or more entries. Here it is important to make the response fit the student's writing. A written response on one journal should not be so general that it can easily transfer to another journal. For example, instead of "interesting" or "I like this," I might write, "This reminded me of when I . . .," or, "It sounds as though you were feeling . . ."

Implicit in written response is no correcting, no red penciling, no grading. Some teachers even feel that any writing on the child's work is unacceptable. They use Post-its to make comments. These may also be used on journal entries in the early grades to transcribe the young child's invented spelling. To respect children's privacy, we tell them if there is an entry they would not like the teacher to read to fold over or fold and staple the page.

Very important, too, is the tone of the response. I believe the main purpose of responding to journals is to give an interested, honest reaction to the message. Any questions or comments should be genuine and come from the teacher's need to know. Questions such as "What else happened?" should be asked only if we really want answers and not just to have the student make the writing "longer." Ownership must remain with the child. While teachers sometimes incorporate correct spelling and grammar in their written responses based on errors the student made, this is never the primary purpose of responding to student journals.

Responding through Publishing

Many of our first-graders use their journals to house all their writing. Teachers recognize children's efforts by making their writing public. Parent volunteers "publish" children's writing, and the published books become part of the classroom library. (See Chap. 11, "Setting Up an In-School Publishing Process.")

Students' Attitudes and Learnings

When journal writing is done well, the writing serves the students' purposes and is valued by the teacher. It then becomes an activity children relish. However, students dislike journal writing when the activity is abused.

A teacher filling in for a first grade teacher on medical leave stated that the students "hated journal writing." That surprised me, because first-graders usually love the opportunities to write their own stories. When I went into the classroom, I asked some of the students how they felt. Sure enough, they hated journal writing. Here were some of their reasons:

- We have to write a long time.
- We have to write a whole page.
- We're not allowed to talk.
- We're not allowed to draw pictures anymore.
- It's hard to think of ideas.

In this classroom, journal writing had been assigned as part of seatwork during reading. There was no oral discussion ahead of time and no teacher demonstrations. Little time had been allocated for sharing, and the expectation was that at least a full page would be filled.

By contrast, in Kathy Wolfe's kindergarten class, journal writing takes place with enthusiasm every day. Kathy greets each child in the morning and talks about what he or she might write about. Children write in a weekly journal that goes home every Friday. Once a week, journal writing is done in a spiral-bound book. There are teacher demonstrations, and several parent volunteers help to ensure that every child has a miniconference and a response to the journal.

After the first year of daily journal writing, we asked Kathy's students to tell us "What We Have Learned about What Good Writers Do." These were their responses in the order the children gave them:

1. Good writers use their imagination.
2. Good writers take their time.
3. Good writers used their brains to think.
4. Good writers read over their stories before they show them to someone.
5. Good writers use lots of detail.
6. Good writers take time to work on their pictures.
7. Good writers always make sure their pictures go with their stories.
8. Good writers check for mistakes.
9. If they need a word, they look around the room, ask a friend, look in their journal or dictionary, or sound it out. They don't worry if they can't spell it.

I think the insights of these young writers are remarkable and apply across the grades. Students involved regularly in personal journal writing—where there is oral sharing, demonstrations, self-selection of topics, collaboration, time to think and write, and respect for the writer—come to value and understand the craft of writing.

Resources

The following limited number of journal articles and sections from texts have proved useful for incorporating journal writing into the classroom. Because writing in the kindergarten is feasible and desirable—yet is often seen as difficult to implement—a number of the resources address writing at that level.

Atwell, Nancie. 1987. "Procedures for Dialogue Journals." In *In the Middle: Writing, Reading and Learning with Adolescents*. Portsmouth, NH: Heinemann, pp. 192–194.

> *Procedures and purposes for dialogue journals, as well as lots of examples, are presented. (See index entry for additional page references.)*

Bode, Barbara A. April 1989. "Dialogue Journal Writing," *The Reading Teacher*, pp. 568–571.

> *The rationale and procedures for using dialogue journals to empower students and teachers—with specific examples from a first and sixth grade classroom—are presented.*

Fulwiler, Toby (ed.). 1987. *The Journal Book*. Portsmouth, NH: Heinemann-Boynton/ Cook.

> *Over forty educators from the elementary grades through college explore the use of journals—especially the learning log—across the curriculum. Most of the articles in this scholarly text relate to secondary and college levels. "Mathematics Journals: Fourth Grade," by Barbara Schubert (pp. 348–358), is a useful source for elementary teachers ready to use "writing to learn" in mathematics. "The Power of Responding in Dialogue Journals," by Jana Staton (pp. 47–63), gives the rationale and specific procedures for using dialogue journals in the elementary school.*

Furnas, Alfreda. 1985. "Watch Me." In *Breaking Ground: Teachers Relate Reading and Writing in the Elementary School*, Jane Hansen, Thomas Newkirk, and Donald Graves (eds.). Portsmouth, NH: Heinemann, pp. 37–44.

> *Using the overhead projector, a kindergarten teacher demonstrates her own writing process and gets many of her students participating and, eventually, writing and reading independently. Very practical for kindergarten teachers who want their children to write but are unsure how to begin.*

Harste, Jerome C., and Kathy G. Short, with Carolyn Burke. 1988. "Journal Writing." In *Creating Classrooms for Authors*. Portsmouth, NH: Heinemann, pp. 153–160 and 280–285.

> *Rationale and procedures for journal writing are clearly presented, with varied and workable options for teachers.*

Hayes, Lynda Fender. March 1990. "From Scribbling to Writing: Smoothing the Way," *Young Children*, pp. 62–68.

> *A kindergarten teacher interweaves the research on young children's natural progression as writers with lots of meaningful and varied writing activities. Kindergarten teachers will find this a particularly supportive and valuable article for promoting all kinds of writing in the classroom.*

Hilliker, Judith. 1988. "Labelling to Beginning Narrative: Four Kindergarten Children Learn to Write." In *Understanding Writing: Ways of Observing, Learning, and Teaching*, 2nd ed. Thomas Newkirk and Nancie Atwell (eds.). Portsmouth, NH: Heinemann, pp. 14–22.

A teacher-researcher examines the development of four kindergarten writers. Supportive for understanding processes children go through.

Hipple, Marjorie. L. March 1985. "Journal Writing in Kindergarten," *Language Arts*, pp. 255–261.

A kindergarten teacher describes the functions, procedures, and observations of journal writing in her classroom.

Kirby, Dan. 1988. "The 'J'." In *Inside Out: Developmental Strategies for Teaching Writing*. Portsmouth, NH: Heinemann-Boynton/Cook, pp. 45–57.

An English teacher describes why the journal works well and gives suggestions for using four different types of journals: the writer's notebook, the class journal, the project journal, and the diary. Included are suggestions for teacher responding. Intermediate through secondary teachers will find this article helpful and specific.

Sowers, Susan. 1985. "The Story and the 'All About' Book." In *Breaking Ground: Teachers Relate Reading and Writing in the Elementary School*, Jane Hansen, Thomas Newkirk, and Donald Graves (eds.). Portsmouth, NH: Heinemann, pp. 73–82.

Before they get into narrative writing, Sowers notes that first-graders prefer to write "all about" books—"a listlike collection of facts, features and attributes of its subject." Helpful for understanding the content and form beginning writers use.

Staton, Jana. February 1988. "ERIC/RCS Report: Dialogue Journals," *Language Arts*, pp. 198–201.

This report by a researcher on the use of dialogue journals defines a dialogue journal and gives the benefits of its use. Many references to sources of information on dialogue journals are included.

Unia, Sumitra. 1985. "From Sunny Days to Green Onions: On Journal Writing." In *Whole Language: Theory in Use*, Judith Newman (ed.). Portsmouth, NH: Heinemann, pp. 65–72.

An elementary teacher reflects on her experiences and personal growth in beginning to implement journal writing. Honest and inspiring.

Zemelman, Steven, and Harvey Daniels. 1988. "Journal Writing." In *A Community of Writers: Teaching Writing in the Junior and Senior High School*. Portsmouth, NH: Heinemann, pp. 99–102.

Gives logistics and possibilities for journal writing for older students.

10

Integrating Spelling into the Reading-Writing Classroom

Grade 2: adding a word to the spelling chart

Implementing a Nontraditional Approach to Spelling

"What makes someone a good speller?"

"I think someone is a good speller if they write a lot and read a lot in school and at home" wrote Ben, a second-grader, on his end-of-the-year "spelling interview."

Ben was one of twenty-one second-graders and twenty-six third-graders participating in a new spelling program at our school, where most teachers were still using a traditional spelling approach.

Elaine Weiner, a second grade teacher, and I had been sharing concerns for several years about having to use a spelling text that teaches words in isolation without any meaningful integration of spelling into the language processes. Elaine's interest in making a change grew as we shared and discussed professional articles and books related to current spelling research and practice. Gradually, Elaine began to reshape her philosophy about the teaching of spelling. She felt the need for a spelling program that would reflect the whole language climate of her reading-writing classroom.

In the fall of 1988, when the spelling workbooks had not yet arrived, I approached Linda Cooper, a respected third grade teacher with a strong whole language background. We discussed the possibility of the three of us instituting a new spelling program. Elaine, Linda, and I then met to discuss the teaching of spelling as an integrated part of the reading-writing process. To us that meant that most of the words children would learn to spell would be chosen by them from their daily writing.

This was the first of weekly meetings that continued throughout the school year. At the first meeting we focused on management techniques, the use of spelling lists versus no lists, setting up our program, and documenting children's progress through daily writing. We continued to meet regularly to work out changes in the program, evaluate progress, and keep a log of our observations and reflections. In addition, this spelling support group provided a forum for the sharing of successes.

concerns, frustrations, and anecdotes. Our regular meetings promoted confidence, collegiality, and risk taking.

After establishing a general plan, we asked our principal, Dr. Bernice Stokes, for permission to implement a spelling program that was philosophically consistent with the way children learn. Dr. Stokes readily agreed, partly because of her own frustration with her daughter's failure to transfer spelling words from weekly tests to daily writing and partly because of her respect for us as teachers. She made it clear that our program should include ongoing assessment in the two classrooms as well as pre- and post-testing with the three other classes at both the second and third grade levels. The hope was that the post-tests would indicate that children in our programs were learning to spell at least as well as children using the traditional spelling programs.

Assessment of our informal integrated spelling program, which began in early October, involved four second grade and four third grade classes. Using twenty-five words from the district spelling curriculum and an additional twenty-five high-frequency words selected by the three of us, we set out to informally measure overall growth from October to June. The mean results from the four classes at each grade level on the October pre-tests were within five to seven percentage points. The grade 2 children spelled from 62 to 69 percent of the words correctly and the grade 3 children from 76 to 81 percent, indicating that the spelling abilities of the classes at each grade level were comparable.

Elaine and Linda gave their classes two more tests of high-frequency words during the school year to assess student growth. The results indicated that their students were mastering high-frequency words as a result of their immersion in a reading-writing classroom. Three times during the school year, Elaine and Linda also prepared paragraphs for proofreading. One score was given for the percentage of misspelled words circled and another score for the percentage of standard spellings written. An informal evaluation noted that students' proofreading abilities were developing.

In June, a post-test was administered to each of the eight classes in the second and third grades to informally measure the year's growth. The mean results among all the classes was again within 7 percentage points, with the range from 77 to 84 percent in both grades. It appeared that there was no advantage to teaching spelling with a traditional spelling text.

Elaine Weiner and Linda Cooper noted that most of the words students misspelled came from the district spelling curriculum lists. Students in their classes did significantly better on the high-frequency words, indicating that words that are seen and written often are learned better. The post-test results—including the better scores on high-frequency words—were also consistent the following year in another building for two teachers who used an integrated spelling approach.

Ongoing evaluation by Linda and Elaine involved keeping anecdotal records of students' writing, conferencing with students using the contents of their spelling and writing folders, giving proofreading exercises, and checking on high-frequency words.

At the end of the school year, the children in the informal, integrated program were administered a "spelling interview" questionnaire to determine their attitudes and what they had discovered about learning to spell (see Figure 10–1). Almost every child answered "yes" to the question, "Are you a good speller?"

Figure 10-1   Spelling Interview

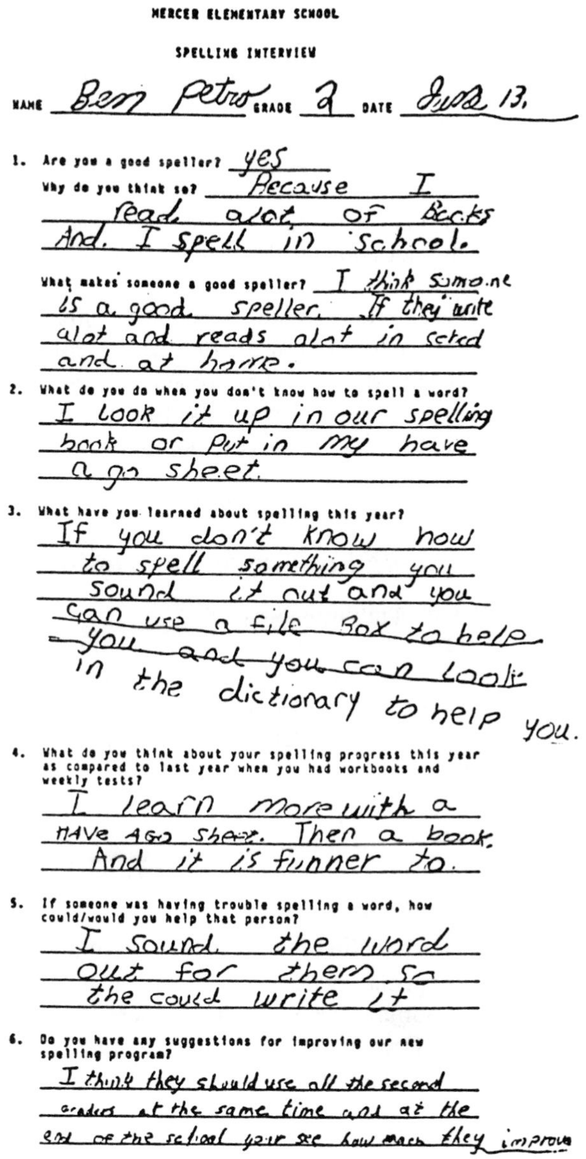

MERCER ELEMENTARY SCHOOL

SPELLING INTERVIEW

NAME *Benj Petro* GRADE *2* DATE *June 13.*

1. Are you a good speller? *yes*
   Why do you think so? *Because I read alot of Books And. I spell in school.*

   What makes someone a good speller? *I think someone is a good speller. If they write alot and reads alot in school and at home.*

2. What do you do when you don't know how to spell a word?
   I look it up in our spelling book or Put in my have a go sheet.

3. What have you learned about spelling this year?
   If you don't know how to spell something you sound it out and you can use a file Box to help you and you can look in the dictionary to help you.

4. What do you think about your spelling progress this year as compared to last year when you had workbooks and weekly tests?
   I learn more with a have ago sheet. Then a book. And it is funner to.

5. If someone was having trouble spelling a word, how could/would you help that person?
   I sound the word out for them so the could write it

6. Do you have any suggestions for improving our new spelling program?
   I think they should use all the second graders at the same time and at the end of the school year see how much they improve

When asked, "What makes someone a good speller?" a number of children responded, "A good speller reads a lot." To the question, "What do you do when you don't know how to spell a word?" a student responded, "I imagine what the word looks like in my mind, and if in writing it, it looks wrong, I try again." Several students responded, "You either look it up in the dictionary, look in your file box, or ask the person next to you."

To the question, "What have you learned about spelling this year?" these were typical student responses:

- To try again if I don't get it right the first time.
- I've learned you don't have to use a spelling workbook to learn to spell.
- I've learned how to correct my own mistakes in spelling.
- You can learn how to spell a lot of words if you really want to.

After the success of our integrated spelling program, four more teachers in other buildings in our district—a second grade teacher, a third grade teacher, and two fourth grade teachers—opted to integrate spelling into the language arts after they secured permission from their principals. At the same time, a small number of first grade teachers in our district continued to incorporate an integrated approach to spelling.

The remainder of this chapter examines a whole language view of spelling and recounts how a group of teachers in our district have translated the approach into classroom practice and evaluation. I believe, based on personal experience working with and observing learning disabled students, that the principles and strategies discussed here are as applicable to at-risk populations as they are to regular education students.

Understanding a Whole Language View of Spelling

A whole language view of spelling focuses on taking risks, teaching and applying spelling strategies, and recognizing and correcting misspellings when students edit or proofread their written work. This viewpoint recognizes first and foremost that spelling is learned and taught in the context of writing and that spelling competence, like all language competence, develops gradually over time.

The following principles apply:

Spelling Principles

1. Spelling should facilitate communication of written language, not limit it.
2. Spelling is developmental.
3. The need for standard spelling should be kept in proper perspective.
4. There should be no special spelling curriculum or regular lesson sequences. (From Kenneth Goodman, Brooks Smith, Robert Meredith, and Yetta Goodman, [Richard C. Owen, 1987], *Language and Thinking in School: A Whole-Language Curriculum*, pp. 300–301)

Spelling Stages

A whole language view of spelling, which is based on research, recognizes that children go through predictable stages in developing spelling strategies but that they go through these stages at their own rate. Invented spelling is not just tolerated; it is accepted and welcomed as a normal part of the process of becoming a competent speller. This view is very different from the traditional approach to spelling which expects perfect spelling from young children and which has all students in a classroom memorize the same predetermined list of words each week.

If one acknowledges the research that clearly demonstrates the stages all children go through in learning to spell, then the question becomes not whether to teach spelling as an integrated, developmental part of the language arts but how to accomplish this goal most effectively. Briefly stated, and based largely on the research of Richard Gentry (1982), the developmental stages learners go through in learning to spell include:

1. Prephonemic spelling Children scribble, form letters, and string letters together but without the awareness that letters represent phonemes or speech sounds. Children do, however, create meaningful messages through their exploration. Prephonemic spelling is typical of preschoolers and beginning kindergartners.

2. Early phonemic spelling There is a limited attempt to represent phonemes with letters, for example, using one or two letters for a word ("m" for "my" and "nt" for "night"). Early phonemic spelling is typical of many kindergarten and beginning first grade children.

3. Phonetic (or letter-name) spelling The child uses letters for phonemes—for example, "lik" for "like" and "brthr" for "brother." The child represents most phonemes, understands the concept of a word but is not quite reading yet. This is where we find many of our ending kindergartners and beginning first-graders.

4. Transitional spelling In this stage, children are internalizing much information about spelling patterns, and the words they write look like English words. For example, the child may write "skool" for "school" and "happe" for "happy." Rules are employed, but not always correctly. With reading and writing practice, children integrate more spelling rules and patterns. This stage usually includes first through third grade children.

5. Standard spelling At this stage, children spell most words correctly. We have found this stage occurs by the middle to the end of third grade or in fourth grade. Children are now ready to learn to spell homonyms, contractions, and irregular spellings, as well as to begin to internalize the rules that govern more difficult vowel and consonant combinations, word endings, and prefixes and suffixes. (We have chosen to use the term "standard spelling" instead of "correct spelling." Even when children have not reached the highest level, they are inventing spelling that is "correct" for their developmental level.)

Because many educators have not read the research on how spelling develops, they continue to employ and support spelling practices that are at odds with current research and theory concerning how children learn to spell. Before we can begin to move away from sequential, highly structured spelling programs, a secure knowledge base of how all language—including spelling—is learned is necessary. As educators, we also need to understand and be able to articulate that philosophy to ourselves, our administrators, our students, and the parents of our students. Even more important, we must already have established reading-writing classrooms in which children are reading and writing meaningful texts each day. Until that time, it is probably best to stay with the commercial spelling programs. (See "Resources" at the end of this chapter, especially Wilde, 1990, for help in putting research into practice.)

Components of an Integrated Spelling Program

The spelling program we developed and continue to modify is based on the principles just discussed, past teaching experiences, careful observation of students, and the current research we read and discuss. Our goal is to produce independent writers who are competent spellers. We believe that the best way to achieve this is to immerse students in a variety of meaningful daily reading and writing experiences.

While the implementation process has been slightly different for each teacher involved, we all continue to share the same philosophy: "Standard spelling is the consequence of writing and reading, not the access to it. . . . standard spelling is of little consequence if you do not write. Writing comes first!" (Bean and Bouffler, 1988, p. 47).

Children in our classrooms learn to spell the words they need, want, and are ready for through a variety of spelling strategies and resources.

Choosing Spelling Words

Words children work on for spelling mastery come from the following sources:

1. Words children misspell
2. Words children ask for
3. Words the teacher knows children need
4. Words relevant to a topic or theme

Emphasizing Spelling Strategies

In traditional programs, emphasis is on memorizing lists of words through repetition and drill. Since all the words for the week usually fit the same pattern or rule, it is not uncommon for students to do well on weekly tests and remain poor spellers. Because they are taught rules and not strategies, often students can spell the words only within the controlled workbook or testing framework. This is true as early as first grade. One insightful first-grader proclaimed, "You memorize the pattern, but you really don't know how to spell the words."

In an integrated approach, emphasis shifts to teaching students to utilize spelling strategies and to think about and apply what they have learned in the process of writing. Such an approach recognizes that the spelling of most words will occur in the normal context of reading and writing. Visual memory, sound-symbol relationships, and morphemic (base word) knowledge are developed implicitly and explicitly in teaching the following strategies:

1. Discovering the Rules

Whenever the teacher notices similar spelling errors being made by a number of students, a minilesson (a five- to ten-minute strategy-teaching session) is used to help students form generalizations about spelling rules. As an example, when children do not drop the "e" when adding "ing" to words such as "come," "write," and "have," the invented spellings ("comeing," "writeing," and "haveing") can be written on a transparency. Using an overhead projector, the teacher highlights the problem area and guides the students toward self-correction. Because students have encountered words in print over and over again when reading, they can usually offer the standard spellings and generate the rule. Specific spelling patterns, grapho-phonic generalizations, prefixes, suffixes, and root words are discussed at this time.

At times, words that fit a specific pattern are written on the overhead. Students are invited to come up one at a time and write another word that fits the pattern. Then the rule is generated by the class. Often a chart is made and kept hanging all week so that students can continue to add words that fit the pattern. Rules that work most consistently are the rules for suffixes (see Figure 10–2).

It has been interesting to note that children will also discover a rule before the rule is introduced in the basal spelling program. For example, "tion" in Figure 10–2 is not introduced until grade 4, yet this suffix regularly comes up in grade 2.

2. Recognizing the Limited Utility of Rules

While commercial spelling programs emphasize spelling rules and look for words to fit the pattern, many English words do not fit a rule. Frank Smith notes, "The 'rules' of spelling can be numbered in the hundreds and still carry only a fifty percent probability of being correct for any particular word" (1988, p. 18). When we discover a rule, we also note the exceptions.

3. Applying the Known to the Unknown

We use this strategy a lot with students. Through wide reading and writing students automatically write many words in standard spelling. Often when a student is working through a word on his Have-a-Go sheet (discussed in the next

Figure 10-2   Suffix Rules for -ion Words as Generated by Fourth-graders

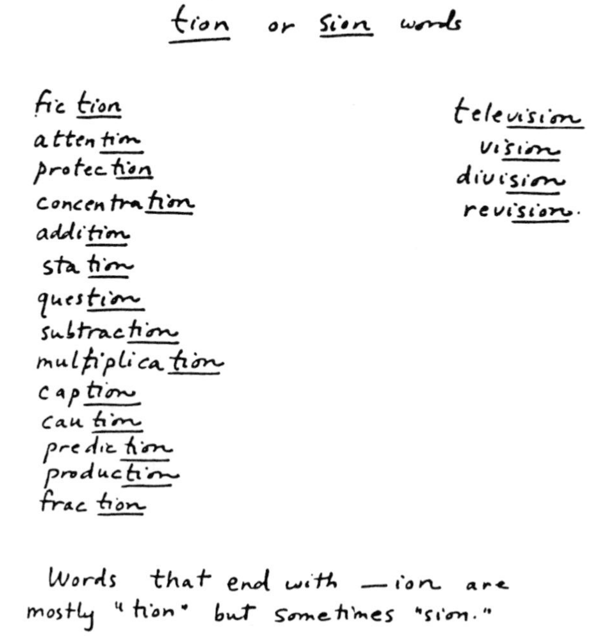

section), we might say something like, "You already know how to spell the word
_____. This word ends the same way." It is important to show students how to
make connections so they can eventually do this on their own.

For example, when a grade 3 student spelled "anyd" for "annoyed," I slowly
pronounced the word and asked, "What word do you know that has the 'oy'
sound?" When he did not respond, I asked, "Do you know 'boy' and 'toy'?" The
student then attempted to write the word and wrote "anoyd." After I asked,
"What do you know about words that have the 'd' sound at the end, like 'stopped'
and 'walked'?" he was able to write his second attempt as "anoyed." Lastly, I put a
caret in "an˄oyed" and asked, "What missing letter could go here? Think about
other words you know." Not only was the student able to write the word correctly,
but because he had worked through the problem areas he would probably not
misspell it again.

4. Proofreading

Proofreading in spelling (which is most often used when a child is ready to edit a
piece of writing that is ready to go to final copy) includes two separate activities:

1. Examination—identifying as many misspelled words as possible
   We have our students circle these words with a colored pencil.
2. Production—correctly spelling as many of the misspelled words as possible
   We expect students to correctly spell at least three to five of the words.

When a piece of writing is being brought to final copy, the child takes a colored
pencil and finds and corrects as many misspelled words as possible. The teacher
then serves as the final editor and uses a different-colored pencil or marker to
identify the misspelled words the student cannot find and correct. The Have-a-Go
sheet is often used with the student as a worksheet in moving from the invented
spelling to standard spelling.

Systematic attention needs to be given to proofreading so students develop
responsibility for this necessary lifelong skill. We have found that students are more
effective proofreaders if there is a lapse of time between writing and proofreading.
I have also found that it works well to suggest that students look for misspellings by
reading one word at a time from right to left, starting with the last word in the last
line of their writing. In that way, they are focusing only on individual words and
not on content.

Initially, placing the responsibility on students to find and correct spelling errors
may seem burdensome to the teacher. Because teachers, especially at the secondary
level, have traditionally found and corrected all errors, students may not take the
activity seriously. However, no real learning takes place if the teacher continues to
make most corrections. In fact, students tend to repeat the errors in subsequent
writing. It is important to remain firm and not to accept papers until students have
done their own proofreading and/or checked their papers with a peer. (This
expectation does not apply in first grade.) Teachers find that when they expect
students to assume responsibility for proofreading and when they have given
enough demonstrations, students can do much more than teachers had previously
thought they could. (See Figure 10–3 for an example of the work of a third grade L.
D. student.) However, once students have done their best proofreading, the teacher
avoids unnecessary frustration by spelling the remaining words "for free."

Figure 10-3   A Third Grade L.D. Student Assumes Responsibility for Proofreading

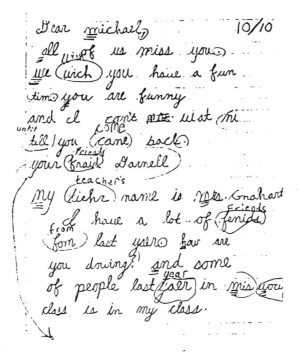

5. Using the Dictionary

We teach the use of the dictionary as the need arises, when the meaning of a word needed for reading is not clear from the context or when students desire specific information or want to expand their vocabulary. If the dictionary is referred to often and meaningfully, and the teacher demonstrates how to use it, students will readily learn about guide words, diacritical marks, accents, pronunciations, variant spellings, and multiple meanings. We have a variety of dictionaries available, including an excellent unabridged dictionary such as *Webster's Third International.* Instead of one set of dictionaries for all children in the classroom, several different sets, with fewer copies of each, will stimulate more interest and provide more information. Also, if a computer with a spelling checker is available, children can be taught how to use it.

Dictionary use can also be combined with vocabulary study and etymology (origin/derivation of words). Older students enjoy searching for the derivatives of a base word and reading word meanings in the dictionary. Some teachers use a challenge word of the day or week and invite students to find and discuss variations. For example, for the base word "cycle," a group of fourth-graders came up with "bicycle," "tricycle," "recycle," "cyclical," "cyclic," "cycling," "cyclist."

Resources for Developing Spelling Strategies

We use the following resources to develop strategies in a print-rich environment that provides students with lots of opportunities for reading, writing, and collaboration.

• ***Have-a-Go sheets*** The Have-a-Go sheet, adapted from Australia (Jo-Ann Parry and David Hornsby, *Write On: A Conference Approach to Writing* [Heinemann, 1988], p. 61), is based on the idea that children, like adults, can usually identify a misspelled word even if they cannot spell it correctly. Children choose misspelled words from their daily writing and attempt to "have-a-go" at standard spellings. The teacher then conferences with the student to guide thinking processes and confirm or help with the final, standard spelling. (See Figure 10–4 for a low-ability second-grader's Have-a-Go sheet.) This is the technique I use the most when I am unsure of a spelling: I write the word several different ways to see which spelling *looks* right.

Teachers that try Have-a-Go sheets are quickly convinced of their effectiveness. Fourth grade teacher Brenda Spivey says,

> After having had the Have-a-Go sheet explained to me for the first time, I enthusiastically tried it out on my class. I was amazed to find out that it really does work. One little girl, a very poor speller, having used the sheet and spelled a word herself, had a look on her face that could only say, "At last I can spell!" The change in this child alone convinced me that there are methods of teaching spelling that work, unlike the weekly test method. I'm convinced that Have-a-Go teaches children to use a tried and true method that adults have always used!

• ***Peer help*** When students don't know how to spell a word and have tried several sources, they will often ask a peer, "How do you spell ______?" Students quickly learn who the good spellers are and seek them out.

Figure 10–4 Low-Ability Second-grader's Have-a-Go sheet

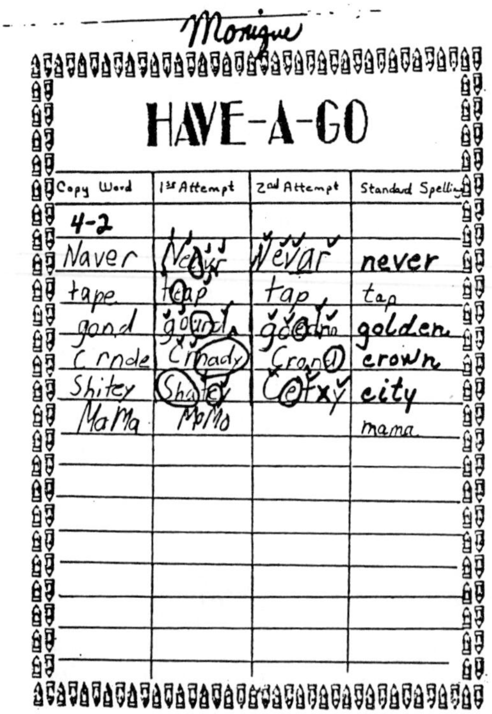

Monique

HAVE-A-GO

Copy Word	1st Attempt	2nd Attempt	Standard Spelling
4-2			
Naver	Naver	Nevar	never
tape	tap	tap	tap
gond	good	gcedn	golden
Crnde	Cmady	Cron	crown
Shitey	Shatey	Cetxy	city
MaMa	MoMo		mama

If another adult is nearby, this is the technique I use most often if I am still unsure of a word after having written it several ways. We need to encourage collaboration as an important spelling strategy.

• *Minilessons*   Minilessons involve direct instruction through demonstration as well as provide opportunities for student participation and practice. They are often done whole class, usually at the end of a weekly time set aside for spelling and usually involving the overhead projector. The lessons are based on the needs of the children and on the belief that students don't just "pick up" all the skills they need. Minilessons also occur one-to-one when the teacher conferences with a child. It helps to keep in mind that only about 25 percent of the children may actually apply the skill that is taught to their own writing. A minilesson will probably need to be demonstrated over and over again. As in all language learning, children will acquire the skill when they are ready.

A typical minilesson involves calling the children's attention to a problem some of the students are experiencing. For example, in conferencing one-to-one with a class of fourth-graders, I noticed many were having difficulty knowing when to double the final consonant before adding "ing" or "ed." I wrote some words on the overhead projector (see Figure 10–5, top) and asked them to give me a rule. I wrote down what they told me, "Before 'ing,' double the consonant." I then challenged

Figures 10–5 and 10–6   Working with the Class on a Double Consonant Rule and Testing Its Validity

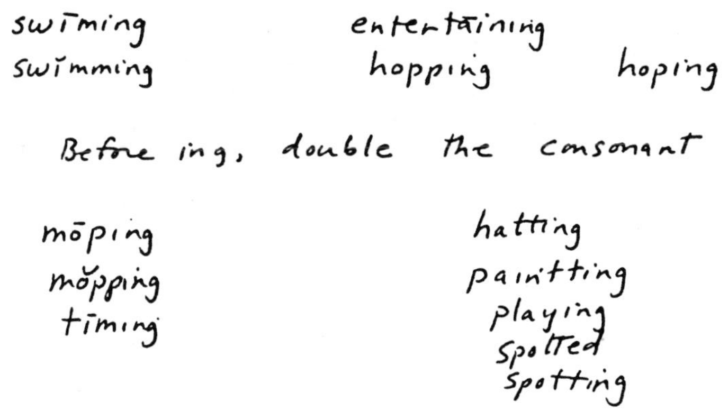

Figure 10–6

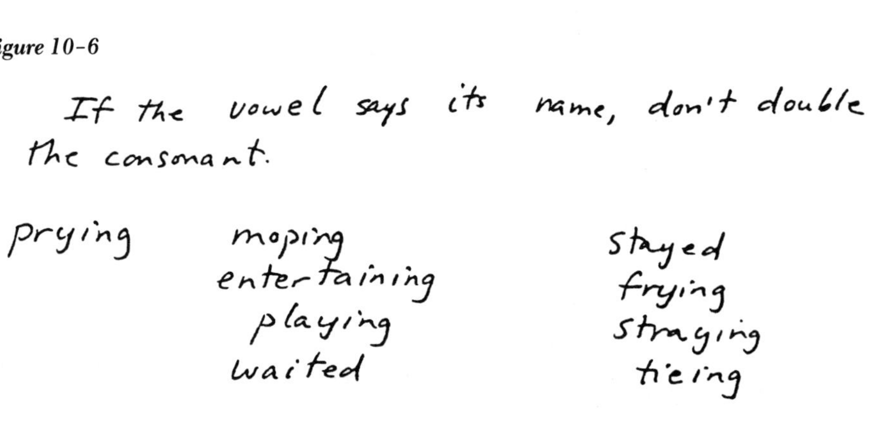

them by writing other words (see Figure 10–5, bottom) and asking, "Are you correct?"

There was heated discussion, and an L. D. student who had spelling difficulties gave the rule, "If the vowel says its name, don't double the consonant." I then asked for, and they gave me, words to test out the validity of the rule (see Figure 10–6). Next, I wrote, with input from the students, several words with doubled consonants before the ending and challenged them to make another generalization. They took about fifteen minutes to come up with the detailed rule (see Figure 10–7). Then a student simplified it all by saying, "When the vowel is short we double."

Finally, I called out words orally one at a time and challenged the students to apply what we had been discussing and to spell the words (see Figure 10–8). There was some hesitation as each student who volunteered gave me the desired spelling, but every student spelled his or her word correctly. Usually a minilesson lasts five to ten minutes, but this one had lasted forty-five minutes! It was time well spent. Attention had never wavered, and a difficult concept had been internalized for most of the students.

A minilesson may also be used to talk about words the teacher feels students should know how to spell. For example, Linda Cooper tells her third grade students that she expects the following often misspelled words to be spelled correctly at all times: "said," "what," "when," "too," "color." Students add these words to their file boxes and are expected to refer to them as needed. First grade teacher Peg Rimedio posts a "Words to Remember" list to call attention to words students are using over and over again in their daily writing.

Marcy Silver, a third grade teacher who has just completed her first year with an integrated spelling program, comments:

> While most of the minilessons came from the context of the students' writing, I also checked the spelling workbook to be sure all the skills were covered. Once in a while, I put in a lesson I just thought they should have. The kids love the minilessons. Hands are flying in the air. Kids gather around to write on the charts. There is lots of excitement.

Figure 10-7   The Final Detailed Double Consonant Rule

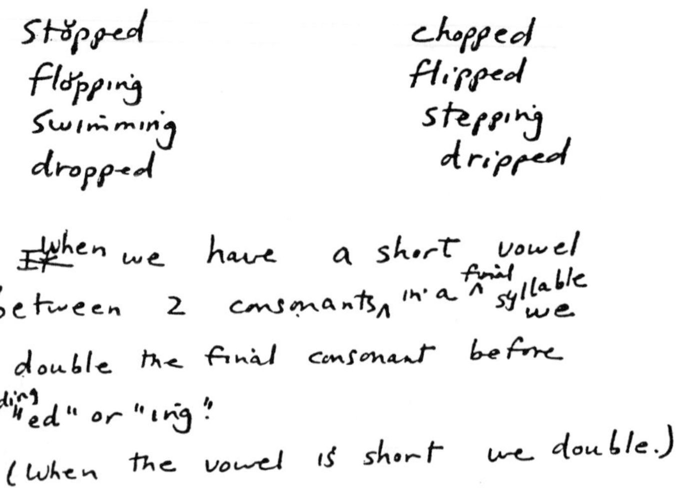

Figure 10-8   Applying the Class's Double Consonant Rule

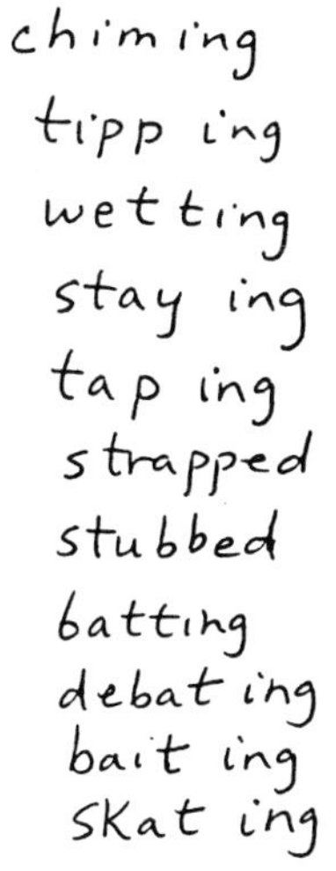

chim ing
tipp ing
wet ting
stay ing
tap ing
s trapped
stubbed
batting
debat ing
bait ing
skat ing

• *Personal dictionary*   Once the child has discovered the standard spelling of a word (usually after it has been worked through on the Have-a-Go sheet), the word is recorded on a 3 by 5 inch card and filed alphabetically in the student's individual file box. Alphabetizing is also taught here as students are expected to file cards in order. Children add the words they want to spell and that teachers expect them to spell. High-frequency words are also recorded in the file box so they are easily accessible. Students frequently use the file box as a reference in their daily writing. There is a lot of excitement as students use their individual file boxes as personal word banks.

Some teachers prefer to have students keep an "I Can Spell" list in the back of their journals. Having a booklet to which pages can be added in alphabetical order would also work well. Each student may also make a personal thesaurus.

• *Wall charts*   Wall charts are used to group words around a theme: key vocabulary from a story, common words that need to be spelled correctly, content words, family words, holiday words, and so on. Lists and charts are also compiled to go along with the seasons, months, and topics of study and interest. In addition to wall charts, words from a theme chart may be typed in large print and put into a report cover for reference. Such lists are especially useful in the primary grades where students do not yet have a large core of words they can spell.

In a first grade room, it would not be unusual to see a variety of lists posted in enlarged print. For example, in February one teacher had lists posted for the following: family words (to aid journal writing), winter words, February words, and guinea pig words (for the class pet), as well as various phonics charts. These lists had all been generated with and by the children.

Additionally, in a minilesson as a rule is generated, a chart is started with the rule stated at the top (see Figure 10–9). The children then supply as many words as they can to fit the rule. The chart is then posted, and children are encouraged to continue adding words they find in their reading. After a period of time, usually a week or two, the teacher and the children review the chart and make needed corrections.

Figure 10-9   Creating a Chart Using a Class-generated Rule

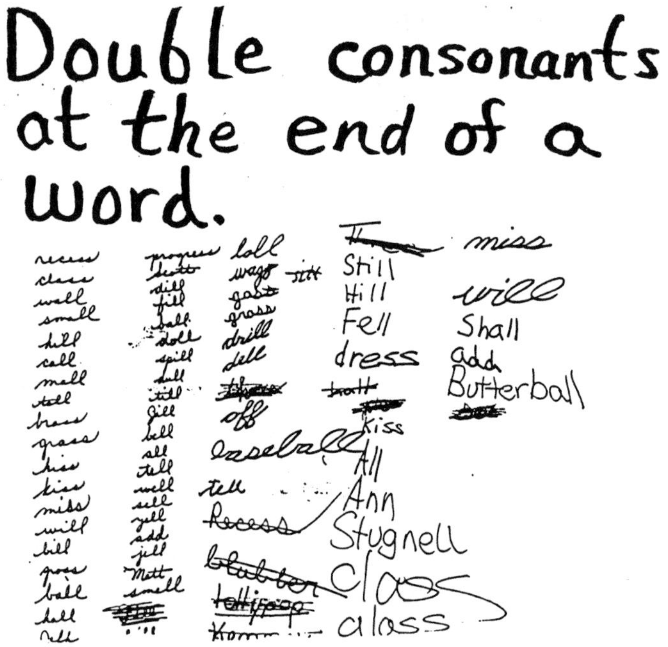

Double consonants at the end of a word.

[handwritten word lists illustrating the double-consonant rule, including words such as: still, Hill, Fell, dress, miss, will, Shall, add, Butterball, Ann, Stugnell, class, recess, kiss, off, tell, baseball]

● *Spelling Big Books*   After a chart is taken down from the wall and corrections have been made, a final alphabetized copy is prepared as a page for the class Spelling Big Book. These pages are usually completed in large, legible print by parent volunteers. Often they highlight the repeated pattern in each word in another color so that it stands out to the students. The Spelling Big Book includes a table of contents and serves as a reference for children to use in their daily writing. Because of the different needs of each group of children, a new Spelling Big Book is created each year.

● *Other spelling references*   A variety of visual references is available to students in the classroom, including commercial dictionaries, thesauruses, textbooks, encyclopedias, trade books, magazines, newspapers, spelling reference books, posters, charts, and topic reference books (for example, for seasons, months, holidays, or events). Our students also have consumable spelling resources for daily personal use. (See pp. 261–262 for a description and ordering information.) In addition, books corresponding to a theme or topic are developed by the class for easy reference. For example, a special presidential election book was compiled that listed words such as "Democrat," "Republican," "politician," "registration," and "majority."

● *Spelling games*   Spelling games—commercial, computer, teacher made, and student made—are available and used regularly. These games aid students in developing standard spellings in an informal setting.

● *Conferencing*   As children are involved in their daily reading and writing activities, the teacher—at times with my help as the language arts resource teacher and/or a parent volunteer—confers with individual students. Usually the teacher guides students on their Have-a-Go sheets. Students select misspelled words from their journals, writing folders, or any other piece of writing they are working on and bring them to standard spelling with the help of the teacher.

Often the teacher intervenes after a first attempt at standard spelling. She points out which parts of the word are correct and which still need to be worked on. She may guide the child to the standard spelling by pointing out previously mentioned strategies. More and more, conferencing is occurring as part of the writing process, when there is a need to bring a piece to final copy and standard spelling is expected.

Organizing and Managing an Integrated Spelling Program

The key to management in spelling is making the environment safe for risk taking. Children develop the confidence and desire to solve their own spelling problems without worrying about getting a word right for the teacher or on a formal weekly test. Children recognize that their best attempts are not just tolerated but are genuinely accepted, encouraged, and congratulated.

The Need for Effective Parent Communication

Parents are initially uneasy about a more relaxed view of spelling. Based on their own schooling and experiences with their other children, they expect and rarely question the traditional approach to spelling with its workbook pages to complete, words to study, and weekly tests. Many parents have welcomed the Thursday night spelling drills for the next day's test as a sure way of participating in their child's education. Furthermore, parents are not generally aware of the research supporting a developmental view of spelling.

In addition, some parents get the message that spelling doesn't matter when teachers talk about accepting invented spellings. One parent told me, "We're producing educated people who can't spell." Her older child, a fifth-grader, was still misspelling words like "they" and "friend" in her journal, and the parent was now understandably quite skeptical about invented spelling. While it is acceptable for older children to use invented spelling in rough drafts, we need to expect high-frequency words to be spelled correctly while at the same time we encourage invented spelling for the more difficult words. We have to be very careful to give the message that standard spelling is important and is expected.

Whenever there is a change in programs, parents must be well informed. A third grade teacher who had not informed all parents of her new spelling program found out just how critical the need is for parental education. A student in her class brought home her spelling book with her Have-a-Go sheets. Her mother erased all the student's attempts and made her write all the words correctly. The student returned to school quite upset.

Sharing our new spelling program with parents continues to be a high priority. Letters go home explaining that the spelling text will not be used and explaining the philosophy and research supporting the new approach (see Appendix J4). Teachers discuss the spelling program during curriculum night (open house) and explain the transition that will occur from invented spellings to standard spellings.

Current research and children's work samples from previous years are used to support teachers' statements and to allay parents' anxieties about invented spelling. Usually teachers share writing samples from an average student from September to June so parents have an idea of what to expect and what is considered typical.

It has been my experience that if the teacher is knowledgeable about spelling development and current research—as well as comfortable with a holistic view of spelling—parents respond positively. In one of our weekly language arts support group meetings that focused on spelling, two first grade teachers shared parents' reactions to invented spelling. One teacher said that the parents of her students were delighted with her spelling program while the other teacher reported that many of her parents had concerns about spelling development. I looked at the two teachers and smiled to myself. One was totally comfortable with invented spelling and one was not. The parents were merely reflecting the messages the teachers had been sending, consciously or not.

Keeping Your Administrators Well Informed

Administrators are busy people who do not appreciate learning about a new program after it has been implemented. One principal was quite embarrassed when she learned from a parent that no spelling workbooks were being used in her child's class.

Consult your administrator before making any major changes in your spelling program. Discuss what you plan to do and share copies of articles and books that support a holistic view of spelling (see pp. 260–261). Invite your principal into your classroom regularly and let him or her know how things are progressing. Let your principal know what spelling lessons have been taught through minilessons. (See Figure 10–10 for a third grade teacher's first semester record, which she duplicated for her administrator.) In that way, when a parent questions the new program or asks how spelling is being addressed, the principal can answer specifically.

Organizing for Success

• *Setting aside time for Spelling*   In getting started, we have found it helpful to designate a consistent, weekly time of forty-five minutes to an hour when children find words from their daily writing to work through on their Have-a-Go sheets. Usually students circle five or more words that they know are misspelled and transfer them to their Have-a-Go sheets. Some teachers choose to do this activity in the editing stage of the writing process when pieces are being brought to final copy. Other teachers prefer to have children choose one new word each day and add it alphabetically to their file boxes. In any case, this is the time when the teacher is available for guidance and instruction.

• *The importance of demonstration*   Before students use the Have-a-Go sheet (or peer conferencing or peer testing), Don Holdaway's developmental model for language learning is employed. Demonstrations will need to take place repeatedly until students understand and can apply the procedures.

To begin with, students are asked to find a word in their writing that they know is misspelled but that they would like to be able to spell correctly. When doing a demonstration, I place a blank transparency of a Have-a-Go sheet (Appendix I) on

Figure 10-10   A Third Grade Teacher's First Semester Spelling Record

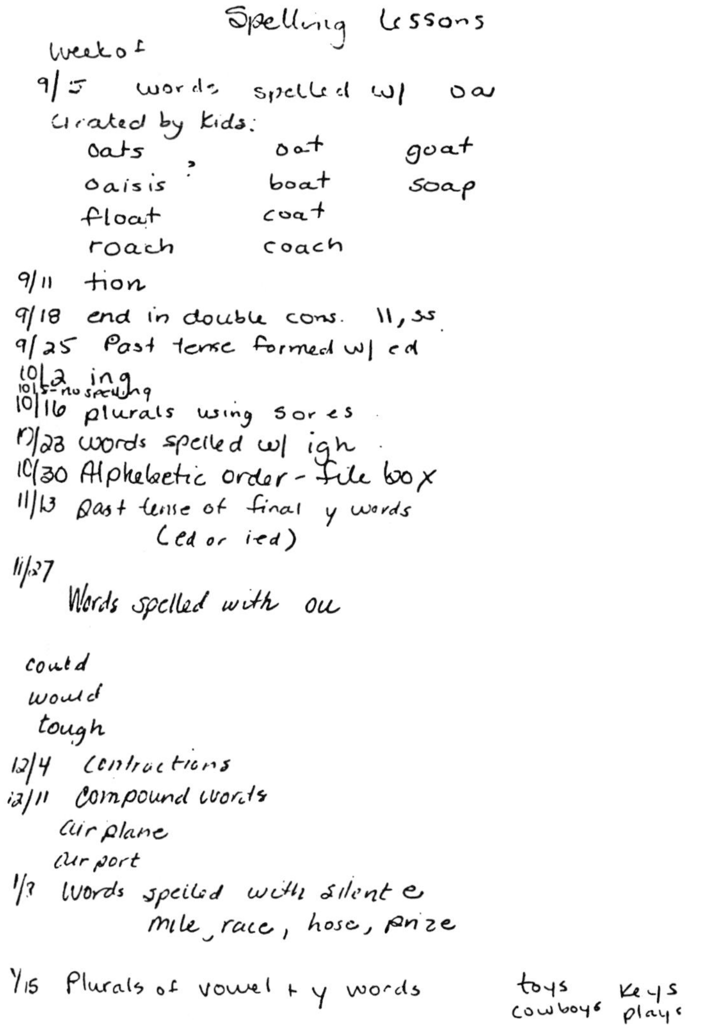

Spelling Lessons

Week of
9/5   words spelled w/ oa
Crated by kids:

oats ,   oat   goat
oasis ?   boat   soap
float   coat
roach   coach

9/11   tion
9/18   end in double cons. ll, ss
9/25   Past tense formed w/ ed
10/2   ing
10/5 - no spelling
10/16 plurals using s or es
10/23 words spelled w/ igh
10/30 Alphabetic order - file box
11/13 Past tense of final y words
        (ed or ied)

11/27
  Words spelled with ou

could
would
tough

12/4   Contractions
12/11 Compound words
       airplane
       airport
1/8   Words spelled with silent e
       mile, race, hose, prize

1/15   Plurals of vowel + y words   toys   keys
                                          cowboys plays

the overhead projector. A volunteer says a word with its invented spelling. Then we talk through and work through various attempts to spell the word correctly. (See Figure 10-11 for a demonstration that took place at the beginning of second grade.)

First, I slowly pronounce the word, stretching out each syllable. Sometimes the correct pronunciation—especially for a student who has difficulty hearing sounds in words—may be enough for the student to find and correct the error(s). Then I ask the student, "Which part looks right to you?" I will often put a check over the letters that are correct. Next, I ask, "Which part looks wrong to you?" Teachers are always amazed that even poor spellers and L. D. students can often identify the part of the word that looks wrong even if they cannot spell the word. I usually circle that part and ask the student to make a first attempt. After the first attempt, I continue to guide the student with prompts such as the following:

Figure 10-11   Talking through the Spelling of Words: Demonstrating Have-a-Go

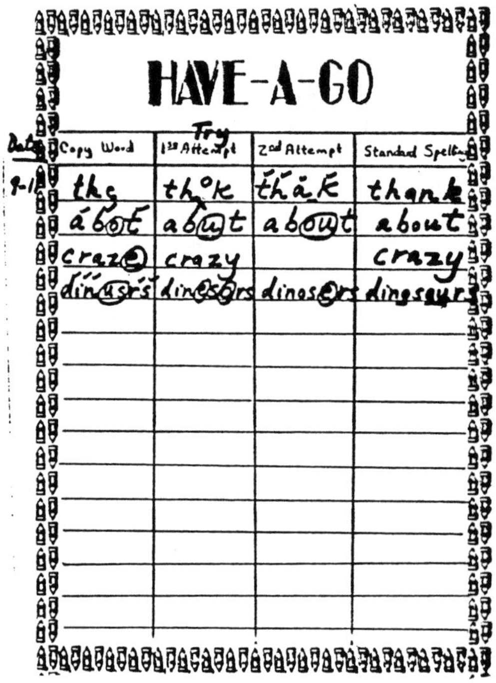

- Does it look right now?
- What else could you try?
- What other letters could you use there to make that same sound?
- What do you know about words that have the _____ (for example, "er") sound at the end?
- How else could you spell that?
- You're missing a letter here. (Put in a caret.) What do you think it could be?
- Do you know how to spell _____? This word has a part that's the same.
- Take a look at the wall chart we worked on the other day. Your word is similar.
- What can you do to help yourself?

I verbalize some approaches that can be used if the student doesn't come up with strategies. Finally, I write the standard spelling in the last column, telling the student to look at the word carefully, "especially the tricky part that gave you trouble" and to come up to the overhead projector and write the word. Because the students have been actively involved in working through the trouble spot, even the poor spellers almost always write their word correctly.

- *Utilizing parent volunteers*   Especially the first year, we have found it essential to have several parent volunteers come in weekly to assist with the editing and proofreading processes and the Have-a-Go activity sheets. Parents have also been helpful in transferring spelling words from wall charts to the class Spelling Big Book. If volunteers are not available, students from higher grades may be used. As the teaching of spelling becomes more and more a natural part of all writing the need for volunteer help will lessen, although this may take several years to occur.

Welcoming parents into the classroom on a regular basis is also good for public relations. One first grade mother who helped weekly with journal writing was openly skeptical about invented spelling. She became convinced only after she *saw* her child, and all children in the classroom, internalizing spelling generalizations and making major spelling gains. This parent, who was active and vocal in the Parent-Teacher Association, shared her positive views with the community.

• *Keeping track of skills*   Teachers that move from a traditional spelling program to an integrated one initially find it useful to list all of the skills lessons covered in the spelling workbook program and to check these off as they are taught. Not only does this give the teacher some needed security; as already noted, the results can be shared with parents and administrators.

Many teachers are beginning to keep anecdotal records that note a student's growth in spelling as part of growth in writing. (See Chap. 13, "Evaluation.")

• *Materials needed*

Spelling organizer. Every student has a spelling organizer that serves as a record of the words she has chosen to learn to spell. This bound booklet takes the place of the traditional workbook and includes at the front a self-check list for learning new spellings, a cumulative record of about twelve to fifteen Have-a-Go sheets with Can You Spell It? sheets on the reverse side, and sheets for periodic peer testing (see Figure 10–12).

With the Have-a-Go sheets, we have found that two attempts at conventional spelling are usually sufficient. Three attempts, which we tried last year, did not work well for second-graders. However, upper grade teachers found that some students liked and needed three or more attempts.

Linda Cooper, who designed our original spelling organizer, now uses a simple pocket folder with Am I Becoming a Good Speller? on one side and Have-a-Go sheets, stapled cumulatively and handed out one at a time as needed, on the other side. As with any management tool, teachers need to make adjustments to suit their own needs.

File boxes. Each student also has a file box that holds 3 by 5 inch cards with alphabetical dividers. These supplies are purchased with student money from the annual supply fee. Some teachers save money and have students make their own dividers. Elaine Weiner has her students purchase their index cards and alphabetical dividers in the class store, thereby integrating math and language.

In first grade, Peg Rimedio uses index cards in an envelope stapled to the inside back cover of the writing journal. After words are mastered and listed on the "I Can Spell" sheet, they are taken home. New cards come from the teacher as she sees the need for specific words or as children request them.

Dictionaries. Each child has a copy of a compact personal dictionary and access to complete commercial dictionaries (see pp. 261–262).

Chart paper. We use large, sturdy chart paper (24 by 35 inches). We punch holes at the top or sides for ring binders so that pages may be added and moved as needed for the Spelling Big Book.

Figure 10-12   Pages from the Spelling Organizer

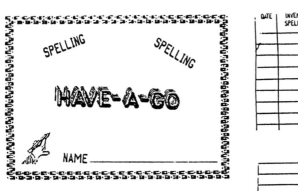

DATE	INVENTED SPELLING	1ST ATTEMPT	2ND ATTEMPT	3RD ATTEMPT	STANDARD SPELLING

CAN YOU SPELL IT ?

PEER TESTING

DATE	WORDS	DATE	WORDS

Am I Becoming a Good Speller? Very likely you are if you can say...

I *care* about spelling

I will need spelling all the time I am in school. My parents want me to be a good speller. When I leave school, people will expect me to spell well.

I *write* often

The more I write, the more I am practicing spelling. I may not stop to check a spelling as I write my first draft, but I always check when I revise the draft.

I *proof-read* my writing

I finally proof-read any writing I will pass to readers. In doing this, I inspect every letter and all punctuation. Sometimes I also get a partner to check my "proofing."

I *read every day*

Reading leaves impressions of spelling in my mind. It also adds to the number of words I may use. While reading, I sometimes pause to notice spellings.

I *explore* words

For example, I notice letter patterns like *tion, ough, qu*. And prefixes (like *dis-*) and suffixes (like *-less*). And meaning stems, as in para*graph*, bio*graphy*, tele*graphic*.

I *check* to be sure

Sometimes while writing I ask for the spelling of a word. But I know that the final way to settle a doubt about a spelling is to consult a dictionary.

I *learn* new spellings

1 Look at the new word and say it softly.
2 Cover it and try to "see" it in the mind.
3 Write it from memory.
4 Check (and if incorrect, repeat the four steps).

There are many other spelling ideas worth trying, such as...

• Keep adding to a personal list of "Words I Have Learned to Spell."
• Find and play spelling and language games that you enjoy.
• Keep improving your handwriting, because that will help your spelling
• Try out every spelling idea your teacher shows you and make a habit of any idea that works well for you, e.g., working with a partner

R. D. Walshe, for The Primary English Teaching Association, Sydney Australia. Reproduced with permission.

Post-it notes. Some teachers like students to add words to the spelling chart on Post-its. In that way, words that are found not to fit the rule or pattern may simply be removed. Post-its are also great for alphabetizing practice. Students work together to put the remaining Post-its words in alphabetical order before a final chart is made.

Colored pencils and pens for editing and proofreading.

What Happens during Spelling Time

• <u>*Choosing words to learn to spell*</u>   Some teachers have children choose words from their journals, while others, who prefer not to use journals at all for this purpose, ask students to select words from other writing. Usually teachers ask students to circle the misspelled words before transferring them to their Have-a-Go sheets.

Students are encouraged to choose "important" words they will need to use again and not words that they will rarely use. Students become quite proficient in choosing appropriate words. We have also noticed that, overall, they choose much harder words than those in the basal spelling program.

We usually expect students to find at least five misspelled words, although sometimes they will choose more. Every once in a while we have a natural speller who has few misspelled words. We can utilize that talent by having the student help his or her classmates in the same way we do.

• *Having-a-Go*   Students put the date in the left-hand margin on their Have-a-Go sheets and work through at least five words. They are encouraged to use all appropriate strategies and available resources to arrive at the standard spelling of a word. Usually we tell the students to make only one attempt on each word and then wait for a conference. In the meantime, students work on drafts and revisions of writing in progress.

• *Conferencing*   Conferencing occurs with the teacher, a peer, or a parent volunteer. After a child has worked through the first or several attempts to spell a word correctly, he is guided in finding the trouble spots. The conference is essentially a one-to-one minilesson. Teachers also take the time to check file boxes and spelling organizers to be sure words are being added and spelled correctly.

• *Can You Spell It? sheets*   After the word has been worked through to standard spelling, the child looks at it carefully and writes it on the Can You Spell It? sheet (on the reverse side of the Have-a-Go). This may take place as part of the conference, and I might say something like: "Now, carefully look at the tricky part. That's right. It's just those two letters that gave you trouble. Good. Now write the word here on your Can You Spell It? sheet." The child then writes the word. "Now check yourself. Did you get it right? . . . Good."

The student now takes a 3 by 5 inch card and adds the word alphabetically to her file box. If the child misspells the word, she is referred to her Am I Becoming a Good Speller? folder and is reminded to go through the four steps for learning new spellings:

1. Look at the new word and say it softly.
2. Cover it and try to "see" it in the mind.
3. Write it from memory.
4. Check (if incorrect, repeat the four steps).

• *Minilesson*   The minilesson, as discussed earlier in this chapter, takes place regularly as needs arise.

• *Peer testing*   While some teachers believe all testing is unnecessary, others opt for peer testing, either when students feel they are ready or on a weekly basis. First grade teacher Peg Rimedio does voluntary testing of students' individual words with the help of fourth grade volunteers. Every Friday Elaine Weiner's second-graders test each other on the words they worked through that week. There is no grading of tests by the teacher. However, any word that is missed automatically goes on the next week's Have-a-Go sheet. Elaine says her students' enthusiasm for peer testing is evident. Many students voluntarily copy down their words and take them home to study. Elaine checks first to be sure they are written correctly.

Teachers note that students who are tested on their own words get almost all the words right. It has also been interesting to note that even the poorest spellers know when they've misspelled a word.

Spelling in Kindergarten and First Grade

First grade teacher Peg Rimedio, a former kindergarten teacher, suggests the following.

Kindergarten   Informally noticing beginning and ending sounds in poems, charts, and stories is all the teacher needs to do at this level. As in grades 1 and 2, students can be asked to predict how a word begins or ends as the teacher is writing an experience chart, journal entry, or group story.

Grade 1

1. Have lots of words around the room for reference.
2. Introduce Have-a-Go sheets, the dictionary, and the editing process in a relaxed, informal way. Emphasize exposure and exploration rather than marking what is correct or incorrect. Don't expect mastery.
3. Call spelling activities (noting word parts, rules, and patterns) "spelling" so that children and parents know they are doing spelling.
4. Explore alternatives to traditional spelling tests that put young children under unnecessary pressure. A procedure could be worked out for voluntary tests so that kids can see what they have mastered if they want to.

Evaluation

Teacher Observations from the First Year of an Integrated Spelling Program

From the time our informal, integrated spelling program was introduced, we teachers noticed that the students were enthusiastic and positive. As they were reading, children became aware of how words are spelled. Occasionally, a child would remark, "Oh, so that's how you spell that word." Students readily added words to the classroom spelling charts as they became aware of words that fit a particular pattern.

It was interesting to see students challenge themselves by choosing to learn to spell words that were more difficult than their teachers might have chosen. (See Figure 10–4 for a second-grader's Have-a-Go sheet in early fall.) Students also came to see the need for proofreading. One third-grader commented, "I finished my story. I'm taking it home to go over it." A majority of the students also enjoyed making classroom spelling games. This led to the unexpected bonus of learning cooperation and collaboration as the children worked in small groups.

Parents were amazed at the growth in their children's spellings. In fact, the initial fear about having to defend this new program never materialized. Positive comments were made to teachers informally and at parent-teacher conferences. Many parents verbalized that they liked the spelling program. "It's more meaningful and a better way for children to learn how to spell" was a typical comment.

There were some unexpected outcomes. Elaine Weiner and Linda Cooper had made a list of the specific objectives introduced in the spelling workbook and district curriculum guide. They were surprised and pleased to find that the children had already discovered about 20 percent of the rules in just the first two months of school. Another surprise was the frequency of invented spellings that was still occurring in rough drafts. We thought standard spelling might occur with greater frequency. Children, however, found and standardized spellings more easily and with greater frequency while proofreading.

Finally, we came to appreciate spelling as a developmental process and felt it was probably unrealistic to expect mastery of certain words in one year, even if the words had been introduced. For instance "too," "two," and "to" remained a difficult concept for second-graders, as did "their," "they're," and "there" for third-graders.

Meaningful Evaluation of Spelling

We believe that evaluation of spelling should be a natural part of the writing process. There are many meaningful ways students, teachers, and parents can note spelling progress without resorting to whole-class testing. Daily writing, including journals, stories, narratives, content pieces, and poetry, can all be used for evidence of spelling growth. Personal spelling records such as dictionaries, Words I Can Spell booklets, and file boxes are all ways for children to record words they are now spelling.

Developing proofreading skills is also an excellent way to build spelling abilities. Even as early as second grade, teachers may reasonably expect students to bring a piece of writing to final copy about once a month and get as close as possible to standard spelling.

To note changes in student attitudes and strategies being used, spelling inventories and interviews may be scheduled at the beginning and end of the school year (see Figure 10–1). An interview may even be done whole class. In Ellen Rubin's second grade during the last week of school in June 1990, I asked the children to tell me what good spellers do. I posed the question orally and then randomly called on students who volunteered. On the overhead projector, I wrote their responses exactly as the students gave them to me and in the order stated:

What Strategies Do Good Spellers Use to Get Standard Spelling?

1. Give the word as many attempts as you need.
2. You have to read the word a lot. You have to see the word a lot in stories.
3. Try to memorize words that you need most.
4. The long words are the easy words, and the short words are the hard words because you can't sound out the short words. You can sound out "paleontologist" easier than "were" or "right."
5. Try writing the word until it looks right to you.
6. You can sound it out.
7. You can look the word up in the dictionary.
8. Ask a friend.

9. Good spellers learn to spell the words they use over and over again in their stories.

10. Good spellers read a lot about what they want to spell. If I'm interested in space and I want to spell "Jupiter," I'd read about it.

11. You could look in your spelling box.

12. You could look for the word on the class spelling charts.

13. You could look it up in your "little dictionary"—personal dictionary.

14. You can use the thesaurus—"word bank."

15. Look for the word on "News of the Day"—newspaper.

This was Ellen's first year implementing an integrated spelling approach, and she and I were both delighted and amazed with the responses. We were very impressed with the reading-writing connection the children made and with the focus on meaning and real-life practicality of their responses. For example, it is often easier to spell a long word you can sound out, as Craig mentioned in (4), but we had no idea Craig not only understood this concept but could apply it. Also, the last statements referred to using charts or the dictionary. Just as adults often use the dictionary as a last resort, the students recognized other strategies as being more useful. Finding a word in the dictionary is difficult unless one already knows the correct spelling of at least the first three letters.

Rethinking the Use of Traditional Spelling Tests

We need to look carefully at the widely accepted practice of requiring weekly spelling tests. Not only do they put unnecessary pressure on young students especially, they take up a lot of time in the home that might be better spent on worthwhile literacy activities. I am amazed at how much time parents tell me they work with their children, helping them study for spelling tests. Even with a first-grader, the parents may spend as much as an hour or more drilling words for the Friday test. I think the reason spelling tests are accepted without question is that parents are familiar with the process from their own schooling, and they think the tests are contributing to their child's progress. Testing also makes grading easy, since all a teacher needs to do to arrive at a student's grade is average the weekly test percentages. We need to rethink whether the time and effort that is being put into spelling tests should be invested in an activity that is of questionable value. If testing is seen as necessary, peer testing of individual students' self-selected words, as described earlier in this chapter, is a more viable alternative.

We also need to question the validity of standardized spelling tests where, typically, the student is asked to choose the correctly spelled word from among four choices. Such tests are really proofreading tests. Unless a child can also write the word, the test is not totally valid as a measure of spelling ability.

Students can be devastated by the pressure and effects of weekly testing. Thomas, a bright fourth-grader, spoke with me about his experiences with spelling tests. In first grade, Thomas had been in Karen Shiba's class where spelling was taught incidentally through immersion in reading and writing activities. He had felt positive about himself as an independent writer despite his poor grapho-phonics abilities. While Thomas' invented spelling was a challenge to read, his journal from September to June showed consistent evidence of steady progress in spelling.

In second and third grades, Thomas was in classrooms that put a high priority on doing well on weekly spelling tests. He told me, "I had headaches and stomach aches a lot. I was always thinking about spelling pretests and spelling tests, and it made me sick. I always did real bad on my spelling tests. I hated them. I still think they're a waste of time and unfair. I could do excellent in the workbook and still mess up on the test."

In fourth grade, Thomas began to relax about spelling. He still struggled but noted, "Spelling will probably always be hard for me. This year I'm doing well in spelling. It's easier for me. My teacher doesn't think spelling tests are that important." No doubt his teacher's relaxed attitude helped his own.

Nora, a first-grader who felt very pressured by weekly spelling tests, told her mother—who also happened to be a first grade teacher—"You should do spelling stuff but you shouldn't have tests because the kids who don't get 100 percent feel bad." Nora also told her mother, who did not give spelling tests, "I think you're real smart because you give kids free choice. Because if kids can choose [the words] they want to do it. But if they have to do it, they don't want to do it." Her statements are evidence of a young child's sensitivity to the need for choice while recognizing the importance of doing "spelling stuff."

Reflections

We are all still in the process of developing and reassessing the teaching and learning of spelling in the classroom. Those of us who have tried an integrated spelling program have all completed the first year with the belief that its implementation has been consistent and relevant for our reading-writing classrooms. We believe our children are spelling at least as well as those using a traditional program, and we know they are greater risk takers. We see our children learning and applying phonics generalizations in their daily reading and writing. And we continue to note that our best spellers are usually our best readers and writers, while the majority of our poor spellers also struggle with reading and writing.

We continue regularly to discuss issues, concerns, research, and professional articles having to do with spelling and to spend much time discussing theory and how to put it into practice. Professional reading continues to provide a needed framework as well as a challenge to continue to improve our spelling instruction. We are presently focusing on developing better techniques in classroom management and evaluation.

We have come to believe that spelling methods and materials are secondary to immersion in authentic reading and writing activities. Eventually, we expect that spelling will be totally integrated into our teaching. We will know that has happened when we stop referring to spelling separately and begin teaching all spelling as needs occur in daily reading and writing.

Resources

The following resources are particularly helpful for formulating theory and practice in the teaching of spelling. A number of the articles and books have been discussed in our weekly language arts support groups as we focused on spelling in depth.

Bean, Wendy, and Chrystine Bouffler. 1988. *Spell by Writing*. Portsmouth, NH: Heinemann.

>*This text (92 pp.) remains my favorite, as well as the favorite of several of my colleagues, on the teaching of spelling. For the teacher who already understands and accepts the theory behind teaching spelling as a part of writing, this book is invaluable. Lots of detailed "strategy lesson plans" for helping children develop as writers are clearly presented.*

Buchanan, Ethel. 1989. *Spelling for Whole Language Classrooms*. Katonah, NY: Richard C. Owen.

>*For teachers who have a well-developed theory base for developmental spelling, this spiral-bound handbook (154 pp.) focuses in depth on the stages of spelling development and gives detailed procedures for analyzing misspellings.*

Gentry, Richard. November 1982. "An Analysis of Developmental Spelling in GYNS AT WORK," *The Reading Teacher*, pp. 192–200.

>*Using Glenda Bissex's case study of her son's language development, Gentry details five stages of spelling development and gives guidelines for helping children acquire spelling competence. Gentry believes teachers need to identify and understand these stages in order to teach spelling appropriately.*

Gentry, Richard. 1987. *Spel . . . is a Four-Letter Word*. Portsmouth, NH: Heinemann.

>*This is a good starting place for teachers and parents. This short (54 pp.), easy to read guide offers the author's personal experience as well as research on learning to spell. Myths about spelling are cleared up; invented spelling is explained; and strategies for teaching spelling are presented.*

Harp, Bill. March 1988. "When the Principal Asks 'Why Are Your Kids Giving Each Other Spelling Tests?' " *The Reading Teacher*, pp. 702–704.

>*This short piece gives a clear rationale for peer testing in an individualized spelling program. Share this with administrators and parents.*

Parry, Jo-Ann, and David Hornsby. 1988. "Spelling in the Writing Classroom." In *Write On: A Conference Approach to Writing*. Portsmouth, NH: Heinemann, pp. 57–66.

>*This is a highly practical chapter that includes the spelling stages learners go through, the necessary conditions for learning to spell, and lots of terrific ideas for teaching strategies and setting up classroom spelling procedures. Visual representations of activities are very helpful.*

Sowers, Susan. 1988. "Six Questions Teachers Ask about Invented Spelling." In *Understanding Writing: Ways of Observing, Learning, and Teaching*, 2nd ed. Thomas Newkirk and Nancie Atwell (eds.) Portsmouth, NH: Heinemann, pp. 62–79.

>*Sowers aptly answers the following questions: (1) "What is invented spelling?" (2) "Why should children be permitted to be inventive spellers?" (3) "Other than being 'wrong' instead of right, how does invented spelling differ from standard spelling?" (4) "Are there stages in invented spelling?" (5) "Does invented spelling get better on its own?" (6) "How do you decide what spelling skills to teach an inventive speller?" This informative piece, particularly helpful for understanding invented spelling, includes important information on communicating with parents.*

Temple, Charles, Ruth Nathan, Nancy Burris, and Frances Temple. 1988. *The Beginnings of Writing*, 2nd ed. Boston: Allyn and Bacon.

>*This excellent text (280 pp.) examines children's writing, ages four to eight, and has complete chapters on invented spelling, learning standard spelling, and making*

progress in spelling. Preschool through grade 2 teachers will find this text very informative.

White, Thomas G., Joanne Sowell, and Alice Yanagihara. January 1989. "Teaching Elementary Students to Use Word-Part Clues," *The Reading Teacher*, pp. 302–307.

> *Applicable for students in grade 3 and above, this is a valuable article for actively involving students in using and understanding prefixes and suffixes. Two tables— "The most common prefixes in printed school English for grades 3-9" and "English suffixes ranked by frequency of occurrence"—are especially useful to the teacher. Possible prefix and suffix lessons are included.*

Wilde, Sandra. 1989. "Looking at Invented Spelling: A Kidwatcher's Guide to Spelling. Parts I and II." In *The Whole Language Evaluation Book*, Kenneth Goodman, Yetta Goodman, and Wendy Hood (eds.). Portsmouth, NH: Heinemann, pp. 213–236.

> *Wilde discusses and analyzes four major principles in holistic spelling evaluation: (1) evaluating through natural writing instead of tests; (2) evaluating analytically rather than just in terms of right or wrong; (3) evaluating by looking at strategies employed instead of looking at words in isolation; (4) evaluating as a knowledgeable professional and not just a scorer of tests. Very useful for teachers ready to analyze invented spellings and observe the spelling strategies children use.*

Wilde, Sandra. January 1990. "A Proposal for a New Spelling Curriculum," *The Elementary School Journal*, pp. 275–289.

> *If you have time to read only one article about spelling, read this outstanding, comprehensive monograph. Wilde examines recent research on children's invented spelling, critiques the traditional textbook model of teaching spelling that has ignored the research, and argues for classroom spelling practice that is consistent with how children learn all language—gradually and with lots of practice in meaningful contexts. Teachers and administrators will receive strong theoretical and practical support as well as learn many specific strategies for developing a spelling curriculum that is part of the reading-writing process.*

Zutell, Jerry. October 1978. "Some Psycholinguistic Perspectives on Children's Spelling," *Language Arts*, pp. 844–850.

> *This classic, often referred to article reaffirms that the research supporting invented spellings and its implications for teaching has been around for a long time. This is a superb article for gaining a clear understanding of how children learn to spell, for a review of the early spelling research, and for practical applications for school and home.*

Consumable Resources for Students

Teachers of integrated spelling programs have found it useful for each elementary student to have a personal spelling dictionary. These short references are easier to use than a regular dictionary, and they contain space for students to add their own words alphabetically. Our teachers purchase these inexpensive handbooks out of the annual student supply fee. The spelling booklets are collected at the end of the year and are passed on to the next grade's teacher.

Holloway, Judy (compiler). 1989. *Writing Dictionary*. Scarborough, Ontario, Canada: Ginn Publishing Canada Inc. ($2.25) (In U.S., order through Steck-Vaughn Co., Austin, Texas.)

> *First grade teachers and special education teachers have found this dictionary invaluable. Our teacher of developmentally handicapped students says, "All the*

words my students need are here and easy to find because there are so few words on each page." This terrific resource has delightful visuals and lots of space for beginning writers to add their own words.

Hurray, Gregory. 1987. *A Spelling Dictionary for Beginning Writers.* Cambridge, MA: Educators Publishing Service. ($2.00)

Second grade teachers especially love this easy-to-use resource with its large, clear type for beginning writers (also applicable for grades 1 and 3). An extensive "Word Bank" at the end includes a mini-thesaurus of common words such as "big," "good," and "said" as well as lists of theme words that include the calendar, numbers, colors, clothes, school, and family.

Sitton, Rebecca, and Robert Forest. 1987. *The Quick-Word Handbook for Everyday Writers.* North Billerica, MA: Curriculum Associates. ($.89)

This is a handy resource for elementary students in grades 3 and above. About one thousand high-utility words are included along with a list of abbreviations, states, numbers, months, and days and a list of homophones and sentences delineating homophone pairs.

11

Setting Up an In-School Publishing Process

*A parent volunteer publishing
a book with a first grade student*

Publishing children's written work in a final copy, printed edition that is shared publicly is a powerful tool for motivating and engaging students in continued reading and writing. However, because publishing in the classroom can be so time consuming, the use of parent volunteers can facilitate and expedite the process. This chapter describes a school-wide publishing effort that has worked well in our district. While the model described might not meet your needs or work for your school or district, my hope is that you can use it to determine your own available resources and possibilities. Perhaps with the support of your Parent-Teacher Association and the school administrator, you may see ways to get the publishing process going in your own classroom or school on a scale you are comfortable with.

A District Publishing Program

Every teacher in every first grade classroom is involved in our district-wide effort to celebrate children's writing and to connect children's writing to reading through publishing. Whether through journal writing, story writing, or writing workshop, children have frequent and regular opportunities to write on self-selected topics. While participation in our organized publishing program is voluntary, any initial reluctance disappeared once teachers have seen the power of publishing.

Since the fall of 1987, we have been extremely fortunate to have Marianne Sopko as the parent volunteer coordinator for publishing in our elementary schools. This volunteer position, which Marianne created, grew out of her involvement in publishing in her son Mike's first grade classroom where she worked closely with me and with first grade teacher Karen Shiba. She was so impressed with what publishing did for the children's self-esteem, as well as for their reading and writing development, that she initiated a district-wide publishing effort. (See Routman, 1988, pp. 110–118 and 194–197, for earlier information on book publishing.)

Our book publishing program places special emphasis on first grade, where the most help is needed and where the power of publishing is most dramatic. For some children publishing promotes a leap into literacy because their own writing may be the first successful reading they do. Additionally, the many books that are published in a school year become a treasured part of the classroom book collection.

For older children publishing remains powerful as a motivation for writing. Many teachers report that the children's published books are the most popular ones in the classroom. Publishing also legitimizes the need for revisions and conventions—correct spelling, grammar, clarity, format—and gives a needed purpose for doing one's best work. Once you "go public," the writing has to be in its best form. There's no question that publishing authentic writing for an audience increases students' willingness to revise.

The Role of Parents

Parents make publishing easy and possible for the classroom teacher by assuming the labor-intensive aspects of the job. In first grade, parents make the book covers and take the stories the children have written in invented spellings—in their journals, notebooks, or writing folders—and transcribe them into standard English with conventional spellings. In some kindergarten classes, parents type stories from the children's journals and take dictation. Always, great caution is taken through training parents and gently reminding them that ownership belongs with the child. Parents are encouraged not to teach or intrude but rather to encourage, support, and guide.

In second through sixth grades, parents make or teach children to make wallpaper book covers. Once teachers learn how to make the books, they take over in guiding students. Many parents also serve as final editors-typists of children's books. Occasionally, after the teacher has carefully demonstrated for them, parents are used in facilitating the revision process.

For the efficient management of the publishing process, each of our elementary buildings has a parent coordinator who oversees the running of the program. The coordinator is responsible for training parent volunteers for publishing, serving as a liaison with teachers and making sure supplies and book covers are maintained and available. We have found the system works best if coordinators are first grade parents. Because their own children directly benefit from the process, the parents recognize the value of publishing and invest their time and effort in it. Marianne Sopko has served as the overall supervising coordinator who trains and coaches each of the building coordinators and meets with them regularly as needed. Past coordinators train incoming ones with support from Marianne.

Even with all of these supports, establishing a comfortable working relationship between teachers and parents takes time, sensitivity, and honest communication on the part of everyone involved. One year, in one building, some well-meaning but overzealous parents organized themselves before teachers were ready. A flyer went out the first week of school asking teachers how many volunteers they wanted and how they wanted them to be used. When teachers showed little immediate interest in getting started with publishing, some of the parents became upset. The teachers, however, were not yet ready to implement a program. They needed the first six weeks of school to establish their routines and get to know their students. Once teachers communicated their needs, the parents understood and respected the teachers' requests.

The Role of Teachers
Asking for Help

For some teachers, it was difficult initially to ask for parent help, perhaps because of their own staunch independence or because they feared parents invading the classroom. However, once teachers give it a try, they find allowing parents to help with publishing is not nearly as disruptive as they had imagined, and they welcome assistance with the editing process. Having parents take care of the mechanical processes of actually making and editing the books frees teachers. Because the parents have been chosen by the teachers and then specially trained by the coordinator, it is uncommon for a parent not to work out to a teacher's satisfaction.

When teachers take the time to be very specific about what they want parents to do, they are particularly pleased with the results. Third grade teacher Donna Brittain gives her parent volunteers a complete set of typed guidelines when her students are publishing their own poetry books.

Record Keeping

It is up to the teacher to keep a record of who has published, completed illustrations to go along with the text, and shared completed books with the class. It is very easy in first grade to overlook a child who has difficulty getting writing down on the page. I was upset one year to learn that one of my Reading Recovery students had published only one book by April. These are the children who especially need the publishing process to foster their literacy skills. Their own language, the most predictable text of all, needs to be used to support their reading development and to build confidence in their abilities. It is necessary, even if it requires that the parent volunteer mostly take dictation, for reluctant learners to have an equal chance. Keeping a class chart and checking off publication dates facilitates an equitable publishing process.

Our first-graders publish an average of six to eight books over a school year. Initially, any or all of their writing may go to publication, but as the year progresses, students are encouraged to choose only their best or favorite pieces. In second grade and above, where much of the transcribing is done by the children, several books per child, per school year, is average. One of these may be a book for the local Young Authors' Conference.

Word Processing

Computers have added a new dimension to children's desire to write. While word processing is available to all students in our district, every fifth- and sixth-grader takes a semester course under the leadership of our computer expert Adrianne Geszler. Students' word processing expertise has aided the publishing process; it is easier and faster for them to do revisions with printed text. Students enjoy the difference in the "feel" of composition produced by word processing versus that done by hand. And students with poor handwriting or learning disabled students who have difficulty reading their own writing find that seeing the piece in type can facilitate the writing process. Finally, when children's rough drafts have been typed exactly as they were written onto a word processing program and printed out double- or triple-spaced, it is much easier for them to see what needs to be edited.

However, word processing is not a panacea. Just because a piece was written on the computer does not guarantee its quality. Unless the writing process is clearly established in the classroom and students understand the teacher's expectations for revision and editing, a story composed on a word processor can be dull or poorly written. Students will not automatically revise just because the word processor is available; they first have to value revision as a strategy. As with all communication and language processes in the classroom, using technology depends largely on the teacher's philosophy and beliefs.

For the last several years, our teachers and students have especially enjoyed the easy workability and large print of "The Children's Writing and Publishing Center" by Learning Company in Menlo, California. However, recognizing how quickly computer programs become obsolete, teachers would do well to check with Learning Company as well as with Sunburst in Pleasantville, New York, and Scholastic Inc. in New York City for reputable word processing programs.

Setting Up the Publishing Program

Space Requirements

Storage space with shelving to house supplies and some designated table space on which to work are necessary. We house all publishing supplies in a corner of our WEB (see p. 452). A round table in our WEB is used for publishing, and supplies are within easy reach. In most of our buildings, tables and chairs are set up in the halls just outside the classrooms for parents and students to work together.

Supplies Needed

Funds for purchasing book publishing supplies are now a part of our school district's annual budget, and our district warehouse now stocks chipboard and rubber cement. As necessary, supplies are replenished by the parent volunteer coordinator. Teachers and parents are welcome to use all supplies but are requested to return items promptly when they are no longer using them. The following supplies are recommended for setting up a publishing program:

- **Wallpaper** (for book covers). A local wallpaper store may be willing to contribute discontinued wallpaper books. It is much easier to work with flat sheets than with rolls, and you get lots of variety. Remove the pages with a razor blade.
- **Chipboard** (for backing the book covers). This cardboard is purchased in quantity at a local paper supply company. One thousand 8 1/2 by 14 inch pieces cost about $25. Each piece, when cut to size, yields a book. To save time and ensure accuracy, we have whole boxes cut at a printer's for about $15.
- **Tape** (for securing the chipboard before pasting). Any cellophane or masking tape works, but Scotch Magic tape is the easiest to use. If you're doing a lot of books, heavy tape dispensers, which permit one-hand use, speed up the process.
- **Rubber cement** (for pasting the covers). There is no subsitiute for rubber cement. A quart of rubber cement will do about one hundred books. (Gallon cans are the most economical and can be used with smaller dispensers.)

Empty cans are returned for refilling. Elmer's glue may be used for the margins that are folded down over the cardboard, but we have found through experimentation that rubber cement works best for getting a smooth result on the front and inside covers.

- **Construction paper** (for the inside covers). A heavier weight (#80) produces a nicer result. Look for the best price, variety of colors, and quality of paper.
- **Labels for book titles** (for the title and author). We use mostly C-Line badges with colored borders (red, blue, green, and gold). If you buy in quantity, you may be able to get a discount. Any self-stick blank label affixed to the front cover will work.
- **Long-arm staplers** (for binding). For books using folded sheets, a long-arm stapler that allows sheets to be stapled at the centerfold is a must.
- **Mimeograph paper** (for book pages). Paper is cut to size by volunteers. With 8 1/2 by 11 inch paper there will be one cut; with legal size paper (11 by 14 inch) there will be two 6 1/2 by 11 inch cuts. (See directions for making wallpaper books.)
- **Paper cutter** (for cutting book pages to size).
- **Erasable pens** (for transcribing by hand).
- **Brass paper fasteners (brads)** (for assembling books of single pages). Look for #3 or #4.
- **Punches** (for making holes in cover and pages). "Ticket" punch size works best; a small hole is more desirable for securing the pages with brads.
- **Dictionary** (for checking spelling).
- **Sets of directions for book publishing** (for making book covers). Directions (see the next section, "Making the Book Covers") are posted on a wall near the supplies. Individual copies of directions are also available for parents to take when they are making book covers at home.

Estimated Costs

If wallpaper and labor are donated and mimeograph paper is used from the school's supply, the cost per book is about 15 cents.

Chipboard	2.5 cents/book
Cutting cost	1.5 cents/book
Rubber cement	4 cents/book
Construction paper	2.5 cents/book
Tape	2 cents/book
Labels for cover	2.5 cents/book

Additionally, you will need to plan on start-up costs of about $150. That amount will buy several half-pint- or pint-size dispensers for the rubber cement (which can be replenished from a gallon can), several heavy tape dispensers, several long-arm staplers, brass paper fasteners, punches, and erasable pens. A heavy-duty stapler that can secure up to one hundred pages may be needed for older grades.

Making the Book Covers

We begin each school year with a large supply (several hundred) of book covers on hand. Many parents are willing to take supplies home and make book covers over the summer. In addition, requests to parents for making book covers occur build-ing- and district-wide during the school year as needed. (See Appendix J6 and J7 for sample flyers that were sent to parents.)

We have found that two types of wallpaper book covers work especially well:

1. Folded sheets of paper are stapled into the centerfold of the book. This type is used for first grade publishing (and sometimes in second grade) where the parent editor hand prints the child's story.

2. Single sheets of paper are secured by staples or brass paper fasteners. This kind of fastener is used if children write out their own books (a page can easily be replaced) or if pages are word processed or typed.

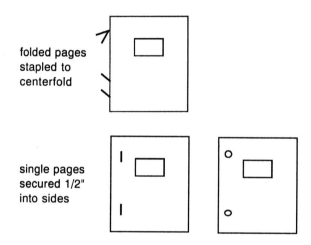

See end of chapter for directions for making the two types of book covers.

Training Parents

Teachers are encouraged to identify parents whom they think would work well with students in the publishing process. These need to be parents who value and understand invented spelling, who recognize the importance of keeping the writing ownership with the child, and who are sensitive and professional about the infor-mation they learn about and from children. However, some teachers are comfort-able using any parents who want to participate. While several parents per class-room is ideal, having even one parent involved can have an impact on the publishing effort. The parents are asked to come in once a week for at least an hour throughout the school year.

Because of the large number of parents working full-time, some years it is particularly difficult to get parent volunteers. Even working parents, however, can make book covers, and they do (see Appendix J6). If getting volunteers proves difficult, you might try recruiting senior citizens, parents without school-age children, or older students.

Marianne Sopko models the publishing process for each building coordinator. She follows Holdaway's developmental model by demonstrating first, inviting parents to try the process while she coaches, and then giving parents time to practice on their own. She begins by bringing in a child the teacher has indentified as ready to publish. (Some teachers write on the board the names of the children who are ready to publish. In this way, the volunteer knows exactly who to take and in what order.)

First, the child is asked to read his writing. Then, questions—as needed for clarification—are asked. Some regrouping of material may be suggested, but the final decision concerning reorganization is the child's. The child selects a book cover, gives his story a title if one is not already in place, and watches while his journal entries or other written pieces are transcribed into book form. The child is then encouraged to read the book. This is especially important for making the beginning reading-writing connection.

After the child returns to class, Marianne discusses the process and answers questions from the observing parent. If the parent feels ready, the parent publishes the next child's writing while Marianne observes and coaches. It takes Marianne a full hour and a half to cover the key elements and mechanics of publishing, publish one child, and observe the parent publish one child.

The coordinators then train the parent volunteers in their respective buildings, and/or former volunteers are used to train new parents. Even without such a coordinated volunteer program, teachers could train their own volunteers to support the publishing process in the classroom.

Teacher Leadership and Administrative Support in Getting Started

Modeled on the publishing process in our district, two teachers in a neighboring school district wrote a proposal to establish publishing centers at their elementary schools. Both teachers felt the program—which was piloted in two buildings—was successful largely because of the strong support of the assistant superintendent of schools and the two school principals.

Funds were appropriated for paying Marianne Sopko as a consultant, for teachers to be released to observe the publishing process in another school district, and for the purchase of necessary supplies. The principals helped identify parent volunteer coordinators who would be knowledgeable, reliable, supportive, and nonthreatening to teachers and other parents. The principals were also helpful in suggesting the names of parent volunteers who could be expected to work well with teachers and children.

In addition to administrative support, this new publishing effort was successful because two teachers were willing to commit time without pay to meet with the parent coordinator, order supplies, discuss future directions, spend time with the principals, and do professional reading and whatever else was necessary to get the publishing effort organized for the two schools.

Evaluation

Once a publishing program is operative, it's a good idea to take an objective look at how well the program is working: How many books are being published? What is the quality of the books? Are book covers and supplies usually on hand? What are the teacher's and children's attitudes toward the process and products?

Publishing Center Evaluation Form

1. Did you use the services of the publishing center this year?

   Yes _____   No_____

   If not, are there any changes which would make the program more useful to you?

2. What was the most helpful or valuable aspect of the program?

3. What, if any, problems did you encounter? (scheduling, availability of volunteers, volunteer-student relationships, book format, other)

4. Were the volunteers adequately trained? Would you suggest additional training in any areas?

5. What suggestions do you have to improve the program?

6. Do you plan to use the center next year? Yes_____   No_____
   In order to have enough book covers ready by September, we would like to know *about* how many books you think you will publish per student._____

Name (optional) _____

(form developed by Nancy Erkkila and Donna Ostberg)

At the end of the first year of setting up a publishing center, one school system gave the above written evaluation to all participating teachers and administrators. Directions and changes for the following year were based largely on information received from the surveys.

Reflections

We were unusually fortunate in our district to have a parent volunteer spearhead a district-wide publishing effort in the elementary grades. Teachers in other districts who have taken the leadership to work with their administrators and parents have also been successful in setting up publishing centers in their own buildings or classrooms.

It is not only the children's excitement at having their writing published that is significant about the publishing process. Once parent volunteers feel comfortable and confident with their role in the process, many say it is the most gratifying work they have ever done in their child's school. As they witness how important publishing is to students, they come to place a very high value on it. Additionally, they see firsthand the literacy development and potential of all children, and they come to appreciate the power of writing for reading and thinking. Welcoming parents into the school for publishing makes them an integral and vital part of the school community.

HOW TO MAKE WALLPAPER BOOKS
FOR FOLDED PAGES

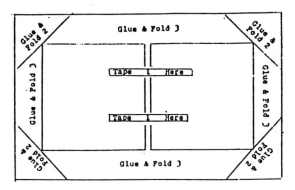

Suggested Dimensions:

Cardboard: 6½" x 7½"
Wallpaper: At least 15" x 9"
Construction paper: 6½" x 12"

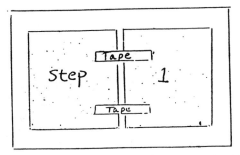

1. Tape cardboard to wrong side of wallpaper, leaving
    about 3/8" gap between cardboad pieces at center.

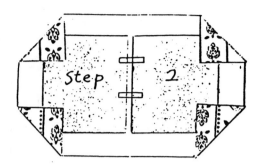

2.   Glue and fold wallpaper corners to cardboard.

3.   Glue and fold wallpaper
     sides to cardboard.

4.   Glue construction paper
     lining to wallpaper sides.

5.   Cut paper for book to fit dimensions of construction
     paper lining and staple to centerfold with long-arm
     stapler.

     -Standard 8½" X 11" paper cut to 6½" X 11" works well.

How To Make Wallpaper Books for Typed Single Pages

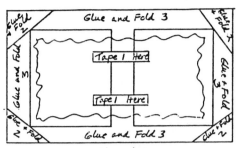

Dimensions:
Cardboard: 6½" x 7¼"
Wallpaper: at least 16" x 9"
Construction paper: 13¾" x 6¾"

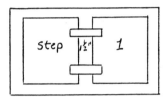

1. Tape cardboard to wrong side of wallpaper, leaving about 1½" gap between cardboard pieces at center.

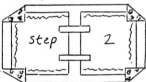

2. Glue outer edges of wallpaper and cardboard and fold wallpaper corners to cardboard.

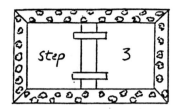 

3. Fold wallpaper sides to cardboard.

4. Glue construction paper lining to wallpaper sides.

5. Cut sheets of paper 6¾" x 6¾" to fit the book. This permits typing individual pages which is much easier than typing folded sheets.

When text and illustrations are finished, insert pages into fold of book cover. Staple on outside. binding close to where the cardboard interfacing lies or punch holes through binding and pages and secure with brass paper fasteners.

 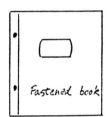

stapled book

Fastened book

If the book has many pages, you may need to use a heavy duty stapler

TYPING LAYOUT FOR WALLPAPER BOOKS

Left margin needs to be 1 1/4 inches
Top, right, and bottom margins look good at 3/4"
Double space

To keep the process simpler, I recommend typing on only one side of the page--if typing on both sides of the page, BOTH RIGHT AND LEFT MARGINS NEED TO BE 1 1/4 INCHES.

OPTION SETTINGS FOR WORD PROCESSING ON 'APPLEWORKS'

IF USING PIN FEED COMPUTER PAPER, enter the following options before typing:

Left Margin (LM): 1.2
Right Margin (RM): 2.2
Top Margin (TM): .6
Bottom Margin (BM): 5.0
Double space (DS)

When the typing is finished, the sheets can be sent back to school to be cut to size to fit the book: 6 1/2" wide by 6 3/4" long.

IF USING SINGLE SHEETS THAT ARE INDIVIDUALLY FED into the printer, use the same options, but add:

Pause Each Page (PE)

As you print, the computer will pause at the end of each page. This allows you to insert the next blank sheet of paper. Then press 'Return' and the printer will proceed with the second page.

Top Margin 3/4 " (Appleworks .6)

CAN CATS PREDICT EARTHQUAKES?

The answer is yes, but we still don't know how. Many cat owners claim that their cats have saved their lives. Before an earthquake, a cat will act strangely, by starting to hiss and growl, or it may carry its babies to safety.

WHY DO WE SAY,

"YOU LET THE CAT OUT OF THE BAG?"

We often say this phrase when somebody gives a secret away. It started back in the eighteenth century when market salesmen would try to cheat people by putting cats in the bags

Typewriter: Left. Margin 1 1/4"

(Appleworks: LM: 1.2)

Right Margin 3/4"

(Appleworks: RM 2.2)

sample page

Bottom Margin: 3/4 " (Appleworks: BM 5.0)

<---------- 6 3/4" ---------->

12

Integration

Teachers must function more like orchestra conductors than like lecturers: getting things started and keeping them moving along, providing information and pointing to resources, coordinating a diverse but harmonious buzz of activity.
(Goodlad and Oakes, 1988, p. 19)

*Note taking in grade 3:
collaboration during the practice phase*

What Is Integration?

Integration is implicit in whole language teaching. Integration, or integrated language arts, is an approach to learning and a way of thinking that respects the interrelationship of the language processes—reading, writing, speaking, and listening—as integral to meaningful teaching in any area. Integration refers to integration of the language arts as well as integration of the language arts across the curriculum. Before the latter can be successfully accomplished, the former needs to be firmly in place. Integration also means that major concepts and larger understandings are being developed in social contexts and that related activities are in harmony with and important to the major concepts.

My convictions about what is meant by integrated teaching and learning were confirmed and extended at an IRA conference where I heard Debbie Powell and Dick Needham of the University of Northern Colorado do an excellent presentation: "Authentic Reading, Writing and Content Learning in an Integrated Curriculum" (symposium at the annual meeting of the International Reading Association, Atlanta, Georgia, May 1990). They stressed that topics of study should be based on the "big understandings" you are trying to get across from your curriculum and that these topics be of critical importance to what children need to learn. The "big understandings," or major concepts to be developed, then become the root of unit planning. "Planning begins with substantive content and then integrates the processes (reading, writing, math, science, art, and so on) as tools for the acquisition, organization, evaluation, and application of knowledge." (Needham, IRA, 1990).

Integration, which can occur on a variety of levels, may take place with the study of just one book or one major concept in mathematics—as long as reading, writing, speaking, and listening are interrelated and are consistent with a whole language philosophy. It has taken many of us at least three to five years to feel we are successfully integrating the language arts through literature. Integration across the curriculum is an area some of us are just beginning to explore. I have yet to be in a classroom that is totally integrated—that is, where language, concepts and content are interconnected across the entire curriculum all day every day. That kind of integration is rare and takes many years to achieve.

I believe literature is the best vehicle to achieve integration of the language arts. One piece of literature or one literature thematic unit can invite comparison, encourage synthesis and analysis of the author's and/or the illustrator's styles, expand vocabulary and thinking, and have an impact on student writing. Quality literature can be a vehicle for meaningful units such as the following:

- Books with similar themes
- Books by one author
- Books by one illustrator
- Books in the same genre (for example, mysteries, biographies, poetry, short stories)
- Books with similar characters
- Versions of folk/fairy tales (see "A Folk/Fairy Tale Unit for Grades 3–6" in Appendix A)

Misconceptions about Thematic Units

Somehow, it has become common to equate thematic units with whole language. Many teachers believe that if they are using thematic units, they are "doing" whole language. Not necessarily. Unfortunately, many of the thematic units teachers buy and create are nothing more than suggested activities clustered around a central focus or topic. The units incorporate some elements of math, science, social studies, art, and music, but there is often little or no development of important ideas. This is correlation, not integration. With integration, the relationships among the disciplines or subject areas are meaningful and natural. Concepts identified are not only related to the topic or subject but are important to them. With correlation, the connections are superficial and forced, and there is no important concept development.

Superficial units or themes that focus on such topics as the circus, cars, bears, animals, monsters, dragons, mice, pigs, and kites are commonly used in the elementary grades and are good examples of correlations. Teachers gather together all the books they can find on a subject and plan lots of activities around the topic. Frequently the activities are creative and interesting. However, while these activities may be fun for kids, often the units lack substance and are not based on major concepts. We need to begin asking ourselves whether such units are worth the enormous teacher preparation and class time that they require and whether they effectively foster the development of important concepts and skills. I believe that we need to be investing most of our time in conscious, deliberate, thoughtful topics and themes that go beyond the literal level.

A case in point is a thematic unit on bears, which is often utilized in the early grades. Teachers and students read lots of books about bears, write stories about bears, make bear cookies, draw bear pictures, and so on—all very entertaining and delightful. However, such a unit is not designed to develop important concepts and provide opportunities for transfer of skills. Even when pretend and real bears are compared, we need to ask, how relevant is this to the child's life? We need always to be asking ourselves, "What are the educational objectives and goals of this unit?"

It is possible to take a theme like bears and make meaningful connections to the curriculum and children's lives. In developing themes, primary consideration must be given to developing attitudes, oral language, perspectives to be covered, opportunities for social interaction, and the interrelationship of important concepts. Loretta Martin, a second grade teacher, recently did a thematic unit on bears. The major concepts that she was consciously developing included "Bears are not the gentle creatures we think they are" and "Bears are a family unit with definite nurturing patterns." After brainstorming what they knew and wanted to find out about bears as a whole class, students chose the topic they wanted to learn about and worked in groups. Students chose to investigate such topics as habitat, body skeleton, food, and bears as an endangered species. Students read, wrote, researched, and used the library to locate information. Each group eventually gave an optional oral presentation to the class or conferenced with the teacher about what they had learned.

Second grade teacher Elaine Weiner took the study of trees and tied it to students' lives. The major concepts she wanted to develop were "We cannot live on earth without trees" and "Trees provide shade, beauty, paper, homes for animals, and more." Students observed trees at the school throughout the year and noted changes, growth, and animal life in and around trees through the seasons. The class also identified all the trees on school property. Each student then adopted one tree and kept a year-long observational record. With the help of parents, students also counted and identified the trees in their own yards. The class then did a tally and prepared a group graph that included over ninety different kinds of trees found in students' yards. Students read books and poems about trees and did bark and leaf rubbings of some of the school's trees. A parent who is an arborist also shared what he does in his work.

A thematic unit is an integrated unit only when the topic or theme is meaningful, relevant to the curriculum and students' lives, consistent with whole language principles, and authentic in the interrelationship of the language processes. When planning thematic units, interdisciplinary connections across the different subject areas are not necessary for integration to be occurring. "The only reason to include some other discipline is if it somehow extends and enriches the learning or is beneficial to the student" (Andrea Butler, conversation, September 1990).

Planning for Integration

In planning for integrated instruction, we need to be asking ourselves several important questions. Even if we feel tied to a single text in a subject area, we need to be asking these questions—or others like them—to make our unit of study as meaningful as possible.

- What important concepts do I want students to learn?
- Why should students learn these concepts? Are they intellectually rich and important? Do they foster critical and creative thinking?
- What learning experiences will help develop these conceptual understandings?

- What skills and strategies am I helping to develop?
- Am I setting up a climate that encourages inquiry and choice?
- Am I putting in place alternative evaluation procedures? (See Chap. 13, "Evaluation.")
- What student attitudes am I fostering?

The following informal guidelines may be helpful in developing a framework for an integrated language unit in literature or the content areas. It would be easy to follow the guidelines and create a superficial unit; integration will occur only if whole language principles of language learning are respected and adopted.

Informal Guidelines

In planning an integrated unit, some teachers prefer to do most of the planning themselves. Planning may also be done collaboratively with students to ensure that they have a voice in the curriculum-making process.

- *Planning the unit*

  Select an important topic or theme that is both developmentally appropriate and important to the curriculum and to children's needs and interests.

  Brainstorm possibilities.
  > Webbing, mapping, illustrating, listing ideas, jotting down concepts
  > > Organize information into categories.
  > > Find out and verify what students already know about the topic.
  > > Separate known information from "What we want to find out."

  Decide major understandings and concepts to be developed. While this is largely the teacher's responsibility, try to include questions students want to explore.

  Determine activities that will help develop conceptual understandings.

  Determine experiences and activities that can be used to help promote problem-solving strategies.

  Gather resources—quality literature and resources from home, school, and community to be used for observation, exploration, researching, reading, and writing. Consult the school librarian, media specialist, and art and music teachers.

  If students will be expected to do factual writing, plan for students to become familiar with this genre.

  Inform parents of the unit study.

  If applicable, arrange speakers, send out letters of inquiry, and arrange field trips.

  Organize the classroom and set up centers, for example, book and resource areas.

- *Implementation*

  Be sure students understand why the topic is being studied.

  Teach note-taking, report-writing, and research skills if they will be needed.

(For specific information on report writing, see Collerson, 1988, and Graves, 1989, 1990.)

Provide time for reading appropriate resources with questions in mind that were determined in the planning stage.

Add new information to categories from brainstorming. Correct misconceptions.

Include individual, partner, small-group, and whole-class activities.

Promote opportunities for collaboration, choice, and creation of varied formats.

Provide teacher guidance and minilessons as needed (using the developmental model for language learning, pp. 9–10).

Encourage the unplanned learnings—the questions and discoveries that occur as a result of immersion in an engaging topic.

Maintain a climate of inquiry: investigating, collecting data, gathering information, problem solving, revising, rethinking.

- *Evaluation*

Organize new information with what is already known. Allow students some choice: oral presentation, debate, written report, published writing, graph, drama, mural, dance, song.

Provide time for sharing, reporting, speaking, and listening.

Discuss and evaluate new learning; relate old to new.

Balance teacher evaluation, peer group evaluation, and self-evaluation (See Chap. 13, "Evaluation.")

Incorporating the Fine Arts

Music teacher Nancy Tuttle and art teacher Jill Wisneski believe that the major concepts that are part of their courses of study can be meaningfully integrated into classroom teaching. Both believe that communication between specialists and teachers is the key when planning for successful integration of disciplines. Both teachers use their disciplines to extend and enrich responses to literature and to take students to another level of understanding. Promoting and valuing oral language, thinking, creating, collaborating, and problem solving are central to concept development in the music and art areas.

For example, Nancy uses some of the core books in our literature study (after they have been read by the students and discussed with the classroom teacher) to guide students to write their own music. Working together as a whole class, students paraphrase the key points of the text, work through a melody, and produce a song with lyrics. Nancy believes that the "rhythm of music is the rhythm of speech" and that the "phrasing of music parallels punctuation." When primary teachers bring her Big Books, she enriches the reading experience by focusing on the rhythm and cadence of the language.

Jill finds that a child's awareness of line, shape, color, and form can be expanded through connecting art to classroom study and the child's life. For example, when a group of fourth-graders read *James and the Giant Peach* by Roald Dahl (Knopf, 1961), she helped students enrich and extend the text by having them create characters from the book out of clay. Students learned how to use clay properly and skillfully while exploring shape, texture, and character interpretation. In addition, students learn to talk about and critique art while connecting with the visual history of art. This experience helps them in their own decision-making processes while at the same time they create their own art.

Another example of successful integration occurs regularly when first grade teacher Donna Zorge and music teacher Carol Spero collaborate. Carol writes original music to go along with favorite Big Books. Donna and the children create dramatic movements to accompany the songs. Both teachers note the children's confidence, joy, and reading fluency when they can sing the text and follow it along visually.

Integration in the Content Areas

Just as basal texts dominate reading instruction, content area texts dominate the major subject areas. Typically, we have taught social studies by saying, "Take out your social studies book and open to page ____." Then there follows a whole-class, round-robin reading, with the teacher stopping occasionally to ask questions and lead the discussion. Often students are expected to complete end-of-chapter questions designed to assess their understanding of the text. Because such exercises are boring and fail to engage many students, comprehension often suffers.

In contrast, when teachers actively involve students and plan for integration—even when they are relying on one text—student learning and engagement are quite different. Some teachers believe the best place to start with meaningful thematic units is in the content areas. Pappas, Kiefer, and Levstik (1990, p. 331) recommend beginning with expanding the content of social studies or science. (See also Richards, 1990, and Balding and Richards, 1990, for samples of broad-based units with "big understandings.")

Note Taking

Before students can be successful in the research process, they need to be able to take notes effectively. Note taking is a necessary lifelong skill that students need to have demonstrated over and over again throughout the school year. Using Holdaway's developmental model for learning—demonstration, participation, practice, and sharing—we carefully go through the process in various contexts, taking notes from texts, interviews, news articles, oral presentations, films, videos.

Third grade teacher Julie Beers and I demonstrated note taking before her students were to begin animal research reports. Using a selection on alligators and crocodiles from *Zoo Books* (Wildlife Education, Ltd., 1986), we reproduced the text of the first page and made a transparency. We left the other half page blank to demonstrate note taking on the overhead projector. As we slowly read the passage aloud, we highlighted key phrases and important information by underlining them in yellow magic marker. We verbalized our thinking processes as we worked, and then we showed students how to make the key phrases into notes (see Figure 12–1).

After we had demonstrated the process several times and invited students to participate in choosing the words we should write down, the students broke into small groups. Each group was given a copy of part of a *Zoo Books* article on

Figure 12-1   Note-taking Demonstration

From *Zoo Books 2: Alligators and Crocodiles*, (San Diego: Wildlife Education Ltd., 1986). Text reprinted with permission.

Alligators and crocodiles have fascinated people for centuries. Many "tall tales" have been told about these giant reptiles with the long tails. They are the original models for many dragons, "serpents," and other fairy tale monsters.

The true story of alligators and crocodiles is even more fascinating. The name "crocodile" was first used about 2,000 years ago by Greek adventurers who were traveling in Egypt. The huge crocodiles reminded them of a tiny lizard called "krokodeilos" that lived back in their Greek villages. So the world's biggest reptile got its name from one of the world's smallest. Alligators got their name in a similar way. Spanish adventurers exploring the coast of Florida gave them the name "el legarto," which means "the lizard."

There is one other animal very closely related to alligators and crocodiles. It is called a *gharial* (GAIR-ee-ul). This word comes from India, where gharials live. It was a name first used for *jars* that were long and thin. In the case of this animal, however, it is the *jaws* that are extremely long and thin.

Together, alligators, crocodiles, and gharials make up the group of animals known as *crocodilians* (CROCK-UH-DILL-EE-UNS). Crocodilians are the world's largest *reptiles*. A reptile is a cold-blooded animal that has scaly skin, lays eggs, and breathes with lungs. Crocodilians continue to grow throughout their lives. Some males grow to be more than 15 feet long (4.6 kilometers). And they may weigh over 500 pounds (227 kilograms). Females are usually smaller than the males.

There are also "dwarf" species of alligators and crocodiles which seldom get longer than 4 or 5 feet (1.2 to 1.5 meters). And, of course, others can grow to gigantic sizes. A Saltwater crocodile captured near the coast of India was reported to be 27½ feet long (8.4 meters) and weighed over a thousand pounds (450 kilograms).

No one knows exactly how old this crocodile was. But we do know that crocodilians can live a long time. An alligator in a zoo once lived for 56 years. But some scientists think that crocodiles living in the wild can live to be over a hundred years old.

This young crocodile is trying to capture a frog, but doesn't seem to have the "hang" of it yet. But like all crocodilians, when it grows up, it will be an excellent hunter.

CROCODILES

original models for fairy tale monsters

name first used 2000 years ago

world's largest reptile

part of a group of animals known as crocodilians.

cold blooded, scaly skin, lays eggs, breathes with lungs

some males more than 15' long may weigh over 500 lbs.
females usually smaller

dwarf - up to 4'-5'

can live in wild over 100 years

elephants and a blank transparency. Students were told to place the blank transparency over the article and underline key phrases and important points, as we had done, and then to write their notes on the right side of the page (see Figure 12–2). Groups then came up to the overhead projector with their transparency and placed it over a transparency of the article they had just read. They then shared their notes and received feedback and guidance from us and from other students. Finally, after

Figure 12-2 *Two Students' Note-taking Exercise*

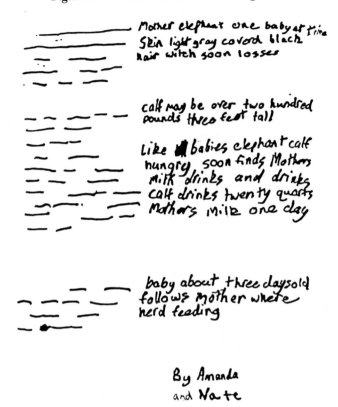

By Amanda
and Nate

we felt students understood the process, they began to apply taking notes to their individual research reports.

We initially had some problems with the process. We found that four students in a small group were too many to work together well. A better plan was for students to work in pairs, with one acting as scribe and the other giving oral suggestions and feedback. Another problem surfaced when we asked students to read through an entire section before beginning to take notes. We found that they largely ignored that request and took notes as they were reading. When we examined our own note-taking processes, we realized that's what we do as adults.

Examining our own processes as adults has helped us make decisions for teaching. For example, some teachers recommend that students take notes after they have read and closed the book as a way to avoid copying. However, as adults we don't do that, so we allow students to take notes with their books open.

Teachers find that demonstrating note taking pays big dividends. Students become proficient at using and applying this skill in all the content areas. The key to success is repeated demonstrations and reteaching throughout the year with various genres and contexts. Also, when demonstrating and practicing, using a short article seems to work best. Fifth grade teacher Jim Servis finds occasionally collecting students' notes is an excellent check. Using the same content handout, students take notes and turn them in. Jim hands the notes back a week later and asks students to write a cohesive paragraph from their notes. Students quickly see firsthand whether their notes are valid and how important it is to take meaningful notes.

An Integrated Social Studies Unit

The unit "Getting to Know Your State" was developed by fourth grade teacher Joan Servis in response to a required part of the social studies curriculum. The thematic unit is integrated with the language arts and takes place over a four-week period. Because it is important for students to know why a unit of study is being undertaken, they discussed the topic and listed the reasons it is important for them to know about their state (see Figure 12–3). Depending on the topic of study, we may need to make explicit why a unit is being studied or has been studied. Students may not be able to articulate the why's until a unit has concluded.

As we are writing and organizing integrated units, we need to stop and reflect on the important, global concepts we want to develop. Both teachers and students should be able to articulate these concepts.

Larger Understandings/Major Concepts/Desired Outcomes

1. Various factors affect our lives in Ohio, for example, natural resources, climate, pollution, and unemployment.
2. We can better understand our world and work to make it better if we have a better understanding of the factors that influence life in Ohio.

Figure 12–3 Understanding the Reasons for a Unit of Study

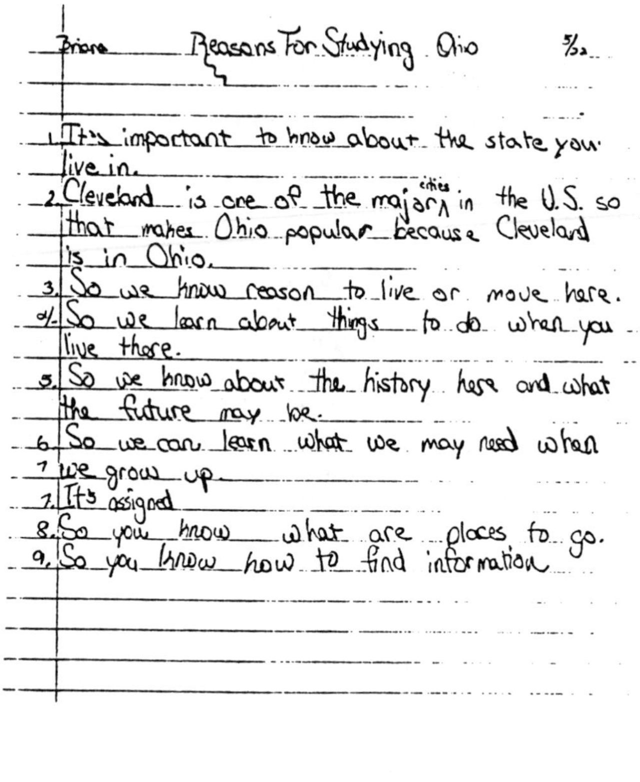

Briana Reasons For Studying Ohio 5/2

1. It's important to know about the state you live in.
2. Cleveland is one of the major cities in the U.S. so that makes Ohio popular because Cleveland is in Ohio.
3. So we know reason to live or move here.
4. So we learn about things to do when you live there.
5. So we know about the history here and what the future may be.
6. So we can learn what we may need when we grow up.
7. It's assigned
8. So you know what are places to go.
9. So you know how to find information

3. Finding out about our state necessitates the use of real-life skills—telephoning, letter writing, interviewing, researching. It is important to do these well to obtain necessary information.

Process/Procedures

1. Web/brainstorm the topic "A web is a kind of visual brainstorm that helps to generate ideas and link them to a theme or central focus" (Charlotte Huck, Susan Hepler, and Janet Hickman, *Children's Literature in the Elementary School*, 4th ed. [Holt, Rinehart and Winston, 1987], p. 652).

Figure 12–4 is an example of a brainstorming map made by a recent class. Each year the map is somewhat different. Many of us have found that webbing works best when done with teacher guidance. While such visual maps look easy to read, a lot of information is omitted, and the reader is expected to fill in the gaps. Because most students have difficulty doing this on their own, webs should be done collaboratively and talked about so that students make connections.

2. Select the topic and prioritize On a card, students list their first, second, and

Figure 12–4 Whole-Class Brainstorming for Social Studies Unit "Getting to Know Your State"

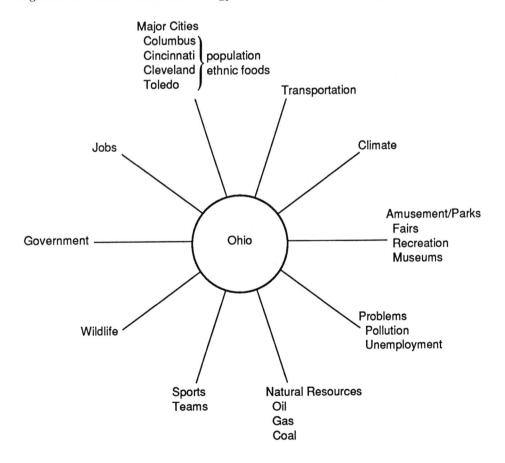

third choices of topics they wish to research. Just about everyone gets their first or second choices.

3. Divide into groups   Up to four students in a group seems to work best for cooperative work. Joan divided her class of twenty-four students into six groups, with four in each of the following topic groups:

- Wildlife
- Amusement parks/recreation/tourist sights
- Problems (present/future)
- Major cities/population
- Climate/jobs
- Government

4. Groups write their own questions to research for their topic of study   For the first few years Joan implemented this unit, she developed the questions and the format for research and study. In a further transition, students now choose their own questions and format. Students also determine the division of labor and how the information they gather will be organized.

5. Conference over questions for study   After each group formulates the questions to answer about their topic, they meet with another group to get its reactions to the substance of the questions. Revisions, additions, and deletions are then made. Finally, questions are turned in to the teacher for final feedback and revision. Conferencing may be necessary to resolve needed changes.

6. Group establishes format   Using the questions they have generated, the group members create a format and decide who will do what and what resources will be needed. Joan checks and okays each format, gives needed suggestions, and assists the groups in gathering what they need—informational books and phone numbers for obtaining information about their state, travel information, and so on.

7. Students take notes on their topics   Students use various resources to find answers to their questions, and they help one another as they are working. Notes are checked by Joan for relevance and proper form. (See "Note Taking" earlier in this chapter.)

8. Students write rough drafts   Notes are organized into cohesive paragraphs. The writing process stops here for this particular project.

9. Groups present information to the whole class   Upon completion of rough drafts, each group decides how it will share its information with the class. Students rehearse their presentations joyfully. Costumes and props are carried in from home, and students get very excited about their performance. Joan advises, "Educate and entertain. Don't bore us." Some past presentations have included radio shows, food festivals, plays, travelogues, quiz shows, questionnaires with audience involvement. Students take notes on one another's presentations.

10. Presentations are evaluated orally   Students begin with positive feedback that includes what they liked and what they learned. At least two positive statements are expected to be made before a suggestion for improvement may be given. The teacher participates as one voice.

11. Group interactions and content learned are evaluated Students are evaluated on group interaction and presentation and are also asked to complete a teacher-made essay test on the unit. Figures 12–5 and 12–6 are examples of students' self-evaluations. (See also p. 321 for the form students use to evaluate the unit.)

Figures 12–5 and 12–6   Fourth-graders' Self-evaluations of Group Work

Self-Evaluation

_____ SS _____ Discussion Group

Name Lindsay   Date 5/21

Book/topic _____ Ohio _____

1. What did I do well today (and/or improve on) during group discussion?

I got alot of roles on problems of Cleveland just by my own knolage.

I also tried to organized my group and get them working. I looked at a book called Undiscovered Ohio, but the only information they had on Cleveland, Columbus and Cincinati was on the Cleveland Metroparks. So I used my knolage.

2. What do I still need to improve on during group discussion?

I am going to call 1-800-Buckeye and I will make sure everyone gets alot of information!! Also I will try to make sure that none of us goof off at any time, like someone I won't mention names did.

Self-Evaluation

_____ SS _____ Discussion Group

Name Adam   Date 5/21

Book/topic Ohio

1. What did I do well today (and/or improve on) during group discussion?

I helped Ginaya do our government format. I didn't work very hard because I didn't have any information about Ohio's governor. I went to the library and didn't know what book I should get. So I didn't get any notes.

2. What do I still need to improve on during group discussion?

I need to improve not talking to much and getting down to buisness instead of not doing anything.

Figure 12-6

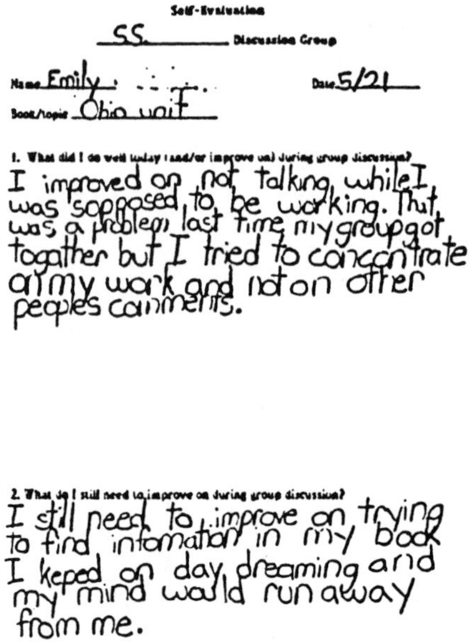

Self-Evaluation

SS _____ Discussion Group

Name Emily _____   Date 5/21

Book/Topic Ohio unit

1. What did I do well today (and/or improve on) during group discussion?

I improved on not talking while I was supposed to be working. That was a problem last time my group got together but I tried to concentrate on my work and not on other peoples comments.

2. What do I still need to improve on during group discussion?

I still need to improve on trying to find information in my book I keped on day dreaming and my mind would run away from me.

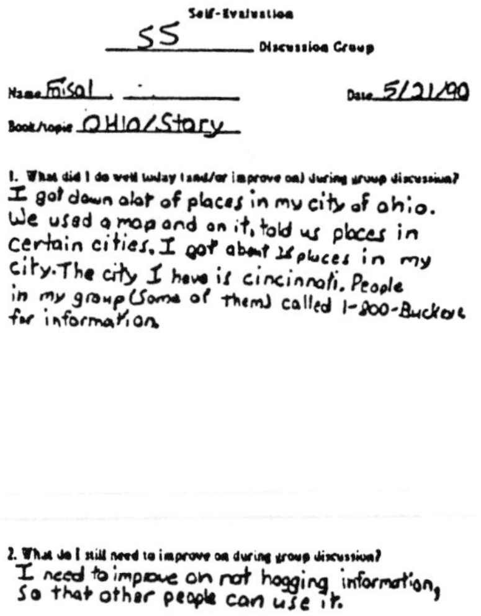

Self-Evaluation

SS _____ Discussion Group

Name Faisal _____   Date 5/21/90

Book/Topic Ohio/Story

1. What did I do well today (and/or improve on) during group discussion?

I got down alot of places in my city of ohio. We used a map and on it, told us places in certain cities. I got about 18 places in my city. The city I have is cincinnati. People in my group (some of them) called 1-800-Buckeye for information.

2. What do I still need to improve on during group discussion?

I need to improve on not hogging information, so that other people can use it.

Outcomes

One positive outcome of collaborative group work is that students help one another and work cooperatively to improve group dynamics. Even though each group has an area of specialization within the topic, students learn that if groups work together, they obtain more complete information and more thorough and balanced coverage of a topic.

Students also come to realize that they have the power to affect change in their own lives. For example, members of the group researching "Problems" began to talk about the need for recycling waste. At the conclusion of an end-of-the-unit party, students independently collected soda pop cans for recycling. Some students also began to urge their parents to begin recycling cans at home.

Moving toward More Meaningful Mathematics Instruction

Most teachers find that while they may be able to make natural mathematical connections to topics and themes, for the most part mathematics needs to be taught as a separate subject area. However, integration of math still takes place as long as the language processes are being used in a meaningful way and mathematical activities are relevant and supportive of the major concepts being developed.

With mathematics, teachers are beginning to see the value of providing students with interesting and relevant problems to think about, concrete materials to work with, and opportunities to find relationships among mathematical concepts. Holistic professional resources are becoming available in mathematics, and it is no longer unheard of to hear students describing the strategies and thinking processes they used to arrive at a solution. Many of the exciting changes that are coming about in mathematics teaching are the result of the issuance of the *Curriculum and Evaluation Standards for School Mathematics* (k–12) by the National Council of Teachers of Mathematics (1989), an impressive document which views mathematics as a means of communication and as a language system.

We need to familiarize ourselves with *Standards* and look at math the way we view reading and writing—as a language process that children learn developmentally with much modeling, exploration, and feedback. The conditions of language learning (see p. 13 and Figure 2–1) apply for mathematical learning as well. Additionally, mathematics needs to become relevant to children's lives by counting and manipulating real objects, measuring, estimating, graphing, classifying, and problem solving across the curriculum. Cooperative learning groups, teacher demonstrations, child-initiated problem solving, risk taking, and written and oral sharing need to be as much a part of the math curriculum as they are a part of the total language program.

Many teachers who no longer use workbooks in reading hang on to supplemental math workbooks and concentrate most of their instruction on computation practice and drill, including word problems that have no relevance to children's lives. While students do learn to compute, it's at the expense of mathematical processes that require reasoning and thinking.

I believe part of the reason the change to more meaningful math teaching has been slow in coming is that teachers in transition to whole language have focused most of their efforts on the language arts. Realistically, there isn't time or energy to revamp everything at one time. Also, most of us don't have the stamina for sweeping change; we all need the security of something familiar. Implicit in this further transition is time for the teacher to be a learner and time for students to learn at their own pace. Additionally, the resources available on teaching mathematics meaningfully—professional literature and staff development opportunities—have been very limited compared with those available in the language arts. Because little information is available for the teacher ready to make math a meaningful part of the curriculum, at the end of this chapter I have listed some recent journal articles and professional books that have proved to be useful resources.

In looking at the need for change, Beth Lazerick, a secular studies principal of a k–6 building whose doctoral studies focused on math education, states: "Kids have been rewarded in math for getting the right answer, not for developing strategies for arriving at the right answer." She believes kids also hang onto their crutches (for example, their fingers as counters) because they continue to be rewarded for their correct answers. Instead, Beth recommends having students do predicting, sampling, and exploring—and then describing how they got their answers. One suggestion she makes is having children write about and solve real-life math problems. Intermediate grade students might look at their family's actual grocery receipts and determine how much was spent on junk food, vegetables, and so on. Primary grade students could sort, estimate, and count the number of items in the many collections most of them have. In most cases, teachers will first need staff development opportunities in order to become comfortable in implementing these kinds of problem-solving activities in their mathematics programs.

Writing in Mathematics

One of the most exciting possibilities and new realities in current math teaching is the idea of students using writing to reflect on their reasoning processes. Writing provides students a way to extend and deepen their understanding of concepts. It gives them an opportunity to reflect on what they have been doing and to formulate and rethink their ideas. When students commit their thoughts to writing, they extend and cement their learning experiences. The teacher also benefits. When a student describes what she comprehends, the information contributes to the teacher's picture of what the student knows and understands and helps in making instructional decisions. Teachers who allow students to choose how they will demonstrate and interpret mathematical understandings are often surprised and delighted by the variety of responses.

Teachers can also use writing in math as part of the ongoing assessment process. Journals, portfolios, teacher observation, anecdotal records, and self-evaluation have as much a place in math evaluation as they do in other language processes. Having students write about the strategies they used to work through a problem and discuss what they learned makes students aware of their own learning. See Figures 12–7 and 12–8 for two fifth-graders' math journal entries done in math consultant Betty Hess's class.

The Need for Change

Conventional mathematics teaching has not immersed children in a rich math environment or encouraged exploration and responsibility. For the most part, math has been a hierarchical skills-driven program with lots of practice exercises from a commercial publisher. In many cases, math has been more about memorizing facts than understanding processes. A process approach to math starts where the child is, provides many opportunities for real-life, open-ended problem solving, and guides learners to construct their own understandings. Conferencing with other students, talking, listening, writing and reading, and explaining and sharing with peers are integral parts of the program. Finally, students begin to understand the role that mathematics plays in their world.

Figures 12–7 and 12–8   Two Fifth-graders' Math Journal Entries

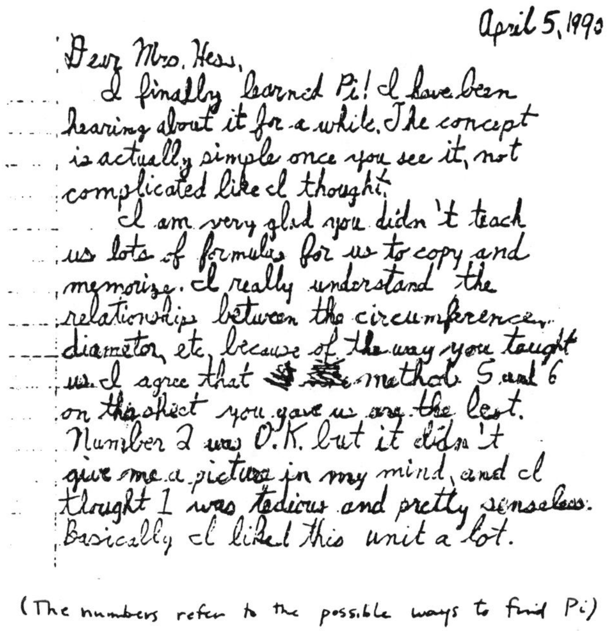

April 5, 1990

Dear Mrs. Hess,

I finally learned Pi! I have been hearing about it for a while. The concept is actually simple once you see it, not complicated like I thought.

I am very glad you didn't teach us lots of formulas for us to copy and memorize. I really understand the relationship between the circumference, diameter, etc. because of the way you taught us. I agree that method 5 and 6 on the sheet you gave us are the least. Number 2 was O.K. but it didn't give me a picture in my mind, and I thought 1 was tedious and pretty senseless. Basically I liked this unit a lot.

(The numbers refer to the possible ways to find Pi)

Figure 12–8

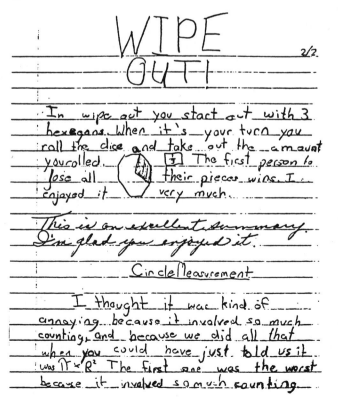

WIPE
OUT!   2/2

In wipe out you start out with 3 hexagons. When it's your turn you roll the dice and take out the amount you rolled. The first person to lose all their pieces wins. I enjoyed it very much.

This is an excellent summary. I'm glad you enjoyed it.

Circle Measurement

I thought it was kind of annoying because it involved so much counting, and because we did all that when you could have just told us it was $\pi \times R^2$ The first one was the worst because it involved so much counting.

Constraints to Successful Integrated Language Programs

While meaningful integration is an admirable and worthy educational goal, we also need to be realistic about how difficult integration is to achieve. This section considers some of the factors that work against successful integrated language programs.

Theoretical Understandings

Before integration can take place, we need an understanding of the theory underlying children's language acquisition, an in-depth knowledge of the literature and resources being used, and an understanding of the curriculum. Without this knowledge of theory and practice, teachers are likely to "basalize" units with only superficial interdisciplinary connections. With a large majority of teachers acting as scripted technicians managing preset commercial programs, we are still a long way from being curriculum decision makers. Ongoing staff development efforts need to include helping teachers to understand integration and develop meaningful integrated language units.

Time

We need to work with our administrators to create uninterrupted blocks of instructional time in daily schedules. On the elementary level, self-contained classrooms—with no switching rooms for various subjects—promote flexibility and offer opportunities for integration. Many teachers find the only way they can tie language arts and reading to the content areas and have time for both is through integration, made possible by large blocks of uninterrupted time.

Additionally, teachers must have release time to plan with colleagues, research topics, write and adjust curriculum, and gather resources. It is unrealistic to expect individual teachers to devote hours of planning on their own time. While common planning time across grade levels is a start, it is not sufficient. Teachers cannot be expected to implement an integrated curriculum without several hours a month of release time for planning. While I noticed that some administrators in Australia were willing to make such a time commitment, I have rarely seen it here in the states.

In one district teachers were expected to meet by grade levels after school every few months to share ideas and plan and write units. One angry teacher commented that because release time had not been provided, many teachers would continue to do "whatever is easier."

Administrative Support

An integrated curriculum requires a fully committed administrator who values and understands the approach and is willing to give teachers time and funds to develop it. Teachers cannot get a budget for curriculum development and the purchase of resources and equipment without administrative support.

Resources

Beyond collections of fiction, there is a need for in-class libraries with quality literature of all types. Nonfiction materials especially—magazines, newspapers, encyclopedias, information books—do not presently exist in most classrooms. There is also a need for flexible, open library times for students—not standard practice in many school libraries.

Curriculum Requirements

Teachers and administrators are constrained by course objectives and state guidelines. Some of these are necessary to ensure that important concepts are developed in logical sequence at particular grade levels. However, many districts further constrain themselves by adopting basal texts and social studies and science textbooks using publishers' guidelines as a total program. These texts should be used as one of many resources—to be referred to, not adhered to.

Reflections

An integrated language curriculum focuses on important concepts through topic and theme development in a manner that is not contrived. Students come to understand their world better through engaging in relevant school experiences. While interdisciplinary integration is a desired long-range goal, we need to begin by working toward integration in smaller areas; we might begin with literature study and then add social studies, science, and math. We need to integrate the language arts and the visual arts—reading, writing, speaking, listening, art, music, drama, dance—into the various subject areas instead of trying to bring every subject into the language arts. The language arts can then be the medium for integrating the subject areas. Finally, as in all difficult transitions, we need to move slowly and allow ourselves time for continuous risk taking, reflection, and rethinking.

Resources for Improving Mathematics Instruction

For full information and annotations for the following titles, see *Resources for Teachers*, "Professional Books" and "Literacy Extension Resources."

Atwell, *Coming to Know: Writing to Learn in the Intermediate Grades*

Baker, *Mathematics in Process*

Griffiths and Clyne, *Books You Can Count On: Linking Mathematics and Literature*

Romberg, *Curriculum and Evaluation Standards for School Mathematics*

Whitin, Mills, and O'Keefe, *Living and Learning Mathematics: Stories and Strategies for Supporting Mathematical Literacy*

Burns, Marilyn. January 1988. "Beyond 'the Right Answer' . . . Helping Your Students Make Sense Out of MATH," *Learning*, pp. 31–36.

Using writing and cooperative learning, Burns details four strategies for promoting thinking and reasoning. Immediate, practical applications to the classroom.

Davison, David M., and Daniel L. Pearce. April 1988. "Using Writing Activities to Reinforce Mathematics Instruction," *Arithmetic Teacher*, pp. 42–45.

The authors discuss and define five categories of mathematical writing activities: direct use of language, linguistic translation, summarizing, applied use of language, and creative use of language. Activities described have application in classrooms at all grade levels.

Ohanian, Susan. October 1989. "Readin' 'Rithmetic: Using Children's Literature to Teach Math," *Learning*; pp. 32–35.

Specific books about counting and numbers are discussed with suggestions for developing mathematical concepts.

Richards, Leah. January 1990. " 'Measuring Things in Words': Language for Learning Mathematics," *Language Arts*, pp. 14–25.

An Australian teacher (of eleven-year-olds) describes how she uses language to develop children's knowledge and confidence in mathematics. Using math themes and subsequent investigations, she sets out the plans, strategies, and evaluation techniques. Samples of children's writing are also given.

Steen, Lynn Arthur. September 1989. "Teaching Mathematics for Tomorrow's World," *Educational Leadership*, pp. 18–22.

A professor of mathematics gives the rationale for the "revitalization" of mathematics education and includes an overview of necessary curricular changes. Valuable reading for teachers, administrators, and policy makers.

13

Evaluation

The most fundamental goal of all educational evaluation is optimal instruction for all children and evaluation practices are only legitimate to the extent that they serve this goal.
(Johnston, 1987, p. 744)

Giving students time to work things out on their own: reading in the kindergarten

Evaluation is a critical issue all teachers struggle with. In an attempt to help clarify some current issues and give theoretical and practical direction to teachers, this chapter examines the effects of standardized testing and considers definitions, beliefs, components, and contexts of meaningful evaluation. This chapter also takes a look at portfolio assessment, confronts report cards and grading systems, offers various means for self-evaluation, and concludes with annotated resource articles that inform the evaluation process. Because standardized testing still dominates assessment, I begin with the effects of standardized testing and attempt to put this issue into perspective.

Effects of Standardized Testing

While eating breakfast one morning, I was reading an article in *The New York Times* entitled "How Two Brooklyn Schools Can Be So Alike and Yet So Different" by Joseph Burger (July 24, 1990). I was struck by the fact that tests still drive all aspects of education. The article described two public schools in poor, black neighborhoods. In one school, over 80 percent of the students read at or above the national average for their grade *based on standardized test scores*; at the other school, less than 40 percent did. The reporter credited the difference to a principal with a strong personal leadership style as well as to a year-long emphasis on test preparation. Teachers at the higher-scoring school were required to have two daily reading lessons: One involved using the basal text and workbooks and the other focused on preparing for reading tests. The principal was quoted as saying: "I would prefer if we could find a different way of evaluating children's progress. But given the reality, I have no choice. Schools are looked at this way. I'm not certain that the instrument is testing what we want to test, but I don't know what instrument would be better."

I did a rough calculation. Based on 180 school days and one hour a day allocated to reading, at least ninety instructional hours were being devoted to passing a fragmented test that would do little to inform the teacher or students of meaningful progress in reading. Yet the results of such tests are used routinely all over the country to judge the effectiveness of schools, to place students in special programs, to track students, to pass or retain students, to decide whether or not certain programs should continue to be funded, to evaluate teachers, and to plan curriculums.

I felt totally disheartened when I finished the article. I believed the students were good test takers, but I was not convinced that the school was producing readers. The article made no mention of anything associated with real reading— reading and discussing authentic literature, reading aloud, choosing books, thinking about books, and finding delight in reading. Reading was defined here in terms of "standard readers," workbooks, and test scores.

Preoccupation with test scores not only robs our students but also harms our teaching. I remember a third grade teacher whose students always had the highest test scores. Not only did she teach to the test but her curriculum was skills-driven, dominated by workbooks, worksheets, and boring drill. When the students went on to fourth grade, where the teacher taught to the students, the test scores always dropped. It looked as though the students lost ground that next year, and the fourth grade teacher felt bad. She believed she was a good teacher, but she knew she was being judged by the students' test scores.

The "worst case scenario" occurred some years ago and involved a teacher who actually changed responses in student test booklets so her class would score well. However, the scores looked so good for a class with many low achievers that it became obvious something was amiss. Something is very wrong when teachers feel driven to go to such extraordinary, and even illegal, lengths to see that their students score well.

As long as we continue to equate reading progress with high test scores, we have little hope of raising a generation of readers: students who are able to read and reason, who are able to relate and apply ideas to their lives and different situations, and who choose to read for pleasure.

Standardized Test Scores: A Look at One Student

Even when we say the tests are not important, we want our students to score well because we teachers are often judged by the results. Recently my principal called me into her office while looking at the standardized test results she had just received. "Did you work with this child?" she asked me. I could tell from the tone of her voice that the news was not good. Doris, a third-grader who had been one of my Reading Recovery students in first grade, had scored in the third stanine in total reading. "Doris is a good reader," I insisted. "Something is wrong with the test. I want to see the test booklet." While I was convinced Doris was a capable reader, nonetheless, I felt quite defensive. Somehow, Doris should have done better.

I spoke with Doris's classroom teacher Linda Cooper, who also saw Doris as a competent reader. We decided to measure Doris's reading by observing her reading processes on an unfamiliar but meaningful text. Doris was asked to read pages 15–17 of *Mr. Popper's Penguins* by Richard and Florence Atwater (Little, Brown,

1938), a lengthy chapter book that is at least at a third grade level. After a brief oral introduction, I asked Doris to read the text. Her accuracy rate was 93 percent, indicating the book was at her instructional level. More significant to us was the definite indication that Doris understood what she was reading. When I asked her, "What was it that *Mrs.* Popper wanted?" Doris responded, "She wanted a clean house!" I had meant to ask her, "What was it that *Mr.* Popper wanted?"—an easier question. Doris, however, had no trouble answering any of the questions or briefly retelling the story. Linda and I felt vindicated: Obviously Doris was a very capable reader.

Because we were puzzled by her low scores on the standardized reading test, Linda and I looked through the test booklet with Doris. We wanted to see if she could give us any insights into how and why she had responded to certain questions as she had. Several factors became apparent. Because Doris thoughtfully used her own background experiences to make sense when reading—as we did in class when reading and discussing a book—she sometimes marked an answer that was correct for her but not for the test makers. For example, in the "Word Reading" section, Doris was supposed to fill in a little circle under the word in each line that goes with the picture. In a picture of a girl in pajamas, sleeping in a bed with a quilt, instead of filling in the circle under "pajamas," Doris filled in the circle under "patches"—"because it's just like my quilt with patches all over," she explained. Following a short "Reading Comprehension" paragraph where a question asks what happened to a mother and son who didn't know which road to take while driving, Doris marked they had gotten "stuck" instead of "lost"—"because when I'm lost I always feel stuck."

The other factor that became apparent was that Doris had been penalized because she was unpracticed with worksheets and word-study skills subtests, which do not measure reading in context. That is, when Doris had to perform a task without the aid of context—the surrounding authentic text, illustrations, and learning setting that help give meaning to a word or groups of words—she was at a clear disadvantage. In many cases where she made an error, she simply did not understand the test format. While we would never spend a whole year preparing for the test, it was obvious that our students would need to have some test taking preparation in—"reading-test-reading" (Reardon, 1990)—if they were to have a fair chance at succeeding in test taking.

Now, about a month before our fall testing, our principal, Bernice Stokes, makes sure students become familiar with test formats. Students receive guidance and practice in analyzing and interpreting the phrasing and structure of the test questions as well as in ruling out unlikely responses and guessing intelligently. One useful strategy on the reading comprehension section is to have students read the questions first. The short, connected paragraphs in this section measure test-taking skills more than they do reading comprehension. Students who have learned how to answer test questions can often do well on this section without ever reading the passage given in the test.

Phonics in Isolation: Looking Beyond the Test Scores

Performance on a subtest can give an inaccurate message about a student's learning abilities and needs. Rather than providing information that could be useful for instructional decision making, the results are neither credible nor reliable. When the results are interpreted literally, low scores on subtests are responsible for placing and maintaining students in adjunct skills-based instructional programs. The message for students and their parents is that mastering a discrete set of skills is of primary importance in becoming a good reader. We need to keep in mind that skills are valuable only to the extent that they can be strategically applied to an authentic reading context.

Doris's lowest standardized test score, a year below grade level, was on the "Word Study Skills" subtest. Here the student was asked to mark one out of three words that had the same sound as the underlined letter(s) in the first word. For example, in the line: "g<u>oo</u>d   tool   found   put," the correct response is "put." (Doris marked "tool.") What is being evaluated here is certainly not reading or even decoding. Never having done an activity like this before, Doris was confused by the directions. Additionally, one reason she wound up in Reading Recovery in the first place was because she had difficulty hearing sounds in words. Doris did well with phonics when she could integrate phonics with semantics and syntax in the context of a meaningful text. Yet her low score on the "decontextualized" subtest pulled her overall reading score way down.

Doris's mother, with whom we had a close working relationship, was upset about her daughter's low score on the subtest and insisted Doris be "pulled out" to work with the Chapter 1 teacher on "phonics skills." She knew Doris was a competent reader, but the test score made her question her own beliefs. Even when we showed her how well Doris had read the passage in *Mr. Popper's Penguins* and talked with her at length about what it means to be a good reader, she still wanted her daughter "to have the phonics she needs." We talked with Doris's mother about the message being "pulled out" for reading help would convey to Doris, and we asked her to trust us. Finally, she gave in.

At the end of the school year Doris's mother said,

> I didn't understand that the test really didn't measure what Doris could do. I'm so glad I listened to you. Doris reads beautifully, and she has no trouble at all with phonics when she has a meaningful sentence or paragraph. She can then figure out almost all the words or put in something that makes sense.

Parents, based on their own education and the way reading has been taught for so many years, overvalue word-study skills tests in isolation. We need to educate parents about the place of phonics in reading, about the unimportance of isolated subtests, and about the failure of standardized tests to assess phonics knowledge accurately. In my own district, since the fall 1990, we have been using a new basis for norming, one that allows a total reading score minus the phonics-structural analysis subtests. At least that's an improvement.

Another reason parents seem to place so much importance on test scores has to do with the amount of time schools devote to standardized testing. At our fall parent conferences, parents traditionally spend quite a lot of time listening to teachers explain how to read the print-outs of the students' standardized test scores. The sheer amount of time we spend on this activity sends the message that "this is important." Since parents perceive test scores as indicators of academic success, we need to educate them about other more legitimate criteria. We need to spend most of our evaluation time on observational measures and to share those with parents as the most valid evaluation indicators of their children's achievement. When teachers have shared portfolios—with multiple samples of student's work in various contexts—parents quickly move away from their preoccupation with test data (Rob Tierney, conversation, August 1990).

What Happens to Test Scores with Whole Language?

There's no question that children like Doris—competent readers who integrate strategies in context but who perform poorly on the various subtests—are handicapped on standardized tests. Nonetheless, most of our students' scores on standardized tests have not been adversely affected by whole language approach to reading instruction. Our director of testing reports that the reading scores in our five k–4 buildings have remained consistent over the past five years.

However, this is not always the case. I have heard stories of lowered test scores during the first years of transition to whole language. Nonetheless, as far as I know, there is no evidence that over the long term students in whole language programs perform less well on standardized tests. In fact, over the long haul, they probably do better, especially if they have had some instruction and practice in test taking.

What is required is that administrators and board of education members have an understanding of whole language and a long-range commitment that goes beyond immediate test results. They must also be willing to consider other indicators as valid measures of success. Norm Smith, a principal of a whole language school in California, commented, "Without the understanding of the Board of Education and their willingness to allow time for the results to show on the tests, a great program might have been stopped in its second or third year." He reported that a longitudinal study showed that "after nearly five years in the program, the overall positive results of whole language are starting to show on tests." At the same time, he acknowledged the immediate success of whole language, as reflected by increased student attendance, a more positive school atmosphere, increased parent involvement, more proficiency in English by students making the transition from Spanish to English, and more positive student and parent attitudes (Bird, 1989, pp. 118–120).

I believe that daily reading and writing with real literature—and instruction that derives from children's interests and needs in the reading-writing process—is the best preparation for testing regardless of the types of tests we are using. Even when a district has a course of study for teaching discrete skills, if teachers teach the skills by immersing students in holistic, meaningful literacy events, the students will do well—as long as they have guidance and practice in "reading-test-reading." The reverse is not true: Teaching discrete skills may yield temporary high scores on isolated subtests, but these results do not necessarily transfer to comprehending meaningful text.

Standardized Testing in Perspective

One needs to look beyond standardized test scores to gather a balanced profile of a student. Testing that relies on one data base from one setting—rather than multiple indicators that look at the student over time—cannot be used to guide the learner.

Standardized tests tell administrators, teachers, and parents how a child compares with his peers, but the tests give very little information that is useful instructionally and no information on learning processes over time. A further hazard is that standardized tests are often relied on more for information about students' deficits than for information about their strengths.

Standardized tests, with their multiple choice question format, do not allow the reader to intepret the text based on personal background knowledge and experiences. The right answers have already been locked in by the test makers. Even with improved standardized tests—such as those in place in Michigan and Illinois, which attempt to move away from a skills-based approach to reading to a more interactive, strategic one—the tests can be used only as one assessment measure. While these states and others are working to improve test formats to include more prediction and inferential questions, the questions and answers remain the test maker's, and none are open ended. While the format and questions are better, they are still used in unnatural settings and require limited input from the learner. Nor do the results reflect the student's learning process over time. The same is true for timed essay tests that expect students, under pressure, to write a perfect final copy in one sitting. Such requirements ignore writing as an evolving, reflective, revising, and editing process.

Perhaps most important, we cannot ignore the very real, lifelong damage to student self-esteem that stems from overemphasis on the results of standardized tests. Most standardized and readiness tests do not consider the language differences among different sociocultural groups, so that many children are placed at an unfair disadvantage. It is well known that Chapter 1 and special education programs have a disproportionate number of minority students, and standardized tests have played a major factor in these placements.

Since there seems to be little likelihood that we as a society will be doing away with standardized tests in the near future, it is imperative we monitor *how* such tests are used and interpreted. As responsible educators, we must begin to use other data to provide more reliable evidence for measuring a student's progress or determining a student's placement in a program. As teachers and educators, we must help parents put tests into a proper perspective. We need to invite parents to join us in actively trying to reduce the emphasis on standardized tests.

Perhaps, most important, we teachers must become evaluation experts so we can trust and rely on our own knowledge to best serve students. When we have a good student who scores poorly on a test, we must convince administrators, parents, and the student that the problem is with the testing instrument and not with the test taker. Teachers can do even more: They can try to reduce the focus on basal book tests and teacher-made tests, which are given even more emphasis than standardized tests.

We must also communicate to administrators, parents, and board of education members the recommendation of many respected educators and of the National Association for the Education of Young Children to end standardized testing (including readiness testing) in grades k–2 (Bredkamp and Shepard, 1989; Kamii, 1990). We can work to improve the attitudes surrounding testing in our own school districts. At the very least, we can advocate testing only in the fall of the year so teachers do not wind up teaching to the test. We can find out when and how often state testing is required. Some teachers have been surprised to learn that their school district is actually doing some optional standardized testing. Some states do not require standardized testing until grade 3, yet their school districts begin testing in the earlier grades. Teachers and administrators who have taken the time to check with their state departments of education for the "standard" requirements in assessment often find there is latitude for district choice.

A few states have already begun to replace standardized testing in grades k–2 with informal, classroom-based evaluation. We no longer test in first grade; in our district the Reading Recovery teachers administer a diagnostic survey (Clay, 1985) to first-graders about whom teachers want more information. At this time, some primary teachers in our district are actively involved in an effort to do away with standardized testing in grade 2.

What Is Evaluation and Why Is It So Difficult?

While teachers may be beginning to feel more comfortable and confident with whole language teaching, just to mention the word "evaluation," and you can feel the tension. Teachers feel inadequate, frustrated, and even terrified about handling evaluation fairly and competently. Most of us have had little training or guidance in assessment and evaluation procedures, and our confidence in relying on ourselves to assess students' progress is shaky, at best. Even when teachers feel ready— both theoretically and practically—to move toward more holistic evaluation, just managing the time and logistics for ongoing evaluation can be overwhelming. Additionally, the whole issue of trust plays a major role in the evaluation process. Administrators, parents, community members, and politicians need to value and respect informed teacher judgment, and teachers first need to learn to trust and value their own observations.

"What about evaluation?" is probably the question asked most often by teachers who have begun to move from a transmission, lecture style of teaching to a more democratic, interactive style. There are no easy answers, and the issue is even more difficult for teachers who have to give grades. Like moving from the basal to literature, where most of us have needed lots of time to teach the literature well, we need to give ourselves lots of time for this further transition to more meaningful evaluation in our teaching. The process is a slow, evolving one that requires lots of risk taking and continuous self-examination. Because evaluation is such a difficult area for most of us, at the end of this chapter I have included an annotated list of journal articles and books on evaluation that have proved to be particularly useful to teachers.

Before meaningful evaluation can become an integrated, ongoing, natural part of teaching, we teachers need to have certain conditions in place:

- A thorough knowledge of developmental learning processes and curriculum
- An examination and clear articulation of one's beliefs and goals about evaluation
- Knowledge and experience of how to collect, record, interpret, and analyze multiple sources of data
- Flexibility and willingness to try out and value multiple evaluation procedures to gain a complete picture of the learner
- A strong commitment to understand and implement a meaningful approach to evaluation

Before we can start incorporating meaningful evaluation methods—most of which are based on observation of students and include things like anecdotal records, interviews, learning logs, and running records—we first need to understand and value why this type of evaluation is integral to the teaching-learning process. We need to guard against simply putting procedures into place without understanding the theory behind them. Otherwise, evaluation becomes very much like the basalization of literature that occurs when only the materials change: Merely putting new procedures and activities into place will not result in meaningful teaching.

Another very real constraint to meaningful evaluation is management. Finding the time to add observational procedures to an already packed day is difficult. Management of evaluation procedures is one of the major reasons more teachers are not actively involved in the evaluation process. It's been my experience that, unless a collaborative classroom is formed, teachers do not have time in their daily schedules to make observations and record and analyze them. Until students and teachers share the responsibilities for teaching and learning, the evaluation task appears overwhelming.

Teachers need blocks of time when students can work independently on worthwhile enterprises without direct teacher supervision so they can take time to observe, conference, interview, and meet one-to-one with students. For that to happen, teachers need to have classrooms in which students are largely monitoring their own learning processes. In other words, they have to already have whole language classrooms. Holistic evaluation is a final step—it happens *after* the management, theory, and knowledge base are in place. That's why it's so difficult. To try to simply fit it in before that doesn't work.

Nonetheless, teachers find that when they begin to observe learners in broader contexts—as will be discussed later in this chapter—they start to initiate more holistic evaluation procedures. For example, teachers report that when they give sustained attention to a child's reading, they can do better analysis and teaching.

Defining Assessment and Evaluation

While the terms "assessment" and "evaluation" are often used interchangeably, they are not exactly the same. The distinction became apparent to me when I participated in a preconvention institute at IRA ("Literacy Assessment: Setting an Agenda for the 90's," International Reading Association annual meeting, Atlanta, May 1990). As I now understand it, assessment is only the beginning of the evaluation process.

"Assessment" refers to data collection and the gathering of evidence. "Evaluation" implies bringing meaning to that data through interpretation, analysis, and reflection and includes the kinds of instructional decisions that are made by careful examination of the evidence. I prefer to use the term "evaluation" in a broader context, to designate both the collection of data and the interpretation and application of it. While the evaluation process depends on assessment, assessment is only the first step in the evaluation process. Data, by itself—without observational components and interpretation—has no meaningful place in instruction or informed teaching. You can't make a value judgment about test scores; they are merely raw data. It's the interpretation of that data which brings one to the evaluation level.

For example, interpreting and analyzing Doris's standardized test scores *along with* observational measures of her reading process enabled us to evaluate her reading and not just assess it. We could not make informed instructional decisions by relying solely on Doris's test scores; we needed information from other meaningful contexts in order to plan a sound instructional program.

Very often assessment takes place apart from teaching, although ideally it needs to be an integral part of instruction. "Assessment should be constructed so good instruction is the best preparation" (Karen Wixon at assessment preconvention institute, IRA, 1990). In other words, assessment procedures should go hand in hand with good teaching. For example, when Doris's reading was assessed through a regularly occurring, genuine reading event—reading literature—she needed no special preparation to do well. Educators need to keep Wixon's statement in mind before they accord so much weight to standardized tests. Assessment needs to be meaningful, multimodal, and ongoing and must occur in authentic contexts.

Authentic assessment is at the heart of the evaluation process:

> Authentic assessment isn't a single method. It includes performance tests, such as conversations in a foreign language; observations, open-ended questions where students tackle a problem but there's no single right answer; exhibitions in which students choose their own ways to demonstrate what they have learned; interviews, giving students a chance to reflect on their achievement; and portfolios, collections of student work. The list is limited only by the criterion of authenticity, is this what we want students to know and be able to do? (Ruth Mitchell, in *Portfolio, The Newsletter of Arts PROPEL*, December 13, 1989).

While the holistic evaluation process begins with assessment and the collecting and recording of data, unless we use the data to inform and guide instruction, we are not evaluating; we are merely amassing bits and pieces of information. Before we can become expert evaluators, we have to be excellent observers, or "kidwatchers," as Yetta Goodman calls it. Through kidwatching teachers begin to develop a stronger and more clearly articulated theory base.

The difficult part is that good observation, the most critical component in evaluation, is only as good as the teacher's knowledge base. Before we can become expert observers, we have to be expert learners. We have to be able to observe and value strengths more than deficits. We have to know what to look for: What are the developmental markers we are seeing or not seeing? We have to be expert listeners: What does the student really mean? We have to be able to recognize an individual student's learning patterns and use them to take the child further. We also have to know how to set up the learning environment to maximize student development. Most of all, we need to value observation as integral to evaluation and be willing to risk adding it to our literacy programs. None of this is easy, and most of us take many years to make our evaluation processes more consistent with our beliefs about learning.

How assessment procedures and information are used is what raises the assessment process to the level of evaluation. If data collection is being used only for accountability, for grading and reporting to parents—as it usually is—meaningful evaluation is not taking place. Instead, what is taking place is simply accountability and data reporting. The goal of evaluation, like the goal of teaching, is to make the learner self-monitoring, self-regulating, and independent. The highest goal in evaluation is to have students and teachers able to reflectively appraise their own work and set new directions for teaching and learning. Ideally, self-evaluation becomes the major evaluation mode.

Traditionally, the teacher has been "in charge" of appraising and setting new directions. Shifting this responsibility to the child can seem like a radical and scary departure from what we have been taught to believe and practice. As with any profound change, we need to start slowly and gradually, take the time to understand the theory and beliefs that support the change, and allow time and latitude to make mistakes. In an attempt to ease the transition to more meaningful evaluation, the remainder of this chapter will examine beliefs, components, and issues in evaluation; demonstrate various observational strategies; and discuss the rationale and procedures for self-evaluation.

Beliefs about Evaluation for Students and Teachers

The word "evaluation" derives from "value." Before evaluation procedures can be changed and improved, we need to be able to identify what we value and state our literacy goals. A clear understanding of our beliefs and goals—along with what we want to do and why we want to do it—precedes putting evaluation practices into place.

Your beliefs and goals will be somewhat different from mine, based on your own philosophy, background, and experiences. I present my list only as a way to begin thinking about what evaluation means to you. In the struggle to work through what evaluation means, it's often a good idea to try to put your beliefs and goals in writing and then try to apply them in your classroom.

These beliefs are as important for teacher-learners as they are for student-learners.

My Beliefs	*My Goals*
Evaluation needs to:	Evaluation procedures should:
• Be consistent with theory	• Be based on daily authentic language experiences; be consistent with what we know about language learning
• Be multifaceted	• Include process and product, informal and formal measures, observational data, work samples, conferences, interviews, reading-writing strategies
• Emphasize informal/observational methods	• Highly value and utilize anecdotal records, retellings, reading and writing logs and journals, writing samples, tape recordings, running records
• Be an integral, ongoing part of the teaching-learning process, not separate from it	• Inform teaching by being a natural part of daily classroom happenings

My Beliefs	*My Goals*
• Respect and trust teacher judgment	• Value teachers' observational data
• Report to students, parents, and selves	• Give useful, clear information that indicates progress and notes needed new directions
• Have expectations clearly defined	• Explain evaluation criteria to students and parents at the beginning of the term or project
• Focus on the learner's strengths	• State first what the learner can do well; avoid negative statements
• Assess interests and attitudes	• Incorporate interest and attitude interviews and surveys and include results in setting instructional goals
• Encourage risk taking and approximation	• Value invented spelling and attempts at self-correction; view errors as natural part of the learning process
• Collect, record, analyze, and share data	• Include record keeping by students and teachers
• Guide the learner	• Set directions for teaching and lead to growth for the learner
• Be noncompetitive	• View the child in comparison with self—not others; reduce emphasis on grades and standardized tests
• Be diagnostic and descriptive note growth note strengths and weaknesses note directions for teaching and future learning	• Incorporate narrative; report to students, parents, and ourselves in a way that promotes social interaction, reflection, and growth
• Promote self-evaluation and self-monitoring	• Involve learners in assessing strengths and weaknesses and in setting goals; promote independence
• Place the final responsibility with the learner	• Eventually enable learners to assess their own learning, develop their own evaluation criteria, and make intelligent decisions for directions in future learning

Components of Evaluation

I see evaluation as involving five components. For evaluation to be meaningful, these components must occur interactively within a naturalistic framework. That is, the observation, activity, test, or task must be relevant, authentic, and part of the teaching-learning process by informing the learner and furthering instruction.

Figure 13-1   Data Gathering Profile

EVALUATION
DATA GATHERING PROFILE
contexts

OBSERVATION

anecdotal records
interviews, probes
conversations
response groups for writing
retellings
participation in mini-lessons
shared reading experiences
shared writing experiences
passage reading in books
running records/miscue analysis
audio tapes, video tapes
note-taking samples
one-to-one writing samples
drafts, revisions, sketches
oral presentations
problem-solving groups
whole-class evaluations
responses through performing arts
reading environmental print (K)
dramatic play
learning centers

responses to open-ended questions
literature response logs
learning/reflection logs
writing journals
self-evaluations
completed enterprises/projects/activi-
    ties/assignments/reports/research/
    graphs/charts/illustrations
student-created questions/tests
notebooks
writing folders
reading records of books read
vocabulary records
writing samples (plays, poems, letters,
    stories, published pieces)
responses through visual arts
portfolios

OBSERVATION OF PROCESS

OBSERVATION OF PRODUCT

CLIMATE OF INQUIRY

CONTEXTUALIZED MEASURES

DECONTEXTUALIZED MEASURES

MEASUREMENT

inventories, checklists
teacher-made tests
proofreading exercises
cloze exercises
informal reading inventories
interest/attitude surveys
unit or book tests
dictations
holistic writing assessments
informal reading/writing evaluations

standardized achievement tests
minimum competency tests
school, district, or state tests
norm-referenced tests
criterion-referenced tests
writing vocabulary (Clay, 1985) (K–2)
letter, letter-sound, and word tests
    (K–2)
spelling tests, vocabulary tests
diagnostic tests/surveys
worksheets

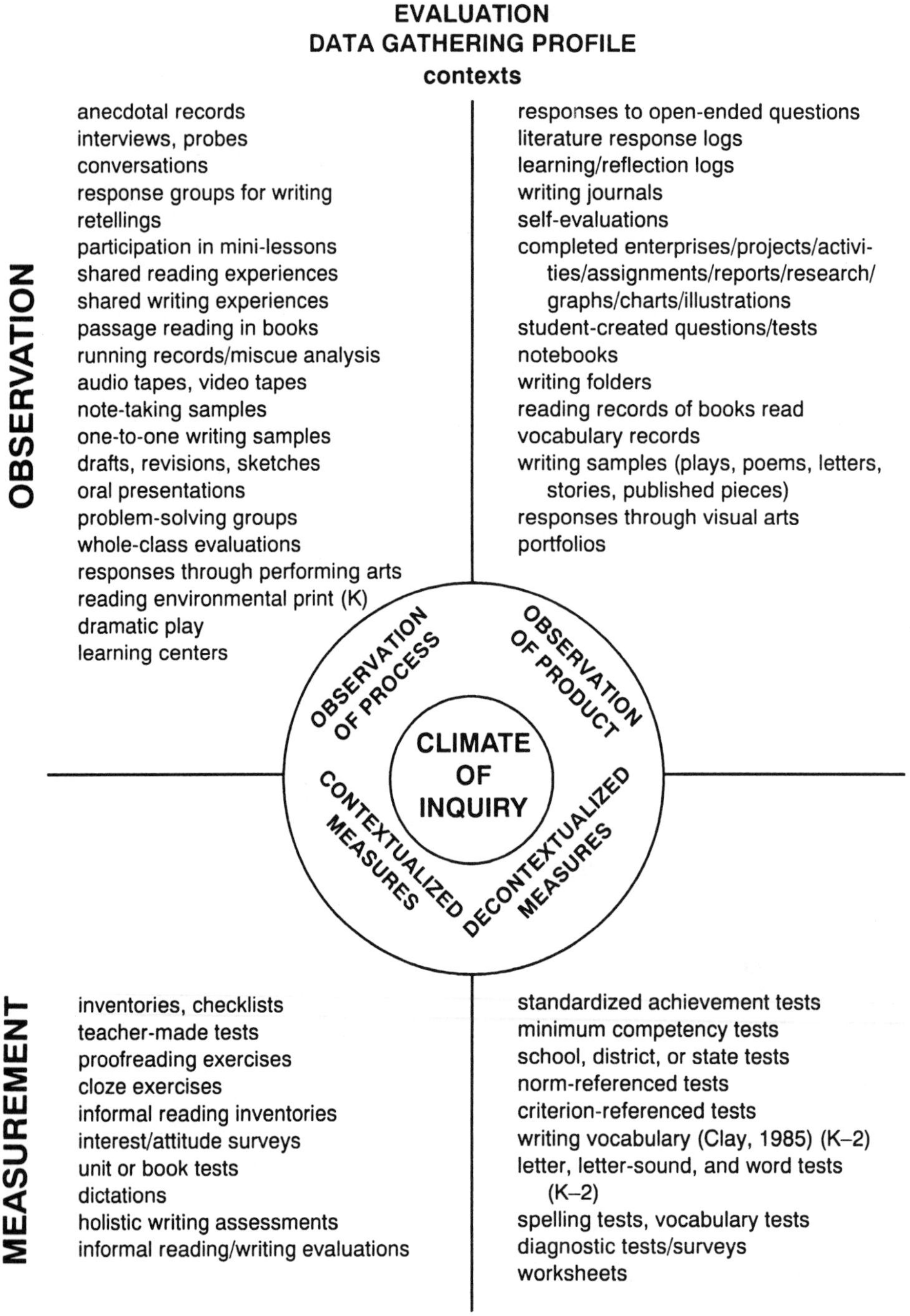

Adapted from a form developed by R. Anthony, T. Johnson, N. Mickelson, and A. Preece, shared at Preconvention Institute, "Evaluation: A Perspective for Change." World Congress on Reading, International Reading Association, Brisbane, Australia, July 1988.

- *Observations of both process and product and collection of data*

    Consider multiple sources of data from varying learning contexts.
    See "Data Gathering Profile," Figure 13–1, for guidance.

    The "Data Gathering Profile" is worth examining carefully both as a way of looking at what is meant by balanced evaluation procedures and as a check on yourself. For example, note that the evaluation profile is divided into four quadrants. The two lower quadrants are composed of more traditional assessment measures. While these are important and valid, we want to be sure that *most* of the data we are using for informed evaluation comes from observational contexts, especially process. You may want to keep the profile handy to use as a self-check list of what you are already doing, to monitor your own evaluation procedures, and to see what other kinds of evidence you might want to consider gathering. Adjust the profile to fit your particular teaching situation.

- *Recording of observations and data*

    See the "Data Gathering Profile," Figure 13–1, especially anecdotal records.

- *Interpretation and analysis of observations and data*

    Requires theory and knowledge about literacy learning
        miscue analysis, running records
        interviews, probes (example of Doris), use of videotapes

- *Reporting of information*

    Reporting to parents—report cards, narratives, conferences, records
    Reporting at district, local, and state levels—test results
    Communicating to others—achievement, process
    Reporting to self; self-evaluation

- *Application to teaching/learning*

    How teaching is informed and new instructional directions set lead to staff development and continuous self-evaluation; without this step, learner has not been served

Evaluation: Putting Theory into Practice

No single behavior, strategy, activity, or task can provide a comprehensive picture of student learning. Only a variety of measures, examined carefully over a period of time, can give an accurate and complete picture of a student's progress, strengths, and needs. Besides the "Data Gathering Profile" (Figure 13–1), Andrea Butler shared with me a questioning framework that has served me well in deciding the kinds of evaluation measures to utilize. "What do I want to know?" and "How am I going to find it out?" are two questions that can help the evaluation process. See Figure 13–2 for examples of how this framework may be utilized.

Figure 13-2   A Framework for Guiding the Evaluation Process

EVALUATION

What do I want to know?	How am I going to find it out?		
	Informal	*Ongoing*	*Formal*
Oral reading	One-to-one observation Paired reading	Shared reading Guided reading in group	Tape recordings Running records
Spelling	Have-a-Go sheets Free writing Pretests	Writing samples Journal writing	Proofreading exercises/paragraphs Weekly tests Dictations
Reading comprehension	Books child chooses Retellings	Contributions in group discussion Reading response logs Evidence provided to support viewpoints	Written tests Standardized tests Cloze exercises
Reading-writing attitudes	Books chooses Amount of reading/writing Interview (oral)	Writing journal, writing folder Responses in discussion/conferences Participation in shared reading and shared writing	Interview /written survey Reading records of books read
How student views self as a reader/writer	Attitude survey—oral Books/topics chooses WEB reading	Choices for portfolio Reflection log Questions asked in conferences Oral and written responses to text	Self-evaluations rubrics narratives report cards

Focusing on procedures and contexts that I and other teachers have used successfully, this section discusses various components from the "Data Gathering Profile," especially those that involve teacher evaluation. Most of these are informal measures. However, just because observation is informal does not mean that it is not highly informed and accurate. Quite the contrary. Teacher observation and judgment, especially of process, are the most valid means to collect and analyze data on children's learning.

Observational Strategies and Informal Evaluation

The following pages highlight some observational processes from the "Data Gathering Profile." The analysis and application of information that needs to accompany meaningful observation of students and recording of data take years of informed practice as well as a solid knowledge of theory and the language processes. Give yourself lots of time to make mistakes, take risks, and try out new procedures. Go slowly. Add one or more contexts from the profile as you feel ready.

At the same time, keep in mind that the "Data Gathering Profile" should not be used as a menu or list of assessment activities but as part of a larger literacy framework. We need always to have an expanded view of literacy assessment— viewing and guiding students to be effective decision makers and active meaning makers who employ reading and writing for a variety of meaningful purposes.

Anecdotal Records

Anecdotal records are dated, informal observational notations that describe language development as well as social development in terms of the learner's attitudes, strengths, weaknesses, needs, progress, learning styles, skills, strategies used, or anything else that seems significant at the time of observation. These records are usually brief comments that are very specific to what the child is doing and needs to be doing. They provide documented, accumulated information over time and offer an expanded view of the student's development of literacy.

Anecdotal records may be taken in a variety of settings, for example: journal writing, dramatic play, oral reading, literature discussion groups, spelling, independent work, and writing. The contexts are limited only by your particular needs

Second grade teacher Ellen Rubin
taking anecdotal records
during a writing conference

and time constraints. While the setting for record taking can be whole class, small group, or individual, most often anecdotal records are taken on individual students, either in a one-to-one setting with the teacher or by the teacher observing the child or the child's work in a particular context. (See Figures 13–3 through 13–7 for variations of anecdotal records. Most of these examples represent first efforts by teachers.)

Figure 13–3 A Kindergarten Teacher's Anecdotal Records of Student's Reading Behaviors

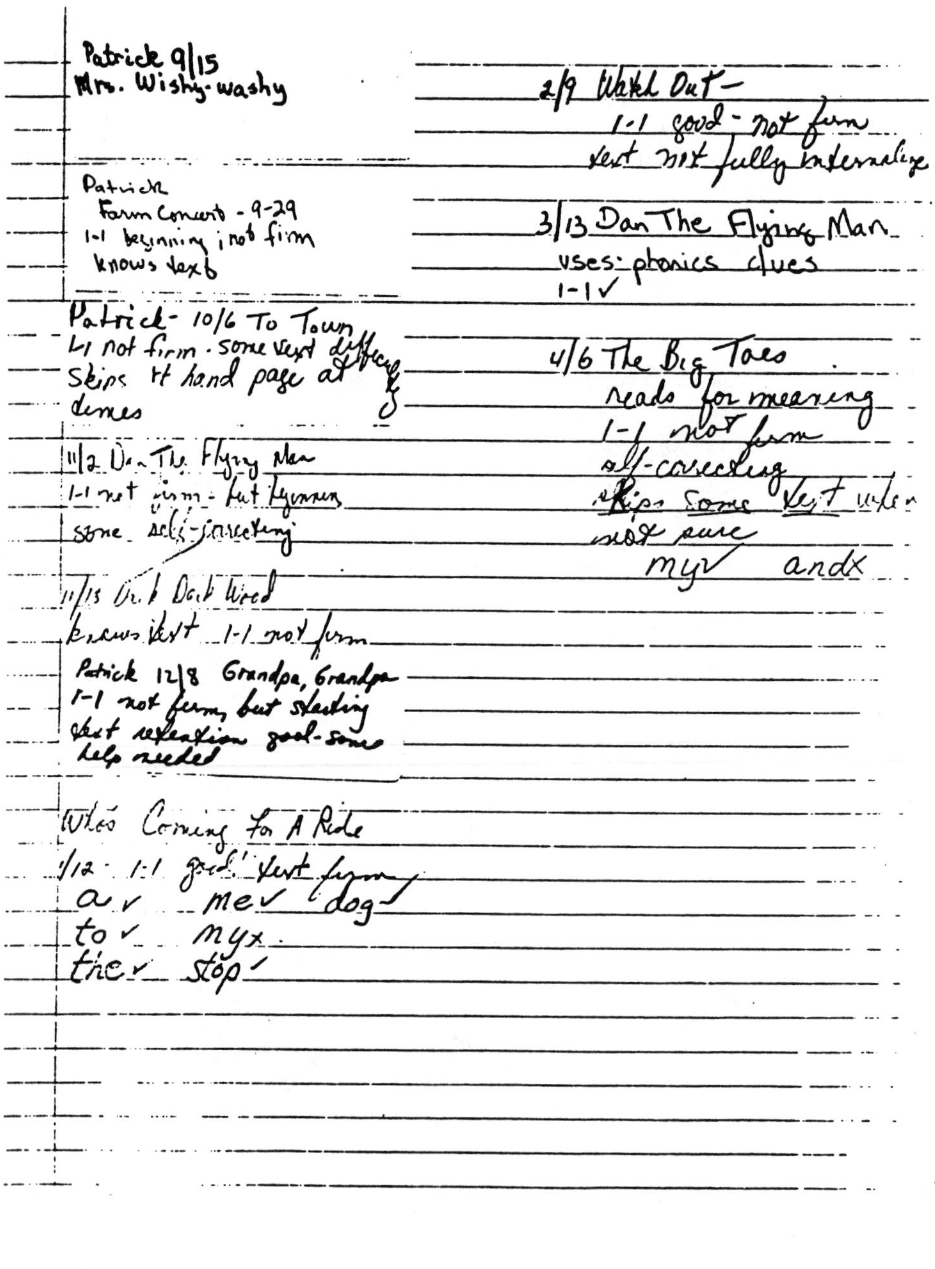

Patrick 9/15
Mrs. Wishy-washy

Patrick
Farm Concert - 9-29
1-1 beginning; not firm
knows text

Patrick - 10/6 To Town
1-1 not firm. some text difficulty
Skips rt hand page at times

11/2 Dan The Flying Man
1-1 not firm - but happens
some self-correcting

11/15 Out Out Weed
knows text 1-1 not firm

Patrick 12/8 Grandpa, Grandpa
1-1 not firm, but starting
text retention good - some
help needed

Who's Coming For A Ride
1/12 1:1 good! text firm
a ✓ me ✓ dog
to ✓ my x
there ✓ stop ✓

2/9 Wake Out -
1-1 good - not firm
text not fully internalize

3/13 Dan The Flying Man
uses: phonics clues
1-1 ✓

4/6 The Big Toe
reads for meaning
1-1 not firm
self-correcting
skips some text when
not sure
my ✓ and x

Figure 13-4 A Grade 1 Teacher's Anecdotal Records of Students' Independent Work

strengths needs

Taylor

10/13
I like Book — ending periods, -er, ēē
short vowels — beg cap. CVe ch -ing

Plane Ride
Strawberry Book -great innovation

10/20
On Halloween

- extended on story; sc-; good sight words — periods - putting hyphens between words
sense of plural; beg./ends consen. — ow; capitals at beg,
ă ĭ

Journal 10-20

ch — tr

Witch book 10/25 good effort illus. — -ed (using -d), periods
-great plot development

Blank book
The Indian Book
- innovation from beg. pattern

blank book _ Haunted House — -confusion over hard/soft g
- good use of written expression "but..."

Figure 13-5 Anecdotal Notes on Third Grade Students' Journal Entries

Allen :

9-6-88   Journal

Very expressive - connected ideas. writes confidently
Getting the idea of paragraphing. Needs to reread for
punctuation or capitals in some places.

Keith   Journal

9-6-88   good effort or detail - story about his dog o how he fetches
i̇/I , He omits endings or some verb tense difficulty

Figure 13-6   A Third Grade Teacher's Anecdotal Notes on One Student's Reading

Name: *Nathan*

READING RECORD   *(grade 3)*

Attitude -
12/6 Enjoyed the book - rate (9¾) told why he did not
     rate it a ten. Boring part. Excited about Chester Cricket.
□/6 Rated (8) liked ending but some parts he didn't understand.
1-9 Excited about book - willing to talk about it.
     Difficult to get him to stop!

Selection of Books-
12/6 Wild Timothy
      Chester Cricket's New Home
1-9 The Secret Garden

Reading Strategies/Comprehension-
12/6 Told about new book - Chester Cricket - described where
he lives. Good details - big ladies - oversized!
Forgot name of boy.
1-9 Told about characters - good detail. Gets the
main ideas and predicts well. - "I think he is like
a doctor.

I have modeled taking anecdotal records for kindergarten teachers who have never gone through the process before and want to learn. With the teacher looking on, I invite the child, or the teacher invites the child, to choose a favorite book to read. I then observe the child "reading" the book and note what the child is doing (see Figure 13–8). I also give positive feedback to the child, telling him what I notice he can do. For early childhood teachers just beginning this process, the checklist of print concepts (Figure 13–13) may be helpful for building an awareness of important behaviors to observe and assess.

Beginning to take anecdotal records is difficult and requires taking a risk. At first, your records may not be particularly informative, but you will improve with practice and your observational skills and use of specific language to match the task will improve. As an ongoing record of students' process and progress, the records will serve you, the students, the parents, and your administrator well. Probably the hardest aspect of taking anecdotal records is finding time in an already full

Figure 13-7   A Third Grade Teacher's Anecdotal Notes on One Student's Writing

WRITING RECORD   *(grade 3)*

Attitude-
10/89 Willing to write. Enjoys writing stories and poems.
3/9 Excellent use of punctuation - detailed
Conversation when writing.

Clarity of Expression-
10/89 Easy to understand. Clear to the reader.
3/9 Clear

Revision and Editing (willingness to change)
10/89 Willing to go back and change around. Needs to
spend more time editing in marking pen. Tends to
erase.

Mechanics (spelling, captials, periods)
10/5/89 Makes paragraphs when needed.
3/9 Mechanics is improving, knows
when to add punctuation + capitals.
Spelling improving.

schedule. In addition, there is the confidence factor for us as teachers. We haven't had much training or encouragement in keeping informal records, nor have we seen them be highly regarded. Valuing informal observational data means trusting teacher judgment.

Despite the constraints of time and effort, taking anecdotal records pays important dividends. The records are useful for conferences with the student, parents, or administrator, serve as benchmarks for noting student progress and setting instructional goals, and become objective sources of factual documentation and of specific information for writing narratives on report forms. Anecdotal records can also be used to promote reflection on student growth by the students, parents, teachers, and administrators. Finally, since only the employment of multiple evaluation measures can assure a representative picture of the student, anecdotal records are a way to observe and note process and product in various contexts.

Figure 13-8   Observational Notes of Kindergartners' Reading of a Favorite Book

Noah

chose Obadiah. pointed to title & title page & read it.
    attempt at 1:1 - pretty close
    looking at text - making sense in retelling - very close to text
    knew finger should come out at end of line - moved finger
        to end when he finished reading a line.
    ready to work on 1:1 matching for greater accuracy.
p. 16 - did perfect 1:1 when asked to reread. & given some modeling
    could locate some specific words: "pot" two times
    could find "black" by going back to beginn. of line.

Keindre   3-5-90

Lazy Mary - read title, held book correctly, reads left to right
    looking at text.   p 3   memorized
                        p 4   "
                        p 5   "
                        p 7   "
    has 1:1 matching pretty well - did some s/c when text
didn't fit.
    ? - could identify it
    p 9 - looked at text - had 1:1 matching.
    1:1 matching became more accurate as went through book
    went back to begin. of text when text didn't fit
    could point to "Mary", "will" several times when asked
    actually reading text.
    ready to do crisp 1:1 matching

Marcy Silver, a third grade teacher who has taken records for two years, says,

> My anecdotal records have been especially useful during parent conferences.
> I can be very specific about each child, and the parents feel good because it's
> obvious I know their child. For example, I might have noted the child's atti-
> tudes and facial gestures when he was talking about a particular book. I'd never
> remember that weeks later if I hadn't written it down. I've also used the
> anecdotal records to conference with students and to write comments on report
> cards. After two years, it's going a lot more smoothly. It's definitely been worth
> the effort.

Organizing for Taking Anecdotal Records To find the time to take anecdotal records, you need to make the process an integral part of your teaching. This is difficult to do unless your classroom is organized collaboratively, with students managing their own behaviors, and you have blocks of time when you are not directly teaching or supervising. Attempting to take observational notes while teaching does not work and serves only to frustrate the teacher. For your first attempts, try involving your students in an activity that you feel confident they can complete independently. Then, call up several students, one at a time, and have them read to you. Use the sample anecdotal records provided in this chapter as a starting framework. With time and experience, you will develop your own style and comfort level and become familiar with the vocabulary that describes language learning.

Many opportunities exist within the normal routines of the classroom when anecdotal records may be taken. When young students are involved in dramatic play, writing at the writing center, or looking at books, the teacher can take five minutes to focus on several students and jot down some notes. When students have assumed a leadership role in a literature discussion group, the teacher can occasionally become an observer and note taker. When you are conferencing with a student, you can jot down relevant comments about what you are noticing or conferencing about. Some teachers who check their students' independent reading daily occasionally use that time to note observations about reading attitudes and strategies used. Once in a while, you can ask several students to join you at a table during sustained silent reading and note what they do in the process of reading. Or instead of scheduling reading groups five days a week, take one day—for example, Friday—to meet with students one-to-one to listen to them read and then make anecdotal comments. Finally, if you have a collaborative classroom where you have provided opportunities for children to work together, you will be able to be a teacher researcher and observer and note the problem-solving strategies students are using and then base instruction on your observations. At the highest level, your anecdotal records can become the basis for self-evaluation, where you begin to note patterns and behaviors that inform your teaching.

For keeping anecdotal records, some teachers use a three-ring binder with dividers, allocating several pages for each student—perhaps one for reading, one for math, and one for writing. Others prefer a spiral-bound notebook with a tab inserted for each student in the class. Some teachers color code their tabs for the five days of the week and divide their class into five groups. On the day they are taking anecdotal records, they focus on the five or six students in a particular color. In that way, you would make observational comments about each student at least several times a month.

One management system that works very well is to use a clipboard while sitting down with the students or while walking around observing. The teacher makes brief notes on an index card or Post-it and adds the comments to the notebook later. An efficient method that many of our teachers favor is to clip a strip of adhesive mailing or package labels to a clipboard and write comments directly on the labels. At the end of the day, the rectangular label is pasted on the child's page. (See Figure 13–9 for a kindergarten teacher's observational comments done on mailing labels that have not yet been pasted onto students' individual records—from "Booklook" setting where students choose books to read independently or with peers.)

Figure 13-9   A Kindergarten Teacher's Observational Notes on Mailing Labels for Pasting onto Student Records

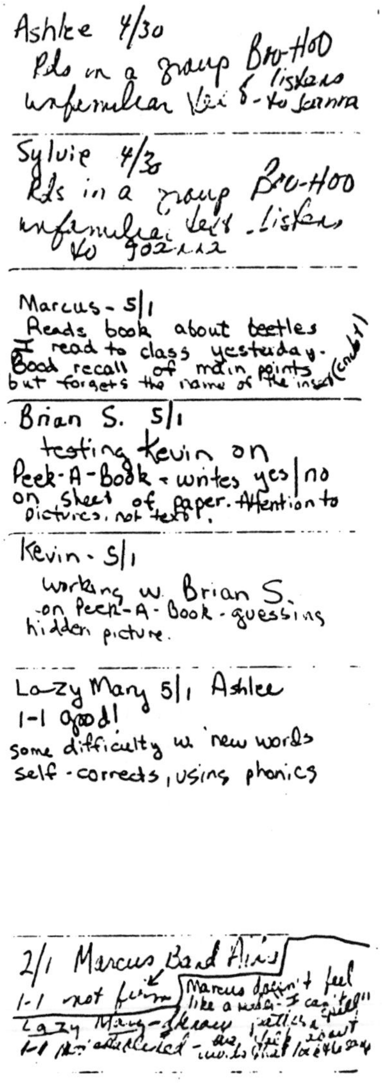

In taking anecdotal records, it is important for all comments to begin positively with something the child *is* doing. This is a difficult adjustment, for most of us tend to begin with what the child is not doing. Focusing on strengths first is important for several reasons. Eventually noticing strengths first becomes a state of mind. Taking a positive view of all children is part of whole language philosophy and all good teaching. In addition, I believe students and parents are entitled to hear about the child's positive behaviors.

Even a young child should be able to take a look at her section in the anecdotal notebook and feel comfortable. This is not to say we don't list the needs and deficits; we do, but *after* we have noted what the child is doing well. A good check is to see if you feel comfortable sharing your records with the student and with her parents. If you don't, you may want to think about your attitudes toward observation. We need to treat our students as we would want to be treated. I know I would be upset if my principal refused to show me her observational notes about my teaching because they are negatively worded.

Before you decide to add anecdotal records to your routines, it's important to look at where you are in your teaching. While lots of talk turns on the need to take anecdotal records, few teachers actually keep such records. In our district, after three years of moving toward whole language, some teachers are just beginning to attempt that additional record keeping. Most teachers seem to need about five years to feel ready to handle and value this additional but crucial responsibility. The exceptions are our kindergarten teachers, many of whom have been taking and utilizing observational notes for years.

While the taking of anecdotal records is of vital importance to the total evaluation process, give yourself time to make this transition. Find the system and time arrangement that work best for you. There is no one right way. As you begin to make taking anecdotal records a part of your teaching, eventually, the task will no longer seem like an extra incumbrance, and you will feel as though you know your students a lot better. Start small, perhaps with one area such as reading or writing. At the same time, you may want to include beginning and ending year interviews or attitude surveys along with anecdotal notes on each child. Keep in mind that your records may be short and infrequent. Some teachers find that taking records as infrequently as several times a quarter (twice in nine weeks) is sufficient help to be worth the effort.

Interviews and Surveys

One-to-one interviews are an ideal way to get to know your students. I prefer interviews to written surveys because students often feel limited by the questions and the space on the page. They tend to respond minimally in writing, and I never feel I have learned much about the student. With a personal interview, you can probe a response and elicit information that reflects attitudes, strategies, preferences, and level of confidence—all in just a few minutes. I think it's worth taking some time at the beginning of school to interview each of your students. If you take just several students a day for five to ten minutes each, you can get through your entire class in two weeks. The specific information you gain will save time later because you will be better prepared to set relevant instructional goals.

You'll probably want to design your own form, survey, or questionnaire based on your and your students' needs. Use the "Reading Survey" (Figure 13–10), "Writing Survey" (Figure 13–11), "Spelling Interview" (Appendix H), and "Writing Interview" (Figure 13–12) as guides.

Here are some additional questions you may want to include. All of these would be too many. Choose those that suit your purposes.

- Where do you read at home?
- How much television do you watch? What are your favorite programs?
- Does anyone read to you at home? Were you read to when you were little?
- Do you sign out books from the public library?
- Name the last book that you read.

- Does anything about reading cause you trouble?
- Who in your family likes to spend time reading?
- Do you like to write stories?
- How do you get your ideas for writing?
- Are you a good listener? Why do you think so?
- How do you feel about speaking in front of others?
- What do you like to do in your free time?
- What is the best present you ever received?
- What is something you think you do very well?
- What is something you think you need to work on?
- What is something you hope to learn this year at school?
- Is there anything you would like me to know that would help you have a good year at school?

Figure 13-10   Reading Survey

READING SURVEY

Name_____   Date_____

1. How do you feel about reading?

2. Do you have a favorite author? Explain.

3. What kinds of books do you like to read?

4. What was your last favorite book? Explain.

5. Do you think it's important to be a good reader? Explain.

6. What do you do when you come to a word you can't read?

Figure 13-11   Writing Survey
Developed by Karen Horton.

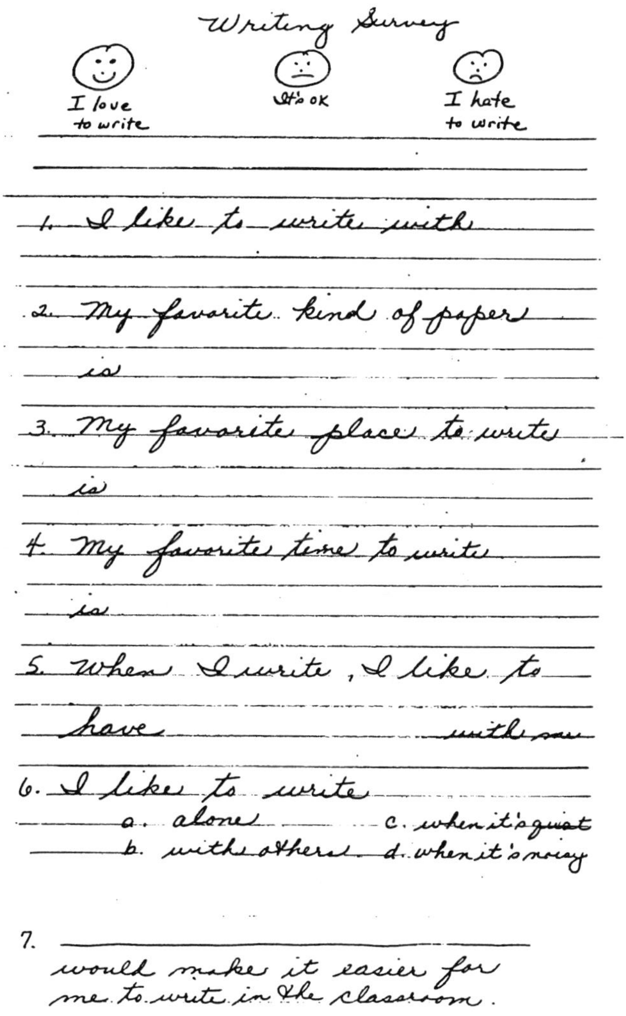

Writing Survey

😊 I love to write   😐 It's ok   🙁 I hate to write

1. I like to write with

2. My favorite kind of paper is

3. My favorite place to write is

4. My favorite time to write is

5. When I write, I like to have _____ with me

6. I like to write
   a. alone   c. when it's quiet
   b. with others   d. when it's noisy

7. _____ would make it easier for me to write in the classroom.

Inspired by Frank Smith's *Joining the Literacy Club*, fourth grade teacher Joan Di Dio designed a "Literacy Express" membership form to make all her entering students immediate members of the "Literacy Club." Her purpose is for all students to feel that if they have read or written anything at all (which, of course, everyone has), they are already members of the club. The requirements are deliberately kept simple so no one can be excluded. The membership application has blank, lined spaces for "I. Books You've Read" (or "That Have Been Read to You") and "II. *Any* Kinds of Writing You've Ever Done." The idea and form could even be adapted to kindergarten by changing the two headings above to "Books You Like," which could include favorite stories children have heard read aloud, and

Figure 13–12 Writing Interview

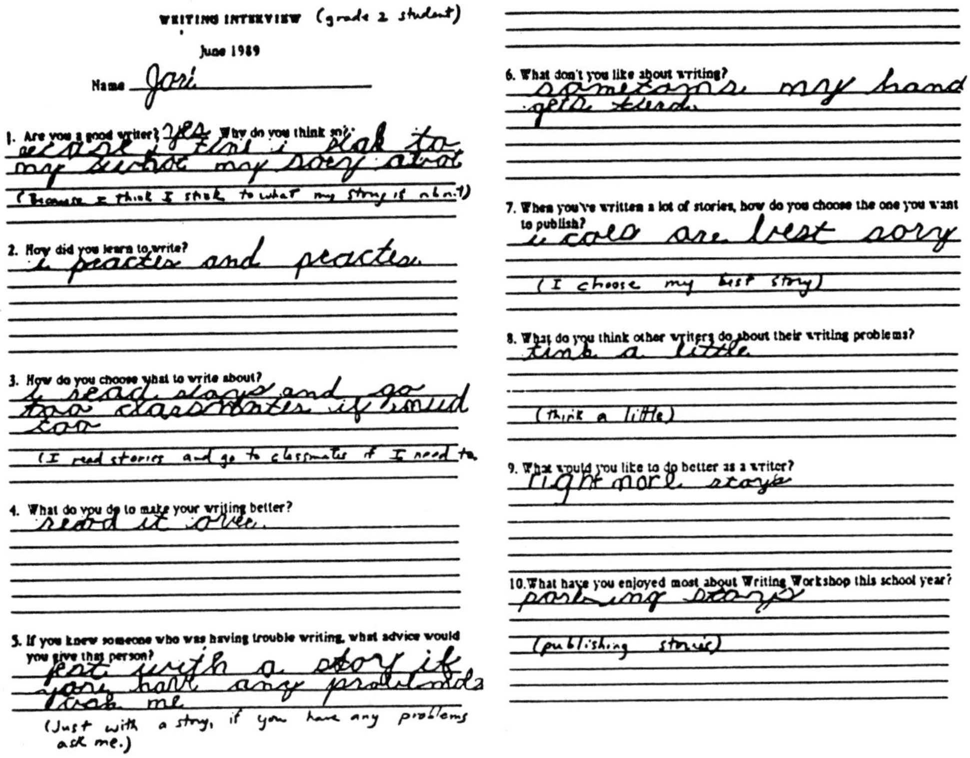

WRITING INTERVIEW (grade 2 student)

June 1989

Name Jori

1. Are you a good writer? yes Why do you think so? because i first i stak to my techer my sory about
(Because I think I stick to what my story is about)

2. How did you learn to write? i peactes and peactes

3. How do you choose what to write about? i read storys and go too classmates if i need too
(I read stories and go to classmates if I need to.)

4. What do you do to make your writing better? read it over.

5. If you knew someone who was having trouble writing, what advice would you give that person? just with a story if you have any problems asck me
(Just with a story, if you have any problems ask me.)

6. What don't you like about writing? sometoms my hand gets tired.

7. When you've written a lot of stories, how do you choose the one you want to publish? i cose are best sory
(I choose my best story)

8. What do you think other writers do about their writing problems? tink a little
(think a little)

9. What would you like to do better as a writer? right more storys

10. What have you enjoyed most about Writing Workshop this school year? posling storys
(publishing stories)

"Writing You Like to Do," with available blank space to affirm that marks on paper that have meaning to the child make the child a writer and club member.

Older students can design their own interview forms as a way for the teacher to get to know them. Students can also interview each other. Important questions for an interview form could also come from a shared writing experience. Completed forms may be posted or bound into a book and read as a way for all students to get to know their classmates.

One-to-one interviews, or written interview surveys the child completes, are also useful at the end of the year for noting changes in attitudes and what the child has learned. After two years of being immersed in a literature program, almost all the children in a third grade class responded positively to the question, "Do you like to read?" on a written interview form. The only exceptions were the students who were new to the school. Note in Figure 13–12 a second-grader's "Writing Interview" after a year of daily "writing workshop" (Calkins, *The Art of Teaching Writing*, Heinemann, 1986).

Interviews or surveys can also be used in the content areas to find out student attitudes toward the content, what students have learned, and their suggestions for improving a unit or course. A sample content interview, based on the work of Rogers (1989), follows:

Content Interview

1. What are the most important things you have learned in _____ (science, health, math, social studies) during this _____ (year, semester, quarter, class)?
2. How did you feel about this course (unit, class) and the way it was set up?
3. What did you like best about the unit?
4. What did you like least about the unit?
5. Do you have any suggestions for how this unit should be taught to next year's class?

Conferences

Conferences are a powerful evaluation tool. By following the lead of the student—and not imposing a teacher agenda—conferences enable us to get to know students as learners and to guide them in making literacy connections. Many teachers are starting to use the conferences they are already having with students as a time to make anecdotal observations. In addition to ongoing writing conferences, we have ongoing reading conferences related to independent reading (see WEB, pp. 43–49).

Checklists

Lots of teachers use checklists effectively and wisely. While on the whole I prefer narratives and anecdotal records, there are times when checklists work well. I like to use a checklist, combined with narrative and observational comments, for checking early literacy behaviors—letter-sound knowledge, basic sight words, and print concepts. See Figure 13–13 for "Concepts About Print," adapted from Marie Clay's "Concepts about Print" (1985). The form can easily be used as a straight checklist by adding verticle lines across the page and writing students' names across the top.

Note the procedures for using the "Concepts About Print" checklist. A real book with simple text and matching pictures would be used to check for understanding of concepts. Under "Letter and Word Knowledge," when checking for understanding the difference between one letter and two letters, one word and two words, and a first and last letter of a word, Clay recommends giving the child two index cards. Choose a page with only one line of print and show the child how to hold one card in each hand, lay them side by side, covering the line of text, and then slide the cards back and forth to expose the print. Once the child can do this, ask him to show you the desired number of letters and words. These are important concepts for checking whether the child understands the difference between a letter and a word. (See Clay, 1985, pp. 27–30, for specific language the examiner uses for checking some of these concepts.)

I also like checklists when they help put students in charge of their own learning, for example, having students check for specific skills before completing and handing in an assignment. (See Figure 13–14, "Proofreader's Checklist.")

The problem I have with most checklists for teachers is that you wind up spending most of your time focusing on the list to be checked rather than on the

Figure 13–13   Concepts About Print Form

Concepts About Print

Book Handling _____

front of book, cover _____

title _____

turns pages left to right _____

notices pictures _____

points to print when reading (telling) _____

holds book correctly _____

Directionality
understands top/bottom
points top left to begin
beginning to have one-to-one matching
   of spoken word to printed word
moves finger left to right and word for
   word, down the page (return sweep)
reads (turns) pages in order

Letter and Word Knowledge
can locate one letter and then two letters
can locate one word and then two words
can locate a first letter and a last letter
can point to a specific word when prompted
can identify a capital letter and then the same
   lower case letter

Higher Level Concepts
understands use of "."
understands use of "?"
understands use of " "
uses beginning letter sounds
uses final consonant sounds
relies on pictures to tell the story
relies on memory for text
uses structural cues

Adapted from "Concepts of Print" test in *The Early Detection of Reading Difficulties*, 3rd ed., by Marie M. Clay (Portsmouth, NH: Heinemann, 1985).

child. By looking for progress on a skills checklist, you can easily miss observing the learning that is occurring. The other problem is that when checklists are devised by someone else, they never quite fit the teacher's and student's needs. My personal advice, based on experience, is to use checklists sparingly and then to devise your own forms based on your children and your needs. Use these and other forms (such as those included in "Resources" at the end of this chapter) as models, but adapt them to suit your purposes and the students' needs.

Figure 13-14   Proofreader's Checklist

Proofreader's Checklist

Name_____   Date_____

Before you consider your paper complete, check to see that you have done the following:

_____ Each sentence begins with a capital letter.
_____ "I" is always capitalized.
_____ Each sentence ends with correct punctuation ("." "?" or "!").
_____ The names of people and important places are capitalized.
_____ Speech marks (") are used to show when someone is talking.
_____ Each new paragraph is indented
_____ I have checked and corrected my spelling to the best of my ability.
_____ I have checked to see that my story makes sense.
_____ My handwriting is clear and legible.

Is there anything else you did in checking over your paper? Note it in the space below.

_____
_____
_____

Retellings

Asking students to give an oral or written retelling of what they have read is an effective strategy for evaluating comprehension and is a viable alternative to teacher follow-up questions. Children are in charge of telling in their own words what they have understood, and the setting is relaxed and informal. Retelling is known to help with oral language skills of students and to improve reading comprehension in less proficient readers (Koskinen and others, 1988).

Retelling literally means asking the child, "Tell me about what you've just read." Some teachers may phrase a request for a retelling as, "Retell this story as if you were telling it to someone who had never read (or heard) it before." I always use the retelling strategy when I am doing an informal reading evaluation with a child. It's a quick and efficient way to assess whether the child has grasped the overall meaning of the text. As they are becoming familiar with the process, some teachers like to use a tape recorder so they don't miss any part of the child's responses.

The teacher can guide the retelling process if the child is having difficulty with such comments as, "Tell me what you remember," "How did the story begin?" or "What happened next?". If these strategies fail, specific story questions may be asked. Poor readers, who lack confidence, benefit greatly from the teacher's probing. Guided questioning forces them to rethink the passage, and their retellings often improve substantially.

The retelling strategy is also an effective way to assess long-range comprehension. For example, one month after a content area study, students can be asked to retell in writing the important concepts they remember. (For other ways of retelling, for example, using picture mapping and sequencing activities, see "Literature Extension Activities," pp. 94–101. See also Koskinen and others, 1988.)

Diagnostic Tests/Surveys

Clay's "Diagnostic Survey" (1985, pp. 16–46), which is used for selecting children for the Reading Recovery program, can easily be adapted in part for end-of-the-year kindergarten and for grade 1 classes. Parts of the survey may also be useful for grade 2 or for entering new students. The "Letter Identification" test asks children to identify fifty-four different characters and includes upper and lower case letters. The "Word Test" asks children to read down a list of twenty basic sight vocabulary words and checks knowledge of high-frequency words. The "Concepts About Print Test" checks important book and print-related concepts. (See Figure 13–13 for a workable adaptation.)

The "Writing Vocabulary Test" asks the child to write down all the words he knows how to write, beginning with his own name and including personal and basic words. It works well to take your class into the gym or a space where there is no print around for reference. The child has ten minutes for the task, and the score is the number of words spelled correctly. Verbal prompts are allowed. For example, the teacher can ask, "Do you know how to write _____?" (See Clay, 1985, p 36, for suggested prompts.) This is an easy test to adapt to whole-class use and a quick way to find out who the readers and writers are. We find the writing score correlates highly with reading ability. Take your papers and rank them from high to low. The high scorers will be the proficient readers and the lowest scorers the struggling readers.

Another of Clay's diagnostic tests that is easy to use whole class is the "Dictation Test." The teacher reads a sentence, and the children are asked to write it. The child is given credit for every sound written correctly. For example, if the child wrote "hav" for "have" or "todae" for "today," he gets credit for correctly writing all the sounds in the word, even though the spelling is not correct. The score gives some information on the child's ability to hear sounds in words, indicating graphophonic ability, and to make sound-letter connections. (See Clay, 1985, pp. 38–40, for specific directions.)

Running Records and Miscue Analysis

Running records are a form of miscue analysis. The teacher observes, records, and analyzes any unexpected words the child says in the process of reading aloud a connected text. Running records are used for instructional purposes to evaluate the child's reading behaviors and set directions for teaching, to check the difficulty of a text for a child, and to monitor progress.

While initially taking a running record seems quite complicated, with lots of practice and attention to detail it becomes second nature. It is very difficult to teach yourself to take a running record, but it is possible. (See Clay, 1985, pp. 17–23.) The easiest and best way to learn is to have a trained Reading Recovery teacher demonstrate for you and practice with you.

As part of my job, I have taught classroom teachers how to take running records, and they have found it enormously useful for reading diagnosis and reporting to parents. Other Reading Recovery teachers in our district have done the same. I recommend combining running records with retellings and using running records with your good readers about three times a year and with your struggling readers about every six weeks.

At some point in your transition to more meaningful evaluation strategies, you will want to include some form of miscue analysis. Again, this is not an easy transition in whole language teaching, especially for those teachers who have had no specialized training and practice in this area, but it is an important component. In order to know what reading strategies students are and are not using—so you can plan effectively for instruction and evaluate intelligently—being able to do an analysis of reading behaviors is extremely useful. Give yourself time to handle this further transition. Connie Weaver (1988) has done a comprehensive job of explaining miscue analysis, building on and referring to the work of Kenneth Goodman, Yetta Goodman, Dorothy Watson, and Carolyn Burke. Once you understand the concepts and procedures of miscue analysis, you may want to work out your own variations of the procedure.

Informal Evaluations of Reading and Writing

When my principal requests information about a child in our building, I no longer obtain the information through formal assessment or norm-referenced testing. I can find out everything I need to know through informal assessment. I always take several running records using book texts. Based on what the teacher has told me about the child, I have a variety of books on hand. Usually I pick one I think might work and say to the child, "Take a look at this book. Does it look just about right for you? Does it seem too easy, too hard?" After the child is comfortable with the book, both in terms of readability and interest, I ask the student to read orally a 100–300 word passage. (I count the words later.) With older children, choosing a passage closer to 300 words is a good idea, because as the reader begins to get a sense of the story, he may read the last section considerably better than the beginning section. This will have a positive effect on the child's comprehension and overall miscue rate. Following the reading, I ask the child to do a retelling of the story as described in "Retellings," earlier in this section.

For writing evaluation, I may ask to see a favorite piece of the student's writing, the child's journal, or a sample of "anything you might like to write about." For young children, I might use the "Dictation Test" and the "Writing Vocabulary Test." The entire informal evaluation usually takes about twenty minutes.

Finally, I share my observations and findings with the teacher and principal and write up an informal summary. (See Figure 13–15 for the informal reading evaluation of a new grade 2 student who entered school in late spring.)

Recently I have begun to add an informal interview (where I talk with the child and record responses) to the informal evaluation as I have become more aware of the importance of including the child's attitudes, behaviors, and understandings of himself as a learner.

Teacher-Made Tests

While most of our comprehension checks in reading center around student responses in logs, discussions, and other related book activities, teachers sometimes

Figure 13-15   Informal Reading Evaluation

INFORMAL READING EVALUATION
(Using running records, retellings, and writing samples)

Name: Myra B.
Grade: 2
Date: 5-19-89
Birthday: 5-21-81
Age: 8-0   Examiner: Regie Routman

READING
Based on three passages in the context of a story, Myra's oral reading and comprehension level are well above grade level. She reads fluently and generally has good word attack skills and understanding of what she's read.

Strengths
1. When in trouble, Myra keeps going and maintains the flow of the story.
2. She reads with good phrasing and cadence.
3. She comprehends main ideas and can do a simple retelling that includes major points of the story in sequence.
4. She sees herself as a good reader.

Weaknesses
1. Her self-correction rate is low, indicating she sometimes reads the words without thinking about overall meaning.
2. She has difficulty with words of three syllables or more.
3. She does not always use the context to help herself when she comes to an unknown word.
4. At times, she ignores punctuation.

WRITING
Based on a writing sample, Myra's writing is below grade level for handwriting, punctuation, content, and maturity—closer to a first grade level for this time of year than a second grade level. Myra reported that almost all the writing she did at her previous school was copying from the board.

RECOMMENDATIONS
1. Recognize Myra's excellent reading ability, and use that strength to connect to the writing areas.
2. Demonstrate to Myra how she can use the meaningful context of a story to figure out unknown words.
3. Continue to give Myra help in cursive handwriting.
4. Conference with her parents regarding the writing process and writing activities that can be encouraged over the summer.

give a written test after a book has been completed in group. Questions are open-ended and are designed to encourage a variety of thoughtful responses. (See Figure 13–16 for a test developed by fourth grade teacher Nancy Schubert and a student's responses.)

When teachers give tests, students need to know what is expected without, at the same time, being given a lot of rigid guidelines. Nancy Schubert gives her students as much time as they need to take tests and also encourages them to use the book. She comments,

> In most of life, you can go back to the source for reference, so why not here? When students can use the book, they think it's not a test. However, you have to know the book to use it well. Also, if I give a test, I no longer say, "Time is up." I might say, "We have gym now, but you'll have time later." I don't want kids to feel pressured. I want them to do well.

In place of a formal test, Nancy sometimes has students write and illustrate the six to eight main events of a book in sequence. Students write sentences or short paragraphs in a booklet format, and accompanying illustrations may be optional. Students enjoy this variation on a test, and the teacher learns a great deal about what the student has understood about the book. As long as students can justify their responses, different interpretations are accepted.

For older students, you may want to include student-developed questions. My favorite final exam in graduate school was in a philosophy of education class where the professor presented several important, global questions but also gave the option for the student to write and answer his own important question. I still recall the fun I had creating and answering my own question.

Passage Reading of a Book

One nonthreatening way to evaluate oral reading is to have students pick a favorite part of a chapter or a book that they have read recently and read it to you. You could also choose to photocopy a section from a book that the students have read as a group and observe a student reading the passage to you in a one-to-one setting.

Journal Writing

Journals may be used to evaluate spelling, phonics, handwriting, and writing abilities, in addition to content and ideas. Some teachers keep a checklist in the front or back of the journal and note the date the child used a particular skill—for example, capitalizing "I" or using question marks or possessives correctly. Other teachers encourage students to look through their journals and note these findings.

Critical Issues in Meaningful Evaluation

Portfolio Assessment

Portfolio assessment is one of the current directions in evaluation. The International Reading Association 1990 conference included many opportunities for teachers to hear about the topic. Articles in professional journals are talking about portfolio assessment as the state of the art in evaluation. And in several states

Figure 13–16   *Teacher-made Test for* James and the Giant Peach *by Roald Dahl*

Name: Natalie   "James & the Giant Peach"

1. Explain how James changed during the story. How did his character develop during the book? In the beginning of the book James was sad. He had two very mean aunts, that hated him. He cleaned, cooked, washed and did all the aunts told him to do. (Not asked him.) At the end when he lived in the peach pit, he had all the playmates in the world. Many came to see James's famous home. The children asked him to tell his story again and again. So he wrote the story in the form of a book by R. Dal.

2. Where in the book did you feel happy about something that happened? Find 2 examples. I felt happy when Aunt Spiker and Aunt Sponge got crushed by the peach. Centipede cut the stem and it rolled off what was called "a ghostly hill!" The two aunts scrambled to save themselves, tripped over each other and "CRUNCH!"
② I was glad when the peach landed on top of the Empire Terminal Tower instead of smashing into a zillion tiny pieces. I was glad nobody was hurt badly.

3. Who was your favorite character in the book? Give at least 3 reasons in your choice.
I think Centipede was my favorite character because
   1. He was smart
   2. He helped the peach   →
   3. He's a rascal
   4. He makes me laugh
   5. He is mistchevous
   6. He says funny stuff

4. Name one hero in this story. Explain why you think this character is a hero.
I think James was a hero because he saved the peach from the sharks. He used the earthworm for bait. He attracted gulls. Then he tethered them to silk, made by the silkworm.

5. What do you think the crocodile tongues really were? Explain. I think the crocodile tongues were really some of Aunt Spiker's dead skin that had fallen off of her hand. Then the old man dipped them in green paint, and then put them in a → brown paper bag.

6. In the next adventure what will happen to James? Explain. His mother and father will not be eaten by a rhino. He will be happy forever. Aunt Sponge and aunt Spiker will be eaten by the rhino. But the two are so gross, the rhino spits them up. They are taken to the cemetery, and put into their graves. The two tombstones say DRIP. (which means Don't Rest In Peace —

7. Pretend you are talking with Roald Dahl. What are some (3 or 4) questions you would like to ask him?
1. How long have you been writing books?
2. How many have you written so far?
3. Is writing fun?
4. Where do you get your ideas?
5. Do you watch TV?
6. Are you rich
7. What is your favorite food? Is it chocolate or peaches? Thank you Mr. Dahl It's been nice meeting you!

8. Will you read this story to your children? Why or why not? Yes I will. It may encourage them to read or write books of their own. And also Roald is a very good author

One day the giant peach will roll down the hill, into the cemetery and squash the two graves. They will sink into to earth and never be seen again!

portfolio assessment is mandated or is in the process of being required. With all of this, one would think portfolio assessment is everywhere. Not so. Most school districts are only just beginning to look at and think about portfolio assessment.

Portfolio assessment, as I understand it, is based on the selection of a representative, ongoing, and changing collection of work samples. Usually the pieces are stored in a large folder or portfolio, much in the same way an artist or writer saves sketches, drafts, and completed pieces. The concept behind portfolios is a powerful one and can be consistent with whole language teaching as long as it is a natural process that serves the students and guides the teacher. Ideally, students look at their work over time and make reflective decisions about what might go into their classroom portfolios. Thus, students are at the center of the assessment process. Through continued student examination, discussion, and reflection, the portfolio can become a vehicle for continued growth in the learning process.

The problem is in carrying out the concept. There is a real danger, especially when the procedure is mandated, that portfolios will become collection silos—storage bins filled with data serving no useful purpose. Just because work is in folders or on tapes, or check marks and grades are in a teacher's record book, does not mean evaluation is taking place.

At present, the notion of portfolio assessment seems to overemphasize collections of things. I think this is probably a normal part of the initial transition process, much the same way as teachers are initially overconcerned about activities when first teaching with literature. However, and this is the important factor, the only way we will move to evaluation in the highest sense—valuing and analyzing the process, the product, and attitudes about teaching-learning—is to make evaluation consistent with our philosophy. What is significant is not the collection itself but what the collection represents, or how it demonstrates the learning process that has taken place and, especially, the insights the learner has gained.

Because I worry about the misuse of the term "portfolio assessment," I prefer "portfolio approach to evaluation." By that I mean using multiple indicators and data sources to inform and guide instruction and to put the learner in charge of the evaluation process. The portfolio as a particular physical holding place need not even exist. What would exist is knowledgeable employment of various observations, measurements, and records that are assimilated to create a profile of students, their progress, and their learning needs. Students would be initially guided in looking carefully at their work over time. Self-evaluation of their work would focus on process and change, on what is significant and not just their best work. A portfolio approach to evaluation assumes knowledgeable teachers who understand and integrate language and learning processes in their teaching and who are ready to give up some control and entrust ownership of the learning-evaluation process to students.

Many of us are already using a portfolio approach in our teaching. We rely on reading records, reading logs, journals, writing samples, discussion groups, collaborative projects, and other authentic reading-writing-listening-speaking activities as responses to literature and content area texts and material. We need to take the approach beyond the response level to the evaluation level. With a portfolio approach to evaluation, students examine their responses and thoughtfully select and appraise representative and significant work samples. This is a sophisticated concept that is not easy to implement. A portfolio approach goes beyond keeping a collection of work samples; it includes a way of thinking about evaluation. This highest level is necessary if students are to become independent learners and critical thinkers.

Probably having students examine and collect selected writing samples over time is a good place to begin with a portfolio approach. In the beginning, or until teachers and students are ready for students to do most of the selecting and evaluating, a compromise might be to balance the selection process, with the teacher sometimes choosing, the teacher and student sometimes deciding together, and the student sometimes selecting. In any case, students and teachers need to know and be able to articulate why they are choosing a particular piece for the portfolio.

For example, in getting started, the teacher could guide the student in verbalizing what is significant about a selected piece. Some questions to help students think about and evaluate their work might include: "Do you notice anything about this piece of writing that is significant for you?" "What are your strengths?" "What do you think you have improved on?" "How might you have made this piece better?" Even a kindergarten student may be guided to look at journal entries over time and note her specific growth as a writer. Eventually, students should be able to identify on their own their progress, strengths, needs, and future goals.

Beginning to adopt a portfolio approach to evaluation is no easy matter. In our district, we struggled this past school year in our weekly language arts support groups trying to decide if and how to implement writing portfolios. The year before, based on an idea from Upper Arlington, Ohio, schools, we had talked about the possibility of saving three "significant" pieces of writing from each child each year. The pieces could be kept in a permanent folder that would follow the child from kindergarten through twelfth grade and be part of the permanent record.

In three of our five k–4 buildings, we spent several months looking at children's writing samples from a school-wide writing prompt (kindergarten used journal samples) in an attempt to establish criteria by which to judge the quality of student writing at each grade level. While the holistic scoring and analysis were valuable for looking at children's writing, we continued to wrestle with how to utilize portfolios, and we came to no consensus or decisions concerning implementation.

After an entire year of ongoing discussion, looking at children's writing samples, and talking about possible implementation procedures, we had not resolved the following issues related to setting up writing portfolios:

- How would the pieces be selected?
- Who would select them?
- How many pieces would be selected?
- How would the portfolio be used in the total evaluation process?

Part of the problem is that many of our teachers and administrators are not yet highly trained or experienced in the writing process. Even establishing criteria for good writing became difficult. At some grade levels teachers wanted to give mechanics equal or greater weight than content. Unless the approach is based on an understanding of how children learn language processes, portfolio assessment is likely to be a "catch-all" folder for work samples. Until teachers are at a point where they are reflective about their own teaching-learning and classrooms are collaborative communities, work samples are likely to be selected by teachers without ownership by students. Teachers need to be asking questions about their own teaching and looking at alternative possibilities in problem solving before they can expect students to do the same.

Another constraint to portfolio assessment is the problem of teacher management—finding time for periodic review of the contents of the portfolio. Optimally, students would take time to look through their portfolios and make judgments about their own learning. Students and teachers would conference with each other and with parents and note progress, changes, and new directions for teaching and learning. For teachers to encourage student self-evaluation and for students to assume responsibility for their portfolios is a big step. Teachers have to be ready and willing to give up some control of the learning process and to guide students toward independence.

Despite these constraints, we probably need to stop discussing and jump in and "have-a-go." Rob Tierney, a professor at The Ohio State University in Columbus, reports encouraging news about teacher change on the basis of a group of Ohio teachers he has worked with over the past several years. He notes that just about all the teachers who became involved in portfolio assessment found enough benefits for students and themselves to choose continuing involvement in the project. Furthermore, by observing students, teachers became more effective decision makers and problem solvers and were able to put in place aspects of evaluation that never existed before in their classrooms. By carefully looking at their students, teachers began thinking about what meaningful evaluation is. The portfolios became a way of grounding assessment in the classroom—facilitating ongoing thinking and talking about evaluation, promoting ownership of evaluation by students, and contributing to ongoing learning.

Whatever a school or district finally decides about a portfolio approach, student self-selection and optional elements must be included along with the required components. All aspects of students' thinking processes, not just written work, need to play a part. For example, if teachers and administrators who decide to go with portfolio assessment decide that three writing samples should be part of each permanent portfolio, students should also have an opportunity to select for their portfolios work samples that are significant to them—whether these are illustrations, sample literature response log pages, or reading records.

Rob Tierney is one of the few U.S. researchers who has collected data on the impact of portfolio assessment on teachers, parents, and students. He has looked at how students view themselves as writers and readers and the extent to which portfolios facilitate the achievement of ongoing learning goals. Rob sees portfolios as a "vehicle that gives students opportunities to get involved in self-assessment." He stresses that student ownership and student self-assessment must be the first priority, but also admits that "the hardest part is the issue of student self-assessment" (conversation, August 1990).

The verdict is not yet in on portfolio assessment. It may be that it's a great idea that many of us are not quite ready for yet. There is no formula for implementation or one best method. Teachers as skilled observers who are highly knowledgeable about language processes have to be ready to place students, even young students, at the center of the evaluation process. Portfolios can then be used as intended—as vehicles for students' self-evaluation, reflection, and learning.

The process could easily fail if it serves only the needs of teachers and administrators. We need to move slowly in setting up thoughtful objectives and guidelines, or we and our students will end up amassing collections of work for somebody else's purposes. If the evaluation process is truly to serve learners and their needs, then the learners must be central to the process.

Report Cards and Grading

Concern about report cards and grading scares off potential whole language teachers. Many teachers already feel tremendous pressure to keep grades and to report to parents four times a year. Having to deal with a new way of reporting can be overwhelming. In my own district, we use a checklist and narrative format for reporting in kindergarten through grade 3 and letter grades for grades 4 through 12. We continue to struggle with the grading process and the design of holistic report cards. One teacher told me, "I understand meaningful evaluation, but I don't understand how I can possibly give grades."

We need to keep in mind that grading is not evaluation. A student's abilities can never be described by a single letter. At best, grading is a narrow, arbitrary measuring system that fosters competition, discourages cooperation, and does little to promote understanding. Like standardized test scores, grades are scores that do not carry any real meaning for instructional purposes. Yet grades continue to drive instruction and learning in our schools. "Grades are the sole reason that most school activities are undertaken, requiring or enticing students to engage in tasks they would never otherwise go near" (Smith, 1988, p. 69).

My preference is to dispense with grades entirely, or at least until junior high school. I constantly hear that we can't do away with grades because the parents want them. The only parents I know who like grades are the parents of the "A" students. I believe the rest would be pleased to consider an alternative, especially if teachers and students took the time to keep records of performance-based evaluation and shared these with parents.

Nonetheless, grading is a fact of life for most teachers. We can work to change the system, but in the meantime, most of us have to deal with grades. While recognizing that the giving of grades is inconsistent with whole language philosophy, teachers can give grades in a fair and holistic manner. When grades are used, they should be used for looking at a child in relation to himself and for comparing and analyzing the child's growth over time.

Consistent with whole language philosophy would be involving the child in the grading process. I recommend using a rubric, a format of criteria that the student and parent see at the start of the grading period. An "A" in a subject must mean more than just that the teacher thought the work was excellent. What specific criteria were used to determine the grade? With a rubric set up ahead of time, every student and parent know the expectations for the course and, technically, every student has the potential to get an "A."

In addition to the teacher filling in the rubric, it is a good idea to have students fill it in at the end of the project or grading period or at interim periods. Where interim reports are required, rubrics can be completed as self-evaluation forms by students and co-signed by the student, teacher, and parent. The teacher and student could then conference—individually or with parents—and note strengths and weaknesses, discuss differences in perceptions, and set realistic goals for the next semester. With the exception of very low-achieving students who may have difficulty perceiving where they are, most students evaluate themselves quite fairly. If anything, they are tougher on themselves than the teacher is.

Following is an example of a rubric for reading based on independent, self-selected reading (WEB) and in-class reading (log, discussion, and related activities):

Rubric for Reading

- Reads and understands nightly WEB book (independent reading)
- Completes WEB folder (record of daily and monthly reading)
- Completes assigned reading on time
- Completes literature response log on time and to the best of his or her ability
- Contributes thoughtful comments to literature group discussion
- Refers to log in discussion—uses text to support statements
- Listens attentively and responds to peer comments in discussion
- Completes literature-related activities and assignments to the best of his or her ability
- Takes good care of books

Grades might be allocated as follows:

A—consistently for all areas	(9 out of 10)
B—consistently for most areas	(8 out of 10)
C—consistently for some areas	(6–7 out of 10)
D—inconsistently for most areas	(5–6 out of 10)
F—inconsistently for all areas	(5 or less out of 10)

Note that on the rubric, "consistently" means "most of the time," or you could define the term more specifically to meet your needs. Teachers and students would support their judgments on the rubric through anecdotal records, work samples, and other evidence from the "Data Gathering Profile." All the evidence could be utilized to complete specific report cards.

See Figure 13–17 for a reading rubric, Figure 13–18 for a sample writing rubric, and Figure 13–19 for a spelling rubric based on an integrated spelling program as described in Chapter 10. While ten categories were selected to make the grading easier, any number of categories could work. See Figure 13–20 for the first-time use of the reading rubric by fourth-grader Doris (discussed at the beginning of this chapter) as a self-evaluation at the end of the first grading period.

A rubric need not be formal. Fourth grade teacher Joan Servis combines the following components, with each worth a certain percentage, to arrive at student grades on a major topic of study in social studies or science. Students and parents are informed at the start of the project about the expectations and scoring system.

- Group work (may account for as much as 50 percent of grade)
    cooperation, collaboration, note taking, research, use of references, participation in group discussion
- Presentation
    explanation of research project to class, optional format, organization, effort

Figure 13-17   Reading Rubric

Name _____   Date _____

READING RUBRIC

Category	Consistent	Inconsistent	Comments
Reads and understands nightly WEB books (independent reading)			
Completes WEB folder (record of daily and monthly reading)			
Completes assigned reading on time			
Completes literature response log on time and to the best of his/her ability			
Contributes thoughtful comments to literature group discussion			
Refers to log in discussion-- uses text to support statements			
Listens attentively and responds to peer comments in discussion			
Completes literature related activities and assignments on time			
Completes literature related activities and assignments to the best of his/her ability			
Takes good care of books			

FINAL GRADE _____

GRADING SYSTEM

A--consistent for all areas (9 out of 10)
B--consistent for most areas (8 out of 10)
C--consistent for many areas (7 out of 10)
D--consistent for some areas (6 out of 10)
F--inconsistent for many areas (5 or fewer out of 10)

- Essay test on understanding of major concepts of topic
    open-ended questions
    complete sentences, best spelling, punctuation, legibility expected

The essay test questions have included:

- Name five facts you learned about _____.
- Choose a presentation you observed and tell what you learned.
- What else would you like to know about this topic?
- What did this unit cause you to think about?

Samples of other informal rubrics (not necessarily used for grades), which are first attempts by teachers, are given in Figures 13–21 and 13–22. Note in Figure 13–22 that third grade teacher Karen Horton has added a column for student self-evaluation two years later.

The examples shown are meant to serve only as possibilities. Notice that they do include both process and product in various contexts and go way beyond workbook pages and weekly or unit tests. The rubrics will undoubtedly need to be revised

Figure 13-18   Writing Rubric

```
Name _____       Date _____

                       WRITING RUBRIC

Category                      Consistent   Inconsistent   Comments

Able to write a coherent draft

Willingly takes suggestions
from peers and teacher

Able to give constructive feed-
back to a peer's draft

Attempts to incorporate
colorful language

Takes responsibility for
revising

Proofreads for _____

Adheres to writing deadlines

Keeps writing folder organized
and up to date

Learning to take meaningful
notes

In content areas, incorporates
and seeks out multiple
references


FINAL GRADE   _____

GRADING SYSTEM

A--consistent for all areas (9 out of 10)
B--consistent for most areas (8 out of 10)
C--consistent for many areas (7 out of 10)
D--consistent for some areas (6 out of 10)
F--inconsistent for many areas (5 or fewer out of 10)
```

after use. For example, they are probably too achievement oriented and need also to include improvement and effort.

For your first attempt at creating a rubric, you may want to do some brainstorming with a colleague. Though your first efforts may require lots of revision, you will get better through trial and error and feedback from colleagues and students. Give it a try. Teachers who begin to use rubrics seem to experience less conflict about having to give grades.

Fourth grade teacher Linda Cooper had this to say after using the reading, writing, and spelling rubrics for the first time: "I was absolutely shocked that the rubrics ended coming up with probably the same grades I would have given. I really didn't expect the results to be appropriate. It was only my trust in you and Dr. Stokes [our principal]—and your support—that enabled me to take a risk."

After employing your rubric for a semester, you may want to ask for student feedback and make revisions. The point is that students and parents have a right to know how grades will be determined at the start of a course. They also should know what is not being graded, because not everything requires a grade. Students need lots of opportunities for ungraded practice. They also have a right and responsibility to be part of the total evaluation process. Even if you have to use grades, you can still promote a climate of reflection and self-evaluation. For

Figure 13-19   Spelling Rubric

```
Name _____        Date _____

                    SPELLING RUBRIC

Category                       Consistent  Inconsistent  Comments
```

Category	Consistent	Inconsistent	Comments
Proofreads for identification			
Proofreads for corrections			
Attempts standard spelling on Have-A-Go sheets			
Consults multiple resources for standard spelling			
Uses file boxes and spells words correctly			
Uses file boxes and alphabetizes			
Takes informal tests -- dictation			
Takes informal tests -- proofreading paragraphs			
Takes formal tests -- high frequency words			
Takes formal tests -- content area words			

```
FINAL GRADE  _____

GRADING SYSTEM

A--consistent for all areas (9 out of 10)
B--consistent for most areas (8 out of 10)
C--consistent for many areas (7 out of 10)
D--consistent for some areas (6 out of 10)
F--inconsistent for many areas (5 or fewer out of 10)
```

secondary teachers, Nancie Atwell provides guidelines for evaluation and grading (see *In the Middle*, Heinemann, 1987, especially pp. 113–121).

In reporting to parents, it works well if you can also meet personally with parents, or provide an accompanying narrative, since grades by themselves tell nothing specific about the student. In our elementary grades, we have required teacher-parent conferences in the fall and optional conferences in the spring. While traditionally the conference has been between the teacher and parents, I believe the student—even a young student—should attend and participate in at least part of the conference. The student's work samples, drafts, processes, and goals could be shared with the parents, and new directions could be set for teaching and learning with the student actively involved in the plan.

With traditional assessment we have often left the student out of the process; with holistic evaluation the student is central to the process. Even when grades are required, this can be done. Dana Noble, a high school English teacher, now includes the writing conference he has with a student along with the child's final papers in determining the writing grade. The student is also expected to turn in all drafts and revisions, not just the completed final copy.

Finally, and perhaps most important, work out an evaluation system you feel is fair and with which you are comfortable. Try to balance your scoring system with

Figure 13-20   Reading Rubric Used by a Fourth-grader

Name Doris   Date 10-24-90

READING RUBRIC

Category	Consistent	Inconsistent	Comments
Reads and understands nightly WEB books (independent reading)	✓		
Completes WEB folder (record of daily and monthly reading)	✓		
Completes assigned reading on time	✓		most of the time
Completes literature response log on time and to the best of his/her ability	✓		
Contributes thoughtful comments to literature group discussion	✓		tries hard
Refers to log in discussion-- uses text to support statements	✓		
Listens attentively and responds to peer comments in discussion		✓	most of the time
Completes literature related activities and assignments on time		✓	need to improv
Completes literature related activities and assignments to the best of his/her ability	✓		
Takes good care of books	✓		

FINAL GRADE   B—

GRADING SYSTEM

A--consistent for all areas (9 out of 10)
B--consistent for most areas (8 out of 10)
C--consistent for many areas (7 out of 10)
D--consistent for some areas (6 out of 10)
F--inconsistent for many areas (5 or fewer out of 10)

observations, interviews, and performance samples. Also, try to make your grades more process-performance-based than product-based.

Improving Report Cards

Report cards in our district have undergone major revisions in the elementary grades, especially in kindergarten through grade 3, where we use a checklist and a narrative. We have a separate report card for each of the k–3 grades and one design that uses letter grades for grades 4–6. Once we moved to more meaning-based strategies in our teaching, the descriptors on the old forms no longer fit the way we were teaching. Committees made up of teachers and administrators worked together to improve our methods of reporting to parents. Then teachers at each grade level had an opportunity to give feedback.

In a three-year period, we have been through two major revisions, and there's no doubt there will be more in the future. Improvements have involved changing, adding, and deleting descriptors and categories, especially as they apply to reading

Figures 13-21 and 13-22   Informal Rubrics

NAME _____   DATE _____

___/10 - NEATNESS

___/20 - GRAMMAR (spelling, punctuation, correct
        usage)

___/30 - ART WORK

___/40 - CONTENT (story, information)

___/100 - total grade

COMMENTS:

Evaluation of a 3rd grade Book

1. Vocabulary appropriate for 3rd graders ☐

2. All papers turned in ☐

3. Written on every other line ☐

4. Illustrations were planned ☐

5. Spelling corrected on dummy copy ☐

6. Sentences corrected on dummy copy ☐

Grade on project - _____

and writing. In our first revision, we added observational categories such as shared reading, reading strategies, and writing process, but we kept the old marking system: "O" (outstanding), "S" (satisfactory), "I" (improving), and "N" (needs improvement). That system did not work well for two reasons. First, the marks did not fit philosophically with our beliefs about language learning; and, second, they fostered competition. Many teachers felt the marks were not developmentally appropriate, and they did not like the way the system fostered comparisons on the part of parents. Some parents whose children had received an "O" during the first marking period wanted to know why the mark wasn't "O+" the next report period. Or parents who saw an "S" (satisfactory) the first marking period wanted an explanation of why the child had not received an "O."

The descriptor terms we are now using include "consistently," "occasionally," "seldom," and "not evaluated at this time." Many teachers and administrators feel this is a significant improvement because the system is more compatible with our philosophy and teaching.

Our second revision encompassed fewer but broader categories, including atti-

Figure 13-22   Informal Rubrics

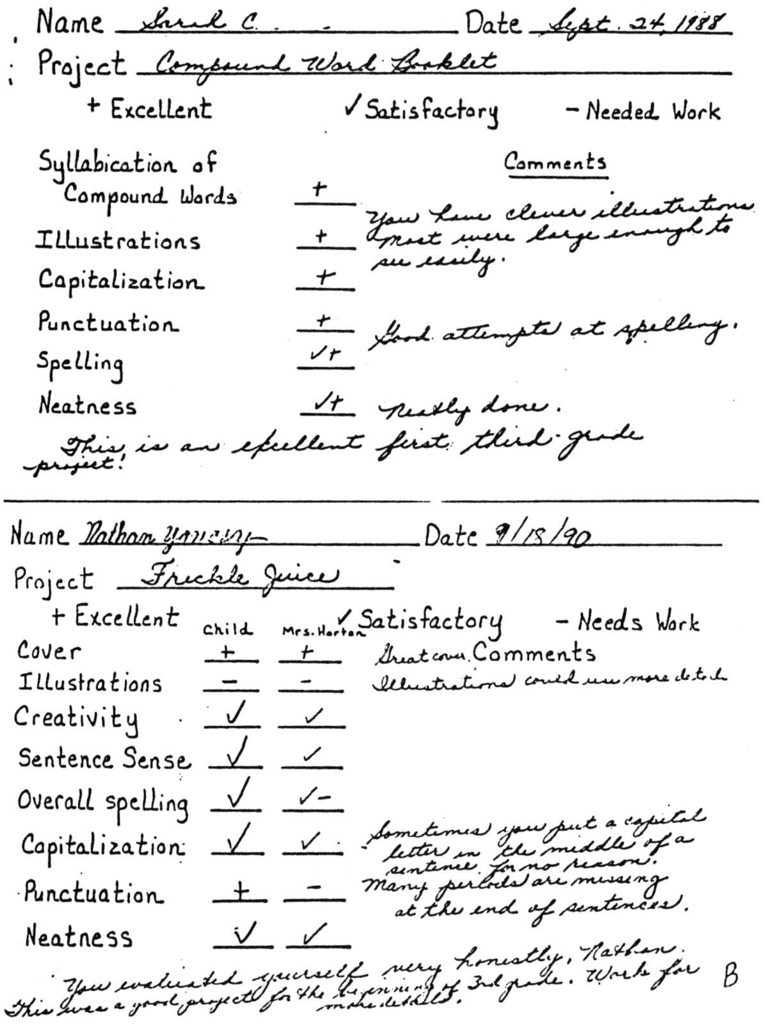

Name *Sarah C.*   Date *Sept. 24, 1988*

Project *Compound Word Booklet*

+ Excellent   ✓ Satisfactory   – Needed Work

Syllabication of   Comments
  Compound Words   +
                                                    You have clever illustrations
Illustrations   +   *most were large enough to*
                                                    see easily.
Capitalization   +

Punctuation   +   *Good attempts at spelling.*
Spelling   ✓+

Neatness   ✓+   *neatly done.*

This is an excellent first third-grade project!

Name *Nathan Young*   Date *9/18/90*

Project *Freckle Juice*

+ Excellent   child   Mrs. Horton ✓ Satisfactory   – Needs Work

Cover   +   +   *Great cover.* Comments
Illustrations   –   –   *Illustrations could use more detail*
Creativity   ✓   ✓
Sentence Sense   ✓   ✓
Overall spelling   ✓   ✓–
Capitalization   ✓   ✓   *Sometimes you put a capital*
                                      letter in the middle of a
                                      sentence for no reason.
Punctuation   +   –   *Many periods are missing*
                                      at the end of sentences.
Neatness   ✓   ✓
                                      You evaluated yourself very honestly, Nathan.   B
This was a good project for the beginning of 3rd grade. Work for more detail.

tudes toward reading and writing, and our language-related categories are now consistent across grades 1–3. We found that our first revised k–3 report card was taking too long to fill out, and parents became bogged down by having to look at so many sections. Figure 13-23 shows the whole language section on the report card for grade 2. The grades 4–6 committee decided to combine reading and writing processes with spelling under the category whole language.

One step that teachers can take, whatever form is in use, is to avoid negative statements, note what the child is doing well, and discuss the child's progress in relation to where he once was and where he is now. Other information, for example, that the child is reading a year below grade level, can be given *after* the teacher's positive statements about what the child can do.

Teachers can also work to change the words that go along with the descriptor lists so they do not foster competition and comparison among students. For exam-

Figure 13-23 Whole Language Section on Grade 2 Report Card

WHOLE LANGUAGE

EFFORT			SPEAKING & LISTENING		
READING STRATEGIES/COMPREHENSION			Can express ideas orally with fluency		
Uses picture clues			Listens and comments appropriately		
Uses context clues			**HANDWRITING**		
Uses structural clues			Forms manuscript letters and numerals appropriately		
Uses phonetic clues			Forms cursive letters appropriately		
Self-corrects			Spaces letters and words appropriately		
Learns, understands & utilizes new vocabulary			Writes neatly		
Recalls main idea, details and sequence			**SPELLING**		
Follows plots & sees relationships between characters			Moves from invented spelling to conventional spelling		
Takes risks in predicting and in discussions			Learns spelling words		
Formulates questions from material read			Applies correct spelling		
Is able to find proof to answer questions			**REFERENCE SKILLS**		
Recognizes different story forms			Uses reference sources for reading and writing		
Reads orally with fluency			**READING/WRITING ATTITUDES**		
WRITING PROCESS			Demonstrates an interest in reading		
Generates topics for personal writing			Chooses to read silently		
Writes with thorough development (beginning, middle,end) to observe unity			Demonstrates an interest in writing		
Makes use of descriptive language			Chooses to write		
Is developing correct capitalization, punctuation & sentence structure					
Is beginning to revise					
Has begun to edit for mechanics					

ple, to indicate that the child is performing at a very competent level, words such as the following may be used: "proficient," "consistently," "usually," "most of the time," "secure," and "effectively demonstrated." To indicate a middle level, these words may fit: "sometimes," "demonstrated some of the time," "developing," "occasionally," and "generally." To indicate that a skill or strategy is not yet understood or mastered, terms such as the following may be used: "not noticed yet," "not yet," "working on," and "infrequently." As much as possible, try to keep the wording positive.

Finally, parents must be informed about any changes in reporting practices. If our most recent changes had not been clearly explained, a parent might easily have interpreted an "O" for "outstanding," whereas "O" now represents "occasionally." Parents also need to understand why the reporting system has been changed so they feel they are part of the evaluation process.

Reflections

As teachers, we need to stop complaining about the evaluation process and start contributing to it. Too often we have complacently given over our power for decision making and change to others. Knowledgeable teachers who use common sense, experience, and a collaborative approach can make the evaluation process more meaningful.

While we are working to improve report cards, we should keep in mind that eventually a total narrative, nongraded report format, or even no report card at all, may be possible. Whole language teachers find that a single report card does not give an adequate or accurate profile of a student. Including a portfolio approach to evaluation provides a more complete student portrait as well as an opportunity for reflection, both for teachers and students.

Reporting to parents can be an opportunity for improved, open-ended communication between parents and teachers. One school I visited in Australia did not have report cards. Parents came to the school four times a year to meet with the teacher and student and discuss the student's progress. All manner of student work samples were shared and discussed. In looking to improve reporting to parents, we need to be asking, "What do we want to achieve with parents in informing them? How can we best achieve this?"

Self-Evaluation for Teachers and Students

The foremost goal of evaluation is self-evaluation, that is, the analysis of our own attitudes and processes so that we can use the information to promote continued growth and learning. The purpose of self-evaluation is the purpose of education— to enable an individual to function independently, intelligently, and productively. This is not just a worthy goal for students. If we are to be expecting self-evaluation by our students, we teachers must also be demonstrating it and practicing it ourselves. Self-evaluation implies trust of ourselves and of our students, and that is often the hardest part of the teaching-learning process.

Self-evaluation by teachers is a difficult, but necessary part of the evaluation process. By taking a look at what you choose to evaluate, you get a picture of what you value. For example, when I filled out "What Do I Want to Know?" (Figure 13–2), initially I had included only oral reading, spelling, and reading comprehension on the grid. I added reading-writing attitudes and the student's view of himself as a reader-writer after talking with Rob Tierney and Andrea Butler. I realized that my orientation was more toward a skills model than I had recognized or wanted to admit. The same is true of my informal reading evaluation (Figure 13–15). I have not connected reading and writing, nor have I taken the time to interview the student to determine how he views himself as a reader. I am now aware that my evaluation process needs to reflect more accurately students' attitudes, behaviors, and understandings.

Good teaching fosters self-evaluation by students. Capable readers self-monitor and self-correct while reading. They self-select much of what they read and often keep records of their reading. Even a first-grader can begin to keep track of books read. A competent writer is able to choose his own topics, effectively proofread, and know why he chose a particular piece of writing for publication. A portfolio approach—student centered and properly implemented—has potential for high-level self-evaluation. Engaging in self-regulation and self-examination of multiple data sources gives the learner the message, "I am better at this today. Here is my evidence."

This section examines various procedures that can be effectively used for self-evaluation by teachers and students. Certainly the list provided here is not exhaustive, but these are procedures that have helped to increase teachers' and students' awareness of attitudes, strengths, weaknesses, areas needing improvement, and directions for future teaching and learning. In this section, too, teachers who have been in transition toward whole language for three to five years share their thoughts on teaching and learning. Finally, some former students in a first grade literacy program (Routman, 1988) share their present attitudes toward reading, writing, and literacy.

Self-Evaluation Procedures

Self-evaluations can take many forms, such as class responses to teachers' evaluation questions, a self-evaluation checklist for teachers, individual evaluative responses for literature-group discussions, reflection logs, weekly evaluations, report cards, self-evaluations by students, and report cards on teachers by students.

Class Responses to Teachers' Evaluation Questions

Individual student and whole-class responses to questions can be used by teachers to evaluate the kind of instruction that is going on in our classrooms. By carefully analyzing students' feedback, teachers can find out whether what they think they are teaching really is what they are teaching. Teachers who are able to value students' opinions about what has gone on in the classroom are truly reflective practitioners.

Some questions we can ask to inform our teaching might include:

- How is reading taught in this class?
- How is writing taught in this class?
- What do you do when you come to a word you can't read?
- What do you do when you want to spell a word you're not sure of?
- How do you decide what to take notes on?
- How do you study for a test?
- What do good writers do?

Ellen Rubin, a second grade teacher who implemented writing workshop (Calkins, 1986) for the first time, wanted to know what her students had learned about writing. I offered to ask her class what good writers do. The purpose of the question was to help guide her self-evaluation of the year's writing program. I called on students in random order and then wrote down their responses. Their first responses (out of many) follow:

What We Have Learned about What Good Writers Do

1. Don't put too many thoughts into the same sentence.
2. Skip lines when you're writing so you have room to make changes.
3. Use punctuation at the end of sentences.
4. Start a new paragraph when you have a new thought.
5. Use capital letters for names and at the start of each sentence.

Ellen and I spoke honestly about what the students stressed first—predominantly mechanics. While how and when they get ideas for stories (such as "asking classmates")—as well as how they write interesting stories (such as "conference with a classmate or the teacher")—eventually surfaced, their first emphasis was on editing. Ellen took a hard look at her teaching. While she believed she had been stressing writing for meaning and content first, the children's responses made her think about the messages she had actually been sending.

She set conscious goals for the second year of writing workshop. She would emphasize content before form, and she would consciously listen to the language she was using. Ellen's growth as a writing teacher is reflected in the students' responses the following year when they were asked what good writers do. There is far greater evidence of writers immersed in writing and concerned about the quality of their writing.

What We Have Learned about What Good Writers Do

1. They think up a story and then they write it.
2. After they write a story, they read over it to see if it makes sense and it's the way they want it.
3. They check their spelling.
4. They use expression—"good words" like Roald Dahl uses; instead of "said"—"muttered."
5. They write good sentences by using interesting words.
6. They write with detail. They tell what happened.
7. They make their writing clear so that people can read it—legible handwriting.
8. They try to improve their story as much as they can—put in different words if they don't like some of the words.
9. They put in words that you might have to ask what they mean—like "grieved"—and they use words that might help it get published. Instead of "she was very sad," use "she grieved."
10. They put capital letters, exclamation marks, and other marks where they need them to make sense.
11. The author sometimes needs to find an illustrator or a photographer, for most information books.
12. Good writers let somebody else read their story. If one part doesn't make sense the reader can suggest how to fix it.
13. On your first time writing a story, you don't worry about spelling. You just write your thoughts down so you don't forget your thoughts.

In another whole-class evaluation, Joyce Pope's first-graders did a shared writing experience following a visit by a doll maker. With their teacher's guidance, the students wrote a story telling about the doll maker and how she made dolls. After the detailed story was completed on large chart paper, Joyce asked the students what they had learned about the writing they had just done. She used the shared writing experience to extend and confirm the learning that had taken place. It is important for students to be able to verbalize what they have learned so they are aware learning has taken place. I believe if we did this more often in classrooms, parents would get fewer "nothing" responses to the question, "What did you learn today?"

What Did We Learn?

- A story needs an interesting beginning and a good ending to show it's over.
- We had to remember the order.
- We couldn't start to write until we started to think.
- When you rough draft, you can cross out.
- If you read aloud, you catch your mistakes.
- The words had to match the pictures.
- We had to print neatly for the reader.
- Apostrophes tell someone owns it, like "Elizabeth's shoes."
- Use a full stop (.) if you tell, a question mark (?) if you ask, and an exciting mark (!) to show you feel strongly.
- We can say good things about ourselves or other kids.
- We can spell by sounding out, writing in chunks, looking in a book, asking a friend, using a dictionary, having-a-go at it, or looking back at a page already done.
- We can use what we know to explain, like "It looks as big as my two-year-old cousin."
- We can investigate to find facts for our story, like using a yardstick to measure the doll.
- We can print in special ways to give a message, like "long-g-g" and "VERY BIG!!!"
- We learned to work longer than ever before.

Second grade teacher Mary Pryor wanted to know what her students thought about the core literature books they had read and discussed so she could effectively plan her reading program for the following year. After Mary discussed and demonstrated good questioning strategies, the students worked in pairs to come up with their own important questions. See Figures 13–24 and 13–25. Then they responded to each other's question formats (see Figures 13–26 and 13–27). In another attempt to look carefully at her teaching, third grade teacher Linda Cooper asked her students for feedback on the reading program (see Figure 13–28).

Self-Evaluation Checklist for Teachers

In looking at our daily teaching, teachers may find having a list of important and desirable teaching behaviors is helpful. You may want to adapt the list I put together (Figure 13–29) for your own purposes.

Individual Evaluative Responses to Literature Group Discussions

Joan Servis and I devised the form shown in Figures 13–30 and 13–31 to use occasionally with students after a literature discussion group. We have tried checklists and more involved formats and find that the simplicity and open-ended quality of this form is both easy for students to use and very informative. The same format works well for evaluation of small-group work in the content areas.

Figure 13–24 and 13–25 Student-generated Questions on Core Literature Books, Grade 2

5-19-89

Reading

Write 5 evaluation questions with a partner.

1. Do you think the words are like poetry?

2 What was your favorite activety in the book?

3. Did you like the chartecters?

A 4. What was your favorite charter?

B Why?

5. What was your favorite chapter?

6. Would you like to read the book again!

Figure 13–25

Najah
5-19-89

Reading

Write five evaluation questions with a partner

1. a What was your favorite charater?
b Why did you choose that person?

2. Was the lanuegue aporpreat in the nine book you read?

3. Were the word's hard for second graders?

4. a Were the nine books exiting?
b Why were they exciting?

5. Do you think kids will like these books? other grades

6. Would you like the book to be made into a video

Evaluation   5-24-89

The Courage of Sarah Noble

1. Yes, I think the words are like poetry because the book has beautiful words.

2. I liked when we wrote what happened to Sarah when she grew up.

3. I liked the charecters because they are kind and loving.

4. My favorite chareder was Sarah because she was nice, loving and caring

4. Her job was to make sure that her father and herself were fed. And take care of the horse.

5. My favorite chapter was FRIENDS becaus Sarah made friends with the indians and wasn't afraid of them anymore.

6. I want to read the book again because it was a true storry, and Sarah was the kind of person who would do anything for her family.

7. Yes. I think they should make the book into a movie becase it would attract a good audience.

Figure 13-27

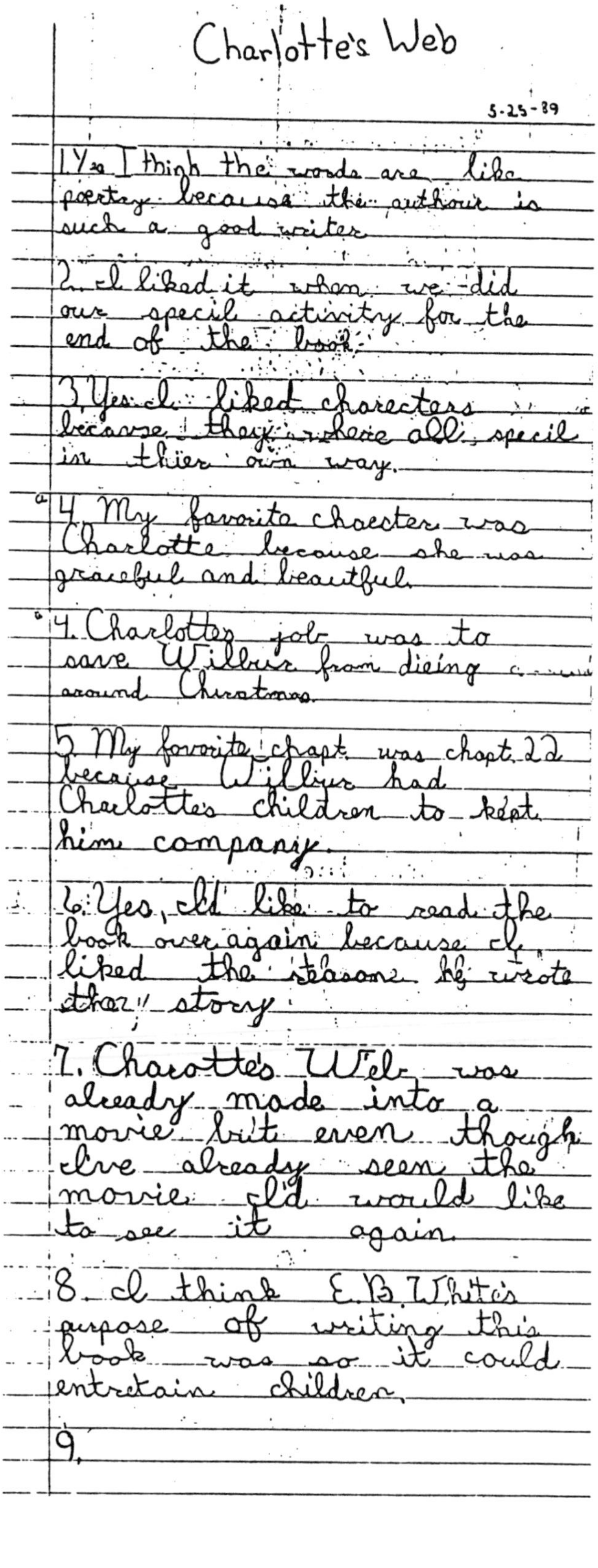

Charlotte's Web

5-25-89

1 Yes I think the words are like poetry because the authour is such a good writer

2 I liked it when we did our special activity for the end of the book.

3 Yes I liked charecters because they where all special in thier own way.

4 My favorite chaecter was Charlotte because she was graceful and beautful.

4. Charlottes job was to save Wilbur from dieing around Christmas.

5 My favorite chapt. was chapt. 22 because Wilbur had Charlotte's children to kept him company.

6 Yes, I'd like to read the book over again because I liked the reasons he wrote that story

7. Charlottes Web was already made into a movie but even though I've already seen the movie I'd would like to see it again.

8. I think E.B. White's purpose of writing this book was so it could entretain children.

9.

Figure 13-28   Students' Feedback to the Teacher on the Reading Program, Grade 3

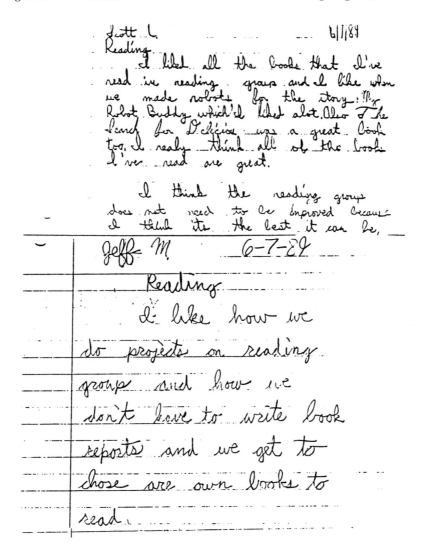

Reflection Logs

Some teachers are finding that reflection logs, a place for students to think about and comment on their learning, are important tools for fostering self-evaluation. Having to put thoughts into writing seems to help clarify what has, or has not, been learned. Not only do students think about their learning; teachers have an opportunity to understand what concepts have been understood and what needs to be retaught. As with all journal writing, no corrections are made in these logs. Reflection logs can be used the last fifteen minutes of the day or week and/or in the content areas. After a while the teacher will not need to ask specific questions, but at the beginning, some guiding questions could be:

- What did I learn today? (new insight or confirmation)
- What am I still confused about?
- What would I like to know more about?

See Figure 13–32 for a page from a fourth grade student's reflection log on what he has learned that day and how he has used his time.

Some teachers also keep personal reflection logs as a way to think about and self-evaluate their teaching.

Weekly Evaluation

Even very young children are capable of looking at their work and progress and putting their thoughts into writing. Weekly evaluations can be a vehicle for students to reflect on their attitudes, strengths, and weaknesses and can be used to communicate with parents and inform our teaching. With regular use, students become conscious of their strengths and what they need to improve. You will first want to demonstrate how the form might be filled out. The overhead projector works well here.

Whatever form or method you use, keep it simple and allow for open-ended comments and flexibility. (See Figure 13–33 for a sample form.) Some space may also be left on the form for teacher and parent comments. After a while, you may want to do a shared writing and design your own format with the students. Adapted for kindergarten, the weekly evaluation form may be used at the end of the week as a whole-class activity and then sent home as a newsletter.

Figure 13-29   A Self-evaluation Checklist for Teachers

A Self-Evaluation Checklist for Teachers

Am I reading literature aloud to students every day?
Am I providing time and choice daily for students to read and write on self-selected books and topics?
Am I noticing and commenting on what students are doing well and are able to do?
Are students in my class excited about learning?
Am I a happy and effective reading and writing model for my students?
Am I taking the time to demonstrate and not just assigning?
Are my questions allowing for varied responses and interpretations?
Am I equally respectful of all students regardless of culture and background?
Are my expectations high for all students?
Do students know and understand how they will be evaluated or graded?
Are my responses to students, both orally and in writing, specific and helpful?
Am I using the "red pencil" sparingly, or not at all?
Are children in my classroom feeling successful, regardless of their abilities?
Do I provide regular opportunities for students to share and collaborate?
Is the work students are doing meaningful and purposeful?
Am I encouraging students to solve their own problems and take ownership of their learning?
Am I providing opportunities for students to reflect on their progress?
Are my evaluation procedures consistent with my philosophy and my teaching?
Am I communicating effectively with parents and administrators?

Figures 13-30 and 13-31   Self-evaluations in Literature Discussion Group

Self-Evaluation

Literature Discussion Group

Name __Briana__   Date __4/17__

Book/story __Fairy Tale__

1. What did I do well today (and/or improve on) during group discussion?

I think that we do well on cooperating together
and contributing to all discussions. We improved
on listening to each other's ideas and
asking questions on them so that we
understand them and aren't just
writing them down on our sloppy
copy.

2. What do I still need to improve on during group discussion?

We need to work on staying
on one subject so we don't get
confused.

Figure 13-31

Self-Evaluation

Literature Discussion Group

Name __Elizabeth__   Date __4-17-90__

Book/story __Fairytale__

1. What did I do well today (and/or improve on) during group discussion?

We talked over if we should change any
titles and the topics. Our group got a little
hectic but we maneged it. I maybe got
a little bossy. I tried to control myself
and respect others when they were talking.
   I think I improved on giving sugestions
on what to do. I think that I'm beging to
feel comfatable in a group.

2. What do I still need to improve on during group discussion?

Maybe not being so bossy when
I'm not captain of the group.

Figure 13–32   A Page from a Fourth Grade Student's Reflection Log

10/26/90

Respect
    I finished all of my work.
We had to do six things: draw
my family, two little worksheets,
traditions, rules at home, and re-
sponsabilities.
        I could have done
my picture better. I didn't
think it looked good. I think I
talked a little bit too much.
All in all, I used my time wisely.
        I learned how your little
work and what they do. I felt
I learned a lot.

Figure 13–33   Weekly Self-evaluation

Weekly Evaluation

Name_____   Date_____

This week I learned

What was most important to me this week was

I did very well

I am confused about

I still need to work on

Student signature _____
Teacher signature _____
Parent signature _____

Report Cards and Student Self-Evaluations

I think it makes sense to have students write a narrative of how they see their progress in a particular subject to go along with the teacher's comments. Certainly that provides a more balanced picture. Students generally enjoy the opportunity to be part of the reporting-to-parents process. Even first-graders can evaluate themselves with some insight (see Figures 13–34 through 13–37).

Some teachers attach the students' evaluations to their own when reporting to parents. Third grade teacher Julie Beers asked her students to evaluate themselves in reading. First she demonstrated on the overhead projector by evaluating her own reading (Figure 13–38). Then students volunteered to write on the overhead projector with her guidance (Figure 13–39). Finally, they were ready to write on their own (Figures 13–40 and 13–41). Sylvia Tallentire, a third grade teacher, has her students design their own report cards when evaluating themselves. (See Figures 13–42 through 13–45.)

Figure 13-34   First-grader's Response to "How I Grew as a Learner This Year"
Format by Peg Rimedio.

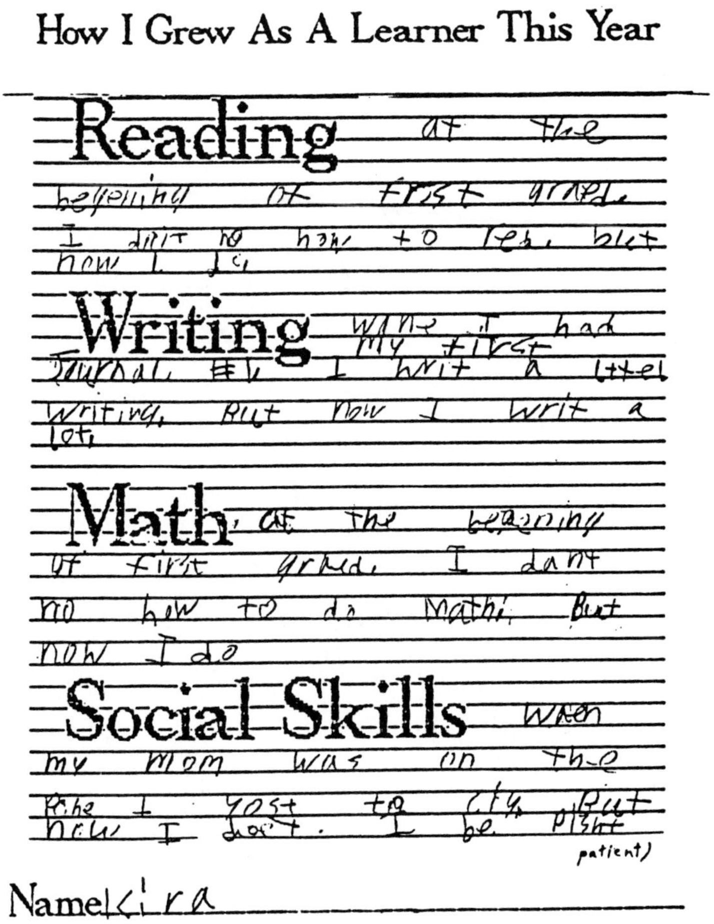

How I Grew As A Learner This Year

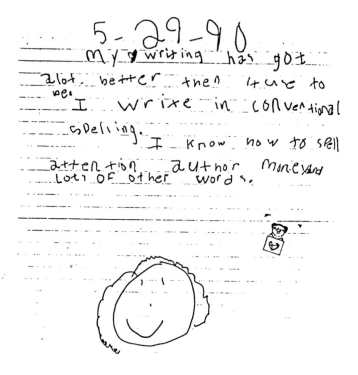

5-29-90

My writing has got alot better then it use to be. I wrixe in conventional spelling. I know how to spell attention author moneyand lots of other words.

Figure 13-36

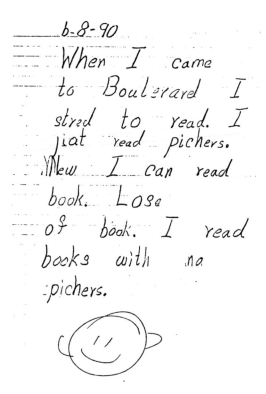

6-8-90

When I came to Boulevard I stred to read. I jiat read pichers. New I can read book. Lose of book. I read books with no pichers.

Figure 13-37

6-8-90
The fert day
I came to school
I cod not read
to good but now
that we have
reading prtners I can
read good. by Lauren

Figure 13-38   A Teacher Evaluates Her Own Reading

Reading
I read very fast. I usuall
read about 1-2 books
per week. ✓I need to
read books other than professional
books. I always read during
RAP but on occasion, I
have not been intrestd in my
book so I'm not too excitea
about reading it.
During reading group, I
actually participate in the
discussions. I listen to
others ideas although there
are times I get distracte
because. I wory too much
about what the other childre
not in reading group are doing.

355

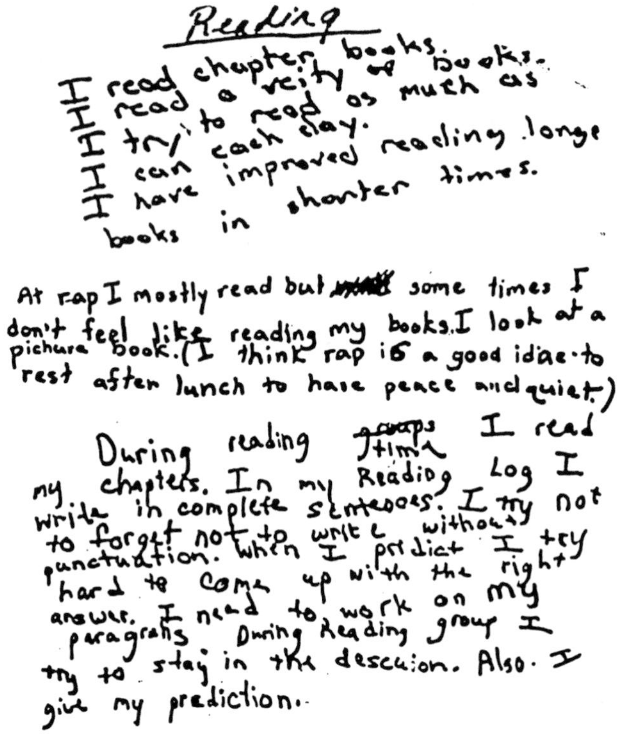

Reading

I read chapter books or books. I read a veity as much as I can each day. I try to read improved reading longe books in shorter times. I have

At rap I mostly read but ~~mostly~~ some times I don't feel like reading my books. I look at a pichure book. (I think rap is a good idae to rest after lunch to have peace and quiet.)

During reading groups I time read my chapters. In my Reading Log I write in complete sentences. I try not to forget not to write without punctuation. When I prdict I try hard to come up with the right answer. I need to work on my paragrahs During Reading group I try to stay in the descuion. Also. I give my prediction.

Figures 13-40 and 13-41   *Third Grade Students' Self-evaluations of Reading Behaviors*

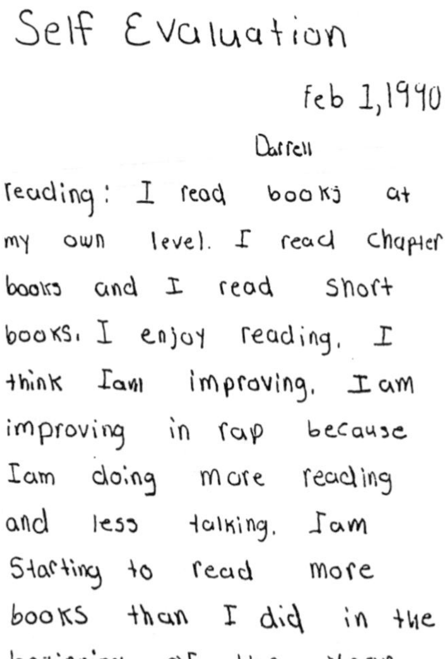

Self Evaluation

feb 1, 1990

Darrell

reading: I read books at my own level. I read Chapter books and I read Short books. I enjoy reading. I think I am improving. I am improving in rap because I am doing more reading and less talking. I am Starting to read more books than I did in the beginning of the year.

Figure 13-41

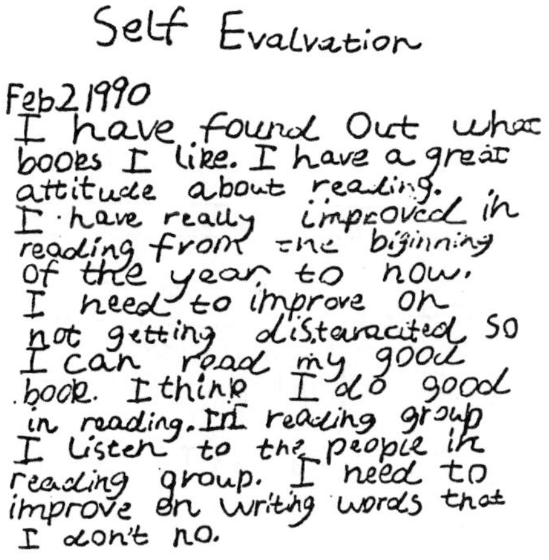
Self Evalvation

Feb2 1990
I have found Out what books I like. I have a great attitude about reading. I have really improved in reading from the biginning of the year to now. I need to improve on not getting distaracited so I can read my good book. I think I do good in reading. In reading group I listen to the people in reading group. I need to improve on writing words that I don't no.

Figures 13-42 through 13-45 Student-Designed Report Cards

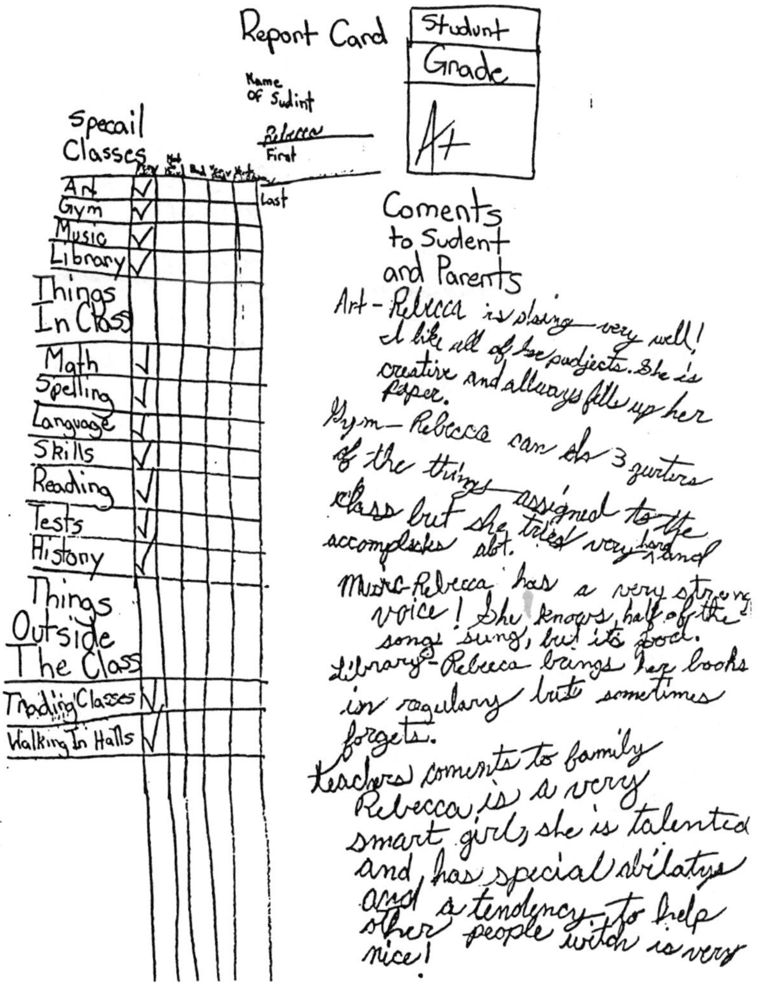
Report Card

Student
Grade
A+

Name of Sudint

Rebecca
First

Last

Specail Classes
Art ✓
Gym ✓
Music ✓
Library ✓

Things In Class
Math ✓
Spelling ✓
Language ✓
Skills ✓
Reading ✓
Tests ✓
History ✓

Things Outside The Class
Trading Classes ✓
Walking In Halls ✓

Coments to Sudent and Parents

Art - Rebecca is ~~doing very~~ well! I like all of her pudjects. She is creative and allways fills up her paper.

Gym - Rebecca can do 3 qurters of the things ~~assigned to the~~ class but she tries very hard and accomplecks alot.

Music - Rebecca has a very strong voice! She knows half of the songs sung, but its good.

Library - Rebecca brings her books in regulary but sometimes forgets.

teachers coments to family
Rebecca is a very smart girl, she is talented and has special abilatys and a tendency to help other people witch is very nice!

Figure 13-43

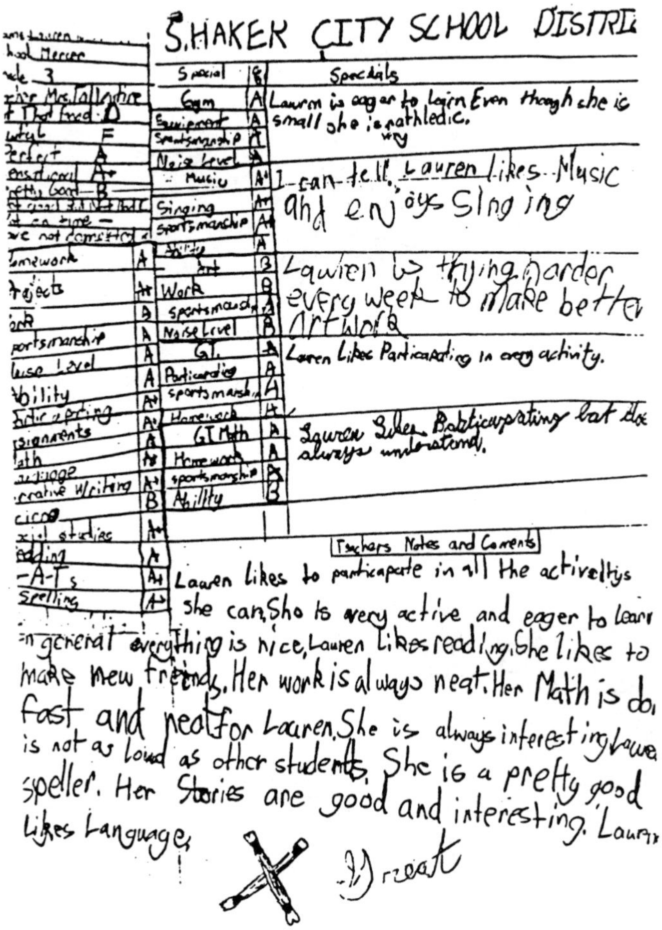

This is a handwritten student report card / evaluation form titled "SHAKER CITY SCHOOL DISTRICT" for a student named Lauren, filled in by a child.

Subject	Grade	Special	Grade	Specials
Mrs. Tallentine	D	Gym	A	Lauren is eager to learn. Even though she is small she is very athledic.
	F	Equipment	A	
perfect	A	Sportsmanship	A	
pretty good	A+	Noise Level	A	
good	B	Music	A+	I can tell Lauren likes Music and enjoys singing
almost perfect		Singing	A+	
on time	—	Sportsmanship	A+	
are not classified		Skills	A	
homework	A	Art	B	Lauren is trying harder every week to make better Art Work
projects	A+	Work	B	
art	A	Sportsmanship	A	
sportsmanship	A	Noise Level	A	
noise level	A	G.I.	B	Lauren likes participating in every activity.
ability	A	Participating	A	
participating	A+	Sportsmanship	A	
improvements	A	Homework	A	
math	A	GT Math	A	Lauren likes participating but doesn't always understand.
language	A+	Homework	A	
creative writing	A+	Sportsmanship	B	
ciroo	B	Ability	B	
social studies	A+			
adding	A			
A-1s	A+			
Spelling	A+			

Teachers Notes and Comments
Lauren likes to participate in all the activeltys she can. She is very active and eager to learn. In general everything is nice, Lauren likes reading. She likes to make new friends. Her work is always neat. Her Math is done fast and neat for Lauren. She is always interesting. Lauren is not as loud as other students. She is a pretty good speller. Her Stories are good and interesting. Lauren likes Languages!   -Great

Figure 13-44

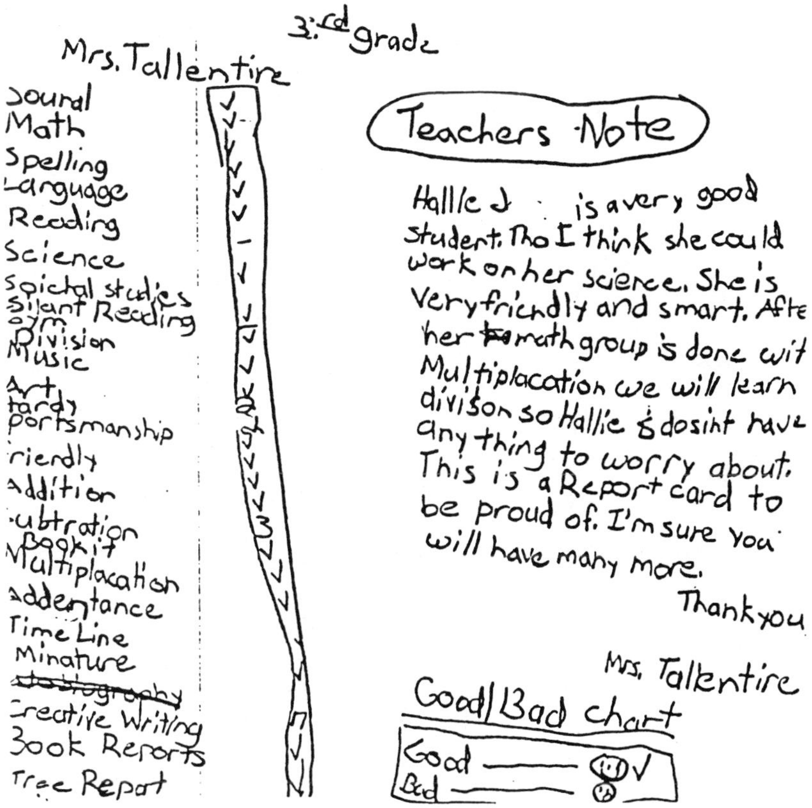

Mrs. Tallentire   3:rd grade

Journal
Math
Spelling
Language
Reading
Science
Spictal studies
Silent Reading
Gym
Division
Music
Art
tardy
Sportsmanship
friendly
Addition
Subtration
Bookit
Multiplacation
Addentance
Time Line
Minature
Stalography
Creative Writing
Book Reports
Tree Report

Teachers Note

Hallie J   is a very good
student. Tho I think she could
work on her science. She is
very friendly and smart. Afte
her math group is done wit
Multiplacation we will learn
divison so Hallie dosint have
any thing to worry about.
This is a Report card to
be proud of. I'm sure you
will have many more.

                    Thank you

            Mrs. Tallentire

Good Bad chart

Good ——— ☺ ✓
Bad ——— ☹

Figure 13-45

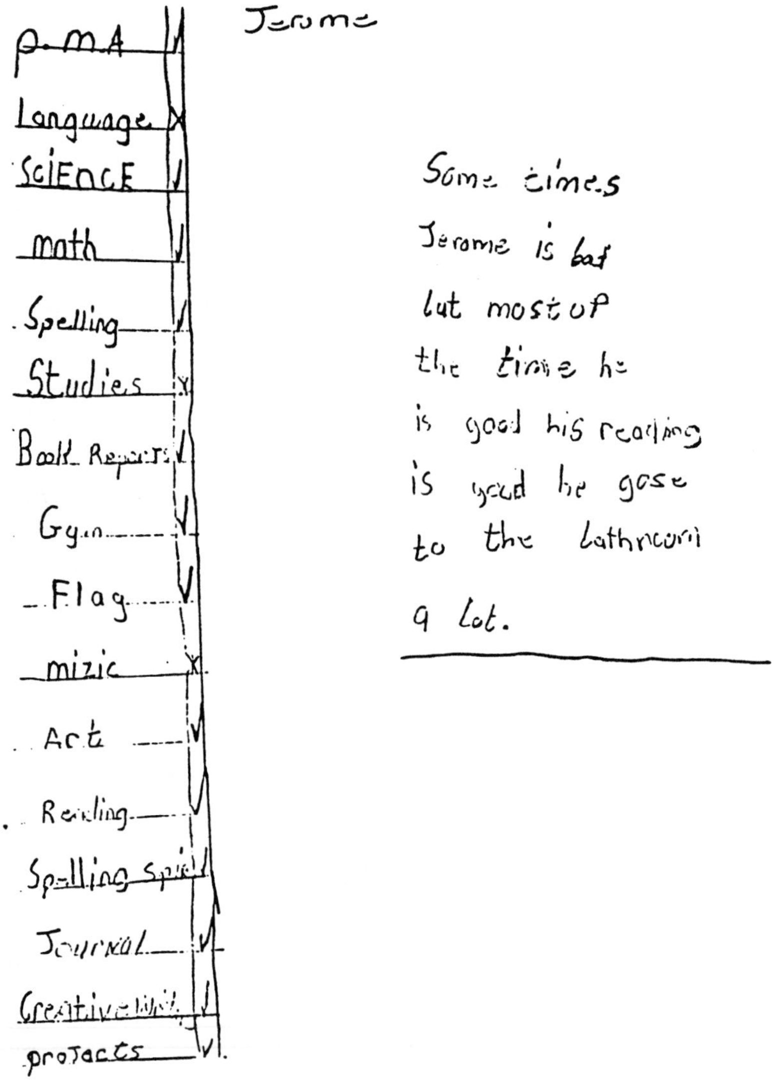

p. m.A

Language

SciEncE

math

Spelling

Studies

Book Report

Gym

Flag

mizic

Act

Reading

Spelling spie

Journal

Creative wri

proJects

Jerome

Some times
Jerome is bad
but most of
the time he
is good his reading
is good he gose
to the bathroom
a lot.

Report Cards on Teachers by Students

Teachers find that when they take the risk and ask students to evaluate their teaching, the results can be informative and insightful. One teacher told me, "The children's comments made me rethink some of my behaviors." A first grade teacher was surprised by the number of "C"'s she received in "fairness." A third grade teacher did not realize that she was not focused on the students in reading group until she read her "N"—"needs improvement" comments. Until teachers saw those comments, they had no idea students perceived them that way. (See Figures 13–46 through 13–51 for samples of report cards on the teacher for grades 1, 2, and 3.)

Figures 13-46, 13-47, and 13-48   Report Cards on the Teacher in Grade I
(Based on an idea and format developed by R. Anthony, T. Johnson, N. Mickelson and A. Preece.)

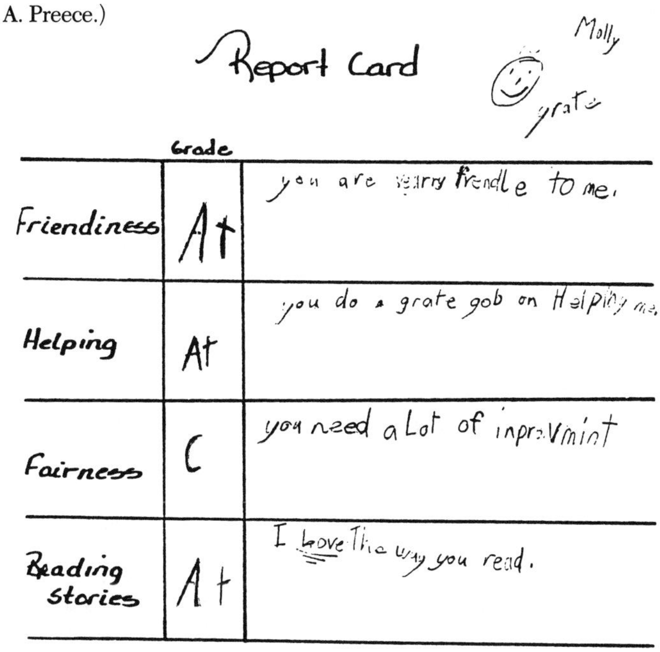

Report Card   Molly
                               grate

	Grade	
Friendiness	A†	you are varry frendle to me.
Helping	A†	you do a grate gob on Helping me.
Fairness	C	you need a Lot of inpravmint
Reading Stories	A †	I love The way you read.

Figure 13-47

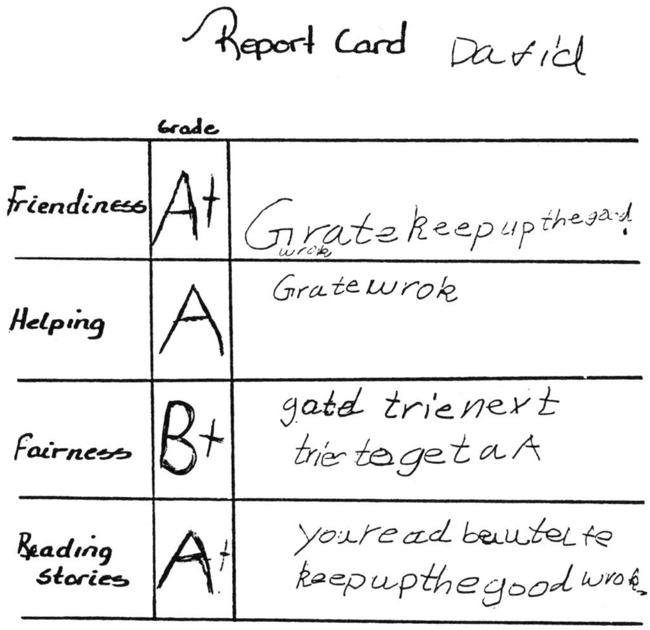

Report Card   David

	Grade	
Friendiness	A†	Grate keep up the good wrok
Helping	A	Grate wrok
Fairness	B†	gatd trie next trie to get a A
Reading Stories	A†	you read beuuteLte keep up the good wrok.

Figure 13-48

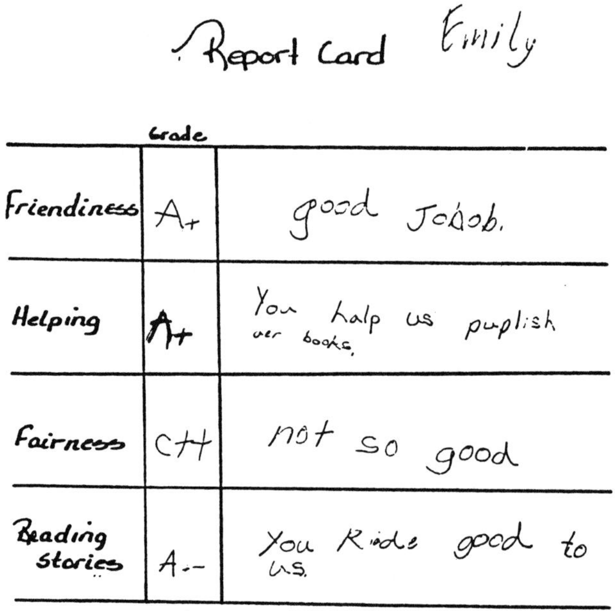

Report Card   Emily

	Grade	
Friendiness	A+	good Jobob.
Helping	A+	You halp us puplish uer books.
Fairness	C+t	not so good
Reading Stories	A.--	You Ride good to us.

Figure 13-49   A Report Card on the Teacher in Grade 2

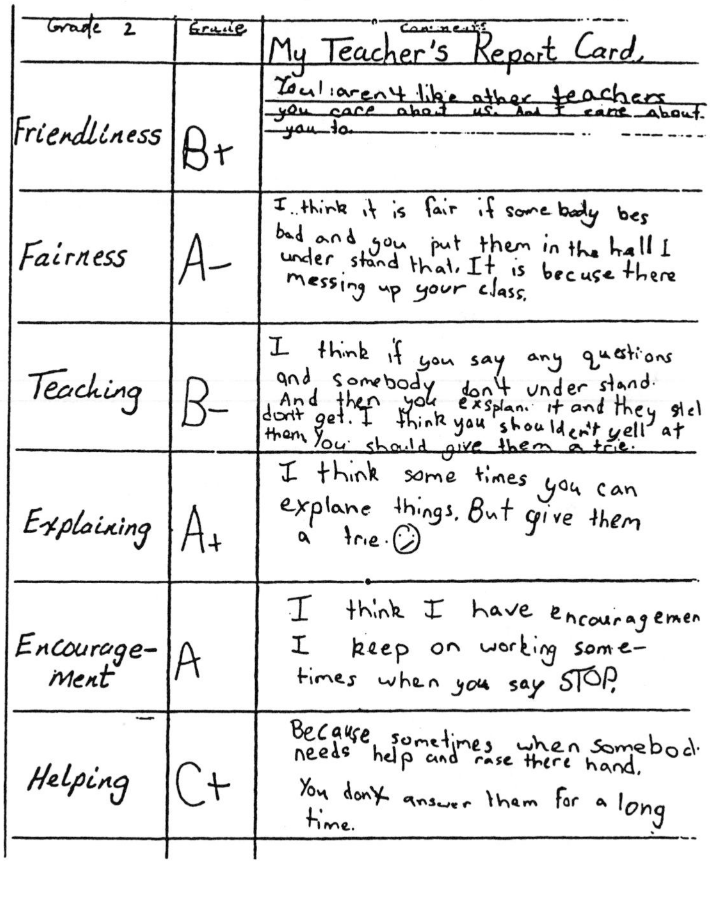

Grade 2	Grade	My Teacher's Report Card. Comments
Friendliness	B+	You aren't like other teachers you care about us. And I care about you to
Fairness	A-	I think it is fair if some body bes bad and you put them in the hall I under stand that. It is becuse there messing up your class.
Teaching	B-	I think if you say any questions and somebody don't under stand. And then you exsplain it and they stel don't get. I think you shouldn't yell at them You should give them a trie.
Explaining	A+	I think some times you can explane things. But give them a trie. ☺
Encourage-ment	A	I think I have encouragemen I keep on working some-times when you say STOP.
Helping	C+	Because sometimes when somebod needs help and rase there hand. You don't answer them for a long time.

362

Figures 13-50 and 13-51   Report Cards on the Teacher in Grade 3

REPORT CARD
ON THE TEACHER

Dane

EXPLANATION OF MARKS
O-Outstanding
S-Satisfactory
I-Improving
N-Needs Improvement

		Comments
1. Demonstrates an interest in books	O	You Demonsrate outstanding interest in books.
2. Teaches the writing process	S	You teach writin. and process very good.
3. Listens in group situations	N	You do not Listen in reading groups well. You need to listen
4. Fairness	N	You are not fair bow to the boys you need to Improve.
5. Willing to help	O	you are willing to help on anything
6. Friendliness	I	You are Improvein. in Friendliness to the boys

Figure 13–51

Alison M.

EXPLANATION OF MARKS
O-Outstanding
S-Satisfactory
I-Improving
N-Needs Improvement

		Comments
1. Demonstrates an interest in books	O	You alwas tells as good book to read and why to read books.
2. Teaches the writing process	O	Alwas explains about writing if someone dosen't understand
3. Listens in group situations	N	Needs to not worry about the other children around.
4. Fairness	S	Some times gets the boys in trouble then the girls.
5. Willing to help	O	Alwas willing to help if you can understand.
6. Friendliness	O	Alwas in the morning you greet like you were our mother.

Taking a Look at Teacher and Student Attitudes

Teachers

Teachers Who Have Been in the Process of Becoming Whole Language Teachers for Three to Five Years

In this section, elementary school teachers who have been immersed in professional reading, literature in the classroom, the writing process, and more meaningful teaching talk about their attitudes, their growth, their frustrations, and their goals. These are experienced, knowledgeable teachers who have been in the process of becoming whole language teachers for at least three to five years. All are active participants in our weekly language arts support groups.

Karen Sher taught first grade in an inner-city school for five years, using dull texts and a heavily phonetic approach to reading. Realizing "intuitively" that the curriculum was not relevant to students' lives, she incorporated art and writing activities into each day's program to make school more interesting. After teaching preschool for three years, she moved into kindergarten, where she has taught for the last four years.

> I'm less tied to programs and teachers' guides now, and this is a new feeling for me. All of a sudden, things are popping into my head—coming from me— and I don't need the security of having to read it somewhere first. I'm starting to trust myself more, and that's a powerful feeling. Teaching has become more fun and creative for me. I was so impatient and frustrated with myself for so long, I never thought I'd get to this place.
>
> I'm also more forgiving of my mistakes. In watching myself grow as a teacher, I have also learned what helps children grow. I used my principal's supportive relationship with me as a model for my behavior with children. Her praise and positive comments left me feeling good about myself, and I thought, "If she can do this to me, I can do this to kids." That kind of positive feedback was instrumental in allowing myself to make mistakes. Because I was given freedom to grow and develop at my own pace, I want to give that to the children in my classroom. When you give someone freedom, you send them the message, "I have faith in you."

Pam Anderson has taught for fifteen years in grades 2, 3, and 6, with the last seven years in sixth grade. While she began as a traditional teacher, she always strived for students to have a say in what was going on in the classroom and to make school interesting.

> I have appreciated that I've had the freedom to slowly evolve. When I heard what was going on in the k–4 buildings, I wanted to learn more about it. I think people thought I was doing more than I was. I see now that I really didn't have a sense of what whole language was.
>
> Now, I feel good that I have a better grasp about what whole language may be about. This past summer, I read Frank Smith's *Joining the Literacy Club*, and I also attended a week-long whole language workshop. That really brought things together for me, for thinking about what I want to be as a teacher. I'm going to try to give my students more choice this year.
>
> I'm fearful that I probably want to do too much. I still feel that I have to do everything to make the day go smoothly. It's hard to let go of some control.

Joan Di Dio has taught for twenty years in grades, 2, 4, 5, and 6, with the last seven years in fourth grade. She began as a traditional teacher but always tried to make her teaching meaningful in spite of reliance on basal texts.

> I feel best about my deeper understanding of whole language. Whenever I get off track and doubt what I'm doing, professional reading helps get me refocused. At the same time, I feel an inadequacy and frustration at not being able to immediately implement everything that I'm reading about. I want to do it all at once, and I realize I can't.
>
> I'm still struggling with a number of issues. I didn't have reading groups last year, and it's bothered me. I had whole class reading and individualized reading. I just couldn't fit in the groups with my fragmented schedule. Management of groups is a concern too—being able to think up meaningful activities that will take kids long enough so I can devote myself totally to a group.
>
> Evaluation is a big issue for me. Grappling with grades is a horrendous burden to a whole language teacher. I feel guilty knowing that what I've done with letter grades is not indicative of my students as readers and writers. I see now if I can work out a rubric, I can tackle it. I'm trying to get the courage to trust myself and look at evaluation differently. As in every school, there are colleagues who have a very different approach in their teaching philosophy. Sometimes, I have a feeling of isolation which makes it difficult for me to implement what I really believe in.

Linda Cooper has been teaching for thirteen years and has spent the last five years in third grade. She began as "a good basal teacher who followed the manual." About five years ago she began to make changes in her teaching.

> When kids started asking me what dictionary definition I wanted for the vocabulary words because the vocabulary was done before the story, and I also saw the amount of time I spent explaining worksheets that were done in one-third the time it took for me to explain them, I knew I was ready for change.
>
> At about the same time, I observed our school's first grade literature program, and I became convinced that there were more exciting ways to teach language arts than what I had been doing. Even though I was scared to death the first year, I moved away from the basal. Having you take a reading group in my room—at the same time I did—was very reassuring. I could hear some of the questions you asked, and that helped me. It made my transition easier and more secure. Also, when a lesson we both thought was wonderful died, I realized I didn't have to know it all. I saw that when we could talk out what went wrong, we could work out the problems. That was most valuable.
>
> Then I started professional reading and getting the philosophy behind my thinking. I slowly gained the confidence to set up my room and interpret whole language my way. I was going along fine till I was just moved to fourth grade. I spent the entire summer in a panic worrying about having to put letter grades into a whole language program. I began feeling better after proofreading your chapter on evaluation and understanding that evaluation and grading are not the same. I saw I was further along in understanding whole language philosophy than I thought. I feel more willing to give evaluation a try now.

Students

Former Students in Our First Grade Literacy Program

At the suggestion of my former principal, Delores Groves, in June 1989 I interviewed fifth and sixth grade students who had been in our first grade in a reading-writing classroom where they had been immersed daily in authentic literature and self-selected writing (Routman, 1988). We were interested to find out what, if any, effect they felt their first grade experience had had on them and how they viewed their education to this point. While initially I asked about twenty students to complete a written interview form, I found their comments—limited to the space and questions provided—gave little in-depth information. I therefore selected seven students of varying abilities, three fifth-graders and four sixth-graders, to interview personally. Four representative interviews follow.

Martin had been in our district Headstart program and had qualified for Chapter 1 in the fall of first grade. His daily journal writing had been a favorite activity and a springboard for his learning to read (see Routman, 1988, pp. 96–103). As a fifth-grader, Martin exuded confidence and a positive attitude about himself. It was clear from his comments that writing was still very central to his life.

ROUTMAN: What are your best memories of school so far?

MARTIN: Grades 1 and 2 because that's when I did the most writing. We don't do so much writing now. I published a whole bunch of books in first and second grade. Now, hardly anything I write gets published.
First and second grade were also important to me because we had a good reading program. I don't remember how I learned to read, but I know I read a lot of books. The books influenced me to write more because I saw all that good writing of authors.

ROUTMAN: I remember you used to prefer writing to reading and most other activities. Is that still true?

MARTIN: I still like writing best because it lets me put my thoughts on paper. Sometimes I write when I'm bored, and then I'm not bored anymore. I write stories and draw pictures. I write mysteries and adventures and everyday life stuff. I write lots of stories at home. I don't bring them in to share because the teacher doesn't read them.
The way I was taught, it was exciting and made me want to write. Ideas came easily to me because of all the stories we read. I always got good ideas for characters. Also I wanted to go to the Young Authors' Conference. When you took me in first grade, I still remember that. I was so proud to share my books. I felt like an author.

ROUTMAN: What's writing in school like for you now?

MARTIN: The teacher chooses most of the topics. Some of them are all right, but I don't like a lot of them. It takes longer to write when she chooses the topic. Like we had to write a myth. I had no ideas but the teacher said we had to write a myth, and get graded on it. It was very hard for me because I didn't know a lot about myths. Other people in my class suggested ideas to me, and that helped.
I don't like to get graded. It makes me nervous. You shouldn't be graded when you're trying to use your imagination. Using your imagination is more fun than something the teacher has thought of. This whole year, I could only choose my own topic once. That story is my favorite because I got to use my own imagination. I think it's the best thing I've written so far. Would you like to see it?

Martin very proudly showed me a story where the cover was a cut-out cardboard from a box of bran flakes. The story was humorous, expressive, and adventurous. The main character was called Natural Flake. Martin had been in school a whole year and felt he had completed only one meaningful piece of writing.

Quita was one of our most remarkable writers in first grade. In second grade, when she was not in a reading-writing classroom, the principal and I noticed little growth and less interest in writing on her part. As a fifth-grader, she was a strong student and was in the gifted math program.

ROUTMAN: What are your best memories of school so far?

QUITA: Probably math has been most significant to me, especially learning division and decimals.

ROUTMAN: What do you remember about your early school writing experiences?

QUITA: I don't remember how I learned to write. I loved the daily journal writing in first grade. But after that, I didn't get to write as much.

ROUTMAN: What about reading? How do you feel about reading, and do you choose to spend time reading?

QUITA: When I get home from school, I read about fifteen minutes or more by choice. I usually pick a novel. I think I became a reader because there were lots of good choices at Moreland. There were no boring books that the teacher made you read. Now, I read at least two or three chapters a day on my own. I go with the emotions of the book. If it's a sad part, I get sad. If it's a happy part, I feel happy.
I like reading, but I'd prefer more choice. With my teacher this year, we have to read each book with the whole class, and we have to read two assigned chapters each night. I'm in a high reading group. We change classes; there's also a middle and a low group. We also have book reports due every two weeks on our free reading. We have to do oral and written book reports. I don't think kids should have to write book reports. It takes away from the fun of reading.

Oscar presented himself as a fairly confident sixth-grader. He clearly saw himself as a "reader." In first grade, he had struggled with learning to read, and he continued to struggle through the grades. For several years he had received Chapter 1 reading support. In third grade, it was suggested he be evaluated for possible learning disabilities. Oscar's parents had refused, saying he just needed to apply himself more.

ROUTMAN: How is school going for you?

OSCAR: Science and social studies are hard for me. I'm a good reader, but I don't like some of the books we're reading in class. I don't like when we have to do summaries and book reports. I like to write stories, especially when I can decide what to write about.
Before I didn't like school at all. Now I do. We play a basketball game when we study for tests. And when we have comprehension assignments, you can work with a partner.

First and second grade were really hard for me. As I got older, I kept
trying and school got easier.

ROUTMAN: How do you feel about reading? What kinds of books do you like to
read, and when do you read?

OSCAR: I like to read books that are funny and have illustrations. I just read
The Little Fishes (by E. C. Hauggard, Houghton Mifflin, 1967).
(*He proceeded to tell me the whole story, excitedly.*) At home I read
before I go to bed, until I fall asleep.

ROUTMAN: What do you remember most about your early school years?

OSCAR: I remember the *Mr. Men* books (by Roger Hargreaves, Price/Stern/
Sloan, 1982) in first grade and liking them. I liked journal writing
and publishing books.

ROUTMAN: What has been the most significant thing in your education so far?

OSCAR: My improvement.

ROUTMAN: What do you do if you can't read something?

OSCAR: When I come to a word I don't know, I try to figure it out. I skip it
and read the next sentence to see if the word will come to my mind.
If not, I'll ask my mother, and she'll tell me. Skipping words and
coming back to them works best for me.

Nicky was a conscientious, achieving sixth-grader; she had been like that since
first grade. Raised by her mother and grandmother, school and learning remained
an important focus in her life. Nicky told me she wants to be a doctor, lawyer, or
basketball player when she grows up.

ROUTMAN: What are your best memories of school so far?

NICKY: This year has been most significant to me. With Mr. H. we go over
everything we don't understand. We switch papers and grade each
other's. Then Mr. H. goes over all the work.

ROUTMAN: Tell me how you feel about reading and writing.

NICKY: I like to read most of the time. I don't like that we have to do so
much writing on every book: summaries, focuses, what we'd change
about the book. Then we have to hand those in every two weeks. If I
were the teacher, I'd have students read the book without interruption and require less writing.

ROUTMAN: When do you read?

NICKY: Most of my reading is done at school. I have no time at home. On
weekends, I have to watch my cousin. Sometimes I pick up a book
when I'm mad at my mother, and I have nothing else to do. I like
fantasy, mystery, and some nonfiction.

ROUTMAN: Do you still like to write, and when do you write?

NICKY: I have written a lot of stories. I spend about an hour a day writing
stories at home. I like writing better than reading. I remember
doing a lot of writing at Moreland. At Moreland I learned how to
write and read books and reading helped writing. If you read and
then write it down, you understand it more. I like to write songs and

stories about people—how kids relate to school and their parents. Some of the stories I wrote were based on *Sixth Grade Can Really Kill You* [by Barthe DeClements, Viking, 1985]. I choose parts I like from books I've read and put them in my own stories. I learned that in first grade at Moreland.

You know, we read lots of books in school, but instead of essays and book reports, we could write our own stories and books. I think that makes more sense.

Observations

From interviewing these students, it became clear to me that being immersed in a reading-writing classroom in first grade was very significant for their view of literacy even four and five years later. In spite of the fact that these students all wished they had more choice in and ownership of their reading and writing, their attitudes about reading and writing remained fairly positive. These students were very aware of the influence of reading on writing, the power and enjoyment of journal writing and publishing, the importance of self-selection in reading and writing, and the need for time set aside for reading.

These positive attitudes and self-awareness seem to indicate that even one year in a whole language classroom can make a difference in a child's reading-writing attitudes and behaviors. That one year—no matter when it comes—is still better than never being in a whole language classroom. This should give some comfort to the teacher who may be the only whole language teacher in a school.

At the same time, it is also quite clear that just because a district makes a written commitment to more meaning-centered approaches and moves from the basal to literature, unless ongoing staff development takes place across all the grades, teachers will teach as they have always taught. What came through from the interviews was that reading was largely whole class, there was some ability grouping for reading, there were lots of required written book reports and summaries, and most writing topics were assigned by the teacher. While choice and ownership were primary to the students, they were not yet highly valued by some of the teachers. That would only come when teachers acquired a strong theoretical understanding of language learning and whole language principles.

Reflections on Evaluation

Balancing evaluation means relying not only on multiple sources to inform instruction but on sources that rely heavily on observation and process. Meaningful evaluation means an extremely knowledgeable teacher looking at how students apply knowledge in different contexts. On the highest level, meticulous documentation would be done largely by the learner. The teacher-learner or student-learner would be observing and talking about his own learning processes—including strategies being used, changes being noticed, progress being made, strengths and weaknesses observed, past and present levels of functioning noted, and new goals needing to be established.

Evaluation will no doubt continue to be an area educators grapple with. Self-evaluation is still the hardest part for me. While I strive to improve my evaluation procedures, it is a struggle. Although I am continually examining my teaching philosophy, behaviors, and methods, I have not yet taken the risk of asking for feedback from my colleagues on how I do my job. I plan to make that one of my new goals.

If evaluation is to move to a place where it is valid and valued by teachers, students, parents, administrators, and policy makers, then teachers need to stop waiting for someone else to make the necessary changes. We can no longer rely on test constructors, state departments of education, and administrators to set evaluation policy. If we want evaluation to be consistent with our theory of how children learn, teachers must get together and actively work for better assessment and evaluation procedures. One teacher working alone is not likely to have much effect, but groups of teachers can write letters, influence administrators and board of education members, share recent research with parents and policy makers, change testing procedures, and work to make evaluation more balanced, informative, and useful. It is an effort worth making. Until meaningful evaluation becomes an integrated part of all teaching and learning, tests and decontextualized measures will continue to drive, misinform, and misguide instruction.

Resources

For professional books dealing with evaluation, see *Resources for Teachers*, especially:

Barrs and others. 1990. *The Primary Language Record: Handbook for Teachers*

Baskwill and Whitman. 1988. *Evaluation: Whole Language, Whole Child*

Clay. 1985. *The Early Detection of Reading Difficulties*, 3rd ed.

Cohen. 1988. *TESTS: Marked for Life*

Goodman, Goodman, and Hood. 1989. *The Whole Language Evaluation Book*

Harp. 1991. *Assessment and Evaluation in Whole Language Programs*

Jett-Simpson. 1990. *Toward an Ecological Assessment of Reading Progress*

Kamii. 1990. *Achievement Testing in the Early Grades: The Games Grownups Play*

Tierney, Carter, and Desai. 1991. *Portfolios in the Reading-Writing Classroom*

The following journal articles, chapters, and booklets have been particularly useful in personal exploration and in our weekly language arts support groups for deepening understanding of evaluation in a meaning-centered classroom.

Ammon, Richard. Fall 1988. "Evaluation in the Holistic Reading/Language Arts Curriculum." *Oregon English. Theme: Whole Language.* Portland: Oregon Council of Teachers of English, pp. 65–69. (An earlier version first appeared in Ulrich Hardt (ed.), *Teaching Reading with the Other Language Arts*, IRA, 1983.)

Teachers will find this a valuable article for understanding holistic evaluation and for gaining specific strategies and ideas for evaluation of the language arts. The article concludes with excellent reflective questions for the teacher. Many of our teachers have found this a particularly useful article for establishing a holistic framework.

Au, Kathryn H., Judith A. Scheu, Alice J. Kawakami, and Patricia A. Herman. April 1990. "Assessment and Accountability in a Whole Literacy Curriculum," *The Reading Teacher*, pp. 574–578.

This informative article addresses teachers' concerns about assessment and accountability with a "whole literacy" approach. Based on their work in the Kamehameha Elementary Education Program (KEEP) in Hawaii, the authors recommend a port-

folio approach incorporating a curriculum framework based on six aspects of literacy: ownership, reading comprehension, writing process, word identification, language and vocabulary knowledge, and voluntary reading. Five major assessment tasks and procedures are suggested for providing information on the six aspects of literacy: questionnaire on attitudes for reading and writing, response to literature task, student's writing sample, running record, and voluntary reading log. Some specific examples of assessment tasks are provided. This is an excellent article for understanding and implementing holistic assessment strategies.

Bailey, Janis, Phyllis Brazee, and others. April 1988. "Problem Solving Our Way to Alternative Evaluation Procedures," *Language Arts*, pp. 364–373.

A group of teachers describe their attempts to move toward evaluation that is consistent with their meaning-centered approaches to reading and writing. This is a terrific article, both for understanding holistic evaluation and for the literacy evaluation forms and checklists that are shared.

Brandt, Ronald (executive ed.). April 1989. *Educational Leadership: Redirecting Assessment.*

Don't miss this comprehensive, provocative, and outstanding issue for perspectives on the current state of assessment and for directions for meaningful assessment. (See "Themed Journals," pp. 27b–28b, for complete information on this issue.)

Bredekamp, Sue, and Lorrie Shepard. March 1989. "How Best to Protect Children from Inappropriate School Expectations, Practices, and Policies," *Young Children*, pp. 14–24.

This important position statement, from the National Association for the Education of Young Children, on the uses and misuses of standardized testing with young children complements and follows the NAEYC position statement on developmentally appropriate practice (Bredekamp, 1987). Based on research findings, the authors address inappropriate assessment-curriculum–related policies in kindergarten and the primary grades: readiness testing, raising the entrance age, transitional classes, increased academic demand in kindergarten, and retention. They note that they are not opposed to all standardized testing—for example, reliable screening measures that are used for instructional planning in meeting children's special needs are valid. However, standardized tests used to exclude, admit, or place children in special classes are viewed as harmful. "If no beneficial outcome for children can be demonstrated, then using a standardized test is not justified" (p. 15). The article concludes with suggested guidelines for decision making in testing and placement. Use these specific guidelines and resources to promote appropriate practice in your school district. Every teacher, administrator, parent, and policy maker concerned with early childhood education should read this powerful article.

Cambourne, Brian, and Jan Turbill. January 1990. "Assessment in Whole Language Classrooms: Theory into Practice," *The Elementary School Journal*, pp. 337–349.

This superb, comprehensive article stresses that a measurement-based view of assessment does not fit with a whole language philosophy. The authors, Australian educators working as coresearchers with classroom teachers, advocate applying "responsive evaluation" (which believes that "the 'human-as-instrument' is as effective and valid as the 'test-as-instrument' when assessing human behavior") to whole language classrooms. Using multiple methods and procedures for data collection and analysis in naturalistic classroom settings, they conclude that responsive evaluation is "trustworthy," "scientific," and advantageous to the learning process. Appendixes give fine examples of anecdotal records, some markers for noting control of language, and language evaluation checklists for reading and writing.

Eggleton, Jill. 1990. *Whole Language Evaluation. Reading, Writing and Spelling*. Bothell, WA: The Wright Group.

This 80-page resource by a New Zealand educator is full of practical ideas for evaluating and monitoring children's progress in the "emergent," "early," and "fluency" stages of reading, writing, and spelling. Lots of sample checklists, forms, suggested approaches, and ideas for use in the early grades.

Fisher, Bobbi. November/December 1989. "Assessing Emergent and Initial Readers," *Teaching K–8*, pp. 56–58.

A practicing kindergarten teacher describes the systematic way she observes, records, and assesses each of her students' early literacy behaviors through a tape recorded reading and writing interview, various reading and writing observations and conferences, and procedures to assess letter, sound, and word-sound identification. Kindergarten and first grade teachers will find this a practical, invaluable article.

Harman, Susan. 1989–1990. "The Tests: Trivial or Toxic?" *Teachers Networking: The Whole Language Newsletter*. Vol. 9, no. 1, pp. 1 and 5–9.

The author, who is project director of the American Reading Council, refutes claims that standardized tests are objective or useful for diagnosis, accountability, and placement. She points out the monopoly of the three major elementary school test publishers who are also the same three (out of four) major elementary basal reading text publishers. Harmon notes the damaging effects of tests on many levels of education and calls for evaluation that respects teachers as professionals and that thoughtfully observes children's performance over time.

Harp, Bill. November 1988. "When the Principal Asks: 'When You Do Whole Language Instruction, How Will You Keep Track of Reading and Writing Skills?'" *The Reading Teacher*, pp. 160–161.

This brief response gives the rationale for more meaning-based assessment, with some specific examples of holistic measures.

Hornsby, David, and Deborah Sukarna, with Jo-Ann Parry. 1988. "Record Keeping and Evaluation." In *Read On: A Conference Approach to Reading*. Portsmouth, NH: Heinemann, Chap. 12, pp. 129–143.

Lots of practical and visual examples are given for evaluation in the classroom along with learning principles supporting holistic evaluation of individual children. Very helpful to the teacher who wants to "see" what holistic record keeping might look like.

Johnston, Peter. April 1987. "Teachers as Evaluation Experts," *The Reading Teacher*, pp. 744–748.

Johnston affirms that the current preoccupation with testing does not further instruction. Instead, he recommends that knowledgeable classroom teachers— interacting with and observing individual students—should evaluate students and make appropriate instructional decisions. He describes what a teacher who is an expert in literacy evaluation would know and be able to do. This article is a personal favorite; read it and discuss it with colleagues for information and inspiration.

King, Dorothy F. 1989–1990. "My Word! Real Kids or Unreal Tasks: The Obvious Choice," *Teacher's Networking: The Whole Language Newsletter*, Vol. 9, no. 1, pp. 14–15.

After getting back low test scores from a thoughtfully literate second grade class, an administrator takes a careful look at the tests and the students and decides to ignore the test results. Share this article with your administrator.

Koskinen, Patricia S., Linda B. Gambrell, Barbara A. Kapinus, and Betty S. Heathington. May 1988. "Retelling: A Strategy for Enhancing Students' Reading Comprehension," *The Reading Teacher*, pp. 892–897.

> *This compact article cites the research that supports the beneficial outcomes of retelling and gives suggested models for how to use retelling in the classroom. Useful for all classrooms.*

Neill, D. Monty, and Noe J. Medina. May 1989. "Standardized Testing: Harmful to Educational Health," *Phi Delta Kappan*, pp. 688–697.

> *Share this carefully researched article on the negative effects of multiple-choice standardized testing with other educators and policy makers in your district. Unfortunately, the authors' research reveals that "the number of states that mandate testing has increased greatly in recent years" (p. 689). Some adverse effects of testing include placing disproportionate numbers of minorities in remedial, special education, and lower-track programs; focusing on basic skills and isolated facts instead of on integration of information and critical thinking. "[T]esting must become an occasional adjunct, used for obtaining basic but limited information about education—and for nothing else" (p. 695).*

Reardon, S. Jeanne. Winter 1990. "Putting Reading Tests in Their Place," *The New Advocate*, pp. 29–37.

> *A first grade classroom teacher acknowledges that while the results of standardized tests are not particularly useful to students or the teacher, the results are used to make decisions about children and reading programs. Therefore, students should be taught "reading-test-reading" as a separate reading genre to prepare them for test taking. The author describes how she manages to weave the reading-test genre into her reading program without compromising the high-level thinking and joy of reading that goes on in her reading-writing classroom.*

Rogers, Vincent. May 1989. "Assessing the Curriculum Experienced by Children," *Phi Delta Kappan*, pp. 714–717.

> *This is a superb and highly useful article for k–12 teachers by the director of the Alternative Assessment Project at the University of Connecticut. Rogers gives many creative, workable strategies and activities for assessing the "curriculum of the mind." To probe and assess what students have actually experienced and learned in the content areas, Rogers describes a range of activities and interview probes that can be applied successfully to any classroom in which the teacher is looking to incorporate alternatives to traditional testing. Don't miss this valuable resource!*

Seidel, Steve. December 13, 1989. "Even Before Portfolios: The Activities and Atmosphere of a Portfolio Classroom," *Portfolio: The Newsletter of Arts Propel*, pp. 6–9.

> *A portrait of a ninth grade portfolio classroom gives valuable insights into the conditions and strategies that put students at the center of their own assessment as writers and learners. Applicable and useful for all grade levels.*

Sharp, Quality Quinn (compiler). 1989. *Evaluation: Whole Language Checklists for Evaluating Your Children. For Grades K–6.* New York: Scholastic.

> *This 38-page booklet provides many useful checklists in various areas: reading behaviors, reader response, writing and spelling, miscue analysis, students self-evaluation, and literary appreciation.*

Teale, William H. November 1988. "Developmentally Appropriate Assessment of Reading and Writing in the Early Childhood Classroom," *The Elementary School Journal*, pp. 173–183.

An expert researcher in emergent literacy cites the theoretical rationale and calls for assessment programs and procedures for four- and five-year-olds that are based mostly on performance samples and observational methods. The major concepts and skills that are significant in children's emerging literacy are identified and ways to assess students' knowledge of those concepts and skills are demonstrated. This is a useful article for prekindergarten and kindergarten teachers who are looking to tie teaching and assessment together in a developmentally appropriate and meaningful manner.

Valencia, Sheila. January 1990. "Assessment: A Portfolio Approach to Classroom Reading Assessment: The Whys, Whats, and Hows." *The Reading Teacher*, pp. 338–340.

A knowledgeable professor describes a portfolio approach to reading assessment, including the physical and instructional organization of the portfolio, and argues that such an approach is authentic, ongoing, multifaceted, and collaborative.

Watson, Dorothy (ed.). 1987. "Valuing and Evaluating the Learners and Their Language." In *Ideas and Insights: Language Arts in the Elementary School.* Urbana, IL: National Council of Teachers of English, Chap. 10, pp. 209–219.

Assessment suggestions are given for literature discussion groups, journal writing, kidwatching, writing, student goal setting, spelling, miscue, analysis, and self-evaluation. Very helpful and practical for the classroom teacher at any grade level.

Weaver, Constance. 1988. "How Can We Assess Readers' Strengths and Begin to Determine Their Instructional Needs?" In *Reading Process and Practice: From Socio-Psycholinguistics to Whole Language.* Portsmouth, NH: Heinemann, Chap. 10, pp. 321–363.

This outstanding chapter will guide the teacher in assessment procedures. Particularly valuable are the detailed procedures and guidelines for miscue analysis.

Wiggins, Grant. April 1989. "Teaching to the (Authentic) Test." *Educational Leadership*, pp. 41–47.

Wiggins, a special consultant to the Coalition of Essential Schools on assessment and curriculum issues, calls for content-based teaching and testing at the high school level that is based on skills of inquiry and expression. In place of classrooms tests, he suggests designing performances in authentic contexts. For a graduation requirement, he suggests a public exhibition of mastery, where the student demonstrates knowledge and synthesis of what has been learned. Read the article to apply the specifics. See page 45 for criteria for authentic tests.

Wolfe, Dennie Palmer. April 1989. "Portfolio Assessment: Sampling Student Work," *Educational Leadership*, pp. 35–39.

The author, a researcher involved with portfolio assessment, advocates making school assessment more in keeping with real life, which is full of long-term projects that need ongoing reflection and monitoring. Modeled on the working processes of musicians and artists, the suggested goal is for students to be guided in taking the responsibility of thoughtfully judging their own work over time. Educators interested in the use of portfolios as part of the assessment process will want to read this article.

Wood, George (coordinator). Fall 1990. *Democracy in Education: Alternatives to Standardized Testing.*

Read and discuss this issue for insights from teachers and students on standardized testing. (See "Themed Journals," p. 29b, for a full description.)

14

The Learning Disabled Student:

A Part of the At-Risk Population

L.D. teacher Margie Glaros noting students' insights during a discussion of Stone Fox *(Gardiner, 1980)*

"I believe there are very few true learning disabled students. We have made them learning disabled by focusing on their deficits, instead of their strengths." There was a loud round of applause. It was obvious I had touched a nerve. No other comment I made as the opening speaker at the whole language conference had aroused so much emotion and support.

I am a certified teacher for children who have been identified as learning disabled (L.D.). For eight years I worked in my local school district as an L.D. tutor where I saw students on a one-to-one pull-out basis for thirty minutes a day. Based on my graduate-level training, I taught reading with a heavy emphasis on phonics. I taught most skills in isolation, and I taught mainly to the students' deficits. I did frequent task analysis, keeping charts and records documenting skills growth, and I used behavior modification techniques to motivate and reward students. I worked hard, and my students made real gains. Yet in all that time, I have very few recollections of dismissing a student from the L.D. program. Almost all students continued to need and receive supportive services throughout their school careers.

It is, therefore, not surprising to me that the number of students identified as learning disabled has continued to increase since 1975 when the Education of All Handicapped Children Act became federal law. The public law, P.L. 94-142, requires that school districts identify and provide appropriate education for all handicapped children. Since the law was enacted, the number of students identified as learning disabled has remained at 6 to 10 percent of the total U.S. school population.

It is interesting to note that the L.D. population is often partly defined by a "definition of exclusion." That is, these are students who are *not* achieving in school in spite of the fact that they are *not* mentally retarded, *not* deaf or blind, *not*

376

emotionally disturbed, and have *not* had inordinate obstacles to learning such as poor teaching and frequent absences.

I do not believe that becoming learning disabled is a predetermined condition. Even with the few students who have been identified as having biological or neurological dysfunctions, the way students are perceived, taught, and interacted with has dramatic effects on achievement. Teachers who view a child as having learning abilities, as opposed to disabilities, will usuallly find a way to be successful in teaching the child.

[margin note: LD not a predeter condition]

I strongly believe the number of children identified as L.D. could be greatly reduced if educators focused on students' strengths instead of on their deficits. While the Individual Education Plan, required for each identified student, is intended to remediate the deficits and teach to the strengths, more often than not the main emphasis on this written plan focuses only on goals and objectives to remediate the deficits.

This chapter takes a close look at some students with learning disabilities and discusses related issues: teaching strategies, evaluation, the pull-out program, changing attitudes of the L.D. teacher, and communicating with parents. Since students with learning problems are a part of every classroom, the intended audience is the classroom teacher as well as the L.D., or Resource Room, teacher and parents. In addition, since the L.D. student is part of the broad at-risk population, the issues discussed are relevant and applicable to the special education population, Chapter 1 students, second language learners, limited-language–proficient learners, and other remedial learners, including illiterate adults. My hope is that while recognizing the problems in dealing with at-risk learners, teachers, administrators, and parents will feel encouraged by the possibilities.

A Look at Three Students

Expectations for Success: Paul

Several years ago, on a mid-January day, I received a call from a learning disabilities teacher in our district. She was very concerned about one of her students and asked if I would work with Paul.

> Paul was a fourth-grader who had entered our school district in second grade and had then repeated that grade. Despite caring teachers and varied teaching strategies and materials, he was a virtual nonreader and nonwriter after nearly four years in our district. In addition, Paul had begun "acting up" in the classroom. These days, he was receiving few positive comments from teachers.
>
> Theo Husband had been Paul's L.D. teacher since second grade, and she and Paul enjoyed a warm and caring relationship. Her classroom was the place where Paul felt most consistently valued and successful. Paul often sought her out at lunch time and after school, when he talked to her for hours. She, in turn, was a good listener and constantly worked at building his self-esteem after a tough day in school. In fourth grade, during one of their talks, Paul spoke about how the kids were teasing him, and then he blurted out, "I really want to learn how to read." It was at

that point that Theo decided to call me. She hoped that together we might make a difference in Paul's learning.

Theo was completely dedicated to seeking the best for Paul. She had tried many programs and methods and consulted colleagues for advice. She had spent years being an advocate for Paul—attending school conferences and keeping in close contact with his mom. Now, mid-year in fourth grade, Theo was experiencing anxieties because Paul would be leaving at the end of the school year to enter another building where all fifth- and sixth-graders were housed. At the same time, Paul's mother was expressing some anger about her son's failure to learn to read and write in the public school and was threatening to send him to a private school.

As the only information I had about Paul at our first meeting was that he was having severe difficulties, I had no preconceived notions about what he could or could not do. I met him with the expectation that he was whole and able and that he could learn. I spoke with him in language and tone uncharacteristic of me. I told him that I was a well-known reading expert and that I had never failed to teach a child to read—*never.* I told him that I would be teaching him in a way that was totally different from what he had experienced so far and that he would be successful.

Paul had agreed to meet with me only after much encouragement by Theo. We spent the first half hour just talking and getting to know each other. I knew that after many years of frustration with reading and writing, he doubted his abilities. Paul's expectations about becoming a successful reader and writer would need to change before any new learning could take place.

In the course of our conversation, I asked Paul about reading in school, and he told me about the basal texts and worksheets he'd had. When I asked him to show me what he was working on now in reading, he brought me his Phonics C workbook. I asked Paul if his own language and stories had ever been used to try to teach him to read. Because he said no, I decided to begin with the most predictable text of all—his own language.

That first day together Paul and I wrote our first book. I folded several sheets of blank, white ditto paper together and asked Paul what he would like his first story to be about. I suggested he write about something he was interested in and knew a lot about. With very little hesitation, he told me he wanted his book to be called *The New Space Shuttle.* I served as his scribe as he dictated the story, told me how much print he wanted on each page, and where the writing and the illustrations would be placed. I began with a title and author page, followed by an information page that included where and when the book was being published. His completed story was forty-two words spread over four pages of text and illustrations. It read as follows. (See Figure 14–1 for reproduction and layout.)

- p. 1: I want to improve space travel so we can get farther away from the earth.
- p. 2: Then we can meet other people.
- p. 3: Technology will improve the way we live.
- p. 4: This is a drawing of the way I think the space shuttle should be.

Figure 14-1   Paul's First Book

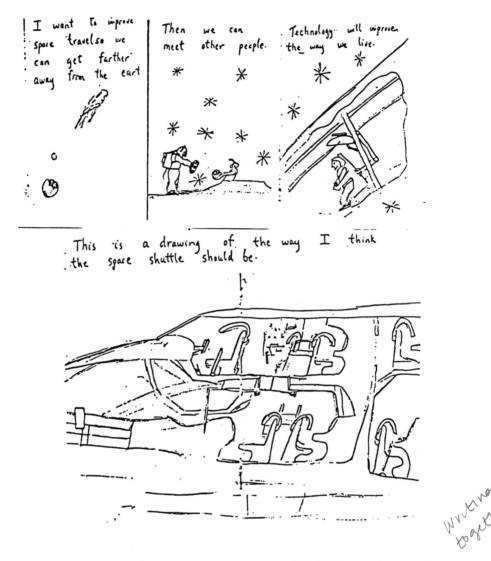

I want to improve
space travel so we
can get farther
away from the eart

Then we can
meet other people.

Technology will improve
the way we live.

This is a drawing of the way I think
the space shuttle should be.

writing together

As Paul dictated one page at a time to me, I had him watch me write as I slowly verbalized and stretched out the sounds of each word. Then I asked him to read the page back to me. Because it was his own language on a topic that was important to him, he read the page without difficulty. We continued, one page at a time. I slowly verbalized each word as I wrote it. Paul carefully observed the process and read each completed page.

Next, I suggested to Paul that it might be a good idea to have an "About the Author" page for this first book. We looked at several book jackets and discussed the kinds of information that might be included. He dictated: "Paul is eleven years old. He is a nice guy. He can be friendly and funny. He likes to draw. He knows a lot about science and history. He wants to be an

Air Force pilot when he grows up. When he retires he will design ships for outer space."

I was surprised that he would risk having that much print on a page (it took up eleven lines when it was handwritten), and despite the fact that there were no picture cues, he was able to read it. I was even more surprised by his last line: "When he retires he will design ships for outer space." That statement told me that Paul was an imaginative and inquiring student.

Working with Paul that first day, I was struck by his strong oral language, his delightful sense of humor, and his knowledge of things scientific. I had expected him to be of normal intelligence; I had not expected him to be above average. Because of my own prejudices about literacy, I assumed that if he was a nonreader and nonwriter after so many years in school, he probably wasn't overly bright. How wrong I was!

After we completed the text and Paul had read each page, we went back and read his book together. He followed my voice so he would know how a story should sound in its pacing, phrasing, and overall fluency. I assured Paul that he would always be able to read his own stories, and eventually these reading skills would transfer to commercial books and other reading materials.

After reading his completed text, Paul began to add illustrations. Paul was an excellent artist, and he loved to draw. Incorporating his artistic ability to complement his story served as a boost to his confidence by acknowledging his special talent.

Before Paul started to draw, we talked about how important it was for the illustrations to match the text, both to help him when reading and to support the story line. We were very specific in talking about how certain pictures would help him remember words in the text. He carefully worked on the illustrations after our visit and had them completed when I saw him the following week.

I encountered a changed student in our second session. Paul, who had never been able to read even his own writing, was bursting with pride at his first reading success. He proudly read me *The New Space Shuttle*, including the author page, which he had practiced and reread in school and at home over and over again. His L.D. teacher, Theo, was absolutely joyful. It was the first time she had ever seen Paul believe that he could read.

Much later Theo told me of the significance of my first session with Paul. "He really felt he accomplished something that day." Paul had carried his book around with him all day, never letting it out of his sight. Even during his math lesson, the book sat beside him on the table, and he kept flipping through it.

I continued to work with Paul, about forty-five minutes every Thursday until the end of the school year in June. If he hesitated when reading a word, we discussed how he could use the context of the whole sentence and his picture to help him work it out. He could also, finally, utilize the phonics he had been drilled on for so many years. To read "Technology" in his first book, *The New Space Shuttle*, all he needed was to see the "T." To

[handwritten margin note: strong oral language]

Figure 14-2   Paul's Second Book

He has a brown shell. He
is fast. He is lazy, but I
keep him in good shape with
an amusement park in my
room.

read "should" on page 4, he needed to be helped to see that it began like
"shuttle." The familiar context and structure of his story, his picture, and
his memory for text would work together to do the rest.

Each week Paul gained a little more confidence and risked putting more
print on the pages of the successive books he wrote. The second book we
wrote together was *My Pet Turtle.* It was, by his choice, 237 words spread
out over eleven pages. (See Figure 14-2 for a sample page.) The book also
included, as did all his new books from that point on, a dedication page.
This one read "Dedicated to George" (his turtle). His next book, written
during our third session the following week, was *How I Would Teach My
Friend to Draw.* The book was dedicated to his friend Yusef, and it took
Yusef, step by step, through sequenced stages in drawing a horse. It was
fifteen pages and 184 words.

In February, over the span of four once a week meetings, Paul composed
My Friend P. J., a charming story about friendship, shared adventures,
and life's happenings beginning in nursery school. The book was eighteen
pages of text and 1,175 words! While Paul's beginning pages had less than
50 words on a page and were carefully illustrated, the last three pages had
well over 100 words on a page with no illustrations. He practiced until he
could proudly read each page.

Child as real author; written as real author

Shortly thereafter, a parent volunteer word-processed *My Pet Turtle* and *My Friend P. J.*, made ten copies of each, and bound them into books. We introduced Paul as the author in several second and third grade classrooms, where these stories were used as reading materials with small groups. Paul was buoyant. What a boost to his self-esteem! He practiced reading these typed versions and began to dictate a science fiction story, *War Adventures*, at our next meeting.

I now sensed that Paul's growing confidence and risk taking would enable him to try reading an unknown book. At our meeting during the third week of February, I brought some trade books with me—three picture books of varying difficulty and several easy chapter books. We looked through them together as I told him something about the story line of each book. When I asked him to choose which book he'd like to read, I had no idea what he would pick. Paul enthusiastically decided on the delightful picture book *Louis the Fish* by Arthur Yorinks, with pictures by Richard Egielski (Farrar, Straus and Giroux, 1980). Paul loved the richly colored graphic illustrations as well as the fanciful text about a butcher who yearns to be a fish. After I read the entire book to him, he was eager to try it. I assured him that with practice he would be able to read it. We began with reading just the first few pages over and over again. Paul never seemed to tire of reading *Louis the Fish*. Four months later, he still seemed to love that book.

At our first session in March, Paul announced that his reading was getting better, but that the school librarian didn't know it yet. He asked me if I would go with him during library time to choose a science fiction book. I told him I would speak to the librarian so she could help him choose more appropriately. At the same time, his mother reported that Paul was beginning to choose to read in his spare time at home, and Theo reported similar behavior in school. He was beginning to see himself as a reader for the first time in his life.

More responsibility

Additionally, Paul's work habits began to change. Whereas previously he would use avoidance behaviors and never attempt any work on his own (except for math computation), Paul now began to complete assignments and to be responsible about bringing back homework. His mom reported coming home from work and being surprised and pleased to find Paul already working on his spelling pages. His usual behavior had been to wait for her help before starting any assignments.

Paul continued to read and reread all his books—at home, with his L.D. teacher, during sustained silent reading in his regular classroom, and with me. At first, during classroom sustained silent reading time, he would only illustrate, but as his confidence in his ability to read slowly began to grow, he gave up drawing for reading.

In early March, I brought Paul *More Stories Julian Tells* by Ann Cammeron (Knopf, 1986). I knew Paul would appreciate the subtle humor in the stories of this black family and identify with the main character, Julian. It was one of our third grade core books, and it would be the first chapter book Paul would read. Sometimes he would reread a page three and four times until he could read it smoothly. By the beginning of April his improved fluency was noticeable. He could read the first two chapters in *More Stories Julian Tells* without help, with reasonable speed, and with about 90 percent accuracy. *IRI?*

At the end of April, Paul signed out his first chapter book from the school library. It was *Russell Sprouts* by Johanna Hurwitz (Morrow, 1987). It was the first book he picked up and started reading on his own without guidance. There were few pictures, yet he tackled it boldly. He was very proud of himself. He had chosen an appropriate book for himself, and he stayed with it until he finished it about four weeks later.

While Paul was feeling some confidence as a reader, it was also necessary that he begin to see himself as a writer. By mid-February, I began writing weekly letters to Paul. I wanted a way to increase our contact, but I also wanted him to begin to risk writing for himself, which, up to now, he had been reluctant to do. I told him not to worry about his spelling, but just to do the best he could and that I would be able to read it. When he received my first letter through the interschool mail, he asked the L.D. teacher for help reading it. But when he received another letter from me the following week, he refused help, read it privately, and didn't want to share its contents with anyone. He began writing to me regularly (see Figure 14–3). *letter writing*

In early April we began writing Paul's sixth book, *My Vacation*, and for the first time, Paul was willing to do the writing himself. I sat right next to him and encouraged him to put down the sounds he heard and to try to remember the way words looked in books. When he made a mistake, I would ask him if the word looked right. Usually he could tell if the word was misspelled. If he was unable to spell the word correctly on subsequent attempts, I wrote the word for him. Whenever possible, I would encourage him to relate the known to the unknown, to use a pattern he already knew in one word and apply it to a new word.

At the same time, Paul continued to reread all his old, familiar books. When he got stuck, he now relied on meaning strategies combined with phonics to self-correct. For example, from his *War Adventures* he read, "We *could* our vehicle Euto 3." He immediately self-corrected "could" for "called." Several lines later he read, "*Both* was coming from his nose." He quickly self-corrected and reread, "*Blood* was coming from his nose." His ability to monitor his own reading was a major breakthrough in his being able to begin to read independently.

In late May there was a conference about Paul to discuss the results of his recent re-evaluation. The school psychologist, speech therapist, L.D. teacher, classroom teacher, Paul's mother, and myself were in attendance. Paul's I.Q. was reported as average. The psychologist indicated that Paul had experienced normal developmental milestones, had average intelligence, evidenced distractible behavior, and suffered from asthma. He was taking ritalin to control hyperactive behavior and medication for asthma.

A language assessment revealed average to above-average vocabulary skills, which served to mask a language disability, making it difficult for Paul to retrieve single words. Tests of auditory processing and written

Figure 14–3   *Increasing Contact with Paul through Letter Writing*

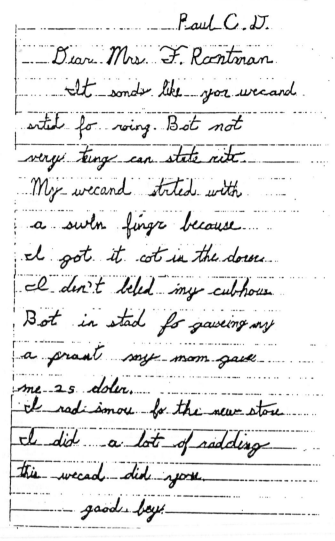

Dear Mrs. F. Routman,

It sounds like your weekend started off wrong. But not everything can start right. My weekend started with a swollen finger because I got it caught in the door. I didn't build my clubhouse. But instead of giving me a present, my mom gave me 25 dollars.

I read some of the new stories. I did a lot of reading this weekend. Did you?

Good by.

language both revealed low average scores relative to his ability. A diagnostic reading test yielded significantly below average scores—two standard deviations below his expected performance level. At the end of the conference, Paul's mother spoke of how proud she was of Paul's progress, explaining, "He will read to anyone now."

I have not worked with Paul since he completed fourth grade and moved to our grades 5 and 6 building. However, we have kept in regular contact through letter writing. As Paul has grown older he has used a word processor with a spelling checker, and he has sent his letters out in edited form. I am always pleased when he refers to books he is enjoying.

Paul and his mother both report that he reads and writes over vacations and in his free time. He still prefers books with interesting pictures and enjoys reading games magazines as well as the movies and comics sections of the newspaper. Vicki Griminger, his present L.D. teacher, notes that Paul willingly picks up books to read in class. As long as Paul chooses to read and write, I feel confident that his literacy skills will continue to develop.

Teaching Skills in Context: Chris

"He doesn't know anything. He doesn't know how to read and write. He's very low." Those were among the first comments made by Chris's mother to his new teacher when Chris transferred to our school district near the end of second semester in second grade.

Chris, who had already been in four other schools, received little support from home. His mother was usually at work, and his older brothers picked physical fights with him. In his new classroom, he was quiet and unmotivated. Still, it was clear he was a capable child. During discussions, his oral contributions, though infrequent, were on target and meaningful.

In the fall of third grade, his L.D. teacher, Margie Glaros, asked me if I could work with Chris on the day I was in her building. Chris was receiving services in the L.D. resource room for up to two and a half hours daily. Margie reported that it seemed as though Chris had been taught reading only phonetically. He had no idea what else he could do when he couldn't figure out a word.

When I first met Chris he seemed ready to learn. He told me, "This is the first school I've been in where anyone really cares." As with Paul, I began with his own language and interests. I acted as scribe for his first book, *My Two Cats*, and for his next two books, *About My Grandpa* and *About My Friend Brian*. For his last book, *About the Gerbils*, he did most of the writing himself. He illustrated each of his books and practiced reading them many times.

At the suggestion of his L.D. teacher, Chris taped himself reading his stories. Margie told me the taping originally came about as a result of Chris's disappointment over a missed session with me. Because he wanted to share his improvement in reading, Chris taped his latest book and sent it to me in the school mail. When I saw him the following week, I complimented him on his efforts. We also talked about how choppy his reading sounded, and I demonstrated what "fluent" reading sounds like. He practiced, retaped himself, and was able to notice his improvement.

I had worked with Chris for only a few months when he suddenly moved to another school district. Working cooperatively with Margie, even in our short time together, I saw a marked change in Chris's attitude and ability. Chris was coming to see himself as a potential reader and writer, and he was beginning to take risks. Relying on context he created, he was beginning to learn and apply literacy skills. His improvement was most noticeable working one-to-one or in a group with younger students. He was still somewhat resistant in groups of grade-level peers.

Margie and I believed that Chris would learn to read and write high-frequency words if they came from the context of his stories. Years of skills in isolation had not contributed favorably to his literacy development. If he began with the whole, he could deal with the parts. Therefore, all work in word analysis came directly from the familiar language of his own text.

Chris's brief story is included because strategies that were working with Chris are applicable for other L.D. and special education students. (See "Selected Reading-Writing Strategies," pp. 391–393, for specific strategies utilized with Chris.) Hopefully, Chris will continue to build on his successes. We know it will not be easy for him. The same school year he transferred, we were contacted by two additional schools. Margie wrote to them and shared goals and methods that had worked for Chris. Margie, I, and the students in Margie's lab also wrote to Chris, but we never received a reply from him.

Focusing on the Strengths: Onajé

When I first met Onajé, he didn't smile. He kind of dragged himself down the hall, shoulders down, with a pout on his face. Onajé was a fourth-grader, and he had been receiving pull-out services for learning disabilities since second grade.

Onajé was presently working one-to-one with a tutor thirty minutes daily. It was clear that he did not see himself as a capable learner. Except for his oral contributions to classroom literature discussions, he did not appear to enjoy school, and he certainly didn't see himself as a reader or a writer.

In early fall, Onajé's L.D. tutor, Ellen Potter, asked me if I would model lessons for her on the day I was in her building. Ellen expressed concern that she was focusing more on what Onajé couldn't do and felt she might be contributing to his continuing lack of confidence. She was also aware of her skills-based orientation and felt ready to include some holistic strategies.

For our first lesson, we took a piece of writing Onajé had completed in the classroom (see Figure 14–4). I began our lesson by telling Onajé how much I liked his piece of writing and how well he had stuck to the topic. Knowing that spelling was a significant problem area for Onajé, I pointed out that most of his words were spelled correctly. I went through his paper, one line at a time, and pointed out each word that was correctly spelled. Out of the seventy words in his story, almost 80 percent were spelled accurately. I shared that information with Onajé and his tutor, and they both looked at me in disbelief. They were used to looking at his papers and seeing only the errors.

Next, I asked Onajé to read orally from *My Robot Buddy* by Alfred Slote (Lippincott, 1975), the science fiction book (in our grade 3 core collection) that he was reading with Ellen. His reading was choppy and hesitant, but based on his oral retelling, he seemed to get the overall meaning. I attended to everything he did well when he read. For instance, when he

Focus on strengths

Figure 14-4   *Writing by Onajé*

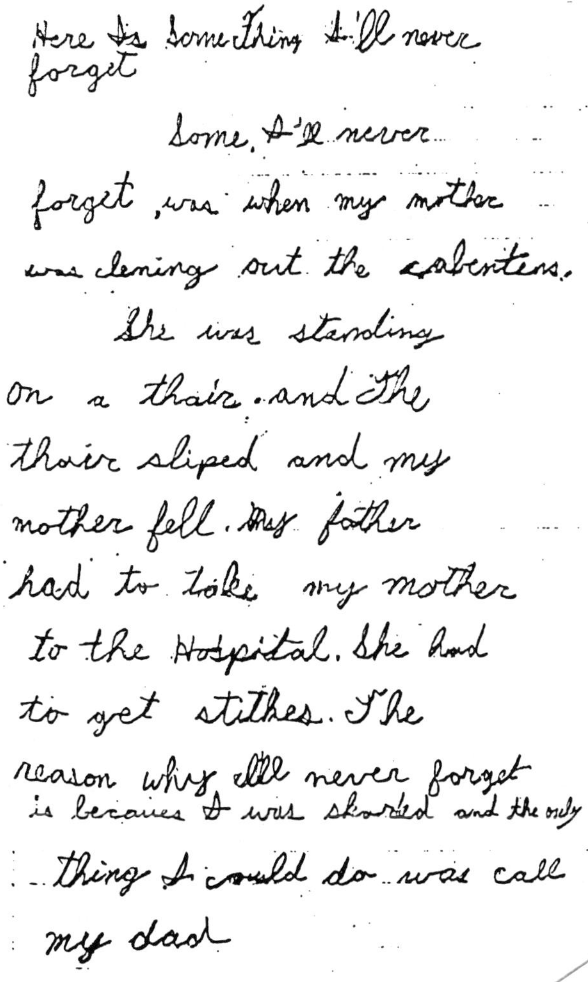

Here is Some Thing I'll never
forget

      Some, I'll never
forget, was when my mother
was cleaning out the caberters.
      She was standing
on a thair. and the
thair sliped and my
mother fell. My father
had to take my mother
to the Hospital. She had
to get stithes. The
reason why I'll never forget
is becaues I was skarded and the only
     thing I could do was call
     my dad

[handwritten margin note:] What did you do that good readers do?

[handwritten margin note:] Praise the good things

substituted a word that made sense for a word he couldn't read, I praised him and told him, "That's what good readers do." Then I asked him, "What did you just do that good readers do?" Onajé was almost unable to talk about a reading strength. I had to restate what he had just done well and prod him to repeat what I'd said. When I came back the second week, Onajé again read orally from *My Robot Buddy*, and I focused once more on the positive things he did while reading. When he had difficulty, I showed him how he might help himself.

     I asked him what kinds of books he might be interested in and he told me "science fiction" and "adventure." We talked about how important it was to read every day in order to become a really good reader.

     The following week I brought three chapter books for him: *The Ghost of the Dutchman* by Cruz Martel (Scholastic, 1979), *The Twits* by Roald Dahl (Knopf, 1980), and *The Magic Finger* by Roald Dahl (Harper &

& Row, 1966). I told him something of the story line of each, and I asked him to choose one for nightly, independent reading. He chose *The Ghost of the Dutchman*.

I asked Onajé to begin reading orally. I wanted to demonstrate what he could do when he got into difficulty. When he couldn't read "rested" on page 1, I said, "Go on. Finish the sentence." Then, on his own, he went back and read the whole sentence from the beginning. I had him verbalize what he had just done. He said, "I skipped the word I couldn't read and read to the end of the sentence."

On page 2, I told him to read silently and "jot down any word that gives you trouble but only if it interferes with the meaning of the story." He read and wrote down "sailor." I asked, "What did you do when you came to that word?" He said, "I read it as 'soldier.'" Again, I stressed that what he had done, substituting a word that would make sense, was an excellent strategy. We did not work on "sounding out" the word "sailor." This would not have been the most efficient use of our time because Onajé's meaningful substitution did not affect his overall comprehension.

We were about to close the book when Onajé asked if he could continue reading. Ellen indicated that during the previous week he had also asked her, "Can I read today?" These were the very first times Onajé had ever requested to read. He was beginning to believe he could be a reader. However, it would still be some time before he chose to read voluntarily.

At about this time, I suggested to Ellen that we invite Onajé's mother in to observe me working with her son. Previously she had communicated to Ellen that she felt "bitter" about "whole language." It was also evident from talking with Onajé that his mom was giving him a lot of help at home. She didn't believe he had the necessary skills to figure things out for himself.

During our session she observed some teaching for strategies. For example, when Onajé circled "anoter" as recognition of a misspelling on a writing paper, I asked him if he knew "brother." He wrote it correctly, and then connected it to writing "another." When reading, he was not interrupted when he made an error. He was given time to self-correct, was guided to incorporate meaning-based strategies, and was asked to verbalize higher-level strategies he was using. He also received lots of praise for his efforts.

Following our session, I asked Onajé's mother how she felt about the way we were teaching spelling and reading. She said with a smile, "Now I understand what you're trying to do, and I like it." She admitted she had found it difficult to notice what Onajé does well: "When I see his papers, I see only the errors. I comment on them, and I want to take over." Gradually, over the coming months, Onajé's mother was able to focus more on the positive and to believe that Onajé was developing the necessary skills to read and write successfully. Her change in attitude contributed to Onajé's growing self-esteem.

After a while, I suggested to Onajé's classroom teacher that he probably didn't need to use the time with his L.D. tutor to work on reading, that perhaps the focus should be on writing while the tutor monitored his reading. What had become clear in working with Onajé weekly was that he utilized enough meaning-based and grapho-phonic strategies to make overall sense of what he was reading. When this message was given to his classroom teacher, she was initially disbelieving. She had heard him read only orally in front of the class, which all of her students were required to do. Based on his public oral reading, he was a poor reader. I told her it was like asking a stutterer to make a speech. I believed he should have to read orally only for diagnostic purposes in a one-to-one setting or if he chose to read orally. I explained that Onajé might never be a fluent oral reader, but all of his required and voluntary reading could be done silently. Silent reading was not only a situation that afforded him the opportunity to work through difficulties at his own pace, it was also the desired goal for all independent readers.

Onajé had become quite proficient in incorporating higher-level reading strategies, and Ellen and I noted his self-correction rate was much improved. For example, in observing him while he read silently, he continued to jot down words interfering with his reading, such as "incredible" and "practice," but more often than not, he would wind up erasing those words. As he continued reading, he seemed to work out the difficult words or make meaningful substitutions. We would also see him move his line marker back to the beginning of a sentence or phrase and then reread to get the meaning. In addition, we observed him skipping a word after softly pronouncing the beginning letters. Then, moving his line marker, he would read on to the end of the sentence and then head back to the beginning of the sentence again. We could tell by his pleased expression that he had figured out the troublesome spot. As Onajé began to see that he could rely less upon his teachers and his mom and more upon himself, his confidence began to grow.

Nonetheless, getting Onajé to invest in reading independently took much encouragement by Ellen, his mother, and me. He eventually finished *The Ghost of the Dutchman* on his own. Although it was only thirty-eight pages, it took him about three weeks. One of the things we had to do was discuss realistic expectations about nightly reading. Onajé complained that because of nightly homework, he had little time to read. He thought if he read one or two pages a day, that was adequate. We said that reading for pleasure was the most important homework he could do and that he should read for twenty to thirty minutes each evening. Eventually, he became convinced. One morning, about a month later, Onajé proudly announced he had completed and very much enjoyed *The Twits* by Roald Dahl. It was the first book he had chosen to read and complete independently. His face broke into a broad smile as he told about the book.

Shortly thereafter, I talked with Onajé about his reading. Looking back on our talk, I see that what struck me most was the pride and success he felt, clearly visible by the ever-present smile on his face. He seemed peaceful, not at all the agitated, moody student from just several months ago. Part of our conversation follows:

ROUTMAN: How are you feeling about reading?

ONAJE: Good. It's not fun when you can't read. You can't stick your
          hand up like the other kids. It's scary when you can't read.
          Now I can read like the other kids, and I don't mind if the
          teacher calls on me. It's fun to read like everyone else.

ROUTMAN: What's different for you now?

ONAJE: I can read better now, and I like to read. I read faster, too. I
          like to read hard words on signs and directions. I read at home
          now sometimes when I don't have too much homework. And
          my mom leaves me alone now to do my work.

ROUTMAN: You seem a lot happier.

ONAJE: Yeah, because I don't need as much help in my reading as I did
          at the beginning of the year.

ROUTMAN: What do you do now when you come to a hard word?

ONAJE: I either go past it and come back to it, or I see what would fit
          there, or I try to sound it out.

Onajé's classroom teacher, always supportive of his efforts, commented that he had begun volunteering to read aloud in class. She noted that though he wasn't fluent, he was no longer a hesitant reader who lacked confidence. Ellen Potter, his L.D. tutor, noted that Onajé was "reading like crazy!" She noted that it used to take Onajé fifteen minutes to "go through" two pages. Now he was much quicker, more fluent, and was integrating cueing systems. Perhaps, best of all, he was excited about starting new books because he believed he could read them. On an author page in a book he wrote, he had written, "I like to read in my spare time."

By the end of fourth grade, Onajé's new Individual Education Plan for the following year reflected his reading strengths. A norm-referenced educational achievement test indicated Onajé had gone from the 3rd to 7th stanine in reading comprehension in one year. He would now be receiving all reading instruction in the regular classroom. Ellen remains convinced that if she had not begun to change her emphasis from focusing on the deficits to building on Onajé's reading strengths, he would still be a learning disabled reader.

Selected Reading–Writing Strategies for L.D. and Other At-Risk Students

This section encompasses selected strategies I and other teachers have used successfully with L.D. and remedial students to teach reading and writing. However, these strategies are not just for the L.D. or special education teacher. The classroom teacher also has the responsibility to teach the L.D. student—usually the major responsibility. As such, the classroom teacher must be knowledgeable and flexible enough to set up a learning environment in which every student becomes literate.

I believe all of us learn language most easily when the language is whole, and when the experiences, contexts, and texts are meaningful and relevant to the learners' lives. Therefore, the strategies for teaching L.D. students and other at-risk learners should be similar to the meaning-based, holistic strategies recommended for teaching all students.

Fragmented instruction is particularly difficult for at-risk learners. While efficient language learners figure out what makes sense regardless of the instruction and ignore what doesn't fit, the at-risk population becomes further handicapped by splintered instruction. These are the students who do not learn language efficiently. They are often unable to filter out what doesn't make sense.

For example, at-risk students may be able to complete phonics or language workbook exercises but still be unable to apply those skills in a meaningful context. When instruction has focused on disconnected parts and isolated skills, students often find the bits and pieces insufficient to enable them to make sense of language and texts. These students need better instruction, more of it, and lots of opportunities to practice and apply meaning-based strategies.

Paul's mother told me,

> If the teacher or I take the time to give Paul an overall sense of what the story is about, or to discuss what the main concepts or questions to be answered are in a social studies or science text, he can pretty much figure things out for himself—even if the reading level is hard for him. But if he is just given an assignment without any background information, he is at a loss to make sense of it.

While the strategies discussed in this section may be used successfully with all students, they are especially helpful for the at-risk children. When applicable, I have used specific examples from working with Paul, Chris, and Onajé, as well as from a group of L.D. students, to demonstrate how a strategy has been used. Although the strategies that follow are presented one at a time, in the actual teaching-learning situation, they are often integrated and used interactively.

Creating Predictable Text from the Child's Language

This is a sure-fire technique that has never failed me. The child's own language becomes his beginning reading material. The approach has worked successfully for first-graders as well as for high school students, and I believe it can also work well for illiterate adults. By encouraging the student to talk and write about what is important to him, and by writing for and with the student, by hand or on the word processor, the student engages in the material. The "skills" are taught as they come up, in the context of reading and writing together. (See "Expectations for Success: Paul," at the beginning of this chapter, for specifics.)

Although the specific examples cited come from working with one student, predictable text can easily come from a group of students. A common experience, a series of books by an author, or a favorite book can all be used as a springboard for a shared writing. The story can then be reproduced so each child has a personal copy for reading and illustrating.

The following techniques have been successfully utilized with a child's natural language, predictable text:

Cutting apart a sentence from the child's story   A sentence from the child's story is written with a marker on a vertical strip. The words, and in some cases the word parts, are cut apart. The student attempts to put the sentence in proper sequence. If necessary, the student goes back to the text to check or correct herself.

With Chris, L.D. teacher Margie Glaros or I would choose a sentence that had one or more basic sight words that we knew Chris would encounter often in other contexts. We would write the sentence from his illustrated story on a sentence strip that had been cut lengthwise from the photocopy paper. Next, we would cut the sentence apart, word by word. (Later some words might also be cut apart to emphasize a teaching point, such as a consonant digraph or blend, for example, *wh en*, *th ird*, *gr ade*.) Although Chris saw words in isolation, they always went back into the context. Chris was expected to put the sentence back together in sequence and read it aloud as he did so. He would then check himself against the written text. If he had made a mistake, he was expected to self-correct using his book's written model.

Chris kept all sentences from each book (cut apart and held with a paperclip in a large envelope labeled with the book title) so he might practice often on his own.

Referring to other texts the child can read   When a student gets stuck reading or writing a word that has been known in another context, he is guided to go back to a familiar source, read the particular word in context, and then apply it to the new situation. Students get very proficient at locating the unknown word, reading it in the familiar context, and applying it to the new context.

When beginning to write *About the Gerbils*, I asked Chris, "Where have you seen 'About' before?" He was able to find his previously written book, *About My Friend Brian*, and read and write "About" for himself in the new title.

Making a "Words I Can Write" booklet   When it appeared that Chris was reading a high-frequency word without any help, I would ask him to try writing it. If he wrote it correctly, he was able to add it to his "Words I Can Write" booklet. He could eventually read all these words in isolation. If he got stuck, he referred to one of his books for help. He was very proud of his growing list of words and seemed eager to add new words to his booklet (see Figure 14–5).

Teaching some short vowels, or other phonics generalizations, through the child's name or other well-known words   Many children like Chris have a difficult time applying short vowels, particularly "e" and "i," to reading and writing words. When Chris was unsure of what letter to put in the middle of words such as "with" and "get," which came from his stories, he referred back to his name, "Chris Jenesin." With guidance, he could make the correct connection. Eventually, he would do this on his own. (For specifics on teaching phonics, see "Phonics in Perspective," pp. 149–155.)

Sharing the scribing process   For some L.D. students, writing has been so difficult that the teacher needs to sit right next to the child to provide emotional and physical support. An environment in which the child feels valued and safe enough to take a risk must already exist. Even students who have been reluctant to write can usually be persuaded to give it a try if the teacher takes over when the child falters. If a word processor is available, the child is even more willing to get started.

Once Chris knew he could read and write some words, he was willing to risk writing for himself with some support. In his third book, *About the Gerbils*, he was encouraged to write as much of each word as he was able and to use all of the above strategies. For his sentence "Sometimes I get to pick them up," he was able to write all of the letters that are underlined.

Sometimes I get to pick them up.

Figure 14-5   Chris's "Words I Can Write" List

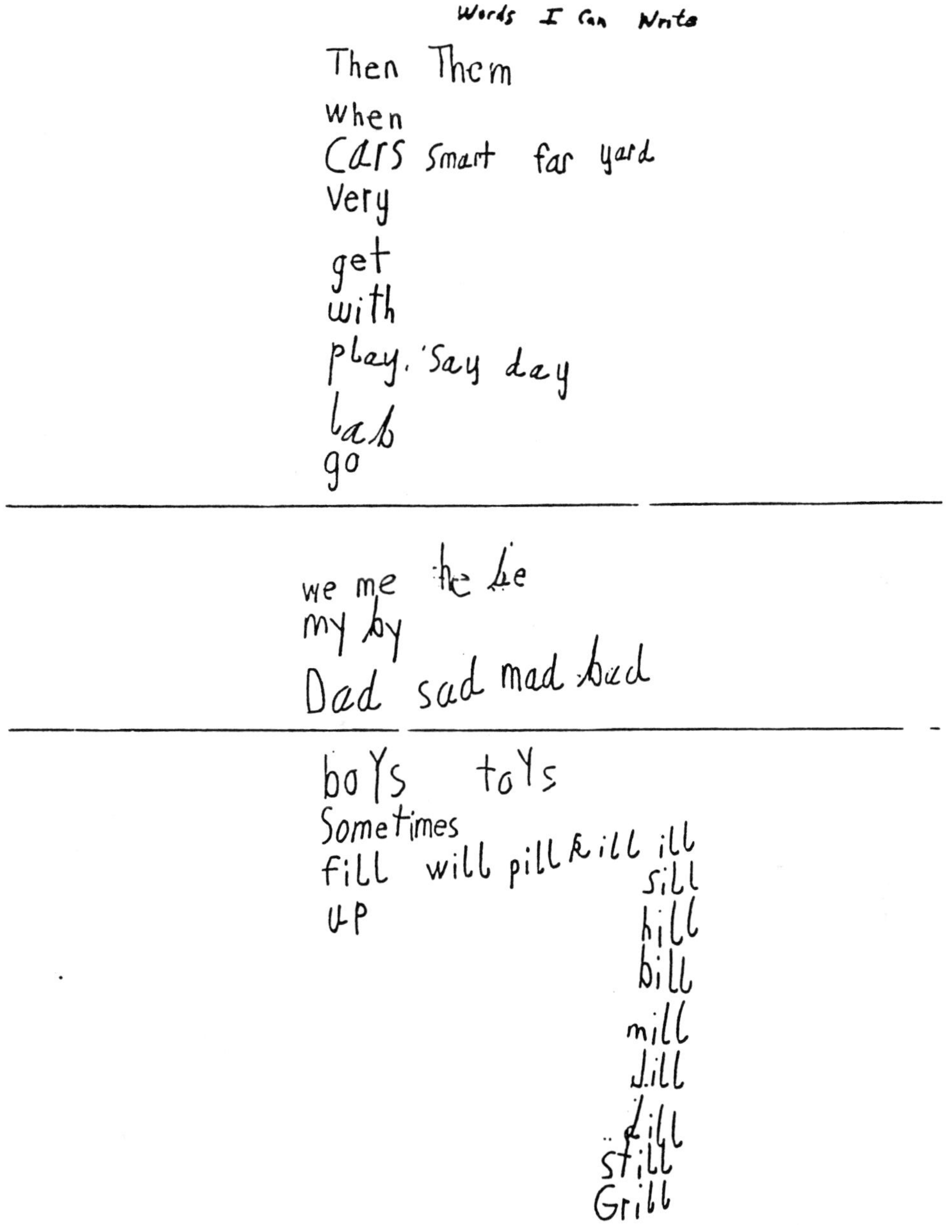

Words I Can Write

Then   Them

When

Cars   smart   far   yard

Very

get

with

play. 'say day

lab

go

---

we me he be

my by

Dad   sad   mad   bad

---

boys   toys

Sometimes

fill   will   pill   Rill   ill

   sill

up

   hill

   bill

   mill

   Jill

   fill

   still

   Grill

On a subsequent page, "Sometimes I get to go down to the boy's bathroom to fill up the bottle," he referred back to the above page and was able to write "Sometimes," "get," and "up" in their entirety.

He decided "sometimes" was a word he wanted to have in his "Words I Can Write" booklet. In spite of its length, he mastered the word after looking at it many times, writing it, and referring back to his stories when he got stuck.

Creating Predictable Text from Patterned Language

Little books that repeat a pattern such as "I can . . ." or "This is . . ." can be used as a springboard for writing and reading original stories. Using simple patterned text with matching pictures, Mary Leo's developmentally handicapped students in grades 2–4 did the first reading and writing they had ever done using an "I Can . . ." text as a model. Prior to that time, all skills and sight words had been taught in isolation. (See *Recommended Literature*, "Books Which Invite Readers into Print" for suggested publishers and titles.)

Using Predictable, Well-Written Literature

Special education teachers who formerly used basal texts report a big difference in interest level and motivation, not only by the students but by the teachers themselves, when quality literature is used to teach reading. Both teachers and students were bored with dull materials. At the secondary level, this also means supplementing the literature of the 1970s with more relevant and interesting texts.

Onajé became a reader only when the emphasis of his instruction shifted from structured texts and skills sheets to predictable texts and books at his interest level. Then the pleasure of reading could be combined with skills instruction arising from his on-site needs.

Allowing the student to self-select reading books is especially important. A high school teacher reported her first success with a student who had a keen interest in all aspects of building. She brought in everything she could find on the subject, and all the student's reading and writing emanated from those books.

Creating Predictable Text from Literature

Working in a small group, students can create their own text to use as reading material. Because the language is their own, students are highly motivated to read it. After students have heard or read several poems, stories, or books by an author, they can be encouraged to create their own text in that author's style. The teacher acts as guide and scribe. Because students are already familiar with the characters, settings, and plots in a series, they feel confident developing a sequel or related chapter or story. A group of second-graders enjoyed writing their own *Nate the Great* text, based on the series by Marjorie Sharmat (Putnam, 1977), while a group of sixth-graders created an epilogue to *The Great Gilly Hopkins* by Katherine Paterson. The text can be written on overhead transparencies or large chart paper for group reading or photocopied so each student has a copy to read. Students' original texts may take the form of a conversation between two characters, a scene in a play, a chapter, or a complete story.

Using wordless picture books   Wordless picture books work wonderfully well with elementary and secondary students as a springboard for developing oral language and for creating original stories to read. (See "Wordless Books" in *Recommended Literature* for appealing selections.) Students begin by orally retelling the story through the pictures. The original text can then be written by the teacher or another student. Older students can create text for younger readers. Students can also work in pairs to create original wordless books, with one student creating the pictures and the other writing the text.

Besides wordless books, familiar picture books can also be used, and the existing text can be covered up. The new text becomes a retelling or new version in students' own language. Even in schools where the basal text is the mainstay of the reading program, students can cover up the text of a dull story, rewrite it, and practice reading the new, improved version.

Reading Aloud to the Student and by the Student

Reading aloud *to* the child—for vocabulary development, literature appreciation, exposure to literary-level language and authors' styles, and comprehension— continues to be of utmost importance for attitude, motivation, and just sheer enjoyment.

Reading aloud by the teacher is important even at the secondary level where lack of vocabulary and word meanings interfere with comprehension. Reading aloud helps build needed vocabulary and lets the student hear what fluent reading sounds like. In addition, it is recommended in a test-taking situation where the student is unable to read the test.

Reading aloud *by* the child, in a one-on-one or small-group setting where the child feels safe enough to take a risk, provides the teacher with information on the strategies the child is using or not using. The teacher can then guide the child to employ various strategies that good readers use. At times, the child's reading aloud can be documented with a running record or tape recording.

Relating the known to the unknown   Whenever possible, it is advisable to use what the child already knows and apply that knowledge to a new situation. When Chris could not read "them," we went back to "then" in one of his stories. When he could not write "by," we used "my," which he already knew. After he was able to read and write "play," we wrote and read "say," "day," "may," and other words that fit the pattern.

Shared Reading

Shared reading, as described on pages 33–38, is an excellent technique for getting the student engaged in reading. I find using a transparency on the overhead projector invaluable for maintaining attention, focusing eyes on the print, and immersing the student in reading without singling her out. Students get to hear and feel the appropriate phrasing and fluency for poems, songs, raps, or excerpts from a book. The reading is always invitational; students are expected to follow the text with their eyes and join in orally if they choose to do so. While the emphasis is always on enjoyment in a social setting, one or two teaching points—such as calling attention to conventions of print—may be made on subsequent rereadings.

Repeated Reading

Reading a selection over and over again increases fluency and improves word-attack skills, building confidence and enabling the student to focus on comprehension. Working alone, with a partner, or with the aid of a tape recorder, the student chooses a paragraph or excerpt and practices it until he can read it fluently. Students can tape record themselves, evaluate where they need to improve, and then rerecord themselves.

Paired Reading

Paired reading occurs when one reader supports another in the reading of the text. The student has a personal copy of the text and follows along visually as he:

> Hears the text on tape
>
> Listens to a peer read the text
>
> Has the support of a peer when needed in reading the text for himself
>
> Follows the voice of the teacher or reader

Once the student is familiar with the text he can try it again on his own. More important, he can be included in group discussion of the text. Paired reading assumes that a reader will be able to understand the text even if he is unable to read it all independently.

Having books available on tape   Many L.D. students who have difficulty reading do quite well understanding text and contributing to oral discussion if they can hear the text and follow along with a tape. Students can then "read" literature that is at their listening comprehension level, even though the text is above their instructional and independent levels. Literature and content area tapes are made by the teacher or parent volunteer or are available free from the local public library through the federally funded "Talking Book" program.

Paul's mother reported that her son experienced success when his L.D. teacher sent home tapes from chapters in his science and social studies texts. When the key vocabulary and focus of the chapter were discussed prior to reading-listening, Paul was able to answer orally questions about the chapter without difficulty.

Sustained Silent Reading of Self-Selected Text

Sustained silent reading, where the student engages in uninterrupted reading of a book of his choice, is one of the most important strategies for increasing fluency, vocabulary, and overall reading ability. Students need to do lots of reading of easy books for pleasure to become fluent, confident readers. Before students willingly and successfully engage in this activity, they must be able to help themselves—beyond "sounding out"—when encountering an unknown word. They must be integrating all cueing systems—using semantics and syntax along with graphophonics.

Promoting independent silent reading and self-monitoring   Using a line marker, verbalizing the strategies used when in difficulty, jotting down important vocabulary that interfered with understanding the text, and connecting the known to the unknown all helped Onajé read more independently.

In reading *My Robot Buddy* by Alfred Slote, Onajé had difficulty with the sentence "I couldn't really believe they'd hear me, but suddenly the air cruiser started its descent onto the road" (p. 58). He could not read and did not know the exact meanings of "cruiser" and "descent." Thinking while reading, he was able to substitute "vehicle" for "cruiser" and "landing" for "descent." Because he had jotted down both those words, we worked on them grapho-phonically and for meaning. For "cruiser" I wrote the word "bruise," which was in his vocabulary, and related it to "cruise." We talked about what kind of vehicle an air cruiser could be. For "descent" he could read "de," but could not apply "sc." I wrote down "science," "scene," and "scent," which he could read, and had him apply what he already knew to "descent." We used "ascend" and "descend" together, and I graphically demonstrated the opposite meanings by moving my body and my arms.

Providing books at Onajé's interest and reading level helped him begin to read on his own. Setting realistic expectations with him and his mother contributed to his success.

Promoting reading comprehension   Some L.D. and classroom teachers note that many at-risk learners have difficulty grasping the major points of a story once they move into longer books where most of the reading is done independently. These children need to understand why we read. They also need to be carefully monitored and held accountable for what they have read. I have found that assigning only a few pages of silent reading at a time works well. In severe cases, silently reading and monitoring one paragraph at a time may be necessary until the student begins to self-monitor and think about what he is reading.

I was recently asked to work with Robert, a third-grader, who could read the words in a grade-level book but could not say what he had read beyond giving some unrelated details. When I asked him, "Why do we read?" he replied, "to know the words." Because he viewed reading only as reading the words, he did not stop when something didn't make sense, and he never went back to reread or refocus.

I asked Robert to read a passage orally (pp. 15–16) from *Mr. Popper's Penguins* by Richard and Florence Atwater (Little, Brown, 1938), a book he had never seen before. Before he began reading, I gave him some general background information about what he was about to read, and then I took a running record of his reading. Although he read with 92 percent accuracy, indicating the book was at his instructional level, when I asked him to tell me what he had just read (what Mr. Popper wanted to do and why), he gave me misinformation. I sent him back to the text to reread. When he again gave me inaccurate information, I sent him back to the specific paragraph and asked, "Where does it say that? Find the line that says that, and read it to me." He finally replied, "It doesn't say that anywhere." I asked him, "What does it say? Now put that into your own words." With prodding, and my insisting he reread, think about his reading, and stop every time something didn't make sense or sound right, Robert could eventually come up with an intelligent response.

By continuing to ask Robert very specific questions that focused on main ideas, by verbally modeling thinking processes aloud, and by guiding him to reread a small chunk of text silently and do a retelling, Robert gradually improved in overall comprehension. Although he had been expected to be reading a chapter book as part of his independent, nightly reading, he had never received guided instruction in understanding what he was reading silently. He was now asked to slow down and read only several pages a night. He knew his teacher would be asking him to do a retelling, and that if he could not do it, he would be asked to reread. He was also asked to verify his oral responses. He would be asked, "How do you know that? Where in the text does it say that?" By being held accountable on a daily basis, by talking through specific passages with his teacher, and by being shown where he needed to reread, Robert gradually improved his comprehension abilities.

Emphasizing Silent Reading as Part of Instructional Time

Typically, most of the reading instruction time for remedial students is spent in oral reading and practice exercises. Even when L.D. and remedial learners use real literature, the tendency is to have students read aloud. Since most of the reading students will do in school is silent reading—and since silent reading is how reading is used in the world outside school—students need to be guided in the transition from oral to silent reading. As teachers, we tend to feel slightly uncomfortable allowing silent reading during "teaching" time, but it is necessary if students are to become successful, independent readers. When students find that they can begin to monitor their own reading and work out trouble spots on their own, their reading confidence, along with the amount of time they spend reading silently, increases.

I was asked to work with a group of third grade L.D. students reading *The Mouse and the Motorcycle* by Beverly Cleary (Morrow, 1965). Up to this time, their reading in the L.D. class had been done mostly round-robin style, with each child taking a turn reading orally. At the same time that I asked them to read several pages silently, I asked them to "write down any words you can't read or don't know the meaning of." Then we took the words they had trouble with and worked them through together. Mostly, they worked them through after I asked them, "What could you try that might help you?" As they worked through their difficult words, I kept asking, "What can you do?" and then, "What did you do to work that out? What could that word mean? Reread that paragraph, and see if you can figure it out." Margie Glaros, the L.D. teacher, and I had already spent a lot of time putting the responsibility for learning on them and emphasizing meaningful language strategies.

Donald had written down the word "automatically" from the sentence "He did not even have to think what to do—he automatically grabbed for the motorcycle and held on with all his strength" (pp. 82–83). When he went back to work it out, he skipped it and got the meaning through the context by predicting what the word could mean. He substituted "quickly." Because what he put in made sense, it was not significant that he could not read the exact word.

Below is the chart that came out of several short sessions and stayed posted in the L.D. classroom for referral. It is shown exactly as the students wrote it.

What to Do When You Can't Read a Word

1. Look at that word again—ending, middle, beginning.
2. Read on, and then come back to the hard word and try again.
3. Stretch out the letters; take the word apart.
4. Think about what would make sense.
5. Think about what would sound right.

6. Substitute a word that makes sense.
7. See if it looks like a word you've seen before.
8. Put word parts together (re lief).
9. Skip the word and go on.

It is very valuable to take the time to get students to verbalize what works for them. The list you and your students come up with will be worded differently but will be even more valid because it will come from your students. If the strategies they come up with are limited, the teacher needs to guide them and demonstrate meaningful alternatives.

When, after several silent reading sessions of short passages, it became clear these students were reading for meaning and using the above strategies, I asked them to read an entire chapter in *The Mouse and the Motorcycle* silently (pp. 79–85). Before they started reading, I explained that we would begin to use a reading log. (See "Literature Response Logs," pp. 103–122, for a complete explanation of the reading log.) The students were asked to answer the following question: "What's the most important thing that happened in this chapter?" They were told they needed to write only one sentence. To help focus their attention, I sat with them and read the chapter silently at the same time. Damon wrote, "Ralph got caught in a vacuum cleaner but he chewed himself out." It was clear from each of their individual responses that they had gleaned the main ideas of the chapter.

After the students had moved almost totally into silent reading during their instructional reading time in the L.D. class, I asked them, "How do you feel about reading silently versus reading out loud?" These were their responses:

"You can go faster."

"I like reading in my mind."

"You don't have to express yourself, or change the tone of your voice."

"I like it 'cause if I don't know a word, I can ask someone who is also reading silently."

"If I don't know a word, I can figure it out myself without anyone helping me."

Self-Selected Writing

For many L.D. children, their own writing—in language that is predictable and familiar to them—leads to their first successful reading. Teaching needs become apparent from a close look at the child's self-selected, frequent writing. Journal writing, as described in Chapter 9, is a powerful vehicle for evaluating the child's phonics, spelling, use of syntax, and ideas. Writing as a response to reading also indicates the thought processing and connections the child is making.

Using Post-its or a copy of an original piece of writing   Students are sensitive to "marks" made by the teacher on their writing. Leaving the original writing intact sends a message of respect and value to the student. I find students more receptive to working out problem areas when the "marks" are made on a copy. Instead of a reproduced copy of the original, some teachers write on Post-its and place them strategically on the original writing to draw attention to particular strengths and concerns.

Using self-selected writing to teach spelling   Onajé's L.D. tutor, Ellen Potter, used his personal writing to teach phonics and spelling. For example, in the piece in Figure 14–4, she took "thair" and "stithes" as an opportunity to teach "ch." They kept a chart of "ch" words as they came across them, and several weeks later we noted the correct usage of "ch" in Onajé's journal writing.

Many L.D. students are able to find their own misspelled words from journal entries or other writing and use the Have-a-Go sheet (see Appendix I) effectively. Ellen often used a Have-a-Go sheet to help Onajé work out his misspellings. First he would find and circle those words that "looked" wrong. Then he would work them out with help from his tutor, a spelling dictionary, and other resources available.

Typing or word-processing the student's writing   Students are more willing to make revisions and corrections when the text is clean and easily readable and spaces are left between lines. In addition, a typed copy sends a message to the student that the writing is appreciated.

Valuing Oral Responses

When Paul had to respond to a test by writing, he stated, "I know the information but it doesn't come out right."

Some L.D. students can really shine when they are encouraged to contribute their thoughts orally. Students need to know that verbal responses are just as valid and valued as written responses. A student who is unable to read and write sufficiently well to complete a test should be given the test orally. When the spelling and handwriting are poor, the student should be allowed to dictate to the teacher or volunteer. In addition, some students find when they can tape their original story or responses and go back to the tape at their leisure, they can write adequate responses.

Using a tape recorder in the content areas   Older students who cannot copy well from the board or take notes quickly or in an organized fashion benefit from taping the discussion in the content areas. On their own, or with assistance, they can work at their own pace to write down necessary information.

Using a tape recorder for a final copy   Some teachers allow students to put their final copy of a story on tape, so that writing and editing are not required.

Writing Aloud

Writing aloud is an excellent, nonthreatening way for students to observe frequently the conventions of writing. Seeing words formed, spaced, spelled, and used in context with correct capitalization and punctuation eventually imprints on the students. The teacher can incorporate and highlight conventions and words that students need or are struggling to learn.

Shared Writing

Shared writing is appropriate and desirable even at the high school level. The teacher, in collaboration with the students, guides the students in the composition of a common interest and demonstrates the process of writing. While the chalk-board may be used, Magic Marker on large chart paper or a transparency on the overhead projector is even more attention getting.

Sustained Silent Writing for Teachers and Students

Typically, because writing is an area of difficulty for L.D. students, much encour-agement is needed. Margie Glaros and I have found students will make a much greater effort and maintain attention longer when teacher and students write simultaneously in a shared setting.

Valuing time for talk and sharing before writing   Margie and I asked a group of five third grade L.D. students to write about their relationship with a sibling or other family member. Our purpose was to get these students, who normally wrote very little and who stopped writing after just a few minutes, to write for a sustained period. We began by sitting around a table with the students. Margie and I each spoke in detail about our relationship with one of our siblings. We then encouraged the students to verbalize their thoughts about a sister, brother, or family member—what they liked about them, what drove them crazy, special interests shared. If they got stuck talking, we asked questions to help stimulate thinking. We allowed about fifteen to twenty minutes just for talking. The students later told us that talking over what they might write about made the writing "easy." Not only did their talking to the group help clarify what they already knew and could write about but listening to their peers triggered memories and gener-ated fresh ideas for their own writing. Later, they were also eager to share orally their completed stories with each other.

Writing while students are writing   When Margie and I wrote with the students, we found that they were less distracted and more willing to invest in their writing. They saw each of us look up as we stopped to think and put out heads down and be seriously quiet as we engaged in the writing. When a student looked up as though she was finished, even though everyone else was still writing, we reminded the student—based on her oral sharing—that she probably had more she could write. Eventually, the student went back to adding to her piece. The students later acknowledged feeling pleased with and surprised by the quantity of their writing. We teachers were surprised that each student was able to stay with the writing for about twenty minutes.

Demonstrating   Once the students were convinced they could write a substantial amount on a topic they knew about, we moved into refining the writing. We asked them to choose one small part of their sibling story and try to develop it in some depth. First Margie and I talked about what parts of our stories we would pick. I told them I was going to expand on one line in my story: "When my sister Adrienne and I were little, we used to fight all the time except when we built cities together in our bedroom." Then I went on to explain in detail how we moved our furniture, spread blankets and bedspreads across desks and beds, fortified our "city" with comic books, games, and snacks, and played happily secluded "under wraps" until our parents insisted we clean up. Margie told about an incident in a restaurant as an example of how her brothers always teased her. Then each of the students, with guidance when necessary, talked about a part that could be expanded into its own story. We then wrote quietly together for about thirty minutes. Again, seeing teachers writing was a powerful inducement for students to write.

Conferencing with Peers

We have found students are more willing to make revisions if feedback is given in a group setting. Working with a group of L.D. students in the middle grades, Margie and I noted that when we demonstrated positive comments and questions to each other about our writing, students were eager to participate and were very willing and able to provide appropriate feedback to each other.

In one situation, we gave the students a choice. Did they want to put the piece away, revise it, or edit it? We were surprised that even though they didn't want to do revisions, they opted to edit their pieces so they could be published. Because the choice was theirs, they were willing to make the required effort.

Since we wanted most of the responsibility to rest with the students, we first spent time making a chart of what to look for while editing. We wrote the chart using their responses in their own language. To our surprise, the students knew what needed to be done in the editing process. After going over their chart, they began by circling all misspelled words, and with guidance and encouragement, they went on to self-edit their pieces with a greater effort and involvement than usual.

Perspectives on Teaching for Strategies

Learning disability teachers who move toward more holistic models do not give up skills teaching. They come to believe that comprehension and meaning must be part of all teaching-learning situations. As such, they incorporate the skills teaching they have always done in meaningful contexts so that students use the skills strategically. Students no longer *practice* skills through exercises and drill. With guidance, they learn how and when to apply skills strategically as they *use* them in authentic contexts.

For example, a traditional, multisensory approach that includes seeing, sounding, tracing, and writing might well be employed, but not with the belief that isolated, decoding skills in a prescribed hierarchy is necessary *before* the child can read or write a story. The structured letter and word study would be related to, and part of, the authentic reading and writing experience. A child needing work in a particular phonics skill would work on the deficit areas in the context of reading real stories and/or writing for real purposes.

Finally, if learning disability students are to become learning ability students, they must receive large doses of meaningful instruction that facilitates their understanding of language. Teaching for strategies, where students learn how and when to apply skills in a thoughtful manner, must become the major instructional approach. Their language arts experiences—in and out of the classroom—must be purposefully integrated and include reading all types of literature as well as writing on a variety of relevant topics. The definitions and expectations of literacy we hold for regular students must also apply to at-risk students.

Evaluation and the L.D. Student

I feel strongly that evaluation techniques for L.D. and other special education students should be the same as they are for all students. (See Chap. 13, "Evaluation.") In this section, I highlight some concerns about present methods of evaluation as well as discuss several holistic evaluation techniques that are particularly useful for L.D. students.

The Multifactored Assessment

For more than fifteen years, I attended before-school weekly meetings as a member of the special services team in my elementary building. Our primary function was to assess the needs of students recommended for special services and to determine whether or not the students qualified for such services. More often than not the student was being assessed for a possible learning disability in one or more areas. And more often than not the student's deficits, based primarily on standardized test scores, were the focus of discussion.

To be eligible for special support services from the L.D. teacher or tutor, a student must demonstrate significant discrepancies between cognitive ability and academic achievement. Prior to beginning a multifactored assessment, a recommendation—usually by the classroom teacher—is formally written stating the reasons for referral as well as the instructional methods and services that have been employed. Then, with signed permission from the child's parent, the school psychologist, classroom teacher, L.D. teacher, speech pathologist, and other members of the special services staff take a careful look at the whole child.

I am pleased to note that special services teams in our district are currently making concerted efforts to look at the child more holistically. They are noting strengths as well as weaknesses and are attempting to obtain a profile of the child that goes beyond standardized test scores. In addition to various standardized tests and assessment instruments (including an individually administered cognitive assessment), informal measures of evaluation and teacher observations are becoming more highly valued as equally important parts of the assessment. Eventually, as more holistic assessment becomes the norm, fewer students should end up diagnosed as learning disabled.

Even so, because of unfavorable classroom practices and the types of standardized tests presently being used, a child with adequate learning abilities may wind up being referred to the special services team. For the child who does not do well with part-to-whole learning and exercises and subtests in isolation, a "learning disability" may show up unnecessarily. In some instances, where the classroom teacher is teaching reading primarily through phonics, a child that could probably learn to read with a holistic, multisensory approach might be labeled L.D. prematurely. In one case, a first grade teacher stated that a particular student would *never* make the transfer to content-reading materials in the middle grades. This prediction was based on the student's difficulty with phonics in isolation and recall of isolated sight words. The student in question is presently functioning well above average in the fourth grade and has been phased out of L.D. after several years of immersion in reading real literature and dealing with phonics and meaning-based strategies in the context of reading.

Further distortions of a student's abilities are common when the diagnostic instruments used to assess the student only measure skills in isolation. Paul, who is discussed at the beginning of this chapter, did extremely poorly on the *Woodcock Reading Mastery Tests—Revised* (American Guidance Service, Inc., 1987). His severely depressed total reading score was a combination of his performance on five separate subtests: letter identification, word indentification, word attack, word comprehension, and passage comprehension. Taking isolated tests and combining them to get a reading ability score is common practice but is of questionable value because the assessed tasks do not constitute meaningful reading. The results cannot be used diagnostically, and they give no realistic picture of what the child *can* do.

Furthermore, when parents are given the information that their child is weak in a subtest such as word-attack skills and they are not given the total picture, the parents often intepret that to mean that the child needs work on word-attack skills in isolation. The parent comes to view reading in segments rather than as a process of constructing meanings.

Taking a Close Look at a Diagnostic Reading Test

Looking closely at the *Woodcock Reading Mastery Tests—Revised*, one sees that this test—and many similar diagnostic reading tests—is of limited use for evaluation purposes. The tasks students are expected to perform do not occur in meaning-based classrooms. The word identification test involves naming words presented in list format. Yet the only time students are expected to read words in list format is on such a reading test.

The word-attack test requires the student to read nonsense, phonetically regular syllables (such as "ift" and "vunhip"). It is significant that the Examiner's Manual states:

> Nonsense words have been chosen as the main stimuli for this test because the task faced by a subject encountering a nonsense word closely simulates the real-life task of a person encountering an unknown—though real—word. A correct response to a real word would not provide evidence that a subject has applied word attack skills to that word, only that he or she has identified it (p. 6).

This is nonsense! The creators of the test are telling us that being able to sound out a word is the most valid way to approach unknown words. Indeed, a full page word-attack error inventory has the examiner target every error by sound and syllable.

Low scores on these two subtests indicate students' difficulty with nonsense syllables and words in isolation. Conversely, high scores indicate a child's facility with nonsense syllables and words in isolation. Such overemphasis on one cueing system—grapho-phonics—reflects a traditional view of reading that does not include important research on how good readers process print. High scores on these tests have nothing to do with real reading and the integrated strategies that good readers use in processing print in meaningful context.

The subtests that purport to measure comprehension are also in question. The word comprehension test consists of three subtests—antonyms, synonyms, and analogies. The Examiner's Manual indicates that these subtests provide "another measure of the subject's comprehension of reading vocabulary" (p. 7). Such tests may well measure a student's ability to read a word in isolation and respond with a synonym or antonym, or to complete a word-pair analogy, but I fail to see how such tests correspond to comprehending meaningful texts. Regarding the analogies task, the manual suggests that the word comprehension task closely resembles "real-life reading." But a format such as

mechanic–vehicle   dentist–

is not real-life reading.

The final subtest on the *Woodcock Reading Mastery Tests—Revised* is the passage comprehension test. It consists of multiple items of one or two sentences with one word missing. The student is expected to fill in a blank space in this context-in-isolation exercise. Certainly such an exercise cannot be considered genuine reading. In the meaning-based classroom, we would never expect a child to read one unrelated two-sentence passage followed by as many as eighty similar sentence passages and call it reading. Yet the manual states: "a correct response demonstrates that the subject has comprehended the entire passage" (p. 8).

I do not have a problem with using such a diagnostic reading test *as long as* real reading is also being assessed. Test reading, with its bits and pieces of unrelated words out of meaningful context, is only test reading. The student encounters such exercises *only* in taking the test. Real reading is what the student does every day, so most of the reading assessment must come from authentic, continuous, meaningful text. Within that text, we need to be looking at how the student samples, predicts, confirms, and self-corrects while in the process of reading.

This kind of assessment is especially important to use with L.D. students, who characteristically do not do well with phonics and isolated skills. Keeping in mind that phonics is a low-level strategy and that poor readers go to phonics while good readers rely on meaning, assessment must become more meaning based. As educators, we must begin to press for more balanced and meaningful assessment; the sum of the testing parts do not make a whole. At the same time, we must also educate parents about what meaningful reading involves and put decoding skills into proper perspective.

The thoughtful and thorough examiner needs to note the strategies—not just the skills in isolation—the reader is using or not using. What else, if anything, does the student use besides phonics when he gets into difficulty? One way to note the strategies the reader uses is to take a running record of the child's oral reading. (See *Early Detection Of Reading Difficulties* by Marie Clay [Heinemann, 1985] for directions on taking a running record.) Taking a running record from meaningful text, where the child has the opportunity to use picture cues with the written context and syntax—as well as grapho-phonic cues—can yield very different results than a standardized test. By noting the stategies the reader is using or not using, the teacher can establish meaningful and realistic teaching goals.

Using the Running Record Diagnostically: Dennis

Dennis was a third-grader who was in a pull-out L.D. classroom for daily reading instruction. Because he was experiencing great difficulty reading in the classroom, his teacher asked me to take a running record of his oral reading.

> I showed Dennis several books and asked him which one he thought "looked about right" to him. He chose *Stone Fox* by John Gardiner, a core book in our third grade literature collection. I asked him to stop reading

after it had become apparent the book was far too difficult for him. He could only read a few small words in the first several sentences.

"Let's try *Nate the Great* by Marjorie Sharmat" (Putnam, 1977), I told him. "This book is about a boy detective who solves cases. Start reading here, and see if you can find out what Nate the Great is up to now." Before Dennis started to read, I asked him how this book "looked," and he said it looked easy. As Dennis read, he relied totally on "sounding out" words. He read the entire passage at a consistent pace and did not stop when he made an error.

This book, which he said was "easy," turned out to be at his frustration level, indicating not only his poor reading skills but his inaccurate perception about his reading abilities. In examining his running record of 192 words, I saw that Dennis had made fifty errors, or miscues, giving him an accuracy level of about 75 percent. His self-correction rate was severely low, with one self-correction for every twenty-five errors.

When I asked him to tell me what the passage was about, I was amazed Dennis could tell me anything coherent about what he'd read. I complimented him on his good comprehension despite his excessive word-attack difficulties and said that it indicated he was smart. I talked honestly to him about how difficult the passage really was for him and about his over-reliance on phonics. I suggested that he slow down, reread for meaning, and think about what makes sense when reading—all strategies that good readers use. The tears he was trying to hold back indicated he was upset by what I had told him. I then showed Dennis how, if he thought about what he was reading at all times, he would be able to figure out most of the words. As an example, he had started (his errors are in italics):

> I am a detective
> I *know*/work *all*/alone.
> Let me tell you about my last case:
> I had just *ate*/eaten breakfast.
> It was a good breakfast.*Pan*/*pick*/*pack*/pancakes, *jus*/juice, *p. . .*/pancakes, *make me*/milk,

His error "ate" for "eaten" did not affect the meaning so I chose to ignore it at this time. I asked Dennis, "What had Nate just done?" He replied, "ate breakfast." I continued, "So what was in that good breakfast? Try this line again." With that guidance, he read the entire line correctly. I praised him and said, "That's what good readers do. They think about what they're reading, and when something doesn't make sense they slow down, go back to the beginning, and try again. You did that. Good for you."

Because I wanted Dennis to begin to see himself as a reader who could read for meaning, I told him I would be back the following week so he could try the same passage again. On the re-evaluation of the same passage the next week, his accuracy level was 93 percent and he had one self-correction for every three errors. We were both pleased with his greatly improved performance.

Because it is important for a child to verbalize what he is doing well so he is conscious of his actions and will repeat them, I asked him, "When you have trouble reading a word now, what else will you do besides sound it out?" He was able to tell me three good strategies:

> If it doesn't make sense, go back and look at it again.
>
> Look at the picture.
>
> Skip over it, and then come back to it, and see what makes sense.

I told Dennis, "There's one more thing you can do. Put in a word that will make sense when you can't figure it out."

When I shared his running records with his L.D. teacher, she said that she had been trying to teach Dennis meaning strategies but that his mother insisted on his "sounding out" every word at home. Nonetheless, several weeks later, Dennis' classroom teacher reported that he had shown increased confidence and interest during free reading time. Dennis was voluntarily reading many of the books in the *Nate the Great* series.

Perspectives

Assessment practices nation-wide continue to focus far too much on students' deficits. In addition, traditional attitudes and practices that overvalue standardized testing results still prevail. While the research and philosophy of how children learn to read and write has evolved and changed, the old assessment paradigm is still firmly in place. Part of the problem is that meaningful standardized tests are not yet readily available. Also, teacher education at both the undergraduate and graduate levels often does not include training in more holistic, informal evaluation measures. Learning how to take anecdotal records, running records, or do miscue analysis is not commonly taught in many universities. Learning how to administer a norm-referenced test is taught as standard procedure. Teachers, psychologists, parents, and administrators must become active in the movement to make assessment procedures and Individual Education Plans (IEP's) consistent with current research and views of the language processes.

In evaluating L.D. students—and all students—we need to get a fair and accurate picture of how the student functions over time. We need to employ and develop assessment and Individual Education Plans that rely not just on standardized tests given on one day but on the student's continuing learning processes. Running records, anecdotal records, oral tapes, journals, writing samples, reading records, retellings, student self-evaluations, and teacher and parent observations need to carry greater weight.

Whatever evaluation techniques we use, they must utilize the whole—the whole functioning student, the whole context, and whole literacy acts. If we continue to focus on the parts in teaching and evaluation, we will continue to identify and maintain a large population of learning disabled students.

The Pull-Out Program

Most students identified as learning disabled in the United States receive daily instruction in reading and language arts from a specially certified teacher. In almost all cases the L.D. teacher works outside the regular classroom in a resource room pull-out setting. Pull-out instruction is also the norm for Chapter 1 and other remedial programs across the country. While in some situations the pull-out program is advisable, too often it is used as a place for children who do not quite fit into the classroom setting and who require attention and instruction the classroom teacher feels unable to provide. More important, the majority of the children that are pulled-out remain in the special education program most of their school careers.

For the truly learning disabled children, estimated to represent not more than 2–3 percent of the population (two to three times less than the actual identified population), a separate setting for part of the day may be advisable. Thus, specific, specialized instruction may be provided for children who are not only unable to function in the classroom but who may feel "different" because they cannot do classroom work. Many L.D. teachers believe that some students must have a highly structured, multisensory approach in a setting with few distractions. Basically, if a student is way behind classmates or feeling too frustrated to confront regular classroom work, a "replacement" program that is offered in another setting may be necessary. Also, in fairness to the classroom teacher (who is already expected to be an expert in reading, math, computers, cooperative learning, current events, social studies, science, health, behavior, and so on), expecting proficiency in yet another highly specialized field may be unrealistic and even unfair.

A pull-out setting may also allow many moments of glory for a child who has few opportunities to shine in the regular classroom. Additionally, some L.D. teachers provide a safe, nurturing environment that may not, unfortunately, be available in the regular classroom. The resource room may be the only place in which the student feels completely comfortable and understood.

Paul's mother told me she preferred having Paul pulled out for reading instruction, but not because she believed he would be served better academically. She stated that Paul is very sensitive about his reading, and she worried about his being teased and feeling embarrassed among his peers. In the resource room, he did not feel uncomfortable about reading an easy book, and he did not have to read aloud in front of his peers.

I do not object to the pull out when it is a highly specialized, interim situation. In my four years as a Reading Recovery teacher working with first-graders, I was completely comfortable with the pull out. These children needed the quiet, intensive, one-to-one setting with very specific teaching techniques. However, once the children were "recovered" after twelve to twenty weeks of instruction, they went back into—and remained in—the regular classroom. The pull out was a stopgap measure, employed just long enough to give the student the skills and confidence necessary to function in the regular classroom. It was not a school lifetime placement, as often becomes the case for L.D. and Chapter 1 students.

The pull-out model is also desirable if the child is receiving skills-based instruction in the classroom but in the resource room setting is meeting success with a more holistic, meaningful model of instruction. In some cases, the L.D. teacher, or supportive services teacher, can share what's working and influence the classroom teacher to make some meaningful changes. In some school districts, the Chapter 1 teachers or reading specialists have initiated the movement toward more meaning-based, whole language teaching. (For a successful model, see Walmsley and Walp, 1990, in "Resources" at the end of this chapter.)

The pull-out program seems to be most successful when the classroom and supportive services teachers work cooperatively and are in agreement in terms of philosophy and methodology. The programs complement each other, with the child receiving similar messages and techniques from both teachers. For example, a child is pulled out during writing workshop time and works on writing while classmates are writing. Unfortunately for the student, this is not the usual case. Too often the pull-out and classroom programs are totally different, so that the child is sent confusing and conflicting messages. These different programs coexist in spite of the fact that regular education initiatives in special education and recent Chapter 1 guidelines point to greater coordination.

For some students, being pulled out of the regular classroom is a greater drawback than it is a support. Mark, who had been identified as learning disabled in third grade and who had been leaving the classroom to work with a tutor daily, rebelled against such treatment after one year. "I never liked it because I missed what was going on in class," he said. "I felt I was always behind. I felt pressure. When you go to the tutor, it makes you feel singled out—like you're not part of the whole class. And it's sort of embarrassing."

Onajé (discussed early in this chapter) also felt embarrassed about leaving the classroom but was never able to express his feelings until his mother observed him one morning in the pull-out setting. She observed that Onajé kept his head lowered and never smiled throughout the lesson. She was surprised when the tutor said this was how he presented himself each day. When she spoke to Onajé that evening about the need to have a good learning attitude, he said he felt ashamed about being pulled out.

Neither Onajé's classroom teacher, nor his L.D. tutor, nor I was aware of his very sensitive feelings until his mother shared them. We then took several steps to partially alleviate his feelings of embarrassment. Onajé's classroom teacher moved his desk from the back of the room to the front, so that when he left and re-entered the room he was less conspicuous. And when possible—for example, when the class was working on writing—his L.D. teacher tried to come into the classroom and give assistance in that setting. As a result of those changes, Onajé began coming to his tutoring sessions more frequently on his own and on time. Previously, his tutor had been having to call for him daily.

Onajé and Mark felt embarrassed about being pulled out in spite of the fact that they were leaving meaning-based classrooms. Their teachers did not expect them to make up work when they returned. For students who are expected to complete the worksheets they missed while they were "down the hall," feelings move beyond embarrassment to resentment.

Then, too, even spending time with a specially trained teacher does not ensure that students will receive more or better instruction. A recent study documents that L.D. students who are being served in a special education program receive more seatwork than active teaching. The L.D. teacher, it said, spends most of the time monitoring progress, checking responses, and recording performances (Richard Allington and Anne McGill-Franzen, "School Response to Reading Failure: Chapter 1 and Special Education Students in Grades Two, Four, and Eight," *The Elementary School Journal*, May 1989, pp. 529–542). If this study is representative of what occurs in L.D. classes, the fact that the L.D. population continues to increase should come as no surprise.

Additionally, much instructional time is lost while the student is in transit—when the student goes "down the hall." The student spends at least fifteen—more realistically thirty—minutes a day in such tasks as packing up, leaving the classroom, walking down the hall, getting settled in the Resource Room, getting ready to read, focusing, exiting the Resource Room, traveling back and re-entering the classroom, refocusing, and figuring out what's going on. That means that instruction in the pull-out program actually has to be accelerated and more efficient to make up for loss of instructional time. In reality, this is rarely the case, contributing to keeping students in special education programs (Richard Allington, "The Redesign of Remedial and Special Education Interventions," presentation at the national Reading Recovery Conference, Columbus, Ohio, February 1990).

The content of instruction for L.D. students is also in question. As I have worked and talked with many teachers around the country, I have found that in teaching L.D. students to read, phonics continues to be the major strategy being taught. Since phonics is a major weakness for most of these students, overemphasis on decoding and skills in isolation practically ensures a student's continued disability. On the surface, it would seem logical that if phonics is the problem for these students, then phonics instruction should be the solution. What happens in many L.D. programs, however, is that phonics instruction occurs as an isolated activity—unconnected to authentic reading and writing. Students neither see the purpose for what they are doing nor meet much success. Many minority students and second language learners (ESL students) have difficulty hearing and identifying vowel sounds. Struggling with daily phonics exercises only heightens their already existing feelings of inadequacy. Eventually, most of them learn to pronounce the words, but they take little pleasure or pride in reading. They rarely choose to read, so that their reading continues to be slow and ineffectual. To become a reader, one has to read continuous, meaningful material. Until the teaching of grapho-phonics strategies is integrated with meaning-based strategies—and until reading is viewed as getting meaning from print and not just reading words—many of these students will fail to reach their potential reading levels.

The lack of reading progress for some L.D. students also has to do with the fact that classroom teachers may use the pull-out program as a way of relinquishing responsibility for reading instruction. If the L.D. teacher is the teacher of record in reading, very likely the student will be pulled out during classroom reading time. If the student is unable to read the words of the classroom reading books, the teacher may assume the student cannot be included in a reading group. However, this deprives the student not only of taking part in a high-level discussion he may be capable of joining but also of participating as a member of a group.

Peter was a fifth grade student with a third grade reading level; his L.D. teacher was the teacher of record for reading. Even though his Individual Education Plan recommended that he be included in a classroom reading group, his inclusion was not mandatory because the classroom teacher was not responsible for instructing or evaluating him in reading. Despite the fact that he had an excellent oral vocabulary and strong listening skills, Peter was never included in a classroom literature group. Had he been paired with another reader or given the opportunity to hear the book on tape, Peter would have benefited greatly from being part of a group discussion of such books as *The Great Gilly Hopkins* by Katherine Paterson and *The Sign of the Beaver* by Elizabeth Speare. Peter missed out on the opportunity not only to read these great books but also to share his personal reactions to the reading, to learn from his peers, and to connect good literature to his life. Then, too, his classmates and teacher missed the unique insights Peter would have brought to the group.

Despite growing concerns about the possible ineffectiveness of pull-out programs, there is little current data to support the practice of the L.D. teacher—or any supplemental services teacher—going into the regular classroom. In addition, in most states, the division of special education does not give local school districts funding at high enough levels to make this a feasible option. The funding is far greater when there is a pull-out program, a situation that in itself helps to perpetuate the traditional model. Unfortunately, L.D. service can depend more on funding organizations than on educational theories and children's needs. Still, in spite of the lack of data and funding, school districts need to be exploring alternatives.

School districts need to consider seriously the implementation of holistic, collaborative models where the L.D. or Chapter 1 teacher works in the regular classrooms in cooperation with the regular teacher. The L.D. teacher would, more likely, be seen as a valid instructor and teacher, not just as an adjunct person, as has often been the case in the pull-out model. In one school district, where administrators and teachers are committed to a language-based integrated day, the L.D. teacher goes into the classroom and team teaches with the classroom teacher. At the secondary level, where much of what goes on in the pull-out setting involves help with assignments, the L.D. tutor or supplemental teacher in the classroom could help students better understand classroom teacher expectations as well as background information and organizational skills needed to complete assignments.

We need to examine those L.D. models of school districts that have been successful in moving from skills-based to meaning-based instruction and from a pull-out to an in-class setting. Finally, we need to be open minded about all possibilities and use what works best for kids. We must place remedial and L.D. students in situations that enhance and increase their learning opportunities. In some cases, for the supportive services teacher to pull out students may be desirable. However, I believe that in far more cases, working within the classroom—providing additional, high-quality instruction coordinated and shared with the classroom teacher—may be the more desirable route.

The L.D. Teacher: Changing Attitudes

> I think the biggest thing is to be willing to try whole language, even if it's just with a few kids. I never got the reading results with the basal and skill sheets. The kids read far better now that I use good literature. And once you see how much more the kids enjoy learning, you become convinced.

Teachers in Transition

Vicki Griminger, a well-respected L.D. teacher in grades 5 and 6 in our school district, who also was Paul's L.D. teacher for two years, made the comments above. As Vicki tells it, she started out as a very traditional L.D. teacher eighteen years ago—lots of worksheets, skills in isolation, heavy phonics emphasis. But she always read aloud to her kids.

She credits her transition to more holistic teaching to being at Moreland School and seeing the first grade program (see Routman, 1988) and to reading and discussing professional books and articles with colleagues. Initially a total skeptic, Vicki became a believer after several years. She says:

> I watched what was happening in the first grade. I saw it working, and eventually I got caught up in the excitement of it all. The kids and teachers were having so much fun, and everyone was learning. Gradually, my thinking began to change. I started slowly, with journal writing. Initially I had the most success with first-graders. It was harder to do with my older kids due to the lengthier books they were reading.

For Ellen Potter, an L.D. tutor, the transition to whole language with L.D. students has been difficult but personally rewarding. An L.D. tutor for three years and a classroom teacher before that, Ellen was entrenched in the skills model. She began to change her thinking when she observed Onajé in a teaching situation in which he was viewed as able to read. She started attending weekly language arts support groups where we were discussing the philosophy behind whole language, and she began to take a critical look at her teaching. One day she told me proudly that she had removed all the dittos from the kids' folders. She had filed them; she wasn't ready yet to throw them out.

Ellen comments,

> I used to do every page, every ditto, and every workbook page in the basal reader when I was teaching second grade. I used to feel kids would learn more if we did every page. Also, I felt it was a way for parents to see what we were working on in class so that they could give help at home if it was needed. When I moved into L.D., whatever I could get my hands on that was tangible, I put in the kids' folders. Even now, when I've moved away from all that, I sometimes find myself sliding back into the skills model when someone gives me materials that look new and exciting. However, I'm able to catch myself, and now I'm able to select the activities that will be most appropriate for the lesson I want to teach.

When Ellen moved into L.D., she continued to rely on dittos and story starters, but she was also beginning to look carefully at students' needs. At the same time, she used literature in her reading program right from the start because she believed she needed to support what was going on in the classroom and because our district had made a commitment to teaching reading with literature.

As Ellen began slowly to examine her teaching, read articles, and talk with colleagues, she made changes in both her philosophy and her teaching. A major shift was in how she taught reading. While she had added trade books to her program, she used to write down every word Onajé missed and would constantly interrupt him when he was reading. A list of missed words was regularly sent home for Onajé to master. Even though she knew Onajé was upset by the interruptions and the home drill with his mom, Ellen believed this drill in isolation was necessary. In addition, she wasn't ready to give up any control. She felt she had to be with Onajé every step of the way.

As she observed Onajé in a reading situation in which he was guided to use strategies to figure out words and meanings for himself, as well as encouraged to read silently, Ellen began to question her methods:

> I used to think if a child could read out loud fluently, that meant he was a good reader. Comprehension came later. But, if it didn't sound very fluent, I assumed he was a poor reader. I never realized Onajé could make mistakes and still understand what he reads. Now, even though he's making fewer and fewer mistakes, I find it difficult to give him wait time, allow him to read silently, and trust he will find his errors. I still stop Onajé and tell him the word. I know I need to improve on how to help him, but I am much better at complimenting him now for what he does well, and that has made a big difference.

Ellen has become reflective in her teaching. She continues to seek answers, try out new ideas, meet with colleagues, and trust herself and her students more. Increasingly, she is using more meaning-based materials and strategies and is making every effort to keep language whole.

Margie Glaros has been an L.D. teacher for seven years. She had been an L.D. tutor for five years and a classroom teacher for three years. As a starting L.D. teacher, she was initially skills-based, with lots of structured phonics work and structured reading texts.

For the majority of the kids a skills approach to reading "seemed to work," but for the really severe kids, "no program worked." As for writing, most of Margie's students were not eager to attempt it in any form. Spelling was taught by drilling the weekly classroom lists. While students might show improvement on the weekly tests, there was no transfer. They were memorizing skills but could not apply them.

A particularly hard-to-reach fourth grade student made Margie think about looking for alternatives. She began to use taped books and repetitive readings. Looking back, she notes, "While there was some improvement, there was no real instruction going on. The student was following the text with his eyes while listening to the teacher or a tape. But that wasn't enough. No strategies were being taught." Margie admits to feeling defeated, incompetent, and terribly frustrated.

At about the same time, our district was in the process of making a commitment to more meaning-centered teaching approaches through literature and whole language. A reorganization closed some elementary buildings and moved many teachers to different buildings. Contact with new teachers encouraged Margie to think about trying new approaches. She began attending the weekly language arts support group and began to view herself as an extension of the classroom.

> I tried to start doing things more like the classroom teachers were doing. Having the same philosophy made it easier to communicate with classroom teachers. I feel it helped me be viewed as a colleague, not "just" a special services person. Teachers began to see me as someone who was interested in doing the same things. And it did seem as though the kids could succeed with similar materials and methods. The whole thing just made sense.

Margie began adding literature to her reading program, and by the following year she was teaching all reading through literature. By observing a colleague pattern lessons from the literature and teach the skills in context, she began to try similar lessons herself. "Before that, I'd never had any instruction in teaching strategies."

At the same time, Margie added journal writing to her program and began pulling all the children's spelling words from their writing. (See Chap. 10 on spelling for specifics.) Writing, spelling, and reading became interrelated activities for Margie and the children.

Walking into Margie's L.D. resource room today, one sees students engaged in reading literature and doing all kinds of writing. The room is filled with wonderful books, cozy corners in which to read them, writing materials, tape recorders, a computer, charts made by and with the children, and displays of children's work. Most important, the children are happy and filled with pride at what they are accomplishing.

Margie's move toward more meaningful teaching has been gradual. Interacting with colleagues at weekly support meetings, working cooperatively with classroom teachers in the building, and doing lots of professional reading and thinking about her teaching have all contributed to her professional growth. Margie is still struggling with the teaching of phonics. Some of her students use a structured phonics workbook, but she is also consistently teaching phonics in the context of real reading.

Theo Husband has been a special education teacher in our school district for twelve years. She believes that each child is entitled to the gift of learning and that we as educators must help students find and develop their strengths. She sees whole language as another way of becoming involved with her students.

> Whole language has forced me to examine my beliefs about learning and teaching. It confirms my beliefs that an eclectic approach to education meets the needs of our students. Learning is multimodal! I'm learning with my kids and looking at them to see what their needs are so I can help them reach their full developmental potential. I'm able to be creative in my teaching, and I find myself enjoying using varied resources.

Best of all, Theo finds that her students are also more excited and motivated about what they are learning. She feels that whole language has helped develop a sense of self-esteem in her students and has allowed them to take risks with their learning.

Parents: The Need for Effective Communication

Parents of L.D. children often feel separated from the educational process. One mother told me she signed all the papers so her child could be serviced but never really understood what she signed. She felt too "embarrassed" to ask the necessary questions.

As educators, we need to take the time to make parents feel comfortable and well informed. Too many parents never really comprehend what L.D. means. One parent told me, "After six years in the L.D. program, I'm still not sure what all the terms mean and what L.D. really is."

Bonnie Daniels, Paul's (see beginning of chapter), mother, is a social worker, well accustomed to group meetings and agency procedures. As such, she has never felt insecure or inadequate at meetings with the psychoeducational team at Paul's school. She has freely voiced her opinions and asked hard questions about her son's Individual Education Plan, but she knows she is not typical. She is concerned that inexperienced parents may just listen quietly and assume the professional team has all the answers.

Bonnie suggests a fifteen-minute preconference for parents with the L.D. teacher or psychologist just before the "big" meeting. She comments, "As a social worker, I would never bring a client into a room without first saying, 'This is what to expect. This is what you're going to hear.' It's too threatening for most people to walk into a room full of professional strangers."

Bonnie Daniels also suggests that teachers focus on specific educational progress when talking with parents. For years she had heard what a "wonderful" child Paul was and what a great personality he had. "The attitude seemed to be that because of his great vocabulary and articulation skills, he would suddenly wake up one morning and be reading. It was never explained to me how this was going to happen."

Other parents feel a sense of exasperation with teachers who fail to recognize the child's disability. One parent said, "Because they can't see the handicap, some don't acknowledge it. At times, they see it as the child's fault." This mother saw her child as making strides, for example, when he got three words right on a spelling test when previously he had never spelled even one word correctly. The parent's praise was not echoed by the teacher. "My son is not getting enough positive feedback for what he's doing well," she said.

Parents really appreciate it when they find their child's efforts are acknowledged by the classroom teacher. One parent told me that out of six teachers her child had had, only one had been sensitive to her child and made him feel good about himself. Among other things, on written tests that teacher had graded the child only on the content of his answers, not on his spelling or handwriting. The teacher had also taken the time to give the child extra help after school.

It is not only teachers who need to send positive messages to students; parents too need to be sensitive about giving criticism. Paul Daniels and his mother related a situation that illustrates this point. Paul had brought home a writing paper, and because his mom immediately commented on his poor spelling (after Paul had been humiliated by a substitute teacher in front of the class for the same thing), he never heard her say the content was excellent. He was mad for days, and his mother had no idea how upset her son was until he finally told her.

Robin Grimes, Onajé's (pp. 386–390) mother, admits to having put a lot of pressure on her son.

> If the teacher sent work home, I felt he *had* to get it. When I looked at his papers, I only saw the errors. Onajé was afraid to make a mistake with all the pressure I was putting on him. Working together, we both ended up in tears. I was feeling very stressed out. Watching you focusing on the positive really turned things around for me. I realized he needed support and that I had to compliment him for doing his best. I'm still involved, but now I try to focus on what Onajé's doing right. That has made all the difference.

Finally, Paul Daniels gives this advice to parents: "Be more positive. Put your-selves in your child's shoes. Encourage them. Congratulate them on what they do well. Listen to your kids 'cause sometimes they have a lot to say." It's good advice for teachers too.

Reflections

Looking closely at Paul, Chris, and Onajé—*all considered by their L.D. teachers to be as severely disabled as any students they had* ever *worked with*—one sees that literacy is possible when the expectations for success are constantly present, when the focus of instruction stems from the student's strengths, when the skills are taught strategically in the context of the learning situation, and when the student is provided additional time and quality education by knowledgeable practitioners.

It is not enough to care about the students, have a trusting relationship, and hope that years of skills instruction will finally take hold. Teachers, parents, administrators, and students must first believe that L.D. students can and will learn. All must work together to find what the student can do and build on those strengths, no matter how small they initially seem to be.

Each student, regardless of age, must be taken at his readiness and interest level, whatever that happens to be. The learning program must then be designed for the child; the child cannot be fitted into a commercial program. And as much as possible, instruction needs to be holistic and strategically based, with educational needs determined cooperatively by the learner, teacher, and parent—in the context of an authentic, reading-writing situation.

In addition, even though difficult to achieve, efforts between regular and remedial programs must be better coordinated in curriculum design and implementation. Administrators need to exert their leadership and take strong initiatives in their local school districts so cooperative and congruent programming between regular and special education programs becomes the norm instead of the exception.

For all of us, the impossible task seems possible only when we begin to believe we *can* do it and appropriate guidance and support are available.

Resources

For more information on holistic approaches to working with at-risk and learning disabled students see the following books and articles.

Bartoli, Jill, and Morton Botel. 1988. *Reading/Learning Disability: An Ecological Approach.* New York: Teachers College Press.

> *The authors propose understanding learners' behaviors through broad social contexts that include the classroom, school, and community. Specific suggestions to support this "ecological model" include an integrated language approach to reading and writing across the curriculum. A substantial portion of this scholarly text (272 pp.) is devoted to strategies for teaching that include specific case studies and lesson plans. Important reading for educators and policy makers ready to question and change traditional understandings of learning disabilities.*

Carbo, Marie. November 1987. "Deprogramming Reading Failure: Giving Unequal Learners an Equal Chance," *Phi Delta Kappan*, pp. 197–201.

> *The author discusses the importance of matching reading instruction with students' learning styles and notes that poor readers have been most successful with teaching that has accommodated their global, tactile, and kinesthetic strengths. Teachers will find the specific recommendations and activities, based on research findings, applicable for increasing students' chances for reading success.*

Church, Susan, and Judith M. Newman. 1985. "A Case History of an Instructionally Induced Reading Problem." In *Whole Language. Theory in Use*, Judith M. Newman (ed.). Portsmouth, NH: Heinemann, pp. 169–179.

> *This is a case history of a ninth grade student reading on a second grade level after years of intensive, supplementary instruction in word analysis (phonics) and word identification (skills). The student learns what he is taught, reflecting his teachers'*

beliefs about the reading process, but he never views reading as a meaning-getting process. Only when the focus of his instructional program shifts to developing strategies in the context of classroom reading materials does this student begin to understand texts. Must reading for teachers ready to look at reading for L.D. students as a constructive process.

Gersten, Russell, and Joseph Dimino. February 1989. "Teaching Literature to At-Risk Students," *Educational Leadership*, pp. 53–57.

The authors describe an instructional approach that uses "scaffolding" and "story grammar" to teach literary analysis to low-achieving secondary students. This is a useful article for incorporating story grammar elements (stating the problem and main characters; noting character clues, reactions, themes, resolution) to improve students' comprehension of literature. The teacher "thinks aloud" and demonstrates his language processes and decision making to the students. Eventually, with guidance, students are able to use this approach on their own.

Hasselriis, Peter. January 1982. "IEPs and a Whole-Language Model of Language Arts," *Topics in Learning and Learning Disabilities*, pp. 17–21.

The author examines the requirements of IEP's (written Individual Education Plans required by Public Law 94-142 for all handicapped students) and suggests that there is nothing in the law that mandates an emphasis on skills-oriented goals and objectives. He states, "Objectives should be written so as to lead to instructional strategies that keep students in constant touch with language (either oral or written) that is unfragmented—language that is interesting, practical, worthwhile, and functional" (p. 19). The practitioner who wants to write IEP's that are reflective of the whole language philosophy and current view of reading will find sample IEP's included.

Maria, Katherine. January 1989. "Developing Disadvantaged Children's Background Knowledge Interactively," *The Reading Teacher*, pp. 296–300.

Various strategies are discussed for helping disadvantaged students understand a text. The teacher selects several main concepts from a text, estimates what kind of background knowledge students will need for comprehension, and then demonstrates one or more prereading strategies to develop background knowledge.

Mills, Heidi, and Jean Anne Clyde (eds.). 1990. *Portraits of Whole Language Classrooms: Learning for All Ages*. Portsmouth, NH: Heinemann.

Five chapters in this text describe whole language in use with remedial students: a resource room setting in an elementary school, an ESL elementary school classroom, a middle school remedial program, an English class of "reluctant learners" at a high school, and a university "Ed Lab" servicing students with learning difficulties. I found the interviewing of peers assignment described by middle school teacher Betty Ann Slesinger and the individually designed final English exams described by reading consultant Donelle Blubaugh working with students in Marianne Dalton's tenth grade English class illustrative of some alternative reading-writing possibilities that work. "[R]eluctant students . . . are not reluctant learners when the school agenda is kid-centered, when they are given time to read and write about things that matter and for authentic audiences, when they are provided with realistic language models, and when their voices are as important as our own" (Donelle Blubaugh, p. 274).

Pogrow, Stanley. January 1990. "Challenging At-Risk Students: Findings from the HOTS Program," *Phi Delta Kappan*, pp. 389–397.

This powerful article with supportive data advocates that the way to develop and apply thinking skills in at-risk students who "do not understand what it means to understand" is through changing the way teachers ask and respond to questions. Instead of typical, brief, recall responses, students should be engaged in high-level, intensive conversation where thinking processes are initially modeled by the teacher. "[T]he constant probing by the teacher gradually increases the students' confidence in their own ability to express ideas, and the quantity and sophistication of their speech increases" (p. 393). Some specific interventions for increasing the learning capability of at-risk students are suggested.

Rhodes, Lynn K., and Curt Dudley-Marling. 1988. *Readers and Writers with a Difference. A Holistic Approach to Teaching Learning Disabled and Remedial Students.* Portsmouth, NH: Heinemann.

See the complete annotation in Resources for Teachers. *See especially instructional strategies for developing reading and writing fluency, pp. 102–121.*

Thistlewaite, Linda L. May 1990. "Critical Reading for At-Risk Students," *Journal of Reading*, pp. 586–593.

The author defines critical reading and offers seven activities for teaching and promoting it. Specific strategy lessons are presented for use of tabloid articles, advertisements, editorials, movie reviews, comparison of a book and movie, and descriptions of two historical events. Very useful for promoting critical reading and thinking for intermediate through college age students.

Trachtenburg, Phyllis, and Ann Ferruggia. January 1989. "Big Books from Little Voices: Reaching High Risk Beginning Readers," *The Reading Teacher*, pp. 284–289.

This article describes how skills instruction can be incorporated through shared book experiences of favorite books. An enlarged text version of Cordoroy *by Don Freeman is used to develop sight vocabulary, phonics, fluency, and self-confidence with a class of at-risk first-graders.*

Walmsley, Sean A., and Trudy Pombrio Walp. January 1990. "Integrating Literature and Composing into the Language Arts Curriculum: Philosophy and Practice," *The Elementary School Journal*, Vol. 90, no. 3, pp. 251–274.

This scholarly, comprehensive article gives the rationale and specifics of an integrated language arts curriculum (reading full-length literature and composing) that extends to students with reading and writing difficulties in remedial programs. Implementation and results in a small, rural school district are described in detail. "The approach to remediation assumes that poor readers and writers need more time and better instruction to accomplish their classroom tasks rather than a separate remedial reading program with its own curriculum" (p. 265).

Wheeler, Nancy S. 1990. "Showing the Way: Using Journal Writing to Develop Learning and Teaching Strategies." In *Coming to Know: Writing to Learn in the Intermediate Grades*, Nancie Atwell (ed.). Portsmouth, NH: Heinemann.

An L.D. teacher in a resource room setting describes how she developed a program of journal writing for both herself and a fourth grade student as the major strategy for improving very depressed reading and writing abilities.

15

Classroom Management and Organization

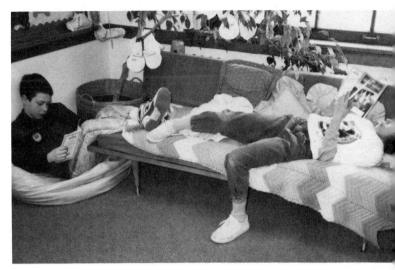

Enjoying the cozy book corner in the classroom

"I'm in a downward spiral. Each day, I feel myself losing more control of the classroom. What's more, I find I keep lowering my expectations for the kids because it's taking longer to get everything done."

A dedicated first-year teacher talked with me after five months into the school year. She had started school full of enthusiasm and with high hopes of having a whole language classroom. Fresh out of the university, she was ready and eager to try out what she had learned about whole language and teaching. She attended our weekly whole language support group, worked long hours trying to create meaningful learning contexts, and dedicated herself to the students and her job.

Now, however, the rules and point systems she had established no longer seemed to work. As soon as her back was turned, someone was out of control. Praising the appropriately behaved students and hoping the rude ones would get the message to fall in line was having no effect. By the end of the day she was exasperated, and lately she had given some thought to changing professions.

While this new teacher understood and could apply many whole language strategies to reading and writing, her management system was based on the traditional belief that children need tight controls set by the teacher. Yet, just as many of us are working to help children take more responsibility for their reading and writing, we also need to help children take more ownership of their behaviors.

Some experts tell us it is no harder to have order in a whole language classroom than it is in a teacher-dominated one. I disagree. I believe it is much harder in the whole language classroom because the children are expected to take responsibility for their own behaviors—even when the teacher is not looking. Having that inner self-control, which is necessary for the free movement and effectively operating learning centers that whole language classrooms often have, does not just happen. It takes many months of modeling, self-evaluation, setting expectations, and trial and error.

Most of us, including myself, have had behaviorist training. As long as we are in control—giving rewards and points, putting names on the board, and granting and taking away privileges—things seem to run smoothly. Many of us have spent years trying to bribe children into being interested by appealing to their stomachs, their sense of competition, and their desire for tangible rewards. But when we are absent, student self-control often disappears. It's as if an entirely different group of children is in the room when a substitute appears. The children are well behaved only when the classroom teacher is present and asserting authority. This teacher-dominated classroom looks orderly, and it is—as long as the teacher functions as overseer.

By contrast, the whole language classroom may well be using rewards but the rewards do not usually foster competition, and they are less likely to be tangible ones. Rewards might include reading to the kindergarten, having extra time on the computer, being a gym helper, writing collaboratively with a partner, or working in the hall.

As opposed to coercion and bribery, the whole language teacher uses persuasion and problem solving. Built into effective classroom management are the principles of whole language, including collaboration, demonstrations, self-evaluation, and teacher as facilitator. Motivation to behave appropriately comes from within the students. Students know what to do, where to find resources, where everything belongs, and what behaviors are acceptable in the classroom. Rather than being a method, management is a way of thinking and an approach that is consistent with whole language beliefs about learning.

For example, instead of "tattling" and relying on the teacher to solve a problem, students will often first problem solve through writing. Writing encourages students to think through a problem independently and to assume some responsibility for the solution. Before the teacher intervenes, the student may fill out a form that lists such questions as the following:

- What is the problem?
- What did I do?
- How can I help solve this problem?

Developing a system of management that is contrary to the traditional teacher-in-control approach is a difficult and slow process for most of us. It takes an understanding of whole language philosophy, the desire to have a collaborative classroom, time, experience, trial and error, risk taking, and trust in students. The transition process can be frustrating, and, in the beginning, it often seems easier to just continue to give orders and set the rules ourselves. However, if the goal of education is independence, then children need to learn to behave and interact without teacher supervision. Initially, constant modeling and role playing are required, and, for a while, it does take longer to get everything done. This is time well spent because once children assume responsibility for expectations and procedures, the teacher is freed to observe and work with children.

To the untrained eye, a whole language classroom often looks less structured than a traditional classroom because there is much talking and movement as well as children involved in different enterprises. However, just the opposite is true. For things to flow well, the teacher is highly organized, students have had a part in setting up the environment, and students understand, respect, and share responsibility for classroom management.

Some visitors to our whole language classrooms have asked, "What is the discipline policy?" They are amazed when we say we don't have one, that we share responsibility with students. Visitors also note, "It seems so natural," referring to the way students converse and work together. What the visitors do not see is that the naturalness, which looks so easy, has taken months of cooperative work and problem solving to set up.

Establishing the Climate of the Whole Language Classroom

The amount of choice students have, the importance of opportunities to collaborate with each other and with the teacher, the number and relevance of teacher demonstrations, as well as other important issues, have already been discussed in "Becoming a Whole Language Teacher" (pp. 12–25). All of these factors, and others related to them, contribute to a supportive, nurturing learning environment in the classroom. Putting theory into practice, however, takes time, experience, and patience.

Setting Up the Collaborative Classroom

Walking into Joan Servis' fourth grade room, one quickly notices that this is a collaborative classroom. Children work cooperatively, problem solving and supporting each other in the learning process. Joan is a facilitator and a learner, guiding and stretching her students to find and support their own meanings. There is a feeling of community and caring between the students and teacher, and one senses that this is a happy and literate environment.

Joan says it takes about five weeks for her to begin to feel that her classroom has become a collaborative community: "I know I have it when I tell the class it is time for physical education or recess and they moan because they would rather continue with math or writing or with whatever academics we're involved in. When that happens, I know I have the cohesiveness going. But at the beginning of the year, without it, I feel very frustrated."

High school English teacher Holly Burgess felt she had the cohesiveness of a comfortable, safe community two months into the school year. She notes,

> After a class of reluctant readers had read and discussed *The Learning Tree* by Gordon Parks, I asked them to write their own questions for a final test on the book. The questions they wrote were all so good I typed up the entire set and asked students to choose four to answer. When time was up, students wanted more time to write. That had never happened before. Students felt nonthreatened because the questions were their own, they had access to the questions and the book, the book related to their lives, and they really wanted to stay involved with the book.

First grade teacher Karen Shiba says that establishing a collaborative classroom requires "consistency and routine." Karen moves slowly and takes the first few months of school to introduce procedures and expectations. She says, "I don't introduce a new center until everything is running smoothly, and the children are working well independently." She and other primary teachers note that the excitement and sense of community in their classrooms often emanates from the daily shared reading experiences. The literature, poems, songs, and chants provide opportunities for innovations on text and other motivational activities that generate success and collaboration.

Joan Servis begins working for collaboration the first week of school by getting children used to working with each other. Her class is a racially integrated one, with children at extreme ends of the scale in terms of economic background, behavior, and academic ability. In working to establish a collaborative community, she notes, "You never get 100 percent, but if you have 95 percent, that's wonderful."

While Joan likes collaborative groups of three and four, she begins by having children work in pairs after she has demonstrated what they are to do, whether the activity is peer conferencing, note taking, or responding in a literature log. After several weeks, the students begin working as a cooperative group. (See Hill and Hill, 1990, for procedures for setting up groups and for establishing a collaborative classroom.)

Joan says that she constantly employs the following strategies to establish a collaborative classroom. She notes, "If the task is worthy of collaboration, that is, if it is interesting and relevant and the materials are engaging and not too difficult, then collaboration works."

• *Expecting self-evaluation of behaviors*   When students finish working together, for example, in math or social studies, they are asked to reflect upon their behaviors. (See Figures 12–5 and 12–6 in Chap. 12, "Integration," and Figures 13–30 and 13–31 in Chap. 13, "Evaluation.") With teacher guidance, orally and in writing students are constantly examining how they might improve the functioning of the group, and gradually they take more responsibility for their behaviors.

I have found that promoting continuous self-evaluation eventually leads students to assume more responsibility for their behaviors. For example, when I am teaching a demonstration lesson and a student misbehaves or the noise level of the class gets too high, I say something like, "I'm having difficulty hearing students in reading group. What can you [rest of class] do that would help the situation?" In the past, I would have said something like, "It's too noisy in here. Jason, you need to be in your seat. Kara, quiet down and get to work." I find that having students problem solve puts the responsibility on them and takes the teacher out of the role of placing blame and taking over. It also makes students more aware of what behaviors are appropriate.

• *Stressing cooperation*   Through oral discussion and shared writing, Joan Servis and her students discuss specific behaviors that foster respect and cooperation, for example, making eye contact, listening to one another, and taking turns.

Additionally, students are encouraged to help each other. For example, Joan does not check daily reading logs (explained in "WEB Reading," Chap. 3) until the group (usually four students) has completed recording in their logs and all raise their hands (an idea she picked up from fifth grade teacher Jim Servis). The stronger students have assisted and encouraged the others, so that when Joan comes over to check, the entire group has completed the logs satisfactorily.

• *Praising positive behaviors*   Orally and in writing, Joan comments on what students are doing well. Commenting on positive behaviors encourages students to repeat the behaviors.

• *Making sure students completely understand the task*   Through repeated demonstrations and specific instructions about what the group is to accomplish, Joan makes sure each group member knows what to do and that each group has a spokesperson.

• *Modeling and role playing appropriate and inappropriate behaviors*   To establish a collaborative classroom, demonstrations are often not enough. With teacher guidance, students need to move from teacher demonstrations to role playing appropriate behaviors and interactions. For example, the class looks on as a group of students role play how to use the reading center. Following their role playing, the teacher guides a class discussion about appropriate and inappropriate behaviors.

Many teachers have found it works best to demonstrate and role play one activity at a time and to take many weeks to establish classroom routines. While initially this can be very time-consuming, following this plan pays dividends later on. For teachers who feel routines have not been well established, it works well to think of the current week as week one, and just start again.

The Physical Climate and Room Arrangement

Along with learning expectations and the emotional climate, the physical layout and setup of the classroom support the teacher's philosophy of learning and teaching. The way we organize our classrooms affects children's views of themselves as readers and writers and has an impact on their attitudes toward school and learning.

A whole language, collaborative classroom has a distinctive look and feel that is noticeable when you walk into the room. There are displays of children's work and books everywhere. There is space for exploration, learning centers, and a classroom library, and the room is full of attractive, purposeful print.

While each whole language classroom is unique, they often have a number of physical factors in common. These physical changes are not easy to implement because they go hand in hand with our development of learning theory. As with the development of theory, we need to give ourselves time to become comfortable with a new physical setup. Most teachers make these changes slowly and gradually over a period of many years. The following are suggestions and alternatives for consideration.

Room Arrangement

In a whole language classroom, the room is set up so students can read, write, and collaborate comfortably by themselves or in a small group. There are open spaces where the class can gather or small groups can meet. There are centers of designated areas where students have opportunities for talk, exploration, writing, reading, and sharing. In a small room, or in a secondary classroom, the hallway is sometimes used for conferences and paired collaboration. See Figure 15–1 for the setup of Joan Servis' fourth grade classroom and Figure 15–2 for the arrangement of Karen Sher's kindergarten classroom.

Figure 15-1   Joan Servis' Fourth Grade Classroom

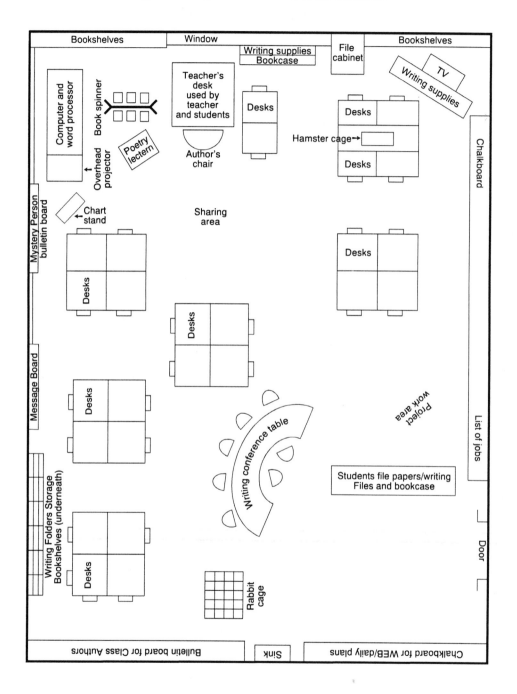

Figure 15-2 Karen Sher's Kindergarten Classroom

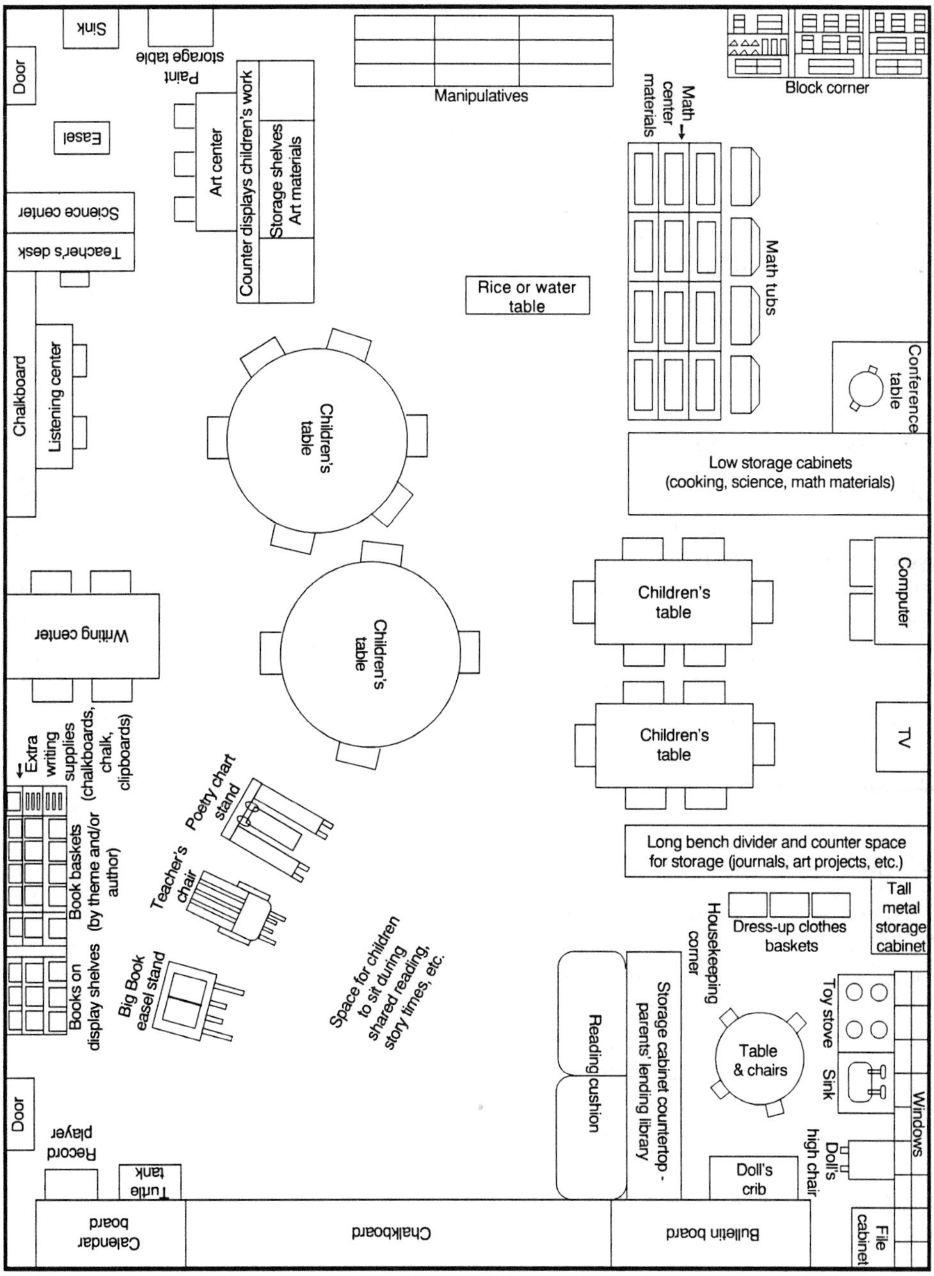

Desks

Desks are usually clustered so students have opportunities to collaborate with a partner and with a small group. Clumps of four desks work well; more than five can be difficult for small-group work. Some teachers have begun to replace all desks with large tables, an arrangement that allows for greater flexibility and more work space for projects but that requires separate storage areas for students' books and materials. Stackable bins or personal baskets have worked well here.

Eliminating the teacher's desk is an option for getting more space since some teachers find that in a whole language classroom they rarely sit at their desks. Adding another file cabinet, with extra file folders and organizers, may be necessary, but teachers who do get rid of their desks find they prefer having an extra table that provides additional space for collaborative work and conferencing. Teachers who keep their desks use them more as a place for a student and teacher to confer undisturbed rather than as the focal point for the teacher in the classroom.

Whole-Group Area

Whole language classrooms, especially at the elementary level, include an area where the whole group can gather. Some teachers define such an area with a carpet; others use furniture to block off space. Some teachers move desks out of the way just before whole-group time and have students sit on carpet squares. An easel for Big Books, a stand to hold enlarged-print poetry charts, a rocking chair, and an author's chair are often part of this space. Sometimes the cozy reading corner is part of this area or adjacent to it.

Secondary classrooms often have mobile, lighter-weight furniture. Some teachers prefer chair arrangements in semicircles, u-shapes, or clusters of armchair desks. Such clustering promotes a feeling of community.

Bulletin Boards

A teacher's beliefs about learning and teaching are evident in the format and content of the classroom bulletin boards. When the classroom is a collaborative one, children's work is everywhere, and the bulletin boards—which are done by and for the students—reflect meaningful and relevant reading-writing processes. By contrast, in traditional classrooms, bulletin boards are most often "done" by the teacher. I still remember the last-minute, time-consuming scramble to have all bulletin boards complete for the first day of school and the constant pressure throughout the year to change the bulletin boards so they would be current and attractive.

By giving students some ownership of the bulletin boards, they take more pride and responsibility for how the room looks and functions. By using children's work instead of commercially prepared materials, the teacher is sending a message that the classroom is student centered. This transition is not an easy one for most of us, and it does not occur until we are ready to share control and responsibility for learning with our students.

However, putting students in charge of the bulletin boards saves the teacher lots of time. In one Australian classroom I visited, the teacher reported starting school with empty bulletin boards each year and saying to students, "This is going to be our room together for an entire year. How do you want to use our bulletin boards? What do you want our room to look like?"

Sixth grade teacher Pam Anderson tried this approach for three out of her five bulletin boards this past fall and found that students did a better job than she had anticipated. She recalled, "I really had reservations about turning over the bulletin boards to the students because I thought it would be difficult to establish cooperative work habits so early in the school year. But most of them took the project seriously and did well." Beginning with a class discussion led by Pam, students decided to have a holiday bulletin board, a calendar bulletin board, and a behavior/rules bulletin board. Then students worked together in groups—based on the bulletin board they wanted to work on—discussing and sketching out their plans, which were subject to Pam's approval.

Some teachers effectively use bulletin boards to feature students' writing. Based on an idea in *Creating Classrooms for Authors* (Harste, Short, and Burke, 1988), Joan Servis uses her largest bulletin board to spotlight the writing of each class member. Each student—and the teacher—has a space on a 9 by 12 inch sheet of colored paper on which a piece of monthly writing is selected by the writer to be posted. Each month a new piece is tacked on top, and a collection of dated writing samples results. Other teachers keep students' writing samples in a transparent, plastic folder and staple it to the wall.

A permanent bulletin board that promotes self-esteem and interpersonal relationships is "Person of the Week" or "Author of the Week." Each week a different student is highlighted with family photographs, writing samples, interviews, and anything significant about the student. With teacher guidance, the student can be in charge of planning and creating the bulletin board. The student is also often the special classroom helper for that week.

Another idea that works well and gives a personal touch to the classroom is to replace the usual commercial borders on bulletin boards with student-designed borders. For example, students can design a class logo at the beginning of the school year and reproduce it on plain borders or paper strips.

At the secondary level, where classrooms are usually shared with other teachers, hallway display cabinets can be used to exhibit student writing. At our high school, a recent hallway display showed students' writing alongside the teachers'. Another display demonstrated high school readers. In the same window case, readers—both teachers and students—displayed favorite books recently read, along with a description of why these books were significant to them.

Message Board

In addition to legitimizing note passing, the message board can serve as a permanent bulletin board that promotes within-class communication, fluency in writing, and self-esteem. At designated times, students write and receive signed messages to and from each other and the teacher. Some teachers use the message board to have students communicate and work out classroom problems. For example, a student who is upset about something or someone may write a message through the message board to the teacher, or a student may be asked to write a message explaining what he has done to try to solve a particular behavior or discipline problem. If a student in Joan Servis' class wants to have her seat changed, the reasons are stated, and the request is put in writing through the message board. Some teachers use the message board as a way to recognize students' positive behaviors. Joan says that about one quarter of her class receives a positive written message from her each morning and that students eagerly await those messages.

The message board was developed by Carolyn Burke of Indiana University, and specific procedures and ideas for its use are given in *Creating Classrooms for Authors* (Harste, Short, and Burke, 1988, pp. 309–312). Some teachers use mail-boxes, especially in the younger grades, to serve the same purposes as the message board.

Display Areas

Children need lots of space to display their own work. To get additional display space for children's work, many teachers have found that fishing line or nylon string, attached to the wall or woodwork with small eyehooks and strung across the room or in levels across the window wall works well. The line is light, transparent, flexible, and easy to put up. Clothespins work well for attaching work samples to the lines. Window shades may also be utilized for posting charts.

Cozy Reading Corner

A whole language classroom usually has an attractive area, not only for display of many books, but a "cozy corner" where students can read in a relaxed, comfortable manner. Just as we adults do not do all our reading sitting upright at a desk, children also need to have space in which to curl up comfortably with a book. Along with attractive book shelves, book racks, and/or book spinners, the corner may include beanbag chairs, cushions, a rocking chair, a throw rug, reading posters, and even a sofa or bench for reading. Many parents are willing to donate some of these items. Books and materials are always easily accessible to students.

The amount of time and effort spent establishing an attractive library center pays off. Researchers Lesley Mandel Morrow and Carol Simon Weinstein found that students, even those who were poor readers, chose to read more during free-choice time and have more interaction with books when there was a well-designed, inviting reading corner (Morrow and Weinstein, "Encouraging Voluntary Reading: The Impact of a Literature Program on Children's Use of Library Centers," *Reading Research Quarterly*, Summer 1986, pp. 330–346).

In addition to all types of fiction and nonfiction books—both commercial and student written—the reading corner may include magazines, plays, poetry, news-papers, reference books, and dictionaries. While many teachers prefer to limit reading workshop, or sustained silent reading time in class, to books, these other resources are available when students have "free" time or when they are working on special projects. For younger children, there will need to be many titles with predictable structures, favorite storybooks, and counting and concept books. In the reading corner there may also be puppets and felt boards to dramatize stories. Books should be attractively displayed, many of them with covers cleary visible.

One hundred to 150 books in various genres is a good number to aim for in the classroom library. Involving students by checking with them for particular titles, authors, and subjects that they would like to see included in the library gives them ownership of reading. Even when funds for books are very limited, teachers can establish classroom libraries by signing out books from the school and public libraries. Often librarians are willing to rotate sets of about fifty titles to help establish classroom libraries. Asking parents to donate books from home that children are no longer reading has worked well in helping many teachers build libraries. Other teachers have checked out local garage sales and library sales for books. Some teachers also accumulate many books for the classroom through bonuses from book clubs such as Trumpet (Scholastic).

Writing Center

The writing center has a table and chairs, pencils, pens, markers, crayons, chalk, all types of paper, booklets, envelopes, book-making materials, a computer or typewriter, and chalkboards. Students know how to use the materials, and the center is open to them. (Some teachers have been able to get parents to donate an old typewriter to the center.) Where space is tight, a small table or ledge that houses writing supplies works well.

Listening Center

An area is set aside for small groups of students (using headphones) to listen to cassette recordings of favorite books while they follow along in individual copies. The listening center may also be used for students to hear a text over and over again before they are about to read, and also to reread a text to gain fluency. The teacher, or another proficient reader, may also record a small portion of text that has already been discussed in reading group, so that students can listen and follow along visually. Additionally, the tape recorder may be used to record student reading of text and original stories. Students enjoy creating a final copy without worrying about editing.

Other Learning Areas /Centers

Depending on what is going on in the elementary classroom, there may also be areas for math manipulatives, science projects, and other curriculum/theme study. While these centers will not be discussed in this book, they are briefly noted so as not to be overlooked.

Messages, Directions, Jobs, and Rules

In a whole language classroom, many of the notices, announcements, and schedules are written by the students. With teacher guidance, even very young children can write appropriate explanatory labels and messages on displays, equipment, cabinets, and other classroom items. Jobs are often designated on a volunteer basis. Students sign up for the jobs they want to do, and because the choice is theirs, they are motivated to do the job well. Other teachers prefer to identify classroom jobs with the students and then rotate the jobs. Many teachers find it works well to co-establish classroom rules through a shared writing experience. There are usually few classroom rules, and they are always stated positively. For example, one rule might say, "Be courteous" (instead of "Don't be rude").

Classroom Organization
Lesson Plans and Schedules

Whole language teachers often find that traditional lesson plan formats are too confining. In addition to the required curriculum, because much of what goes on in the whole language setting springs from the children's needs and interests— which are always subject to change—a flexible framework seems to work best. For the teacher, this requires a solid theory base, confidence in oneself and the children, and a flexible, supportive principal who understands whole language.

Many whole language teachers design their own formats for lesson plans. Sometimes these plans are done in pencil and may be "messy" because of ongoing changes and additions teachers make. Instead of traditional lesson plan books, some teachers use three-ring notebooks, large spirals or oversized blank books in which they can create their own formats and spaces. Often the major components or areas of study are blocked out for the day or week, with the specifics to be filled in one day at a time (see Figure 15–3). For example, there may be blocks for shared reading, guided reading, independent reading, sustained silent reading, and writing workshop. Often there are separate folders for each area of study. For example, under reading-writing workshop or language arts, the plan might indicate a biography unit. The objectives and specifics are listed in the particular folder. The folder also may contain reproduced samples of well-done projects by students from past years to use as demonstrations.

Kindergarten teacher Karen Sher has designed an innovative, flexible lesson plan format that works well for her and may be easily adapted across the grade levels. Karen writes a broad, comprehensive plan for the week and then writes daily on large Post-its (which she overlaps in the corner of her large spiral notebook) what she specifically hopes to do that day. The weekly plan and Post-its give her freedom. If a project is not finished one day, it easily carries over to the next day (see Figure 15–4).

Flexible planning represents a major change for Karen. She says,

> If I used to breathe, I wrote it down. As I became more secure, I relaxed and wrote down less. But I was still spending a lot of time trying to fit everything into those little boxes in the plan book. I felt so frustrated by my plans, but, at the time, I didn't know why. Now my lesson plans match my teaching. My plans provide me a framework so I can easily weave everything together. I always have at least several units or themes going on at one time, perhaps an author study, a unit on feelings, and a science unit that has arisen naturally from the children's interests.

First grade teacher Jim Henry also uses a flexible format. While Jim has a broad, overall weekly plan, the bulk of his planning is done daily on a 3 by 5 inch pad of paper. He notes, "Our class projects and successful motivational activities stem from our daily shared reading experiences. The planning of these experiences often hinges upon the previous day's efforts, so that planning for the next session happens at the end of each day."

Teachers I have worked with have taken at least three to five years to develop a schedule and lesson plan format they feel comfortable with. All of these teachers expect their daily plans to change. Joan Servis calls her daily schedule a "forecast."

Figure 15-3   Susan Mear's Grade 1 Schedule/Plan

MONDAY

9:05	Entry Bell - Meet children at Front Door
9:10	Begin reading poems and jokes
9:15-9:20	Announcements and Pledge on PA
9:20-9:45	Reading to and with Children and Calendar (Calendar information in substitute folder) Story: Optional Big Book: Poem: Objective: To immerse children in literature, to see reading demonstrated, to point out conventions of language, punctuation, sentence structure, phonics in context, etc. Evaluation: Are they involved? Do they read poems later by their choice and use the strategies? Do they transfer knowledge to their own writing using language conventions, punctuation, phonics and sentence structure correctly?
9:45-11:10	Reading in Small Groups - Guided Reading (20-25 min. per group). The reading material for the groups is contained in the folders in the basket behind my table marked Reading. Please be flexible with the order of the groups because of the pull-outs. Some groups may be reading independently. (During this time later in the year the children can put their things to share on my chair -- stories they wrote, Journal page, etc. -- About six children will have time at the end of reading period.) Objective: To match children and books, to demonstrate reading strategies, language conventions, phonics and grammar in context and develop reading competence. Evaluation: Children will read independently, transfer strategies to new material, understand what they have read and appreciate the author's craft. Seatwork:
11:10-11:15	Restrooms (Recess Optional)
11:15-11:50	Math Their Way and Box It, Bag It - Children are doing hands-on activities contained in Tubs at the Math bookcase - The children are familiar with this and can set it up and proceed on their own. Objective: Evaluation:
11:50-12:15	Story Writing for Publication (Folders contained in tub under cubbies.)
12:15	Lunch (Mrs. Mims will come to the room and pick them up.)
1:05	Entry Bell
1:05-1:20	Quiet Time/Reading (SSR) Objectives: To allow for choice, to establish regular reading habits, to enjoy reading, etc. Evaluation: None Read with:
1:20-1:30	Story:
1:30-2:10	Social Science -- Text: Objective: Evaluation:
2:10-2:30	Box It, Bag It - hands on addition and subtraction contained in the school boxes on the math shelf - Number Operations Objective: To use computational skills Evaluation:
2:30-2:45	Handwriting either on desk with chalk, on transparencies, on paper or with shaving cream on desk.
2:45-3:15	Physical Education
3:25	Dismissal

Theme of the week:

Figure 15-4   Proposed Weekly Schedule for Karen Sher's Kindergarten Class

Proposed Weekly Schedule for Kindergarten
Karen Sher, Teacher
week of October 1, 1990

LANGUAGE ARTS ACTIVITIES	MATHEMATICS
Poetry → Turtle Poem ⎫ on chart stand; Autumn Poem ⎭	Graphing: 1. graph Rosemary Wells books; 2. Apple Tasting Party → graph favorite kind
Shared Reading → ① Read class made book: Our Trip to Sage Fruit Farm; ② Introduce: The Monster's Party (Big Book); ③ Sing song & read Big Book: Miss Mary Mack	Free Exploration: Add tubs: mirrors, tiles, toothpicks
Phonics, Penmanship: Focus → Tt - relate to our turtle; Penmanship → Practice writing our first names; the letter Tt; Reinforcement → Ff → make class book Our Favorite Food Book; Cooking - fruit salad	Stuffed Animal Theme Activities: Counting/Estimation: Count stuffed animals (use graphing mat) with numeral cards: Children estimate first. Story Problems: develop with stuffed animals
Phonics (Tt) reinforcements: 1. Draw pictures beginning with Tt; 2. note Tt items brought in by children & Tt words in reading & conversation; 3. Toothpick art; 4. Cut magazine pictures beginning with Tt; 5. Invite children to play 'teacher'	Comparing: weight & height of children's animals with mine. Use balance scale. Vocab: heavier/lighter, taller/shorter, the same. Concept Instruction: Pattern: ① Introduce people sorting: the pattern a/c categories used for sorting; ② Snap/Clap patterns → translate to words, shapes, letters, etc; ③ Pattern fruit salad on skewers
Literature: ① Closure on Rosemary Wells - graph our favorite; ② New author - Pat Hutchins; ③ Get from library → Fall Books, Turtle Books; ④ Book Look → daily opportunity for children to enjoy books alone or with friends. Writing: ① Journals → model diff. ways of writing; ② encourage writing during activity time; ③ photograph children engaged in writing	New Tubs: ① Begin to introduce pattern tubs: stamp & ink pad patterns - unifix patterns

She notes, "Like the weather, it is subject to change." See Figures 15–4 through 15–6 for three elementary teachers' schedules/plans.

Plans for the Substitute

Since it may be difficult to have a substitute who does not understand or accept whole language principles, whole language teachers try not to be absent a lot. Of course, the reality of life is that we are sometimes absent. Some teachers keep a set of alternative, more traditional plans in a substitute folder. Others try to find a substitute who understands whole language and works well with the class. Then, they request that same substitute consistently.

Some teachers find that having separate folders of procedures for the substitute works well—for example, folders of explanation for WEB reading, sustained silent

Figure 15-4 Continued

Social Studies / Science	Art / Music
S.S.: Developing an understanding of ourselves and others (OUSO) Obj: To become aware that we do things to achieve goals; to examine our own purposes & to determine results Stories - ① *Frowny Brown* - people who are dejected are not fun to be with ② *The Box* - dealing with rejection	1. Flip Face - relate to OUSO themes - children will express times when they felt happy or sad and flip face to appropriate expression
	2. Toothpick Art
	3. Fancy Foil Magnets } Ff
	4. Make flowers to decorate room)
	5. Begin giant leaf mobiles - FALL
	6. Nature Collage - after our walk
Science ① Apple Experiments - lemon juice; covered vs not covered ② FALL - (literature) - Walk in Southerly Park : collect signs of Fall Begin leaf & seed collections, SORT A/C different attributes	7. Music ① introduce children to Raffi and his music ② rest to Firebird Suite (Stravinsky)

10-1-90 Monday - Tentative Plan
Special Classes - Art - 9:20 - 10:15
                 PE - 11:15 - 11:45

<u>A.M.</u>
- Greet children, take attendance, gym shoes, snacks
- ART
- Calendar
- Group Time
    - Poetry → Turtle Poem, Fall Poem
    - read Apple Farm Book together
    - Sing & read Miss Mary Mack
- SNACK, BATHROOM, BOOKLOOK
- Physical Education
- Math - Free Exploration Tubs
    - small groups will work with me comparing stuffed animals (Height & weight)
- STORYTIME - non-fiction - Box Turtle book
    - discuss difference between fiction & non-fiction
    LUNCH
- Shared writing → LUNCHTIME STORIES
- Literature/Math - review book by Rosemary Wells. Which was your favorite? Why? Graph
REST → music - Firebird Suite
SCIENCE → Walk in Southerly Park - observe and collect signs of fall
Independent Activities - children choose room centers. Include at art center - making flowers to decorate room.

Figure 15-5   Ellen Rubin's Flexible Schedule

Flexible Schedule for Heterogeneous Class   Grade 2   Ellen Rubin

9:05–9:30 A.M. *Taking Care of Business*
  •write note to classmate and put in classmate's mailbox
  •write daily "News of the Day"
    large piece of newsprint is posted daily, and students can write their news throughout
      the day. For example, "My tooth came out last night." (1 or 2 sentences on anything
      important to student.)
  •read
  •class meteorologist does weather report   } Jobs change
  •class mathematician takes self-designed class survey } every 2 weeks

9:30–10:00 *Reading Aloud* (and occasional Shared Reading)
    teacher reads excellent literature to class—content oriented (social studies/science);
      theme oriented (author, seasonal, mystery, nonfiction); predicting, reasoning, dis-
      cussing—focus on author's "voice" (style, individuality)

10:00–10:30 *Independent Reading*
  •using self-selected books, students read alone (SSR) or "buddy read"—books, peers'
      published pieces, magazines
  •student records selection in daily reading log
  •teacher holds individual reading conferences

10:30–11:30 *Reading-Writing Workshop*
  (opening)   •mini-lesson (modeling, usually whole class, 5-10 minutes)
               •class continues with work in progress
                 free choice 90% of time (1/2 of time within teacher specified parameters
                   [genre writing, content area writing, focused writing—setting, devel-
                   opment, using interesting words, proofreading, etc])
  (ongoing)   •peer conferencing
               •small group and/or individual conferencing with teacher (anecdotal
                 records taken)
               •word processing
               •special projects (plays, puppetry, book projects, content area projects)
  (closing)   •sharing circle (students can share any writing)
[Note: Spelling is integrated with writing {see Chap.10}. Once a week, parent volunteers
assist.]

11:30–12:00 *Guided Reading*
    whole class and/or small group reading using core books

12:00–12:10 teaching mechanics of cursive handwriting or working on final copy of piece

1:05–1:30 *Whole Class Project Sharing*
    students share favorite poems, talk about favorite books, share published books,
      share content area projects

1:30–2:15 *Mathematics*
    Math textbook program supplemented with open-ended problem solving and monthly
      graphing from weather reports (meteorologist) and math surveys

2:30–2:50 *Science/Social Studies/Health*
    Content areas are integrated into literature program and writing as much as possible.
      This is "spillover" time for what has not been integrated.

2:30–3:10 *Day Books (Journals)*
    "Capture the day—you'll never get it back again." Students write about their day, and of-
      ten refer to this journal for writing ideas; occasionally, journal is used as a literature
      response log.

3:10–3:15 *"News of the Day" and Wrap-Up*
    Students read what they have written throughout the day

Figure 15-6   Joan Servis' Grade 4 Class Schedule

Schedule for Heterogeneous Class—Grade 4

Joan Servis

MONDAY	TUESDAY	WEDNESDAY	THURSDAY	FRIDAY
9:15–9:45 W.E.B. — Independent reading and bookcheck. See Chapter 3 for procedures.				
9:45–10:00 Class announcements. Children and teacher plan activities for the day.				
10:00–11:00	**10:00–11:00**	**10:00–11:25**	**10:00–11:00**	**10:00–11:25**

Opportunities/Independent Worktime/Process Writing

From list on the board which was generated from teacher and students, the students select an opportunity. Teacher circulates, holds writing conferences, and provides needed materials and guidance. Some examples of opportunities are: projects relating to current literature books (see Reading below), teacher and peer writing conferences, journal writing, pen pal letters, writing drafts or final copies of current book/story/article/letter, and editing revised stories. (Spelling is taught as part of writing; see Chap. 10.)

11:00–12:00	**11:00–11:45**	**11:25–12:10**	**11:00–11:45**	**11:25–12:10**
Social Science	Social Science	Physical Education	Social Science	Physical Education

Social Studies and Science are combined. Students work in interest groups, reading, researching, and presenting orally to the class the results of their findings. Some units of study have included: Prairie Life and Land, the Amazon Basin, Ohio, and Life in the Deserts of the U.S.

12:00–12:15	**11:45–12:15**		**11:45–12:15**	
Sharing	Music	Physical Education	Music	Physical Education

Sharing—Whole class gathers for oral sharing of successes accomplished in the morning.

12:15–1:05   Lunch/Recess

1:05–1:15   Poetry

Class poet (volunteer job) reads aloud previously selected poetry to the class

1:15–2:15   Reading

Students read (independently, in pairs, or occasionally teacher reads aloud) the current class selection from core literature. Children read with 1 or 2 open-ended questions in mind (questions are on board). Procedures are followed for Literature Response Logs and Literature Discussion Groups (see Chap. 6).

2:25–3:15	**2:15–2:45**	**2:15–2:45**	**2:15–2:45**	**2:15–2:45**
Art	Mathematics	Mathematics	Mathematics	Mathematics

Mathematics—Students primarily work on problem solving of word problems in groups of four. Computation is assigned as homework. Concepts are taught in class.

	2:45–3:15	**2:45–3:15**	**2:45–3:15**	**2:45–3:15**
Art	Teacher Readiing Aloud	Teacher Reading Aloud	Teacher Reading Aloud	Teacher Reading Aloud

Reading aloud by teacher—picture books, novels, various genres. Class makes predictions, reacts to selection read with comments and discussion.

3:15–3:25   Self-evaluation

Oral or written, of contributions to the class either as a team member or as an individual. (See Figures 13-30 and 13-31 in Chap. 13, "Evaluation," for sample written self-evaluations.)

3:25   Dismissal

reading, spelling, literature response logs, and literature discussion. If a collaborative classroom has been established in which children work well together and take responsibility for their behaviors, tasks, and routines, a substitute may be able to carry on the regular program.

High school English teacher Holly Burgess notes, "The first time I had to be absent this year—three days all together—I created substitute plans and then scrapped them! How could I encourage and trust students to follow the reading/writing plan I had taken such pains to establish if I were still in such rigid control of who could do what, when?!" The note from the substitute indicated that most of the students had stayed committed to the usual tasks for most of the period.

Getting around Time Constraints

Especially at the secondary level, where rigid time frames (forty-five- to fifty-minute periods) affect the "flow" of the curriculum, some teachers and schools have begun experimenting with more flexible time blocks in order to establish some continuity. For example, ninth grade teacher Dana Noble schedules writing workshop daily for several weeks and then moves to responding to literature for several more weeks (see Figure 15–7). Additionally, some teachers and administrators are working to create larger time frames by scheduling classes twice or three times a week but for longer time periods, as is the practice at some colleges and universities. Middle school English teacher Mary Krogness says, "Think of class time as being on a continuum versus its being so many little parcels used rigidly."

Most whole language teachers at the elementary level prefer to keep their classes

Figure 15-7   Dana Noble's Grade 9 Writing Workshop and Response-based Literature Study Schedules

Schedules for Writing Workshop and for Response-Based Literature Study
Grade 9   English

Dana Noble

Each schedule of a 50-minute period is in effect for approximately a two-week span, intermittently throughout the year. (Or schedules could alternate M,T,W [writing] and T,F [literature study]) Time spans are approximations only. In actuality, schedule reflects a daily routine which flows together as one time block.

I   **Schedule for Writing Workshop** (based on model by Nancie Atwell, 1987, *In the Middle*)

MONDAY	TUESDAY	WEDNESDAY	THURSDAY	FRIDAY
8:05	Students have picked up their writing folders before the bell rings.			
8:05–8:15	Mini-lesson: Rehearsing, writing leads, giving response, paragraphing, editing, common punctuation errors, etc.			
8:15–8:20	Silent write: Read your piece in progress, consider the next step in the process of writing, and begin writing, revising, editing and thinking.			
8:20–8:25	Schedule the day: Each student announces his/her progress in the current piece: Draft 2, ready for response, editing for final draft, starting a new piece, etc.			
8:25–8:50	Writing time: Writers write, get and give response in conference area, edit, finish pieces of writing.			
8:50–8:55	Group share: A student reads work in progress or talks about problems and asks for ideas in whole group session.			
8:55	Students place drafts in their folders on their way to next class.			

Individual reading and response

At home, students read books they have chosen from book talks, book sharing, or other sources. Students write responses in journal: comments on plot, personal connections, observations about author style and story structure, and ideas for writing in writing workshop.

II   **Schedule for Response -Based Literature Study**   (See Chap. 6.)

MONDAY	TUESDAY	WEDNESDAY	THURSDAY	FRIDAY
8:05	Students reread journal responses to prompts about current literature they are studying.			

8:10	Students form groups to read their responses, compare and discuss ideas.
	  Groups are formed by various factors: common book choices, common prompt choices, or common interests.
	Other small group activities may include the following:
	  1. Students exchange journals, read another student's response to the same or different prompt, (or an undirected response to the literature) and write a reaction to their response: confirming facts, providing an opposing viewpoint, or contrasting their reading.
	  2. One small group discusses their responses while the rest of the class carefully listens and observes without interrupting. At a signal from the teacher, other students are invited to offer new or contrasting observations about the literature.			

8:30	Students rejoin the whole group for discussion, dramatic interpretation of the literature, brief writing assignments using the literature as a model, individual reading, etc.			
8:50	In the last five minutes, students write down a prompt written on the board for the night's reading or discuss and choose one question from a list of open-ended questions.			

Note: Be flexible! Setting up a definitive time schedule has been done only for the purpose of giving some time-management guidance to teachers.

Figure 15-8   Encouraging Self-Evaluation

```
Name of project _____
    ☐ My pictures go with my story.
    ☐ I have used my best handwriting.
    ☐ I have used capitals and periods.
    ☐ I practiced reading this once.



    _____
                signature
```

self-contained (and to avoid switching classes). This plan affords maximum flexibility, with time to establish a collaborative classroom community and to build in opportunities for integration across the curriculum. Teachers also try to work with their principals to obtain blocks of uninterrupted time.

Setting Aside Time for Sharing

Many teachers in reading-writing classrooms find there is never enough time for children to share. Students, creating their own projects and stories, want to share everything. We have found it works well to set aside time daily and/or weekly (at the end of the morning, afternoon, or week) for students to share their work. Even at the secondary level, sharing is important.

Holly Burgess, a high school English teacher, plans time after a writing prompt, especially with all-class reads, for students to either read their journal responses or tell about what they wrote. She notes, "Surprisingly, I have about 95 percent of students sharing, even with reluctant readers/writers. All gain from each others' insights."

Jim Henry found that in his first grade classroom he had to move away from allowing students to share everything. Being allowed to share everything seemed to encourage students to rush through their work. Then, too, students became frustrated because there was never enough time for everyone to share. Instead, Jim put in place a whole-class weekly share where students had an opportunity to share one piece every week or every other week. The specialized sharing invited children to do and choose their finest work and also encouraged self-evaluation. Jim also developed a simple form that encouraged his first-graders to do their best work on all required and optional projects (see Figure 15–8).

Providing Reading-Writing Opportunities That Allow for Choice

Planning for Unstructured or Independent-Choice Time

A critical component of whole language is allowing and promoting student choice and decision making. We need to provide and value time for students to select options. Peg Rimedio, a first grade teacher, notes, "The most important thing in first grade is to plan the unstructured time. If you give children constant activities to do, they are not going to have time to explore. Everything doesn't need to be checked and marked by the teacher. The main thing that kids need—that we don't give them—is time and choice." Peg has built many student-selected activities into her daily program. However, before giving students options for their unstructured time, she sets up materials and procedures and carefully explains how they may be used.

Most teachers find it takes at least the first six weeks of school to set up routines and procedures with students. In setting up learning centers and explaining optional and expected activities, teachers find that when activities are introduced slowly, one at a time, week by week, and when the use of centers and activities is carefully and repeatedly demonstrated, role played, and monitored, students learn to use them appropriately.

First grade teacher Karen Shiba has a daily block of time when students have unstructured, independent choice time. During most of that time, Karen is meeting with reading groups or conferencing with students. Students not in group are involved in optional reading, writing, or listening activities. Available options are gradually introduced and explained. For the first two weeks, students are expected to spend the entire independent work time reading Big Books and little books, independently or with a friend anywhere in the room as long as they use "inside voices" and do not disturb the teacher. The third week Karen introduces and demonstrates the use of the mailboxes. The following week she introduces the listening center with its tape recorders and headphones. The fifth week, Karen demonstrates the use of the computer, with two students working collaboratively. At the same time, students also have the option to continue journal writing or illustrate their published books. The only requirement is the illustration of the week's poems (from shared reading) that become part of each student's poetry notebook. Self-evaluation is a big part of the successful management of unstructured time. If a student is off task, Karen will ask, "Are you reading, writing, or listening?" The student has to say what she is doing and could be doing. (For more specifics on Karen's first grade reading and language block that allows for flexibility and choice, see Routman, 1988, pp. 36, 37, 200, and 319.)

Even with careful planning, we will often need to demonstrate more than once. One high school teacher found that after many weeks she finally had reading workshop functioning well. Then she introduced writing workshop, only to find that some students forgot about completing their reading journal. While she had expected students to continue doing their reading journals (along with writing workshop), she had not made that expectation explicit.

Involving Students in Planning

In planning, in addition to meeting the requirements of the curriculum, students in whole language classrooms have options. Kindergarten teacher Karen Sher asks her students, "What do you want to learn about today?" and includes her own input and direction. An author study of Steven Kellogg emerged initially from the children's hearing the story *Can I Keep Him?* and wanting more books by the same author. The study of Kellogg included obtaining information and photographs of the author, finding lots of books by the author for reading aloud and independent reading, making a whole-class graph of favorite books by Kellogg, and discussing the language the author uses and how he does his illustrations.

Karen also uses Friday mornings and many afternoons as opportunities for students to choose "meaningful educational" activities. Children decide what art, reading, writing, math, manipulative, or curriculum-related acvitity they want to do, and Karen is available to provide materials, set up the environment, conference with students, and give help as needed.

Giving students more options connected to what they are interested in is a recent change for Karen. She notes that the half day of flexible time or "independent choice" allows her to observe children and then set directions in her teaching. She states, "I have found that children will take me where they need to go."

Karen also provides unstructured time through daily sharing. At the beginning of the year, children are assigned their day of the week for sharing, and approximately four to five children have an opportunity to share daily. Sharing time sometimes leads to a curriculum focus. One afternoon a student brought in two beetles in a paper bag. A lively class discussion led Karen to bring in books about beetles. One student chose to make an elaborate beetle out of art supplies found in the room.

Examples of Reading-Writing Opportunities

Joan Servis' fourth grade students have daily reading-writing opportunities, and Joan is available during that time to conference with students. See Figure 15–6 for Joan's weekly schedule.

The following were the opportunities listed on the chalkboard one morning early in the school year just before Halloween and again near the end of the school year when a folk/fairy tale unit was in progress (see Appendix A). Asterisks (*) designate required activities.

Opportunities—October 25

1. *Halloween book (original Halloween story for first-graders)
2. Reader's Theater (poem or picture book)
3. Cleveland Electric Illuminating Company Contest (poster on how electricity affects our lives)
4. Letter to Robert Munsch (follow-up reading-hearing many of his books)
5. Memorize Halloween chant to do with first-graders
6. Message for message board
7. Letters to American servicemen and servicewomen in Saudi Arabia (during the Middle East crisis in Kuwait)
8. Newspaper activity (to go along with local daily newspaper)
9. Rods (cuisennaire rod puzzles)

<u>*Opportunities—May 15*</u>

1. *Young Authors book—finish
2. Fairy tale—choose new one to read
     Storymapping
     Picture of characters and setting
     Sloppy copy of original fairy tale
3. "Once Upon a Time" project
     Optional activities to go along with fairy tales (see Appendix A)
4. Read—independently or with a partner
     Books for Young Authors that have been completed by other students
     Optional activities to go along with fairy tales
5. Messages for message board
6. News articles for "Onaway Outreach"
7. Journals

See Figures 15–9 through 15–11 for additional examples by other teachers.

Figure 15-9   *One Day's Invitations to Meaningful Independent Activities in Grade 1*
From Jim Henry's first grade classroom.

<u>Today's Invitations</u>   5-31-90

Continue journal
Listening Center
Reading Center
Letters to:
                    Jake the Snake (garden snake)
                    Nipper ⎫
                    Cuddles ⎭ guinea pigs (classroom pets)

Projects   (literature adaptations)
     The Tenth Good Thing About _____
     Frog and Toad Are Friends
                         chapter 6
     The Longest Journey in Shaker Heights
     Jake The Snake Manual
     Blueberries for _____

Figure 15-10   Independent Work in a Grade 3 Classroom

From Linda Cooper's third grade classroom.

The following appears on the chalkboard
and the items shown below are on a table under the chalkboard

LANGUAGE WORKSHOP

Independent Worktime Activities *(required)*

1. Reading Assignment
2. Homonyms
3. Thesaurus
4. Personification Story
5. Riddle Book

Book Projects *(optional)*

Make a diorama
Write a letter to/from
   a character
Make a mobile
Make a puppet show
Write a reaction to the book
Make a poster advertising
   · the book
Write a commercial
Make a book jacket
Make up your own extension
   project (clear it first)

1. Reading Assignment - the assignment made in reading group which may be a reading and/or a written activity.

2. Homonyms - (skill project) - every day for about two weeks four new homonyms were solicited from the students. Each pair of homonyms was recorded on the pears in alphabetical order. The students then used each homonym correctly in a sentence. (Dictionaries were used as references). Another class period was given to cutting out all the pears, punching a hole in each, and arranging them in alphabetical order on a ring. (This project is evaluated by the homonym being used and spelled correctly, and the proper use of capitals, punctuation and alphabetical order).

3. Thesaurus - Each day a new word is added to the thesaurus. This word is usually an "overused" word from their writing. They may use dictionaries, reading group books, library books, or any other written material as a resource to complete this activity. The thesaurus is then used by the student as a reference.

4. Personification Story - After studying an author and his/her books, such as William Steig's picture books leading up to the core reading book, Abel's Island, each student then writes his/her own personification story.

5. Riddle Book - On each page of the book, three clues and an illustration about a main character are given so that we can guess the character and novel.

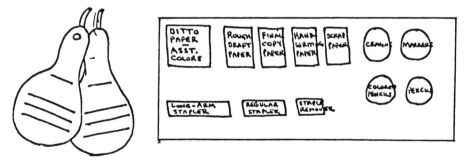

Figure 15–11   Suggestions for Independent Activities
From Julie Beers's third grade classroom.

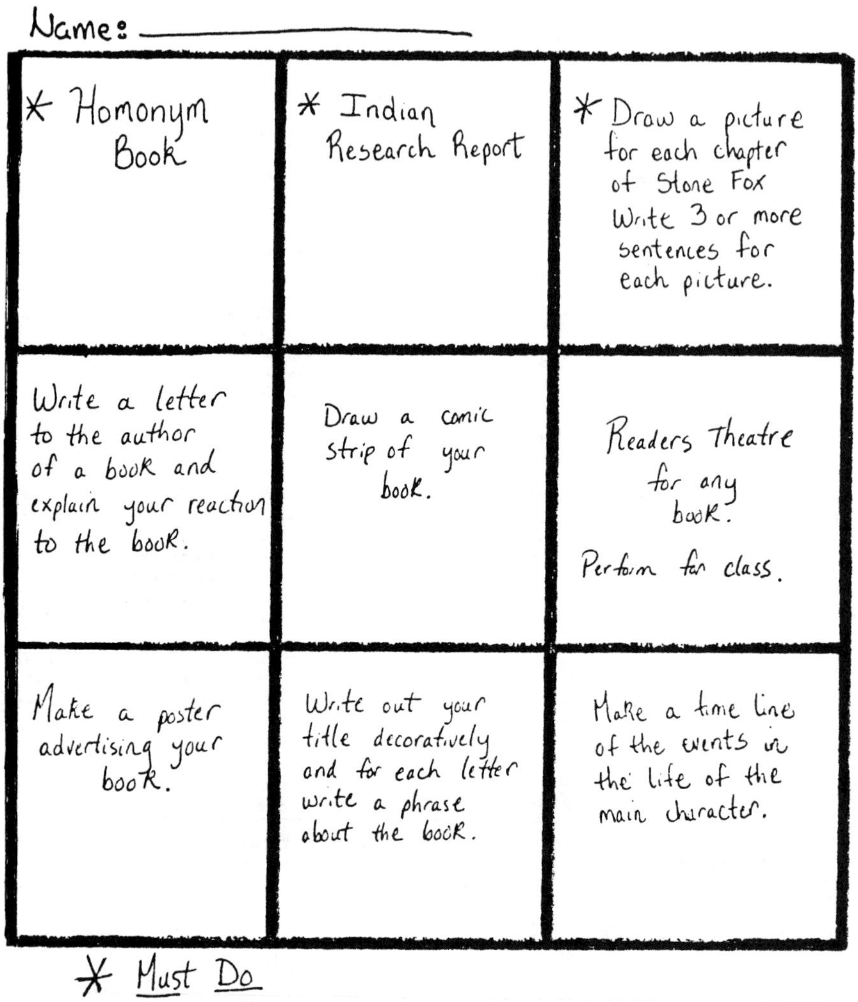

Name: _____

＊ Homonym Book	＊ Indian Research Report	＊ Draw a picture for each chapter of Stone Fox. Write 3 or more sentences for each picture.
Write a letter to the author of a book and explain your reaction to the book.	Draw a comic strip of your book.	Readers Theatre for any book. Perform for class.
Make a poster advertising your book.	Write out your title decoratively and for each letter write a phrase about the book.	Make a time line of the events in the life of the main character.

＊ <u>Must</u> <u>Do</u>

Managing Multiple Reading Groups

Teachers who are accustomed to teaching literature with a whole-class approach panic at the thought of juggling multiple reading groups. Especially worrisome is the independent work, the seatwork component. How to design reading time so students are productively involved in meaningful activities when the teacher is meeting with a reading group has been a challenge for all of us.

We are constantly reminded how difficult the transition is from workbooks and packaged activities to more meaningful independent work when we have visitors. Third grade teacher Linda Cooper and I have noticed that many visitors to her classroom spend most of their time examining the independent work the children are doing, even when they could be observing her facilitating an interesting reading group discussion. We are reminded that until teachers feel they can manage the independent work component, multiple reading groups do not seem possible for many teachers.

Organizing for Reading Groups

We find that we can meet with three reading groups in about one hour. When getting started with groups and using three different books, some teachers find that rotating the three books among the heterogeneous groups works well to give everyone a chance to read each book. Most of us try to meet with groups daily. Others work out a system they are comfortable with, for example, meeting with reading groups three days a week and conferencing with students individually two days a week. As long as students have lots of daily opportunities for reading and writing, with teacher guidance and independently, there is no one right or best way to set up groups. Because reading groups are used mostly for discussion once the child is reading fluently, all the important points about the reading surface in a fifteen-minute period. (See Chap. 6, "Responding to Literature: Later Transitions," for specific procedures and management of the reading group.)

In addition to heterogeneous grouping, it is also important to meet with the student or a small group of students who are experiencing difficulty reading the common text. While heterogeneous grouping works well for discussion and collaboration, it is still our job to teach students at their instructional level. We need to take time daily to guide students in figuring out unknown vocabulary, attacking new words, integrating all cueing systems, and practicing reading for fluency.

Multiple Reading Groups in Grade 1

As previously mentioned, until children are reading easily, I like to meet with homogeneous groups for at least the first several months of school. I find that we go through about one book a week per group and that most of the independent activities spring from the books and from the children's own ideas. When the classroom is child centered, the students are deeply involved in developing activities and creating projects right along with you.

I have found it works well to do as much as you can during group time so you are not spending a lot of time on outside planning. In addition to on-the-spot teaching, independent work can be created in group. For example, the final copy of an innovation on a text can be done during group time. This also has the advantage of students seeing the teacher modeling and writing in front of them. As an example, early in the school year, after a group of struggling first-graders had read *I Climb* (DLM, 1976), using blank ditto paper we did a shared writing modeled on the simple text. The students decided to write an *I Jump* book following the same pattern and number of pages but using the names of students in the group. (" 'I can jump,' said Katie" was a typical page.) Reproducing the completed booklet so students could illustrate it and use it as another reading text took only five minutes. (See "Teaching for Strategies," pp. 138–144, for examples of strategy lessons in primary grade reading groups.)

Reading Group Rules, Grade 1

- Don't tell another person a word. Give the person time to try to figure it out.
- Follow along even if it's not your turn to read.

Finding a Comfortable Noise Level

Moving from a silent classroom to a classroom full of conversation is an adjustment for most of us. When I am with a reading group, I cannot concentrate if there is loud talking. I am comfortable only with students whispering, and I make that an expectation of students. With young children who have difficulty keeping their voices to a whisper, role playing seems to help.

Independent Work Time

As the whole language classroom evolves, students know what is expected of them and how and where to seek help when they need it. Usually there are some required activities, but there are choices as well. Many of us have found that a good plan is to expect the reading assignment to be done first. Above grade 1, this assignment frequently involves silent reading and response in the literature response log. There may also be a required project connected with the read-aloud book or curriculum. For example, activities may be related to a field trip or care of classroom pets, or communicating-writing to parents or people relevant to a topic of study. Included also are optional activities, such as are described in "Literature Extension Activities" (pp. 87–102), or skills booklets connected to literature (pp. 135–138). See Figures 15–9 through 15–11 for three teachers' expectations during independent work time while reading groups were taking place and pages 439–440 for samples of "opportunities."

Some choices and opportunities have included, but are not limited to, sustained silent reading, writing a draft, journal writing, listening to a tape of a story, using the overhead projector (placed on the floor with the week's poems on transparencies), responding to literature (through the reading log or literature extension activities), editing, peer conferencing, working at the computer, following a filmstrip, and making a tape.

While demonstrations will be necessary for some of what will be done during independent work time, most of reading time will be spent reading and writing. With traditional seatwork, it typically takes at least fifteen to thirty minutes daily just to explain what students are to do. We need to be questioning that kind of time being spent on activities of questionable value.

A difficult transition for many of us has been to think of the time children spend reading and listening to books during their independent work time as valuable. Used to seeing products and completed pages, teachers need time to value activities where the results are not so concretely visible. Even more difficult for many of us is the concept of allowing children choice in the work they do. Providing choice allows children to pursue a highly engaging activity without interruption.

First grade teacher Jim Henry notes that when his students were given more choice during independent work time—including choosing the format and the project—more students became engaged with their work, more time was spent on the task, and the quality of work improved. Jim moved from mandatory projects, where he set up the format and was requiring a certain number of completed pages a day, to offering students "invitations" to choose from a variety of options. Jim comments, "Looking back, I see that I was giving kids a lot of 'busy work.' I spent a lot of time trying to convince them that the dittos and fragmented writing were important when they weren't."

Jim notes that students did not automatically monitor their time well. A weekly form we developed proved to be an effective management tool (see Figure 15–12). Students kept all their contracts and work in a folder Jim looked at daily and collected weekly. He took anecdotal notes on students' projects and conferenced with students as needed. (See also Figure 15–13 for a daily management plan developed by second grade teacher Elaine Weiner to put students in charge of their work.)

Another effective management tool for promoting appropriate behavior during independent work time is first to do a shared writing of behavioral expectations. I find it works well to treat the shared writing as a draft and make modifications with students as problems arise. The following was a first draft from a grade 2 class.

Rules for Independent Work

1. Work quietly.
2. If you have a question, use a whisper voice and ask someone at your table.
3. Work at your seat on
   reading
   journal
   any other assignment given.
4. When you finish your work
   read free choice book
   listen to a tape
   go to art center
   use the computer
   practice cursive handwriting
   work on Have-a-Go sheet
   illustrate published book
   get a game to play quietly (up to four people).

Organizing for Visitors

We have many visitors that come to find out more about whole language and a literature approach to reading. We are very careful to tell all visitors that we are in transition, that we are still at the beginning stages of moving toward whole language, and that we are all learners too. After several years of trial and error, we have worked out a system for visitors that works well for both the visitors and us teachers. I share our procedures so that you may adapt what is useful to your own school.

Visiting teachers and administrators are first invited to attend our weekly whole language support group with the hope that they may see it as a possibility for

Figure 15-12   Weekly Plan: Two First Grade Students

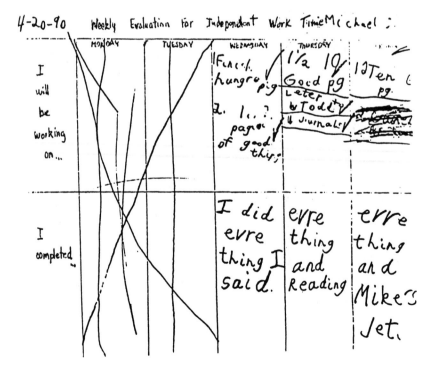

Figure 15-13   A Second-grader's Daily Management Plan

MY WORK PLANS   *(daily)*

NAME _____ *alexander* _____

DATE *June 7* _____

THIS IS WHAT I NEED TO DO:

1. *Science Experiment* _____
2. ✓*Fairy tale* _____
3. ✓*Reading* _____
4. ✓*Reading log* _____
5. *Wether Experiments* _____
6. ✓*Wether Puzzle* _____

Check off all items that you have finished.

Take home any work that is not finished for homework.

Please have your parents initial this paper after your homework is finished.

support and staff development in their own building. Then visitors have the opportunity to visit classrooms and explore the WEB, where our literature collection is housed. Finally, the principal, myself, and whatever teachers are available meet with the group of visitors to answer their questions, clear up any confusions, and to learn from each other.

While at the beginning certain teachers were selected to have visitors, in the last few years any teacher who chooses to have her classroom open may do so. In keeping with whole language philosophy, which respects all learners, no matter where they happen to be in the process, this more democratic format presents a realistic picture of the change process and is fair to and respectful of all teachers.

Also in keeping with whole language philosophy, our visitors are not assigned to particular rooms but may choose the classrooms they want to visit. They receive a welcome letter describing the makeup of the building and school district, some general information about whole language in our district, a map of the building, a schedule, and a brief description of what will be going on in the classrooms that are open for visitation.

Additionally, some visitors also receive a detailed description of what is going on in a particular classroom. Some teachers have taken visitations as an opportunity for an authentic writing experience. The teacher and students do a shared writing of what visitors can expect to observe in the classroom. Some of these pieces are detailed and include an explanation of procedures in reading, writing, and other areas. These handouts—along with encouraging visitors to talk with students about their questions—allow the teacher to continue teaching without interruption. The descriptions of language learning also allow the visitor to better understand what is happening in the classroom. These shared writings may also serve as self-evaluations for teachers. Teachers note how their students are perceiving reading, writing, and other language-curriculum processes in the classroom.

Utilizing Library Services

Librarians are valuable resources available in every community. They are aware of the latest and best books published and have a wealth of information on these books. They are experts at finding the books and resources teachers need.

Even if your school does not have a library or librarian, you can use your public libraries to enrich your curriculum and support your teaching. Susan Scheps, supervisor of the children's department at one of our local public libraries, says, "I have never met a children's librarian from a public library who wouldn't be thrilled to be approached by a teacher for any kind of help at all—read-alouds, special projects, research, anything."

In addition to our public libraries, we are fortunate in our district to have libraries and librarians in every school building as well as a district library media office that supports and facilitates the operation of all our libraries. Most book and media orders and requests for laminating and spiral binding of Big Books and blank books go through the district library office under the leadership of Ellen Stepanian.

While the services discussed in this section relate to our district, my hope is that you will see possibilities and options for your own school and district.

• *Check your public library resources.*   Most public libraries will arrange for you to sign out multiple copies of books for your literature program if given sufficient notice. With limited school or district budgets, the local public library system may be used to supplement the school and library resources. In an effort to support literature-based reading, some public libraries now have available twenty or so paperback copies of many titles, and often the books can be signed out for three or four weeks. If such a service is not yet available in your area, you may want to work with your local schools and public libraries to make it a reality.

• *Communicate with your librarian.*   Let your librarian know what kinds of books and resources you need. For example, if you are looking for predictable books or various versions of a familiar tale, your librarian can alert you to books already existing in the collection as well as new and recently acquired books.

Share bibliographies from workshops and professional books with librarians. Many of the books you are interested in may already be in the library collection, and your librarian can locate them for you.

Also, share articles and information from workshops about whole language. Include librarians in staff development efforts. Librarians will be better able to assist you if they understand the principles of whole language and how those principles apply to teaching and learning in the classroom.

• *Establish a classroom library.*   Support your independent reading program by using your school and/or public library to bring books into the classroom. Often books may be borrowed for an extended period of time, and you will probably be able to sign out thirty to fifty books at once.

• *Begin a professional library.*   If you do not already have a professional library for teachers in your school, be the impetus for starting one. You might want to begin by subscribing to newsletters and journals. (See *Resources for Teachers* for recommendations.) If a professional library already exists, recommend to the librarian outstanding new titles for purchase.

• *Find out about available media.*   Check with your librarian for video, filmstrips, cassettes, public television programs, and other resources to enrich literature and content area study. Find out about programming and scheduling for "Reading Rainbow," "Long Ago and Far Away," and other exceptional public broadcasting opportunities.

• *Become familiar with authors.*   Librarians can gather many books by one author, information about authors, and addresses to write to authors, and they may be willing to help arrange an author visit or a Young Authors' conference in your school or local area. Public librarians also inform teachers of author visits to local schools and bookstores.

• *Incorporate nonfiction books into your reading program.*   Consult your librarian to learn about and to incorporate nonfiction into your reading program. With a literature approach to reading, most of the emphasis has been on fiction, but children also need to appreciate nonfiction as an important genre. Fortunately, more and more high-interest, beautifully illustrated and easy to read nonfiction books have been published. Librarians are more likely than teachers to be familiar with the latest and best in nonfiction—including books in enlarged print, books with outstanding illustrations, and books on timely topics. Your public library budget will usually allow for a more extensive nonfiction collection than your school library.

• *Let librarians know what your classroom needs are several weeks in advance.*

Multiple copies of books   If your school district has libraries in each building, often your librarian can get you multiple copies of a desired title by borrowing from other buildings. Your local public library may be able to do the same and may even be able to extend the usual loan period.

Resources for a unit of study   Librarians are terrific resources for planning and implementing thematic units. Not only will they help gather resources, but often they are willing to come into classrooms and work with teachers if the teacher requests it. Some school librarians will also prepare written bibliographies for content areas or thematic units. For example, a librarian can compile a list of math-related literature, books on handicapped people, environmental issues, or whatever topic is being studied.

When the local public library is notified ahead of time that a teacher will need lots of books for an upcoming project, the librarian can temporarily extend the loan period on books related to the topic and can designate certain titles as reference books for a set amount of time. In that way, more students have access to the books, and librarians can provide better service to students.

• *Talk to your public librarian about the arrangement of easy readers.*   Our local public libraries have recently changed the way beginning reading books are organized. All grade-level designations have been removed from books. Books—up to chapter books—are now categorized to reflect readability levels based on multiple factors, rather than just readability formulas. Books for children are divided into three sections—"Get Ready" (easier), "Get Set" (medium), and "Go" (harder) —roughly based on the readability and book-leveling system given in *Transitions* (Routman, 1988). Picture books and chapter books are organized into separate sections.

Local librarians were finding that strict adherence to grade levels to categorize books was inconsistent with what the schools were trying to promote with literature use and was giving parents the wrong message. Parents were coming to the library asking for "hard" books, believing their children would become better readers with books at a higher level. The librarians find that the new organization system supports what librarians have always done when helping connect children and books. With a young reader, they are likely to ask, "What have you read lately?" and then suggest, "Take a look at this book. Read this sentence." Librarians find that this more natural approach to books has promoted wider reading among students and a more relaxed approach to book selection with parents.

• *Support a summer reading program.*   Our school librarians publish an annual annotated reading list that goes home with students at the end of the school year. Such a list gives guidance to children, parents, and teachers and narrows the selection when there are so many books to choose from. Most public libraries sponsor motivational summer reading activities. Invite your local public librarians into your classroom to talk about summer reading and the programs they offer. We find that when students read widely over the summer, they make gains in fluency, vocabulary, and comprehension. Communicate with parents to make them aware of summer reading opportunities.

Organizing a Book Collection

Getting Money for Books

Jean Sylak, our director of elementary education, notes that the cost of moving from a basal-workbook reading program to a total literature program initially cost approximately the same amount as adopting a new basal series. In addition, the thousands of dollars that used to be spent annually for workbooks have gone toward replacing books and updating the schools' collections. However, our district budget for art supplies doubled after we made a commitment to move toward whole language.

Some teachers in other districts have been able to use the money that used to go for consumable workbooks and worksheets to purchase paperback literature. Other teachers have written grant proposals for books and/or enlisted the help of their Parent-Teacher Association to raise funds.

My recommendation is that whatever your budget, put most of the available funds into books, not programs. Except for the very early levels, where children need lots of easy reading material that is not always available as literature, books are your best investment. We have also chosen to invest in paperbacks that have not been specially coated for durability—and cost more—so that we can buy as many books as possible.

Selecting Titles for Purchase

Before ordering books for a literature collection, it is important to be familiar with the best of children's literature. The "Recommended Literature" by grade levels (k–12) and categories (blue pages) will be helpful in guiding you in organizing and ordering your own classroom, building, or district collection. Also, use your own personal favorites, and check with your librarian and other teachers for suggestions.

A collection of quality literature has become a priority in our district. We started with a core collection of books in each elementary building, which included approximately seven titles per grade level with enough copies to be used whole class or in small groups. (Each kindergarten class also received *The Story Box* [Stage 1, The Wright Group], which included twenty-four Big Books and accompanying little books.) In general, if there were four classes at a grade level, then enough copies of a title were purchased for two full classrooms. In addition, a supplemental collection, based on teacher and librarian recommendations—and titles suggested in *Transitions* (Routman, 1988)—were purchased for each k–4 building. Ten copies of more than 300 titles were purchased. The quantity was less for Big Books. The grade level assigned to the books is based on teacher input and is determined within each building. While the core books are used only at the designated grade level, or at a higher grade level, the supplemental books are used by the entire building.

We continue to meet by grade levels several times yearly to discuss the use of the books and to update our collections. Based on the recommendations of teachers and librarians, our district library media office orders books to be evaluated for possible purchase. For example, grade 1 teachers felt they needed a nonfiction book in the core collection. Thus, *Chickens Aren't the Only Ones* by Ruth Heller was purchased in Big Book and little book form after first grade teachers had had an opportunity to discuss possible titles. In grade 4, teachers decided they no longer wanted to use one core book that had been originally selected. In its place, teachers chose to use Cynthia Rylant's book of short stories, *Every Living Thing*, and copies were ordered through the library media office.

In addition to the common core collection in each building, every building orders titles, through each principal's budget, to meet student and teacher needs. For example, in the building where I am based, teachers sought more multicultural titles, especially African-American literature. Several teachers took the responsibility for recommending quality titles, and approximately twenty new books, in multiples of ten, were ordered. We have also been able to secure new titles through the generosity of the Parent-Teacher Association.

Housing the Collection

Each of our elementary buildings has a central location for housing the literature collection and a committee that is responsible for managing the collection. Often it is parent volunteers who oversee the organization of the book room. In the building where I am based, we house all our books in a former book storage room, and we call the room the WEB. Conduit pipe, secured by eye bolts, has been installed to hang our Big Books on skirt hangers. "Notes on the Use of the WEB" are given to all teachers the first week of school. (See Appendix F for specifics on our WEB procedures and organization.)

I believe that a central storage area, open equally to all teachers, is necessary for the successful functioning of a literature program. In the building where I am based, our literature collection—which includes core books, commercial books, teacher-made Big Books, and supplemental literature in various genres—is open to all classroom teachers, the L.D. teacher, the L.D. tutor, the Chapter 1 teacher, tutors, parent volunteers, and the teachers of the behavior-disordered class and the developmentally handicapped class. Books are signed out as needed. Teachers looking for a particular book need only look at the sign-out book (see Figure 15–14 for a sample page) to see who has the title and how long it has been signed out. All books are returned to the WEB at the end of the school year.

That all teachers should have equal access to all books cannot be emphasized enough. In that way, all teachers have an equal opportunity to sign out as many books as other teachers, and new teachers to the building—or teachers who have just moved into a literature approach—are not at a disadvantage. In one building a lot of resentment built up when a teacher refused to house "her" books (which had been purchased with district funds) in the central book area. One teacher even

Figure 15-14 A Page from the "Literature Collection" Sign-out Book

MERCER SCHOOL LITERATURE PROGRAM PAPERBACK BOOK COLLECTION

Note: Title* indicates reading group book.
Big Book* indicates teacher-made book.

GRD	TITLE	#	TYPE	Initial	# Books	Date Out	Date In	Initial	# Books	Date Out	Date In	Initial	# Books	Date Out	Date In	Initial	# Books	Date Out	Date In
1	I Was Walking Down the Road	1	BB																
1	I Was Walking Down the Road*	19	Fic																
1	I Wish I Was Sick Too	13	Fic																
1	I'll Be the Horse If You'll Play With Me	3	Fic																
1	I'll Fix Anthony*	10	Fic																
4	Ida Early Comes Over the Mountain	9	Fic																
	If A Poem Bothers You	9	Poetry																
1	If I Had*	7	Fic																
2/3	If I Were in Charge of the World	10	Poetry																
	If Kids Could Ask the President One Question	2	NFic																
2	If the Dinosaurs Came Back	1	BB*																
2	If the Dinosaurs Came Back	13	Fic																
1	If You Give A Mouse...	9	Fic																
1	If You Meet A Dragon	10	Fic																
2	If You Sailed on the Mayflower	3	NFic																
3	Iggie's House	2	Fic																
1	In a Dark Dark Wood	1	BB																
1	In a Dark Dark Wood*	7	Fic																

transferred to another building the following year, largely because of the negative feelings of inequity that resulted. Even though the teacher with all the books said that anyone could borrow those books from her room, it is a lot easier to take books from a central location where no special permission is needed.

Caring for and Repairing Books, and Book Sign-out

Without special handling and attention, our core books have on average lasted three years. Where teachers have taken time to talk with students about book care and handling and have made caring for and repairing books a priority, titles have lasted much longer. In the school where I am based, most of our collection is still in use after seven years of heavy use. That extra durability is due to the responsibility teachers put on students to take care of books and to the dedication of parent volunteers who spend many hours repairing our books.

Most book repairs involve the use of transparent book tape of various widths to reinforce bindings, covers, and inside covers. To facilitate the repair process, we have several tape system applicators (ordered from an office supply company) for volunteers and students to use. Additionally, our Parent-Teacher Association recently purchased us a plastic binding system that allows spiral binding of books where the pages are still usable but the binding cannot be repaired. The binding system is also used extensively in the publishing process in grade 2 and up and for school-wide publishing needs.

Under the leadership of Judy Heiskell, our parent volunteer WEB room coordi-

End of year book repair

Parent volunteer Judy Heiskell organizing the WEB

nator in the building where I am based, all books in our collection are inventoried, repaired, and reshelved at the end of the school year. Other volunteer parents and some older students work with Judy for several weeks in this time-consuming but worthwhile effort. For easy storage and handling, books are grouped by title with rubber bands. Books that can no longer be repaired and need to be replaced are returned to the library media office with a request for new copies.

Our school secretary, Bev Scoby, has entered our entire collection on computer, and she updates it each summer and prints out a new sign-out book for the upcoming school year. We are also extremely fortunate that Judy Heiskell continues to assume the responsibility for putting the new sign-out book together and to have it ready for the first week of school.

Ordering Paperback Books

Wholesalers

If you are fortunate enough to have two or three hundred dollars or more, you probably want to order from a book wholesaler in order to receive a sizable discount. Also, even though you may be ordering books from many different publishers, it is a great time saver to be able to place your entire order with one source. Most wholesalers will special order titles when they are not in stock. Additionally, many wholesalers are now stocking Big Books. Plan to order about 25 percent more book titles than the money allotted to allow for titles currently out of print and out of stock. You can often expect delivery on your order within a few weeks.

There are hundreds of reputable wholesalers across the country, and many have regional locations as well. Before choosing a wholesaler, check with your school librarian and find out who the school uses to purchase its books. Check to see if there is already a catalog available for you to look at. You may want to place your order directly through your school or district library to save opening up a new account. Also, if your order is included with a library order, you may be able to get a greater discount. Three reputable wholesalers with relevant information are listed below. Wholesalers usually have toll free 800 numbers for obtaining information and offer free catalogs on request. Inquiries should be directed to the school marketing department

THE BAKER & TAYLOR CO.
652 East Main Street
Bridgewater, NJ 08807-0920
(800) 775-1800

- Stocks over 50,000 titles in paperback—includes mass market and trade books
- Will create customized lists according to subject needs; call or write customer service
- Minimum order—ten assorted books
- Discount—negotiable, based on volume, with the following minimum level discounts:
  30% trade and hard cover
  10% single copies
- Ships within 48 hours of receipt of order

THE BOOKMEN INC.
525 North Third Street
Minneapolis, MN 55401
(800) 328-8411

- Well-organized catalog *Paperbacks for Young People* and monthly update includes over 3,000 titles for k–12; minimum order of twenty-five assorted books; will also special order titles not in catalog with a five-copy minimum (allow about four weeks)
- Books shipped within twenty-four hours of receipt of order
- Discount—40 to 43% plus freight, or 36% with free delivery

H. P. KOPPELMANN INC.
Paperback Book Service
P.O. Box 145
Hartford, CT 06141
(800) 243-7724

- K–6 catalog includes Big Books from several publishers; grades 7–12 catalog also available; stocks about 20,000 titles; school and library oriented
- Quality literature titles, some arranged in collections by recommended grade level, authors, and various categories
- Special orders accepted with a minimum of five of same title

- Well-done teacher book guides (by notable educators) for over 100 titles; teacher guides may be requested free with an order of 20 copies or more of a title or purchased for $1.00 each
- Videos available for many titles
- Discount: 30%, 5 or more of same title, $1,000 minimum order
    25%, 5 or more of same title, minimum order 25 books
    20%, 15 or more of same title, or 25 or more assorted titles
    10%, less than 25 assorted titles
- Shipping within 72 hours of receipt of order

Transitional Resources for Literature

For teachers and school districts that need a guided framework in the change process, the following commercial programs contain high-quality, balanced anthologies that use unabridged, authentic literature and also have helpful accompanying and management teacher resource books. While these collections are useful for organization in getting started in whole language, teachers are advised to supplement these programs with quality trade books.

DELMAR PUBLISHERS INC.
Two Computer Drive West
Box 15-015
Albany, NY 12212-5015
(800) 347-7707

> *Publishes* Early Bird Teacher Resource Book *for k-1 (geared more to k).*

GINN PUBLISHING CANADA INC.
3771 Victoria Park Avenue
Scarborough, Ontario MIW 2P9
(800) 359-5980

> *Publishes* Journeys *(k–6). Accompanying teacher resource books are excellent. See* Tuinman *in Resources for Teachers, "Literacy Extension Resources."*

HARCOURT BRACE JOVANOVICH INC.
Orlando, FL 32887
(800) 237-2665

> *Publishes* Impressions *(k–8) through Holt, Rinehart and Winston, Canada.*

HOUGHTON MIFFLIN COMPANY
One Beacon Street
Boston, MA 02108
(Write for your regional sales office and the 800 number that serves your state.)

   Publishes Houghton Mifflin Literature *(k–8).*

SCHOLASTIC INC.
P.O. Box 7502
Jefferson City, MO 65102
(800) 325-6149

   Publishes Bookshelf *(k–2).*

Reliable Sources for Literature for the Reading–Writing Classroom

The following selections have been found to support a literature approach to reading. Other materials from each publisher will need to be carefully examined to determine whether they are consistent with a whole language philosophy.

DLM
P.O. Box 4000
1 DLM Park
Allen, TX 75002
(800) 527-4747

   DLM publishes literature by Bill Marin, Jr., including a wonderful selection of poetry, Big Books, and a recent edition of the original Sounds of Language *series with teachers' editions for grades k–4 (editions for grades 5–6 will be available in 1992). Audio cassettes are available for k–2. Predictable science books in 9 by 12 inch format for grades k–2 are beautifully photographed and written. Poetry by Leland B. Jacobs is available on 12 by 18 inch posters and in small books. Two sets of six–eight-page predictable books for emergent readers,* This Is the Way I Go *and* Can You Do This? *are excellent for practicing early reading strategies.*

HARCOURT BRACE JOVANOVICH INC.
Orlando, FL 32887
(800) 237-2665

   Especially notable are the beautifully illustrated Bill Martin Big Books, which include such classics as Brown Bear, Brown Bear, What Do You See? *and* The Longest Journey in the World. *Each Big Book is sold only with eight small books, an audiocassette, and a teacher's guide. "Lap Books" (12½ by 16³/₁₆ inches)—high-quality wordless books and picture books by notable authors—are available for k–1 with accompanying small books and cassettes. HBJ also packages trade book libraries for grades k–6.*

HOUGHTON MIFFLIN COMPANY
One Beacon Street
Boston, MA 02108
(Write for your regional sales office and the 800 number that serves your state.)

   Houghton Mifflin Literature is a collection of multiple copies of six to ten quality paperback books for grade levels k–8, with Big Books included for k and 1. The program is a good transition for teachers moving away from the basal who still want some structure and guidance with authentic literature.

Author Videotapes of six authors (Lois Lowry, Bill Peet, James Marshall, David Macaulay, Scott O'Dell, and Elizabeth George Speare) give students a glimpse of how authors go about creating their books. Houghton Mifflin also publishes over thirty titles by Bill Peet, available in paperback.

MODERN CURRICULUM PRESS
13900 Prospect Avenue
Cleveland, OH 44136
(800) 321-3106

Content Big Books from Australia with accompanying standard-size books are beautifully illustrated and packed with interesting information. They include Earthworms, Five Trees, and Nikki's Walk (wordless) and are useful through the intermediate grades. Check the catalog for other quality Big Books. "Content Connection" is a fine collection of content trade books centered around a theme. "Folklore" contains a variety of folk tale titles.

NELLIE EDGE SEMINARS AND RESOURCES
P.O. Box 12399
Salem, OR 97309
(503) 399-0040

Nellie Edge is the creator and distributor of predictable Big Books of folksongs, rhymes, and chants for kindergarten and grade 1. Each spiral-bound Big Book—at an average cost of $13—is constructed of black and white tagboard for teachers to color. Every Big Book order also includes a black line master, allowing teachers to make accompanying personal copies for each student to "read." The company also has high-frequency word stamps for use with young children getting started with writing. Sponsors workshops for grades k–1.

RICHARD C. OWEN PUBLISHERS INC.
135 Katonah Avenue
Katonah, NY 10536
(800) 336-5588

Richard C. Owen is the distributor for Ready to Read books, a core program of real books — the national reading program in New Zealand — intended for five-, six-, and seven-year-olds. For the upper elementary grades, a quality collection of Canadian poetry and literature — as well as School Journals, a periodical with a variety of genres from New Zealand — is available. A delightful selection of Big Books and an excellent selection of professional books for teachers are also available. The company also sponsors high-quality whole language workshops.

RIGBY EDUCATION
P.O. Box 797
Crystal Lake, IL 60014
(800) 822-8661

This is a reliable source for quality Big Books and accompanying little books. "Contemporary Stories and Traditional Tales" are popular titles for shared book experience. Particularly appealing are "The Informazing Books" by Steve Molene, beautifully photographed informational texts for the elementary grades in Big Book *format and accompanied by an extensive teacher resource guide. Eight-page books, for guided and independent reading at the earliest levels, are very useful for gaining fluency and confidence at the emergent reader stage. "City Kids," natural language texts about everyday children's happenings, are delightful books for reading and for serving as writing springboards in the early grades.*

SCHOLASTIC INC.

P.O. Box 7502
Jefferson City, MO 65102
(800) 325-6149

Scholastic is the largest source of instructional paperbacks in the United States. Titles include predictable books, chapter books, multicultural books, "Reading Rainbow," and many award-winning books as well as over 120 Big Books. Scholastic also packages trade book libraries for classrooms and publishes excellent professional resources and concise, practical booklets for teachers. Sponsors classroom book clubs for children to purchase paperbacks at substantial discounts.

SHORT STORY INTERNATIONAL

6 Sheffield Road
Great Neck, NY 11021
(516) 466-6091

Short Story International is a nonprofit organization that publishes high-quality, multicultural short stories by authors from countries all over the world. These well-written, contemporary stories—often accompanied by illustrations—appeal to both reluctant and avid readers and are a nice change of pace from full-length chapter books.

There are three separate ongoing series. Annual subscriptions, single issues, or back issues are available. With an order of twenty or more subscriptions, a teacher's guide (which may also be ordered separately) is included.
Seedling Series—*geared to grades 4–7 (may be used in grade 3 as a read-aloud or for independent reading); includes seven to eight individually illustrated stories per issue; published four times a year.*
Student Series—*aimed at junior high to high school, grades 8–12; includes ten to twelve stories per issue; published four times a year.*
Short Story International—*for high school advanced placement, college, and adult readers; includes twelve to fifteen stories per issue; published six times a year.*

21ST CENTURY EDUCATION INC.

496 La Guardia Place #367
New York, NY 10012
(800) 866-5559

This source provides k–8 integrated, literature-based units of excellent titles in various genres, grouped by theme and grade level. The typical thematic teaching unit is priced between $100 and $200 and includes books, audios (if applicable), and instructional resources. On average, a unit contains thirty books (six to twelve individual titles) in hardcover and paperback. Units are customized and are meant to be used flexibly across grade levels and special groups. This is a very valuable source for teachers who want to use high-quality literature but are unsure of titles to choose and need support to develop an integrated instructional program centered around literature.

THE WRIGHT GROUP
19201 120th Ave. N.E.
Bothell, WA 98011
(800) 523-2371

> *The Wright Group is the publisher of* The Story Box, *a collection of Big Books and accompanying little books from New Zealand. Especially delightful are the predictable titles for kindergarten and grade 1, Level 1, Emergent Level. Many eight-page little books, which are good for beginning reading practice and developing fluency, are included in the* Sunshine Series *and nonfiction TWIG books. The Song Box includes traditional children's songs (such as "The Eensy Weensy Spider" and "She'll Be Comin' 'Round the Mountain")—available as Big Books with accompanying small books. Various resource books for teachers are available. The Wright Group offers integrated language workshops, k–6.*

16

Establishing Support Networks

*Using older students: a fourth-grader
helping a first-grader with his reading*

I believe teachers must take the lead in staff development and in establishing support networks in their districts. Traditionally, staff development has been undervalued in this country, with many school districts having no long-range plans for professional development. In order to move forward in our teaching, however, we must become knowledgeable practitioners. We need to understand sound staff development practices so we can put our theory and potential resources into effective practice.

This chapter explores effective staff development as well as support resources for teaching. While the examples given come from my school district and experiences, my hope is that you will be stimulated to think about investigating possible resources for staff development and support in your own school and district. No doubt, your available resources will be somewhat different. Nonetheless, you can use this chapter as a way to think about your own workable possibilities for establishing support networks.

Staff Development

We are a society conditioned to the quick fix, the one-shot workshop led by the expert from out-of-town. In education, change has traditionally meant new materials with, perhaps, some in-service on the use of those materials. Then, the following year, the focus usually shifts to a new subject. Rarely has change in school districts focused on an ongoing commitment that emphasizes educational philosophy and how we teach. Rather, the emphasis is usually on methodology and what we teach. Since whole language implementation necessitates a strong evolving theory base, the one-shot approach is particularly ineffective. For change to be effective, comprehensive, and lasting, staff development must occur cohesively over an extended period of time.

461

Staff development has traditionally been done *to* teachers and *on* teachers instead of *with* teachers and *by* teachers. My own personal philosophy views teachers as knowledgeable professionals who should be actively involved with planning and implementation. Teachers have a clear sense of what they need for growth and development; these needs must be seriously considered. Besides aiming at increased professional knowledge, staff development programs should include opportunities for teacher leadership, collegial interaction, decision making, and problem solving. Most important, effective staff development should lead teacher-learners toward continued inquiry and independence.

The terms "in-service" and "staff development" need clarification because they are sometimes used interchangeably. However, they do not refer to the same thing. While in-service may encompass more than one session and be a part of staff development, its goal is to provide specific information to staff with little or no follow-up. Usually the information is transmitted to the audience with minimal opportunities for interaction. On the other hand, staff development is an ongoing program that focuses on specific needs—for example, the district's, the students', or the teachers'. Staff development provides not only information but the time to process and integrate knowledge and practice. The goal of staff development is to improve conditions, whether it be the climate of the school or skills of the teacher.

My Beliefs and Goals about Staff Development

Because I believe it's important to be able to articulate one's philosophy, I state my personal beliefs and goals as an example of how you might explore your own. As you read this, I hope you will reflect on your own beliefs and develop your own theoretical framework.

Beliefs	*Goals*
• Staff development must be ongoing.	• Establish support groups that meet regularly. Put in place a three- to five-year staff development plan.
• Teachers must have choices.	• Allow voluntary attendance at support groups. Provide options in required staff development.
• Program change must be research and knowledge based.	• Read and discuss professional literature, attend conferences, and provide other opportunities for acquisition of theory.
• Teachers should be encouraged to attend professional conferences and participate in professional organizations.	• Allocate adequate discretionary funds, and make professional growth a priority. Have clear expectations for resourcing these opportunities.
• Teachers should be involved in district decision making.	• Include teachers in curriculum design, district evaluation procedures, and hiring new teachers.

Beliefs	*Goals*
• A teacher-to-teacher component is desirable and necessary.	• Recognize and utilize talented classroom and resource teachers for potential teacher leaders, staff developers, and coaches.
• Teachers need support in the change process.	• Give release time for in-service, and provide support staff to facilitate the change process.
• First-year teachers need additional support.	• Provide a mentor teacher/internship for at least one year.
• Teachers need opportunities to observe and interact with other teachers.	• Provide release time for peer observation and collaboration. Provide training for peer coaching.
• Teachers need time for collegial reflection during the school day.	• Use specialists, paraprofessionals, and parents to create blocks of time for discussion and planning.
• Effective change takes lots of time.	• Establish reasonable time lines for both staff development and teacher change.
• Different people need different support and time expectations.	• Make provisions for individual differences.
• All of these beliefs and goals also apply to administrators.	• Provide staff development opportunities for administrators. Expect administrators to participate actively.

Components of Effective Staff Development

Bruce Joyce and Beverly Showers, well-known researchers on effective teacher change, have outlined principles and components of effective staff development that have been widely accepted. They have found that for new concepts and strategies to transfer to classroom teaching, the components discussed below need to build on each other and be used in combination (Joyce and Showers, 1980). The following discussion applies their components to whole language teaching.

1. Presentation of Theory

Understanding the research and theory of literacy learning provides the rationale for a whole language instructional approach to teaching and learning. In-service by "experts" can fit here. Interactive discussion of professional reading and theory takes place regularly at our weekly language arts support groups. Development of theory is ongoing.

2. Demonstration or Modeling

Demonstrations show the learner how to do the skill or strategy and also increase understanding of the theory. Usually multiple demonstrations are necessary.

Teachers demonstrate for each other at our weekly language arts support groups as well as view effective professional videotapes. A major part of my job is demonstrating strategy lessons for teachers.

As a language arts resource teacher, I go into classrooms and demonstrate how shared reading, shared writing, journal writing, literature discussion, or any other component of whole language might be taught. I first meet with the teacher to discuss her needs and where she is in the change process. After the teacher has observed the demonstration lesson or specific intervention strategies, we discuss what has gone on and what the teacher is comfortable with and has questions about.

3. Practice under Simulated Conditions

The teacher tries out the new strategy when circumstances do not require managment of the whole class. Peer coaching is very effective here. In my role, I encourage and attempt to give the teacher confidence while she is trying out a new strategy. Then she takes time to practice on her own. Repeated practice will be necessary.

4. Structured Feedback

Structured feedback through careful observation gives the teacher an opportunity to reflect on teaching behavior. Structured feedback should be presented in a way that encourages teachers to draw their own conclusions. Feedback can come from peers, administrators, or self. I often observe a teacher trying out a new approach, and, afterwards, I meet with the teacher to give constructive feedback. I try to avoid the one-shot deal. For effective change, practice-feedback on the new instructional practice needs to happen at least several consecutive times. Before this can happen, there has to be a high level of trust between teachers.

5. Coaching for Application

For maximum transfer of new learning, coaching is the critical component. I define coaching as a collegial process where support, assistance, and companionship are given along with demonstrations and constructive feedback. Without coaching, strategies that have been tried out may never reach the application-to-teaching stage. This is what is inherently wrong with a one-shot approach to staff development; there are no personal support systems built in for employment of new knowledge.

Coaching is the largest and most satisfying part of my job. As a nonjudgmental coach, I try to be an encourager, cheerleader, and supportive and empathetic assistant. While I may try to guide the teacher in analyzing and interpreting teaching behaviors, I am not an evaluator or supervisor in any way. I am a peer working and collaborating with peers.

Coaching does not work if it is tainted by "evaluation," actual or implied. The "threat" of evaluation can hinder or destroy the mutual trust needed for effective change.

Teacher Support Groups

One of the most effective staff development vehicles that employs some of the principles just listed is the teacher support group. All over the country teachers are getting together and forming groups to support and encourage each other as they move toward meaning-centered, whole language teaching. In these meetings, teachers talk frankly about issues and concerns in their teaching and try to integrate theory and practice. Many of us have found that meeting with our peers has lessened our anxiety, fostered collegiality and collaboration, and promoted and confirmed professional growth. Perhaps, above all, we find out we are not alone; others have struggled along with us.

There are now many state and local understanding whole language networks, and even a Confederation of Whole Language Support Groups, called the Whole Language Umbrella, which provides a network for groups across the United States and Canada. Many of these groups are called TAWL (Teachers Applying Whole Language). I prefer the designation used by some California teachers I met; their TAWL stands for Teachers Attempting Whole Language. I also like the TAWL that stands for Teachers Approaching Whole Language and the one that translates to Talking About Whole Language. We have simply called our school and district groups Language Arts Support Groups or Whole Language Support Groups. Whatever name is used, it should be inclusive and welcoming to all interested teachers.

Getting Support Groups Going

Weekly Building Support Groups

When I first began my job as a teacher supporting other teachers in transition to whole language, I saw a need for teachers to have time to be together to share issues and concerns and to support each other. In addition, there was no way I could provide full support to all interested teachers in the school district. By meeting collegially, we could all learn from each other and grow professionally. Our meetings are a form of peer coaching. Through ongoing dialoguing and sharing with each other in the change process toward more effective teaching, we have become supportive communities.

Our weekly language arts support groups have been in place in each of our k–4 buildings since the fall of 1987. Since school does not begin until 9:15 A.M., we meet from 8:30 to 9:00 A.M. in the library or in a classroom. I serve as facilitator at four of the buildings; fourth grade teacher Joan Servis serves as facilitator in her building. For me this has meant five meetings a week. For teachers who choose to attend, this means one morning a week. Attendance ranges from about 50 to 90 percent of the staff, depending on interests, needs, and time demands. Some teachers attend faithfully every week; others have never come. This open door policy is an important aspect. It protects teachers' rights to attend voluntarily; it treats teachers as adults. The focus and agenda are set by the group, based on teachers' expressed needs. A copy of the agenda and applicable articles are distributed with the principal's weekly bulletin. The time and location of the meeting is announced over the public address system by the school secretary just before it is ready to begin.

We began haphazardly. The first year our district made a commitment to more meaningful approaches to reading and writing through literature, our agenda was fragmented and scattered, reflecting our own confusion and disorganization. Most of our concerns were related to practical and organizational matters—materials, activities, and management. One week we talked about one issue; the following week the agenda would be totally different. Looking back, that seems quite normal for the change process. We needed time to find our own way. That first year principals did not generally attend the meetings. They were sensitive to the fact that teachers needed time to express concerns and insecurities.

Getting started did not always go smoothly. At the first meeting in one building, a teacher dominated the half hour with complaints about teaching and students and almost sabotaged the entire effort. Not wanting to dominate or interfere, I let the teacher continue speaking. Teachers left very depressed, and several expressed unwillingness to return the following week. I wrestled with what to do. While I didn't want to quell free speech, the purpose of the group was teacher support, and this clearly wasn't happening. The next week, when the teacher returned and again tried to preside with negative comments, I intervened and said, "I'm sorry, I appreciate your concerns. However, what you're talking about are building concerns. The purpose of this group is teacher support." While I was sorry the teacher never came to another meeting, my intervention allowed the rest of us to move ahead in positive directions.

By the second year, we knew our needs better and, quite naturally, each building chose to focus in depth on an issue of concern. By the second or third years, principals were making an attempt to attend meetings, and most teachers welcomed their presence, input, and support. For the second and third years, a building focus might go on for several months. Usually I gathered journal articles, professional books, and resources and made copies of articles for interested teachers. Often we would begin by discussing a journal article that had been "assigned" the week before. An interest in and examination of whole language theory began to evolve in the second and third years.

Recently, we have focused on such issues as explaining whole language to parents, integrating spelling, portfolio assessment and evaluation, writing process, schoolwide holistic writing and scoring criteria, vocabulary and questioning, using a core literature book, taking a close look at standardized testing, strategies for at-risk students, and phonics. We have also used this time to share ideas and materials from conferences and to discuss activities and concepts that are effective and ineffective as well as to give feedback about new professional books and significant upcoming conferences.

One of our most successful focuses took place this last school year. All teachers and administrators in the k–4 buildings had an opportunity to view and discuss four whole language videotapes by Andrea Butler. This was the third year teachers were moving toward whole language, and there seemed to be a readiness to understand the theory better and relate it to classroom practice. Attendance was high, not only by classroom teachers and administrators but by special teachers, who agreed that Brian Cambourne's conditions of learning also apply in math, art, music, and physical education.

The art teacher said that she was becoming more conscious of children's needs to have some choice. The music teacher confirmed that if she wanted her students to do a research report on a composer, it was her responsibility to demonstrate report writing in music. The physical education teacher began to add writing to his program. For example, he asked students to write about their experience with the wind chimes, and when he talked about a forward roll with first-graders, he wrote "forward roll" on the chalkboard. Amazed first-graders told their classroom teacher, "Gosh, he can write too!"

One of the surprising outcomes of our weekly meetings has been seeing ourselves as experts. In one building, we focused on evaluation for three months. The interview forms, anecdotal records, and evaluation procedures we talked about, created, tried out, and eventually came up with were as good as any I have found in books on evaluation. Of course, we did our homework first. We observed our students carefully, and we read and discussed relevant journal articles before adapting many of the idea we came upon.

Another unexpected outcome has been finding out that when teachers act responsibly, we have some power. The push to do away with standardized testing in first grade began in one of our support groups and picked up momentum throughout the district. We continue to be activists on the standardized testing issue. One of our groups wrote a letter to the head of the corporation that publishes the standardized tests we use. We asked some hard questions about why the reading tests were not more compatible with recent research findings about reading as an interactive, constructive process. In addition to a detailed response, several representatives from the company came to one of our meetings, did a slick presentation, and answered our questions. When we learned that the company's newest tests could be normed for reading comprehension only—without the fragmented word study skills and phonics-in-isolation—we were vocal and successful in making that change a reality in our district. Based on research that calls for no standardized testing before grade 3 (Kamii, 1990), some of us hope to be influential in doing away with testing in grade 2.

Perhaps most important, we have become teacher researchers—reflective inquirers who have enough theoretical knowledge to look at our own teaching, ask and explore our own questions, and begin to trust and value what we are observing and finding. Our practice has continued to change as our theory has grown, so that now theory and practice seem less separate. Becoming a teacher researcher—with resulting effective and long-lasting change—may very well be the highest form of staff development we can hope for.

It is not difficult to get a support group started in your building. Even if there is only one other teacher to begin with, set up a regular time to meet. Keep your doors open and invite others to join you. Try to meet weekly, but even meeting monthly—or every few months—is better than not meeting at all. The hardest part is getting started for the first time.

An example of a weekly language arts support group   Two months before school ended, teachers in one k-4 building requested a meeting devoted to "sharing." A second grade teacher started that meeting by talking about, and passing around, the letters her students wrote from the point of view of Sarah as part of their literature study of *The Courage of Sarah Noble* by Alice Dalgliesh. She commented that all the important points of the story came out in the letters.

A third grade teacher then shared a new poetry book she had just read, *Sunrises and Songs* (McClure, Harrison, and Reed), and told how she was going to have her students keep poetry journals the next year. She also spoke about the influence of the book *For the Good of the Earth and the Sun* (Heard) on her teaching of poetry this year and how encouraged she had been by the poetry writing of children who had had no previous experience. She passed around poetry anthologies by her students.

A second grade teacher concurred and talked about what had happened since she had begun to immerse her students in poetry. Another second grade teacher told how she begins each day with a child (or teacher) reading aloud a favorite poem and how sometimes the whole class memorizes a preferred poem.

A third grade teacher expressed a need to talk about our new report cards. She felt further revisions were still needed. Discussion followed, and several teachers also spoke of the need for our district to come to some decision regarding portfolio assessment.

A fourth grade teacher shared resources and ideas from a hands-on science and environment conference she had attended the previous week.

Finally, we discussed future directions for our group. Several teachers requested a bibliography of recommended professional books for summer reading. (I shared with them the list and the books several weeks later.) One teacher spoke about the influence of Frank Smith's *Essays into Literacy* on her teaching and recommended we continue to read articles and discuss theory as it applies to our teaching. In closing, we decided to leave time near the end of school to discuss setting up the whole language classroom in the fall.

Looking at the diverse agenda of the meeting, it would be easy to dismiss it as unfocused. While most of our meetings tend to stay fairly focused on a topic we are exploring in depth, occasionally devoting whole meetings to the sharing of ideas and concerns fills an important need. Teachers request and enjoy the opportunity to share valuable teaching ideas based on reading and experience. Often books and ideas we share wind up being used and applied by other teachers. Allowing time to express concerns helps us understand each other's needs, redirect meetings so they stay meaningful to the group, and set new focuses. All of this is important for meeting the needs of the support group.

Sampling of support group agendas   Following are some notices of recent meetings that appeared in weekly bulletins in our k-4 buildings and which may be helpful for your own groups. It is important to keep the tone invitational and nonthreatening. On one bulletin, I had written, "Please come prepared to discuss . . . ," and some teachers took that to mean they were expected to do methodical readings of the attached journal article. After I have received feedback from some teachers, I was careful to say in the future, "We will be discussing . . . ." Even if teachers did not have the time to read the article, or had read only part of it, it was important that everyone felt welcome to attend.

- In continuing our focus on the writing process, we will be discussing the attached article, "Encouraging Meaning Making in Young Writers" by Juliebo and Edwards. Starting with kindergarten, we will also begin sharing expectations and processes by grade level.

- Come celebrate the writing process with your colleagues! We will begin going through the process as adults. Bury your fears, take a risk, and join the process movement. Everyone welcome!

- In our continuing focus and critical discussion and questioning, we will begin discussing *Danny the Champion of the World* by Roald Dahl. Please come prepared with questions and strategies for Chapters 1, 2, and 3 as well as with ideas for how you might introduce the book. We will begin promptly at 8:30 A.M. You may obtain a personal copy of this book from the office. That way you can write in it and keep the book.

- The Whole Language Support Group has been discussing the need for writing folders to be passed on to the next grade at the end of the school year. These folders would contain samples of the students' writing (probably three or four samples). To help us select samples, we have been discussing common criteria for evaluating writing. On January 31, the group will meet at 8:30 A.M. to develop broad criteria for evaluation. We will be developing criteria specific to each grade level, after examining students' writing samples on a topic that has been agreed upon across grades 1–4.

- Based on the concerns which emerged about testing and the group discussions on October 25, we will begin to work on organizing our ideas about having standardized testing consistent with whole language teaching. Please read the attached article, "Evaluation in the Holistic Reading/Language Arts Curriculum" by Richard Ammon.

- We will be viewing the first of four Andrea Butler videotapes on elements of whole language. This 35-minute videotape discusses Brian Cambourne's conditions of learning. Following the viewing, there will be small-group discussions. This is an excellent tape that is applicable to all teachers across the curriculum. You are always welcome to attend.

  In order to view the tape and have follow-up discussion, we need to begin promptly at 8:15 A.M. Those that attend may leave school fifteen minutes early. Your attendance is encouraged.

- We will begin demonstrating how to take a running record of a child's oral reading. This will be our focus for the next four weeks. If you are interested in this topic, it would probably be most beneficial to plan to attend all four sessions.

A District or Local Support Group

In addition to our weekly building support groups, we also have a district support group. Since the early 1980s, a group of teachers from across the district have been meeting about every six weeks. While our meetings began over lunch hour in one elementary building, we now meet in homes in the evening, and attendance averages twenty to twenty-five teachers. Recently, what has been particularly encouraging and exciting is the high school involvement. We now have at least several high school teachers and a professor from a local university in attendance regularly.

For our first district home meetings, invitations went out only to those teachers we felt were interested and committed. After a while, that approach seemed exclusive, and we now invite all professional staff in the district. Joan Servis has continued to act as secretary and to ensure that the meeting notices are sent out.

She sends a flyer to a representative in each school building, who duplicates and distributes the invitation to the staff. People who are planning to come let the host/hostess know. We also count on about five or six people showing up without having responded.

We also open our meetings to any teacher in any outside district who needs support and does not have a local group. At most meetings, we have teachers from three to five other school districts, occasionally from several hours away. Everyone is made to feel welcome. We have gained much from the experiences of our fledgling members, who keep us humble by reminding us how difficult and scary the starting process is. After a while we encourage visiting teachers to start their own local groups. At times, we have calls requesting on-the-spot help in starting a new support group. We invite the teachers requesting help to one of our meetings to see how the group functions, and usually they feel confident enough to go back and start their own group.

Our meetings have a relaxed, conversational format. We have no set agenda, and we charge no dues. We begin at 7:30 P.M. and end at 9:00 P.M., with a new meeting date set and someone volunteering a home for the next meeting. We alternate evenings of the week to allow people with commitments on a particular evening to be able to attend most of the time. While our meetings are very informal with no preset agendas or speakers, you may well prefer a more structured approach with topics planned for each meeting and occasional speakers. Use what works well for your group.

We usually begin by sharing a new professional book or two and passing it around. I, or another member, act as facilitator, which means only that we make sure everyone who wants to gets a chance to speak. Teachers share frustrations, concerns, activities, journal articles, techniques, questions, and anything that seems relevant to them. The small group size has allowed for lots of talk and exchange of ideas. The hour and a half format has encouraged high-level discussion.

Particularly exciting has been the sharing among cross-grade level teachers k–12. One English teacher commented, "I hear an idea from a second grade teacher, and I think, I could do that at the high school." A learning disabilities teacher shared how she had successfully tried working in the regular classroom after listening to a discussion on the harmful effects of pull-out programs.

During one meeting, high school English teacher Bill Newby shared his frustration with not being able to get many senior high school students to invest time in the revision process. He stated, "I'm working at trying to create an attitude, a tone for revision, but it's very difficult." Susan Mears, a first grade teacher, suggested Bill try a technique she uses. First, Susan has a parent come into her classroom and, in front of the children, the parent asks Susan questions and makes suggestions for a piece Susan has written. Then Susan models her revision process on the overhead projector. Students see two trusting adults talking knowledgeably and honestly about a piece of writing. Six weeks later, at our next meeting, Bill shared how, based on Susan's idea of adults modeling the writing process, he had invited high school teacher Dana Noble into his classroom to respond to his own writing. Students saw the struggle of two adults giving and receiving feedback. After the demonstration, Bill noted that more students were willing to share and respond to their own writing without feeling they were being criticized.

As a direct result of attending our district support group, a small group of our fifth and sixth grade teachers began a support group in their elementary school. Additionally, as a follow-up to a workshop he presented on whole language to the secondary English faculty, Bill Newby took the initiative to purchase Tom Romano's *Clearing the Way* for members of the high school English department who began devoting some of their meetings to discussing the book. Furthermore, influenced by the success of our weekly language arts support groups, math support groups have begun to meet every other week in several of our elementary schools.

Teachers' attitudes   Nan Bonfils, an American teaching in Malaysia, was visiting with me and other teachers in one of our schools recently. As visitors often do, she attended our langauge arts support group and commented on how struck she was by the level of commitment and reflective inquiry of our teachers. When she asked teachers why they come to these meetings, they spoke eloquently about the opportunities for inspiration, refocusing, rethinking, reflecting, and sharing successes and failures.

Darla Carlson, a first grade teacher, says she found the weekly support group meetings in her building "solid" and very helpful. She commented,

> At first, as a new teacher, I was too self-conscious to ask questions and speak up at our meetings. When I heard other people talk about their concerns and what wasn't going well, it helped to know I wasn't the only one. Probably what was most helpful were the other colleagues on my grade level who were so willing to be supportive.

Kindergarten teacher Karen Sher comments,

> Without question, the weekly support groups have been one of the most important stimulants for my growth. Sharing ideas and concerns with peers on my grade level and other grade levels has been invaluable. The literature—books and articles—that came my way, via the support group, helped to satisfy an intellectual hunger and provided me a framework to connect practical classroom teaching to theory. I appreciated having the readings spread out over time so I did not feel overwhelmed. Understanding the *why* in my teaching has helped me define where I wanted to go next.

Often at our meetings, teachers' confusions about an issue are cleared up. For example, one teacher said she was relieved to hear she could allow kids to read more than one chapter at a time or just let them read and discuss. She had been feeling guilty for not having more seatwork. On another occasion, a fourth grade teacher admitted she no longer felt guilty reading aloud to her class, but she was still struggling with whether it was all right to read aloud sometimes in place of having reading groups. Third grade teacher Lee Sattelmeyer comments, "One of the reasons the support groups worked is because once the idea of support was broached, teachers were able to acknowledge their own needs and confusions without feeling guilty."

Teachers also share positive happenings. Fourth grade teacher Janet Houk acknowledged her appreciation for the fine job primary grade teachers were doing in reading and writing. She noted, "I have no nonreaders. I've never before had a group of kids who all love to read. They like to write, too."

Finally, we still have our frustrations. Some teachers feel that having dialogues about theory and philosophy through reading and discussing journal articles and professional books needs to be a far greater priority. One teacher told me, "Far too few of our group see the value in understanding the theory behind whole language. I think we're still too activity focused." Some mornings teachers arrive late, and it seems as though we have barely gotten started when our time is up. Other teachers say they have felt threatened occasionally when a peer has disagreed with them. Some weeks teachers have been so busy that few have read the "assigned" journal article. Our meetings are not perfect. We are in process and probably always will be. We will continue to have dialogues and to meet and share our beliefs, frustrations, concerns, and goals.

Reflections   Undoubtedly, in spite of our occasional frustrations, the weekly support group has been one of our best staff development efforts. It is relevant, teacher centered, and voluntary, and development occurs slowly and deliberately over long periods of time. The support group attempts to address our needs as teacher learners and to promote leadership in our teaching as well as in district decision making. It has given us a chance to talk with each other, share ideas, and get to know each other better. The support group has diminished the isolation of teaching and fostered respect for colleagues. Cross grade-level sharing has given us an appreciation and understanding of the learning and language processes from grade to grade. While we recognize we have lots of room for growth, our support groups have been an important impetus for change for many teachers.

Administrators as Staff Developers

While support groups make a significant impact on teachers' professional growth, teacher growth and change are even more powerful when strongly supported by the building administrator. The most effective administrators are staff developers. They have frequent, nonthreatening communication with their staff, work with their teachers on a collaborative plan of action, and raise teachers' self-esteem by recognizing and valuing their individual strengths and teaching styles. They also are actively involved in the change and learning process. They read professionally, attend workshops, make an effort to demonstrate effective teaching strategies, and take a leadership role in the change process. Additionally, the most effective administrators have moved away from the traditional boss-employee relationship to a collaborative partnership based on shared decision making.

Elementary principal Rebecca Kimberly is an effective staff developer. Literally, she provides opportunities for her staff to develop to their full potential. When she reads professional journals, she thinks of her teachers' interests and abilities. If she reads an article that she thinks will particularly interest one of her staff, she makes a copy for that teacher. She lets her staff know of upcoming conferences, encourages their attendance, and attends conferences with her teachers. She also attends conferences to promote her own development as an effective administrator. She is frequently—as are the other administrators in our district—an active participant in our weekly language arts support groups. Additionally, she encourages and provides opportunities for peer observation. She has facilitated teachers' interest in learning from one another by hiring a substitute teacher for a half day so a teacher can spend the morning observing in classrooms in the building or in another building.

In place of the traditional faculty meetings that deal solely with details of running the school, Rebecca's bimonthly faculty meetings include opportunities for professional growth. Teachers report on conferences they have been to and share successful teaching strategies. An advisory committee, composed of grade-level representatives and others, meets with her monthly to resolve building issues. A written weekly communication provides detailed information of events, policies, and procedures.

Rebecca also involves teachers in the hiring process. When three kindergarten aides were to be hired, all three kindergarten teachers participated in the interview process and gave feedback. Each of the three teachers received the aide that was his or her first choice. When there are openings for new teachers, Rebecca uses a committee process that includes and respects her teachers' recommendations.

Finally, every few years she asks her staff to do an extensive, anonymous evaluation of her performance and to make recommendations. Based on that feedback, she sets goals for her own professional development. This past year, based on that feedback, Rebecca made a greater effort to spend more time in classrooms and provide feedback to teachers about progress toward their goals.

Jean Church is another example of an administrator who has taken a leadership role in the staff development process. As a curriculum coordinator in Indiana, she has been instrumental in getting her district to make a five-year staff development plan for the implementation of whole language. Starting with a district-wide language arts committee, workable long-range goals were established, and specific goals were outlined for the first three years. The goal for the first year was to build a knowledge base of whole language theory among teachers, administrators, parents, and students. To back up that commitment, the district bought a professional library for every school with at least a dozen current titles, some in multiple copies. Every faculty member was expected to read one self-selected professional book each semester and to try to implement some of the book's ideas. One faculty meeting a month was devoted to discussing and reacting to those professional readings. The second year's goal was continued reading and study at building levels as well as implementation of a process writing approach through trained peer colleagues. Goals for the third year included continued reading and study, refinement of the process writing approach, and implementation of a literature-based conference approach to reading. To accommodate the specific needs of teachers and principals, all participants completed a survey at the start and close of each school year to help identify needed revisions in the staff development plans.

Valuable Resources for Support

The reality is that whole language, or any effective approach to teaching and learning, cannot be fully implemented without administrative support. Unfortunately, that support is not always available. This section looks at the importance of administrative support and how to foster it and examines other available and valuable resources for teachers and schools, including peer tutoring, older students, Reading Recovery, parents, and grants. The chapter concludes with some thoughts on teacher education and future directions for whole language.

Getting Administrative Support

I believe that significant curricular and social change in a school environment cannot be put in place without administrative understanding and support. I think one of the reasons support from administrators has traditionally been slow in developing is that most administrators lack university training and experience in early childhood education. In general, while the literacy movement in schools has evolved in the primary grades, most principals have had experience and training at higher grade levels. Even when administrators seem to understand whole language philosophy, moving beyond mere knowledge of whole language to providing effective support is sometimes difficult to achieve. However, unless administrators become actively involved, whole language cannot survive.

We teachers can do several things to try to facilitate support from administrators.

• *Attending workshops and conferences*   Make every effort to get your administrator to join you at conferences. Often what happens is that teachers attend workshops, come back to school excited about new possibilities, and then try to convince their administrators of the changes they want to make. The change process is a lot easier if you can get your administrator involved at the ground level. If your administrator says there are too many things to be done at school, and she cannot take the time, offer to assist with a task or two so "time" can be created. If administrators are unable to attend, try to bring back tapes of presentations and share handouts and books. Take time to share aspects of the conference with your administrator; the importance of open communication cannot be overstated.

In my experience, it's the rare administrator who goes to conferences with her teachers. Ann Scholl, a principal of an urban elementary school with 800 students, attends conferences with her teachers several times each year. When I asked her how she was able to leave such a large building, she said, "I just make it a priority. Staff development is one of my major goals, and I find supporting my teachers in this way pays big dividends in the long run. It helps us work and plan as a team and become more effective educators."

Another exception is assistant superintendent of schools Bob Justice. When Bob invited me to facilitate a three-day workshop on the implementation of whole language, not only was he very involved in the planning, he also attended all the sessions. Based on my experience, this is quite exceptional. Typically, central office administrators are present for the introductions, and then they are in and out briefly at various points during the day. Bob's uninterrupted attendance gave a powerful message to teachers: He valued the workshops; he too was a learner; he was interested in teachers' questions and reactions; and he would be there to support the change process.

Some conferences have made attendance by the principal or an administrator a prerequisite for teacher attendance. This is not a bad idea. Some reluctant administrators have come to understand some of the theoretical basis for whole language through mandatory attendance.

• *Keeping administrators informed*   Make it a point to invite your administrator into your classroom regularly to see the reading-writing-speaking-listening process in action. Make your principal aware of any curricular changes you are thinking of making. Make copies of noteworthy journal articles, with your underlinings and highlighting, and let your administrator know a discussion of the articles would be welcomed.

I am constantly putting important articles in my principal Bernice Stokes's mailbox and sharing with her new ideas, current research, and information about upcoming conferences. Such sharing is a way for us to have a continued dialogue about news of the profession and possible educational directions. Bernice is interested and knowledgeable and seems to appreciate this opportunity for us to grow in understanding and applying whole language principles.

When I returned from the annual Reading Recovery conference in Columbus, Ohio, in January 1990, I shared in detail (through my notes and a tape I purchased) the research Richard Allington had presented on the negative effects of most pull-out programs on at-risk children. Based on that research and on our common interest in better serving the at-risk population, I proposed that I work with small groups of children as a supportive teacher *in* primary grade classrooms for the next school year. This proposal became a reality. I don't believe it would have happened without our close communication.

I am also careful to keep my principal well informed about daily happenings. If I am having a visitor, if a parent has contacted me, or if I am having a problem with a student, I place a brief note in my principal's mailbox. In that way, she is kept up to date, and she has no chance of being embarrassed by lack of knowledge of a situation.

It is not only principals whose support we need. Invite your superintendent and board of education members to in-services and support groups. As they come to understand the theory underlying whole language, they tend to commit more moral and material support.

Support for Administrators: What to Look for in Classrooms

To support their teachers, administrators often want to know what to look for when observing in whole language classrooms. One principal told me, "The teachers are leading, and I am following." Many teachers are currently more knowledgeable about whole language theory and practice than their administrators. However, in a sincere effort and desire to be better able to support their teachers, administrators have asked, "What are some evidences I might look for in a brief classroom observation to assess the application of whole language principles?" What follows are some questions that may be helpful to keep in mind during a classroom observation. In just ten or fifteen minutes, an administrator would be able to "read" the whole language climate of the room. Teachers may want to share these questions with their administrators and may also want to think about them for their own self-evaluation.

• *Who's doing the talking?* Is the teacher's voice the main voice, or are students doing most of the talking? Does every child have an opportunity to be heard? Are teachers directing with authority or guiding and leading from behind?

• *Do the students know the routines and procedures?* Do the students go to the teacher every time they have a question, or do they know the routines, assume responsibilities, use peers as helpers, and assume some self-management? Do things seem disorganized, or is there a well-planned flow from one activity to another?

• *Are the bulletin boards by and for the children?*   Is children's work displayed everywhere? Are the bulletin boards done by the children, with samples of writing, illustrations, and projects, or are they commercial, perfect, and cute?

• *Does the seating arrangement and teacher control allow for collaboration?*   Are students isolated in rows, or are they grouped so they can conference and assist each other?

• *Is the teacher with the children?*   Is the teacher always standing front and center or sitting at his desk, or is he mostly among the children, demonstrating and guiding as needed?

• *Is there an orderly hum of activity?*   Is the classroom silent, or are students quietly talking with each other and actively engaged in various enterprises?

• *Is reading time focused on comprehension and understanding?*   Are children spending most of reading time oral reading, working on "skills," and responding to literal level questions, or do they have frequent opportunities for responding to open-ended questions and participating in high-level discussion?

• *Is the independent work the children are doing meaningful?*   Are worksheets and workbooks being used with fill-in-the-blank formats, or are there other purposeful activities that encourage open-ended responses that require thinking and application of experience and knowledge?

• *Do the children have choices?*   Is everyone doing the same activity, or are there opportunities for children to make decisions about their work for the day? Are there self-selected reading and writing activities?

• *Are there opportunities for students to work together?*   Are all activities being completed individually, or are pairs and groups of children reading, writing, and problem solving together? Is there time for sharing?

• *Is there a classroom library and cozy reading corner?*   Are there all types of literature attractively displayed and easily accessible? Are there reference books, dictionaries, and thesauruses available? Is there a pleasant reading area where children can read in a comfortable position and with a friend?

• *Are there learning centers, especially a writing center?*   Is there an area where children can find different kinds of paper and writing supplies? Are there many opportunities for writing? Are there opportunities for exploration on topics of study?

• *Does the teacher use anecdotal records and observational data in evaluation?*   Does the teacher use only checks and grades in a grade book? Is there also evidence of informal, observational data?

• *Do the students seem happy and actively involved?*   Are the children passively completing assignments, or are they excited about the opportunities for learning in their classroom?

Peer Tutoring

When small groups of children learn how to work together cooperatively, teachers sometimes reap great benefits. However, putting students in groups does not automatically result in productive learning or successful group interaction. With peer tutoring, a child who has grasped an idea helps a child who has not mastered the concept. Peer tutoring, which is carefully organized by the teacher, may have the most potential as a paired reading technique. With paired reading, the student to be tutored selects any book or reading material to read out loud, and a trained tutor provides needed support and positive feedback in a relaxed setting. In addition to children's positive attitudes toward paired reading, the evaluation research confirms strong gains in reading for both the tutor and the student who is tutored (Topping, 1989; for organization and procedures, see Topping in *Resources for Teachers*).

Paired reading can occur within a class or between classes on the same grade level or across grade levels. We use paired reading on a regular basis in our literature program. Many teachers, believing that all students should have the opportunity to discuss the literature being read whole class or in small groups—even if it is above their reading level—pair students as needed. The more able student reads the text aloud while the less able follows along visually, or the students read out loud together, or the less able student listens to the book on tape and follows along in the book. Paired reading is also used simply for enjoyment, anytime two students choose to pair up to read a book.

Using Older Students within the Support Network

When first grade teacher Peg Rimedio had exhausted all possible resources for getting reading support for the large number of at-risk children in her room, she enlisted the help of Nancy Schubert's fourth grade class. Peg felt that if each of her students had an interested partner willing and able to listen to him or her read, students would become more engaged and competent in their reading. Peg reflected, "I was desperate. I wasn't reaching all the kids, and this partnership provided the vehicle."

Peg and Nancy began by carefully pairing their students. Then Peg showed the fourth-graders how to introduce the book the student had selected, how to guide the student in reading, and how to record the book in the child's reading folder once it had been read successfully. Fourth-graders also wrote books for first-graders to read. Toward the end of the school year, the tutoring sessions were expanded to help first-graders locate books and complete their individual animal research reports. The partner sessions took place twice a week for thirty minutes and were so successful—for both the younger and older students—that the teachers decided to repeat the program.

The surprise dividend was the positive impact the sessions had on the fourth-graders. While it was expected that the first-graders would thrive on the special attention, the fourth-graders enjoyed an equal sense of importance and purpose. Before the shared sessions, Nancy Schubert reviewed the strategies students might use to help the first-graders. Not only did the fourth-graders learn to ask good questions ("Look at the picture. What could it be?"), Nancy noticed a carryover to their own work. In addition, several fourth-graders who had difficulty with interpersonal relationships seemed to become more confident and outgoing. Students also expressed a new appreciation of their teacher. They spoke of how hard it was to be a teacher; many came back exhausted after the thirty-minute one-to-one session.

Another successful first grade–fourth grade partnership was created when first grade teacher Kay Dunlap teamed up with fourth grade teacher Maria Padovani. Kay, a highly experienced teacher who had writing workshop well established in her classroom, engaged the fourth-graders in supporting the editing component of the writing process. Again, the teachers carefully paired the students and established guidelines for the fourth-graders. Teacher modeling was a critical aspect of the initial phase of this partnership. Kay discussed editing with the fourth-graders and gave them a sheet of items to look for, including punctuation, capitalization, and coherence. Besides editing, partners occasionally collaborated on writing stories together. Editing-sharing conferences took place every other Friday for forty minutes.

Once again, benefits for both first- and fourth-graders included empowerment. The fact that teachers let first-graders "go at it together" without imposing ideas seemed to give them much confidence. Fourth-graders were surprised at how well first-graders could write, and that seemed to motivate and assist the fourth-graders in refocusing on their own writing. Maria Padovani noted that her students became more attentive to mechanics and took more responsibility for their own writing. She comments, "I was surprised at how well they could edit. They took it more seriously than with their own writing. The kids also felt very important; the first-graders looked up to them. My kids would get upset if there was a Friday when we couldn't meet."

Another surprise was an excellent management solution that came from a fourth-grader. A mid-year survey of students indicated much concern about the noise level with the two classes working in one room. A student's suggestion of using both classrooms proved remarkably effective. Students that needed to be with their classroom teacher (mostly for behavioral reasons) stayed in their own classroom. Other student pairs were divided between the two rooms. While the new arrangement meant the two teachers had to find a separate time to communicate with each other, they believed the new arrangement was worth that extra effort. The noise level was substantially lowered, and teachers felt they could give more and better assistance to students.

At the end of the school year, first- and fourth-graders filled out a written evaluation form that Kay Dunlap had developed. The evaluations indicated that every student but one liked working with his or her partner. Asked what they had learned about doing writing workshop with partners, first-grader Claire Long responded: "I learned how to make stories better by using things you know about and your imagination and when to put in periods and questions marks" (see Figure 16–1). A number of the fourth-graders' comments pointed to affective outcomes:

"I have learned that my partner has good ideas and different ideas that I could write about."

"I have learned to be patient with my first-grader because this is very hard for them."

"I have learned how to cooperate with my partner."

"I have learned to work better with children younger than me."

Figure 16-1   A First-grader's Evaluation of Writing Workshop with a Fourth Grade Partner

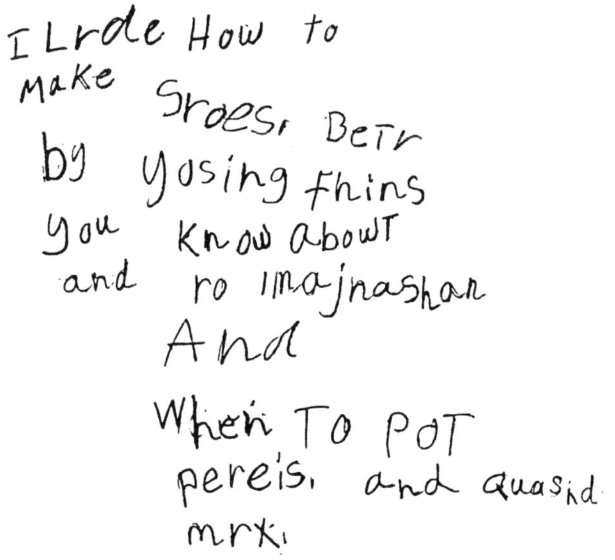

> I Lrde How to
> make Sroes, BeTr
> by yosing fhins
> you Know abowT
> and ro Imajnashan
> And
> Wheri To PoT
> pere's, and quasid
> mrx,

Reading Recovery: Support for At-Risk First-graders

Reading Recovery is an exemplary model of a short-term early intervention designed to reduce and prevent reading failure. Starting where the child is and building on existing strengths, the child is skillfully guided to make accelerated progress in reading whole predictable texts and writing self-generated sentences.

To qualify for the program, the lowest 15 to 20 percent of a beginning first grade population (in the United States) is identified through teacher observation, the results of an individually administered Diagnostic Survey (Clay, 1985), and, in some cases, standardized test results. Then Reading Recovery teachers, who have received highly specialized training from a teacher leader who has participated in a year-long academic training program, provide daily one-to-one instruction for fifteen to twenty weeks. The thirty-minute lessons, meticulously tailored to the child's responses, consist of reading and rereading "little books" and applying reading and writing strategies in the context of authentic reading and writing. In every lesson, the Reading Recovery teacher also takes and analyzes a running record of the child's oral reading of the book introduced the day before. The teacher notes the strategies the child is using and neglecting to use and carefully plans instruction based on the child's needs. The instructional sessions are noteworthy for their rigorous pace, time on task, and independence-fostering behaviors. The goal of the program is to accelerate the student to the average level of his classroom peers, make him an independent reader with a continuing self-improving system, and make further intervention unnecessary.

The program was developed in New Zealand in the 1960s by child psychologist and researcher Marie Clay. In 1979, after twelve years of longitudinal data indicated that once children were "recovered" about 85 percent rarely needed reading support again, the program became nationally funded. Reading Recovery sites

Regie Routman teaching a Reading Recovery lesson

spread to Australia in the mid-1980s and to the United States in 1985 when it came
to Ohio through the The Ohio State University. As of 1990, the results of five years
of research on Reading Recovery students in Ohio have supported the original
findings, and these findings have remained consistent across diverse populations.
The program continues to expand; as of the summer of 1990, sixteen states and
several Canadian provinces had at least one training site. Being designated a
training site means that a teacher-leader, who lived and worked at The Ohio State
University in Columbus for one year, was educated to train and supervise new
Reading Recovery teachers in his/her home state.

For four years I worked as a Reading Recovery teacher every afternoon in the
school where I was based. These teaching experiences were among the most
satisfying and the most demanding I have ever had. I saw firsthand the power and
potential of Reading Recovery for changing how a student is perceived and for
positively affecting an entire school career.

Daniel was one of the last students I worked with. I started seeing him in early
February after he had been in first grade for five months. At that time he was a
nonreader, the lowest-functioning child in his class, and a severe behavior problem.
Daniel was very immature, was easily distracted in a group, and had poor gross
and fine motor control. His limited ability to form letters appropriately and hear
sounds in words made it difficult for him to write in his journal. His Diagnostic
Survey indicated he could identify almost all the upper and lower case letters of the
alphabet; he could read three words ("and," "the," and "yes"); he could write five
words ("Daniel," "mom," "no," "yes," and "my"); he knew print contained the
message in a book, and he had one-to-one matching of spoken words to printed
words on a page; he could hear and write a limited number of beginning and

ending consonants in words; and he could use picture cues and memory to "read" a simple text if he heard part of the story pattern first.

Like all Reading Recovery lessons, every lesson began and ended with books that were carefully selected to meet Daniel's instructional needs and interests. We began with Daniel rereading several books he had previously read with 90–100 percent accuracy. I then took a daily running record of the new book introduced the previous day by observing, recording, and analyzing his oral reading—his accuracies, errors, and self-corrections (see Clay, 1985, for taking a running record). Each lesson also ended with reading a book, a new text carefully introduced through talking about the pictures and language in the story before Daniel attempted reading. In each lesson, reading instruction included making just a few teaching points by focusing on observed strengths and weaknesses. Unique to the Reading Recovery lesson, and all good teaching, are noticing and commenting on what the child has done well. By commenting favorably on Daniel's reading behavior, he was being encouraged to repeat it, and his confidence grew. Typical comments I used, and that Reading Recovery teachers often use, were:

"I like the way you worked that out."

"I saw you looking at the picture to check yourself. That's what a good reader does."

"You went back to the beginning of the sentence and tried again. Good for you."

Also typical of Reading Recovery is the implied message, constantly given to the child, that he needs to take responsibility for most of the problem solving. While the teacher utilizes opportune moments to make relevant teaching points, she is careful to leave sufficient wait time and intervene only when necessary. In a Reading Recovery lesson, the child rarely looks to the teacher; independence is fostered from the very beginning. Some regular prompts I used to get Daniel going on his own were:

"What can you do to help yourself?"

"Can you find the tricky part? Go back and look for it."

"Go back to the beginning of the sentence and try that again."

"Look at how that word starts. Get your mouth ready to say it. Now try it."

"What else can you do?"

With specific guidance, Daniel learned to effectively use meaning and structure cues in reading text. It took longer for him to integrate grapho-phonic cues and orchestrate all three cueing systems interdependently. Once that happened, he was on his way toward independence.

Following the familiar rereadings and the taking of the running record, with my support Daniel dictated and wrote a short message each day. I would then write his message on a sentence strip, cut it apart, and ask Daniel to put it back together. It was in this part of the lesson that Daniel focused heavily on visual cues (graphophonic) and on bringing high-frequency words to fluency.

In our beginning writing lessons, Daniel and I had to spend much time on letter work. See Figure 16–2 for his practice and story page in his second lesson. (The connected boxes are formed to help him hear sounds in words.) Even though he

Figure 16-2   Daniel's Practice and Story Page in His Second Reading Recovery Lesson

could already write "mom" and "my" independently, Daniel was confused about upper and lower case letters and direction in letter formation. Note his writing page at the beginning of May (Figure 16–3). Although his writing vocabulary was not yet keeping pace with his reading, he independently spelled and correctly formed the letters for all the words except "when" and "get."

Daniel was discontinued from Reading Recovery after fourteen weeks and fifty-seven lessons. He was reading *Clifford* books by Norman Bridwell fluently in class, was writing independently in his journal daily, and was just beginning to read *Frog and Toad* books by Arnold Lobel with me. His success had been a joint effort among Daniel, his mother, his classroom teacher Karen Shiba, Cindy Brodsky (a tutor who took her own time to listen to him read regularly), and myself.

When I first met Daniel, he kept his head lowered and seemed very sad. Now he was a happy, confident student. Initially a nonparticipant in reading group, he now prodded his teacher daily, "Is our group next?" He was still a behavior problem but never in reading group.

When Daniel was about to be discontinued, I interviewed him.

Figure 16-3   Daniel's Practice and Story Page in May

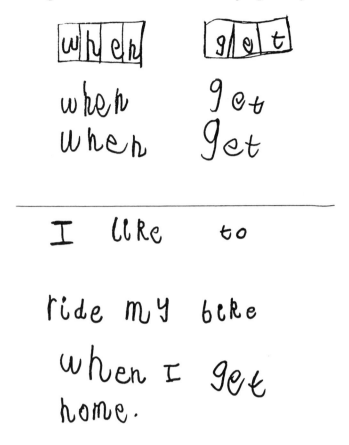

ROUTMAN: What was it like for you when you couldn't read?

DANIEL: Not too good. I couldn't read, and all the other kids could read. I was thinking, I'm not smart. I felt really bad, *real* bad. The teacher would say, "You can read a book," but I couldn't read!

ROUTMAN: Were you worried?

DANIEL: I was thinking I would never be able to read. I was really scared.

ROUTMAN: When did things change for you?

DANIEL: When I came into Reading Recovery, I started to read better, write better. I began to feel proud of myself because I was doing good.

ROUTMAN: Do you feel like you're smart now?

DANIEL: I feel much better because I can read now. I'm a good reader. I think I'm a smart person.

Daniel's mother, initially very upset about her son's nonreading, was enthusiastic about his progress and confidence. Some excerpts from a long letter I received from her follow.

June 12, 1990

Dear Mrs. Routman,

I just wanted to take some time before the school year is out, and the possibility that we may never see each other again, to extend my thanks to you. . . .

Daniel's reading and writing has improved *110%*. He can now pick up books that he has around the house and read them without much help, if any. As you were helping him, you were helping me as well. I love Daniel very much and as I told you before he is my best friend.

I am a single parent and at times it is hard to sit down and work with him as much as I should. Before Daniel started working with you, I was very worried about his reading and writing, and when he came home and told me he was going to be working with a special teacher, and I began to see the results, you cleared away one less worry.

I wish you much luck in your career, and I hope that you continue to help other children as you have helped my son. May God bless and keep you always! Thank you!

Darlene Goodwin

Reading Recovery is not a panacea; it does not work for every child. No program does. It is, however, the best early intervention program I have ever seen, and school districts would do well to investigate its implementation. Reading Recovery is an expensive program that requires at least a three-year commitment, but it is cost effective in the long run. The program also requires strong support, education, understanding, and flexibility on the part of administrators. Administrators must be willing to release teachers part of the school day to work one-to-one with students, and they must be able to look at more than standardized test scores to judge reading success.

Some states now say they have Reading Recovery and that they can train teachers, but this is not so. The Reading Recovery training program is a year-long commitment and includes the theoretical underpinnings upon which this program is built. This critical training can be guaranteed only through the National Diffusion Network for Reading Recovery. Program developer Marie Clay has authorized The Ohio State University in Columbus as the only official U.S. site to educate trainers of teacher leaders.

Finally, besides reducing early reading failure, one of the greatest benefits of Reading Recovery is improved reading instruction. Reading Recovery teachers often have an impact on the way reading is taught in the classroom and in the school. When Reading Recovery teachers are able to work cooperatively with classroom teachers, classroom teachers with a skills-based approach to reading begin to approach the teaching of reading more strategically and more analytically.

This discussion of Reading Recovery is only a brief conceptual framework. For more complete information on the program, see the following resources:

Clay, Marie. 1985. *The Early Detection of Reading Difficulties*, 3rd ed. Portsmouth, NH: Heinemann.

> *Marie Clay describes the procedures for early assessment, intervention, and observation of at-risk beginning readers. Procedures for administering the Diagnostic Survey (observing early literacy skills and book behaviors) and for taking a running*

record (observing and analyzing a child's oral reading behaviors) can be applied to the classroom and will be very helpful to the teacher in making instructional decisions. While I had read this difficult and extensive text before becoming a Reading Recovery teacher, it was most useful to me after I had received the teacher training.

Lyons, Carol. Director of the National Diffusion Network for Reading Recovery, The Ohio State University, 200 Ramseyer Hall, 29 West Woodruff Avenue, Columbus, OH 43210–1177. (Write for information.)

Ohio Department of Education and The Ohio State University. *Reading Recovery Conference.* Columbus, Ohio; held annually in early February.

This high-level conference for teachers, administrators, parents, and policy makers offers sessions on the research, funding, and implementation of Reading Recovery as well as on related issues and strategies for early literacy. Barbara Watson, Director of Reading Recovery in New Zealand, and/or Marie Clay, Developer of Reading Recovery, have often attended and given presentations. (For conference information, write to Hilda Edwards, Division of Inservice, State Department of Education, 65 Front Street, Columbus, OH 43266–0308.)

Pinnell, Gay Su, Diane E. DeFord, and Carol A. Lyons. 1988. *Reading Recovery: Early Intervention for At-Risk First Graders.* Arlington, VA: Educational Research Service.

This 84-page monograph describes the Reading Recovery program and summarizes the research on the program's long-range effects after four years in Ohio.

Pinnell, Gay Su, Mary D. Fried, and Rose Mary Estice. January 1990. "Reading Recovery: Learning How to Make a Difference," *The Reading Teacher,* pp. 282–295.

The authors, all trained in Reading Recovery—a teacher trainer and professor, a state coordinator, and a teacher—describe the program, the components and teaching procedures in a Reading Recovery lesson, the teacher-training model, the program's research base, and the pilot study in Ohio. A case study documents one student's success with the program.

Promoting Parent Education and Involvement

Strong parent involvement is not a question of "Should we?" but rather a question of "How should we?" The importance of ongoing, well-planned involvement of parents is backed by the research on effective schools. Effective parent involvement programs—all of which have elements in common—positively affect school achievement across diverse populations. (Henderson, and Williams and Chavkin, 1988).

We need to welcome parents into our schools and classrooms and keep them well informed about their children's education. We need to create opportunities for parents to see themselves as a vital, continuing part of their children's education. We need to keep the lines of communication open and to build trust. Not only will parents be better able to support the learning process at home but the message will get out to the community and to the principal that the students are learning and happy and that the teachers care. Parents are our best public relations agents. They can do more to sell whole language, or any educational program, than anyone else in the school district. They have far greater power to effect change than the teacher does. Parents are a resource we must use wisely.

Some things we can do to promote education, understanding of whole language, and cooperation among parents include the following:

● *Recognize what parents have done well.*   When we are explaining whole language to parents, a good plan is to start by congratulating parents for what they have done well. We can begin by explaining how parents have successfully taught their children to speak. The research and theory behind whole language are based on the language learning that has taken place in the home. Parents relate easily to the notions of demonstration, approximation, practice, and learning over time when these issues are explained in relation to their child's learning how to talk. Then the transition to applying the same principles to invented spelling and learning to read is a natural one for parents.

● *Provide opportunities for parent education.*   Use open houses, conferences, parent newsletters, and Parent-Teacher Association meetings to increase parents' understanding of the language processes. Besides the regular curriculum statement given to parents at our annual fall open house, third grade teacher Lee Sattelmeyer hands out a language arts philosophy statement (see Figure 16–4 for a recent statement). Also, as much as you feel comfortable with the idea, have your classroom open to parents. Bring them into the literacy process by inviting them to help with journal writing, editing, special projects, and field trips.

Our school sponsors an annual "Family Literacy" night, a workshop on effective strategies for helping parents help their children become successful learners. After a

Figure 16-4   Language Arts Philosophy Statement Given to Parents

LOMOND SCHOOL
SHAKER HEIGHTS, OHIO

THIRD GRADE

I. LANGUAGE ARTS (Whole Language Approach)

Premise

* Language is a composite of three systems: semantics (meaning), syntax (grammar), and graphophonemics (letter-sound correspondence). Learning to read becomes more difficult when systems are taught in isolation. Language is best learned through its use.

* Learning to read requires sharing, interaction, and collaboration involving parent/child, teacher/child, and child/child relationships.

* Placing importance on reading for meaning and reading for enjoyment will develop life long readers.

* When applicable, choice and self-selection in reading and writing activities are important factors in building confidence in language experiences.

* Reading involves an interaction between the reader and the text. Meaning is constructed by the reader based on prior experience.

* Literature can be used as a springboard for writing experiences.

* Learning to write is facilitated when writing exercises are purposeful and communicate ideas rather than practicing isolated skills.

* Where possible, other curriculum areas, e.g., science and social studies, are integrated with the language arts program.

* As much as possible, skills are taught in the context of the literature as the need arises.

brief presentation by several teachers, parents and teachers meet in small groups by grade level to ask questions and discuss concerns about working with their children at home. Some of our kindergarten and first grade teachers sponsor their own classroom literacy workshops as a way to educate parents and make them a welcome part of the literacy process.

The first year that our district made a commitment to whole language, each building devoted a Parent-Teacher Association meeting to explaining whole language and allowing time for questions and answers.

• *Provide parents suggestions for what they can do at home.*   Send home a communication that gives parents a framework for worthwhile home activities. (See "Parents as Allies in Children's Education," Appendix J5, for a model.) Probably most important is getting the message out that parents should continue to read to their children, serve as reading role models themselves, and provide quiet time and space for leisure reading.

• *Start a library for parents.*   Easy access to books about language learning is one way to clarify and expand parents' understanding of language develoment and the language processes. See if your public or school library will fund, organize, and reserve a corner for parents. Use relevant book titles in this book and in Routman (1988) for recommended educational resources for parents. Also check with your local libraries and book stores for recommended titles. Scholastic Inc., and the American Reading Council in New York City, and the International Reading Association in Newark, Delaware, all publish pamphlets, brochures, and books for parents.

• *Utilize parent volunteers.*   Parents may be used in the publishing process to listen to children read, as supports for journal writing, to put together projects for teachers, or for a host of other tasks. Be sure parents are clear on what you want them to do and that they understand the program philosophy. If parents from your classroom are not available, contact grandparents, other relatives, or senior citizens.

• *Let parents know when their child does something well.*   Some teachers make it a point to telephone or drop a short note to parents during the first week of school and, on occasion, throughout the year to note something positive about the child. If parents are contacted when their child does something well, not only are good relations established between the parent and teacher but the parents are likely to be more receptive if you call with a problem.

• *Explain standardized testing and evaluation procedures.*   Jerry Harste of Indiana University recommends having parents take part in the standardized tests their children take. For example, one of the subtests could be given at fall open house. Once parents actually go through the testing process themselves, they are less likely to place so much significance on the test results. Be sure your grading and evaluation procedures are clear to parents, and make parents part of the process. (See Chap. 13, "Evaluation.")

• *Explain how reading is being taught.*   Teachers need to explain how reading is being taught—to the children as well as to the parents—especially when there has been a major change in philosophy. Robin's mother was feeling a lot of anxiety when her first-grader wasn't using "sounding out" as a major strategy. She also expected to see lots of phonics worksheets coming home. It had never been explained to this mother that meaning-based strategies were being emphasized in the classroom, that phonics was being taught in the context of reading and through journal writing, and that phonics sheets were not being used. See Appendix J2, "Ways to Help Your Child with Reading at Home," which gives parents meaning-based strategies to use with their children in the reading process.

It's also a good idea to communicate to parents the kinds of high-level questions that teachers are trying to ask in order to foster the same kind of question asking at home.

• *Explain the writing process.*   Talk to the children about the writing process so they can talk about it to their parents. Some parents think the teacher has shirked responsibility when papers come home with mistakes. Many of our teachers have a stamp, marked "unedited," and we stamp papers that have not gone to final copy. When a final product does go home, you may want to also attach the drafts. See Appendix J1 for a letter to primary parents explaining invented spelling.

• *Communicate regularly in writing.*   A newsletter written by you and/or the students lets parents be part of the learning process. Use the newsletter to communicate class happenings, strategies being taught, and successes to celebrate.

English teacher Dana Noble guides his reluctant ninth grade readers and writers in writing a newsletter to parents describing what's going on in the classroom. Students choose their own format and events, and engagement and interest are high in this authentic writing project. Third grade teacher Julie Beers's students also write a monthly newsletter to parents (see Appendix J9). Julie also writes a newsletter to parents at the start of the school year to explain her philosophy, curriculum, and goals (see Appendix J8 for the reading-writing portions).

• *Encourage good book selection.*   Many parents need guidance in choosing books for children or in helping their children choose. Let parents know about *The Read Aloud Handbook* by Jim Trelease, *The New York Times Parents' Guide to the Best Books for Children* by Eden Ross Lipson, *Choosing Books for Children* by Betsy Hearne, and *Comics to Classics: A Parent's Guide to Books for Teens and Preteens* by Arthea Reed, all published recently (see *Resources for Teachers*). If you use a book club so children can buy trade books inexpensively, recommend some good titles (see Appendix J10). Also, let parents know about favorite authors and popular series for your particular age group so they can look for them with their children at the local library.

• *Avoid any negative reinforcement or reactions to students whose parents are not involved for some reason.*

Support through Grant Money

Many teachers have been resourceful in getting funds for trade books, materials, equipment, additional personnel, curriculum design, and staff development by applying for special grants. Unfortunately, most teachers are unaware that money exists—in some cases big money.

In my own school district, some teachers, with strong administrative support, have been highly successful in the leadership role they have taken in writing proposals and getting approval for grants, in amounts ranging from several hundred dollars to one hundred thousand dollars. Some recent grants include:

- A private foundation grant for a summer literacy outreach program for entering first-graders deemed at risk by their kindergarten teachers
- An effective schools grant to assess building needs—guiding philosophy, teaching-learning climate, expectations, leadership, delivery of instruction
- A matching funds grant with a commitment of equal hours from community leaders in private business and industry to develop a math program more congruent with the new math *Standards* (see Romberg, p. 16b) and real-life needs
- A state grant to fund a language enrichment program for at-risk kindergartners in every school
- A foundation grant to bring in resource personnel to support middle school teachers in working with at-risk students

Check with your administrators, superintendent, and other teachers who have been successful in obtaining grant money. Contact community groups and service organizations, as well as private corporations, to determine whether grants are available. Also check out local, county, federal, and state resources, including your state department of education. See if your city has a library for obtaining information on grants, and check to see what public and private foundations in your town offer educational grants.

Some districts, including my own, have begun their own foundations to further educational development. In addition, our Parent-Teacher Association and our Teachers' Association also offer small annual grants for teacher projects that will enhance teaching and learning.

Some Thoughts on Teacher Education

One would expect recruitment of teachers with a whole language background to become easier as more and more colleges and universities are providing the underlying theory. However, unless universities also move from the traditional transmission model of lecturing truths to an interactive model of sharing understandings, espousing the theory won't be enough. Teacher educators must begin to employ the whole language model in their undergraduate and graduate classes. We teachers need to exert our influence with our local colleges and universities to make sure this begins to happen.

Specifically, for university professors, this means conducting their undergraduate and graduate classes as whole language classes. Just as classroom teachers cannot expect students in their classes to go through processes they have not sufficiently demonstrated, university professors cannot expect their students to become whole language teachers without being whole language teachers themselves. I see that changing the traditional model would mean:

- Employing Holdaway's "Developmental Model of Language Learning" (pp. 9–10)—not just lecturing and giving assignments
- Allowing teachers choices (based on their interests) in required professional reading—for example, choosing any two out of five approved texts

- Journal keeping by students and teachers to record reactions to reading
- Using class time for sharing and collegial interaction
- Encouraging teachers to demonstrate their new knowledge in a variety of forms
- Evaluating university students from a multifaceted perspective

When Jerry Harste of Indiana University visited our district in May 1990, I was impressed with the commitment he told us he has made to changing his own teaching. He gives teachers a choice of professional texts to read, has them keep a journal of their reactions, and devotes class time to discussion of issues raised. He puts his students through the literature discussion process by having them read adult literature and then break into small groups for discussion. In that way, teachers come to understand the process they want to facilitate with their students. In addition to his own evaluation of students, Harste places high value on both peer evaluation and self-evaluation. For example, students are required to turn in a paper describing the classmate they learned the most from. Because this requirement is made clear at the start of each course, students take listening to and learning from each other quite seriously.

In addition to the fact that few educators at the university level employ a whole language teaching model, there is also a scarcity of whole language classrooms in which to place student teachers. To aid the placement process, some universities are pairing up and working closely with teachers and local school systems that have made commitments to whole language. Universities and colleges should then take the opportunity to ask supervising teachers what they think is needed for better preparatory education for classroom teaching. Professors and teachers need to respect and utilize one another's knowledge in looking to create better teacher education models.

Finally, some states are now requiring a four-year liberal arts degree and a fifth year for teacher certification. This makes sense. If teachers are to be models of knowledge and critical thinking, they must have a broad education in the liberal arts as well as basic education courses.

Future Directions

While our school district has made some commitments to furthering whole language on an ongoing basis, we are still working on putting a long-range plan into effect. On the plus side, our teachers are involved in curriculum design, writing new report cards, and ongoing committee work related to the language processes. Reading Recovery is in place in every k–4 building, and classroom teachers are expressing interest in learning how to employ Reading Recovery strategies and assessment procedures. Our weekly language arts support groups are vital and active. Many of our teachers have made presentations at local, state, and national conferences. A small number of our teachers have initiated new programs through obtaining grants and receiving special funding and approval.

We have much room for growth. While our teachers are encouraged to attend conferences, it has been rare for administrators to attend with us. For the most part, workshops with "experts" still tend to be the one-shot deal. Most of our staff development has been in the form of the voluntary efforts of teachers meeting and collaborating. Release time during the school day for staff development has been rare. Teachers are still generally not included in the hiring process, and teacher-administrator relationships often need to be more collaborative. Nevertheless, we are slowly but surely moving forward, and there is no turning back.

On the national scene, existing TAWL groups are active and networking, and new groups are springing up in every state. A national networking exists through the Whole Language Umbrella, which began sponsoring annual conferences in the summer of 1990. Coaching and mentoring programs are being tried out in many districts. Some districts have begun to make hiring of new teachers conditional on their having a whole language background. Districts are also offering early retirement incentives to encourage weeding out more traditional teachers.

There is much work still to be done. Teacher education needs an overhaul, and we need to be doing more as a society to attract the best and the brightest to the teaching profession. In most school districts, reading instruction is still driven by basal readers, skills sheets, and standardized testing. Administrators need to become more involved in understanding and supporting whole language theory and practice if it is to become an approach to teaching and learning that is here to stay. Teachers need to take the initiative to be afforded their rightful and responsible place as decision makers and leaders in the staff development process.

Resources: Staff Development Opportunities

E.L.I.C. (EARLY LITERACY INSERVICE COURSE)
Robyn Platt, Director
760 Industrial Drive
Carey, IL 60013

> *Based on the staff development program that has trained the majority of teachers in Australia since 1983, this literacy course for groups of up to twelve teachers in grades k–3 offers school districts a proven model for effective teacher change. The course includes taking a close look at language learning, reading and writing processes and strategies, evaluation, and more. Teachers meet weekly for twelve weeks with a trained facilitator for one two-hour interactive session, usually after school. Teachers discuss that week's assigned professional readings and specific classroom-based tasks. In addition, the facilitator is available on request to work in classrooms with teachers.*
>
> *In place in Colorado and Upstate New York since 1989, and in Illinois since the fall of 1990, E.L.I.C. has had an impact on teachers' literacy beliefs, attitudes, and practices. E.L.I.C. training also benefits districts already using Reading Recovery by ensuring that students, working with trained Reading Recovery teachers, have a supportive classroom environment. Teachers learn about children's reading-writing processes and how to become kidwatchers.*

FRAMEWORKS
Staff Development Office
Wayne-Finger Lakes BOCES
3501 County Road 20
Stanley, NY 14561

> *Frameworks is a whole language staff development program that has been designed by Australian educators Andrea Butler, Brian Cambourne, and Jan Turbill to support literacy learning in grades k–8. Frameworks uses the same interactive,*

teacher-facilitator model as E.L.I.C.; teachers closely examine many aspects of learning, language, reading, and writing in making connections between their beliefs and their practices.

STAFF DEVELOPMENT SERIES ON WHOLE LANGUAGE
Andrea Butler, Presenter
Rigby Education
454 South Virginia Street
Crystal Lake, IL 60014

These four videos—conditions of natural learning, application of those conditions to the classroom, components of a whole language classroom, and shared book experience—have application in k–12 for understanding the theory and practice behind whole language. A facilitator's guide, several handouts, and recommended professional reading are included. For districts desirous of understanding whole language principles, these videos provide an excellent staff development package.

See also "Reliable Sources for Literature for the Reading-Writing Classroom" in Chapter 15 for publishers that offer whole language workshops.

17

Any
Questions?

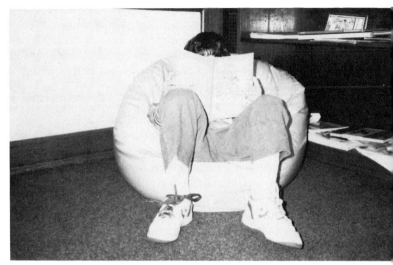

A reader

The following questions are representative of teachers' concerns that have come up repeatedly at workshops and through letters I have received.

What are your feelings and experiences regarding retention?

Unfortunately, years ago I was unaware of the unequivocal research against holding back low-performing students. When I was coteaching language arts in the first grade, I was responsible for the retention of Sheila. Sheila arrived at school late on most mornings, had trouble learning to read and write, and always seemed disorganized. I remember calling several conferences with her mother and trying for hours to persuade her that Sheila needed to be retained. I have no doubt that my convincing arguments finally persuaded Sheila's tearful mother to agree to retention.

While Sheila appeared to do well the first months repeating first grade, she slowly fell further and further behind until by third grade she was not only one of the lowest-achieving children in her class but also one of the unhappiest. That retention decision continues to haunt me. I have never recommended retention since that time.

Under the guise of raising educational standards, we hold back 5 to 7 percent of public school children each year and contribute to even more negative academic achievement, a higher drop-out rate, and damaged self-esteem. While there are rare cases of students who benefit from retention, they are the exception. Current research on retention concludes that there is no benefit in just about every case from kindergarten through high school (see Shepard and Smith, 1990). As responsible educators, we must take this research seriously.

It seems that handwriting of students has gotten poorer with whole language and its acceptance of invented spelling. Do you agree? How do you feel about the need for teaching formal handwriting?

I do think we are seeing less beautiful penmanship these days, but I don't think that's all bad. Some of that perfect penmanship came at the expense of lots of board copying and vacuous writing. We need to remember that, like spelling, the only reason handwriting is necessary is for writing. Writing must come first.

I have relaxed on my teaching and acceptance of handwriting. If it's legible, and neat, I accept it. I have the poorest handwriting of anyone I know, but if I need something to be carefully handwritten, I can do it. Otherwise, I make sure it's typed. Legible writing will always be important, as the current use of handwritten fax communications demonstrates.

If a child can form the letters so they're readable, I leave the handwriting alone. However, I believe it's important to demonstrate the formation of all the letters. This can be done in group minilessons and individually as needed—to encourage legible and attractive letter formation and help with specific problems. For very young children, demonstrations are appropriate as long as mastery is not the goal. I would keep practice handwriting exercises to a minimum and make sure children have lots of opportunities to use handwriting through purposeful writing experiences.

What are your beliefs about homework? Are we assigning too much or not enough? How much should parents have to be involved?

I believe that homework should be based on concepts the student already understands. It should be a practice time, to confirm and extend learning, and, as much as possible, homework should be self-checking. Above all, it should be worth doing, and students and parents should see the purpose of it. Unfortunately, that is not what usually happens.

When I was reading *Growing Up Literate* by Denny Taylor and Catherine Dorsey-Gaines, I remember being very struck by the authors' descriptions of children doing their homework. What struck me was how seriously these children and parents took this work. Homework was done right after school, and parents took the time to check it and give feedback. What disturbed me was how meaningless the exercises were—mostly workbook pages, dittos, and penmanship papers. The parents received no explanation about the work; it just came home and was expected to be completed. It was clear that homework was considered important, so it was done despite its questionable value.

Because many parents and students do take homework seriously, we must be sure that what we are sending home is worth doing. Instead of narrow and boring tasks, we should be providing opportunities for problem solving that are relevant to the children's lives. We must also be cautious about the amount of time we expect children to spend on homework. There is no reason to assign fifty math problems when a student can demonstrate his understanding with ten.

Most of the research on homework (Cooper, 1989) suggests that no more than fifteen to forty-five minutes of homework a week should be assigned students in grades 1–3. I was relieved to have that confirmed. Many of our primary teachers do not assign homework except for the expected, nightly independent WEB reading (p. 43). However, many parents question why more homework is not assigned.

Regarding homework in the elementary grades, Cooper (1989) states,

...homework for young children should help them develop good study habits, foster positive attitudes toward school, and communicate to students the idea that learning takes place at home as well as at school. As such, homework assignments in elementary grades should be short, should employ materials commonly found in the home environment and should lead to success experiences (p. 90).

At the high school level, where one to two hours of homework a night is recommended, it is still necessary that assignments take the form of practice and review to extend and confirm what the student already understands. Harris further recommends that, at all levels, parental involvement and grading be kept to a minimum.

Unfortunately, few school districts and teachers subscribe to the policies the research promotes. Martha Anderson, a parent with a son at a public middle school, has this to say:

My ideas about homework crystallized the year my son Derrick changed schools because of reorganization in our district. Previously my son had little homework, and he was quite positive and self-sufficient about doing it. Then, in his fourth grade year, he had a significant amount of homework—the usual worksheets but also a lot of what I call showcase projects: reports, posters, games, maps, dioramas, the sort of work always in evidence at open house. It was not Derrick's happiest year in school, and more than once his teachers found his work deficient, although in the preceding years he had been a happy and successful student.

What I finally put together spring of that year was that *parents* were doing the projects as much as the children. I came to that conclusion after Derrick and a friend's child had been partners on a project, had to my knowledge worked diligently on it, and had been criticized by the teacher for carelessness and poor presentation. By comparison with projects done with and by parents, work done solely by children looked sloppy and immature. Derrick received a very false and possibly damaging message about his work during fourth grade; his own efforts weren't good enough; he wasn't competent to do his assignments himself and do them successfully.

This had not been the case in earlier grades. Perhaps because Derrick's previous school was the poorest in the district in terms of family income (which means not only families less able to buy supplies, but also parents who may be less available because of shift work or being single parents, who may have less access to transportation, who may have less knowledge of how to use libraries or where to buy supplies, and who may have fewer resources within the home), and because teachers in that school were very sensitive to their students' situations, the assignments he had there didn't presuppose a lot of parent involvement.

As far as homework goes, I am in a bind I have yet to resolve. Many of Derrick's classmates' parents become very involved with their children's school work. While interest is appropriate and, I think, valuable to the child, I don't think it should extend to taking an active role in the child's homework. To do so confuses the matter of whose work it is; I don't think it benefits the child who is "helped." It also plays havoc with the evaluation of children's work, rewarding and penalizing children on the basis of their parents' resources rather than on the children's own efforts. But the bind: given that other parents are helping their children with homework, do I disadvantage my son by taking myself out of it because I have sound reasons for thinking that he is better off doing it himself?

Only teachers and administrators can cut the knot. I have the impression that homework, especially in k–6, is something that the various adults—teachers, administrators, and parents—pass around among themselves to impress each other. The child's interests and how the homework enhances the child's learning appear to be the last considerations. No one can prevent a parent from helping his/her child with homework. However, screening each assignment against the question, Can a child in this class successfully complete this assignment *by him/herself?* would go a long way toward correcting the well-intentioned but mistaken perception that more homework, complicated homework, and inappropriately advanced assignments are the hallmarks of a rich school experience.

We need to take this parent's comments seriously, examine our own homework practices, and make sure they support what the research recommends.

My greatest roadblock has been the concern of parents who feel their children are somehow not receiving their full complement of education when the "trivial pursuit" daily drill pages do not come home. How do you overcome this when workbook pages are replaced with more significant independent activities?

Parents, used to basing education on visible products, have to be reeducated and reoriented to a process approach to learning. The first year our district made a commitment to move toward whole language, each elementary school had a Parent-Teacher Association meeting devoted to explaining whole language, the research it was based upon, the use of literature and accompanying meaningful activities, and the change in the way phonics would be taught. Parents also had opportunities to ask questions and raise concerns.

Even for parents who do not attend Parent-Teacher Association meetings, ongoing communication is possible through weekly newsletters, open house, conferences, and phone calls. We find that when teachers and administrators have taken the time to explain a whole language philosophy of teaching, parents are very quick to embrace this style of teaching. Parents are delighted that their children are reading real literature at school and at home, completing worthwhile projects, and are excited about school. I have never had a parent ask for worksheets once they have understood what whole language is all about.

If I am already doing shared reading, journal writing, and reading literature and poetry daily to my class, what would be a good next step or two?

If you are already doing shared reading, shared writing is a natural next step. You may also want to think about doing some guided writing and allowing more choices for students in both reading and writing activities. You may be ready to add an individualized and independent reading component, as described on pages 41–50. You may also want to think about moving into heterogeneous discussion groups if your literature has been taught mostly whole class. Also, you may want to look at your evaluation procedures and think about adding some observational, process-based aspects.

Continue to do professional reading to stay vibrant as a professional and to question how your theory ties into meaningful practice. Perhaps most important, just focus on one or two new aspects each year. Remember, you don't have to do everything at once. Everyone I know is still in transition—even after many years.

Is there such a thing as a whole language program or whole language text?

There is no such thing as a whole language program or text. Since whole language is a philosophy and approach to teaching and learning, each teacher—with the collaboration of students—creates a program based on curriculum requirements and children's needs and interests. The best commercial text or program can be used only as one resource.

Scheduling still plagues me. How do I fit it all in? I'm afraid, too, that giving children large blocks of time to write may lead to chaos in my classroom.

Scheduling is a problem for most teachers. Even when teachers manage to get uninterrupted blocks of time in their day, they are often disrupted by students leaving and entering from special programs. Many teachers find the only way to fit it all in is to have reading and writing go across the curriculum. For example, if your children are doing research reports in science, the reading and writing they are doing in science could take place during language arts time, with students receiving guidance and practice in reading and writing informational texts.

Allowing time to write means setting up an environment that is structured but not rigid and controlling. Teachers that establish writing workshop or extended writing periods take many weeks and months to demonstrate procedures, set expectations, and give students time and practice to take responsibility for their topics, drafts, revisions, and completed pieces.

I still have trouble with the idea of everyone doing somewhat unstructured activities while I'm conducting a reading group. How can the teacher come up with enough daily activities to keep them all busy? It seems as though it would take so much time.

You are right. It would take too much of the teacher's time to try to "think up" daily activities. However, we are not looking to keep students "busy." We are looking to keep them productively involved with text and responding to it in a way that enriches them and brings deeper connections to the literature. Moving to more unstructured activities is a gradual process. Give yourself time. Teachers find that once they have internalized a whole language philosophy of teaching and learning, ideas come naturally, and options for students make sense. Also, once you begin to share responsibility for learning with the students, they come up with many ideas.

I'm having a hard time moving away from homogeneous grouping. You mentioned it took you ten years. What are some intermediate steps I could take?

Even if you are not comfortable with moving away from ability grouping most of the time, you could still provide some opportunities for heterogeneous grouping. For example, take one month out of your usual reading program, choose a book that will appeal to your students, and divide the class into mixed ability groups. Pair your less able readers with better ones for the reading of the text so everyone can then participate in discussion. Try adding shared book experience, as described on pp. 33–38, to your program. Also, begin to take a careful look at the research on grouping practices (see pp. 71 and 77–78) and then try to examine your own beliefs in light of the research. Change is slow and difficult for most of us, but eventually you will be able to make your theory and practice congruent.

It seems as though I have a noisier classroom as I begin to work with whole language activities. Although in most cases I find it to be productive noise, I worry what others will think as they come into my room. Is this a normal feeling?

Perfectly normal. It seems to take most of us several years to adjust to a noisier classroom. I remember worrying for years about the noise level. I used to query visitors, "Does the noise level bother you?" Most commented on how engaged the children were in their activities, and I would feel relieved. One first grade teacher was particularly bothered because the first grade class next to hers was always quiet. I asked her, "Which classroom would you rather have your own child in?"

Language does not flourish in a silent space. Students need and enjoy opportunities to discuss, share, listen to one another, and communicate. However, go with a noise level with which you are comfortable. For example, when I am guiding a literature discussion, I expect students not in group to work quietly because I find too much noise distracting. I am comfortable with students working together as long as the noise level stays very low. However, if I am not working with a particular group and students are collaborating on various projects where I am available for guidance, I can accept a higher noise level.

I'm trying to eliminate some of the basal drill and skill worksheets but worry that I'll eliminate something that is really important and will cause problems down the line for the students. Are there any guidelines on what to eliminate?

Gradually, as you develop and can articulate your own philosophy of teaching and learning—through observing children, professional reading and reflecting, staff development, sharing with colleagues—you will also develop confidence and trust in yourself to decide what to keep and what to eliminate. I find it always helps when I ask myself, "What is the purpose of this activity? Why am I giving it to students? What do I hope to accomplish? Could this be done in a more meaningful way?" If the skills sheet is not meaningful, don't use it. Keep in mind that mastering a set of skills has nothing to do with being a thoughtfully literate person.

Go slowly. Many teachers hang on to phonics worksheets for years until they become convinced that phonics can be taught more meaningfully and naturally in context. Especially during the first years teachers are moving from the basal to literature, they want the assurance that the "skills" are "covered." This is a normal part of the transition process.

What many of us did initially to ease our worry about "covering" all the skills was to list all the skills required by the curriculum course of study. Then, as we taught those skills through the literature, we checked them off. After a while we relaxed as we saw we could teach all the skills through our daily authentic reading and writing activities.

Once you trust yourself and become a knowledgeable, observant, and reflective teacher, you won't need the skills sheets as an insurance policy that learning is really occurring.

I'm enjoying working with "books" in my classroom but still have that feeling of doubt when the skeptics in the teachers' lounge say that the whole thing is just a fad that will be gone in a year or two. Do you think whole language is here to stay?

Whole language, or whatever one chooses to call meaningful teaching and learning that respects principles of language learning, is not a fad because it is based on solid research over the last several decades on how children learn language. I find the only people that see whole language as a fad are those that are tied to "programs" and mistakenly view whole language as another program instead of as a way of thinking about learning and teaching. However, I believe that unless administrators and policy makers get behind whole language, unless teachers become highly knowledgeable, and unless parents are well educated about whole language, it could well disappear and be considered another passing fad.

I have a couple of gifted students who read several years above the other kids. However, when I did some pretesting, I found that they did not have a few of the skills. Does it matter if they can read fluently with good comprehension but may not know a few of the skills?

If reading is viewed as a constructive, interactive process in which the reader gets meaning from text, being able to "do" isolated skills exercises is meaningless. Take a close look at what the student *can't* do on a test and see whether the student *can* apply the same skill in a meaningful context. If a student is using and applying a skill in a meaningful context, I don't worry about the results of isolated subtests.

I remember a gifted kindergarten student who was a fluent, comprehending reader. As a fluent reader, she had to be integrating the three cueing systems—semantics, syntax, and grapho-phonics. However, when presented with daily phonics worksheets, she rebelled. She could not and would not do them. It became a battle of wills between the teacher—who insisted the child needed phonics to read—and the child, who grew increasingly unhappy in the classroom. I believe it was the teacher's lack of knowledge of the reading process that caused the problem. The teacher was not phased by the fact that the child was already an excellent reader. To be a proficient reader, the child was effectively using and applying skills on a strategic level. However, to that teacher reading meant being able to do the skills on isolated tasks.

When is it okay to teach grammar and parts of speech?

I believe that the same principles apply to teaching grammar as apply to phonics teaching and formal handwriting. It makes more sense *after* you are already reading and writing. Once you have the fluency and conceptual understanding, you can benefit from analysis. It is not necessary to be able to define and label parts of speech in the elementary grades in order to use them appropriately. Students seem to be ready for this by junior high. In the elementary grades, students *internalize* the structure of language through immersion and guidance in authentic daily reading and writing experiences. It takes most of us years to believe this, but once teachers can articulate and apply beliefs about language learning, they find this latter statement to be true.

18

Final Reflections

District whole language support group: an evening meeting in a teacher's home

Becoming a whole language teacher is no easy journey. There is no blue-print, recipe, or formula for success. There are few shortcuts and no ready solutions, and each teacher's route is slightly different. There is no best class to take or classroom to visit to get all the answers. There is not even a commonly understood definition, for whole language is a philosophy, a way of thinking. Becoming a whole language teacher is more about learning than it is about teaching. It is more about asking questions than it is about finding answers. Most of all, it is about making a profound philosophical shift in beliefs about learning and teaching. It is a highly personal, intellectual, and thoughtful endeavor.

Recently I was struck by the sense of frenzy in a group of visiting teachers. Spurred on by their district's new commitment to whole language, these dedicated and hard-working teachers were expected to attend workshops, implement new techniques and literature, take running records and anecdotal records, and revise the report cards—all in one year! There was no time set aside for professional reading and teacher collaboration. Neither was there time for thoughtful reflection about their teaching. Concern with accountability and rapid change was the district's first priority.

In talking with these earnest teachers, I understood that they had little idea why they were doing what they were doing. Instead of operating from a firm theory base, they were simply implementing a new set of procedures and activities. In the district's conscientious efforts to have them become whole language teachers imme-diately, these teachers had lost the joy of teaching and learning. They were going through the motions of change but without personal commitment and understand-ing. Allowing and valuing time for change in the process cannot be overstated. Unless teachers are encouraged to take time for reading, risking, and reflecting, no meaningful change will occur.

501

It takes most of us a long time to feel confident about the changes we have made and are making in our teaching and to begin to trust ourselves. In the process of becoming whole language teachers, most of us find that we are continually struggling and questioning what we are doing. Just when we think we have some answers, new questions arise.

It has taken me about ten years to feel confident with my own philosophy and teaching. I am kinder to myself now when one of my lessons doesn't succeed. I use the failure as an opportunity for reflection, and I often solicit feedback from students as well as other teachers. Based on such ongoing evaluation and reflection, I know there is a lot of learning going on, and I know that this learning is relevant and connected to the students' lives. I am no longer upset when I provide choices and some students abuse them. I no longer believe that time has been poorly spent when there is a lot of conversation between students, and some students seem to be off task. I have realized there is no perfect democracy or perfect classroom.

In the continually evolving process of becoming whole language teachers, my colleagues and I continue to read professionally, think about our teaching, observe our students, attend conferences, and collaborate with each other. We are feeling more courageous in our risk taking, more confident in the decisions we make, and more tolerant of our mistakes. It is a joyful struggle that keeps us energized and excited about our teaching and learning. I wish you continued success and risk taking in your own joyful struggle. I hope that you move slowly and thoughtfully enough to savor and appreciate the lifelong learning process.

RESOURCES
FOR TEACHERS

Resources for Teachers

The following annotated resources—professional books, journal articles, themed journals, journals, newsletters, and literacy extension resources—have been carefully selected to support teachers in continued professional growth in teaching and learning. A (•) before a title indicates a resource that has been found to be particularly useful, thought provoking, and outstanding in quality.

Most resources listed here have publication dates of 1988 and beyond. For other recommended resources, up to and including 1988, see *Resources for Teachers* (Routman, 1988).

Professional Books

Annotations with Vera Milz

The following is an annotated bibliography of books other teachers, Vera Milz, and I have found helpful in furthering our knowledge of language learning, literacy, and teaching. Vera Milz, a highly talented elementary teacher and reviewer of professional books, has annotated many of the titles, and her initials (V. M.) appear after the annotations she has written. All titles, unless otherwise noted, are available in paperback.

Allen, JoBeth, and Jana M. Mason (eds.). 1989. *Risk Makers, Risk Takers, Risk Breakers: Reducing the Risks for Young Literacy Learners*. Portsmouth, NH: Heinemann.

This is a thought-provoking book with chapters by classroom teachers and university researchers who discuss how schools and parents can provide the most effective support for children labeled at-risk. Stereotypes about social class and educational expectations are examined in light of new evidence of early literacy

acquisition by these children. The book is divided into four sections, moving from detailed accounts of successful individual children to descriptions of teachers and their positive learning environments to strategies for parental support and, finally, to suggestions for literacy policies and practices designed to reduce risks for all children. The book is important reading for anyone developing programs that will increase the potential of every young child to be successful in becoming literate. (V. M.)

• Atwell, Nancie (ed.). 1990. *Coming to Know. Writing to Learn in the Intermediate Grades*. Portsmouth, NH: Heinemann.

Practicing teachers in grades 3–6 in Maine enthusiastically describe fresh approaches to writing in the content areas. Social studies, science, math, and art are integrated with reading and writing through the use of learning logs based on personal experiences and observations. Teachers looking for alternatives to traditional book reports and research reports will find well-documented alternative methods. The 70 pages of appendices, which include "Genres for Report Writing," "Prompts for Learning Log Entries," "Bury Yourself in Books: Children's Literature for Content-Area Study," and "Resources for Writing and Reading to Learn," are wonderfully helpful.

Atwell, Nancie (ed.). 1989. *Workshop 1 by and for Teachers: Writing and Literature*. Portsmouth, NH: Heinemann.

This first annual, written by and for classroom teachers, focuses on the teaching of reading and writing. Themes for 1991 and 1992 include "The Politics of

1b

Process" and "The Teacher as Researcher in the 1990's." (Teachers are invited to submit manuscripts to the editor for future annual editions.)

I found the voices of knowledgeable practicing teachers k–8 inspiring. Thomas Newkirk's interview of fifth grade teacher Jack Wilde gave me a lot to think about in the teaching of writing. Donna Skolnick's work with elementary students gave me ideas for connecting literature to writing. Cora Five's sharing of her fifth-graders' original poetry and Marna Bunce's connection of prose to poetry helped me revalue immersion in poetry and wonderful literature as a vehicle for teaching the language of poetry. Read the entire book for the thoughtful insights of teacher-researchers.

Atwell, Nancie (ed.). 1990. *Workshop 2 by and for Teachers: Beyond the Basal*. Portsmouth, NH: Heinemann.

This second annual volume written by and for teachers of grades k–8 is for the "reflective practitioner" who enjoys thinking about and examining meaningful teaching and learning, especially as it applies to literature. I was delighted with (and jealous of) author Cynthia Rylant's description of how easily writing comes to her and her implications for how writing should be taught in school. Marni Schwartz, a middle school teacher, personally describes the value of returning to favorite stories. Kathleen Moore convinces the reader of the value of fairy tales in teaching reading. An interview of Jack Prelutsky by Kathy Hershey and an interview of first grade teacher and writer Carol Avery by Jane Hansen provide insights into their characters and thinking. Kindergarten teacher Bobbi Fisher elaborates on her interview-research process as a way of evaluating students in her reading-writing classroom. Adele Fiderer's piece about book discussion groups with her fourth- and fifth-graders provides an excellent model for any classroom. This is but a sampling of the eloquent voices of teachers who have moved "beyond the basal" to make literature a central part of their lives.

Baghban, Marcia. 1989. *You Can Help Your Young Child with Writing*. Newark, DE: International Reading Association.

This pamphlet is part of a series designed to provide parents with practical ideas to use to support young learners. Beginning with anecdotes of young children writing, it describes how the child's understanding of the writing system differs from that of the adult writer. Answers to possible parent questions, such as "What about correctness?" are given, along with recommended readings for more information. A helpful guide to hand to a questioning parent! (V. M.)

Baker, Ann, and Johnny Baker. 1990. *Mathematics in Process*. Portsmouth, NH: Heinemann.

Elementary teachers who are ready to apply the conditions and principles of whole language to the teaching and learning of mathematics will want to read this book. The authors, Australian educators, advocate applying the writing process and shared book experience to a process approach to mathematics. Lots of examples of open-ended math activities in which children have opportunities to experiment with ideas, develop their own strategies, and communicate and reflect about their experiences are presented.

Barron, Marlene. 1990. *I Learn to Read and Write the Way I Learn to Talk*. Katonah, NY: Richard C. Owen.

Based on whole language theory and practice, this concise booklet (32 pp.) simply and clearly explains early reading and writing behaviors. Excellent to share with preschool through grade 1 parents.

Barrs, Myra, Sue Ellis, Hilary Tester, and Anne Thomas, all of the Centre for Language in Primary Education, London. 1989. *The Primary Language Record: Handbook for Teachers*. Portsmouth, NH: Heinemann.

This handbook is another tool for educators who are interested in developing holistic evaluative records of a child's progress in language development. It has a detailed explanation of procedures, *along with many examples of evaluations of actual children. Copies of the assessment forms are given with permission to photocopy. A unique feature of the suggested evaluation is the involvement of parents throughout the procedure. Primary teachers considering the use of observation-based, anecdotal record-keeping, will find this book to be very helpful for organizing their gathered information to provide a detailed picture of a child's literacy development. (V. M.)*

• Baskwill, Jane. 1989. *Parents and Teachers. Partners in Learning*. Richmond Hill, Ontario: Scholastic Canada.

The author, who is a whole language teacher, parent, and principal, honestly shares how she went about improving parent-teacher communication. Using the "family model" built on trust, understanding, and open communication, Baskwill describes the projects and procedures she initiated in her move toward a reciprocal communication model. Specifics are given in the text and the appendix for how she used a survey, booklet for parents, notes to parents, dialogue journals, newsletters, book bags, parent bags, "lunch box launchers," special kits, and more. An extremely valuable resource for any teacher wishing to significantly improve parent-teacher communication. Be sure your school library and administrator have a copy of this book.

Baskwill, Jane, and Paulette Whitman. 1988. *Evaluation: Whole Language, Whole Child*. New York: Scholastic.

This slim volume is full of tools that allow teachers to describe the development of their students as readers and writers. The authors found that most of the current evaluation methods in use today did not give them the information they needed to help individual children. To find answers, they looked for ways in their own classrooms to observe and interpret and finally to report to parents. What they discovered was helpful to themselves and also is a good starting point for other teachers who want to go beyond the statistical evaluation often used in today's schools. (V. M.)

Bayer, Ann Shea. 1990. *Collaborative-Apprenticeship Learning: Learning and Thinking Across the Curriculum, K–12*. Mountain View, CA: Mayfield. Co-distributed by Richard C. Owen, Katonah, NY.

This terrific text (156 pp.) discusses, demonstrates, and applies a collaborative teacher-learner model that is relevant for teachers at the kindergarten through university level. Teachers ready to shift more responsibility for learning to students and to use language and writing as a tool for learning—especially in the content areas—will find much support here. Specifics for management, eliciting prior knowledge (especially through focused free writing), focused reading, writing to learn, and peer interaction are invaluable for revising approaches to planning and implementing curriculum.

Bird, Lois Bridges (ed.). 1989. *Becoming a Whole Language School: The Fair Oaks Story*. Katonah, NY: Richard C. Owen.

This is an inspiring story of how a school in California, with a majority Hispanic, low socioeconomic population, made the transition to a successful bilingual, whole language school. What is unusual about this story is that the change efforts are led jointly by the principal, superintendent, and a school board member working alongside the students, teachers, consultants, and researchers. All of their voices come through. I found the last section, "How We Got Started," to be particularly moving.

Bissex, Glenda L., and Richard H. Bullock (eds.). 1987. *Seeing for Ourselves: Case-Study Research by Teachers of Writing*. Portsmouth, NH: Heinemann.

Bissex defines a teacher-researcher as "an observer, a questioner, a learner, and a more complete teacher" (pp. 4–5), while Bullock discusses the power of teacher research to change the way teachers regard their students, themselves, and their professsion (p. 27). Case-study research is described as a powerful tool to discover what is happening to the children we teach, as well as a way of looking at both ourselves and our profession. Classroom teachers from first grade to university level then present their findings from their studies of poetry usage, writing process, writing conferences, journal usage, and so on. An especially interesting chapter brings the various authors together for a roundtable discussion on their research. (V. M.)

Bloome, David (ed.). 1989. *Classrooms and Literacy.* Norwood, NJ: Ablex.

Twenty researchers examine literacy activity and learning in natural settings—classrooms in elementary schools. The researchers explore the relationships between classrooms and literacy through four related issues: the classroom community, intellectual consequences, access to literacy, and distribution of power. Educators and teacher-researchers interested in how the functions and functioning of classrooms affect students' literacy will be interested in these long-term, descriptive studies.

Two quotes:

" . . . children from low-income and working class communities tend to have a literacy curriculum different from that of their middle and upper class counterparts" (Bloome, p. 19); "In order to move into a higher group, students must not simply work harder and learn more; they must also learn qualitatively different reading skills, participation styles, and teacher orientations" (Borko and Eisenhart, p. 124).

Bredekamp, Sue (ed.). 1987. *Developmentally Appropriate Practice in Early Childhood Programs Serving Children from Birth through Age 8,* expanded ed. Washington, DC: National Association for the Education of Young Children.

This position statement (91 pp.) has become a highly acknowledged document for looking at appropriate and inappropriate practices for infants, toddlers, preschoolers, and primary grade students. It is an outstanding reference for all teachers, administrators, parents, and policymakers who want to ensure the development of favorable early childhood practices in language and literacy

learning. Be sure your school library has a copy of this publication.

Bruner, Jerome, and Michael Cole. 1990. *Early Literacy. The Developing Child.* Cambridge, MA: Harvard University Press.

In this 173-page resource, the authors closely examine children's meaning making in their talk, play, writing, and reading, and they describe the wide range of literacy activities that young children engage in before formal literacy instruction in school. For parents and educators interested in gaining a greater understanding of children's early literacy development as well as ensuring continuity from the child's literacy experiences at home to school, this is a valuable text.

Butler, Dorothy, and Marie Clay. 1987, 1988. *Reading Begins at Home. Writing Begins at Home.* Portsmouth, NH: Heinemann.

These companion books are very useful in helping parents to understand how young children learn to read and write, and even more important, to help them to support the process before their children enter school. Both are helpful to give to parents of first grade children, and they are especially appreciated by parents with younger children at home. (V. M.)

• Calkins, Lucy McCormick, with Shelley Harwayne. 1991. *Living between the Lines.* Portsmouth, NH: Heinemann.

This is an unusual, personal, and thoughtful book on the teaching of writing. There is no index to look up minilessons, conferencing, or specific procedures to follow. Instead, the reader is completely immersed in the recent work, thoughts, images, and writings of the teachers and students of the Teachers College Writing Project in New York City and is asked to rethink the teaching of writing.

In this sensitively and beautifully written text, the reader gets a feel for what the promise of writing can hold when writing workshop moves from writing folders and published pieces to notebooks and projects. We are asked to re-examine the writing workshop in broader, more flexible ways so we provide—among other elements— "silent spaces," "commitment," "genre study," "longer, slower conferences," ourselves as joyfully literate role models, real-life connections and purposes for writing, and lots of opportunities to help children develop their most promising "seed ideas." "In a sense, everything in this book addresses how we can help youngsters write with an intensity and life force. . ." (p. 271). The changes Calkins has made in her own thinking and teaching since she wrote The Art of Teaching Writing *(Heinemann, 1986) are humbling and inspiring for us all.*

• Cambourne, Brian. 1988. *The Whole Story: Natural Learning and the Acquisition of Literacy in the Classroom.* Richmond Hill, Ontario: Scholastic-TAB.

In whole language circles, Brian Cambourne is to Australia what Don Holdaway is to New Zealand and Ken Goodman is to the United States. For teachers ready to take the time to understand the theory behind whole language, this text (201 pp.) offers detailed insight into the language learning process. The in-depth discussion of Cambourne's eight conditions of learning is thought provoking and applicable to the classroom. While mostly a theoretical text, the reader is taken into a grade 5 Australian classroom and given a picture of theory into practice. There is a useful section on evaluating literacy development. There is no index.

Clay, Marie M. 1985. *The Early Detection of Reading Difficulties,* 3rd ed. Portsmouth, NH: Heinemann.

Educators interested in Reading Recovery will find this text explicit for defining the program's assessment procedures and intervention strategies.

Cohen, S. Alan. 1988. *TESTS: Marked for Life?* Richmond Hill, Ontario: Scholastic-TAB.

This 58-page book clearly explains norm-referenced and criterion-referenced tests and notes the limitations of the former. Share this book with parents and administrators.

Collerson, John (ed.). 1988. *Writing for Life.* Portsmouth, NH: Heinemann.

I found this Primary English Teaching Association publication a very welcome addition to books on the teaching of writing. This practical, readable, 120-page book goes beyond the process-conference approach and gives specific suggestions for teaching writing across the curriculum. There are lots of ideas for teaching children to write in different genres: reports, scripts, descriptions, and factual accounts, as well as narratives. The point is well made that we need to demonstrate expository as well as narrative forms of writing to have a balanced writing program. Applicable for secondary school too.

Collins, James L. (ed.). 1990. *Vital Signs 1: Bringing Together Reading and Writing.* Portsmouth, NH: Heinemann.

Designed to be an annual publication, Vital Signs *is addressed to teachers in junior high school through the first year of college. The first collection of articles is concerned with literature, why it should be read, and practical ideas and strategies for its use. Susan Ohanian's opening piece, "Literature Has No Uses," should be read by teachers of any grade level. Another piece, by Marni Schwartz, discusses storytelling as a means of interacting with literature. Last, Susan Beth Pfeffer, a noted YA author, takes readers behind the scenes to show how she writes her books. (V. M.)*

Cullinan, Bernice E. 1989. *Literature and the Child,* 2nd ed. San Diego: Harcourt Brace Jovanovich. (hardbound)

This is a reference book that I have come to enjoy, and that I have found to be useful even to my primary age students. They often refer to it as we are developing thematic units or studying an author or illustrator's work. As with Charlotte Huck's Children's Literature in the Elementary School, *a landmark anthology of children's books, books are described, and many suggestions are given for their use in the classroom. Yet this book has several unique features, which make it especially useful in the class-*

room, such as a chapter describing literature of many cultures and thematic descriptions within various genres. Brief
profiles of authors/illustrators are placed
throughout the book, as well as a list of
their birthdays in one of the appendices.
I also like the listing of various awards
given to books and authors/illustrators.
Though the book is expensive for a
teacher to purchase singly, it is well
worth requesting as an addition to the
school library. (V. M.)

Davidson, Jane L. (ed.). 1988. *Counterpoint
and Beyond: A Response to "Becoming a
Nation of Readers"*. Urbana, IL: National Council of Teachers of English.

This publication was written to explore concerns that the NCTE Commission on Reading found in the highly pub-
licized BNR (Becoming a Nation of
Readers), which was released in 1985.
They believed that while BNR presented
some sound theoretical positions and offered practical suggestions, it had several
serious faults that needed to be addressed
in a new publication. Commission members felt BNR was biased, did not present
a full picture, and was inconsistent in the
theory of reading presented and in the
suggestions made for beginning reading
instruction. BNR blithely dismissed
whole language theory and research with
the statement, "In the hands of very skill-
ful teachers, the results can be excellent.
But the average result is indifferent when
compared to approaches typical in American classrooms, at least as gauged by
performance on first and second grade
standardized reading achievement tests"
(p. 45, BNR). Several chapters describe
how minority concerns were largely ignored in BNR. The place of literature in
the reading program was barely mentioned beyond suggesting that parents
should read to their children. Another
problem was the relationship between
phonics and comprehension. In one statement, BNR stressed that children construct meaning from their first experiences with reading, while the report
stressed that children be taught basic
letter-sound relationships first, or they

would be unable to comprehend. Both
the original report and Counterpoint
should be read together and the dialogue
continued! (V. M.)

• Doake, David B. 1988. *Reading Begins at
Birth*. New York: Scholastic.

Doake believes that the best time to
introduce a child to books is on the date
of birth, and this volume is a testimonial
to the effectiveness of reading to young
children. He details how his own son
heard stories within six hours of birth
and was "hooked" before his first birthday. The book is filled with vignettes of
parents reading to their children and the
results of this shared time. It is a great
resource for teachers to use with parents
in developing partnerships between
school and home and a reminder that
"children learn to read by reading." As a
bonus, it's a wonderful gift for any new
parents you might know. (V. M.)

Edelsky, Carole, Bess Altwerger, and Barbara
Flores. 1991. *Whole Language. What's
the Difference?* Portsmouth, NH: Heinemann.

This book has been written with the
intention of helping educators become
more knowledgeable about the theoretical bases of whole language. For the
teacher who already has some understanding of whole language, the detailed
theoretical framework that is presented—
as well as the scenes from whole language
classrooms—makes whole language theory very explicit.

Fisher, Bobbi. 1991. *Joyful Learning: A Whole
Language Kindergarten*. Portsmouth, NH:
Heinemann.

This book describes what an observant, knowledgeable kindergarten teacher
does in her classroom in a typical day and
why she does it. It is a remarkably clear
and pragmatic explanation of a classroom based on Don Holdaway's Natural
Learning Model. Each chapter highlights
a specific aspect of the classroom. The
chapters on assessment, dramatic play,
and questions teachers ask are especially
strong. Although the book is focused on
the kindergarten level, teachers from

prekindergarten through grade 2 will find many ideas, routines, themes, and record-keeping suggestions which will directly apply to their whole language classrooms.

Fletcher, Ralph, 1991. *Walking Trees: Teaching Teachers in the New York City Schools*. Portsmouth, NH: Heinemann.

This is a sensitively written, honest account of the author's struggles and successes during one school year when he worked as a staff developer for the Teachers College Writing Project. In a book that reads like a novel, Fletcher poignantly describes his daily experiences in teaching the writing process to administrators, teachers, and children in the New York City Schools. Compelling reading.

• Forester, Anne D., and Margaret Reinhard. 1989. *The Learner's Way*. Winnipeg, Canada: Peguis.

This outstanding text (315 pp.), based on the belief that children learn from models and by being immersed in doing, combines a strong theory base with very specific practice. For the primary teacher, especially in k–2, who wants to visualize the whole language classroom and make it a reality, there is no book that is more helpful. Teachers will find the details and scheduling of actual classroom teaching presented in a clear, relaxed, applicable manner.

Activities and strategies such as storytime, book time, reading groups, unison reading, individualized reading, writing workshop, author's circle, and news time are fully explained. News time is viewed as "our most comprehensive way of modeling all of the writing skills" (p. 90). During news time, children share their news of the day orally as the teacher writes and demonstrates the reading-writing connection through spelling, phonics, handwriting, punctuation, capitalization, and rereading.

Gibson, Linda. 1989. *Literacy Learning in the Early Years: Through Children's Eyes*. New York: Teachers College Press.

The four sections of this book allow the reader to look at early literacy issues at various age levels, birth through two, the three-, four- and five-year-olds, and the primary years. Chapters within the sections contain titles such as "Emergent Literacy: A World of Print," "Building Classroom Culture," "Teaching Reading in the Kindergarten," and "Building a Community of Readers." Each chapter abounds with language stories—both oral and written—in home or school settings. The Epilogue, "Shaping New Images of Literacy Education," really stresses the importance of the teacher. Overall, the book presents a solid theoretical base in fostering language development. (V. M.)

Goodman, Kenneth, Yetta Goodman, and Wendy Hood (eds.). 1989. *The Whole Language Evaluation Book*. Portsmouth, NH: Heinemann.

This powerful book encourages teachers to value their students and to find ways to help them—instead of showing them they have failed. Whole language practitioners across the United States and Canada contributed the various chapters describing alternatives to traditional evaluation techniques. They believe that evaluation should be a way of documenting the learning growth occurring daily—never as an assessment of decontextualized, abstract skills unrelated to the functional use of language. A variety of evaluation strategies, such as anecdotal records, learning logs, miscue analysis, journal samples, portfolios or folders, writing samples, and teacher notes, are described as they are implemented by the authors in various classroom settings from elementary to senior high school, adult education, and with bilingual and special education students. Many useful suggestions are given for record keeping. The book is an excellent resource for persons who are grounded in whole language practices and who are now interested in making student evaluation an integral part of the learning process. (V. M.)

• Goodman, Kenneth S., Patrick Shannon, Yvonne S. Freeman, and Sharon Murphy. 1988. *Report Card on Basal Readers*. Katonah, NY: Richard C. Owen.

Basal reading programs are used in 90 percent of U.S. classrooms—accepted and rarely questioned until recently. This is a book that has been accused of "basal bashing," but it has raised some serious questions. It examines the history of basal readers, how they are produced and marketed, the content of the program, and possible changes/alternatives to the basal. Most shocking to me were the many examples of how teachers have become scripted technicians, encouraged to let the program teach reading. Recommendations for teachers, administrators, teacher educators, researchers, basal authors and publishers, and policy makers are given. This is a provocative book that should be read by anyone choosing materials for children to read. (V. M.)

Goswami, Dixie, and Peter R. Stillman (eds.). 1987. *Reclaiming the Classroom: Teacher Research as an Agency for Change*. Portsmouth, NH: Heinemann-Boynton/Cook.

This exciting collection of essays addresses the "how's" as well as the "why's" of classroom research. The importance of teacher-researchers can be summed up in James Britton's statement, "What the teacher does not achieve in the classroom cannot be achieved by anybody else." Though the book is not a step-by-step procedure manual, a teacher can gain valuable information on how to carry out classroom research. Essays such as "A Quiet Form of Research," "Research as Odyssey," "Class-Based Writing Research: Teachers Learning from Students," and "Planning Classroom Research" were quite useful to me. The final section of the book documents the practices and insights of seven teacher-researchers learning in their classrooms. (V. M.)

Graves, Donald. 1989, 1990. *The Reading/Writing Teacher's Companion: Investigate Nonfiction, Experiment with Fiction*, and *Discover Your Own Literacy*. Portsmouth, NH: Heinemann.

This series of books brings together Graves's current thinking since his landmark book Writing: Teachers and Children at Work (1983). Whereas his earlier work focused more on the process of writing, these books explore the richness of reading and writing together. Examples of children and teachers sharing the books they enjoy and exploring writing in the various forms are given. Graves stresses that teachers must be readers and writers themselves if they are ever going to encourage literacy among their students. Many classroom language stories are shared as teachers are encouraged to reach out and extend their own growth as literate individuals. (V. M.)

Hall, Nigel. 1987. *The Emergence of Literacy*. Portsmouth, NH: Heinemann.

For the educator who wants to examine the worldwide research behind emergent literacy but who doesn't have time to read all the primary sources, this 101-page volume provides a solid foundation. This is a very important book for increasing your knowledge about language learning and for implementing meaningful literacy instructional practices.

Hansen, Jane. 1987. *When Writers Read*. Portsmouth, NH: Heinemann.

This comprehensive text brings writing and reading instruction together based on insights found in writing process classrooms. It begins with Hansen's own questioning as she learned new methods of reading instruction while observing in Ellen Blackburn Karelitz's first grade classroom. However, much of the book is based on her research at Mast Way, a public school in New Hampshire. Guidelines are given for structuring the classroom, evaluation, the teacher's role, the place of phonics, and basal readers based on real happenings in the classrooms where Hansen was working. Chapters are devoted to the ways that librarians, administrators, Chapter 1 teachers, and even college professors can support the classroom teacher. Teachers who are looking for alternatives to basal programs will find this book an invaluable resource. (V. M.)

• Harp, Bill (ed.). 1991. *Assessment and Evaluation in Whole Language Programs.* Norwood, MA: Christopher-Gordon.

This state-of-the-art comprehensive text on theory, history, principles, issues, directions, and strategies of literacy assessment and evaluation is important reading for all educators. Each of the twelve chapters provides a wealth of specific, in-depth information. "Evaluation in Reading—Miscue Analysis" by Dorothy Watson and Janice Henson offers a clear and thorough introduction for teachers ready to apply miscue analysis procedures. In "Whole Language Assessment and Evaluation in Primary Grade Classrooms," S. Jeanne Reardon describes in detail how she uses observations, informal and formal reading and writing conferences, students' writing, and reading records to understand a child's literacy development. Chapters on evaluation in special education classes—as well as bilingual, multicultural classrooms—illustrate how whole language evaluation procedures can be applied here as well. In "Record Keeping in Whole Language Classrooms," Jean Church skillfully discusses and demonstrates the purposes of record keeping, the kinds of records that provide needed information, and what needs to be recorded. The entire text is outstanding for its thoughtfulness and practicality.

Harste, Jerome C. 1989. *New Policy Guidelines for Reading. Connecting Research and Practice.* Urbana, IL: National Council of Teachers of English.

This excellent resource (80 pp.) evaluates recent research in reading comprehension and reading instruction and arrives at recommendations and guidelines for improving the teaching of reading. Any educator or researcher involved in policy making in reading instruction will want to read this handbook to ensure that school reading practices effectively reflect what is known and understood about the reading process. Some quotes to think about:

"Almost anything teachers do beyond a basal reading program significantly improves reading comprehension" (p. 23).

"There are no ethnographic studies of reading that verify a subskills model of reading instruction" (p. 27).

"Our best research evidence suggests that most regular education students learn in the same way as most special education students, and vice versa" (p. 47).

• Harste, Jerome C., and Kathy G. Short, with Carolyn Burke and contributing teacher-researchers. 1988. *Creating Classrooms for Authors: The Reading-Writing Connection.* Portsmouth, NH: Heinemann.

This is an in-depth text (403 pp.) for the experienced reading-writing teacher who already applies the theoretical knowledge of language learning in the classroom along with effective management techniques. The authors view "The Authoring Cycle" as a model for all learning in a curriculum that focuses on life experiences. The reader is given much direction to get and keep the cycle going. Teachers will find the second section of the book, where many specific classroom activities are described, especially valuable. "Author's Chair," "Classroom Newspaper," "Family Stories," "Learning Logs," "Literature Circles," "Reader's Theatre," "Save the Last Word for Me," "Sketch to Stretch," and "Written Conversation" are among some of the curricular activities delineated.

Heald-Taylor, Gail. 1989. *The Administrator's Guide to Whole Language.* Katonah, NY: Richard C. Owen.

This is a handy text (189 pp.) to give to the administrator who wants to know more about whole language and how to facilitate its implementation. Especially useful is the extensive section on the research supporting whole language teaching, the comparison between whole language and skills-based approaches, the activities and strategies principals should expect to see in whole language classrooms, the suggestions for informing and educating parents about whole language, and the section on assessment. Excellent for teachers as well.

- Heard, Georgia. 1989. *For the Good of the Earth and Sun. Teaching Poetry.* Portsmouth, NH: Heinemann.

  A practicing poet and teacher with a love of language and respect for students takes us "inside" the process of poetry writing by describing her own thinking-writing-reading processes. In so doing, she makes reading and writing poetry seem natural, desirable, and possible for us all. The book is practical, inspiring, and lovely to read. For the classroom teacher, there are suggestions and strategies for reading poetry, getting started writing poetry, creating visual images with words, choosing original words, revising, conferencing, and creating linebreaks and white spaces as well as examples of various minilessons. Although Heard sees a place for rhymed poetry, as well as haiku and cinquain, which she calls "the hamburger and hot dog of American poetry classrooms" (p. 96), she goes beyond formula writing to encouraging exploration with various forms and ideas in a poetry-rich environment. Lots of examples of what actually transpires in her poetry workshops with children are included along with many poems by children. There are also useful bibliographies of poetry books for children and reference books for teaching poetry. Reading this extraordinary and powerful book will change the way you approach the teaching of poetry.

- Hearne, Betsy. 1990. *Choosing Books for Children. A Commonsense Guide,* revised and expanded ed. New York: Delacorte.

  Building on her first edition published in 1981, Hearne provides valuable insights and suggestions for choosing and using all kinds of literature—as well as many organized listings with brief annotations of recommended books—for ages one through young adult. Very useful to parents and teachers seeking quality literature.

- Hickman, Janet, and Bernice E. Cullinan (eds.). 1989. *Children's Literature in the Classroom: Weaving Charlotte's Web.* Norwood, MA: Christopher-Gordon. (hardbound)

  Designed as a tribute to Charlotte Huck's teaching and her philosophy about literature for children, this book reflects the influence this remarkable teacher has had on her students. Following the opening tribute describing Huck's career and her vision of literature as the heart of the school curriculum, the book is divided into three sections: understanding the uses of literature in the classroom; celebrating books and authors in the picture book, fantasy, historical fiction, and poetry genres; and developing literature-based programs. The various chapters are contributed by her former students and several children's authors. The Epilogue, "No Wider Than the Heart Is Wide," is a piece by Huck herself. The entire volume is a rich and unique legacy for all of us to savor and treasure. (V. M.)

Hill, Mary W. 1989. *Home: Where Reading and Writing Begin.* Portsmouth, NH: Heinemann.

  This book is written specifically for parents and extends the idea of parents as partners in literacy development. Many examples of the developmental nature of children's reading and writing are given. Children's literature titles fill the pages, along with many practical suggestions for parents who want to reflect and consider how they can encourage their children as readers and writers. It is a great one to hand to parents in answer to their question, "How can I help my child?" (V. M.)

Hill, Susan, and Tim Hill. 1990. *The Collaborative Classroom.* Portsmouth, NH: Heinemann.

  Based on the cooperative learning work of David and Roger Johnson, the authors present lots of detailed examples of activities for successful cooperative group work. Very useful for the teacher who wants children to work together but who needs specific classroom management information to set up the collaborative classroom.

Jenson, Julie M. (ed.) 1989. *Stories to Grow On: Demonstrations of Language Learning in K–8 Classrooms*. Portsmouth, NH: Heinemann.

This book is one of the outcomes of an invitational conference held in Maryland in 1987. Planning for the teaching of elementary school language arts into the 21st century was a major purpose of the conference, and the insights that came from the meeting are described in the opening chapter. More important, eight elementary teachers who participated in the English Coalition Conference in 1987 contributed chapters to this book. Their classrooms show the diversity found in today's schools, and they invite teachers to consider curriculum and environment in light of what is known about how children know language. In these stories, children actively engaging in listening, talking, reading, and writing are carefully described from the first day in a first grade in which children read and create books to a middle school classroom whose children entered as very rote, disengaged learners. As they reflect on their practices, these teachers enable us to make connections and launch further change in our own classrooms. (V. M.)

Jett-Simpson, Mary (ed.). 1990. *Toward an Ecological Assessment of Reading Progress*. Schofield, WI: Wisconsin State Reading Association.

This impressive 119-page text for teachers, administrators, and policy makers deals with the major issues related to accountability and literacy in a straightforward, organized manner. Lots of specific, useful information is provided for making assessment consistent with the current, interactive view of reading. "Ecological assessment combines authentic texts and tasks so that students are involved in activities which real readers and writers do" (p. 19).

Jewell, Margaret Greer, and Miles V. Zintz. 1990. *Learning to Read Naturally*, 2nd ed. Dubuque, IA: Kendall/Hunt.

Written for educators from preschool through the primary grades, this com-prehensive, academic text (397 pp.) advocates a whole language instructional approach to literacy as the most effective foundation for building on the natural language acquisition of young children. Part 1 includes the theoretical base for "natural" reading and writing. Part 2 cites the need for change in literacy instruction from a skills and subskills approach to an emphasis on actual reading and writing activities. Part 3 describes an instructional program for the development of "natural" readers and writers. Extensive appendices list literacy resources, especially bibliographies of books.

Kamii, Constance (ed.). 1990. *Achievement Testing in the Early Grades: The Games Grown-Ups Play*. Washington, DC: National Association for the Education of Young Children.

The contributing authors to this thoughtful text (181 pp.) give research and rationale to demonstrate the harmful effects of achievement testing in kindergarten through second grade. In place of standardized testing with its emphasis on fragmented skills, they recommend evaluation (with teachers in charge) that is rooted in classroom practice and that informs us of students' thinking processes over time. Provocative, important reading for teachers, administrators, parents, and policymakers.

Kobrin, Beverly. 1988. *Eyeopeners! How to Choose and Use Children's Books about Real People, Places, and Things*. New York: Penguin.

Kobrin views fiction and nonfiction as "literary coequals" and states that children need TLC—the total literature connection. Asserting that children have natural curiosity and are fascinated by facts, she discusses over 500 engrossing nonfiction books and groups them by categories such as biographies, dinosaurs, grandparents, and holidays, to name a few. Each book annotation includes a brief summary, recommended age ranges, and teaching tips. This valuable resource book for teachers, parents, and librarians also includes criteria for eval-

uating nonfiction as well as an extensive "Quick-Link Index" to aid the teacher looking for specific topics or themes.

Lipson, Eden Ross. 1988. *The New York Times Parent's Guide to the Best Books for Children*. New York: Random House.

This guide of almost a thousand "best books" published in the United States has been written "to help you look for the next book to give to your favorite child." Book titles, accompanied by brief descriptions, are listed alphabetically by title in each of the following categories: wordless books, picture books, story books, early reading books, middle reading books, and young adult books. Thirty-four indexes allow looking up books in multiple ways. Preschool through middle school (through grade 9) teachers will find this a useful reference to share with parents.

Lloyd-Jones, Richard, and Andrea A. Lunsford (eds.). 1989. *The English Coalition Conference: Democracy through Language*. Urbana, IL: National Council of Teachers of English.

Don't be put off by the title! This book is an important report of a conference held for three weeks at the Wye Plantation in 1987. It brought together 60 English teachers from elementary to college level who listened, discussed, and reflected on where English language arts was, is, and will be going as we head into a new century. Making literacy a possibility for all students emerged as a priority, and many recommendations were considered. The report provides a good starting point for our own personal reflections. (V. M.)

McClure, Amy A., with Peggy Harrison and Sheryl Reed. 1990. *Sunrises and Songs*. Portsmouth, NH: Heinemann.

The reader is taken through a school year in a fifth and sixth grade whole language classroom where students are immersed in poetry daily. The teachers, avid readers and writers of poetry, inspire their students to read and respond to poetry; to write, critique, revise, and publish poetry; and to write daily in their poetry journals. For teachers ready

to connect poetry meaningfully to children's lives, this text is a valuable resource.

Mills, Heidi, and Jean Anne Clyde (eds.). 1990. *Portraits of Whole Language Classrooms: Learning for All Ages*. Portsmouth, NH: Heinemann.

Whole language teachers in varied settings—home day care, preschool, elementary, middle school, high school, university education lab—describe their experiences with students in their classrooms. The book assumes the reader already has a good understanding of whole language theory and classroom management. The final chapter, by John McInerney and Jerome Harste, nicely clarifies some beliefs about whole language. For description of chapters dealing with holistic teaching in remedial settings, see "Resources" at the end of Chapter 14.

Moir, Hughes, Melissa Cain, and Leslie Prosak-Beres (eds). 1990. *Collected Perspectives: Choosing and Using Books for the Classroom*. Norwood, MA: Christopher-Gordon.

Since 1984, Hughes Moir and his staff at the University of Toledo have published a journal, Perspectives, with reviews of current books written by practicing teachers who are using books with children and young adults. This collection pulls these reviews together into one volume that enables teachers to learn about many fine books for children. It also gives tried and tested suggestions to extend the books into various areas of the curriculum—none of which are the monotonous pages of worksheets found in guides that ultimately can beat a wonderful book to death. A feature in these reviews that I find especially useful is the listing of related books to the one cited. This often enables me to extend a child's interest beyond the one that is being read. (V. M.)

Mooney, Margaret E. 1990. *Reading to, with, and by Children*. Katonah, NY: Richard C. Owen.

Teachers, especially k–2, who want a full description and understanding of ap-

proaches to reading (reading aloud, shared reading, language experience, guided reading, and independent reading) and how these approaches can be used in the classroom will treasure this guide (92 pp.). Sample lessons for emergent, early, and fluent readers model strategies and questions teachers can use to get children to enjoy literature as well as predicting, sampling, confirming, and self-correcting on text.

Morrow, Lesley Mandel. 1989. *Literacy Development in the Early Years.* Englewood Cliffs, NJ: Prentice Hall.

For educators interested in current research and theory in early literacy development and how to apply that knowledge to the preschool through grade 1 classroom, this academic text (255 pp.) discusses the development of early literacy in depth and includes strategies for promoting oral language development and reading and writing development. Chapter 5, dealing with recreational reading and organizing well-planned library corners, and Chapter 6, dealing with strategies for using children's literature, are particularly useful. Pages 114–117 are very specific for how to guide a child's story retelling.

Murray, Donald M. 1989. *Expecting the Unexpected: Teaching Myself—and others—to Read and Write.* Portsmouth, NH: Boynton/Cook-Heinemann.

This is a diverse collection of twenty-four pieces full of introspection and sharing. Divided into four sections— Listening to the Page, Learning by Sharing, Exploring Form, Sitting to Write—it reveals Murray's thinking about his own process of writing and teaching writing to others. Along with essays and speeches, he even includes handouts used with his students—one of which was a piece written to describe revision by revealing it, "Revision as Visible Craft." He shares how he wrote and later revised a very personal piece, which he submitted to the Boston Globe for his "Over Sixty" column. In another piece, he answers questions from high school students. In paging through the book, I'm

sure that you will feel the joy of learning through his writing by this distinguished teacher/writer. (V. M.)

- Murray, Donald M. 1990. *Shoptalk: Learning to Write with Writers.* Portsmouth, NH: Boynton/Cook-Heinemann.

As a teenager, Murray was fascinated by writers talking about their writing, and he began a collection of quotations that eventually filled twenty-four thick notebooks. This book is a selection of his favorites organized into sixteen categories, such as "Why Write," "The Beginning Line," "Waiting for Writing," and "The Writing Habit." However, it is not just a book of quotations, for each section begins with a personal essay on Murray's own experiences with the topic. Both we and our students can join the company of writers as we browse through this book. Murray described it well: "I am comforted by what they say to me as we leave the writing desk together. My collection of quotes allows me to learn from fellow writers, to laugh and mourn with them, to know that others have experienced what I have often thought was eccentric or inappropriate." I'm glad that he took the time to share his quotes and insights with us! (V. M.)

- Nagy, William E. 1988. *Teaching Vocabulary to Improve Reading Comprehension.* Urbana, IL: National Council of Teachers of English and Newark, DE: International Reading Association.

This concise book (42 pp.) is the best I have read for combining research and practice in the teaching of vocabulary on a conceptual level. While the author states that "the single most important thing a teacher can do to promote vocabulary growth is to increase students' volume of reading" (p. 38), he also makes it clear that there is an important place for intensive instruction. Three necessary properties of vocabulary instruction are defined: integration ("tying in new words with familiar concepts and experiences"), repetition (having many encounters with a word), and meaningful use. Many useful activities for classroom application are included.

Nathan, Ruth, Frances Temple, Kathleen Juntunen, and Charles Temple. 1989. *Classroom Strategies That Work: An Elementary Teacher's Guide to Process Writing*. Portsmouth, NH: Heinemann.

This book is written by educators who have helped teachers who wanted to use process writing in their classrooms but needed detailed suggestions to begin. It gives very specific directions for setting up a supportive classroom and ways to help children with various aspects of the writing process. Focused lessons on such topics as narrowing topics, characterization, and descriptive writing are given for teachers to present to their students. It is a very basic book designed to get teachers started, and the authors suggest that teachers look to Graves, Calkins, and others for more theoretical information. (V. M.)

Nelms, Ben F. (ed.). 1988. *Literature in the Classroom: Readers, Texts, and Contexts*. Urbana, IL: National Council of Teachers of English.

This informative book reasserts the central place of literature in the school curriculum. Examples of classroom approaches to the teaching of literature are shown from first grade through college. The book is organized to focus on ways to encourage student response, how to explore possibilities of meaning in texts, and, finally, how to use literature to broaden our students' global views. (V. M.)

• Newkirk, Thomas. 1989. *More Than Stories: The Range of Children's Writing*. Portsmouth, NH: Heinemann.

Every once in a while I find a book that makes me think, "Ah, that says what I am thinking, but I haven't been able to put it into words yet." This book is one of that kind for me. Newkirk clearly explains the semiotic position on language development in the opening section, and then he carefully describes the diversity of writing done by young children as they develop the ability to write expository prose. An especially meaningful chapter is an interview of Kathy Matthews, a second grade teacher, who focuses on the many uses for writing found in her classroom. The book blends theory and practice in a way that stretched me as a teacher and gave me a lot to think about. (V. M.)

Newman, Judith M. (ed.). 1990. *Finding Our Own Way: Teachers Exploring Their Assumptions*. Portsmouth, NH: Heinemann.

In this collection of short essays, elementary and secondary teachers examine and question their theories and attitudes about learning and teaching. For all of us struggling to make meaningful change, the personal reflections in this text encourage us to think about how we can better connect our beliefs to our practices.

Pappas, Christine C., Barbara Z. Kiefer, and Linda S. Levstik. 1990. *An Integrated Language Perspective in the Elementary School: Theory into Action*. White Plains, NY: Longman.

Educators wanting to plan and implement thematic units will find much support in this scholarly, comprehensive text (352 pp.). The authors present the theoretical and practical aspects of an integrated language perspective that includes integration of the language arts as well as integration across the curriculum. Marginal notations throughout the text cite references, note useful resources, and highlight and explain concepts. Chapter 4, "Prototypes for Integrated Language Classrooms," includes eight prototypes (thematic units). Each prototpye includes a WEB, a weekly schedule, a typical day in an actual classroom, a summary, and a bibliography of children's literature and resources. The one thing I found missing in the prototypes were the major concepts and understandings. Teachers will find the thematic units excellent models but will need to be sure to put the "big understandings" into their own integrated language units. I found the chapters "More Ideas to Integrate Curricular Areas," "More on How-to: Ideas for Implementation in Integrated Language Classrooms," and "An Integrated Language Perspective Effecting

Change" to be particularly useful for the classroom teacher.

• Peterson, Ralph, and Maryann Eeds. 1990. *Grand Conversations: Literature Groups in Action.* Richmond Hill, Ontario: Scholastic-TAB.

For teachers who are already comfortable with a literature approach to reading, this 80-page text dealing with literature study of "books that have layers of story action and meaning" (p. 26) gives inspiration, organization, specific techniques, and lots of examples for constructing meaning through dialogue and interpretation. Developing children's awareness of, and response to, literary elements—story structure, plot, characters, place, tensions, point of view, mood, time, symbols and metaphors, theme—is fully discussed and demonstrated with examples from excellent literature. Examples of teacher-developed forms for organization and evaluation are also cited. A terrific, high-level resource.

Pinnell, Gay Su, and Myna L. Matlin (eds.). 1989. *Teachers and Research: Language Learning in the Classroom.* Newark, DE: International Reading Association.

This is a collection of articles by educators who share their complex, interrelated roles of teacher, researcher, and teacher educator/staff developer. Knowledge of language learning and the creation of supportive classrooms must come from insightful teachers who are willing to change. Several teachers contribute pieces that document their experiences as they grew in their understanding of how children become literate. Other articles show how teacher educators, consultants, and administrators have rethought their roles in order to support teachers. This is a book supporting change from the inside—not imposed from the outside. It will be of interest to teachers who are questioning language/literacy programs and those wanting to engage in their own teacher research. (V. M.)

• Probst, Robert. 1988. *Response and Analysis: Teaching Literature in Junior and Senior High School.* Portsmouth, NH: Boynton/Cook-Heinemann.

This book brings literature into students' lives. Probst believes literature should be a vital, personal experience and not presented as the object of tests and exercises. Drawing heavily on Louise Rosenblatt's work of almost 50 years ago, this text tries to show that literature should be personally significant, that readers be respected as they respond in different ways, and that readers acknowledge the role of literature in their world. The book is organized into three parts: a rationale of response-based teaching, literature choices, and the overall program. Many suggestions for the classroom are given, and there is an excellent listing of literary works that will stimulate students to think. Two sensitive themes, sexuality and violence, are discussed in detail, while representative books are listed under various themes. Other useful chapters include suggestions for response-based evaluation, as well as one in which film and television are considered as visual literature. Lots of practical and theoretical information for a teacher wanting a response-based literature program. (V. M.)

Reed, Arthea J. S. 1988. *Comics to Classics: A Parent's Guide to Books for Teens and Preteens.* Newark, DE: International Reading Association.

This book is useful to both parents and teachers. It contains a comprehensive list of fine books for children, organized according to topics, such as "Coming of Age," "Black Heroes," "Careers," "Survival," and so forth. The first three chapters discuss the stages of adolescent development in relation to reading, and the final chapters help parents to locate the desired books and give techniques to encourage reading and discussion of the books. (V. M.)

Rhodes, Lynn K., and Curt Dudley-Marling. 1988. *Readers and Writers with a Difference. A Holistic Approach to Teaching Learning Disabled and Remedial Students.* Portsmouth, NH: Heinemann.

For the teacher ready to look at teach-

ing learning disabled and remedial students holistically, this well-documented, comprehensive text (329 pp.) provides a wealth of information on all aspects of language learning. The authors discuss many instructional approaches for assessing, teaching, and extending meaningful reading and writing. The chapter "Developing Fluency in Reading and Writing" provides specific, detailed instructional strategies such as assisted reading, repeated reading, Readers Theatre, choral reading, sustained silent reading, free writing, journal writing, and written conversation. Most of the strategies and activities recommended are appropriate for all learners. An extensive list of predictable trade books for young children is included.

• Romano, Tom. 1987. *Clearing the Way. Working with Teenage Writers.* Portsmouth, NH: Heinemann.

"*Our responsibility as writing teachers is to help students learn personal processes for creating writing that enable them to create their best writing*" (p. 52). Drawing on his own experiences as a high school English teacher, Tom Romano eloquently describes how in a safe writing workshop, he enables students to use language to discover thought and to find their individual voices and styles. Romano demonstrates his craft with samples of his own and students' writing—drafts, revisions, and finished pieces in which meaning comes before correctness and form—examples of purposeful writing prompts, and meaningful ways of evaluating and grading with the goal that "*above anything else, we want them to write again*" (p. 128).

I began this book because I had been invited to speak with interested secondary teachers in our district. I had intended to skim the book, to get a feel for it. The power of Romano's voice grabbed me and never let up until I had ingested every word. I was surprised to find many references to Don Graves and Lucy Calkins and to see high school practice in an effective writing workshop very similar to what we are striving for at the elemen-

tary level. I savored fresh insights, new visions, clear writing by a teacher-learner, and validation that the writing process is inherently the same from kindergarten through grade 12. This is a remarkable book that should be read by every serious teacher of writing.

Romberg, Thomas A., Chair. 1989. *Curriculum and Evaluation Standards for School Mathematics.* Reston, VA: National Council of Teachers of Mathematics.

This comprehensive document (266 pp.) recognizes and addresses the need for major instructional reform in the content and emphasis in mathematics k–12. Fifty-four standards are delineated and divided into four areas: K–4, 5–8, 9–12, and evaluation. Embedded in the Standards *is the belief that "First, 'knowing' mathematics is 'doing' mathematics. A person gathers, discovers, or creates knowledge in the course of some activity having a purpose" (p. 7). Also in each standard are the expected student activities associated with doing mathematics. The document bases its curriculum and evaluation of mathematical literacy on five goals for all students: learning to value mathematics, becoming confident in one's own ability, becoming a mathematical problem solver, learning to communicate mathematically, and learning to reason mathematically. All educators interested in improving the quality of school mathematics will want to become familiar with this highly impressive and workable document.*

Routman, Regie, 1988. *Transitions: From Literature to Literacy.* Portsmouth, NH: Heinemann.

A personal, honest account of a public school teacher's transition from basal texts and worksheets toward literature-based reading and process writing. Some of the topics that are fully discussed include the use of predictable books, how to teach reading and writing with children's books, the place of phonics in the reading-writing program, journal writing, parental involvement, and evaluation. While the book's emphasis is on the primary grades, the theory, ideas, and extensive annotated resources are applicable across the grades. Educators beginning to move toward whole language have found this book both practical and inspiring.

Rudman, Masha Kabakow. 1989. *Children's Literature: Resource for the Classroom.* Norwood, MA: Christopher-Gordon. (hardbound)

Every major issue related to the use of children's literature in the reading program can probably be found in this guide. Experts in the field, ranging from authors to editors to teachers of children's literature, share their insights. Censorship, multicultural literature, and technology are discussed in various chapters. Two chapters present a behind-the-scenes look at how books are created by several talented authors and illustrators (Katherine Paterson, Ed Young, Tomie DePaolo, etc.). This is a reference book that belongs in the library of every school that would like to bring literature into the hands of children. It is helpful for teacher information as well as for sharing with your students. (V. M.)

Shannon, Patrick. 1989. *Broken Promises: Reading Instruction in Twentieth-Century America.* Granby, MA: Bergin & Garvey.

A must for every classroom teacher and administrator to read! The message is that commercially packaged basal reading materials control reading instruction and are doing a "good job of teaching students to decode words and to reproduce the meaning of texts." However, this goal is preventing children from becoming fully literate—"able to understand the connections among their lives and those of others, and to act on their new knowledge to construct a better, a more just, world" (p. viii). Shannon describes the technologizing and marketing of reading in a detailed history of the basal reader and shows how these systems have actually de-skilled teachers by their detailed instructions on how to manage the worksheets, reading selections, and the students. He cites research, some of it his own, as to why so many teachers rely

on basal materials and follow their directions, yet want to be professionals able to make critical judgments to meet student needs. Finally, he devotes the last chapter of the book to the "possibilities of constructive change," such as collective seminars in which teachers analyze their dependence on basals or conduct research in their own classrooms. Although he believes that it will not be easy, Shannon thinks that it is possible for teachers and students to resist the management of their literacy and lives and to "gain their rightful place in reading programs." (V. M.)

• Shannon, Patrick. 1990. *The Struggle to Continue: Progressive Reading Instruction in the United States.* Portsmouth, NH: Heinemann.

This book was written to describe the underlying practices and promises of the child-centered and critical literacy programs—mentioned as positive alternatives to the controlling technological management of literacy decried in Broken Promises. Shannon also gives an historical perspective to the whole language movement by noting it as a recent development of a hundred-year-old movement to provide literacy programs based on the child within a social context. This is a challenging book but worthwhile reading for any teacher who has lived with the domination of reading instruction by the basal reader industry and is attempting to struggle with alternatives. As he helps teachers make connections with the rich progressive past, Shannon encourages teachers to continue to work for better and more compassionate literacy programs for their students and future generations. (V. M.)

• Short, Kathy Gnagey, and Kathryn Mitchell Pierce (eds.). 1990. *Talking about Books: Creating Literate Communities.* Portsmouth, NH: Heinemann.

Fourteen teachers and teacher educators share their experiences with literature study. This is a very thoughtful text for the teacher who already has a collaborative atmosphere in a whole language classroom. Literature circles, which in-

clude small-group discussions in which students read and react to the same book or small-group discussions on text sets in which students read different but thematically related texts, are discussed fully. Lots of specific examples are given, not only for individual books but also for integrated literature study across the curriculum. The introductory chapter by Charlotte Huck sets the tone for the power of literature.

• Smith, Frank. 1990. *To Think*. New York: Teachers College Press.

The process of thinking is examined from all angles in this comprehensive book. As with his previous books, Smith celebrates the power of humans to learn! He expresses concern about complaints that students are unable to think, and, therefore, must be carefully taught, and believes that attempts to teach "thinking skills" can actually hamper the development of thinking. Two especially interesting chapters, "Thinking Creatively" and "Thinking Critically," demystify these aspects of thinking and show how they are not so difficult and distinctive after all. Finally, he looks at educational implications for both teachers and students. He suggests, "Students—and teachers—must learn to doubt. . . . Certainty stunts thought, in ourselves and others. . . . Thought flourishes as questions are asked, not as answers are found" (p. 129). Smith also stresses the importance of functional, relevant reading and writing when he states, "Reading and writing are two activities that promote thought—provided that what is read is worth thinking about and that writing is used for extending the imagination of the writer" (p. 128). Last, he warns that "thinking cannot be broken down into parts, specified in objectives, and taught in isolated exercises and drills. All of this interferes with thought" (p. 128). This is a relevant, challenging book with implications affecting the entire school curriculum. (V. M.)

Smith, Frank. 1988. *Understanding Reading*, 4th ed. Hillsdale, NJ: Lawrence Erlbaum.

This book is about how reading is learned, not taught, as an essentially meaningful activity and how readers are active, not passive, in seeking meaning dependent on their prior knowledge and expectations. It is not a book in which reading is treated as decoding print to sound but rather as a matter of making sense of written language. The book provides a theoretical analysis of the reading process and gives ways to support learners' reading until they are able to read enough for authors to take over. Smith states, "Literacy is not accomplished through the external controls of prescribed programs and formalized tests, but through sensitive teachers who understand what they teach and who also understand the students for whose learning they are responsible." (V. M.)

Stewig, John Warren. 1990. *Read to Write: Using Children's Literature as a Springboard for Teaching Writing*, 3rd ed. Katonah, NY: Richard C. Owen.

The book describes ways to help children grow as writers by introducing them to quality literature and helping them to build their understanding and appreciation through discussion and writing experiences. It is an excellent resource for finding appropriate literature for minilessons that will help children understand the elements of writing, such as characterization, using figurative language, describing a setting, and so on. (V. M.)

Stillman, Peter. 1989. *Families Writing*. Cincinnati, OH: Writer's Digest Books. Distributed by Heinemann Educational Books, Portsmouth, NH. (hardbound)

This is a delightful book about writing for the very best of reasons—for the family's sake—and pure enjoyment. Beginning with reasons for writing, the book is filled with suggestions for a lifetime of family writing activities. It's not a textbook, but a plea to tell your story—to capture family happenings in words to be cherished, enjoyed, and passed on to future generations. Stillman's pleasure in writing shines through the many pieces of his family history that are scattered throughout the book. It's a book that I *want to share with parents, and one I want to return to for ideas and inspiration. (V. M.)*

- Strickland, Dorothy S., and Lesley Mandel Morrow (eds.). 1989. *Emerging Literacy: Young Children Learn to Read and Write*. Newark, DE: International Reading Association.

    If I had to recommend one book to preschool–grade 2 teachers for developing a meaningful literacy program, this would be it. Kindergarten teachers, especially, will find this book particularly helpful for tying theory and practice together and for incorporating appropriate classroom practices. In addition to gaining a current and broad understanding of issues and principles of early literacy, teachers are presented with a wealth of practical ideas and activities. The importance and application of oral language experiences, storybook reading, and all kinds of writing for promoting children's language and literacy growth are clearly delineated.

- Taylor, Denny, and Catherine Dorsey-Gaines. 1988. *Growing Up Literate: Learning from Inner-City Families*. Portsmouth, NH: Heinemann.

    This poignant, moving ethnographic study of urban black families living well below the poverty line focuses on families who have first grade children successfully learning to read and write. Through their carefully documented observations, the authors dispel the common myths and stereotypes of poor, black families. We see overwhelming confirmation that the families effectively use reading and writing daily for their survival, to communicate with others, to fulfill educational requirements, and for pleasure. The authors state, "it is evident that the families with whom we were working are more than the fillers in of forms—they are active members in a print community in which literacy is used for a wide variety of social, technical, and aesthetic purposes, for a wide variety of audiences, and in a wide variety of situations" (p. 200). Educators, researchers, and policy makers are urged to take a close look at these families—and other functioning families—to begin to close the wide gaps between home and school literacy.

Tierney, Robert J., Mark A. Carter, and Laura E. Desai. 1991. *Portfolios in the Reading-Writing Classroom*. Norwood, MA: Christopher-Gordon.

Based on research and practice, k–12, of the use of reading and writing portfolios in several school districts, this scholarly and practical text provides teachers with a flexible framework for implementing and using portfolios in the classroom. The text fully discusses and gives specific examples for topics such as the following: getting started with portfolios, selecting pieces for the portfolio, involving parents in the portfolio assessment process, understanding the teacher's role in the portfolio process, fostering students' self-evaluation of selected items in the portfolio, sustaining portfolios over time, and using portfolios to evaluate students. Everything you ever wanted to know about portfolios but didn't know where to look is located here. Lots of specific examples and ideas.

Tompkins, Gail E. 1990. *Teaching Writing: Balancing Process and Product*. Columbus, OH: Merrill.

Many practical strategies for teaching writing are found in this comprehensive text on the writing process. However, it is not just a recipe book! The author worked closely with classroom teachers and has included many vignettes to show how the ideas are implemented in classrooms. Many student samples are used to show possible outcomes of the various lessons and projects suggested in the book. (V. M.)

Trelease, Jim. 1990. *The New Read-Aloud Handbook*. New York: Penguin.

The author of the inspiring and popular The Read-Aloud Handbook *offers his newest edition for parents and teachers. The first half of the book deals with the need to read aloud to children and how and when to carry through. Trelease offers valuable suggestions to teachers and*

*parents to promote and implement read-
ing aloud and reading for pleasure at
home and in the classroom. The second
half of the book, the "Treasury of Read-
Alouds," presents an extensive listing of
picture books and novels that includes
brief annotations, related books, and
other books by the author. A small listing
of poetry books and anthologies is also
included. As great read-alouds are most
often memorable literature, this text is
also an excellent resource for choosing
books for children to read with teacher
guidance or independently.*

Watson, Dorothy, Carolyn Burke, and Jerome
Harste. 1989. *Whole Language: Inquir-
ing Voices.* Richmond Hill, Ontario:
Scholastic-TAB.

*This 71-page volume, a companion
book to Ken Goodman's* What's Whole in
Whole Language?, *sees teaching as inquiry as the necessary direction for whole
language teachers. Teachers are guided
to reflect on their own learning in order
to foster a community of inquiring
learners. Conditions of inquiry—vulnerability, community, generation of knowledge, democracy, and reflexivity, are discussed and demonstrated. This is a very
readable and sophisticated book for the
teacher who already has a whole language foundation.*

• Weaver, Constance. 1988. *Reading Process
and Practice: From Socio-Psycholinguistics to Whole Language.* Portsmouth, NH: Heinemann.

*For the educator who wants to thor-
oughly understand and apply the reading
process in the context of what is currently
known about language learning, this superb, detailed text (483 pp.) ties theory
and practice together in a very useful
manner. The book includes in-depth,
thoughtful discussions on phonics, word
identificaton, the use of context, reading
strategies, miscue analysis, whole language, reading in the content areas, reading styles, and dyslexia, as well as extensive resources, activities, annotated
readings, and bibliographies. See also annotation (Dorothy Watson and Paul
Crowley) at the end of Chapter 2.*

Weaver, Constance. 1990. *Understanding
Whole Language: From Principles to
Practice.* Portsmouth, NH: Heinemann.

*Weaver provides an extensive research
and theoretical background to support a
whole language approach to teaching
and learning and discusses how whole
language principles can be applied to the
classroom. For educators who already
have a rudimentary understanding of
whole language, this thorough, scholarly
text (329 pp.) provides as in-depth an
understanding of whole language as can
be found. Weaver devotes 58 pages to
phonics–comprising as complete an overview of the research as exists (including
research from whole language classrooms), the implications of the research,
and suggestions for teaching. An extensive section on assessment (79 pp.) includes current information regarding
standardized testing, reading assessment,
and a variety of meaningful assessment
procedures.*

White, Connie. 1990. *Jevon Doesn't Sit at the
Back Anymore.* New York: Scholastic.

*This book launches a new series of
professional books focusing on the
teacher-as-researcher movement. The
author's journey as a teacher who noted
what children could not do to one who
celebrates what children know—and
gives them control over the learning
process—is the main point in this small
book. She documents the progress of
Jevon, who began and repeated kindergarten in her classroom. Even at the end
of his second year, the standardized test
results did not tell how he learned about
reading—yet his teacher was able to
counter this negative image with a report
that demonstrated what he knew, how he
got there, and how he had been supported in his learning. It is a powerful
document supporting anecdotal and observational records. (V. M.)*

Whitin, David J., Heidi Mills, and Timothy
O'Keefe. 1990. *Living and Learning
Mathematics: Stories and Strategies for
Supporting Mathematical Literacy.*
Portsmouth, NH: Heinemann.

This text brings the reader into a tran-

sitional first grade classroom where children learn about mathematical principles through daily exploration and sharing of their own problem-solving strategies. Mathematics is explored through children's interests, curricular themes, classroom events, children's literature, as well as through graphing. Numbers are used for real purposes as children write original mathematical stories about such everyday concerns as losing and growing teeth and fish living and dying in the classroom. The primary grade teacher will find this a useful resource for meaningfully connecting mathematics to the lives of children.

Zemelman, Steven, and Harvey Daniels. 1988. *A Community of Writers: Teaching Writing in the Junior and Senior High School.* Portsmouth, NH: Heinemann.

The authors, codirectors of the Illinois Writing Project, have written a thoughtful and practical text (286 pp.) for teachers of grades 6–12. Drawing on the research of the integrated language arts movement of the 1970s and 1980s, the authors present a complete theoretical and practical framework for the implementation of a process writing classroom. While they honestly acknowledge the obstacles of implementing process writing at the junior and senior high levels, they also stress its necessity "because this is the part of school we most desperately need to reform" (p. 11). Teachers from the upper elementary grades onward will find a wealth of usable ideas for developing classroom management techniques, sensitizing students to working in groups, structuring and designing many types of writing activities, and evaluating student writing beyond copyediting. Three approaches to writing are advocated and explained in depth: student-initiated writing (journals, writing workshop), teacher-assigned writing, and writing to learn. A strong rationale and specific suggestions are given for prewriting, drafting, revising, and conferencing. Teachers will find this book very supportive, realistic, and filled with meaningful writing activities.

Journal Articles

For other annotated journal articles related specifically to spelling, whole language, journal writing, evaluation, and learning disabilities, see "Resources" at the end of respective chapters.

• Atwell, Nancie. Spring 1989. "The Thoughtful Practitioner." *Teachers Networking: The Whole Language Newsletter,* Vol. 9, no. 3, pp. 1, 10–12.

Atwell encourages us to become teacher researchers, that is, "thoughtful practitioners" who constantly examine and evaluate our own teaching and learning. Terrific for thoughtful discussion.

Babbitt, Natalie. November–December 1990. "Protecting Children's Literature." *The Horn Book Magazine,* pp. 696–703.

Children's author Natalie Babbitt eloquently reminds us that good fiction is meant to be enjoyed on a human, personal level. She warns against the lessons and discussions designed "to teach" that often accompany the use of literature in the reading program: "Because if we weigh the stories down with the baggage of unrelated lessons, they will sink and disappear . . ." (p. 703).

Braddock, Jomills Henry II, and James M. McPartland. April 1990. "Alternatives to Tracking." *Educational Leadership,* pp. 76–80.

Citing the harmful effects of tracking, the authors offer specific modifications and alternatives. Among them are postponing and limiting tracking, experimenting with different placement criteria, and providing support for teachers in untracked classes.

Bruce, Joyce, and Beverly Showers. February 1980. "Improving Inservice Training: The Messages of Research." *Educational Leadership,* pp. 379–385.

Many successful staff development programs still base their models on the Joyce and Showers paradigm, which evolved from a review of over two hundred research studies. This classic article by two well-respected researchers gives the components of successful staff development programs—presentation of theory, demonstration of skill, practice, feedback, and coaching. Educators wanting to design effective staff development programs will find this a very useful article.

Burchby, Marcia. Spring 1988. "Literature and Whole Language." *The New Advocate*, pp. 114–123.

An elementary teacher describes how and why she changed from a basal reader approach to a whole language approach. A very supportive article for educators who want both the rationale for change and some specifics for the teaching of reading with literature.

Cooper, Harris. November 1989. "Synthesis of Research on Homework." *Educational Leadership*, pp. 85–91.

Cooper reviews and summarizes almost 120 research studies on the effects of homework. He concludes that homework has a neglible effect on achievement at the elementary level, a moderate effect at the junior high level, and a positive effect at the high school level as long as the material is not too complex or unfamiliar. Cooper includes a useful recommended homework policy for districts, schools, and teachers. Share these policy guidelines with parents and administrators.

Cudd, Evelyn T., and Leslie Roberts. February 1989. "Using Writing to Enhance Content Area Learning in the Primary Grades." *The Reading Teacher*, pp. 392–404.

This excellent article is full of specific demonstrations, ideas, and examples for writing in the content areas in grades 1–3. Very useful to teachers who want to move beyond narrative writing.

Daiute, Colette. October 1989. "Research Currents: Play and Learning to Write," *Language Arts*, pp. 656–664.

The importance of collaborative writing and the benefits of playful talk for children's writing development are emphasized. The research indicates that collaborative composing (especially on the

computer) is "productive and enriching" and that a "little noise and laughter" contribute to writing.

Dowhower, Sarah L. March 1989. "Repeated Reading: Research into Practice," *The Reading Teacher*, pp. 502–507.

The benefits and procedures of repeated reading ("multiple readings of connected text") are discussed and demonstrated. Specific, practical, and useful for all teachers.

Farris, Pamela J. Summer 1989. "Story Time and Story Journals: Linking Literature and Writing." *The New Advocate*, pp. 179–185.

The author details specific ways to link literature with writing through story journals, literary journals, and dialogue journals. Useful for the primary grade teacher.

Five, Cora Lee. Spring 1988. "From Workbook to Workshop: Increasing Children's Involvement in the Reading Process." *The New Advocate*, pp. 103–113.

A fifth grade teacher describes how she moved to a reading program that complemented her writing program in which students had "time, ownership, and response." Very useful and specific for teachers who want to use literature in a reading workshop approach.

• Glasser, William. February 1990. "The Quality School." *Phi Delta Kappan*, pp. 425–435.

A provocative, thought-provoking article on how to manage our teaching so that the majority of students do high-quality schoolwork. Excellent for discussion, k–12.

• Goodland, John I., and Jeannie Oakes. February 1988. "We Must Offer Equal Access to Knowledge." *Educational Leadership*, pp. 16–22.

"Study after study reveals the dominance of telling, lecturing, questioning the class, and monitoring seatwork. The inquiring, questioning, probing, hypothesizing kind of intellectual endeavor often associated with learning is not usually found in classrooms" (p. 17). Furthermore, poor and minority children,

overrepresented in the lowest groups, and with little chance of access to the highest groups, receive the most inferior schooling. Educators are urged to examine tracking practices and consider different ideas: implementing small cooperative learning groups, providing concept-based (rather than fragmented skills) curriculums, and altering the way we perceive individual differences.

Goodman, Kenneth S. Winter 1988. "Look What They've Done to Judy Blume!: The 'Basalization' of Children's Literature." *The New Advocate*, pp. 29–41.

Goodman reiterates that authentic text, the way the author wrote it, is the easiest to read and to learn to read. He decries common tampering with stories by well-known authors to fit basal schemes. Teachers and administrators desirous of using real literature instead of basal texts will find this a supportive article.

Henderson, Anne T. October 1988. "Parents Are a School's Best Friend." *Phi Delta Kappan*, pp. 149–153.

Henderson reviews long-term research findings across diverse populations and reports that "parent involvement in almost any form appears to produce measurable gains in student achievement." While training of parents of at-risk children in home teaching proved significant, the average level of achievement for a school rose only when parents were involved in the school. Important findings for raising achievement levels in effective schools through long-term, comprehensive, well-planned parent involvement.

Henke, Linda. Winter 1988. "Beyond Basal Reading: A District's Commitment to Change." *The New Advocate*, pp. 42–51.

For school districts ready to look at alternative reading program options, this article describes how a district that decides against a new basal adoption implements a program that accommodates use of the old basal while adding lots of trade books, daily independent reading, and daily writing workshop time, as well

as staff development and parent communication.

• Hepler, Susan. Summer 1988. "A Guide for the Teacher Guides: Doing It Yourself." *The New Advocate*, pp. 186–195.

This gem of an article gives specific guidelines to teachers who want to work together to develop meaningful guides for specific books. Meaningful questions, responses to literature, and appropriate activities are discussed and demonstrated. The article is not only useful for making your own guides for books but it is also valuable for looking at commercial guides critically.

Herman, Patricia A. and Janice Dole. September 1988. "Theory and Practice in Vocabulary Learning and Instruction." *The Elementary School Journal*, pp. 43–54.

The authors discuss three approaches to vocabulary instruction—definitional, contextual, and conceptual—while also acknowledging that most words are learned incidentally; "an average reader learns the meaning of 800–1,200 words per year through free reading alone" (p. 44). A combination of the three approaches is recommended, and specifics are provided. The definitional approach, by itself, is seen to be mostly ineffective. With the contextual approach, the importance of teacher demonstration is illustrated through an example of a teacher verbalizing thought processes to figure out the meaning of a word in natural context. A series of activities that demonstrates a conceptual approach to learning a word is clearly delineated. Current research about vocabulary and its effect on reading comprehension is also discussed. An excellent article for gaining perspective on vocabulary acquisition.

• Juliebo, Moira, and Joyce Edwards. January 1989. "Encouraging Meaning Making in Young Writers. " *Young Children*, pp. 22–27.

The authors demonstrate what happens when writing tasks are artificially created by the teacher. They concur with *already existing studies that support the need for topic choice, real purpose, and a varied audience for obtaining children's best written work. Although the writing samples discussed are from primary children, the characteristics that are found to encourage—or restrict—written composition apply to all the grades. An important article for understanding the need for authentic writing experiences.*

Lambert, Linda. May 1988. "Staff Development Redesigned." *Phi Delta Kappan*, pp. 665–668.

Lambert urges expanding the teacher's role in staff development from "passive receiver" to leadership and inquiry. Teachers ready to take an active, decision-making role in restructuring staff development in their school will find lots of support and valuable information in this thought-provoking article. Great for discussion.

Manning, Maryann, Gary Manning, and Constance Kamii. November 1988. "Early Phonics Instruction: Its Effect on Literacy Development." *Young Children*, pp. 4–8.

The authors describe what happened to one six-year-old (who entered school reading predictable books) when she received a heavy dose of phonics instruction in kindergarten. "With the exception of digraphs and consonant blends, the instruction caused confusion and reduced her confidence in her own ability to figure things out." The authors are not against phonics instruction, but they do question an imposed, time-consuming phonics program that may not fit the child's stage of development. Rather, they urge an emphasis on meaning with lots of time for reading and writing so children can work out their own system of rules.

• Ohanian, Susan. Fall 1988. "My Word! A Plea for More Disorderliness." *Teachers Networking. The Whole Language Newsletter.*

Ohanian argues that rather than trusting kids to become readers and celebrating children's literature, many

teachers and publishers ruin the literature for kids by trying to extract as many skills as possible. Must reading for teachers tempted to have kids do lots of activities to go along with books!

Rasinski, Timothy V. May 1989. "Fluency for Everyone: Incorporating Fluency Instruction in the Classroom." *The Reading Teacher*, pp. 690–693.

This highly practical, research-based article gives the classroom teacher specific strategies for promoting and supporting reading fluency of students. Repetition, modeling, direct feedback, tape recording, choral reading, and use of easy materials are fully discussed. I have found this article to be especially useful for helping at-risk students become more proficient readers.

Reardon, S. Jeanne. Winter 1988. "The Development of Critical Readers: A Look into the Classroom." *The New Advocate*, pp. 52–61.

An intermediate grade classroom teacher describes the necessary elements for development of critical readers. Her specific demonstrations of how she reads to her class every day and how she conducts a small-group literature discussion are extremely helpful to the teacher who wants insight into promoting high-level thinking by connecting authors' purposes to literature. Applicable for all the grades.

Reimer, Becky L., and Leslie Warshow. April 1989. "Questions We Ask of Ourselves and Our Students." *The Reading Teacher*, pp. 596–606.

Teachers who have made meaningful and major changes in their teaching tell their personal stories. Supportive, informative, and inspiring to all teachers in the change process.

• Shannon, Patrick. October 1989. "The Struggle for Control of Literacy Lessons." *Language Arts*, pp. 625–634.

The author argues that, in a democratic educational and social setting, the control of literacy lessons should be properly shared by teachers and students. Even when materials are substantially improved over traditional basal texts, publishers still maintain control by pre-determining the possible choices. Shannon raises weighty questions about control of literacy lessons and suggests that as long as a commercial program is used, it is the publisher's choices that control the lessons.

Shepard, Lorrie A., and Mary Lee Smith. May 1990. "Synthesis of Research on Grade Retention." *Educational Leadership*, pp. 84–88.

The authors note that "the large body of research on grade retention is almost uniformly negative." Given that 5 to 7 percent of children in public schools in the United States are retained annually at a cost of almost $10 billion a year, this is an article to be taken seriously. Retention leads to increased risk of dropping out of school, poor self-esteem, and lower achievement in later grades. The authors recommend "promotion plus remediation" and suggest alternative ways to provide specific and additional instructional help.

Slavin, Robert E. September 1988. "Synthesis of Research on Grouping in Elementary and Secondary Schools." *Educational Leadership*, pp. 67–77.

Slavin, perhaps best known for his comprehensive research analysis on ability grouping ("Ability Grouping and Student Achievement in Elementary Schools: A Best Evidence Synthesis." Review of Educational Research, *Vol. 57, no. 3 [1987], pp. 213–336) summarizes the research on achievement effects of ability grouping at the elementary and secondary levels. This scholarly article is important reading for all educators. It calls into question many common grouping practices for regular, gifted, and special education students.*

• Smith, Frank. January 1989. "Overselling Literacy." *Phi Delta Kappan*, pp. 353–359.

"Individuals become literate not from the formal instruction they receive, but from what they read and write about and who they read and write with" (p. 355).

Smith cautions against the promotion of literacy as a cure-all for society's ills and reminds us that literacy is most valuable and productive when it is meaningful and carried out in association with literate people who read and write for pleasure. Rather than relying on instructional programs and evaluation, school environments need to foster collaborative relationships that free the imagination and empower both teachers and students. A great article for group discussion.

Taylor, Denny. November 1989. "Toward a Unified Theory of Literacy Learning and Instructional Practices." *Phi Delta Kappan*, pp. 184–193.

The author argues that "reductionist" and "hierarchical" research views of children's early literacy development do not take into consideration the complex individual and personal ways children have been observed to learn and use language, and, therefore, these views are too narrow to be taken seriously. Taylor urges educators to establish theoretical frameworks that broaden and enhance children's opportunities for dynamic reading and writing experiences. "Our task is to insure that the voices of children become embodied in the ways in which we teach" (p. 193). An important article for thinking about our own understandings and beliefs about literacy.

Throne, Jeanette. September 1988. "Becoming a Kindergarten of Readers?" *Young Children*, pp. 10–16.

A well-respected kindergarten teacher in our school district argues that good kindergarten teachers have always taught reading—not through formal, decontextualized materials—but through all kinds of authentic language experiences. Throne discusses how she fosters reading through shared book experiences, repeated readings, creative dramatics, related writing and art activities, and group discussions about stories. An excellent article for early childhood educators who want a developmentally appropriate curriculum.

Topping, Keith. March 1989. "Peer Tutoring and Paired Reading: Combining Two Powerful Techniques." *The Reading Teacher*, pp. 488–494.

The author, an educational psychologist who developed a parent-child paired reading procedure that is widely practices in the United Kingdom, discusses the benefits, organizational procedures, and evaluation research of paired reading programs in classrooms, in which a more able child assists a less able one in reading. "All the major research reviews on the effectiveness of peer tutoring in reading have shown that the tutors accelerate in reading skill at least as much as, if not more than, the tutees" (p. 489). This very specific article gives complete information to the k–12 teacher who is interested in setting up a paired reading program.

Tunnell, Michael O., and James S. Jacobs. March 1989. "Using 'Real' Books: Research Findings on Literature Based Reading Instruction." *The Reading Teacher*, pp. 470–477.

For educators desirous of research supporting whole language approaches to literacy, this article notes some studies that support a literature-based approach to reading. Share this article with your administrator.

• Turner, Richard L. December 1989. "The 'Great' Debate—Can Both Carbo and Chall Be Right?" *Phi Delta Kappan*, pp. 276–283.

An educational researcher responds to two extreme positions on the teaching of phonics in beginning reading: "Debunking the Great Phonics Myth" by Marie Carbo (Phi Delta Kappan, November 1988) and "Learning to Read: The Great Debate 20 Years Later—A Response to 'Debunking the Great Phonics Myth'" by Jeanne Chall (Phi Delta Kappan, March 1989). In reviewing the research literature on the place of phonics in beginning reading instruction, Turner reviews the "best evidence" studies—those "that were free from bias, that directly addressed the research question of interest, and that inspired confidence in the results" (p. 276). He concludes, "If

systematic phonics influences reading vocabulary and comprehension at all, it does so very, very slightly" (p. 283). Read all three articles for perspectives on phonics in beginning reading.

Wason-Ellam, Linda. March 1988. "Using Literary Patterns: Who's in Control of the Authorship?" *Language Arts*, pp. 291–301.

The author warns against overuse of literary patterns from predictable texts and suggests that beginning writers need to focus on communicating ideas. While innovating on patterned text can be meaningful (especially in oral language activities), often it is overworked and restrictive. "At times, this is carried to such an extreme that the task often resembles workbook activities" (p. 292). Teachers who are spending a lot of time having children extend specific patterns should read this article for perspectives and for suggestions of how predictable books can serve as models to promote authentic writing.

Wiggington, Eliot. February 1989. "Foxfire Grows Up." *Harvard Educational Review*, pp. 24–49.

The developer of the "Foxfire approach," a democratic, experiential, and hands-on approach and philosophy of education describes Foxfire's core educational practices and how he and others work with teachers to achieve them. The approach believes that all-age students "benefit from examining the culture, traditions, and history of their communities, urban or rural, and then documenting and publishing what they found . . ." (p. 24). The Foxfire approach has much in common with whole language in that education is student centered and connected to the real world. Texts are used as resources as the need arises; group work and collaboration are highly valued; the teacher is a facilitator and guide; self-evaluation is intrinsic to the learning process. A provocative article for educators interested in learning about the Foxfire approach.

Williams, David L., and Nancy Feyl Chavkin. October 1989. "Essential Elements of Strong Parent Involvement Programs." *Educational Leadership*, pp. 18–20.

Seven essential elements from successful parent involvement programs in a five-state area are identified and described: written policies, administrative support, training, partnership approach, two-way communication, networking, and evaluation. A list of parent involvement resources is included. A useful article for schools intent on improving parent involvement.

Yaffe, Stephen H. March 1989. "Drama as a Teaching Tool." *Educational Leadership*, pp. 29–32.

The benefits of drama as a response to literature for gifted as well as at-risk students k–12 is discussed and demonstrated.

Themed Journals

These themed journals are wonderful springboards for thinking about practices, processes, and changes in literacy learning and teaching k–12. Many of the articles in these journals have been discussed in our weekly language arts support groups. It is recommended that your school library have a copy of each journal for your reference.

Baumann, James F. (guest ed.). May 1990. *The Reading Teacher: Whole Literacy*. Newark, DE: International Reading Association.

This issue explores possibilities and challenges in implementing whole language. The introductory article, " 'Possibilities, Daddy, I Think It Says Possibilities': A Father's Journal of the Emergence of Literacy" by Lester L. Laminack is both scholarly and delightful for taking a look at a preschooler's attempts to interact with print in his world. Preschool, kindergarten, and grade 1 teachers will find "Dramatic Play: A Context for Meaningful Engagements" by James F. Christie valuable for noting the importance of providing opportunities for literacy-related dramatic

play and for specific suggestions on theme centers and teacher involvement. "Language, Literature, and At-Risk Children" by Nancy L. Roser, James V. Hoffman, and Cynthia Farest describes how a literature program was successfully organized and implemented in a large, impoverished county school system. "Whole Language in the Middle School" by Anna M. McWhirter, which describes a reading workshop approach, will be instructive for middle and high school teachers seeking alternatives to traditional language arts teaching. "Assessment and Accountability in a Whole Literacy Curriculum" by Kathryn H. Au, Judith A. Scheu, Alice J. Kawakami, and Patricia A. Herman will be very useful to teachers, administrators, and school districts looking for accountability incorporating holistic measures for monitoring and documenting learning. Other fine articles discuss the use of computers, parent involvement, reading-spelling links, and how a grade 1 teacher incorporated whole language in her classroom.

Brandt, Ronald (executive ed.). April 1989. *Educational Leadership: Redirecting Assessment*. Alexandria, VA: Association for Supervision and Curriculum Development.

If you are interested in improving evaluation and assessment, don't miss this outstanding issue. Lorie Shepard's opening article, "Why We Need Better Assessments" addresses the limitations of standardized testing and points the way to more authentic assessment. "High-Stakes Testing in Kindergarten" by Samuel J. Meisels discusses the harmful effects and misuse of readiness testing for labeling, placing, and retaining children. "There are presently no readiness or achievement tests sufficiently accurate to serve the high-stakes functions they are being asked to perform" (p. 20). "On Misuse of Testing: A Conversation with George Madaus" by Ron Brandt addresses the concerns of the director of the Center for the Study of Testing, Evaluation, and Educational Policy and is a terrific article for group discussion. Among other things, Madaus notes that high test scores do not correlate with high skills levels; measurement-driven instruction makes teaching easier but "deprofessionalizes" it; ranking school districts by test results uses tests in a way that was never intended. In "Testing and Thoughtfulness," Rexford Brown notes that thinking skills cannot be broken down and tested. He calls for more thoughtful tests such as those that students create themselves. Dennie Palmer Wolf's article, "Portfolio Assessment: Sampling Student Work," is outstanding for understanding the concepts behind portfolio assessment. In a very significant article, "Teaching to the (Authentic) Test," Grant Wiggins calls for a redesign of assessment procedures at the high school level that reflects authentic literacy behaviors. "Theory and Practice in Statewide Reading Assessment: Closing the Gap" by Sheila Valencia, David Pearson, Charles Peters, and Karen Wixon describes the new statewide reading comprehension tests in Illinois and Michigan that are based on current reading theory. "How Do We Evaluate Student Writing? One District's ANSWER" by Melva Lewis and Arnold Lindaman gives specifics on how a district measures students' growth as writers in grades 1–12 using fall and spring writing samples, student and parent evaluative responses of those samples, and holistic assessment of the samples.

Froese, Victor (guest ed.). April 1989. *The Reading Teacher: Empowering Both Teachers and Students.* Newark, DE: International Reading Association.

Each of the articles in this thought-provoking journal is noteworthy for thinking about how literacy is taught and learned in schools and for incorporating recent research into practice. I was particularly impressed by "Building Communities of Readers and Writers" by Trevor Cairney and Susan Langbien, who stress the importance of the social and collaborative nature of learning in all learning environments. "Empowered Students; Empowered Teachers" by William T. Fagan is a very important article for understanding the crucial role teachers play in determining whether or not reading and writing are meaningfully connected to children's lives. "Questions We Ask of Ourselves and Our Students" by Becky L. Reimer and Leslie Warshow describes the struggles and breakthroughs of specific classroom teachers in trying to teach reading and writing with "real life connections." "The Teacher's Role in Students' Success" by Mariam Jean Dreher and Harry Singer calls upon teachers to move from activity managers who follow teacher manuals to professional decision makers who determine goals, materials, and methods.

Good, Thomas L. (ed.). November 1989. *The Elementary School Journal: Special Issue on Whole Language.* Chicago: University of Chicago Press.

This is a superb issue for examining the theory, history, and applications of the whole language movement as well as for getting perspectives and implications for teaching and learning. Yetta Goodman begins the issue with a scholarly article that gives a history of the whole language movement. Kenneth Goodman discusses characteristics of whole language and the strong research base for whole language, as well as research possibilities. Other articles define and describe whole language, Reading Recovery, and current and potential views of teacher education. Two commentaries on whole language respond to the articles in this issue and give varying perspectives. The concluding article by Jerry Harste addresses the future of the whole language movement and is important reading for all those concerned with schooling in a democratic society.

Hardt, Ulrch H. (ed.). Fall 1988. *Oregon English.* Theme: *Whole Language.* Portland: Oregon Council of Teachers of English. (Available for purchase through National Council of Teachers of English, Urbana, IL.)

Favorite articles that are cited elsewhere in Invitations include "Reflections on Whole Language: Past, Present and Potential" by Dorothy Watson, "Evaluation in the Holistic Reading/ Language Arts Curriculum" by Richard Ammon, "Whole Language Teaching: Support from Instructional and Research Models" by Jane B. Braunger. Other articles deal with curricular change, integrating fairy tales into language arts, teaching skills, organizing a student publishing company, integrating letter writing across the curriculum, using children's literature (including picture books) with junior high students, incorporating the arts to reach turned-off high school students, thinking beyond biased textbooks in teaching U.S. history. This entire journal is outstanding for deepening understanding of whole language theory and practice.

Shannon, Patrick, and Kenneth S. Goodman (guest eds.). Autumn 1989. *Theory into Practice: Perspectives on Basal Readers.* Columbus, OH: The Ohio State University.

This journal presents varying viewpoints about basal reading materials and raises philosophical questions about literacy learning and teaching. The volume goes way beyond basal texts and raises critical questions about assessment, textbook adoption, reading programs, students' perceptions about reading, reading comprehension, and more. Important reading for all teachers, administrators, and policy makers who are interested in the effects of reading programs on literacy instruction and development and in bringing about constructive change.

Wood, George (coordinator). Fall 1990. *Democracy and Education: Alternatives to Standardized Testing.* Athens, OH: Institute for Democracy in Education at Ohio University.

Don't miss this powerful, thought-provoking issue! This outstanding journal includes articles that discuss how standardized testing demeans and disempowers educators and students by devaluing classroom teachers' judgment and by overrelying on test makers, and it offers alternatives for authentic evalua-

tion. The lead article, "Toward Authentic Assessment," by the editorial board of Democracy and Education, is a clear statement about standardized testing that contains what's wrong with standardized testing (including a statement from Fair Test, the National Center for Fair and Open Testing) as well as options open to teachers to deal with testing. The second essay is a position statement on standardized testing from the National Association for the Education of Young Children. Educators in early childhood programs will find much support here for restricting test use. The remainder of this issue includes inspiring articles by elementary and secondary teachers and students—and a parent—who offer personal and practical insights into the necessity of valuing and involving students in an authentic evaluation process.

Journals

Democracy and Education
4 issues per year/subscription $12
The Institute for Democracy and Education
College of Education
119 McCracken Hall
Ohio University
Athens, OH 45701-2979

A quality journal written by and for teachers that focuses on issues related to democratic practice. For example, recent themed issues have addressed tracking and ability grouping, democratic management, and alternatives to standardized testing.

Educational Leadership
8 issues per year/subscription $32
Association for Supervision and Curriculum Development
1250 North Pitt Street
Alexandria, VA 22314-1403

A journal for elementary, middle school, and secondary teachers and administrators interested in being on the cutting edge of current educational theory and practice. For anyone interested in being well informed about good ideas regarding today's educational practices.

Elementary School Journal
5 issues per year/subscription $45
(institutions); $28.50 (individual);
$21.25 (NAESP); $19.50 (students)
University of Chicago Press
5720 South Woodlawn
PO Box 37005
Chicago, IL 60637

Geared toward a more scholarly audience, this journal contains studies, research reviews, and analyses of ideas for elementary teachers, administrators, teacher educators, and researchers.

- **English Journal**
8 issues per year/subscription $35
(includes membership in NCTE)
National Council of Teachers of English
1111 Kenyon Road
Urbana, IL 61801

By teachers for teachers in middle, junior, or senior high school, English Journal *contains quality, thought-provoking articles about theory, practice, and new ideas in learning, reading, and writing in the classroom.*

The Horn Book Magazine
6 issues per year/subscription $36
14 Beacon Street
Boston, MA 02108

For anyone interested in quality writing for children and young adults, The Horn Book *provides the most complete, responsible, and thoughtful coverage. Contains announcements of forthcoming titles; reviews of children's and young adult literature, poetry, and nonfiction; biographies; articles from authors about their work; and articles on using literature in the classroom.*

Journal of Reading
8 issues per year/subscription $30
International Reading Association
800 Barksdale Road
PO Box 8139
Newark, DE 19714-8139

Peer-reviewed articles on research, theory, and practice for those interested in teaching reading at middle school, junior high, high school, college, and adult levels. Material may be geared toward a more academic audience. Contains conference announcements. April issue is guest edited and themed.

- **Language Arts**
8 issues per year/subscription $35
National Council of Teachers of English
1111 Kenyon Road
Urbana, IL 61801

Theory and practice in language learning are combined with exceptional literary style in monthly themed journals. This official journal of NCTE (for the elementary grades) notes its new publications, forthcoming conferences, and reviews of children's and professional books.

Learning
9 issues per year/subscription $18.00
Springhouse Corporation
1111 Bethlehem Pike
Springhouse, PA 19477 (correspondence)

PO Box 2580
Boulder, CO 80322 (subscriptions)

This lively journal contains creative suggestions from teachers for teachers, practical applications for the classroom, activities, tips, and a reader exchange. For those interested in teaching k–8. Teachers new to the field should be aware that articles cover a broad spectrum from traditional to whole language approaches.

- **The New Advocate**
4 issues per year/subscription $28
The New Advocate
PO Box 809
Needham Heights, MA 02194–0006

Noted authors, illustrators, and educators share their perspectives on children's literature and related issues in this outstanding literary journal. Book and media reviews are included.

Phi Delta Kappan
10 issues per year/subscription $30
Eighth & Union
PO Box 789
Bloomington, IN 47402

Concerned with issues relating to leadership, research, trends, and policy, Phi Delta Kappan *(named for the educational fraternity) is a must for those truly interested in what's happening in our schools today. Contains an annual Gallup poll of this country's attitude toward public schools.*

• **The Reading Teacher**
9 issues per year/subscription $30
International Reading Association (IRA)
800 Barksdale Road
PO Box 8139
Newark, DE 19714–8139

This practical journal for preschool and elementary teachers focuses on teaching approaches and techniques and also includes reviews of children's books, professional books, tests, and other teacher resources. Subscription includes "Reading Today," a bimonthly newspaper on news of the profession.

Note that IRA sponsors an annual conference, a World Congress, as well as state and local conferences; publishes professional publications and brochures for teachers and parents; and identifies and distributes "Children's Choices"—a yearly list of books children vote as their favorites.

Young Children
6 issues per year/subscription $30
National Association for the Education of Young Children
1834 Connecticut Avenue Northwest
Washington, DC 20009–5786

Preschool and early elementary teachers will find this journal to be thought provoking, informative, and supportive in the area of professional growth. Major issues and ideas in the field are discussed. Contains such items as a calendar of conferences, book reviews, Washington updates, and a section of reader commentary.

Newsletters

The Five Owls
6 bimonthly issues per year/subscription $18
The Five Owls, Inc.
2004 Sheridan Avenue South
Minneapolis, MN 55405

This publication is intended for teachers and parents interested in staying involved and current with the best of children's literature. Includes in-depth book reviews; practical ideas for using books with children; specialized bibli-

ographies; and thoughtful articles, essays, and interviews.

The Kobrin Letter. Concerning Children's Books about Real People, Places and Things.
7 issues per year/subscription $12
The Kobrin Letter
732 Greer Road
Palo Alto, CA 94303

This is the only publication that deals exclusively with the review and recommendation of children's nonfiction. Several themes or topics are dealt with in each issue. For example, one issue dealt with "Trees" and "About AIDS" and included information from approximately six books for each topic.

Portfolio, The Newsletter of Arts PROPEL
[five back issues published from 1987–1989 (Vol. I, nos. 1–5)/$2 (nos. 1, 2, and 4); $2.25 (no. 3); $2.50 (no. 5)]
Harvard University, Graduate School of Education
Harvard Project Zero
323 Longfellow Hall, Appian Way
Cambridge, MA 02138

This outstanding, occasional newsletter of the Arts PROPEL project (the five-year collaborative effort involving artists and researchers from Harvard Project Zero and Educational Testing Service, as well as students, teachers, and administrators from the Pittsburgh Public Schools) shares experiences from the project and offers insightful articles on creative approaches to learning and assessment and evaluation in middle and senior high school classrooms. Lots of terrific information on portfolio assessment.

• **Teachers Networking: The Whole Language Newsletter**
4 issues per year/subscription $15 (U.S.); $18 (Canada)
For group membership at one address, each subscription over six ordered is half price.
Richard C. Owen Publishers, Inc.
Box 585
Katonah, NY 10536

Features thought-provoking articles by leading whole language educators as well as reviews of professional and children's literature, suggested teaching strategies, issues of concern and interest to parents and educators, and a whole language calendar of upcoming conferences. A particularly well-done newsletter.

The Whole Idea
4 issues per year/subscription $12 (U.S.); $15 (Canada)
The Wright Group
18916 North Creek Parkway
Suite 107
Bothell, WA 98011
   Practical articles, activities, and ideas for teachers interested in whole language. Includes ideas from practicing teachers as well as well-known educators. Very useful for the elementary classroom teacher.

Whole Language Special Interest Group of IRA Newsletter
2 issues per year with membership/$5 (U.S.); $6 (Canada)
WLSIG Newsletter
Grace Vento-Zogby
125 Proctor Blvd.
Utica, NY 13501
   This thoughtfully literate newsletter has lead articles by well-known whole language educators as well as reprints of newsworthy articles about whole language. Also includes news of the teaching profession as related to whole language, reviews of recent whole language materials, and a calendar of future events.

The Whole Language Umbrella Newsletter
3 issues per year/subscription $2 with membership in the Whole Language Umbrella, a confederation of whole language teacher support groups and individuals ($25 plus $.25 per U.S. member; $30 plus $.30 per Canadian member).

The Whole Language Umbrella
Dorothy Watson, President
University of Missouri
225 Townsend Hall
Columbia, MO 65211
   *The newsletter describes the activities and business of the Whole Language Umbrella, primarily helping whole language teachers and support groups to network with each other. Includes articles and news about whole language is-*sues and teaching, information about other newsletters and support groups in the United States and Canada, support group publications, and upcoming conferences, including the Whole Language Umbrella conference.*

• **The WEB: Wonderfully Exciting Books**
4 issues per year/subscription $10
The Web, Ohio State University College of Education
200 Ramseyer Hall, 29 West Woodruff
Columbus, OH 43210–1177
   Comprehensive book reviews, which include excellent teaching ideas, are presented by teachers and librarians. The center spread in each issue—a teaching web focusing on activities centered on a book, group of books, genre, or theme—is especially helpful for integrating literature across the curriculum. For more examples of well-done "webs," back issues of The Web *are available for purchase.*

Literacy Extension Resources

Bare Books. 1987. Racine, WI: Treetop Publishing.
   Publishes reasonably priced blank books (about $1 each) and sturdy line guides for writing in the blank books. Each Bare Book *contains twenty-eight blank white pages and a hard cover that measures 6⅜ by 8⅛ inches. Minimum order ten books. Adds a nice touch for special projects.*

Barrett, Norman. 1990. *Picture Library Paperbacks.* New York: Franklin Watts.
   This series of about twenty nonfiction books (can be ordered individually) is packed with information, beautiful photographs, and clear, simple text for grades k–4 and is a welcome addition to the classroom library. Some titles include Polar Animals, Elephants, Bears, Airliners, Trail Bikes, *and* Helicopters.

Baskwill, Jane, and Paulette Whitman. 1988. *Moving On: A Whole Language Sourcebook for Grades Three and Four.* Richmond Hill, Ontario: Scholastic-TAB. (hardbound)

Building on their earlier work, Whole Language Sourcebook *(for grades 1 and 2, Scholastic-TAB, 1986), the authors have created a useful resource divided into four main topics: classroom management, routines, themes, and evaluation. A final section on bibliographies supports the main topics. Themes, with both starter and completed plans for four weeks, make up the largest portion of the resource and include "It's a Mystery," "Incredible Edibles," "Superheroes," "Of Another Age," "Amazing Animals," "On the Move," "Step into Time," and "What's So Funny?". I found the sections on classroom management and routines especially helpful and applicable to any elementary grade teacher. Three-ring binder format. Expensive.*

Blossom, Kate. 1987–1990. *Literature Discussion Resource Packets.* Glens Falls, NY: Blossoms Unlimited.

For teachers making the transition from the basal to literature, thoughtful questions and activities are provided for quality titles from the primary grades through junior high. While there are too many questions and activities to go along with each book chapter, the questions and activities can serve as a model until teachers feel confident to create their own. Expensive.

Bryant, Patricia, and Luceille Werner. 1988. *Reading and Writing . . . Can Be a Child's Talk Written Down,* rev. ed. Peotone, IL: Early Prevention of School Failure.

Written to assist kindergarten and first grade teachers to connect reading and writing through language experience and whole language approaches, this sourcebook is full of activities, thematic ideas, and projects for teachers who want to move away from programs and worksheets. Lots of photographs and visuals make the book a functional resource.

Butzow, Carol M., and John W. Butzow. 1989. *Science through Children's Literature.* Englewood, CO: Teacher Ideas Press.

This useful resource geared to the elementary grades connects fiction books with scientific concepts by describing many activities to go along with specific books. Activities for each science topic are centered around a work of fiction. Related books and references are cited.

Charles, Linda Holden, and Micaelia Randolph Brummett. 1989. *Connections: Linking Manipulatives to Mathematics (Grades 1–6).* Sunnyvale, CA: Creative Publications.

Each grade-level resource contains twenty manipulative lessons that connect to important mathematical topics. Each lesson is structured to be used with the whole class as well as with a small group interaction. As part of each lesson, students discuss, organize, report, display, and write about their findings. A fine resource for teachers looking to encourage more active learning experiences to help build understanding in mathematics.

Chevalier, Tracy. 1989. *Twentieth-Century Children's Writers,* 3rd ed. Chicago: St. James Press. (hardbound)

This useful teacher reference features over 800 contributors in literature. For each author, there is a lengthy, interesting narrative biographical account and a list of publications. Lots of information for in-depth author study.

The Children's Book Council, Inc. 568 Broadway, New York, NY 10012.

Publishes a newsletter with information about children's books, book publishers, and inexpensive publishers' materials. Sells pamphlets, posters, and bookmarks that support reading and writing; sponsors an annual Children's Book Week and distributes accompanying materials. Distributes annually: "Children's Choices" (a yearly selection of newly published books that children prefer), "Outstanding Science Tradebooks for Children" (first published in spring issue of Science and Children*),* and *"Notable Children's Trade Books in the Field of Social Studies"* (*first published in spring issue of* Social Education).

• Commire, Anne (ed.). 1990. *Something about the Author*. Detroit: Gale Research. (hardbound)

Written for teachers and students, this is the most complete and extensive resource on children's authors and illustrators. Most entries are autobiographical and include the following information: personal, career, writings, and sidelights. Updated every year since 1972, there are over sixty volumes in this reference series, and each volume includes a cumulative index. If your school district does not own this outstanding series, check with your local public library.

Cutting, Brian. 1990. *Getting Started in Whole Language*. Bothell, WA: The Wright Group.

This is an excellent, all-purpose, highly practical resource (120 pp.) to see, feel, and read about how a whole language classroom looks and functions. Although this resource is based on the commercially produced "Sunshine Books," the verbal and visual examples for shared reading experiences, writing connections, language experiences, paired reading, independent reading, scheduling, and evaluation are very useful to any k–1 teacher interested in whole language.

Cutting, Brian, with Helen Dupree. 1988. *Language Is Fun. Teacher's Book*. Level 2. Bothell, WA: The Wright Group.

This practical collection of ideas for k–2 whole language classrooms extends to drama, art, and literature. Particularly useful are the colorful photographs and samples of children's work from New Zealand classrooms. While many of the literature extension ideas stem from specific books in a reading series, ideas on the resource's theme "I Can . . ." are applicable across the curriculum.

Elleman, Barbara, Editor-in-Chief. *Book Links*. Booklist Publications, The American Library Association, 50 E. Huron St., Chicago, IL 60611.

Aptly described by its subtitle, Connecting Books, Libraries, and Classrooms, this bimonthly magazine is for teachers, librarians, parents, and anyone else who works with books and children. Each issue explores the connections between literature and the learning experience for children preschool to grade eight, and contains articles, recommended reading lists, and interviews that provide strategies for using books effectively in teaching.

Fox, Carol, and Margery Sauer. 1989. *Celebrate Literature*. Logan, IA: The Perfection Form Company.

These spiral-bound comprehensive resource books for each grade level from kindergarten through grade 6 promote the use of a literature curriculum. Each literature unit is presented by genre—poetry, picture books, traditional literature, fiction, nonfiction, biography—and includes goals and objectives, background information, author study, featured books and resources, lots of student activities, and evaluation activities. Lots of good ideas for the classroom teacher.

• Gilles Carol, Mary Bixby, Paul Crowley, et al. (eds.). 1988. *Whole Language Strategies for Secondary Students*. Katonah, NY: Richard C. Owen.

This 208-page resource is very useful to the middle school and secondary teacher wishing to understand and apply whole language teaching strategies in the classroom. The first section of the book lays the theoretical foundation for whole language. The second section consists of specific strategy lessons from whole language classrooms that tie theory and practice together. Each full-page strategy lesson contains the rationale for the lesson, specific procedures, and extensions and variations on the lesson. Strategy lessons encompass literature, the content areas, reading and writing, computers, and other areas.

Griffiths, Rachel, and Margaret Clyne. 1990. *Books You Can Count On: Linking Mathematics and Literature.* Portsmouth, NH: Heinemann.

This resource for the primary grades takes first-rate children's literature and outlines activities for developing mathematical concepts. Books are presented individually as well as thematically. Two final sections on classroom organization and evaluation are very useful.

• Hamilton, Martha, and Mitch Weiss. 1990. *Children Tell Stories: A Teaching Guide.* Katonah, NY: Richard C. Owen.

The authors, professional storytellers, demonstrate how to teach children to tell stories—especially simple folk tales—and to make storytelling an essential part of the curriculum. The benefits of storytelling by children, including improvement in self-esteem, expressive language skills, group dynamics, and new learnings are convincing. Many exercises and strategies for teaching children all aspects of storytelling are clearly delineated. Handouts for students and parents, as well as extensive bibliographies, are included. The book is so well organized and specific, you will feel storytelling is possible and desirable for your classroom. An outstanding resource for all grade levels.

Holtze, Sally Holmes. 1989. *Sixth Book of Junior Authors and Illustrators.* New York: H. W. Wilson.

This teacher reference, the sixth in the series, offers complete and interesting autobiographical and biographical sketches of about 250 noted children's authors and illustrators. A new volume is published every five to six years.

Hurst, Carol Otis. 1990. *Once Upon a Time . . .: An Encyclopedia for Successfully Using Literature with Young Children.* Allen, TX: DLM. (hardbound)

This comprehensive, spiral-bound resource (370 pp., 8½ by 11 inches) by a highly knowledgeable children's librarian is written and compiled to assist teachers who don't have time to research authors, illustrators, and themes. The

book is well organized into four sections: "Authors and Illustrators," "Individual Picture Books," "Themes," and "Special Pages." Each prominent author and illustrator listing (there are about 45) includes a mailing address (when available), biography, books published, awards received, relevant topics to "notice and talk about," and activity ideas for selected books. The "Special Pages" section includes annotated listings of patterned books, wordless books, Big Books, whole language and children's literature resource books, poetry resources, children's records and tapes, children's magazines, books about color, math, social studies, science, the seasons, and more. A wealth of valuable and useful information. Expensive.

Irvine, Joan. 1987. *How to Make Pop-Ups.* New York: Morrow Junior Books.

For teachers who are interested in making different types of pop-up books, this resource gives easy-to-follow instructions with clear illustrations. The book includes needed materials, directions for cutting, folding, and measuring and many examples of pop-up projects.

Jett-Simpson, Mary (ed.). 1989. *Adventuring with Books. A Booklist for Pre-K–Grade 6,* 9th ed. Urbana, IL: National Council of Teachers of English.

Annotated titles are organized by category, such as wordless picture books, science fiction, fantasy, biography, social studies, nonfiction, and contemporary realistic fiction in this excellent resource (571 pp.). See also other quality booklists from NCTE that are continually updated: Your Reading *(middle school/junior high),* Books for You *(senior high), and* High Interest/Easy Reading *(junior/senior high reluctant readers).*

Kaufman, Ronne L. (executive ed.). 1990. *Innovations: Experiencing Literature in the Classroom.* New York: Scholastic.

Lesson plan guides have been developed to go along with quality books such as The Hundred Dresses *by Eleanor Estes,* Nettie's Trip South *by Ann Turner, and* Lon Po Po *by Ed Young. Each guide (there are about 50 available) includes a story overview, information about the genre and the author/illustrator, and many suggested activities for reading and reacting to the book. While there are too many activities suggested, teachers can choose the ones that will work best for them.*

Killen, Rosemary (project director). 1988. *The Author's Eye.* Santa Rosa, CA: American School Publishers.

Each complete program—available for authors Roald Dahl and Katherine Paterson—includes an excellent video of the author in his or her writing setting, twenty-five "Author's Notebooks," a poster, and a teacher's resource book. The terrific "Author's Notebooks," which are sold in packages of twenty-five and can be ordered separately, include letters written by the author, first drafts, notes, jottings, and favorite phrases and words. Inspiring for understanding how a writer works and for stimulating students' own writing. Very expensive.

• Marcuccio, Phyllis R. *Science and Children.* Washington, DC: National Science Teachers Association.

This informative and practical science journal for elementary and middle school teachers and administrators is published eight times a year and is available with membership to NSTA. Provides thoughtful articles, practical and creative teaching suggestions, reviews of books and resources, colorful posters, and inserts as well as the annual "Notable Science Tradebooks for Children" in a spring issue.

• Moss, Joy F. 1990. *Focus on Literature. A Context for Literacy Learning.* Katonah, NY: Richard C. Owen.

This practical text connects theory and practice and offers in-depth literature units around the following focuses: transformation tales, Baba Yaga *tales, devil tales, cat tales, magic object tales, bird tales, wish tales, horse tales, Cinderella tales. Each unit includes plans for daily sessions, meaningful literature extensions, and bibliographies or tales.*

Natoli, Salvatore J. (ed.). *Social Education.* Washington, DC: National Council for the Social Studies.

This scholarly journal on the teaching of social studies is published seven times a year. Includes position statements, research, articles, and practical ideas for the teaching of social studies. The annual April/May issue includes "Notable Children's Trade Books in the Field of Social Studies," a specially selected annotated bibliography for children in grades k–8.

Norby, Shirley, and Gregory Ryan. 1989. *Famous Children's Authors. Book Two.* Minneapolis, MN: T. S. Denison.

A grade 2 teacher and a children's librarian have written twenty author stories for young readers to enjoy and gain information about popular authors. Each two-page entry ends with a bibliography of the authors' books. Sequel to Book One.

• *NOVA Books.* 1990. New York: Simon & Schuster Books for Young Readers.

Produced in association with the award-winning public television series "NOVA," these outstanding informational paperback science books are a visual delight. Garbage: Where It Comes from, Where It Goes *by Evan and Janet Hadingham documents the growing problem of garbage disposal.* Airborne: The Search for the Secret of Flight *by Richard Maurer traces the discovery of the principles of flight from the 1600s to the present.* Radical Robots: Can You Be Replaced? *by George Harrar is an in-depth examination of robots—how they are built and what they are capable of.* The Great Butterfly Hunt: The Mystery of the Migrating Monarchs *by Ethan Herberman examines the migration patterns of the monarch butterfly. All books include an index, and all are fascinating reading for intermediate grades upward.*

O'Toole, Christopher, Keith Porter, Neil Curtis, Malcolm Perry, and Jennifer Coldrey. 1990. *Discovering Nature Paper-*

backs. New York: Franklin Watts. (First published by The Bookwright Press, New York)

The beautifully photographed natural history series geared for the intermediate grades through junior high includes six books, each dealing with one species at a time (ants, bees and wasps, butterflies and moths, snakes and lizards, spiders, and worms) and taking an investigative look at how they live, eat, and survive in their environment. Each book is crammed with information, is clearly written, and includes a glossary and index.

• Peck, David. 1989. *Novels of Initiation. A Guidebook for Teaching Literature to Adolescents.* New York: Teachers College Press.

This excellent guidebook for secondary teachers contains analyses of twelve American novels commonly read in secondary English classes. Each of these novels is connected by the theme of initiation, that is, the main characters move on a "perilous passage" from childhood to adulthood. Each chapter discusses a different novel and includes an analysis of the novel that encompasses story and setting, characters, themes, style, and language; teaching suggestions for discussion and writing; and other related literary works that can be used with the particular novel. The useful appendices list other American novels of initiation as well as other thematic unit possibilities with suggested novels to fit each theme.

Petty, Kate. 1985. *First Library Paperbacks.* New York: Franklin Watts.

This information-packed picture book series for the primary grades includes six nonfiction books: Crocodiles and Alligators, Dinosaurs, Frogs and Toads, Sharks, Snakes, *and* Spiders.

Raffi. 1989. *The Raffi Everything Grows Songbook.* New York: Crown.

For early childhood teachers who want to connect reading and singing, this spiral-bound book contains the printed

music and words of fifteen songs to go along with Raffi's album Everything Grows. *See also* Raffi Songs to Read *for other materials on the singing-reading connection.*

Raines, Shirley C., and Robert J. Canady. 1989. *Story S-t-r-e-t-c-h-e-r-s: Activities to Expand Children's Favorite Books.* Mt. Rainier, MD: Gryphon House.

This resource presents lots of creative arts teaching ideas and activities as extensions for ninety well-known children's books. The book is organized around common themes such as families and friendship. Useful for preschool, kindergarten, and grade 1.

Roettger, Doris. 1989. *Reading Beyond the Basal Plus.* Logan, IA: The Perfection Form Company.

Written for middle grade teachers, each of these teacher guides on such well-known novels as Bridge to Terabithia *by Katherine Paterson and* Sarah, Plain and Tall *by Patricia MacLachlan presents various meaningful activities to choose from for use before, during, and after reading. Each guide (about twelve are available) also includes a brief book summary, information about the author, and an annotated bibliography of other books with a related theme.*

Scarffe, Bronwen, and Lorraine Wilson. 1990. *You Can't Make a Book in a Day.* Albany, NY: Delmar Publishers.

This book focuses on the publishing or book-making part of the process writing program and is chock-full of ideas and visual aids for publishing in the elementary school classroom.

Seminoff, Nancy E. 1990. *Using Children's Magazines in the K–8 Classroom.* Logan, IA: The Perfection Form Company.

This 284-page handbook suggests many ways to enrich the total curriculum through the use of children's magazines. The author begins with a lively description of about thirty high-quality magazines. The rest of the text is devoted to "across-the-curriculum activities" for grades k–2, 3–5, and 6–8. Publishers' addresses for children's magazines, newsmagazines, and newspapers are included in the final section.

Smith, Jennifer. February 1988. "Periodicals That Publish Children's Original Work." *Language Arts*, pp. 202–208.

> *This informative journal article features twenty-two children's magazines that publish children's original writings and art work. Magazines cited are easily accessible and intended for children preschool through grade 6. Information for each magazine listed includes the title, address, subscription price, frequency of publication, intended audience, and the type of material accepted from children.*

• Stewig, John Warren. 1989. *Reading Pictures: Exploring Illustrations with Children.* New Berlin, WI: Jenson Publications.

> Reading Pictures *provides children with opportunities to study and appreciate the work of six well-known illustrators: Marcia Brown, Nonny Hogrogian, Ezra Jack Keats, Robert McCloskey, Gerald McDermott, and John Steptoe. A detailed guide and four large, quality posters that highlight the art of each illustrator accompany each illustrator unit. The guides, which can be ordered separately, provide a wealth of information and activities for visually interacting with picture books. A parent letter at the end of each guide describes the illustrator unit and gives additional titles for parents to share with their children.*

Stoll, Donald R. (ed.). 1990. *Magazines for Children.* Glassboro, NJ: Educational Press Association of America and Newark, DE: International Reading Association.

> *This publication includes an annotated list of over 100 magazines for preschool through secondary age/grade levels. Each magazine annotation includes the intent of the magazine, its subject matter, and complete ordering information. An introduction by Bernice*

Cullinan *gives a rationale and suggestions for using children's magazines, and a subject index lists magazines by topics. Be sure your library has this useful resource.*

Sylvester, Ron (consultant author). 1988. *Interaction: Teachers' Resource Book.* Auckland, NZ: Shortland Publications. Distributed in the United States by Rigby Education.

> *A series of teacher resource books for grades k–3 with excellent activities and illustrations for integrating the teaching of social studies. While the entire series includes informational books as well, the resource books can stand alone. Some focuses include the community, the family, and learning new tasks.*

Thomas, Rebecca L. 1989. *Primaryplots: A Book Talk Guide for Use with Readers Ages 4–8.* New York: Bowker.

> Primaryplots, *by a librarian in our school district, focuses on 150 current and exemplary picture books for preschoolers to middle grade students. The book is organized into chapters: "Enjoying Family and Friends," "Developing a Positive Self-Image," "Celebrating Everyday Experiences," "Finding the Humor in Picture Books," "Exploring the Past," "Learning about the World around You," "Analyzing Illustrations," and "Focusing on Folktales." Especially useful with each book annotation are the "Book Talk Materials and Activities" and "Related Titles." Teachers and librarians will find this a very helpful guide in planning book talks and various reading activities. [For a similar format of recommended literature for the middle grades through high school, see* Introducing Bookplots 3 *(1988),* Juniorplots 3 *(1987), and* Seniorplots *(1989). Also check with R. R. Bowker for other useful annotated book guides.]*

Tuinman, Jaap, and others. 1988–1990. *Teacher's Resource Book.* Scarborough, Ontario: Ginn Canada.

> *These resource books, created to support the publisher's* Journeys *program,*

stand on their own as useful guides for extending and enriching a literature program. The beginning section, "A Whole Language Learning Environment," is excellent for setting out principles and strategies of language learning as well as supplying a full professional bibliography. Each resource is packed with suggested activities that can be used with any literature program.

- Walsh, Huber M. *Social Studies and the Young Learner.* Washington, DC: National Council for the Social Studies.

A relatively new quarterly journal for k-6 teachers to support the creative teaching of social studies. Some issues are devoted to a specific theme. Includes related children's literature, reviews of books and resources for the classroom, discussions of contemporary issues, and practical ideas and strategies for the elementary teacher. Very informative journal with lots of applicable information.

Whisler, Nancy, and Judy Williams. 1990. *Literature and Cooperative Learning: Pathway to Literacy.* Sacramento, CA: Literature Co-op.

K-8 teachers who want some structured, yet meaningful, activities to use with literature will find this 176-page resource very valuable. Lots of sample lessons that include strategies for cooperative learning and for moving through literature—before, during, and after reading—are included.

- Zarnowski, Myra. 1990. *Learning about Biographies. A Reading-and-Writing Approach for Children.* Urbana, IL: National Council of Teachers of English.

Written for elementary and middle school teachers, the author demonstrates how to actively engage students with the nonfiction genre of biographies. Suggestions and examples are given for reading and discussing biographies and encouraging children to research a particular historical figure and then write their own biographical versions. Includes annotated sources for teachers to locate quality biographies, some recommended children's biographies, and samples of biographies written by students.

Recommended Literature by Grade Level, K–12, and Supplemental Lists

Annotations for grades K–8 and supplemental lists by Susan Hepler
Annotations for grades 9–12 by Dana Noble

As much as possible, each grade level collection is balanced to reflect a wide variety of literature—picture books, poetry, folktales, realistic fiction, historical fiction, science fiction, humor, multicultural literature, and nonfiction. Books have been selected for both their high literary quality and outstanding illustrations. When a folktale has been included, a "best version" has been chosen—that is, a version that is prize winning, easily available, and beautifully told.

With the exception of the kindergarten list in which books are meant to be read *to* the child, all books are meant to be read *by* and *with* the children in the guided reading program. Books have been chosen for suitability for guided reading and literary appreciation—that is, these are books that have the power to evoke high-level discussion and personal connections to children's lives.

We tried to avoid repeating titles wherever possible. Be sure to check the supplemental lists, which include "Books Which Invite Writers to Write" (grades 1–6), "Books about Our Diverse Population" (grades k–3, and 4–6), "Wordless Books" (grades k–6), "People in Other Lands" (grades k–3, and 4–6), and "Life Stories" (grades 2–6) to be sure you have books from other important categories. A library media specialist will also be able to suggest additional titles and update the lists. You may also want to check with reading specialists and resource teachers for suggestions on the use of these books.

So that teachers and schools can afford to purchase multiple copies of books, these lists are almost completely limited to titles that are available in paperback. (A + next to a title means the book is also available as a Big Book.) The word "Series" after an annotation means that there are sequels or at least one more book dealing with the same characters in the same setting. The paperback publisher is noted within the parentheses following the original publisher and date. If the parentheses are empty, the book was not available in paperback when *Invitations* went to press. Paperback books often go in and out of print and sometimes change publishers, so if a book is not available at a particular time, it may well be available at a later date. It is recommended that six to ten copies of each title be purchased so books can be used for guided reading in a small-group disscusion.

Kindergarten

This list features a selection of excellent and near-classic titles with strong story lines, themes powerful to five-year-olds, and good read-aloud possibilities. Some titles introduce popular series, as well.

1. *Bread and Jam for Frances* by Russell Hoban, illustrated by Lillian Hoban. New York: Harper & Row, 1964. (Harper Trophy)
   Like many young children, Frances the badger has narrow food preferences but changes her mind with the help of parents and an adventurous friend. Ex-

cellent discussion starter on the advantages of and difficulties we have in trying new things. (Series)

2. + *The Carrot Seed* by Ruth Kraus, illustrated by Crockett Johnson. New York: Harper & Row, 1945. (Scholastic)

 This classic story fulfills a child's need to feel important and successful by showing how a boy plants a seed and raises a huge carrot despite his family's doubts. Works well with The Great Big Enormous Turnip *and* Titch *in a theme of "planting."*

3. + *Chicken Soup with Rice* by Maurice Sendak. New York: Harper & Row, 1962. (Scholastic)

 A month-by-month rhyming account of one boy's humorous uses for chicken soup that invites children to follow the pattern in making up their own verses.

4. + *Each Peach Pear Plum* by Janet and Allan Ahlberg. New York: Viking, 1979. (Puffin; Scholastic)

 Characters from Mother Goose and well-known folktales appear in an "I Spy" text pattern. As with B. G. Hennessy's The Missing Tarts *(New York: Viking Kestrel, 1989), children enjoy reviewing the familiar characters while seeing a story unfold.*

5. + *Freight Train* by Donald Crews. New York: Greenwillow, 1978. (Scholastic)

 This introduction to what a freight train is and what it does also teaches children specific car names and reinforces the naming of colors. With airbrushed illustrations that seem to move across the page, this is one in a series of Crews's books about transportation.

6. *The Gingerbread Boy* by Paul Galdone. New York: Clarion Books, 1975. (Clarion)

 This well-told version of a familiar cumulative tale makes a good flannel board story, mural, or story map of the action. It also reintroduces the tricky fox, a standard character of many folktales which children may already know.

7. *The Great Big Enormous Turnip* by Leo Tolstoy, illustrated by Helen Oxenbury. New York: Franklin Watts, 1968. ( )

 In cumulative pattern, the animals, children, and the old woman line up behind the old man to try to pull the turnip out of the ground. Excellent for a classroom drama or a flannel board story.

8. "Mother Goose."

 Kindergartners enjoy repeated hearings and chantings of these rhymes. Many collections by well-known illustrators such as Tomie De Paola, Brian Wildsmith, Arnold Lobel, and James Marshall entertain children for hours with these cornerstones of literature. See, too, Each Peach Pear Plum.

9. *The Napping House* by Audrey Wood, illustrated by Don Wood. San Diego: Harcourt Brace Jovanovich, 1984. ( )

 In cumulative pattern, this humorous story pictures a snoring granny who shares the bed with her grandson and an assortment of animals until a pesky flea climbs aboard. Children enjoy chanting the rhythmical text, noticing the flea draw closer to the sleepers in each picture, and the gradually lightening palette of colors as dawn approaches.

10. *Read-Aloud Rhymes for the Very Young* edited by Jack Prelutsky, illustrated by Marc Brown. New York: Knopf, 1986. ( )

 Over 200 poems selected from both old and new poets to enjoy all year long. Poems, which match children's concerns about loose teeth or friendship or their awareness of the seasons, animals, or holidays, are nicely balanced for humor and thoughtfulness.

11. + *Rosie's Walk* by Pat Hutchins. New York: Macmillan, 1968. (Scholastic)

 One long sentence with many prepositional phrases tells of Rosie's walk before dinner. But the illustrations beg to be talked about as another tricky fox is foiled in his attempt to catch his dinner. Children can tell alternative stories, provide dialogue for the many animals pictured, or experiment with patterned shapes in their own art work.

12. + *Ten Nine Eight* by Molly Bang. New York: Greenwillow, 1983. (Scholastic)

An African-American girl and her father get ready for bed in a countdown counting book. Talk about bedtime rituals and solve the mystery of where the missing shoe from the "seven shoes" page has gone.

13. *The Three Bears* by Paul Galdone. New York: Clarion, 1973. (Clarion)

    A cornerstone of children's literary experiences, this story is told in a straightforward manner and illustrated with plenty of wee, little, middle-sized, and great big items or print to encourage children to notice them. Compare treatment of the characters, the household, and humorous touches by looking at other versions of the story illustrated by David McPhail, Lorinda Bryan Cauley, James Marshall, Jan Brett, and Anne Rockwell.

14. *Titch* by Pat Hutchins. New York: Macmillan, 1971. (Puffin)

    Titch, the littlest in his family, always gets the short end of things until he plants a seed and his plant is the envy of his siblings. Good start for encouraging children to talk about aspects of being small or little or young. See also The Carrot Seed. *(Series)*

15. + *The Very Hungry Caterpillar* by Eric Carle. New York: Putnam, 1969. (Scholastic)

    A hungry caterpillar eats his way through various foods during one week, spins a chrysalis (here called erroneously a "cocoon"), and emerges as a beautiful butterfly. Children can retell with the actual book as pictures with die-cut holes provide prediction clues.

16. *Where the Wild Things Are* by Maurice Sendak. New York: Harper & Row, 1964. (Harper Trophy)

    In this reassuring classic, Max, sent to his room for making mischief, dreams he travels to a land where he controls things. Children can notice how the pictures change, or create a wild rumpus complete with animal masks, but the most powerful aspect of the story is still parental forgiveness and love for children even when they misbehave.

Books Which Invite Readers into Print

The following texts, many of which are only eight pages, are recommended for beginning emergent readers. These texts have consistent and simple structure, familiar and repetitive language patterns, very limited print, which is consistently and clearly placed on each page, and illustrations that are highly supportive of the text. These books are excellent for guiding students in developing one-to-one matching (1:1 correspondence) of spoken to printed word, correct directionality skills, and utilization of pictures that depict most of the text. Even at this simplest level, each of these stories ends with a twist to delight the reader. Many of these stories also encourage readers to create their own versions.

1. + *Across the Stream* by Mirra Ginsburg, illustrated by Nancy Tafuri. New York: Greenwillow, 1984. (Scholastic)

    Rhyming text tells of a hen's dream of escaping a fox by crossing a stream on a friendly duck's back. Notice the tiny symbols next to each page number, the many other animals in the illustrations, and discuss whether this is a dream or not. See how many other stories children can recall in which a hen or chicken and a fox appear.

2. *All Fall Down* by Brian Wildsmith. New York: Oxford University Press, 1983. (Oxford)

    "I see" one animal standing upon another until "All fall down." Like 1 Hunter, *this book can be read easily because the pictures make the text predictable. Compare with "Pardon?", Said the* Giraffe *and make your own falling-down story.*

3. + *Brown Bear, Brown Bear, What Do You See?* by Bill Martin, Jr., illustrated by Eric Carle. New York: Henry Holt, 1983. (Harcourt Brace Jovanovich)

    Children enjoy chanting this chain-structured story of an animal of one color who sees another animal of a different color, and so forth. Change the animals to children in the class for a new chant or make another book of differently colored bugs, other animals, or birds.

4. + *The Bus Ride* by Anne McLean, illustrated by Justin Wager. Glenview, IL: Scott, Foresman, 1971. (Scott, Foresman)

    "A girl got on the bus. Then the bus went fast." These first two pages are repeated over and over again, but with different characters—a boy, a fox, a hippopotamus, a goat, a rhinoceros, a horse, a rabbit, and finally a bee, which forces everyone off the bus.

5. *The Cat Sat on the Mat* by Brian Wildsmith. New York: Oxford University Press, 1982. (Oxford)

    Pictures clearly show a cat on the mat but each page turn adds another animal until the annoyed cat says "Sssppstt" and everyone leaves.

6. *The Chick and the Duckling* by Mirra Ginsburg, illustrated by Jose and Ariane Aruego. New York: Macmillan, 1973. (Macmillan)

    "Me, too," says a chick as it follows an adventurous duckling's lead until disaster nearly results and the chick finally thinks for itself: "Not me!".

7. *Have You Seen My Duckling?* by Nancy Tafuri. New York: Greenwillow, 1984. (Puffin)

    An adventurous duckling leaves his family but is visible in each picture as a mother duck asks various pond animals, "Have you seen my duckling?" Children enjoy the visual game of hide-and-seek. Other books by Tafuri that work at this level include Who's Counting? *(New York: Greenwillow, 1986) and* Spots, Feathers, and Curly Tails *(New York: Greenwillow, 1989).*

8. *I Like Books* by Anthony Browne. New York: Knopf, 1987. (Firefly)

    A gorilla mentions the kinds of books he likes; among them are scary books, books about pirates, funny books, and alphabet books. Ask children to talk about "kinds of books." Create a book display on a table in the classroom based on children's categories of books they like.

9. *Mary Wore Her Red Dress and Henry Wore His Green Sneakers* by Merle Peek. New York: Clarion, 1985. (Clarion)

    The verses in the song repeat what critters wore "all day long" when they attended a birthday party. The chantable or singable text is enhanced by humorous illustrations that augment the story line; the story reviews colors cleverly, as well.

10. *My Book* by Ron Maris. New York: Viking Penguin, 1983. (Puffin)

    Half-pages inserted change the look of each picture as a child invites the reader to go through "my gate" and finally into "my room." The text, if not the format, invites readers to make their own book of possessions, routes to favorite spots, and so forth.

11. *1 Hunter* by Pat Hutchins. New York: Greenwillow, 1982. (Mulberry)

    Clues to the next page's minimal text are found on each preceding page of this counting book. Children enjoy being able to predict by finding the hidden animals.

12. *What a Tale* by Brian Wildsmith. New York: Oxford University Press, 1986. (Oxford)

    Five tails, "spotted," or "bobbed," and so forth, turn out to be animals riding in a kangaroo's pouch. Silly with one small pun on the word "tail." See, too, Tail Toes Eyes Ears Nose *by Marilee Robin Burton (New York: Harper & Row, 1989) for more readable fun with animal parts.*

Because it is difficult to find "literature" at this earliest emergent level and because budding readers need lots of practice on easy books, the following simple patterned texts, all in paperback, are also recommended:

1. *Expressways* II, *Reading Corner* 1. Toronto: Gage Educational Publishing, 1986. Available in the United States through Dormac, San Diego, CA.

    A set of eleven books of eight pages each with titles such as I Read, I Have a Pet, I Like to Eat, *and* Baby Animals. *Fanciful illustrations support the short, predictable text.*

2. *This Is the Way I Go.* Allen, TX: DLM, 1976.

    A set of six books emphasizes common action words (climb, fly, run, swim, crawl, and play) in consistent, predictable language patterns. For example, in I Jump, *one page reads, " 'I can jump,' said the horse." Also a good springboard for writing similar texts based on the same pattern. Works well to begin with shared writing in a small group and duplicate the new text for each student to read and illustrate.*

3. *Tiger Cub Readers* by Robert and Marlene McCracken. Winnipeg: Peguis, 1989.

    A set of eight books of fourteen pages each depicts basic concepts and familiar experiences. For example, in What Is This? *each animal page says, "This is a duck" or "This is a pig" with a colorful, clear illustration directly under the text.*

4. *Twig Books* by Rebel Williams. Bothell, WA: The Wright Group, 1990.

    Twig Books, *Sets A, B, C and D, each contain eight nonfiction books of eight pages each. Well done for simplicity, picture match with text, and content material. For example,* Champions *(Set A) shows the symbol and a picture of the Olympics on the cover and title page. The text, spread over eight pages, reads, "People running. People jumping. People swimming. People diving. People lifting. People throwing. Champions!"*

Developing Early Reading Strategies

These are highly predictable books, many with rhyme, rhythm, and repetition that make them especially predictable. Familiar sentence patterns are repeated; illustrations provide excellent support to the text; the print is very clear, sizable, and consistently placed on each page; the language structure and story line are familiar and make sense. In contrast to the highly structured "Books Which Invite Readers into Print," these texts have more words on a page, longer sentences, more descriptive language patterns, and more narrative development. These titles are also

easier to read than titles on the "First Grade" list.

Repeated readings of such books help young readers develop sight vocabulary, fluency, and confidence as well as strengthen early reading strategies such as 1:1 correspondence, left-to-right line sweep, use of picture, meaning, and structure cues and use of beginning and ending consonants. (See also "Recommended Literature for Beginning Readers: Rhyme, Rhythm, and Repetition," Routman, 1988, pp. 285–290, for additional titles.)

1. *Cookie's Week* by Cindy Ward, illustrated by Tomie dePaola. New York: Scholastic, 1988. (Scholastic)

    On each day of the week, a mischievous cat manages to create a new household upset. Predictable, repetitive, natural language pattern. Excellent for understanding cause and effect and for creating original stories based on the book's format and pattern.

2. + *Crocodile Beat* by Gail Jorgensen, illustrated by Patricia Mullins. Crystal Lake, IL: Rigby Education, 1988. (Rigby)

    This colorful animal story of a crocodile in search of his dinner naturally lends itself to drama and movement. Children love chanting the rhythmic beat of this story and seeing the surprise ending. The illustrations, comprised of collage made from tissue paper, are superb.

3. *Dear Zoo* by Rod Campbell. New York: Four Winds Press, 1982. (Puffin)

    A child who writes to the zoo requesting a pet receives various animals and returns them all as unsuitable until a puppy arrives. Each animal is packaged in a pop-up that invites children to predict and see what the zoo has sent. Limited print on each page, consistent pattern, and colorful lift-up feature make this a children's favorite.

4. *Gone Fishing* by Earlene Long, illustrated by Richard Brown. Boston: Houghton Mifflin, 1984. (Houghton Mifflin)

    A father and son spend a quiet, satisfying day fishing and being together. While there are some complex language structures, most of the text is quite simple with supportive illustrations. "A big fish-

ing rod for my daddy" (p. 8). "A little fishing rod for me" (p. 9).

5. + *Greedy Cat* by Joy Cowley. Wellington, New Zealand: Department of Education, 1983. (Richard C. Owen)

    Children delight in Greedy Cat who continually loots "Mum's" shopping bag and who finally gets what he deserves. "Along came Greedy Cat. He looked in the shopping Bag. Gobble, gobble, gobble, and that was the end of that," is spread out over four lines and repeated seven times in the story.

6. *Hush Little Baby* by Aliki. New York: Simon & Schuster, 1968. (Simon & Schuster)

    Popular folk lullaby is easily and enjoyably sung by young readers. This favorite version is gently illustrated with muted colors to support the text.

7. + *In a Dark Dark Wood* by June Melser and Joy Cowley. Auckland, New Zealand: Shortland Publications, 1980. (The Wright Group)

    Children love the suspense of finding out what's in the "dark, dark box" in the "dark, dark house." Compare with Ruth Brown's A Dark, Dark House (New York: Dial, 1981).

8. + *Is Your Mama a Llama?* by Deborah Guarino, illustrated by Steven Kellogg. New York: Scholastic, 1989. (Scholastic)

    A humorous story in rhyming verse follows a baby llama on visits and inquiries to various animals in a quest to determine if his mama is a llama.

9. *It Looked Like Spilt Milk* by Charles G. Shaw. New York: Harper & Row, 1947. (Harper & Row)

    "Sometimes it looked like Spilt Milk. But it wasn't Spilt Milk./ Sometimes it looked like a Rabbit. But it wasn't a Rabbit." Consistent language pattern and simple, accompanying cutouts of the objects make this easy to read and suitable for beginning patterned writing.

10. + *Joshua James Likes Trucks* by Catherine Petrie. Chicago: Children's Press, 1988. (Children's Press)

    Joshua James, a young African-American boy, likes all kinds of trucks—

big, little, long, short, red, green, yellow, and blue and trucks that go up and down. Very predictable text with large, clear print and matching picture cues.*

11. *Just Like Daddy* by Frank Asch. New York: Simon & Schuster, 1981. (Simon & Schuster)

    A gentle story of a young bear who emulates his daddy—and his mommy. Repetitive phrases and clear illustrations make this an appealing, easily readable book.

12. + *More Spaghetti I Say* by Rita Gelman. New York: Scholastic. 1987. (Scholastic)

    Although the pictures are barely more than cartoons, children love this playful, rhyming book about the eating antics of Minnie and Freddy. (Series)

13. + *Mrs. Wishy-Washy* by Joy Cowley, illustrated by Elizabeth Fuller. Auckland, New Zealand: Shortland Publications, 1980. (The Wright Group)

    "Oh, lovely mud," say the cow, the pig, and the duck before Mrs. Wishy-Washy cleans them all up. But back they go into the puddle again. Children will sympathize with these mud-lovers. Retell the story with different animals or make a giant mural mud puddle with a variety of dirty or about-to-be dirty animals.

14. *Mud* by Wendy Cheyette Lewison, illustrated by Maryann Cocca-Leffler. New York: Random House, 1990. (Random House)

    Whimsical pictures match the short, rhyming verse describing a boy and girl who are covered with mud everywhere.

15. *My Bike* by Craig Martin. Wellington, New Zealand: Department of Education, 1985. (Richard C. Owen)

    Realistic photographs show a boy riding his bike each day of the week. The story is cumulative with a new episode being added for each day of the week. Good for reinforcing direction words: "over," "under," "around," "through," "up," and "down" and for writing a similar patterned story. (See pp. 142–143 for examples.) Check other titles in this Ready to Read series.

16. + *Noisy Nora* by Rosemary Wells. New York: Dial, 1973. (Scholastic)

   Young readers love the rhythm and rhyme of this popular tale. Children relate to the angry frustration of young Nora who "had to wait" because her mother and father were busy with her younger siblings. Discuss other, more appropriate, ways Nora could have gotten attention.

17. + *Oh, A-Hunting We Will Go* by John Langstaff. New York: Macmillan, 1974. (Houghton Mifflin)

   This popular rhyming chant with music included on the final page is a favorite classic. In addition to singing the text, children enjoy adding their own original verses.

18. *"Pardon?" Said the Giraffe* by Colin West. New York: Lippincott, 1986. (Harper Trophy)

   " 'What's it like up there?' asked the frog . . . 'Pardon?' said the giraffe." These two language patterns alternate for most of the text as a persistent frog tries repeatedly to talk to a tall giraffe. Children enjoy the humorous ending and finding the frog on the colorful end pages. See, also by West, Not Me, Said the Monkey (*Lippincott, 1987*) and Have You Seen the Crocodile? (*Lippincott, 1986*).

19. + *Pumpkin Pumpkin* by Jeanette Titherington. New York: Greenwillow, 1986. (Scholastic)

   A boy and his grandfather plant a pumpkin seed and raise, harvest, and carve the pumpkin after carefully saving some seeds for next year's pumpkin in this life cycle book. Identify the animals that watch the pumpkin grow, and plant seeds or carve a pumpkin. (Series.)

20. *Things I Like* by Anthony Browne. New York: Knopf, 1989. (Knopf)

   A chimpanzee tells what he likes to do: painting, riding a bike, playing with toys, dressing up, and much more. Humorous illustrations strongly support the text of one to five words on each page.

21. *Wheels on the Bus*. Raffi Songs to Read. Illustrated by Sylvie Kantorovitz Wickstrom. New York: Crown, 1988. (Crown)

   This well-known song invites children to sing the words and follow the people on the bus as they ride to a park. Final page includes the music and additional verses. Other books in the series with pictures by different illustrators bring other well-known songs to life, allowing children to sing their way toward literacy. (Series)

22. *Who Said Red?* by Mary Serfozo. New York: Margaret K. McElderry Books, 1988. (Scholastic)

   Vibrant watercolor illustrations by Keiko Narahashi complement the rhyming and repetitive text. Imaginative use of language for primary color words.

23. + *Who's in the Shed?* by Brenda Parkes. Crystal Lake, IL: Rigby Education, 1986. (Rigby)

   Increasingly enlarged cutouts give additional clues to "Who's in the shed?" Children love predicting as they go along and rereading many times. The recurring pattern is "So the sheep (and other animals) had a peep through a hole in the shed. What did she see?"

Grade 1

Books on this list include titles with strong themes, a variety of genres within the picture book format, interesting literary patterns, and illustrations that invite notice. Many series are included on this list as new readers like to keep reading without having to change settings and characters with each new book.

1. *A Chair for My Mother* by Vera B. Williams. New York: Greenwillow, 1982. (Mulberry)

   A child and her waitress mother save coins to buy a comfortable armchair after their belongings are destroyed in an apartment fire. The community helps them get back on their feet, and the story provides an excellent start for a discussion of how people help each other in neighborhoods, in classrooms, and in the world. Notice Williams' selection of small pictures to highlight aspects of the larger ones. (Series)

2. *Alexander and the Terrible, Horrible, No Good, Very Bad Day* by Judith Viorst, illustrated by Ray Cruz. New York: Atheneum, 1972. (Aladdin)

Alexander has numerous "terrible things" happen to him and considers moving to Australia. Good discussion or story starter about our own terrible, or even very good, days. (Series)

3. *Amos & Boris* by William Steig. New York: Farrar, Straus & Giroux, 1971. (Sunburst)

Like Aesop's "The Lion and the Mouse," this story shows how a seagoing mouse is saved by a whale but then the beached whale is saved by a mouse. Notice the interesting language of the story, write a diary as if you were the mouse or the whale, make a tiny mouse museum of things important to Amos, and ask children to compare Steig's story with Aesop's fable. (See Teacher's Guide, Appendix B.)

4. + *Chickens Aren't the Only Ones* by Ruth Heller. New York: Grossett & Dunlap, 1981. (Scholastic)

Accurate paintings illustrate the rhyming text about all the animals that hatch from eggs: birds, reptiles, fish, insects, and even the extinct dinosaur are mentioned. An excellent discussion starter for ways scientists categorize the world and a fine introduction to a classroom study of animals.

5. *Every Time I Climb a Tree* by David McCord, illustrated by Marc Simont. Boston: Little, Brown, 1967. (Little, Brown)

The title poem invites readers to do their own dreaming from a high place and other poems play with words, sounds, feelings, and sights. A fine introduction to a major American poet; Simont's bold illustrations seem just right for the selections.

6. *Frog and Toad Together* by Arnold Lobel. New York: Harper & Row, 1971. (Harper Trophy)

The steadfast Frog helps his impatient friend Toad through a series of humorous incidents in this popular series. Children enjoy laughing at Toad's impetuous acts and discussing what they would do in similar situations. Occasionally, Lobel's gentle tales provoke readers to discuss theme, or "big ideas," as well. (Series)

7. *George and Martha* by James Marshall. Boston: Houghton Mifflin, 1972. (Sandpiper)

The first collection of small stories about two large friends introduces children to this popular hippo pair. (Series)

8. *Henry and Mudge* by Cynthia Rylant, illustrated by Sucie Stevenson. New York: Macmillan, 1987. (Aladdin)

In an easy-reader format with full-color illustrations, Rylant and Stevenson tell about Henry, a boy who finally gets a pet dog. Mudge grows to 180 pounds, accompanies Henry to school, and gets lost and is found all in seven short chapters. Like Lobel, Rylant packs a lot into few words, and readers will be moved, will laugh, and will want to talk about the story. There are many books in this excellent series. (Series)

9. *Ira Sleeps Over* by Bernard Waber. Boston: Houghton Mifflin, 1972. (Sandpiper)

The universal problem of how to save face even though you want your teddy bear with you is explored in this family story. Ask why Ira decides to take his bear after all. Most children have bedtime rituals and special toys or blankets which they enjoy comparing. (Series)

10. *Little Bear* by Else Holmelund Minarik, illustrated by Maurice Sendak. New York: Harper & Row, 1957. (Harper Trophy)

One of the very first early-reader books and one of the finest presents Little Bear and his friends to children. Elegantly told but with a controlled vocabulary, the stories have endured for over thirty years. Ask children how Little Bear is like and unlike human children.

Jean Van Leeuwen's series beginning with Tales of Oliver Pig, *illustrated by Arnold Lobel (New York: Dial, 1979), provides some of the same reader satisfactions with its humanized pig family growing up. (Series)*

11. *The Little Red Hen* by Paul Galdone. New York: Clarion Books, 1974. (Scholastic)

    If you don't do any of the work, then you don't get any of the hen's bread. Notice the words "Not I" cleverly illustrate and encourage retelling with pictured seeds, wheat, flour, bread, and the four folk tale characters.

12. *Little Red Riding Hood* by Trina Schart Hyman. New York: Holiday House, 1983. (Holiday)

    This classic folktale features the hungry wolf and the helpful huntsman as well as wonderfully illustrated borders and small vignettes. Watch the cat. See Self-Portrait: Trina Schart Hyman (Addison-Wesley, 1981) and tell children about the importance of this story to the author. Compare Lisbeth Zwerger's illustrations for the same story.

13. *The Random House Book of Poetry for Children*, edited by Jack Prelutsky. New York: Random House, 1983. (   )

    Over 500 poems are divided into sections on nature, seasons, children, humor, people, and food ("I'm Hungry!"); other poems invite children to enjoy poetry. An excellent selection from which to choose all year long.

14. + *Time for a Rhyme*, illustrated by Marjorie Gardner, Heather Philpott, and Jane Tanner. Crystal Lake, IL: Rigby, 1982. (Rigby)

    Nursery rhymes, some well known and others not, are presented with lively illustrations for children who may not be familiar with Mother Goose. (See also annotation for "Mother Goose" on the kindergarten list.)

15. *Wiley and the Hairy Man* by Molly Bang. New York: Macmillan, 1976. (Aladdin)

    In this traditional African-American folktale, the Hairy Man threatens Wiley and his mother until they trick him three times.

Trickery and the number three are common motifs in folktales, and children might think of other stories with either of these two patterns.

Grade 2

This list includes some cornerstones of traditional literature, several chapter books for more advanced readers, and an echo from the first grade list, another country's version of "Little Red Riding Hood."

1. *The Adventures of Spider* by Joyce Cooper Arkhurst, illustrated by Jerry Pinkney. Boston: Little, Brown, 1964. (Scholastic)

   Told with the rhythm, sounds, and cadences of African oral tradition, these tales reveal the trickster nature of Anansi, the spider. Look for the interesting features of African folktales. Compare the character of Anansi and the language of the story in Gail Haley's A Story, a Story (New York: Atheneum, 1970) or Gerald McDermott's Anansi the Spider (New York: Holt, Rinehart and Winston, 1972). Invite children to write their own tales. (Series)

2. *Charlotte's Web* by E. B. White, illustrated by Garth Williams. New York: Harper & Row, 1952. (Harper)

   This beloved animal fantasy has become a classic because of its timelessness. A spider's efforts to save a young pig are chronicled in graceful prose. The gentle humor, development of the animal characters, Fern's growth from young child to young girl, the themes of friendship, growing up, and the cycle of life and death make this a powerful book for young readers.

3. *Cinderella, or the Little Glass Slipper* by Charles Perrault, illustrated by Errol Le Cain. New York: Bradbury, 1973. (Puffin)

   The traditional story is cleverly illustrated to show children clearly what a transformation is. Compare text and pictures with versions illustrated by Marcia Brown, Paul Galdone, or Susan Jeffers.

Laugh at Bernice Myers' Sidney Rella and the Glass Sneaker *(New York: Macmillan, 1986), or compare two of the oldest-known variants of the story:* Yeh-Shen *by Ai-Ling Louie, illustrated by Ed Young (New York: Putnam, 1983) and* The Egyptian Cinderella *by Shirley Climo, illustrated by Ruth Heller (New York: Crowell, 1989).*

4. *The Courage of Sarah Noble* by Alice Dalgliesh, illustrated by Leonard Weisgard. New York: Scribner, 1954. (Aladdin)

    Eight-year-old Sarah's courage is proved in many ways when she accompanies her father into the wilderness to cook for him while he builds a cabin for their family. A realistic picture of part of life in "olden days" and a fine discussion of what bravery and courage are.

5. *Do Not Open* by Brinton Turkle. New York: Dutton, 1981. (Dutton)

    When Miss Moody opens a blue glass bottle she finds at the seashore, an evil genie is let loose. But it proves no match for the tricks of Miss Moody and her cat. Recall the trick and ask children to think of other stories, such as "Puss in Boots" or "The Brave Little Tailor," in which trickery is important.

6. *Dr. De Soto* by William Steig. New York: Farrar, Straus & Giroux, 1982. (Sunburst)

    A clever mouse dentist tricks a fox patient. Notice the many contrivances that help the dentist in his office, elicit children's knowledge of the fox character from other folktales, and introduce children to other modern tales by this popular author.

7. *Honey I Love: and Other Poems* by Eloise Greenfield, illustrated by Leo and Diane Dillon. New York: Harper & Row, 1978. (Harper Trophy)

    Greenfield presents a jump-rope rhyme, chants, observations on people and the neighborhood, and thoughts in the voice of a young African-American child. Illustrations in warm browns and sepias are as sensitive as these poems that celebrate a child's world.

8. + *How Much Is a Million?* by David M. Schwartz, illustrated by Steven Kellogg. New York: Lothrop, Lee & Shepard, 1985. (Scholastic)

    Help for the reader in conceptualizing large numbers. Follow up with estimating, finding funny illustrations, inventing rules for the game suggested in Kellogg's humorous illustrations, and read the sequel by the same team, If You Made a Million *(New York: Lothrop, Lee and Shepard, 1989). (Series)*

9. *I Want a Dog* by Dayal Kaur Khalsa. New York: Crown, 1987. (Scholastic)

    May badgers her parents for a pet dog but they are firm in their refusal. So May puts a leash on her white rollerskate and treats it like the longed-for pet. Dog lovers will admire the many dogs crowding the pictures, but children will respond to May's persistent "Try, try, try again," which eventually wins her parents over. The "Henry and Mudge" series by Cynthia Rylant (see grade 1 list) fits well with stories about children who want pets.

10. *Lon Po Po: A Red-Riding Hood Story from China* by Ed Young. New York: Philomel, 1989. (Scholastic)

    Unlike the story most familiar to children, this one presents three daughters who, in disobeying their mother, let an old wolf into the house. But the eldest outwits the wolf in this Chinese story. Locate China on the map, discuss how this older version and Hyman's (see list for grade 1) compare, and wonder over the mysterious dedication. Young has also illustrated a Chinese "Cinderella" variant, Yeh Shen.

11. + *Ox-Cart Man* by Donald Hall, illustrated by Barbara Cooney. New York: Viking, 1979. (Scholastic)

    This lyrical journey from fall to spring in the life of one early nineteenth-century family in New England is a paean to a self-sufficient life. Compare a child's life in this book with that portrayed in The Courage of Sarah Noble, *or with modern children's lives.*

12. *Owl Moon* by Jane Yolen, illustrated by John Schoenherr. New York: Philomel, 1987. (Scholastic)

    A girl's owling trek with her father late one winter night is beautifully evoked in stunning watercolors and poetic prose. Children might enjoy writing or telling of their own memorable experiences with the natural world.

13. *The Patchwork Quilt* by Valerie Flournoy, illustrated by Jerry Pinkney. New York: Dial, 1985. (   )

    Tanya, an African-American child, has a new understanding of the importance of family when she and her mother finish a patchwork quilt her ailing grandmother had started. Discuss how families help each other and the special "gifts" people in families share with each other.

14. *Sam, Bangs, and Moonshine* by Evaline Ness. New York: Holt, 1966. (Holt)

    Samantha's imaginative fantasies are almost responsible for the loss of her friend Thomas when she sends him out to a rock at high tide to see a mermaid. Discuss imagination's values and misuses.

15. *A Toad for Tuesday* by Russell E. Erickson. New York: Lothrop, Lee and Shepard, 1974. (Listening Library Inc.)

    The unlikely friendship that develops between a cranky, messy owl and a good-tempered, orderly toad works well as a springboard for other books about friendship. Readers ready for short chapter books will enjoy the first of four adventure stories featuring the toad brothers Morton and Warton. (Series)

16. + *Where the Forest Meets the Sea* by Jeannie Baker. New York: Greenwillow, 1987. (Scholastic)

    Through striking collage illustrations, readers explore with a modern boy a tropical rain forest in Australia. Throughout, the pictures of ghostly images of past life in the forest as well as ghostly images of possible futures for this forest raise questions about how humans value rain forests and wild land in general. A thought-provoking and beautiful book. See, too, Lynne Cherry's The Ka-

pok Tree *(New York: Harcourt Brace Jovanovich, 1990) to develop an ecological theme.*

17. *Wump World* by Bill Peet. Boston: Houghton Mifflin, 1970. (Houghton Mifflin)

    This delightfully illustrated tale of grass-eating Wumps, peaceful creatures whose world is ruined by pollution and the misuse of natural resources, is both a clever tale and a catalyst for discussion of the pollution of our world. Be sure to check for other Bill Peet titles (over twenty in paperback).

Grade 3

This list includes several fantasies and inviting realistic novels, which introduce readers to popular authors and series, and two nonfiction examples, which suggest to readers how information may be interestingly conveyed in a variety of formats.

1. *Amazing Spiders* by Alexandra Parsons, photographs by Jerry Young. New York: Knopf, 1990. (Knopf)

    With beautiful full-color photographs that reveal multiple details, this informational book series is organized around a dozen topics listed in the contents. Other books in the series invite readers to talk about birds, mammals, and snakes. The parent volumes are "Eyewitness Books," a more densely packed series for older readers. (Series)

2. *The Comeback Dog* by Jane Resh Thomas, illustrated by Troy Howell. Boston: Houghton Mifflin, 1981. (Bantam Skylark)

    Daniel rescues a near-dead dog from a ditch, revives it, and tries to make it love him. Subtly the author gives the reader clues as to Daniel's feelings in this graceful and poignant story of what loving is all about. (Series)

3. *The Cricket in Times Square* by George Selden, illustrated by Garth Williams. New York: Farrar, Straus & Giroux, 1981. (Dell Yearling)

    A city mouse and cat initiate a country cricket into life in a newsstand in

New York City. Introduction to a well-known animal fantasy series and a lovingly illustrated treatise on friendship and its rewards. *(Series)*

4. *Danny the Champion of the World* by Roald Dahl. New York: Knopf, 1975. (Bantam)

    Danny's father's secret poaching in Victor Hazel's wood provides the opportunity for controversial discussion on the morality of poaching. Children enjoy this adventure of a loving, fun-filled relationship between a father and son as told by a master storyteller. See The Author's Eye, *p. 36b, for information about how Dahl works as a writer.*

5. + *Earthworms* by Keith Pigdon and Marilyn Woolley, illustrated by Sadie and Suzanne Pascoe. Cleveland: Modern Curriculum Press, 1989. (Modern Curriculum Press)

    Clear illustrations in a variety of formats with labels, cross-sections, examples, cutaways, and graphs help readers understand earthworms. By discussing how information is conveyed in nonfiction texts, teachers can help children be better users of reference material. Directions for making a wormery are included.

6. *I'll Meet You at the Cucumbers* by Lilian Moore, illustrated by Sharon Woodring. New York: Atheneum, 1988. (Skylark)

    Adam Mouse considers his own country world the ultimate until his pen pal Amanda invites him to the city. There, Adam discovers that he is a poet. This simple animal fantasy novel asks children to consider what poetry is and does. Pair with poetry or with a version of the fable "The Country Mouse and the City Mouse."

7. *Koko's Kitten* by Francine Patterson, photographs by Ronald H. Cohn. New York: Scholastic, 1985. (Scholastic)

    In this nonfiction photo-essay, Dr. Patterson tells how she began to teach Koko the gorilla to speak in American Sign Language (ASL). Talk about how gorillas communicate in the wild and what Patterson has taught here. Discuss what the pictures show us, or perhaps give them captions. How might understanding animals be important to humans? *(Series)*

8. *Miss Rumphius* by Barbara Cooney. New York: Viking, 1982. (Puffin)

    As a child, Miss Rumphius wishes to see faraway places, live by the sea, and make the world more beautiful. As a grown-up, she accomplishes all three in this picture book set in the previous century. Consider how each of us could make the world more beautiful; talk about dreams we have. Read about others who made some part of the world beautiful, such as Johnny Appleseed, George Washington Carver, or The Man Who Planted Trees *by Michael McCurdy (New York: Chelsea Green, 1986).*

9. *Molly's Pilgrim* by Barbara Cohen, illustrated by Michael J. Deraney. New York: Lothrop, Lee and Shepard, 1983. (Skylark)

    The girls in her turn-of-the-century class make fun of her imperfect English, and Molly thinks she will never belong. When she brings her Pilgrim doll dressed like a Russian immigrant to school for the Thanksgiving project, her teacher saves the day. Touching story, based on a true incident, and a good discussion book.

10. *Mufaro's Beautiful Daughters* by John Steptoe. New York: Lothrop, Lee and Shepard, 1987. (Harper)

    The king is choosing a wife, and two beautiful sisters journey to his village. But the mean-spirited sister does not pass the three tests while the kind and gentle Nyasha naturally succeeds. Notice the lush flora and fauna of Zimbabwe. Ask children to compare the good sister/bad sister pattern found in The Talking Eggs, *by Robert D. San Souci, illustrated by Jerry Pinkney (New York: Dial, 1989).*

11. *Poem Stew* edited by William Cole, illustrated by Karen Ann Weinhaus. New York: Lippincott, 1981. (Harper Trophy)

    Over fifty poems celebrate food, funny eaters both real and weird, and our fascination with what we eat. Finger-snapping rhythm, catchy rhymes, and a variety of topics make this an excel-

lent collection for chants, choral reading, before-lunch laughing, and pure enjoyment.

12. *Ramona Quimby, Age 8* by Beverly Cleary, illustrated by Alan Tiegreen. New York: Morrow, 1981. (Dell Yearling)

Ramona deals with changes in her life and grows up a little. Children identify with Ramona's trying to be a third-grader, a younger sister, and a decent person all at once. (Series)

13. *Stone Fox* by John R. Gardiner, illustrated by Marcia Sewell. New York: Crowell, 1980. (Harper Trophy)

Ten-year-old Willy enters a sled dog race against the legendary Indian Stone Fox in order to pay off the back taxes on his grandfather's Wyoming farm. Readers will never forget this masterfully told and moving story set in the 1800s.

14. *The Stories Julian Tells* by Anne Cameron, illustrated by Ann Strugnell. New York: Knopf, 1981. (Knopf)

Six chapters introduce the imaginative Julian, his younger brother Hugh, and their friend Gloria. Strugnell's pictures of this loving African-American family and their often funny encounters are an added plus. First book in a popular series. Compare Julian's imagination with Sam's in Sam, Bangs, and Moonshine *(see grade 2 list). (Series)*

15. *Toad Food and Measle Soup* by Christine McDonnell, illustrated by Diane de Groat. New York: Dial, 1982. (Puffin)

Five short funny episodes chronicle Leo's encounters with vegetarianism, a pet lizard, a lost dog, and his wild imagination. See how many titles children can identify from the class "Book Report Day," or hold a similar festival. Make a class list of other characters with wild imaginations. (Series)

16. *What's the Big Idea, Ben Franklin?* by Jean Fritz, illustrated by Margot Tomes. New York: Coward, McCann & Geoghegan, 1976. (Coward)

Jean Fritz has the knack of making facts lively, interesting, and even funny in her series of well-illustrated biographies of famous people. Create a time line of Franklin's life, marvel over his achievements, or compare information in this book with a fiction account, such as Robert Lawson's Ben and Me *told by Ben's mouse companion (Boston: Little, Brown, 1939). (Series)*

Grade 4

This list introduces picture books for older children, an outstanding collection of short stories, fantasy with larger themes, and historical fiction that both builds and demands a deeper knowledge of the setting.

1. *Anastasia Krupnik* by Lois Lowry. Boston: Houghton Mifflin, 1979. (Bantam)

Anastasia, a budding poet and a thoughtful fourth-grader, is initially annoyed at her parents for having a new baby. But the death of her grandmother, the arrival of baby Sam, and her increasing sense of the importance of family help her change her mind. Anastasia's lists at the end of each chapter suggest by inference her gradual changes of heart in this first Anastasia story. (Series)

2. *Animal Fact/Animal Fable* by Semour Simon, illustrated by Diane deGroat. New York: Crown, 1979. (Crown)

In a clever guessing game format, Simon presents simple statements about animals that may be true or false. When the reader turns the page, his prediction is confirmed or not by a paragraph of facts and two factual illustrations, one usually a close-up. In addition to provoking children to reconsider "common knowledge," this book also provides a lively format children may use in their own report writing. See numerous other books by Simon, one of the foremost writers of nonfiction for children.

3. *Beauty and the Beast* by Michael Hague. New York: Holt, 1989. (Holt)

This classic story of a beast transformed by love invites children to talk about how and why people change both in stories and in real life. Encourage critical thinking by comparing this version with others such as Beauty and the Beast by Mordicai Gerstein *(New York: Dutton, 1989); by Marianna Mayer, illustrated by Mercer Mayer (New York: Macmillan, 1978); or by Jan Brett (Boston: Houghton Mifflin, 1989).*

4. *Bunnicula* by Deborah and James Howe. New York: Atheneum, 1971. (Camelot)

   What if a pet rabbit really is a vampire? Chester the cat believes he has discovered one and sets out to prove to the human family that he is right. Told by the laconic family dog Harold with doglike observations and concerns for food, this first story in the series is humorous and fast-moving. Children enjoy comparing the vampire lore in this book with traditional lore. (Series)

5. *Every Living Thing* by Cynthia Rylant, illustrated by S. D. Schindler. New York: Bradbury, 1985. (Aladdin)

   Twelve challenging but never sentimental short stories invite readers to consider little moments of growth in children and adults. The first story, "Slower Than the Rest," reminds readers of the wonder of human diversity as it aligns a child with special needs and a turtle against a hurried world. The last, "Shell," uses a common metaphor in a symbolic way that young readers can understand.

6. *The Green Book* by Jill Paton Walsh, illustrated by Lloyd Bloom. New York: Farrar, Straus & Giroux, 1982. (Sunburst)

   Vivid writing tells the story of a family from the future who must leave Earth to colonize a new planet. How do they survive? What is the importance of stories in a new land? This thought-provoking short novel begins and ends with the same sentence, a magical discovery for fourth-graders. The paperback omits the illustrations, so be sure to secure at least one hardbound edition for the classroom.

7. *The Hundred Penny Box* by Sharon Bell Mathis, illustrated by Leo and Diane Dillon. New York: Viking Penguin, 1975. (Puffin)

   Michael's great-great-aunt Dewbet is 100 years old and keeps an old box full of pennies to help her remember each birth-

day. *When Michael's mother wants to throw out the box, Michael tries to save all the stories of her life. This moving story of emotions in an extended African-American family is a catalyst for talking about our own family histories. What would children tell for each year or penny in their lives so far?*

8. *Knots on a Counting Rope* by Bill Martin, Jr., and John Archambault, illustrated by Ted Rand. New York: Holt, 1987. (Holt)

   Stunningly illustrated, this picture book tells of a blind Indian boy who loves to hear his grandfather recite his birth story and other stories of the boy's life. For each telling, the old man ties one knot on a rope; when the rope is completely knotted, the boy will be able to tell the stories from his own memory. A perfect catalyst for telling our own birth stories but a fine discussion book, too, for its many layers of meaning.

9. *The Lion, the Witch and the Wardrobe* by C. S. Lewis. New York: Macmillan, 1950. (Collier)

   Four children free Narnia from the spell of the White Witch in this first of a seven-book series. A modern classic. (Series)

10. *The Real Thief* by William Steig. New York: Farrar, Straus & Giroux, 1973. (Sunburst)

    While stretching the vocabulary of readers, Steig tells the story of Gawain the goose, guard of the Royal Treasury, who is wrongly accused of stealing, until a repentant mouse confesses. A good introduction to a popular illustrator. Be sure to have Steig's Dominic (New York: Farrar, Straus & Giroux, 1984) and Abel's Island (New York: Farrar, Straus & Giroux, 1985) on hand as well.

11. *Sarah, Plain and Tall* by Patricia MacLachlan. New York: Harper & Row, 1985. (Harper Trophy)

    In spare prose, Anna tells how Sarah came from Maine after her father places an ad for a wife in an eastern newspaper. Colors and music form a continuous thread through this touching story of family life on the pioneer prairie. See also Brett Harvey's stories of her grandmother's prairie days in My Prairie Year *(New York: Holiday House, 1986)* and My Prairie Christmas *(New York: Holiday House, 1990),* both illustrated by Deborah Kogan Ray.

12. *Sunken Treasure* by Gail Gibbons. New York: Crowell, 1988. (Harper Trophy)

    In this nonfiction book, Gibbons tells of the sinking in 1622 of the ship Atocha, its discovery and the raising of the treasure, its preserving, cataloguing, and distribution, and other famous treasure-laden shipwrecks. Text is succinct, and information-bearing illustrations invite talking over. See, too, other works of nonfiction by this prolific author on such topics as lighthouses, the building of sky-scrapers, the post office, and a host of other subjects.

13. *A Taste of Blackberries* by Doris Buchanan Smith, illustrated by Charles Robinson. New York: Crowell, 1973. (Harper Trophy)

    A young boy describes his friendship with Jamie and his feelings about Jamie's sudden death from a bee sting. Pair this with Mavis Jukes's sensitive and subtle Blackberries in the Dark *(New York: Knopf, 1985; Dell) for another boy who carries on after the death of someone special, in this case, his grandfather.*

14. *Trouble for Lucy* by Carla Stevens, illustrated by Ronald Himler. Boston: Houghton Mifflin, 1981. (Clarion)

    Based on actual journals of pioneers, this story chronicles Lucy's trip with her family, a runaway puppy, her encounter with friendly Indians, and her life on the Oregon Trail in 1843. A good introduction to journals as well as a lively, true-to-life historical account of an important time in American history.

15. *The Whipping Boy* by Sid Fleishman, illustrated by Peter Sis. New York: Greenwillow, 1986. (Troll)

    The theme is like "The Prince and the Pauper" with a light, humorous touch as Jemmy, whipping boy to Prince Brat, leads his prince through a series of adventures. Fun to read aloud and a good introduction to an author whose quasi-historical settings pique our interest while his humor makes us laugh.

Grade 5

This list increases demands on readers to understand more complex characters dealing with varying degrees of success with a variety of issues, both in the present day and in historical settings. In addition, a medieval "theme" is begun.

1. *A Blue-Eyed Daisy* by Cynthia Rylant. New York: Bradbury, 1985. (Dell Yearling)

    Like short glimpses into someone else's life, these chapters present a picture of Ellie's eleventh year. Understated prose, the telling phrase, and a way of letting readers see people truly characterize Rylant's writing.

2. *The Borrowers* by Mary Norton, illustrated by Beth and Joe Krush. San Diego: Harcourt Brace Jovanovich, 1953. (Odyssey)

    This classic asks readers to take another point of view, that of people merely inches tall. A believable story with well-drawn characters and aptly described miniature settings. (Series)

3. *Bridge to Terabithia* by Katherine Paterson, illustrated by Donna Diamond. New York: Crowell, 1977. (Harper Trophy)

    A friendship between an impoverished boy and a girl whose parents have come to the country to re-examine their values grows, then ends abruptly when one dies in a flash flood. A catalyst for discussion of friendship, the story also examines many sorts of bridges: across cultures, across ages, between sexes.

4. *Dear Mr. Henshaw* by Beverly Cleary, illustrated by Paul O. Zelinsky. New York: Morrow, 1983. (Dell Yearling)

    Readers must draw inferences from this story told completely in letters written by sixth-grader Leigh Botts to the author of his favorite books. This honest portrayal of a child in a single-parent family also suggests that readers might discuss the making of a writer and a problem solver.

5. *Door in the Wall* by Marguerite de Angeli. New York: Doubleday, 1949. (Dell Yearling)

   Few books introduce life in the Middle Ages to children as well as this inspiring story of a boy with a handicap who nonetheless makes his own way. Confirm details of life in the 1400s by having such titles as these in the classroom: David Macauley's Castle *(Boston: Houghton Mifflin, 1971), Aliki's* A Medieval Feast *(New York: Crowell, 1983), Joe Lasker's* Merry Ever After: The Story of Two Medieval Weddings *(New York: Viking, 1976), and Jonathan Hunt's* Illuminations *(New York: Bradbury, 1989).*

6. *The Fighting Ground* by Avi. New York: Lippincott, 1984. (Harper Trophy)

   Caught by Hessian soldiers, thirteen-year-old Jonathan begins to wonder if war really is grand. The novel is divided into short chapters and takes place in about one day in 1778. While the book looks simple to read, it makes complex demands on the understanding and emotional maturity of readers.

7. *Journey to Topaz* by Yoshiko Uchida, illustrated by Donald Carrick. New York: Scribner, 1971. (Creative Arts Book Company)

   Based on the incarceration in camps of 110,000 Japanese-Americans, this story is told through the eyes of Yuki. See Behind Barbed Wire *by Daniel S. Davis (New York: Dutton, 1982), for more information as children discuss the emotional and political aspects of this moving story. (Series) (See Teacher's Guide, Appendix C)*

8. *My Side of the Mountain* by Jean Craighead George. New York: Dutton, 1975. (Puffin)

   A stirring story about one boy's survival in the Catskills. Authentic details, nature closely observed, and a character who is very much like a fifth-grader make this a powerful discussion story and a natural for follow-up with activities.

Be sure to have on hand the sequel, On the Far Side of the Mountain *(New York: Dutton, 1989), for interested readers.*

9. *Number the Stars* by Lois Lowry. Boston: Houghton Mifflin, 1989. (Dell Yearling)

   Set during World War II, this tells of one girl's small brave act in saving Jews from the Nazis. Children indentify with the main character, and the story serves as an introduction to the historical period as well. See also Journey to Topaz *(above).*

10. *On My Honor* by Marion Dane Bauer. Boston: Houghton Mifflin, 1986. (Dell Yearling)

    What is honor? When Joel's best friend Tony goads him into swimming in a dangerous river and Tony drowns, Joel is left to ponder that question. Honor, a sympathetic and honest father, and a responsible boy who makes one mistake he'll have to live with make this a powerful catalyst for discussion.

11. *The People Could Fly* by Virginia Hamilton, illustrated by Leo and Diane Dillon. New York: Knopf, 1985. (   )

    African-American folk tales, divided into four sections of animal, fanciful, supernatural, and slave tales of freedom, are richly told and powerfully illustrated. Part of everyone's multicultural American heritage.

12. *The Pinballs* by Betsy Byars. New York: Harper & Row, 1977. (Harper Trophy)

    Three foster children learn to care for each other in this humorous but also moving account of one summer in the Masons' home. Note the way characters remember events, the apt use of figurative language, and how and why Carlie especially changes her attitude.

13. *Saint George and the Dragon* by Margaret Hodges, illustrated by Trina Schart Hyman. Boston: Little, Brown, 1984. (Little, Brown)

    In addition to telling a story popular in the time of Door in the Wall, *this version is painstakingly illustrated to reflect the rich symbolism of medieval art. Look, too, for the author delivering the* manuscript to the illustrator on the back cover.

14. *Spin a Soft Black Song* by Nikki Giovanni, illustrated by George Martins. New York: Farrar, Straus & Giroux, 1985. (Sunburst)

    Poems in free verse with no punctuation or capital letters read like thoughts about African-American families, children in the city, and life in general. A joyful and thoughtful book.

15. *A Stranger Came Ashore* by Mollie Hunter. New York: Harper & Row, 1975. (Harper Trophy)

    Finn Learson says he is a survivor of a shipwreck, but Robbie and his grandfather don't trust him. Rightly so, because Finn Learson is a Selkie, a man upon the land but a Selkie in the sea and he is out to steal Robbie's sister in this well-written mysterious fantasy. Foreshadowing provides many clues. Keep a class-compiled glossary of Shetland Island terms and clues to help readers stay located in the story.

16. *Tuck Everlasting* by Natalie Babbitt. New York: Farrar, Straus & Giroux, 1975. (Sunburst)

    Overprotected Winnie Foster makes a decision to help the Tucks, and her life is changed forever in this fantasy, which considers what it might be like to live forever. With a preface and an afterword that introduce readers to the layers of meaning and symbolism a well-written story may have, this story is a modern classic.

Grade 6

Survival in many settings is a theme of this list: Who survives? How? What do they learn? What do they need beyond satisfying food and shelter needs? Fine writing, use of figurative language, and the continued introduction of some of the best writers of fiction for children also characterize this list.

1. *All the Small Poems* by Valerie Worth, illustrated by Natalie Babbitt. New York: Farrar, Straus & Giroux, 1987. (Sunburst)

    Four of the poet's books in one volume. Valerie Worth has the knack of condensing the essence of things and making the apt or often amazingly right comparisons between the animate and inanimate. A magnet trades "secrets with the North Pole"; a jack-o'-lantern has a "vegetable skull." This disciplined free verse might encourage students to look closely, make connections, eliminate excess words, and create their own small poems.

2. *The Dark is Rising* by Susan Cooper, illustrated by Alan Cober. New York: Atheneum, 1973. (Aladdin)

    On his twelfth birthday, Will discovers he is the last of the old ones and must join the battle outside time against the dark. With many echoes of Welsh myth and legend to ground it, this fantasy draws on many familiar patterns children know from television or movies as well as from other books: the old mentor, the young and unready hero, magical talisman, and old magic. The second in a five-book series. (Series)

3. *Cracker Jackson* by Betsy Byars. New York: Viking Penguin, 1985. (Puffin)

    What should eleven-year-old Cracker do when he discovers that his favorite former babysitter is being abused by her husband? Byars is an author every fifth- and sixth-grader should know for her understanding of what it is like to be a kid becoming a young adult, her excellent writing, her humor, and her way of dealing with difficult topics sympathetically and fairly.

4. *Dicey's Song* by Cynthia Voigt. New York: Atheneum, 1983. (Fawcett)

    In Homecoming *(New York: Atheneum, 1981), a near-orphaned Dicey and her three siblings walked from Connecticut to the Maryland shore to live with their grandmother. This story deals with the prickly peace they must make and with Dicey's maturity, independence, and understanding about family. There are many other books in the Tillerman family saga. (Series)*

5. *The Great Gilly Hopkins* by Katherine Paterson. New York: Crowell, 1978. (Harper Trophy)

   Smart-aleck Gilly finally meets her match in Maime Trotter, the last of a series of foster parents Gilly is placed with. Gilly's gradual change of heart and the hilarity of some scenes impel readers to the story's conclusion. Readers may need some help in discussing the ending as Gilly gets exactly what she has wanted . . . but it is not to stay with Trotter. Is this happy or not?

6. *Hatchet* by Gary Paulsen. Bradbury, 1987. (Puffin)

   After a plane crash, thirteen-year-old Brian spends fifty-four days in the wilderness learning to survive with only the aid of a hatchet given him by his mother. He also reconciles his parents' divorce. Group with other survival stories across genres to compare which qualities make a survivor; how a survivor changes; what beyond food, shelter, and safety (e.g., companions, art, music) helps a survivor; and so forth. (Series)

7. *Homesick: My Own Story* by Jean Fritz, illustrated by Margot Tomes. New York: Putnam, 1982. (Dell Yearling)

   A famous author writes of her childhood in China and her longed-for trip back to the United States in a humorous and authentic voice. Be sure to discuss why the book is titled "homesick."

8. *Island of the Blue Dolphins* by Scott O'Dell. Boston: Houghton Mifflin, 1960. (Dell Yearling)

   A California Indian girl, Karana, survives on an island for eighteen years. Based on fact, this popular story raises many questions about whether "rescue" by Spanish priests was necessarily a good thing. (Series)

9. *Lincoln: A Photobiography* by Russell Freedman. New York: Clarion Books, 1987. (Clarion)

   Quoting often from Lincoln and using a variety of primary sources, Freedman makes the man come alive. Readers learn "the facts" about this President and come to understand the ideas for which he stood, his background and the tenor of the times, and the legacy he has left. Biography at its finest.

10. *Mrs. Frisby and the Rats of Nimh* by Robert C. O'Brien, illustrated by Zena Bernstein. New York: Atheneum, 1971. (Aladdin)

    Where can rats with human intelligence find a place that does not rely on theft and that won't be discovered and destroyed by humans? This complex and fast-moving story deals with the themes of courage and self-determination. Two sequels written by O'Brien's daughter, Jane Conly, continue the story. (Series)

11. *Roll of Thunder, Hear My Cry* by Mildred Taylor, illustrated by Jerry Pinkney. New York: Dial, 1976. (Bantam)

    Being an African-American family in rural Mississippi in the 1930s has rewarding moments as well as grim ones for the Logan family. Nine-year-old Cassie observes racial tension, her mother's struggle to maintain her teaching job, and her own father's dramatic rescue of an African-American teenager from a lynch mob. This story invites children to make links between Lincoln's time, the Depression era, and the present in the lives of African-Americans. (Series)

12. *Sadako and the Thousand Paper Cranes* by Eleanor Coerr, illustrated by Ronald Himler. New York: Putnam, 1977. (Dell Yearling)

    A story based on the life and death from radiation poisoning of a real Japanese girl who lived in Hiroshima during World War II. This short novel is often children's first literary introduction to the consequences of war and is a catalyst for thoughtful discussion. Japanese children remember Sadako with streamers of paper cranes.

13. *The Sign of the Beaver* by Elizabeth Speare. Boston: Houghton Mifflin, 1983. (Dell Yearling)

    Left to attend his family's wilderness cabin in Maine, Matt cannot cope without the help of Attean, a woodland Indian. Consider what gifts each boy leaves with the other, who is freer, what qualities help Matt survive, and whether this story portrays Indians fairly. Compare the character of Matt with that of Brian in Hatchet.

14. *Where the Red Fern Grows* by Wilson Rawls. New York: Doubleday, 1961. (Bantam)

   Billy trains his dogs to be a fine hunting team in the Ozarks in this heartwarming and sentimental tale of the devotion between animals and humans. A long-time favorite with both adults and young readers.

Books Which Invite Writers to Write (Grades 1-6)

This list presents books whose content suggests writing possibilities, either because of strong story models, definitive formats, or inviting organizational patterns. Many of these books can be read by primary children and reread on a different level by upper elementary children.

1. Alphabet Books

   Numerous alphabet books suggest ways for children to organize writing. Illuminations by Jonathan Hunt (New York: Bradbury, 1989) provides medieval information from "alchemist" to "zither," suggesting that children could organize information from a thematic unit study in this manner. Aster Aardvark's Alphabet Adventures by Steven Kellogg (New York: Morrow Junior Books, 1987) is told strictly by the letters: "After Aster applied herself and achieved an A. . . ." Chris Van Allsburg's sinister The Z Was Zapped (Boston: Houghton Mifflin, 1987) or Mary Azarian's woodcut A Farmer's Alphabet (Boston: David Godine, 1981) are other provocative compendiums. Assemble a number of alphabet books, look at how they are organized, and invite children to try their hands at the ones that are appropriate to this grade level.

2. *The Book of Pigericks* by Arnold Lobel. New York: Harper & Row, 1982. (Harper Trophy)

   Zany pigs in all sizes parade through these imaginative limericks. Children can laugh at Lobel's efforts and create their own using this familiar pattern. Be sure to share a few limericks by the masters, Edward Lear and Ogden Nash.

3. + *A House is a House for Me* by Mary Ann Hoberman, illustrated by Betty Fraser. New York: Harper & Row, 1978. (Puffin)

   What constitutes a house? There are obvious ones in this rollicking rhyming text, but there are also unique ones: a carton is a house for a cracker, or peaches are houses for peach pits. Children's illustrated examples of other literal or metaphorical houses make a good class book and help introduce figurative language.

4. *Everybody Needs a Rock* by Byrd Baylor, illustrated by Peter Parnall. New York: Scribner, 1974. (Aladdin)

   Ten "Rules for finding a rock" guide this poetic text. Parnall's black-line illustrations evoke the landscape of special places, as well. Suggest to children that they find a special rock, seashell, flower, or tree and write new rules. Try illustrating in shades of one color and black line as Parnall does. Other titles by this team, such as Your Own Best Secret Place *(New York: Scribner, 1979) or* The Way to Start a Day *(New York: Scribner, 1978) also provide models.*

5. *Fables* by Arnold Lobel. New York: Harper & Row, 1980. (Harper Trophy)

   Following the models of Aesop and La Fontaine, Lobel has created twenty original fables with morals such as "Even the taking of small risks will add excitement to life." It is often easier to start with the moral and work backwards to create the story. Using Aesop, for instance, borrow morals and ask children to create another version that suits this moral. Children who have read such excellent fable collections as Tom Paxton's Aesop's Fables *(New York: Morrow Junior Books, 1988), Harold Jones's* Tales from Aesop *(New York: Watts/Julia MacRae, 1982), or Eve Rice's* Once in a Wood: Ten Tales from Aesop *(New York: Greenwillow, 1979) will have more to bring to this.*

6. *Faint Frogs Feeling Feverish* by Lilian Obligado. New York: Viking Penguin, 1983. (Puffin)

    Alliterative phrases tickle the tongue in this collection of tongue twisters. Susan Purviance's and Marcia O'Shell's Alphabet Annie Announces an All-American Album *(Boston: Houghton Mifflin, 1988) is loaded with alliterative sentences. Nicola Bayley's counting rhyme,* One Old Oxford Ox *(New York: Atheneum, 1977), presents a dozen animals actively engaged. A Snake Is Totally Tail by Judi Barrett (New York: Atheneum, 1983) includes clever alliterative and figurative descriptions of animals. By introducing children to this literary device, teachers help them notice alliteration and provide them with a useful way of enlivening writing. Expect some overuse first!*

7. *Fortunately* by Remy Charlip. New York: Macmillan, 1964. (   )

    Fortunately, Ned got a party invitation; unfortunately, the party was in Florida and Ned lives in New York. In this strongly patterned story, Ned meets each setback with improbable innovation. Using this model, children can create their own preposterous adventures with dinosaurs, at the circus, under the earth, and so on.

8. *Hailstones and Halibut Bones: Adventures in Color* by Mary O'Neil, with new illustrations by John Walner. New York: Doubleday, 1989. (Doubleday)

    O'Neil describes not only things that are red or blue or gray; she also evokes the smell or taste or sounds of a color. While children try their hands at their own color poems, return to the book frequently to help writers see how the poet works. An earlier edition illustrated by Leonard Weisgard (Doubleday, 1969), provides more subtle pictures for the same text. See, too, Eve Merriam's "A Yell for Yellow" in Jamboree: Rhymes for All Times *(New York: Dell Yearling, 1984).*

9. *The Important Book* by Margaret Wise Brown. New York: Harper & Row, 1949. (Harper Trophy)

    What is important about⬛ *This book asks readers to look at*⬛ *Children can generate their own*⬛ *tant attributes for a favorite ar*⬛ *something in nature, or a special time.*⬛

10. *In a Pickle and Other Funny Idioms* by Marvin Terban, illustrated by Giulio Maestro. New York: Clarion Books, 1983. (Clarion)

    "In a pickle" and thirty other common American idioms are presented and explained. Other titles in the series introduce a variety of literary devices. The riddle approach entices a reader to Try Your Hand *(by Jane Thayer, illustrated by Joel Schick. New York: Morrow, 1980) at guessing which "hand" idiom is being defined. Ask children to glean idioms from everyday use, such as expressions using body parts ("have a heart") or using "line" ("line by line," "lining track," "line of vision"). Activities such as this make children much more sensitive to figurative language in their own as well as others' writings. (Series)*

11. *The Jolly Postman, or Other People's Letters* by Janet and Allan Ahlberg. Boston: Little, Brown, 1986. (   )

    A postman delivers letters to fairy tale and folk tale characters. Actual letters in a variety of formats (e.g., advertising circular, invitation, postcard, announcement, lawyer's letterhead, etc.) may be removed from real envelopes. After a study of folktales, brainstorm who might write what sorts of letters. Provide various sizes of envelopes, card stock, different sizes of stationery, and plenty of time for drafts.

12. *The Mysteries of Harris Burdick* by Chris Van Allsburg. Boston: Houghton Mifflin, 1984. (   )

    Fourteen mysterious stories are each suggested with a title, picture, and a single line of text. "Archie Smith, Boy Wonder" shows a sleeping boy observed by five shining lights while the text states, "A tiny voice asked, 'Is he the one?'" Van Allsburg's provocative phrase invites children to provide the beginning and end of a story as they make their own whole stories. On another plane, ask children to

...ve sentences,

...de Paola.
...8. (Scho-

...orn is con-
...ormats suggesting
...ght frame their reports in
...g other than straight narrative:
"...y report is about . . . ." Labels under pictures, cartoons, conversational balloons, and a recipe are some of the features. See, too, Seymour Simon's Animal Fact/Animal Fable *(New York: Crown, 1979) and Joanna Cole's "Magic Schoolbus" series for other challenging informational formats.*

14. *Someday* by Charlotte Zolotow, illustrated by Arnold Lobel. New York: Harper & Row, 1965. (Harper Trophy)

    While many children write their own "someday" stories as wishes for the future, others are able to catch the irony of "Someday . . . my brother will introduce me to his friends and say 'This is my sister,' instead of 'Here's the family creep.' "

15. *Stringbean's Trip to the Shining Sea* by Vera B. Williams and Jennifer Williams. New York: Greenwillow, 1988. (Scholastic)

    This story of Stringbean's trip with his brother in a camper looks like a book of bound postcards. Readers construct Stringbean's trip, his adventures, and his feelings from what the two boys write on the backs of the postcards. Clever stamps, funny pictures on the cards, and the whole novelty of having to infer the story make this a winner with children. Simply retelling the story is a challenge. To recast the format, ask what if some other character who went on a physical or psychological journey wrote back periodically to her family.

16. *The True Story of the 3 Little Pigs* by A. Wolf as told to Jon Scieszka, illustrated by Lane Smith. New York: Viking Kestrel, 1989. (Scholastic)

    For introducing point of view, there is no better book. The wolf tells of how his bad cold and the pigs' rudeness forced him to act. This hilarious story suggests other folk tale characters who might tell their story if children would be their voices: Jack's giant, Gretel's witch, or Wiley's hairy man. Build on this experience by asking children to consider another character's point of view in a novel.

Books about Our Diverse Population (Grades K-3)

Chosen to represent the diversity of American populations today, these titles present contemporary or historical children in a variety of situations. Many have issues worth discussing: the problems encountered when two cultures meet, ways in which people solve problems, the importance of individual action, or the value of collective action, and so forth. Other titles reflect diverse situations in a variety of settings, without dealing with particular issues. See lists by grade level, too, for additional listings.

1. *Angel Child, Dragon Child* by Michele Maria Surat, illustrated by Vo-Dinh Mai. Milwaukee, WI: Raintree Publishers, 1983. (Scholastic).

   Nguyen Hoa, a new Vietnamese-American, has a difficult time getting used to school until she befriends a boy. Together they plan a fund-raising fair to bring her mother from Vietnam to this country.

2. *Annie and the Old One* By Miska Miles, illustrated by Peter Parnall. New York: Little, Brown, 1971. (Little, Brown)

   Parnall's sensitive illustrations match this story of a Navajo girl, Annie, and her denial and gradual acceptance of her grandmother's eventual death.

3. *The Dream Stair* by Betsy James, illustrated by Richard Jesse Watson. New York: Harper & Row, 1990. (   )

   In rich and evocative illustrations full of Hispanic and American symbols, an Hispanic girl is lovingly put to bed by her grandmother. In her imagination, she climbs the dream stair to a special attic room and then descends to the dark warm cellar room before returning to bed.

4. *Friday Night Is Papa Night* by Ruth A. Sonneborn, illustrated by Emily A. McCully. New York: Viking, 1970. (Puffin)

    Pedro and his Hispanic family wait for Papa, who is working at two jobs, to come home on Friday. When Papa finally arrives, it is after midnight but the family gathers for a joyous celebration because Friday is "the nicest night." Children might talk of their own family celebrations or special times after hearing this story.

5. *How My Parents Learned to Eat* by Ina R. Friedman, illustrated by Allen Say. Boston: Houghton Mifflin, 1984. (Sandpiper)

    A girl recounts how her American father and her Japanese mother each learned to eat with an unfamiliar utensil, which explains why in their house they sometimes eat with knives and forks and sometimes with chopsticks.

6. *I Hate English* by Ellen Levine, illustrated by Steve Bjorkman. New York: Scholastic, 1989. (Scholastic)

    Mei-Mei, a recent immigrant from Hong Kong, refuses to speak English until an astute new teacher helps her by reading to her and taking her places. How does it feel to be in a new place? How do people learn to speak a new language?

7. *If I Had a Paka: Poems in Eleven Languages* by Charlotte Pomerantz, illustrated by Nancy Tafuri. New York: Greenwillow, 1982. (   )

    By featuring Hispanic, Vietnamese, Swahili, Samoan, and other words, these poems give small glimpses of other cultures and other languages. Interesting to discuss how we learn the meaning of words in context and not in isolation.

8. *Jamaica's Find* by Juanita Havill, illustrated by Anne Sibley O'Brien. Boston: Houghton Mifflin, 1986. (Sandpiper)

    An African-American girl finds a stuffed dog and contemplates keeping it.

But when she takes it to the park office, she makes a new friend. Also read the sequel, Jamaica Tag-Along (Boston: Houghton Mifflin, 1989).

9. *Knots on a Counting Rope* by Bill Martin, Jr., and John Archambault, illustrated by Ted Rand. New York: Holt, 1987. (Holt)

    This emotional story with magnificent watercolor illustrations tells of a blind Indian child who loves to hear his grandfather recite the story of the boy's life. This loving and hopeful story is set in the American Southwest in a nurturing Indian community.

10. *Me & Neesie* by Eloise Greenfield, illustrated by Moneta Barnett. New York: Harper & Row, 1975. (Harper Trophy)

    Janell's imaginary friend, Neesie, causes trouble as Janell deals with anxiety over starting school. But new friends at school solve some of the problem in this African-American girl's small moment of growing up.

11. *More Stories Julian Tells* by Ann Cameron, illustrated by Ann Strugnell. New York: Knopf, 1986. (Knopf)

    Julian, who is about eight or nine, his younger brother Huey, and his friend Gloria, think of interesting ways to overcome summer boredom with a little help from the boys' dad. Warm, African-American family with typical family exchanges and the second book about Julian. (Series)

12. *Nettie's Trip South* by Ann Turner, illustrated by Ronald Himler. New York: Macmillan, 1987. (Scholastic)

    This simple but eloquent illustrated story is presented as a letter from a white ten-year-old girl to her friend about what she has felt and discovered about slavery in the pre-Civil War South.

13. *Wagon Wheels* by Barbara Brenner, illustrated by Don Bolognese. New York: Harper & Row, 1978. (Harper Trophy)

    In easy-reader format, the beginning settlement of Nicodemus, Kansas, is seen through the eyes of two African-American boys as they walk toward their new prairie home.

14. *Yagua Days* by Cruz Martel, illustrated by Jerry Pinkney. New York: Dial, 1976. (Dial)

    Adan, a boy from New York City, celebrates a family reunion in Puerto Rico. Spanish words, customs, and city life make this a rich reader experience.

Books about Our Diverse Population (Grades 4–6)

Chosen to represent the diversity of cultures and ages that interact in this country, these titles are set in both contemporary and historical settings. These stories enable children to talk about what it is to be an American or a hyphenated American, how groups of people came to settle here, or what life is like for the ever-growing number of bicultural people in this country. We do not presently have a great number of novels that reflect contemporary America's cultural diversity, but this list is a start. See grade level lists for additional titles.

1. *Child of the Owl* by Lawrence Yep. New York: Harper & Row, 1988. (Harper Trophy)

    When the very American Casey is sent to live with her Chinese grandmother in San Francisco's Chinatown, she begins to realize and finally to accept her family heritage as well as her own unique strengths.

2. *How Does It Feel to Be Old?* by Norma Farber, illustrated by Trina Schart Hyman. New York: Dutton, 1979. (Dutton)

    In dialogue between a young girl and her grandmother, the pleasures, longings, and some of the anger and fear of growing old are discussed. Sepia overlays on black and white drawings set off the grandmother's memories from contemporary scenes.

3. *In the Year of the Boar and Jackie Robinson* by Bette Bao Lord, illustrated by Marc Simont. New York: Harper & Row, 1984. (Harper Trophy)

    Twelve chapters chronicle the year (1947) that Shirley Temple Wong, newly arrived in Brooklyn from China, becomes an American. Baseball's great Jackie Robinson is an important catalyst in Shirley's Americanization. Teammates by Peter Golenbock and illustrated by Paul Bacon (San Diego: Harcourt Brace Jovanovich, 1990) presents the importance of Robinson to the integration of major league baseball in picture book format.

4. *Journey to Topaz* by Yoshiko Uchida, illustrated by Donald Carrick. New York: Scribner, 1971. (Creative Arts Book Company)

    Young readers are surprised to learn of the 110,000 Japanese-Americans held in internment camps during World War II when they read this fictionalized story of Uchida's childhood. Daniel S. Davis' nonfiction Behind Barbed Wire *(New York: Dutton, 1982) provides photographs and further information about the fate of the Japanese-Americans following Pearl Harbor. (Series)*

5. *The Lucky Stone* by Lucille Clifton, illustrated by Dale Payson. New York: Delacorte Press, 1976. (Dell Yearling)

    The shining black stone, like a family story, has been passed down through four generations from slave times to the present day, and finally it rests in Tee's hands. Told in four short chapters.

6. *Spin a Soft Black Song* by Nikki Giovanni, illustrated by George Martins. New York: Farrar Straus & Giroux, 1985. (Sunburst)

    Poems about African-American children in families, living and playing in the city and loving life are explored. No punctuation or uppercase letters make readers work a little harder for the ample rewards.

7. *Song of the Trees* by Mildred Taylor, illustrated by Jerry Pinkney. New York: Dial, 1975. (Bantam)

    A short chapter book that depicts an African-American family in the Depression who protect the family's stand of giant old trees from the dishonest white loggers. This introduces the Logans, whose larger story is told in Roll of Thunder, Hear My Cry. *(Series) (see grade 6 list)*

Wordless Books (Grades K-6)

Wordless books must rely on the illustrations to do the work. All of these titles provide excellent discussion possibilities, and some present children with the opportunity to create narratives. They suggest that children become adept at "reading the pictures" and noticing how the illustrator engages us.

1. *The Angel and the Soldier* by Peter Collington. New York: Knopf, 1987. (Dragonfly)

   While a young girl sleeps, her toy angel rescues her toy soldier from the clutches of pirates who live in a ship on top of the piano. Richly evoked by the soft, colored pencil drawings and seen from the perspective of tiny beings, this suggests how we might see the world through someone else's eyes.

2. *Anno's USA* by Mitsumaso Anno. New York: Philomel Books, 1983. (Philomel)

   Anno's lone traveler makes his way from Hawaii to California and across the country moving freely in time. Each double-page spread may show bits from a region's history, famous people and landmarks, fine arts allusions, and well-known characters from children's literature or from "Sesame Street," as well as Anno's trademark optical illusions. Older children, with their greater knowledge of the world, spend hours pondering, naming, and laughing over their discoveries. (Series)

3. *Changes, Changes* by Pat Hutchins. New York: Macmillan, 1971. (Aladdin)

   Entirely with block shapes, Hutchins shows a man and woman who build a block house and dismantle it to produce a fire engine, a boat, and various other things.

4. *Deep in the Forest* by Brinton Turkle. New York: Dutton, 1976. (Dutton)

   This is a mirror of "The Three Bears" but it is a little bear cub who crawls into a Colonial log cabin to wreak havoc. Notice the bear crawling into and out of the pictures which neatly frame this clever story.

5. *First Snow* by Emily Arnold McCully. New York: Harper & Row, 1985. (Harper Trophy)

   The mouse family goes sledding but the littlest mouse is afraid to go down the hill. When she finally gets up her courage, the family can't get her off the slopes. Other books in the series chronicle the arrival of a new baby, a family picnic, a Christmas celebration, and the beginning of school. All have strong narrative possibilities. (Series)

6. *Frog Goes to Dinner* by Mercer Mayer. New York: Dial, 1967. (Dial)

   Chaos results when a boy discovers his pet frog has ridden in his pocket to a fancy restaurant. Jealousy is the theme of One Frog Too Many (New York: Dial, 1975). (Series)

7. *Is It Red? Is It Yellow? Is It Blue?* by Tana Hoban. Greenwillow, 1978. (Mulberry)

   Hoban's colorful photographs of common city scenes, children doing things, and articles invite talk, not only about colors but about what is going on, about shapes, or about associations. Good for introducing children to this prolific creator of photo compendiums.

8. *Jungle Walk* by Nancy Tafuri. New York: Greenwillow, 1988. (   )

   In a dream, a girl follows her cat out the open window and into the jungle surrounding their house. The cat, now a tiger, sees many animals while the girl lurks near the edges of the pictures, until they return/wake up in the morning.

9. + *Niki's Walk* by Jane Tanner. Cleveland: Modern Curriculum Press, 1987. (MCP)

   Niki and his mother go for a walk in this urban setting; celebrate someone's birthday in a park; and see a variety of sights such as a construction site, boats on the river, a tow truck removing a wrecked car, and so forth. Much to talk about with early elementary children.

10. *Peter Spier's Rain* by Peter Spier. New York: Doubleday, 1982. (Doubleday)

    A brother and sister explore their wet neighborhood and engage in hundreds of activities before returning home for a hot bath and cocoa. Writing possibilities in-

63b

out the day from the
one of the children or
you would like to do

...uver Pony by Lynd Ward. New
York: Houghton Mifflin, 1973.
(   )

This long story depicts a lonely farm
boy who fantasizes about the trips he
takes on his beautiful winged pony.
When his family finds him lying ill outside, their present of a real pony helps the
boy bring his fantasy and his real world
together. Older children can better sustain the narrative possibilities of this
story.

12. *The Snowman* by Raymond Briggs. New
    York: Random House, 1978. (Random)

    A small boy has a wonderful night-
    time adventure with his snowman who
    can fly. In the morning, though, his
    friend has melted. Observant children
    may notice that the story takes place
    in Britain when they see landmarks and
    other clues.

13. *Sunshine* by Jan Ormerod. New York:
    Lothrop, Lee and Shepard, 1981.
    (Mulberry)

    A small girl's morning routine as she
    prepares for school is speeded up when
    she shows her parents what time it is.
    The same warm family feeling is created
    in the sequel Moonlight *(New York:
    Lothrop, Lee and Shepard, 1982. (Mul-
    berry)*

People in Other Lands (Grades K–3)

These picture books depict children in a variety of settings other than the United States.
They give young children a glimpse of other
lives lived. Some children may enjoy being
cultural detectives to notice clues in text and
illustration that reveal geography, customs,
plants, animals, foods, games, dress, ways of
living, or settings of the story. While folktales
may reveal other cultures to readers, they are
numerous and not a part of this list.

1. *Ashanti to Zulu: African Traditions* by
   Margaret Musgrove, illustrated by Leo

and Diane Dillon. New York: Dial, 1976.
(Dial)

Alphabetically organized, this stunningly illustrated book introduces readers
to twenty-six African peoples by depicting a custom important to each. Readers
who locate each people on a map of Africa would gain an appreciation for the
vastness of the continent. Muriel and
Tom Feelings' two books, Moja Means
One: Swahili Counting Book *(New York:
Dial, 1971)* and Jambo Means Hello:
Swahili Alphabet Book *(New York: Dial,
1974),* similarly organized, include much
information on the East Africa region.

2. *Count Your Way Through . . . Mexico* by
   Jim Haskins, illustrated by Helen Byers.
   Minneapolis, MN: Carolrhoda, 1989.
   (   )

   Spanish numbers from 1 to 10 introduce such Mexican topics as the four
   sides of the Pyramid of the Sun or the six
   "Los Niños Heroes." With lively illustrations, the series introduces aspects of geography, history, culture, and customs in
   areas such as Korea, Japan, Canada, or
   Africa. (Series)

3. *Crow Boy* by Taro Yashima. New York:
   Viking, 1955. (Puffin)

   Chibi is too shy to participate in
   school in this Japanese village until a
   sympathetic teacher helps him to
   blossom and metamorphose—beautifully
   symbolized as flower and butterfly by
   the book's endpapers. In Sayonara, Mrs.
   Kackleman *by Maira Kalman (New
   York: Viking Kestrel, 1989)* Japanese life
   from a more modern era is enthusiastically depicted as two children take an
   imaginary trip with a Japanese guide.

4. *Galimoto* by Karen Lynn Williams,
   illustrated by Catherine Stock. New
   York: Lothrop, Lee and Shepard, 1990.
   (Mulberry)

   Kondi lives in Malawi and spends a
   day constructing a galimoto, a vehicle
   made from bits of wire. This story of
   resourcefulness, determination, and enterprise is glowingly depicted in water-
   colors and reveals much about contemporary village life on the shores of Lake
   Malawi.

5. *I Am Eyes Ni Macho* by Leila Ward, illustrated by Nonny Hogrogian. New York: Greenwillow, 1978. (Scholastic)

   All that a boy sees, including giraffes, flowers, and Mt. Kilimanjaro, are depicted in this book set in Kenya.

6. *Jafta* by Hugh Lewin, illustrated by Lisa Kopper. Minneapolis, MN: Carolrhoda Books, 1983. (Carolrhoda)

   A South African boy compares his attributes to animals of the region: He can laugh like a hyena or grumble like a warthog. In other books in the series, his father returns from his job in the city, and other aspects and details of village life are warmly realized. (Series)

7. *The Great Kapok Tree* by Lynne Cherry. San Diego: Harcourt Brace Jovanovich, 1990. (   )

   When a woodcutter falls asleep in the Amazon rain forest before beginning his work, animals appear to him and tell why he should not cut down the tree. Jeannie Baker's Where the Forest Meets the Sea *(see grade 2 list) sets an ecological theme in the Australian forests.*

8. *My Little Island* by Frane Lessac. New York: Harper & Row, 1985. (Harper)

   Joyful paintings and an exuberant text portray the visit of two boys to the Carribean island of Montserrat. Text and pictures are detailed and provide plenty for readers to discover about life in the islands. The Chalk Doll *by Charlotte Pomerantz, also illustrated by Lessac (New York: Lippincott, 1989), depicts a Jamaican mother's reminiscence to her daughter of a poor but loving island childhood.*

9. *Not So Fast, Songololo* by Niki Daly. New York: Atheneum, 1985. (Puffin)

   A boy is treated by his granny Gogo to a trip into a large city. The chance to be away from his family is as much a treat as the new tennis shoes, or "tackies," he receives. There are few clues to the South African setting but alert readers will notice money called "rand," which makes this an ethnographic adventure for older readers.

10. *Very Last First Time* by Ja[...] illustrated by Ian Wallace. [...] McElderry, 1986. (   )

    While her mother watches, an [...] girl in northern Canada goes under [...] ice to gather mussels as the tide retreats. An unusual and eerie book that depicts a moment of growing up.

11. *The Way We Go to School: A Book about Children Around the World* by Edith Baer, illustrated by Steve Bjorkman. New York: Scholastic, 1990. (Scholastic)

    In rhyming text, schoolchildren in twenty-two different settings are shown going to school. End pages include a world map of the locations and a helpful sentence locating the exact city.

People in Other Lands, (Grades 4–6)

Mostly novels, these books give readers a perspective on life in other lands. See annotation, p. 64b.

1. *Anno's Italy* by Mitsumasa Anno. New York: Philomel, 1982. (Putnam)

   Anno's lone traveler journeys freely in history through the countryside and cities of Italy. Alert readers will spot famous landmarks and people, images borrowed from fine art, and literary allusions. See also Anno's Britain *(New York: Philomel, 1982). (Series)*

2. *Hating Alison Ashley* by Robin Klein. New York: Penguin, 1985. (Puffin)

   Sixth-grader Erica Yurkin feels clumsy and resentful of her own chaotic household when she compares herself with the elegant Alison and her serene and empty house. But in their rocky road to friendship, the two Australian girls find some mutual respect following a school camping trip.

3. *Homesick: My Own Story* by Jean Fritz, illustrated by Margot Tomes. New York: Putnam, 1982. (Dell Yearling)

   With humor and emotion, Fritz tells about a part of her childhood spent in China in the 1920s and the surprise of returning to the United States and to school.

African Story
ated by Eric
ncott, 1985.

65b

n Andrews,
ew York:

Inuit
the

...ecomes ill,
...neys from
...orking in
...ders may gain
...ining of the painful strug-
...res South Africans are undergoing. The
sequel, Chain of Fire *(New York: Lippin-cott, 1990), follows Naledi in her fif-teenth year.*

5. *The Land I Lost: Adventures of a Boy in Vietnam* by Huyn Quang Nhuong, illus-trated by Vo-Dinh Mai. New York: Harper & Row, 1982. (Harper Trophy)
   The author tells of his boyhood in a Vietnamese hamlet with his college-educated father, his work with a water buffalo named Tank, and the daily life where crocodiles might threaten, monkeys could cause mischief, and the threat of war was imminent.

6. *The Most Beautiful Place in the World* by Ann Cameron, illustrated by Thomas B. Allen. New York: Knopf, 1988. (   )
   Seven-year-old Juan struggles with poverty and parental abandonment but is supported by his own intelligence, de-termination, and the love of his grand-mother. Set in Guatemala, this is a uni-versal story of growing into your own skin and up to your own potential.

7. *Number the Stars* by Lois Lowry. New York: Houghton Mifflin, 1989. (Dell Yearling)
   Ten-year-old Annemarie summons up surprising courage and bravery in many small acts, which result in the saving of her Jewish friends from the Nazis in World War II Denmark. Mary McSwigan's Snow Treasure *(New York: Dutton, 1942), set in this same time period, tells how a brave group of chil-dren smuggle gold out of Norway under the Nazis' noses.*

8. *Ordinary Jack* by Helen Cresswell. New York: Macmillan, 1977. (Puffin) (Series)
   In the first book of this witty series set

in modern-day Britain, Jack tries to de-velop the skill of foretelling the future in order to compete with his extraordinary family, including a father who is a TV writer, a mother who writes an advice column, and siblings who paint well or are near-pros at tennis.

9. *Sadako and the Thousand Paper Cranes* by Eleanor Coerr, illustrated by Ronald Himler. New York: Putnam, 1977. (Dell Yearling)
   Based on the true story of Sadako Sasaki, who died of radiation poisoning when she was twelve. The heroine to the children of Japan is commemorated by a memorial in Hiroshima Peace Park where children leave paper cranes made in her honor. A short but thoroughly moving story.

Life Stories (Grades 2–6)

With the many fine picture book and novel-sized autobiographies and biographies avail-able, children are no longer confined to the often dry series books of individual lives. This list introduces authors of biographies and in-volves children in the lives of some people who made the world a different place because of their actions. Many kinds of biographies as well as a partial autobiography are included here.

1. *A Weed Is a Flower: The Life of George Washington Carver* by Aliki. Englewood Cliffs, NJ: Prentice Hall, 1977. (Simon & Schuster)
   In brief, easy-reader format, Aliki captures simply the story of a man born a slave who became a great research scien-tist. See also her simplified biographies of Benjamin Franklin and Johnny Ap-pleseed.

2. *The Double Life of Pocahontas* by Jean Fritz. New York: Putnam, 1983. (Puffin)
   This complete biography covers the short twenty-one years of Pocahontas' life lived in the early 1600s. Fritz writes ele-gantly about the encounters of the Native Americans with Captain John Smith and

the early Virginia settlers. See, too, other titles about Stonewall Jackson, James Madison, and Benedict Arnold by our foremost writer of biographies for children.

3. *The Great Alexander the Great* by Joe Lasker. New York: Viking, 1983. (Puffin)

    The vividly illustrated life of Alexander, who ruled the land from Greece to India, is highlighted with particular emphasis on his bravado, imagination, and his friendship with his horse, "Bucephalus." See, too, Lasker's The Boy Who Loved Music *(New York: Penguin, 1979) for an imaginative rendering of how Haydn came to compose the "Farewell" Symphony.*

4. *The Glorious Flight: Across the Channel with Louis Bleriot* by Alice and Martin Provensen. New York: Viking, 1983. (Puffin)

    With many historical and background details that invite readers to speculate about life in 1909, the authors involve children in this famous flight.

5. *Indian Chiefs* by Russell Freedman. New York: Holiday House, 1982. (   )

    Aspects of the lives of six Indian leaders who led their people in moments of crisis in the middle 1800s. This collection of partial biographies, illustrated with photographs from the period, enables older readers to see the settling of the West from multiple perspectives.

6. *Johnny Appleseed* by Steven Kellogg. New York: Morrow, 1988. (Morrow)

    The life of John Chapman is based on fact, but many legends surround this famous planter, as well, in this exuberantly illustrated picture book. Children might separate the fact from the fiction here and compare Kellogg's version with Aliki's The Story of Johnny Appleseed *(Englewood Cliffs, NJ: Prentice Hall, 1963) or with Reeve Lindbergh's poetic* Johnny Appleseed, *illustrated by Kathy Jakobsen (New York: Joy Street/Little, Brown, 1990).*

7. *Keep the Lights Burning, Abbie* by Peter and Connie Roop, illustrated by Peter E.

Hanson. Minneapolis, MN: Carolrhoda Books, 1985. (First Edition Books)

In easy-reader format, this fictionalized biographical sketch tells of one month in Abbie Burgess' life when a storm left her father on the mainland and Abbie took care of her sick mother, her siblings, and kept the Maine lighthouse working in 1856. A note tells readers more about Abbie's life.

8. *Laura Ingalls Wilder* by Gwenda Blair, illustrated by Thomas B. Allen. New York: Putnam, 1981. (Putnam)

    In more demanding vocabulary than the type size would suggest, Blair rounds up details that cover but expand upon this well-known author's life as portrayed in her "Little House" books.

9. *Once Upon a Time: A Story of the Brothers Grimm* by Robert Quackenbush. Englewood Cliffs, NJ: Prentice Hall, 1985. (   )

    This light-hearted simplified biography introduces readers to the two brothers who collected folklore and enabled many now-familiar tales to be rendered into print in the early 1800s. Quackenbush has written and illustrated many simplified biographies of such people as Thomas Edison and Peter Stuyvesant. (Series)

10. *The One Bad Thing About Father* by F. N. Monjo, illustrated by Richard Cuffari. New York: Holt, 1974. (Harper Trophy)

    In easy-reader format, readers see Theodore Roosevelt through the eyes of his son Quentin, who maintained that the only bad thing about his father was that he was President, and so his whole family, including the irrepressible Alice Roosevelt, had to live at the White House. See other simplified biographies by this author of such people as Thomas Jefferson and Benjamin Franklin.

11. *Shaka, King of the Zulus* by Diane Stanley and Peter Vennema, illustrated by Diane Stanley. New York: Morrow, 1988. (   )

    The famous leader of one of the largest African armies ever assembled at a period when European explorers were "discovering" the continent is seen in dramatic detailed illustration and text. This picture book biography does not ignore Shaka's cruelty but sets it in the context of tribal beliefs of the time. See, too, books about Good Queen Bess *(New York: Four Winds, 1990)* and Peter the Great *(New York: Four Winds, 1986)* by this team.

12. *Self-Portrait: Trina Schart Hyman* by Trina Schart Hyman. New York: Harper & Row, 1989. (   )

    In her familiar bold black line and color, Hyman reveals her personal connection with the folk tales she has illustrated and discusses her training as an illustrator, her marriage, and her country household. Bound to send children back to her books for another look, and an inspiration to budding artists, as well. *(Series)*

13. *Where Do You Think You're Going, Christopher Columbus?* by Jean Fritz, illustrated by Margot Tomes. New York: Putnam, 1980. (Peppercorn)

    In lively but entirely factual detail, Fritz captures the man's courage and pride, as well as the attitudes of his times. Information-bearing illustrations, end notes, and a helpful index introduce children to the use of these valuable tools. *(Series)*

Grade 7

Books on this list reflect depth both in theme and in demands on the reader. Several titles consider African-Americans in historical and contemporary settings. Many deal with complex themes about love or survival, ambiguous adult characters, and near-adolescents trying to understand each other, or ask readers to consider some consequences of a wartime existence. Several books let readers laugh, too, at themselves, at the well-turned phrase, and at funny events.

1. *A Girl Called Boy* by Belinda Hurmence. New York: Clarion, 1982. (   )

    While fingering a family soapstone carving, a sarcastic African-American girl is transported back to the past where her short hair and blue jeans cause her to be mistaken as a runaway slave. This time-slip fantasy is historically accurate but framed within a contemporary viewpoint.

2. *The Burning Questions of Bingo Brown* by Betsy Byars. New York: Viking Penguin, 1988. (Puffin)

    Bingo wonders about girlfriends, his use of mousse, his teacher's sanity, and his family. Byars combines humorous dialogue and adolescent concerns deftly and believably. *(Series)*

3. *A Day No Pigs Would Die* by Robert Newton Peck. New York: Knopf, 1972. (Dell Yearling)

    In the Depression, thirteen-year-old Rob comes to understand his Vermont father's quiet dignity, his willingness to admit to errors, and his ability to do what must be done for the family to survive.

4. *The House of Dies Drear* by Virginia Hamilton, illustrated by Eros Keith. New York: Macmillan, 1968. (Collier)

    Weird and terrifying but ultimately explainable happenings threaten an African-American professor staying in a house that was a former Underground Railroad stop. Thomas Small and his family finally solve the mystery in this fast-paced story. *(Series)*

5. *Jacob Have I Loved* by Katherine Paterson. New York: Crowell, 1980. (Avon)

    Louise develops from a jealous and bitter twin sister to an emotionally healthy adult on an island in the Chesapeake Bay in the 1940s. Rich with well-developed characters and multiple themes.

6. *Julie of the Wolves* by Jean Craighead George. New York: Harper & Row, 1972. (Harper Trophy)

    Miyax, a thirteen-year-old Eskimo girl, runs away on the tundra and survives with a pack of wolves. Themes of coming of age and ecology, and details of the true behavior of wolves.

7. *Lizard Music* by Daniel M. Pinkwater. New York: Dodd, Mead, 1976. (Bantam)

    Left on his own, eleven-year-old Victor is determined to track down the lizard band he sees on late-night TV. A good introduction to a writer of bizarre, hilarious, and popular fantasy.

8. *The Middle of Somewhere: A Story of South Africa* by Sheila Gordon. New York: Orchard Books, 1989. (   )

    The struggle of an African family to continue to live in their home village, which white South Africans want for a suburb. A story with strong values of brotherhood and persistence ending with the release of Nelson Mandela. See, too, Beverley Naidoo's Journey to Jo'Burg *on the grades 4–6 list.*

9. *My Brother Sam is Dead* by James Lincoln Collier and Christopher Collier. New York: Four Winds, 1974. (Dell Yearling)

    Conflicting loyalties and the injuries inflicted on the innocent during the Revolutionary War are seen through the eyes of Sam's younger brother Tim. See also the Colliers' trilogy about African-Americans during this war, which begins with Jump Ship to Freedom *(New York: Delacorte, 1981).*

10. *Prairie Songs* by Pam Conrad. New York: Harper & Row, 1985. (Harper Trophy)

    Louise's simple pioneer existence is changed forever by the arrival of a doctor and his elegant, though mentally unbalanced, wife. Figurative and descriptive language, as well as a balanced picture of pioneer living, bring this time closer. See, too, Conrad's My Daniel *(New York: Harper & Row, 1989), told in two settings, present and pioneer days.*

11. *The Shooting of Dan McGrew* by Robert W. Service, illustrated by Ted Harrison. Boston: David R. Godine, 1988. (   )

    Life at the Malamute Saloon, as told by Dawson City's resident poet, is boldly brought to life by Harrison's vivid paintings. See, too, Harrison's treatment of Service's The Cremation of Sam McGee *(New York: Greenwillow, 1987).*

12. *Summer of My German Soldier* by Bette Greene. New York: Dial, 1973. (Bantam)

    Told from the viewpoint of a twelve-year-old Jewish girl in a small Arkansas town who befriends a Nazi POW. Amid prejudice and anger, he leaves her to grow up with knowledge that she is a "person of worth."

13. *Village by the Sea* by Paula Fox. New York: Orchard Books, 1988. (Dell Yearling)

    With her father facing surgery, Emma goes to visit her quixotic aunt at the seashore and learns something about love, envy, rage, and finally forgiveness in this powerful psychological novel.

14. *Where the Lilies Bloom* by Vera and Bill Cleaver, illustrated by James Spanfeller. New York: Lippincott, 1969. (New American Library)

    A fourteen-year-old Appalachian girl keeps her family together after her parents' death by trying to teach them "wildcrafting" and the art of being close-mouthed in this survival story. (Series)

15. *Z for Zachariah* by Robert C. O'Brien. New York: Atheneum, 1965. (Collier)

    Ann Burden, the sole survivor in her valley after a nuclear explosion, contemplates a solitary existence. Her discovery of a sick man brings her initial hope, but her diary in which she tells the story chronicles her disillusionment and her final departure with hope of finding other survivors.

Grade 8

Patterns in this list include many titles that help readers consider how a family in any setting can help or impede the growth of its members. Two compelling fantasies deal with individual responsibility and possibilities in a future setting or in an imagined world. As in the previous list, complex themes, characters, and literary presentations put new but not unmanageable demands on young adult readers.

1. *All Together Now* by Sue Ellen Bridgers. New York: Knopf, 1979. (Bantam)

While spending the summer with her grandparents, twelve-year-old Casey makes friends with a retarded man and begins to consider responsibility, friendship, and the nature of families in this richly characterized, often humorously told, novel.

2. *I Will Call It Georgie's Blues* by Suzanne Newton. New York: Viking, 1983. (Dell Yearling)

    Controlled by the conservative views of his minister family and expectations of his small southern town, fifteen-year-old Neal secretly studies to be a jazz pianist. A coming-of-age story compellingly told.

3. *Borrowed Children* by George Ella Lyon. New York: Orchard Books, 1988. (Bantam Starfire)

    Mandy knows her ticket out of her Kentucky hill house is education and is broken-hearted to have to stay home to care for the latest addition to her siblings in the 1920s. But a well-earned trip to Memphis relatives becomes a journey of self-discovery and gives her a new perspective, both on her family and on her dreams.

4. *Eva* by Peter Dickinson. Delacorte, 1989. (   )

    In a future time, a girl's brain is transplanted into a chimpanzee's body, partly to save her life but partly to further research. This passionate and eloquent story raises questions about ecology, responsible science, and the nature of humankind.

5. *The Highwayman* by Alfred Noyes, illustrated by Charles Keeping. New York: Oxford University Press, 1981. (   ) Also illustrated by Charles Mikolaycak (New York: Lothrop, Lee and Shepard, 1983).

    This tragic narrative poem of love and loyalty is dramatically illustrated. Keeping reverses his striking pictures from black on white to a ghostly white on black after the highwayman's death. Comparing these two editions should win the attention of even the most jaded and reluctant poetry readers.

6. *The Moves Make the Man* by Bruce Brooks. New York: Harper & Row, 1984. (Harper)

    A white boy and a African-American boy form a tenuous friendship based on their admiration for each other's sports prowess, one in baseball, the other in basketball. Themes of overcoming prejudice, dealing with mental illness, and of growing up, as well as near-poetic descriptions of playing "hoop."

7. *The Outsiders* by S. E. Hinton. New York: Viking, 1967. (Dell Yearling)

    In this classic gang novel, "Greasers" face death and struggle with peer relationships, poverty, and a search for self. Realistically written and fast paced.

8. *Scorpions* by Walter Dean Myers. New York: Harper & Row, 1988. (Harper Keypoint)

    When Jamal inherits gang leadership and a gun from his imprisoned brother, he can't seem to find a way out. Gritty portrayal of the consequences of impetuous action set in Harlem.

9. *Shabanu: Daughter of the Wind* by Suzanne Fisher Staples. New York: Knopf, 1989.

    At twelve, the youngest daughter of a modern-day Pakistani camel herder knows that she must be married but chafes against her fate. A vivid portrayal of life and death in the desert world and a dramatic coming-of-age story of a brave young girl.

10. *A Solitary Blue* by Cynthia Voigt. New York: Atheneum, 1984. (Fawcett)

    The gradual development of a loving relationship between Jeff and his divorced father takes place only after Jeff, too, has been wounded by his irresponsible mother. Dicey Tillerman, from Voigt's other novels, figures in Jeff's healing as well. (Series)

11. *Traitor: The Case of Benedict Arnold* by Jean Fritz. New York: Viking, 1981. (Puffin)

    Arnold's enthsiastic, impetuous, and reckless personality leads him finally to disappointment and treason. A gripping biography of a complex personality seen against the Revolutionary War period.

12. *A Wizard of Earthsea* by Ursula LeGuin, illustrated by Ruth Robbins. New York: Parnassus Press, 1968. (Bantam)

    Pride and arrogance cause Ged, a young wizard, to call up a shadow that threatens all of Earthsea until Ged can face what he has done. Powerful themes of maintaining balance and harmony, personal responsibility, and self-knowledge, as well as an elegant telling make this fantasy a standard against which others are measured. (Series)

Grades 9 and 10

The concerns, conflicts, pain, and discoveries of adolescents dominate the literature on this list. Characters struggle with pressure from their peers and parents and with the harsh realities of twentieth-century society. Traditional classics and very current fiction are both represented for students to discover great literature and models for their own writing.

1. *Bless the Beasts and the Children* by Glendon Swarthout. New York: Doubleday, 1970. (Pocket Books)

    A group of emotionally handicapped adolescents grow in maturity and self-esteem through their sensitivity to the plight of the buffaloes near their Arizona camp. Readers are challenged by the storytelling through dream sequences and flashbacks in this coming-of-age novel and drawn to its conservationist theme.

2. *The Catcher in the Rye* by J. D. Salinger. Boston: Little, Brown, 1951. (Bantam)

    This classic young adult novel presents the conflicts of innocence and experience and adolescent angst in an irreverent, touching way. Students identify with Holden Caulfield through his run-ins with authority, parents, and insensitive people everywhere. Invites discussion of issues of sexuality, individuality, ethics, and moral values.

3. *The Chocolate War* by Robert Cormier. New York: Pantheon, 1974. (Dell)

    A powerful story of a high school boy who refuses to sell chocolates for his Catholic high school. Jerry stands up against the cold and calculating Brother Leon and the school's secret society. Encourages students to question the uses of power and authority and the responsibilities of the individual to "dare to disturb the universe."

4. *Eight Plus One* by Robert Cormier. New York: Pantheon, 1980. (Bantam)

    Cormier's nine short stories are glimpses into the daily lives and concerns of young people: the mystical world of fathers, the shifting of adolescent friendships, discoveries about love, and the mistakes of youth. Cormier's brief stories are mirrors for students to look into and see themselves.

5. *Fahrenheit 451* by Ray Bradbury. New York: Ballantine, 1953. (Ballantine)

    Told with poetic power, a classic science fiction tale filled with technological wonders and a chilling warning of the dangers of censorship. Montag is a fireman in the cold and ominous future where fires are not extinguished but used to destroy books, the enemy of people in a world where thinking is dangerous. Connects with current issue of language censorship.

6. *The Girl in the Box* by Ouida Sebestyen. Boston: Little, Brown, 1988. (Bantam)

    A sixteen-year-old girl writes notes to the world from a small cellar room where she is being held after a kidnapping. Her only solace is a typewriter; with it she attempts to make sense of the crime, her fear, and, in the process, her life as a teenager. Unusual style and "audience" make for interesting writing model. Issues of mortality and the enduring human spirit may prompt discussion.

7. *A Hero Ain't Nothin' But a Sandwich* by Alice Childress. New York: Coward, McCann & Geoghegan, 1973. (Avon)

    Benjie is a young African-American boy struggling for identity in the ghetto and rapidly becoming addicted to heroin. Told by a variety of narrators and viewpoints, this short novel offers insights into the roles of friends, teachers, and family in their efforts to help Benjie and the complex forces that propel the boy toward his escape from the bleak world around him.

8. *The Hitchhiker's Guide to the Galaxy* by Douglas Adams. New York: Crown, 1979. (Pocket Books)

    A comic science fiction story of the end of the world and one human's consequent outer space adventures. Adams' characters are as likely to say something significant as absurd in this satire of our bureaucratic systems and materialistic values. Readers enjoy the word play and wit of this hip, well-written story, the first of a series by Adams.

9. *Home before Dark* by Sue Ellen Bridgers. New York: Knopf, 1976. (Bantam)

    Vivid characterization pulls readers into the world of a family of migrant workers searching for roots. Excellent writing models for teenage writers in this story of a girl's strength and love. It may prompt reactions to issues of sexual desire and family loyalties.

10. *The Island* by Gary Paulsen. New York: Franklin Watts, 1988. (Dell)

    Very unusual style and structure make this novel of self-discovery an interesting study for young readers. At fifteen, Wil Neuton finds an island one summer that wakens him to nature, meditation, art, and writing as a way to his own growth. Each chapter opens with an entry from Wil's journal, and interspersed with the traditional narration are Wil's own pieces of writing. Students may be led to ask questions about the meanings of their own existence through their reading.

11. *Kaffir Boy* by Mark Mathabane. New York: Macmillan, 1986. (New American Library)

    Autobiography of an African-American boy growing up with the horrors of poverty and racial persecution in modern South Africa. The experiences of Johannes and his family give students a real glimpse into the struggles that continue to dominate the headlines.

12. *The Miracle Worker* by William Gibson. New York: Atheneum, 1960. (Bantam)

    Inspiring dramatization of the story of Helen Keller and her remarkable teacher Anne Sullivan. Students are fascinated by the violent struggle between Anne and Helen. Gibson's focus allows students to see the handicaps of each member of the family, and readers gain insight into how we all handicap ourselves. It also invites the study of stagecraft.

13. *Night* by Elie Wiesel. New York: Hill & Wang, 1960. (Bantam)

    A personal account of a teenage boy's terrifying experiences in the Nazi death camps of World War II. Students identify with Elie through the first person narrative. The stark reality of the events of the holocaust promote study of survival behavior and provoke student interest in this important historical event.

14. *Night Kites* by M. E. Kerr. New York: Harper & Row, 1986. (Harper Keypoint)

    Seventeen-year-old Erick is an average teenager facing the adolescent concerns of dating, friendships, and school, but must come to terms with a much more devastating problem when he learns that his older brother has AIDS. Readers are presented with realistic conflict for discussion of family reaction to homosexuality and disease.

15. *Of Mice and Men* by John Steinbeck. New York: Viking, 1938. (Bantam)

    Classic American novel of the Depression era in our history and a very readable book. Students are drawn into the friendship between the mentally retarded Lennie and his companion George. Offers readers both an important view of America and an opportunity to examine their own needs for attention, love, and friendship.

16. *Reflections on a Gift of Watermelon Pickle* edited by Stephen Dunning et al. New York: Lothrop, Lee and Shepard, 1966. (   )

    A now classic collection of modern verse by a wide variety of well- and little-known poets arranged in short thematic sections or grouped by subject matter. A wealth of poetic forms and ideas for student writing or talking.

17. *Running Loose* by Chris Crutcher. New York: Morrow, 1983. (Dell)

    The humorous, gently sarcastic tone of the narration pulls readers into this book about adolescent pressures to succeed and be popular. Struggles of conscience of the main character provide excellent entries into discussion and self-questioning for teenage readers.

18. *Sheila's Dying* by Alden R. Carter. New York: Putnam, 1987. (Scholastic)

    Story of a teenager dying of cancer realistically presents the stages of emotional trauma and the very difficult day-to-day problems for the victim and her friends and family. Students will also grapple with such moral questions as how much responsibility should we have for one another in times of intense need. Very engaging and well written.

19. *Visions* edited by Donald R. Gallo. New York: Dell, 1987. (Dell)

    Nineteen short stories by authors familiar to and loved by young adults explore issues of acceptance by peers, asserting independence, desire and longing, a full range of adolescent and human concerns. Variety in tone is from tragic to comic, in subject from fantasy to gritty reality. Valuable source to engage teens in literature and the genre of the short story.

Grades 11 and 12

War and survival, mental illness, social injustice, and personal versus societal responsibility are some of the many themes explored in the literature from this list. Students nearing adulthood may satisfy their needs to answer questions about the world through their reading of serious, thought-provoking literature.

1. *After the First Death* by Robert Cormier. New York: Pantheon, 1979. (Avon)

    Political thriller about terrorists who hijack a busload of children. Readers view the situation through the eyes of Miro, a young well-trained killer, Katie, the teenage bus driver, and Ben, the son of a patriotic general. These young views bring into a public drama the issue of what matters more, human life and emotion or political systems and loyalties.

2. *Black Voices* edited by Abraham Chapman. New York: New American Library, 1968. (New American Library)

    A lengthy anthology of poetry, short stories, fiction, and nonfiction by African-American writers, with biographical sketches. Provides serious readers with a survey of African-American literature. Also offers humor, engaging narratives, and thought-provoking short pieces for important discussion of racial conditions in this country.

3. *Fallen Angels* by Walter Dean Myers. New York: Scholastic, 1988. (Scholastic)

    Told by a young African-American man from the streets of New York, this story of a tour of duty in Vietnam evokes the boredom and terror of soldiers thrown into a war they do not understand or know how to fight. Racial conflict mixes with the conflicts of conscience and courage that characterize war novels. Provides valuable context for understanding contemporary American history.

4. *I Know Why the Caged Bird Sings* by Maya Angelou. New York: Random House, 1969. (Bantam)

    An African-American woman tells her moving story of childhood and adolescence. Angelou's writing is fresh, engaging, and poetic. She offers insights about African-American values and culture as well as the pain and joy of being young. Invites personal response from students.

5. *In Country* by Bobbie Ann Mason. New York: Harper & Row, 1985. (Perennial)

    Coming to terms with the scars from the Vietnam War in small-town Kentucky during the 1980s, this book shows the pain and confusion of vets and their families. *Well-drawn characters and an interesting narrative style. Provides students with insights about conflicting attitudes toward this war and may prompt comparisons to current global events.*

6. *A Little Love* by Virginia Hamilton. New York: Putnam, 1984. (   )

    Unusual and touching portrait of a teenager. Overweight, poorly educated Sheema attends the joint vocational school and gets through her daily fears of nuclear disaster and tough punks with the help of her boyfriend Forrest. Students will relate to her experiences in school and her search for her father, missing since her birth.

7. *Lord of the Flies* by William Golding. New York: Putnam, 1954. (Perigee)

    Classic British novel of the ancient struggle between civilization and chaos. Rich details of setting offer students opportunities for seeing craftsmanship while physical and moral conflicts provide for discussion topics.

8. *Memory* by Margaret Mahy. New York: Macmillan, 1987. (Dell)

    Students may empathize with the plight of the elderly in this story of a teenager's reluctant involvement with an Alzheimer's disease victim. From the New Zealand setting readers also get a glimpse into political unrest there. Especially well-drawn characterization will engage students and spur inquiry into their social responsibility to the elderly.

9. *Midnight Hour Encores* by Bruce Brooks. New York: Harper & Row, 1986. (Harper & Row)

    Offers readers a glimpse into the life of a young musical prodigy through authentic details. Ideals of the hippie movement of the 1960s contrast with present-day realities of divorce and materialist values and raise worthwhile questions for young readers.

10. *The Nick Adams Stories* by Ernest Hemingway. New York: Scribner, 1972. (Bantam)

    Hemingway's stories of the young Nick in Michigan bring up issues important to young people: friendship, loyalty, love and sex, and peer pressure. Very *readable, Hemingway's powerful narratives are filled with the ambiguity and mystery of adolescence. An excellent source for discussion and writing ideas.*

11. *One Flew Over the Cuckoo's Nest* by Ken Kesey. New York: Viking, 1962. (New American Library)

    Kesey's antihero, R. P. McMurphy, is both a scoundrel and a saint as he helps a group of beaten men overcome the system that has destroyed their manhood. The uses and misuses of power and the belief in oneself are important questions for students to consider in this classic contemporary novel.

12. *Ordinary People* by Judith Guest. New York: Viking, 1976. (Ballantine)

    Story of a teenager's struggle to accept his brother's death and find his own identity. Conrad learns to face the demons of guilt and rejection that torture him and face up to his family, which is falling apart. Catalyst for study of family dynamics and pressures on young people today.

13. *A Raisin in the Sun* by Lorraine Hansberry. New York: Random House, 1959. (New American Library)

    The voices of an African-American family struggling against poverty and with one another's needs pull readers into this drama. Family loyalty, the need for a strong black identity, and the frustration of the American dream just beyond the grasp of the Younger family are relevant for discussion.

14. *Remembering the Good Times* by Richard Peck. New York: Delacorte, 1985. (Dell)

    First-person narrative of a young man recalling his bittersweet memories of junior high and high school, the powerful bonds of friendship forged with two friends, and the horror of dealing with the suicide of one. Very engaging prose style will pull readers into the story. May inspire study of psychological pressures of family life and society.

15. *A Separate Peace* by John Knowles. New York: Macmillan, 1959. (Bantam)

The global conflict of World War II is the backdrop of this story of prep school students discovering their own sources of conflict. Shifting friendships and loyalties, peer pressure, and confusion about identity complicate the last days of youth before the war. High school students faced with pressures of the real world connect with these lives powerfully.

16. *Slaughterhouse-Five* by Kurt Vonnegut, Jr. New York: Delacorte, 1969. (Dell)

The story of Billy Pilgrim's life, affected as it is by the devastation he witnessed in the bombing of Dresden, Germany, in World War II. The horrors of war and issues of government hypocrisy, individuality, and family appeal to students, and Vonnegut's humorous, offbeat style is engaging to young sensibilities.

17. *Soul Catcher* by Frank Herbert. New York: Putnam, 1972. (Berkley)

An American Indian takes revenge against the white man for his oppression of his people by kidnapping the son of a state official. Authentic details of Indian culture and philosophy invite comparison to popular American thought and values. Narrative techniques of multiple first person, letters, and news reports may offer students models for their own experimentation.

APPENDICES

A Folk/Fairy Tale Unit for Grades 3-6

Folk/fairy tales are stories that have been handed down through the years in oral or written form.

Older students may enjoy and appreciate a unit focusing on comparative analysis of variants of popular folk and fairy tales. Tales such as *Cinderella, Rumpelstiltskin, Sleeping Beauty, Beauty and the Beast, Hansel and Gretel*, and *Little Red Riding Hood* have popular versions from different countries. Check with your librarian for titles.

Younger students also enjoy listening to and comparing different versions of favorite fairy tales such as *The Three Bears, Little Red Riding Hood*, and *Stone Soup*.

Rationale for Doing a Unit on Folk and Fairy Tales

1. Folk/fairy tales are a literary genre that are part of children's cultural heritage.
2. Folk/fairy tales deal with important themes: good triumphs over evil, perseverance and hard work pay off; lucid thinking solves problems; unselfishness is rewarded; justice will be done.
3. While some fairy tales are very violent, they provide an acceptable way for children to deal with violence.
4. Children feel connected with parents and grandparents by reading the same tales that past generations have read.
5. Folk/fairy tales have a wonderful, rich vocabulary.
6. Folk/fairy tales are appealing to all children.
7. Folk/fairy tales stimulate children's imagination.
8. Children of varying abilities are exposed to different levels of meaning.
9. Folk tales are important for understanding various customs and cultures.
10. A large selection of fairy tales is readily available from the school and/or public libraries, making it easy for the teacher to gather a classroom collection. (You do not need special funds to do a folk/fairy tale unit.)
11. If your school mandates the basal text, you can still supplement it—or set it aside for a month—with an authentic literature unit.

Larger Understandings/Major Concepts

1. Folk/fairy tales can be interpreted many different ways depending on point of view, country of origin, and culture.
2. A clearly defined differentiation between good and evil—as presented in folk/fairy tales—can heighten awareness of consequences of behavior and help students make connections to problems in our society that are not so clearly defined.
3. Some things in life, like folk/fairy tales, have remained consistent through the ages for parents and grandparents and can be a vehicle for connectedness between generations.

Planning

Plan on four to six weeks for an in-depth study. Divide the class heterogeneously into three groups for literature discussion, and be sure each student has a literature response log for recording reactions to the folk tales. (See "Literature Response Logs" and "Literature Discussion Groups" in Chap. 6 for procedures.) While some books will be read aloud by the teacher, most will be read silently by the students. Students keep a record of all folk/fairy tales read in their literature response log or in a separate folder (see Figure A–1).

Gather a collection of folk/fairy tales for the classroom, allowing at least four books per student. A class of twenty-five students should have about one hundred books. Some of these should be duplicate copies to allow for paired reading and small-group discussion. Try also to get as many different-quality versions of the tales as you can to allow for comparative analysis. See the bibliography at the end of this appendix for a sampling of folktales from our libraries that have worked well. You may also want to consult the following resources for specific titles, ideas, and other recommended resources. The unit presented here acknowledges the following valuable resources for some of the ideas and activities.

Figure A–1   Record of Folk/Fairy Tales Read by a Student

Briana Hensold
              Fairy Tales I Have Read

1. The Little Mermaid - Freya, Littledale
2. Cinderella - Marcia Brown
3. The Wild Swans - Amy Ehrlich
4. Rumplestilkstin - Paul O. Zelinsky
5. The Frog Prince - Paul Galdone
6. The Girl Who Loved The Wind - Jane Yolen
7. The Weaving Of A Dream - Marilee Heyer
8. The Paper Bag Princess - Robert N. Munsch
9. Tattercoats - Flora Annie Steel
10. Vasilisa The Beautiful - Thomas P. Whitney
11. Petronella - Jay Williams
12. Mufaro's Beautiful Daughters - John Steptoe
13. Princess Furball - Charlotte Huck
14. The True Story of The Three Little Pigs - Jon Scieszka
15. Cinderella - The Brothers Grimm
16. Hansel and Gretel - The Brothers Grimm
17. The Legend of Scarface - Robert San Souci
18. How Rabbit Stole The Fire - Joanna Troughton

Resources

Bosma, Bette. 1987. *Fairy Tales, Fables, Legends, and Myths: Using Folk Literature in Your Classroom*. New York: Teachers College Press.

Lots of ideas for developing units on folk literature are clearly presented. Suggested activities include reading, writing, and the arts.

Huck, Charlotte S., Susan Hepler, and Janet Hickman. 1987. "Traditional Literature," in *Children's Literature in the Elementary School*, 4th ed. New York: Holt, Rinehart and Winston, Chap. 6, pp. 251–307.

Various types of folk tales are discussed, such as cumulative tales and beast tales. Characteristics of folk tales, including plot structures, characterization, style, themes, and motifs are elaborated. Variations of popular folk and fairy tales from around the world are shared.

Huck, Charlotte, and Janet Hickman (eds.). "Folk and Fairy Tales Web," in *The WEB: Wonderfully Exciting Books*. Columbus: Ohio State University College of Education, Vol. I, no. 3, pp. 5–25, and Winter 1986, Volume X, no. 2, pp. 7–21.

These two issues of the WEB discuss and list various folk and fairy tales and provide a "Web of Possibilities" that gives the teacher lots of creative and meaningful ideas. A valuable resource.

Hurst, Carol Otis. "The World of Once Upon a Time." November–December 1985. *Early Years/K–8*, pp. 26–31.

Carol Hurst presents thirty-five wonderful activities to go along with fairy tales. Pick and choose what will work for you and your students.

Moss, Joy F. *Focus on Literature: A Context for Literacy Learning*. 1990. Katonah, NY: Richard C. Owen.

This practical text connects theory and practice and offers in-depth literature units around the following focuses: transformation tales, Baba Yaga tales, devil tales, cat tales, magic object tales, bird tales, wish tales, horse tales, Cinderella tales. Each unit includes plans for daily sessions, meaningful literature extensions, and bibliographies of tales.

Moss Joy F. 1984. *Focus Units in Literature. A Handbook for Elementary School Teachers.* Urbana, IL: National Council of Teachers of English.

"Folktale Patterns: A Focus Unit for Grades Three and Four," pp. 107–124, offers suggestions for connecting folk tales from different countries. References and teaching ideas are presented for three patterns: the theft of magical objects, the use of super-powers by helpful characters, and stories where greedy characters wind up with little ("circle tales").

Spritzer, Daune Rebecca. Fall 1988. "Integrating the Language Arts in the Elementary Classroom Using Fairy Tales, Fables, and Traditional Literature." *Oregon English*. *Theme: Whole Language*, pp. 23–26. (Journal available for purchase through National Council of Teachers of English, Urbana, Illinois)

The author shares a workable four- to six-week unit on folk tales with lots of thoughtful ideas and activities for the classroom teacher. Included are examples of questions to promote critical thinking.

Trousdale, Ann. Fall 1989. "The True Bride: Perceptions of Beauty and Feminine Virtue in Folktales." *The New Advocate*, pp. 239–248.

The author notes variants of fairy tales in which the virtues of the female characters go beyond beauty. For example, in Mufaro's Beautiful Daughters *by John Steptoe, the heroine emerges for her character, not her beauty. Other tales cited have truthfulness, generosity, and loyalty as virtues held above beauty. This is an important article for giving students balanced perspectives of heroines in fairy tales.*

What follows are sixteen instructional plans that have been used successfully in a hetero-geneous fourth grade class. An instructional plan may be used one day, several days, or as long as several weeks. You will find that certain plans will need to be repeated to allow enough time for a concept or activity to be understood and fully discussed.

Allowing about one hour and thirty minutes each day for the folk/fairy tale unit has worked well. This time includes following through on the instructional plan as well as sharing problems and successes. For example, students and teacher may take the time to respond to a written draft of an original fairy tale or share completed storymaps or fairy tales. Note that samples of students' work that have been included come from average students.

The following plans are meant to be used only as a guide. You will want to change the sequence to suit your class needs, to delete some activities, and to add others.

Instructional Plan One   **Characteristics of Fairy Tales** (whole class)

Brainstorm with the class the characteristics of familiar fairy tales. Have a student act as scribe and list them on chart paper. Post the chart where it is easily visible and accessible. The chart is revised throughout the unit as new insights appear.

Characteristics usually mentioned include:

1. Happens in the past—time period not defined
2. Usually has a happy ending
3. May involve the supernatural
4. Often has a clear conflict between good and evil
5. Often begins with "Once upon a time"
6. Often includes a task, which if completed, brings a reward
7. All have plots and problems
8. Often includes a magic object/person to protect or help the main character
9. Often have brave heroes who rescue a helpless maiden
10. Main character sometimes gets fooled
11. Usually has to do with royalty
12. May have a fairy godmother, fairies, elves, or a witch

Instructional Plan Two   **Characteristics of Fairy Tales** (independently)

From the classroom collection of fairy tales you gathered, have the students select a fairy tale to read independently. Instructions to students: "Read your fairy tale silently. As you are reading, take notes in your literature response log on the characteristics you find that make this a fairy tale. Use the characteristics we listed on our chart, as well as any we may have missed."

After students have individually read the books or worked in pairs—jotting down the characteristics they found in their liteature response logs—meet in literature discussion groups. Students share their discoveries.

Instructional Plan Three   **Characteristics of Fairy Tales**

As a whole-class activity, revise the list of characteristics on the chart. Students then select a new book and follow procedures for Instructional Plan 2. Sharing can be whole class, in pairs, or in discussion groups.

Instructional Plan Four   **Comparative Analysis of Fairy Tale Variants** (ongoing activity, can be combined with other plans)

Over a period of several weeks, read to the students, or have available for them to read silently, as many versions of one fairy tale as you can locate. Students note some of the points of difference in their logs. *Cinderella*, which has many variants, is one tale that works well. Students' favorites have included:

Princess Furball by Charlotte Huck, illustrated by Anita Lobel (Greenwillow, 1989).

Vasilisa the Beautiful by Thomas Whitney, illustrated by Nonny Hogrogrian (Macmillan, 1970).

Tattercoats by Flora Annie Steel, illustrated by Diane Goode (Bradbury, 1976).

Cinderella by Charles Perrault; Amy Ehrlick, reteller; illustrated by Susan Jeffers (Dial, 1985).

Mufaro's Beautiful Daughters by John Steptoe (Lothrop, Lee and Shepard, 1987).

A comprehensive listing of *Cinderella* variants is included in *Focus on Literature* by Joy Moss, pp. 183–185. Check with your librarian for other well-known tales with multiple variants.

Instructional Plan Five   Settings in Fairy Tales

As a whole class, discuss what a setting is. Note the settings in tales read so far, and ask the children to be prepared to describe the setting in the tale they read today. In their logs, students write a paragraph describing the setting of their tale. After the tales have been read silently and paragraphs written, students meet in literature discussion group(s) and focus on the settings in their tales.

Instructional Plan Six   Use of Storymapping Format (demonstration)

Read aloud a favorite fairy tale and demonstrate, with input from the students, how to construct a storymap. This can be done on the chalkboard, on the overhead projector, or on large chart paper. This activity is done whole class with teacher guidance that invites student participation. Each student fills in his own copy of the storymap, which is kept and used as a reference model for constructing other storymaps (see **Figure A–2**).

> *Storymapping Format*
>
> Title of story
> Author
> Setting (where and when)
> Characters (who)
> Problem
> Action: 1, 2, 3 . . . (as many as needed)
> Resolution (use key words from the story)

Instructional Plan Seven   Storymapping (practice phase; repeat this activity two or three times)

Pair the children within a literature discussion group. Assign them the task of reading a self-selected fairy tale with their partner and mapping it according to the format (see Figure A–3). This activity can also be done individually or as a small group.

Instructional Plan Eight   Comparing/Contrasting Fairy Tales (optional; depends on availability; check with your librarian)

Show a film or filmstrip of a folk or fairy tale. Then read the book to the class and compare main character, setting, illustrations, and outcomes.

Figure A-2   A Storymap Done Whole Class with Teacher Guidance

Lindsay Kathleen
Campbell

STORY MAPPING FORMAT

Title of Story   Hansel and Greatal By The Brothers Grimm

Setting (where and when)   Large Forest, witches house, long ago

Characters (who)   Hansel and Gretal and Woodcutter and
witch

Problem   Getting away and back home

Action

1. stepmother kicking them out

2. Lost in woods (2 times)   6. Getting home

3. Captured by the witch

4. Deal with the witch

5. Money / jewels

Resolution   (use key words from the story)

Jewels/stepmother gone/Kill Witch/
Get home

Note: Resolution will tell how the problem was solved.

Actions will be main happenings in the story.

Which was more exciting? Which let you sense what was going to happen next more clearly? Which used more descriptive language? What elements of the fairy tale were different?

Instructional Plan Nine   Focusing on Magic

As a whole class, the element of magic is discussed as it has occurred in fairy tales read up to this point. Every student then selects and reads a new fairy tale independently. The students take notes in their literature response logs on:

- What if the magic didn't work?
- Find the magic moment in the fairy tale and speculate on what would happen if the magic failed.

Students share their speculations in literature discussion groups.

Instructional Plan Ten   Dramatizing Fairy Tales

Since several fairy tales have been read by now, ask the children to name some that would be good for dramatization. List the tales on the board. Divide the children into small groups of four or five. Let each group select a tale from the list and prepare to act it out for the rest of the class. The groups should be instructed to keep the tales fairly simple. No costumes or scenery are necessary. Items on hand in the classroom can be used as props. After about thirty minutes, the students give their presentations.

Figure A–3   *A Student's Storymap of* **The Girl Who Loved The Wind**

The Girl Who Loved. The Wind
by Jane Yolen

Title: The Girl Who Loved The Wind
Setting: couple hundred years ago (400500) on the
beach in the garden on the wind in the house
Characters: Danina, Father, Wind, 3 maidservants
3 menservants
Problem: Leave garden and house to find what
her life really is.
Actions 1. moves into house
2. meeting the wind
3. finds out about the world
4. father gets upset
5. meets wind again
6. father takes greater cautions
7. 1ˢᵗ time walking on the beach
8. 2ⁿᵈ " " " "
9. escaping her enclosed life

Resolution: flying away with the wind to
see what the world is really like

Instructional Plan Eleven   Math Activity

Read aloud a version of *Little Red Riding Hood*. Then give the following homework assignment:

"How many miles is it to your grandmother's (or grandparents') house?"

The next day, have students push pins on a world map to show where grandmothers (or grandparents) live. Make a graph showing how many miles away most grandmothers live. This makes an interesting bulletin board.

Instructional Plan Twelve   Comparative Analysis of Fairy Tale Variants (may take several days)

Based on the many fairy tales students have now heard and read, brainstorm, whole class, the main categories that could be compared in the fairy tale variants. List the categories on the chalkboard. Some categories that fourth-graders came up with for variants of *Cinderella* included: personalities of main character; qualities of Cinderella, stepmothers, or trouble-makers; why Cinderella was chosen as bride; helpers; ending.

In small groups of four or five have the students work together to make comparison charts. Students list the variants across the top of the chart. Each group chooses the categories it thinks are important to compare and lists them down the left side of the chart. See Figure A–4 for charts that resulted from two different groups. Each group then presents its findings to the entire class. Discussion with agreement and disagreement will result. Acting out favorite variants, for peers and other classes, can also follow this activity.

Figure A-4   Comparison Charts for "Cinderella" variants: Two Different Group Interpretations

	Grimm's Cinderella	Perrault's Cinderella	Mufaro's Beautiful Daughters	Princess Furball	Vasilisa The Beautiful
Personalities of Main Character	Clever, Sometimes depressed, Kind	nice/Kind, smart, sensitive, mostly happy	Kind, willing, helpful, giving, generous	smart, Kind, clever, tricky,	beautiful, Kind, loving, sweet, giving, willing
Why Prince or King chooses her	She's beautiful, Kind, she's got nice clothes	She's pretty, has beautiful clothes, Kind, considerate	helpful, past test, Kind, gentle, willing, beautiful	makes good soup, beautiful, giving	beautiful, good weaver, good helper, cooperative
Helpers	Animals	fairy God mother	Nyoka and father	nurse	magic doll
Stepmother's Trouble-makers / Family History	Mother dies, replaced by step mother, step mother brings two step sisters	Mother dies, God mother helps Cinderella, Cinderella has two stepsisters	no mother, loveable father, mean, picky, greedy sister	mother died	mother dies, father remarries, leaves town, mother gives Vas. a magic doll
Ending	Gorry happily	There's a wedding happily ever after	prove sister wrong, Marriage, Happy Ending	marriage happy	wedding, happy ending "unedited"

	Grimm's Cinderella	Princess Furball	Mufaro's Beautiful Daughters	Tattercoats	Vasilisa The Beautiful
Personalities of Mischief-Makers	Stepsisters-greedy, spoiled, jealous, Stepmother-jealous, evil	father- promises hand in marriage to an Oger	Manyara-selfish, imiture, selfcentered, impolite, rude, consided	Maids-inconsiderate, grandfather-stubborn	Babayaga-1/2+1/2, stepsisters-jealous, rude, cruel, inconsiderate, selfish, stepmother-self centered, self concieted
Qualities of Cinderella	Kind and pretty, extremly Good	smart, Kind, beautifull, genours	Kind, genours, caring, beautiful	beautiful, sad, getting happer every day	beautiful, Kind, genourss, Tough
Why chose Cinderella as bride	Because the shoe fit and beauty, and the blood was running from the stepsisters feet	Food, Trickery + beauty.	Beautiful + kind to everyone.	He loved - Tattercoats for her beauty	Because she was beautifu and her very beautiful clothing
ending	doves-pecked out eyes of stepsisters. happily ever after for Cinderella	Happy ending for Furball	Happy ending for Nyasha	sadly ends for grandfather, happily ends for Tattercoats	Vasalisa kept doll in pocket all the time, stepsisters burnt to ashes
helpers	Birds	Nurse	Snake	goose Header, geese	Doll "unedited"

Instructional Plan Thirteen   **Recognizing Different Points of View**

This lesson will focus on recognizing a different point of view in fairy tales. Features of satire and parody can be included for older students. The teacher reads aloud *The True Story of the 3 Little Pigs* by A. Wolf as told to John Scieszka. This humorous tale convincingly presents a wolf's reasons for the misfortunes of the three pigs. Differences between this tale and the traditional tale elicit a lively discussion. Among other things, students note that point of view can make a difference in how a character is perceived.

Then ask the children to tell you the characteristics of a traditional prince and princess fairy tale. List them on the chalkboard. Next, read the nontraditional tale *The Paper Bag Princess* by Robert N. Munsch to the class. This is a facetious story of a modern-day princess who saves the prince and then decides he's not to her liking. (If you have multiple copies, students can read in pairs.) Following the reading, have the students answer the following question in their literature response logs: "What different points of view does the author present?"

Meet in response groups, or whole class and share the contrasts between the traditional prince and princess tale and *The Paper Bag Princess*. See Figure A–5 for a chart that resulted from a whole-class discussion.

Day Fourteen   **Developing a Good Lead for an Original Fairy Tale** (may take several days)

Today students will concentrate on the way storytellers begin their stories. The teacher, or students working individually or in pairs, rereads just the first paragraph of several familiar fairy tales. Ask the students: "Which beginning makes you curious about what is going to

Figure A–5   Comparison Chart from Whole-Class Discussion

**Comparing Traditional Tales with Princes and Princesses to
The Paperbag Princess by Robert Munsch**

Traditional Tale	*The Paperbag Princess*
Usual point of view	Different point of view
beautiful princess, beautifully dressed	beautiful, not well dressed (in paper bag)
helpless princess	independent princess, not helpless
kind prince	conceited prince
prince saves princess	princess saves prince
prince and princess get married	princess refuses to marry prince
not much humor	very humorous
evil person fought	evil force outwitted
ball, helping person	no ball, no helping person
happy ending	not happy about break-up, but happy to be
illustrations—clear, beautiful	separated from prince
begins "Once upon a time..."	illustrations—modern, humorous
ends "...happily ever after."	not usual beginning or ending words

happen? Why? Which beginning tells you the most about the story? What information does the author give in the first paragraph?

Brainstorm a topic for the beginning of a fairy tale that the class could write about. Create several beginnings as a shared writing. Analyze each one. Which one would make you want to read on? Why? (Use the overhead projector or large chart paper so students can refer back to the shared writing.)

Have the children work in partners and write the beginning of a fairy tale or rewrite a new beginning for a favorite fairy tale. Share these beginnings in a response group format, having students and the teacher noting what is well done and offering suggestions for improvements.

Instructional Plan Fifteen   **Revising a Good Lead** (whole class)

Using a student's fairy tale beginning (with the student's permission) on the overhead projector, revise for content and clarity as a whole class. Then have students work in pairs revising their fairy tale beginnings. Share in response groups.

Instructional Plan Sixteen   **Storymapping an Original Fairy Tale**

Have students storymap the fairy tales they have started writing. This will cause them to plan the characters, the problem, the action, and the resolution. To clarify their storymap, students can also draw a picture of the characters in the setting. This enables the students to be descriptive in their writing. Have a sharing time at the end of the period. This activity will take more than one period.

Instructional Plan Seventeen   **Writing an Original Fairy Tale**

When students have mapped out their fairy tales and conferenced with the teacher or peer group, they may begin writing their fairy tale. The tale will go through the writing process: rough draft, conference, revision, editing, final copy. This will take several weeks to bring to completion. Completed tales are shared and displayed in the classroom.

Optional Activities (allow student choice)

(For students who have completed fairy tales and/or for end of unit projects)

- *Math activity*   Write down the fairy tales read in class. Have children select their favorites. (Pass out a survey or interview classmates.) Graph the results on a large chart.

- *Diary*   Write a diary entry as if you were the fairy tale character after a major event has occurred, for example, the Beast after Beauty fails to return, Cinderella after the ball, Little Red Riding Hood after she meets the wolf in the woods.

- *Filmstrip*   Using a kit for filmstrips that contains blank film and markers, have students make a filmstrip of a fairy tale. Students also prepare an accompanying script, which they read when presenting the filmstrip to the class.

- *New fairy tale*   Create a new version of a well-known tale. Have students storymap the tale first, and note how this version will be different. Also encourage tales from different points of view. For example, students could choose to write *Little Red Riding Hood* from the wolf's point of view, *Beauty and the Beast* from the vantage point of the Beast, or *The Three Billy Goats Gruff* from the troll's point of view.

- *Newspaper*   Use a newspaper format to write headlines, articles, classified ads, and editorials about fairy tale characters. For example, an ad might be written looking for

Figures A–6 and A–7   Two Students' Mock Classified Ads

> WaNT AD
> WANTeD. PRince MUST Be: HandsoME,
> Good WORKER, CaRiNJ, INTElliGeNT,
> GOOD MANNERED, Good, Natured,
> GallanT, GeNeROuS, and MiNdful.
> Most of all Rich and PoweRFuL.
> REWaRd: PRiNcess NaMeD PeTRoNella
> IN MaRRiage. Beutiful, KiNd,
> HeaRty, and GeNtle, INtelliyent,
> Good Natured

Cinderella's lost slipper; a headline might read: "Children Foil Witch and Reap Bounty"; an editorial might call for the arrest of the wolf after he has demolished two pigs' houses. Captions and illustrations could be included (see Figures A–6 through A–8).

• *Riddle book*   Write riddles about characters from fairy tales and share them with other classes. Each page would have an illustration and a riddle, for example, a picture of a cat in hat and boots. The riddle might say, "He was a very clever cat. Who was he?" The back page would list the answers to the riddles. (The answer to the above riddle is Puss from *Puss in Boots*.) These riddle books can be made clear and easy enough for first- or second-graders to enjoy.

Figure A–7

> LOST
> A slipper, a pure glass slipper. A very, small, pure glass slipper. With high heels and very narrow. It was lost at the ball on May 7, 1800. The prince at the castle is looking for it. REWARD: dance one dance, your choice with the prince. You should return the slipper to the castle immediately.
>
> by Lindsay

Figure A–8   A Student's Mock Newspaper Article

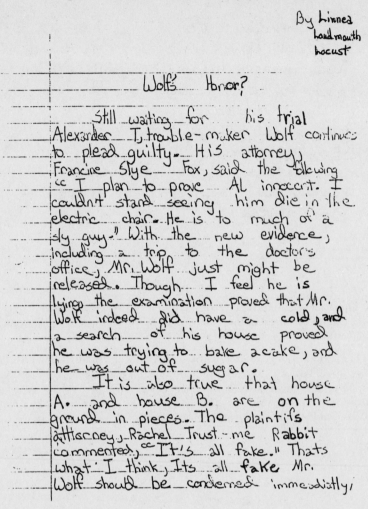

By Linnea
Loudmouth
Locust

Wolf's Honor?

Still waiting for his trial Alexander T. trouble-maker Wolf continues to plead guilty. His attorney, Francine Slye Fox, said the following "I plan to prove AL innocent. I couldn't stand seeing him die in the electric chair. He is to much of a sly guy." With the new evidence, including a trip to the doctor's office, Mr. Wolf just might be released. Though I feel he is lying the examination proved that Mr. Wolf indeed did have a cold, and a search of his house proved he was trying to bake a cake, and he was out of sugar.

It is also true that house A. and house B. are on the ground in pieces. The plaintiffs attorney, Rachel Trust-me Rabbit commented, "It's all fake." Thats what I think, Its all fake Mr. Wolf should be condemned immeadiatly.

• *Crossword puzzle* Design a fairy tale crossword puzzle using words frequently used in fairy tales, such as: prince, princess, prince, witch, Hansel, wolf, pigs, forest, stepmother, spell, magic (see Figure A–9).

• *Dramatization of point of view* A small group of students plan a dramatization of *The Three Little Pigs* from the wolf's point of view, using and adapting the dialogue from the book *The True Story of the 3 Little Pigs* by John Scieszka. Before presenting the drama, the group reminds the audience of the traditional tale by recalling specific events in the familiar version. This dramatization could be presented to other classrooms.

• *Dialogue* Two students write a conversation between two fairy tale characters. It can be taped, written in dramatic form, or read orally as Reader's Theatre.

• *Game* Keeping the theme of a familiar fairy tale, students enjoy designing original games with cards and directions. Students use tagboard and make colorful drawings of events and motifs from the fairy tale. This is an excellent activity for a pair of students.

Figure A-8   (Continued)

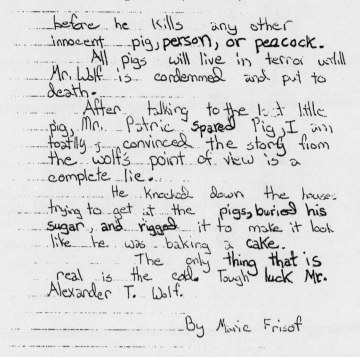

before he kills any other innocent pig, person, or peacock.
All pigs will live in terror untill Mr. Wolf is condemmed and put to death.
After talking to the last little pig, Mr. Patric spared Pig, I am toatlly convinced the story from the wolf's point of view is a complete lie.
He knocked down the houses trying to get at the pigs, buried his sugar, and rigged it to make it look like he was baking a cake.
The only thing that is real is the cold Tough luck Mr. Alexander T. Wolf.

By Marie Frisof

When the game is completed, the students put it to the test by having other students play it.

• *Crafts/arts*   Make a gift for a fairy tale character. The gift could be something the fairy tale character could use to get out of a difficult situation.

• *Fairy tale party*   Under the supervision of the teacher, plan a fairy tale party for another class to attend. The students design and send out invitations. Refreshments are planned, and volunteers bring them in. Students are asked to give presentations such as: the filmstrip, dramatization of the fairy tale books written by the students, and art projects completed. This party is held near the end of the unit (see Figure A–10).

Fairy Tales/Folk Tales

Anderson, Hans Christian. 1987. *The Snow Queen*. Illustrated by Bernadette Watts. New York: North-South Books.

Anderson, Hans Christian. 1981. *The Wild Swans*. Pictures by Susan Jeffers. Retold by Amy Ehrlich. New York: Dial.

Beaumont, Madame del. 1978. *Beauty and the Beast*. New York: Bradbury.

Berson, Harold. 1972. *How the Devil Gets His Due*. New York: Crown.

Brown, Marcia. 1954. *Cinderella*. New York: Macmillan.

Cauley, Lorinda Bryan. 1986. *Puss in Boots*. New York: Harcourt Brace Jovanovich.

Diamond, Donna. 1981. *The Pied Piper of Hamelin*. New York: Holiday House.

Gipson, Morrell. 1984. *Rip Van Winkle*. New York: Doubleday.

Grimm, The Brothers. N.D. *The Elves and the Shoemaker*. Retold and illustrated by Bernadette Watts. New York: North-South Books.

Figure A-9   Fairy Tale Crossword Puzzle

Adam G.
Dina L.   Fairy Tale Crossword Puzzle

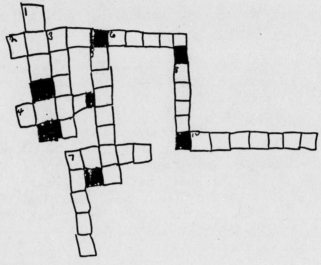

Down

1. One of the seven Dwarfs
3. A poison food that Snow White Ate
5. Cinderella lost her glass _____ .
7. Jack sold his cow for some magic _____ .
9. Rumple Stilskin _____ straw into gold.

Across

2. A reptile, that was turned to a prince.
4. It ate Little Red Riding Hood.
6. The opposite of Beauty.
7. Goldilocks went into this animals house
8. Mirror, Mirror, on the _____
10. Little Red Riding Hood picked _____ , for her Grandmother.

Grimm, The Brothers. 1986. *Grimm's Fairy Tales.* Illustrated by Richard Walz. Racine, WI: Western Publishing.

Grimm, The Brothers. 1981. *Hansel and Gretel.* Illustrated by Anthony Browne. New York: Knopf.

Grimm, The Brothers. 1980. *Hansel and Gretel.* Pictures by Susan Jeffers. New York: Dial.

Grimm, The Brothers. 1983. *Little Red Cap.* Illustrated by Lisbeth Zwerger. New York: Morrow.

Grimm, The Brothers. 1983. *Little Red Riding Hood.* Retold and illustrated by Trina Schart Hyman. New York: Holiday House.

Grimm, The Brothers. 1982. *Rapunzel.* Retold by Barbara Rogasky. Illustrated by Trina Schart Hyman. New York: Holiday House.

Grimm, The Brothers. 1983. *Rumpelstiltskin.* Illustrated by Donna Diamond. New York: Holiday House.

Figure A-10 A Student's Welcome Note to a Fairy Tale Party

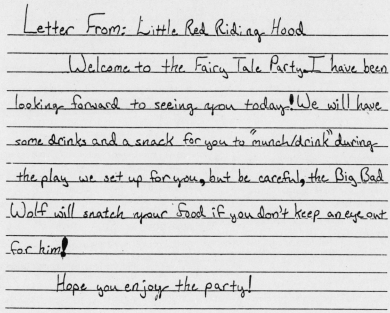

Letter From: Little Red Riding Hood

Welcome to the Fairy Tale Party. I have been looking forward to seeing you today! We will have some drinks and a snack for you to "munch/drink" during the play we set up for you, but be careful, the Big Bad Wolf will snatch your food if you don't keep an eye out for him!

Hope you enjoy the party!

Grimm, The Brothers. 1978. *The Twelve Dancing Princesses*. Illustrated by Errol Le Cain. New York: Viking Penguin.

Grimm, Jacob and Wilhelm. N.D. *Snow White and Rose Red*. Retold and illustrated by Bernadette Watts. New York: North-South Books.

Haley, Gail. 1986. *Jack and the Bean Tree*. New York: Crown.

Hodges, Margaret, 1984. *Saint George and the Dragon*. Illustrated by Trina Schart Hyman. Boston: Little, Brown.

Huck, Charlotte. 1989. *Princess Furball*. Illustrated by Anita Lobel. New York: Greenwillow.

Hyman, Trina Schart. 1977. *The Sleeping Beauty*. Boston: Little, Brown.

Littledale, Freya. 1986. *The Little Mermaid*. Illustrated by Daniel San Souci. New York: Scholastic.

Magnus, Erica. 1986. *The Boy and the Devil*. Minneapolis, MN: Carolrhoda Books.

Mayer, Mercer. 1980. *East of the Sun and West of the Moon*. New York: Four Winds Press.

Munsch, Robert. 1980. *The Paper Bag Princess*. Toronto: Annick Press.

Ransome, Arthur. 1968. *The Fool of the World and the Flying Ship*. New York: Farrar, Straus, and Giroux.

San Souci, Robert. 1978. *The Legend of Scarface*. New York: Doubleday.

Scieszka, Jon. 1989. *The True Story of the 3 Little Pigs*. Illustrated by Lane Smith. New York: Viking Kestrel.

Steel, Flora Annie. 1976. *Tattercoats*. Illustrated by Diane Goode. New York: Bradbury.

Steptoe, John. 1987. *Mufaro's Beautiful Daughters*. New York: Lothrop, Lee, & Shepard.

Whitney, Thomas. 1970. *Vasilisa the Beautiful*. Illustrated by Nonny Hogrogian. New York: Macmillan.

Williams, Jay. 1973. *Petronella*. Illustrated by Friso Henstra. New York: Parents' Magazine Press.

Yolen, Jane. 1987. *The Girl Who Loved the Wind*. Illustrated by Ed Young. New York: Crowell.

Appendix B

TEACHER'S GUIDE
by Susan Hepler

AMOS & BORIS
by William Steig

SUMMARY

In this story, similar to "The Lion and the Mouse", a sea-going mouse falls off his boat and is helped by a whale. The mouse returns the favor later. Steig's elegant telling of the story is matched by his dramatic illustrations.

INITIATING ACTIVITIES

1. What can you tell about the story from looking at the cover and the title page?
2. Read the first page. How can you tell this story is going to be unusual? What do you notice about the words?

THINKING CRITICALLY

1. How did Boris the whale help Amos? How did Amos

return the favor? Does this sound like any other story you know?
2. What kinds of things did Amos put in his boat before he set out? What use might he make of each of these things?
3. What happened when Boris "sounded"? What does it mean when a whale "sounds"?
4. Make a chart of interesting words or groups of words from the story. Beside each word or groups of words, put in your own idea of what they mean.
5. Why do you think Amos and Boris were sad to part? Why would they "never forget each other"?

READ SOME MORE!

Other stories of little and big animals helping each other are The Lion and The Rat, illustrated by Brian Wildsmith, and The Lion and The Mouse, illustrated by Ed Young. Other modern-day fables include Marcia Brown's Once a Mouse, Leo Lionni's Frederick, Arnold Lobel's Fables, and John Ciardi's John J. Plenty and Fiddler Dan.

H.P. Kopplemann Inc., P.O. Box 145, 140 Van Block Ave., Hartford, CT 06141-0145   203-549-6210   1-800-243-7724   IN CT 1-800-842-2165

DO IT YOURSELF

1 Make a display of the things Amos took along in the Rodent. Label each one and make a title for your display.

2 Make a mouse-sized model of the Rodent. Write a description of how you made the model or tell something about it.

3 Pretend that you are Amos telling your grandchildren about your wonderful adventure. Tell or write this story for them.

4 Write a newspaper article telling how "Whale Is Saved During Hurricane Yetta".

5 Paint a picture of your favorite part of the story. Write or tell about your picture.

6 Make a picture of another meeting Amos and Boris might have. Write or tell about your picture.

7 Keep a diary as Amos or Boris would have kept it and report each day's adventures.

by William Steig

Reprinted with permission of H.P. Kopplemann Inc., Hartford, CT.

TEACHER'S GUIDE
by Susan Hepler,

JOURNEY TO TOPAZ
by Yoshiko Uchida

ABOUT THE STORY

Eleven-year-old Yuki Sakane and her family are evacuated to a Japanese internment camp at the beginning of the United States' war against Japan. This restrained story is based on the author's experiences during World War II and reflects the quiet dignity, courage, and loyalty with which Japanese-Americans dealt with this unjust treatment.

INITIATING ACTIVITIES

1. What can you predict about this story by looking at the front cover and the Contents. What feelings does the cover try to show?

2. Read the first paragraph of the Prologue aloud. What do you know about World War II? (Read aloud the whole Prologue before reading the story, or after finishing, depending on the level of students.)

3. Do you know any people now, or in times past, who have been forced to leave their homes and live in guarded camps? What feelings might these people have had?

THINKING CRITICALLY

Chapter 1: "Strangers at the Door" (Pages 1-9)
1. Who is in Yuki's family? What can you tell about them? How are they like families you know? How are they different?

2. Why does the FBI come to Yuki's house? What do they do there?

Chapters 2-3: "The Long Wait" and "A Lonely Christmas" (Pages 11-29)
3. Why does Mother serve tea to the FBI men? How do you think the FBI men feel about the Sakane family? Why do you think that?

4. Besides serving tea, what other Japanese customs does Mother keep?

5. What are Issei? Nissei?

6. What has happened to Father? Why do you think this has happened? Is Father guilty of any crime?

7. What is the "evacuation"? Who ordered it? Why? How does the Sakane family feel about this? How does Mrs. Jamieson feel about this?

Chapter 4: "Ten Days to Pack" (Pages 31-39)
8. What things do Japanese-Americans have to give up or stop doing before they are to be evacuated?

9. What preparations do the Sakane family make before going to the evacuation camp? What do you think is hardest for each person to give up?

10. Do all Caucasian people feel that the Japanese-Americans are being treated fairly?

Chapters 5-6: "Inside the Barbed Wire" and "Home is a Horse Stall" (Pages 41-58)
11. How does the Sakane "apartment" compare with their former home?

12. What small things give the Sakane family comfort at Tanforan?

Chapters 7-8: "A New Friend" and "Ken Spoils a Party" (Pages 59-74)
13. If the Sakane family had made a list of their complaints about the situation at Tanforan, what things would be on that list?

14. Why is Chapter 8's title a good one? What does Ken's decision mean for Yuki and her Mother?

Chapters 9-10: "A New Rumor" and "Goodbye, Tanforan" (Pages 75-91)
15. Why do you think Yuki is glad to be back in school? Have you ever felt that way?

16. Yuki and Emi play "Jan Ken Po." What game does this sound like? What do you call "zoris"?

17. What is Yuki trying to tell Ken when she gives him not a half but a whole candy bar?

18. Mr. Kurihara says America is making prisoners of its own citizens. But Mother has an answer for him (Page 90) beginning, "Fear has made this country do something . . ." What do you think Mother means?

Chapters 11-12: "A Home in the Desert" and "Dust Storm" (Pages 93-109)
19. On a map of the western United States, locate and label: where Father is; the Sakanes' former home town; Tanforan; and the route to Topaz. The last two may take some detective work.

20. Is Topaz a better place than Tanforan? Why or why not?

21. What is a trilobite, the gift Yuki gave to Emi?

Chapters 13-15: "A Last Visit," "Tragedy at Dusk," and "Good News" (Pages 111-129)
22. How have Yuki's feelings changed toward Mr. Kurihara? How does he die? Why? How does the camp show their grief? What does Yuki do? Why?

23. What happy occurrences make Yuki feel a little more hopeful?

24. Why do you think Ken feels so distant from his family?

Chapters 16-17: "Another Goodbye" and "Hello, World" (Pages 131-149)
25. What are the arguments for Ken's joining the all-Nisei army unit? What are the arguments against it? What is Father's advice? What would you have done? Why?

26. Why does Mr. Toda feel so bad?

27. Why can the Sakane family go free in Utah but not in any West Coast state?

28. The Sakane family has many friends both in and out of camp. Which ones help them through the hard times? How? Who do you think helps the most? Why?

29. Do you think this experience may change Yuki? How?

DO IT YOURSELF

1 Pretend you are a friend to Yuki, like Mimi or Mrs. Jamieson, and fix a box of things you'd send to her in Topaz to cheer her up. Make a table display and label your gifts.

2 Mimi gave Yuki a red-covered diary in which to keep her thoughts. Write four or five entries Yuki might have made during some of the difficult or happy times in the story. Don't forget details to make it interesting.

3 Look up "Japanese Internment Camps" in magazines from 1942. What else can you find out from these articles?

4 Write the letters Yuki would write to Mr. Toda or to Emi after she and her family settled in Salt Lake City. What do you imagine might happen next?

5 Invite a Japanese-American person into your classroom to talk about Japanese customs they still keep. Or locate someone who may know about internment camps and ask them to talk about them to the class.

6 Make a book of Japanese customs that were followed by the Sakane family, such as Dolls Festival Day, paperfolding, using certain words, serving tea, and so forth. Do some research on other Japanese customs and report your findings to the class using your informational book.

READ SOME MORE!
Journey Home is a sequel to this story, and The Eternal Spring of Mr. Ito by Sheila Garrigue tells of a Japanese-Canadian family's difficulty during this time. Yoshiko Uchida has also written many other books about the experiences of Japanese-Americans. An excellent informational book about the internment camps with many illustrations is Behind Barbed Wire by Daniel S. Davis.

Appendix D

_____ **Discussion Group**

Name_____   Date_____

Book/topic _____

1. What did I do well today (and/or improve on) during group discussion?

2. What do I still need to improve on during group discussion?

Appendix E

A Sliding Mask

I keep two sizes on hand, one to use with Big Books and the other for regular-size text on the overhead projector or in the small-group or one-to-one reading situation. The slide fits into the slot and is moved to mask, gradually expose, and highlight features of text. Below are two sizes that I use. I outline the windows with black Magic Marker to make the print stand out. Check the text size of your books to determine what sizes will work well for you. Construct with tagboard or file cards.

(actual size)

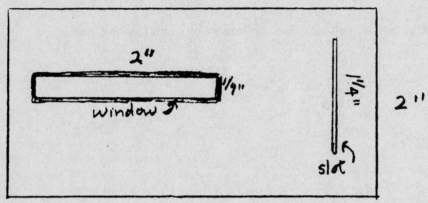

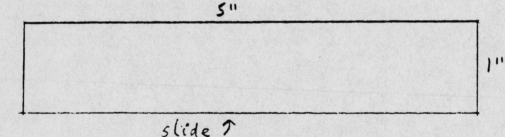

Big book size: 6 ½" x 2 ½" (shown reduced)

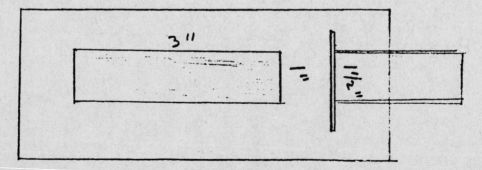

A "Flag"

I use tongue depressors and tagboard to construct flags of different sizes. I usually keep three sizes on hand. I tape or glue the rectangular size tagboard onto the tongue depressor. Experiment to get the sizes that work for you. The size of the flag determines how long a word you can highlight.

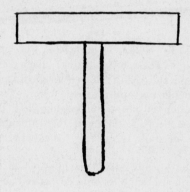

Use
With the overhead projector and screen, you can use a "flag" to call attention to a word. Place the flag on the screen behind you (not on the transparency on the overhead projector) directly over the particular word you want to highlight. Slowly and steadily move the flag away from the screen. The flag lifts the word off the screen and moves it onto the flag. The word is taken out of context so it can be studied or highlighted. Then the word goes back into context by moving the flag back onto the word on the screen. This is a dramatic visual technique that is easy and effective to use with students of all ages.

Notes on
Use of the WEB

Organization of WEB

Books are organized from floor to ceiling by grade level. First grade books are organized by level of difficulty. For your reference there is a listing of these books by level in the first grade section. Kindergarten, second, third, and fourth grade books are shelved alphabetically by title. There are separate designated areas for Biography, Teacher Resources (including professional books, information on specific books, and file folders on core books), Poetry, and Picture Books for older students. Additionally, there are multiple copies and designated areas of supplemental titles for grade 1, books on the environment for grades 1 and 2, and animal and science books.

Big Books are shelved alphabetically by title and hung on rods for easier access.

A Book Publishing corner houses supplies/book covers and all necessary tools for publishing. Please remind your parents that are helping with publishing to return all supplies (staples, scissors, labels, pens, punches, brads, etc.) to the WEB.

Notices of upcoming "whole language" workshops are posted on one wall.

Periodically, you may want to check in the file folders for each of the core books. The folders are continually being updated with additional information/activities about these books.

Book Sign-Out and Return

All WEB books are listed alphabetically by title in the sign-out book and include notations for the grade level, suggested use as a literature discussion group book, the number of books in the collection, and the type of book. Note that the sign-out book also includes a separate section on Teacher Resources as well as a separate reference listing of all books in these categories: Big Books, Ruth Chew, Biography, Bill Peet, Poetry, William Steig.

It is *necessary* that all books be signed out and signed in with your initials, number of copies taken, and dates so teachers know where books are and so we can maintain an accurate record-keeping system. If you are signing out *many* titles at one time and need assistance recording the titles in our WEB sign-out book, please make a list of all titles and give them to Regie or Judy Heiskell, WEB Room Coordinator. She will arrange for a parent volunteer to help you.

To be considerate of others, where a book is designated a reading group book and there are 6–10 copies, please leave the group of books intact, or don't hesitate to ask the teacher who has signed out a few copies of a multiple-copy set if you need them for a reading group.

- Please note where you take books from so you can return them to their proper place and grade level. Please return books bound with rubber bands as it makes for easier storage.
- For all books except for first grade, be sure you return books in alphabetical order. This includes all Big Books.

Also note the list of core books per grade level is posted on one wall. Those titles may be used only at the designated grade level or at a higher grade level.

Each teacher is supposed to have a personal copy of each core book to use as a teacher's guide. See Dr. Stokes if you need any titles.

Classroom Procedures

Each book has a number and school stamp on the inside front cover. To ensure that students take responsibility for core books and WEB books, be sure to note the number of the book each student receives.

Book Repairs

The care and handling of our books is a high priority and needs to be discussed with all students. You may want to invite an older student in to talk about this with younger students.

As best as we were able, most books were repaired in June and are in good shape. Core books that were cancelled have been replaced. In some cases, you will need to have students or parent volunteers repair the books before you use them. It is necessary that we all assume responsibility for book repair to ensure long life for our books. Please be sure books are repaired before you return them.

Book mending tape is available in the WEB. Fourth-graders, previously trained in book repair, can be used to demonstrate book repair to students in grades 2 and 3. Some teachers have found that it works well to assign specific students to this ongoing task. Kindergarten and first grade teachers may want to get some parent volunteers or upper grade students to keep up with book repair.

Lost and Damaged Books

If a book is lost, encourage the student to purchase a replacement copy (it is tedious work to order and replace single copies). Otherwise the student should be charged a $3.00 replacement fee for the lost book.

Monies collected for lost books should be turned into the office along with the title of the lost book. Please keep a record of all books that have been lost and paid for (and give that list to Regie in June) so we know what books to replace.

Fines should be assessed for damaged books. Repair charges can range from $.25 to $1.00. The money will be used for book replacement and WEB supplies.

See Regie for any assistance/concerns/suggestions. We are better organized this year, due to everyone's input and cooperation.

7/90

Appendix G

General Guidelines to Students for Submitting Stories, Poems, or Manuscripts to Publishers

- The writing should belong to you, the student. While adults may respond to the writing, ownership and authorship must remain with the student.
- Conference with your teacher and peers as you go through the authoring cycle. Allow plenty of time for thinking, creating, sharing, revising, and editing.
- Check to see that your material fits the format of the publication to which you are submitting. If unsure, write to the publisher with specific questions.
- Make as many of your changes as possible in the revising and editing stages prior to submitting your finished manuscript. In that way, the voice of the author can be completely respected.
- If you are interested in including illustrations, check with the publisher to see if illustrations are accepted. Be sure to acknowledge the illustrator if you are collaborating with another person in the process.
- Send only your best stories or manuscript.
- Submit to only one publisher at a time. Keep a copy of your submission with the name of the publisher and date sent.
- Acknowledgment of those who have helped you is recommended.
- Submissions should be typed, word processed, or in your very best handwriting.
- All manuscripts submitted should be copyrighted by the use of the "c" with a circle around it, the date, and the name of the author. It's also a good idea to seal the original in an envelope, mail it to the author's home address by registered mail, and keep it sealed, as proof of authorship.
- Enclose a self-addressed, stamped envelope for future correspondence.
- The publisher will notify you if the manuscript is accepted. While royalties are not usual, the publisher will discuss any business aspects with the author.
- The publishing time period varies with each book. Usually publication occurs within six months to eighteen months after a submission is received by the publisher. Just as the authoring cycle takes time, so does the publishing cycle. If a submission is accepted, any necessary conferencing will usually occur by telephone or letter.
- Don't be discouraged if you are rejected. Most writers receive multiple rejections before getting an acceptance.

Regie Routman gratefully acknowledges the input of children's publisher Billie White Price of Quality Publishing, Inc. in Conway, South Carolina.

Spelling Inverview

NAME:_____ Grade _____ Date _____

1. Are you a good speller? _____

   Why do you think so? _____

   _____

   _____

2. What makes someone a good speller?_____

   _____

   _____

   _____

3. What do you do when you don't know how to spell a word?

   _____

   _____

   _____

   _____

4. If someone is having trouble spelling a word how could you

   help that person? _____

   _____

   _____

   _____

5. Describe your spelling program last year. Did you like spelling?

   _____

   _____

HAVE-A-GO

Copy Word	1st Attempt	2nd Attempt	Standard Spelling

Communicating with Parents

J1: Getting Parents Involved

~~ GETTING PARENTS INVOLVED ~~

Children who take pride in expressing their ideas in writing may become discouraged if parents criticize their approximations, particularly the use of temporary spellings. The more knowledgable parents are about the writing process, the more supportive and enthusiastic they are likely to be about their children's work. The following letter may be copied or paraphrased to help parents better understand the writing process.

Dear Parents,

Some parents have been wondering why children in early primary grades are bringing home papers with temporary spellings that haven't been corrected.

Do you remember when your child learned to talk? S/he probably made many "mistakes", or approximations, in speech, and they didn't bother you much. You may have corrected a few, now and then, but mostly you included the child in the events of everyday life, encouraged the child to talk, and enjoyed the conversations. You probably knew, as parents do, that children learn to talk the way they learn to sit up and crawl and walk - they learn to talk by talking.

Learning to write works the same way. For example, early in the year, one child wrote:

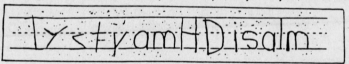

Now this doesn't look like your writing any more than a child's early words sound like your speech. But it's a tremendous piece of work! First of all, and most important, this child knows that written language is supposed to mean something, and he knows exactly what it means:

I was watching TV at my house. Then I saw a little mouse.

Just about every letter stands for one word in the story.

```
I y s        tv a m H     D i s   a l   m
I was (watching) TV at my house.  Then I  saw  a  little mouse.
```

Some developmental stages in writing come before this one, and others come after. From this sample we see that the child knows the following:
  . print proceeds in a straight line from left to right across a page
  . print is made up of letters
  . letters come in upper and lower case
  . letters stand for sounds in the words he wants to write.

Later on the child wrote the following response to a story about two friends playing together

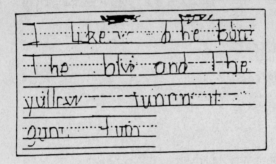

I like the part (where)
the blue and the
yellow turn into
green. from (author's name)

The writing still doesn't look like yours, but it's closer.

Since writing the earlier sample, this child has learned that:
.   written language is made up of words separated by spaces
.   each word between spaces stands for one word in speech
.   written words are made up of a number of different letters
.   there are a number of letter/sound combinations in each word (both beginning and
    ending sounds are included here)
.   when you 'know' a word (The), you spell it the same way every time
.   if you don't 'know' a word, you can use what you do know about letters and sounds to say
    what you mean until you learn the dictionary spelling
.   you self-correct your own writing when it doesn't look right to you, just as children
    self-correct their own speech
.   punctuation is part of written language.

That's a lot to have learned, and the child has doubtless learned more that cannot be documented
by looking at this one sample alone.

Teachers help children learn to write the way parents and families help them learn to talk. If
we put all our energy into correcting temporary spellings, children get discouraged and lose a
natural desire to write. They learn from heavy correction that meaning is less important than
spelling the words right.

If we invite them to use their oral language in their writing, even though they can't spell all
the words correctly, we free them to say what they mean. And, in fact, as the examples show, they
learn a lot about writing in general, and spelling in particular, from the risks they take along the
way. Children learn to write by writing, and we are most helpful to them when we appreciate and
encourage their "best attempts".

Is there a time for teaching particular points of spelling, grammar, punctuation, and
handwriting? **Yes.** Full group and individual conferences address such points as the need is noted in
the childrens' own writing.

Is there a time when children correct their work and turn out finished copy? Yes - when
publishing or 'going public.' In very early grades the children do the hard work - writing the
stories - and we make the corrections. As children become more experienced, they begin to take
responsibility for this work, too.

I hope this letter helps you to share some of your child's joy in writing, much as you share
his/her pleasure in speaking.

Sincerely,

Fall 1988 Newsletter, Whole Language Teachers Association, 16 Concord Road, Sudbury, MA 01776.
Reproduced with permission.

J2: Ways to Help Your Child with Reading at Home

Setting the Atmosphere
Help your child find a quiet, comfortable place to read.
Have your child see you as a reading model.
Read aloud to your child. Reread favorite stories.
Read with your child.
Discuss the stories you read together.
Recognize the value of silent reading.
Keep reading time enjoyable and relaxed.

Responding to Errors in Reading
Based on the way most of us were taught to read, we have told the child to "sound it out" when he comes to an unknown word. While phonics is an important part of reading, reading for meaning is the primary goal. To produce independent readers who monitor and correct themselves as they read, the following prompts are recommended *before* saying "sound it out."

- Give your child wait time of 5 to 10 seconds. See what he attempts to do to help himself.
- "What would make sense there?"
- "What do you think that word could be?"
- "Use the picture to help you figure out what it could be."
- Go back to the beginning and try that again."
- "Skip over it and read to the end of the sentence (or paragraph.) Now what do you think it is?"
- "Put in a word that would make sense there."
- "You read that word before on another page. See if you can find it."
- "Look at how that word begins. Start it out and keep reading."
- Tell your child the word.

Most important, focus on what your child is doing well and attempting to do. Remain loving and supportive. When your child is having difficulty and trying to work out the trouble spots, comments such as the following are suggested:

- "Good for you. I like the way you tried to work that out."
- "That was a good try. Yes, that word would make sense there."
- "I like the way you looked at the picture to help yourself."
- "I like the way you went back to the beginning of the sentence and tried that again. That's what good readers do."
- "You are becoming a good reader. I'm proud of you."

Regie Routman, language arts resource teacher

J3: Letter to Parents Explaining Independent Reading Program

September 4, 1990

Dear Parents,

W. E. B. (Wonderfully Exciting Books) is an important component of our reading program. The student self-selects books from our classroom, school, public, or home library for independent reading.

Your child and I will have frequent opportunities to discuss what has been read independently. The W. E. B. book will be used for reading at home and may also be used for independent reading during language arts time or during S. S. R. (Sustained Silent Reading.) A record of your child's daily reading and a list of completed books will be kept in the classroom.

Your child's responsibility is to read for about thirty minutes each evening and to carry the book back and forth to school each day in a waterproof bag. Your child is also expected to take good care of this book. There will be a fine for damaged books or a replacement fee for lost or severely damaged books.

Over the school year, consistent daily reading will expose your child to various author's styles and will improve your child's fluency, vocabulary, comprehension and writing. Our main goal is that your child will enjoy reading and choose to read for pleasure.

Please join with me in helping to create an environment where our children can enjoy books for a lifetime. Together we can build a community of readers.

Thank you for your help, support, and cooperation with our W. E. B. program.

Sincerely yours,

Please indicate that you have read this letter.

_____

(signature of parent or guardian)

J4: Explanation of Integrated Spelling Program

September 20, 1989

Dear Parents,

The purpose of this letter is to introduce our spelling program to you. We support the philosophy that views spelling as an integral part of the total language arts program. We believe children develop spelling strategies through purposeful daily reading and writing. Therefore, your child will be creating personal spelling lists from daily writing, high frequency words, and content area words in the curriculum. Through research and our own teaching experiences, we have found that children are most interested in learning to spell words they need to use to communicate. We have also found that the more children read and write, the better they read, write, and spell.

We will emphasize three strategies in helping your child become a better speller:
- discovering and applying the rules and patterns
- proofreading
- using the dictionary and other resources

These are the same strategies adults use when trying to spell a word.

When your child asks you how to spell a word, here are some questions you can ask that may help him/her figure out the correct spelling:
Does it look right?
Can you try writing it another way?
How does the word start? How does it end?
Have you seen that word somewhere else?
    Can you find it for me?
What sounds do you hear?

After your child's attempts, verify the spelling by confirming the correct spelling or supplying it. Encourage your child to write the word as a whole, from memory, rather than copying it one letter at a time. Also use the attached sheet "Am I Becoming a Good Speller?", which your child has in his spelling folder, as a guide.

Keep in mind that the goal is not perfect spelling, which we as adults are still developing. The goal is to have children become more aware of spelling strategies and to be able to express themselves legibly, competently, and confidently when writing. Remember, there is no reason to learn to spell if you don't write; writing must come first.

Here are some suggested writing activities to promote writing at home:

notes to each other
greeting cards and invitations
lists for shopping, trips, gifts, parties
letters to grandparents, relatives, and friends
signs
posters
bumper stickers
recipes
songs
phone messages
post cards
puzzles
imaginative stories
jokes and riddles
cartoons
menus
map for a planned trip
diary of a trip
captions for photo pictures

We welcome your cooperation, participation, and questions concerning the spelling program. Please feel free to contact us.

Sincerely,
Elaine Weiner, second grade teacher
Linda Cooper, third grade teacher
Regie Routman, language arts
resource teacher
Dr. Bernice Stokes, principal

J5: Parents as Allies in Children's Education

Parents as Allies in Children's Education

"How can I help my children learn to read and write?"

Parents who ask this question can become valuable allies — all we need do is encourage them to take active roles in helping with their children's education. In particular, parents can be especially helpful in conveying to children the idea that there are good reasons for learning to read and write.

The following are some of the ideas my colleagues and I have suggested to parents in our community, ideas that they say have worked well for them and that they have enjoyed using:

1. *Be a role model for reading*
• Let your children see you reading different materials for different reasons and encourage them to do the same.
• Join a book club.
• Give your children books or magazine subscriptions as gifts.
• Visit the library on a regular basis.

2. *Read to your children every day*
• Find a quiet spot.
• Choose interesting material.
• Encourage your children to read to you, to each other and to other members of the family.

3. *Provide opportunities for listing to audio tapes and for watching selected TV programs*
• Encourage your children to listen to recordings by authors or storytellers.
• Make your own recordings of your children's favourite selections.
• Allow your children to select from the program guide appropriate TV programs for viewing. Their viewing time may constitute one full evening a week, or one or two programs each night. Ask for a written schedule showing times, channels and selected programs. (Make it a rule that they have to vary the times and/or channels.)

4. *Provide opportunities for reading*
• Collect simple recipes and allow your children time to do some cooking.
• Always leave lots of notes for your children. Place them on the fridge door or in their lunch boxes. Sometimes it's fun to leave notes about tasks and include promised rewards for tasks that are completed. An example might be: "Please clean your rooms when you get home from school. When you're finished we'll all go out to eat at the shopping centre this evening."
• Play board games that encourage reading or word play.

5. *Be a Role model for writing*
• Allow your children to see you writing every day for different reasons, business and pleasure.
• Be positive. Don't overemphasize errors in your children's grammar, punctuation or spelling.

6. *Provide opportunities for writing*
• Set up a writing corner. Have a good selection of materials available. Vary the paper (lined and unlined) by size, colour, texture and shape.
• Purchase blank books or make your own by sewing pages together. Wallpaper scraps make good covers.
• Encourage your children to share what they've written.
• Encourage your children to proofread what they've written.
• Provide an incentive for your children to write by typing out some of their writings. If possible, allow them to use a typewriter or word processor themselves.
• Encourage your children to keep a special diary for private writing where they can freely express feelings and opinions. Promise them you will respect their privacy.
• Keep a communal journal when travelling as a family so all the members can write about what they see and discover.

• Have your children assist you in writing out grocery lists. If your children come with you when you go shopping, have them check off items as you pick them out.

7. *Encourage the writing of letters*
• Encourage your children to write thank you notes for presents received.
• Encourage your children to write to grandparents and other relatives and friends.

8. *Encourage Creativity*
• Encourage your children to rewrite TV commercials — or make up new ones.
• Encourage your children to perform commercials or plays that they've written.
• Encourage your children to illustrate their writing — start a file of pictures, photos, illustrations and cartoons for your children to use in illustrating their writing. (Such a file can be a great tool in helping to motivate the reluctant writer.)

Above all, let your children know that reading and writing are meaningful activities. It's true that we learn to read and write for practical reasons, but it's also true that reading and writing are tremendous sources of enjoyment.

By Shary Rea, B.Ed. (elementary school teacher, Alberta, Canada).

J6: *Letter to Parents to Help Make Book Covers*

SHAKER HEIGHTS CITY SCHOOL DISTRICT

MERCER SCHOOL
23325 Wimbledon Road
Shaker Heights, Ohio 44120
(216) 921-1400

BERNICE STOKES, Ph.D   April 13, 1989
Principal

Dear Parents:

    I am writing to you to request your help with an urgent need for the
publishing program for the first and second grades. We have run out of book
covers! A wonderful emergency! Our estimation is that the children in the
school have used over 1500 covers since the beginning of school and most of
those have been in the first and second grades. (Most book covers for the
upper grades are made as part of a classroom project.)

    I would like to ask for volunteers to help us with the covers. I will
package for you the supplies and directions necessary to make 10 covers. All
you will need to do is to provide glue and about one hour of your time. The
covers can be returned in the manila envelope we send home with your supplies.

    If you are interested in helping us please fill out the tear sheet below and
return it to your classroom teacher.

    Thank you for your help in making this important program a success.

                        Susan Long
                        Parent Volunteer Coordinator
                        Mercer School

- -

NAME _____

Classroom teacher _____

I will do _____ packet(s) of book covers.

                Thank you.

**1989 is the
Year of the
Young
Reader**

J7: Request to Parents to Make Book Covers

BOOK-MAKING WORKSHOP

Wednesday, May 31, 1989
District Library Media Center
Woodbury School
9:30 a.m.--3:00 p.m.

This is a "drop in" workshop for
kindergarten and first grade parents
on making wallpaper book covers for
the district's first grade publishing
program.

Come when you can, for as long
as you can, and learn the easy craft
of book-cover making. We need to
make hundreds of book covers to
replenish our stock so that the
Boulevard, Fernway, Lomond, Mercer,
and Onaway Publishing Companies are
ready to go next fall.

We plan to have as much fun as
quilters at a quilting bee so please
join us if you can.

--Marianne Sopko

J8: Communicating with Parents about the Reading-Writing Program

PARENTS NEWSLETTER

ONAWAY ELEMENTARY SCHOOL – GRADE 3

October 3, 1990

My goals for this school year are:

- to continue to promote a positive self image in each student;

- to foster a learning environment which focuses on cooperation and respect for each other; and

- to individualize educational approaches in order to fit the child to the program vs. the program to the child.

My thoughts on education:

- I am process oriented.

- I have total respect for individuals.

- I believe in cooperation vs. competition.

THE CURRICULUM

I.   READING PROGRAM

Components of the Reading Program:

A.   Intensive Reading

The core book we are reading now is More Stories Julian Tells by Ann Cameron.

1.   Whole Class Reading

We read the stories in different ways –
- I read to the students.
- The students read in pairs.
- The students read silently.

2.   Literature Response Groups

The children are divided into three groups according to the book they choose. Also, at times we read the same book and divide into three groups. This allows for small group interaction and discussion.

The students keep a reading log where they respond to the books they read.

I group the children heterogeneously, which promotes self-esteem and discourages competition.

3.   Read Aloud Daily to the Children

B.   Extensive Reading

1.   WEB Program

WEB stands for Wonderfully Exciting Books. The goal of the program is to help the children become lifelong readers by providing them with quality literature and encouraging them to read.

The students are required to read for at least 20 minutes each night. They keep a record of the books they read in their WEB log. At the completion of a book, I interview the student.

2.   RAP

RAP stands for Reading Any Place. Each day the students read for 20–30 minutes silently. This has become a favorite part of our day! The goal is to educate their imaginations and grow as individuals.

3.   Reading Aloud to Younger Group of Children

We read with a kindergarten class each week.

4.   Literature Extension Activities

The students often do activities that extend the literature they read in reading group or that is read aloud to them daily. Some examples are:

- Readers Theatre
- Wanted Posters
- Book Sales
- Murals/Dioramas

II.   COMPONENTS OF THE WRITING PROGRAM

I teach the writing process through:

A.   Writing Workshop

The goal is to teach the students the steps of the writing process. During this time we write stories, reports, pen-pal letters, classroom newspaper. The students keep writing folders of all writing, including drafts and final copies.

B.   Poetry Workshop

The goal is to open up a world of feelings and give a voice in an experience of life. During this time we read, share and discuss poetry. We also write poems using different styles of poetry in our poetry log.

C.   Journal Writing

Our goal is to become effective users and learners of language. We work on this activity two to three times per week.

-2-

By Julie Beers, grade 3 teacher.

J9: Communicating with Parents Through a Student Newspaper

ONAWAY TIMES NEWS

Nov./Dec. 1989   Ms. Beers' class

Reading

In Miss Beers class we read <u>Stone Fox</u>. Stone Fox is an Indian. He won all of his races. Little Willy just ran one race. He won $5,000. Grandfather got better. We read the book in reading groups. Miss Beers put questions on the board, and we answered the questions in our reading log.

Article by
Joseph Simon
Jr. Editor

Hi. My name is Sarah VanAken, your Onaway Times reporter. In reading group we read <u>Stone Fox</u>. <u>Stone Fox</u> was about a boy named Little Willy and his grandfather and how Willy fought to win the race for the money to pay back the taxes to keep the farm. After we read the book, Mrs. Douglass' class came and watched the movie with us. After the movie we got into groups and made a small Venn diagram to show how the book and the movie were the same and different. We talked about things only in the movie, things only in the book, and things that were in both. Then we put it all together and made a big Venn diagram and that's what we did for Stone Fox.

I.W.T. Stands for independent work time. The teacher gave us a folder and gave us some sheets of paper for a homonym book shaped like pears. Then we write sentences. She gave us a sheet of activities to work on too. She gave us a poster to make. We are drawing pictures and writing sentences about <u>Stone Fox</u>.

Article by
Siquia Whitley

Cover page, grade 3, Julie Beers's class.

J10: Letter to Parents Guiding Book Club Selection

Dear Parents,

    Attached is the current Lucky Book Club order form. Lucky Book Club provides you with the opportunity to purchase good literature for your child at very reasonable prices. You are not obligated , however, to purchase anything.

    If you do choose to take advantage of this opportunity, I would recommend the following books from this month's selections.

    Please return the order form and your payment to school by_____. Make checks payable to Lucky Book Club.

    Thanks.

Adapted from an idea developed by Nellie Edge.

Index

- Page numbers in boldface indicate pages on which full publishing information is given.
- Entries for blue pages are not included unless a person or reference is already cited in the text.